Gerry Frank's

Where to

Find It,

Buy It,

Eat It

in

New York

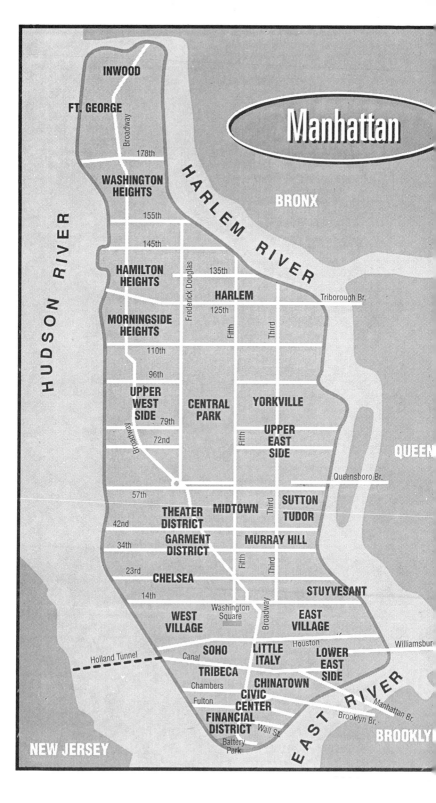

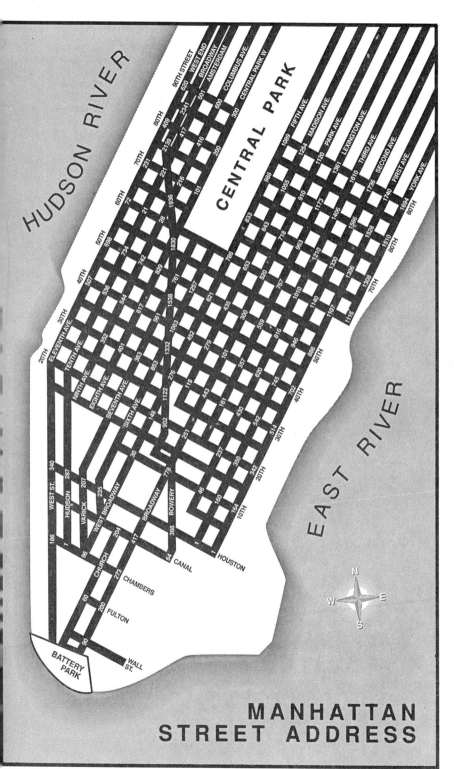

MANHATTAN
STREET ADDRESS

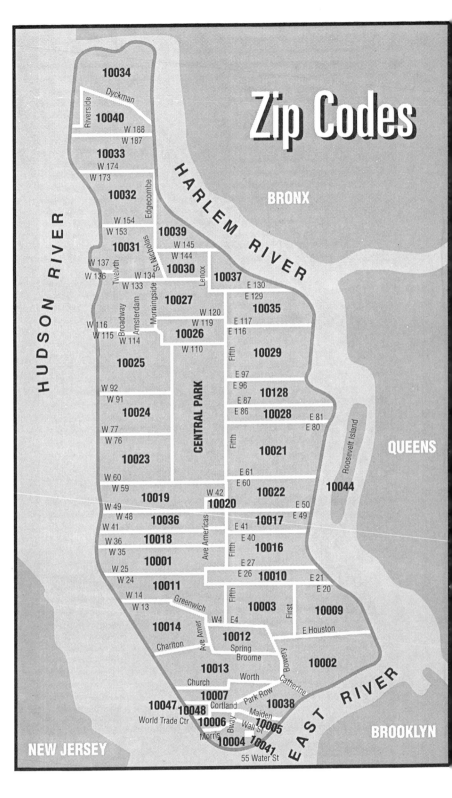

Gerry Frank's
Where to
Find It,
Buy It,
Eat It
in
New York

For additional copies (special quantity prices available),
write or call:

Gerry's Frankly Speaking

P.O. Box 2225
Salem, Oregon 97308
503/585-8411
800/NYC-BOOK (800/692-2665)
FAX: 503/585-1076
E-Mail: gerry@teleport.com
Visit our website: www.tapas.com

Preface

Welcome to the Tenth Anniversary Edition of *Where to Find It, Buy It, Eat It in New York,* New York's favorite and most complete guidebook. There are over 600,000 copies in print, and I thank you, my readers, for this show of confidence. In return, I have tried to give you updated, useful, and thorough information on this great city with each new edition in a style that is personal, helpful, and readable.

This tenth edition is an occasion to look back on the city we have chronicled and loved over the years. Perhaps because I am both a visitor to the city and someone who has walked virtually every block, I am in a unique position to notice major and minor distinctions from the first edition until today.

New York was initially known as the gateway to the American melting pot. Every schoolchild knew this, and periodically the city schools would have "ethnic heritage days" to show off the diversity of the student body. But even the most casual observer will note that nowadays New York (and perhaps the entire country) is less a melting pot and more a mosaic. Forget heritage. The city's students are increasingly first-generation themselves. That, in turn, impacts on the diversity. The residents of Manhattan are increasingly young, unattached, and driven. Families increasingly migrate to the outer boroughs and the suburbs, which leaves newer residents occupying public-school classrooms.

This mosaic can be seen in the retail world as well. In the first several editions we talked of districts and areas where specific wares were sold. This was a unique phenomenon New Yorkers took for granted. On the other hand, seeing a street lined with bridal headpiece shops or a row of sewing-machine repair stores made no sense to folks from out of town. But increasingly there are distinct ethnic merchants who are no longer selling in specific geographical areas but rather from specific market niches that they have claimed throughout the city. Merchants and retailers represent specific immigrant communities. The Greeks have delis, the Koreans are greengrocers, the Indians run newsstands, and the perennial (and quintessential) streetcorner umbrella salesmen are from East Africa. Even some major department stores are foreign-owned.

Since all of these small business people must eat, sleep, and live near their shops as well, the boundaries of Little Italy, German Yorkville, Chinatown, and Spanish Harlem are blurring. While there are nostalgic and sentimental traces of these areas, small mom-and-pop neighborhood stores are being replaced by giant "super stores" or generic chains.

In one of the early editions we talked about the psychological differences between the East Side and West Side. While there are still some differences, if you were dropped on a street in Manhattan without significant markers (like the Empire State Building), such ubiquitous retail installations as Blockbusters, the Chinese takeout, the Korean vegetable market, and maybe even the local health club, none would give a clue if you were in Turtle Bay or Morningside Heights. Nor would the lifestyle.

Some things remain the same. New Yorkers are still people on the move who walk, talk, and eat fast and are perennially short on space. (The sofa that turns into a bed is still the city-dweller's ultimate necessity.) In the first edition we made the statement, "Don't worry about your accent. Everyone has one." Today, accents really are nothing to worry about. They are badges of pride, and virtually every service provider from doctor to waiter proudly retains his. That's the *new* New York! And, happily, it is cleaner, safer, and friendlier than it has been in decades.

Visitors and New Yorkers alike have found this book to be indispensable. All of this would not have been possible without the great cooperation of hundreds of New York eating establishments, food shops, services, stores, hotels, museums, attractions, and all the rest who have allowed me to present what I think is the best of this great city. It is indeed "the book that New York lives by"!

The question I am asked most often is, "How did a fellow from Salem, Oregon, come to write the most popular guide to New York?" I believe my answer makes sense. I was born into an Oregon department-store family, spending 17 years in the retail business plus numerous short stints during school vacations. I often traveled to New York—where we had our own buying office—with store buyers, spending time in the various markets and becoming entranced with the excitement and energy of this great city. I love New York!

After the family business was sold, I joined forces with U. S. Senator Mark Hatfield from Oregon. I served as his assistant and chief-of-staff in Washington, D.C. for 26 years, and left that position in the spring of 1992. During that period I spent two weekends a month in New York, walking the neighborhoods, inspecting the stores, dining in the restaurants, sampling the food shops, trying out the services, and just generally exploring. I continue to do so. What I've found I now share with you.

My qualifications? As a former retailer I have an eye for the value and service that are essential for a successful operation. I have had the privilege of traveling to over 140 nations, so I am able to identify good food, good accommodations, and good value. As the proprietor of a restaurant and specialty food operation in Oregon, I have developed an eye for what customers are seeking for in the ever-changing food world. I have eaten in over 2,000 restaurants of all descriptions in Manhattan. All the walking around has allowed me to keep a moderate waistline, but that is becoming increasingly difficult!

I'd like to point out what differentiates this book from the dozens of other guides to this city. First and foremost, this one is complete. You need nothing else. There are excellent specialty volumes available on various aspects of life in this sometimes overwhelming city, but this one alone combines all the ingredients in which residents and visitors are interested. Whereas many books of this nature are the combined product of people who write different sections, this book is almost exclusively my evaluation only. (I have had specialized advice on some sections where I do not feel qualified, like beauty shops.) You may not agree with all of my comments, but rest assured that I am being honest and forthright. Remember also that no one pays to get in this book, and no one tells me what should or should not be included. Believe me, many have tried! You are obviously aware that a city as dynamic as this one changes almost overnight. Therefore I am able to bring you hundreds of new and exciting places in each edition. The majority of write-ups have some new information in each edition. But this reality also has a downside. It is impossible to keep a book like this absolutely up-to-date. The day it is printed, a store or restaurant might close. However, because I self-publish, my deadline is much closer to its appearance in bookstores than that of major publishers, so what you are reading is the most current information possible. Every entry is checked and updated with each new edition.

The story of the book has become a legend in the publishing business. I had no idea that I would write a book. My only previous experience in journalisn had been publishing a newspaper when I was a youngster. I presently write a column for *The Oregonian,* a major newspaper in the Pacific Northwest, and I have been a special correspondent for *Northwest Reports,* a weekly prime-time television news magazine on KPTV-12 in Portland, as well as a commentator on eating, shopping, and traveling for that station's morning news show. People who knew that I spent a great deal of time in New York would always ask where to eat, stay, shop, and so on. I collected and assembled all the data I'd compiled from years of exploration and took it to the New York book publishers.

Their reaction could not have been more negative. The attitude was, "What is some hick from Oregon doing writing a book on New York?" They wouldn't give me the time of day. I am not the sort of person who likes to be told "no," so I decided to publish and distribute the volume myself. It was a lot of work, and the enterprise had its share of problems and discouragements, but the end product has been worth it. Not only are we the top-selling title in this highly competitive market, but some of the same publishers who originally turned me down now want to publish the book. One of my greatest joys is to be able to say, "Thanks, but no thanks. Where were you when I needed you?"

This book is also published in a convenient pocket-sized abridged edition (for $7.95) that deals mainly with the food and restaurant scene. It is often used by groups visiting Manhattan. There is also a hardcover limited edition ($25). Special prices on quantity lots of all editions (limited, regular, abridged) are available. Please contact me by phone (800/NYC-BOOK or 503/585-8411), fax (503/585-1076), by mail (P.O. Box 2225, Salem, OR 97308) or email (gerry@teleport.com).

The consistent input from you, my readers, has been invaluable. Hardly a day goes by that someone does not tell me about some special find. (Sometimes they don't want me to mention them!) If you have questions or disagree with an evaluation, I want to hear about it. I take each comment very seriously and often reevaluate an entry's inclusion in the book as a result.

A book like this would not be possible without the administrative help of a number of people. I am particularly indebted to my very talented researcher, Carrie McMillan Klein; to my editor, perfectionist Parke Puterbaugh; to my extremely able book assistant, Cheryl Johnson; to my incredibly organized executive assistant, Linda Wooters; to my inspiration, Esther Benovitz; and to my support personnel, Jeryme English and LaVelle Blum. Tim Prock, a talented young local artist, did the cover.

This volume is *not* the Yellow Pages. It is, however, the best and most interesting guidebook about what is out there in the most fascinating city in the world. Enjoy!

Contents

I. THE WORLD'S GREATEST CITY

II. WHERE TO EAT IT: MANHATTAN A LA CARTE

III. WHERE TO FIND IT: MUSEUMS, TOURS, AND OTHER EXPERIENCES

IV. WHERE TO FIND IT: NEW YORK'S BEST FOOD SHOPS

V. WHERE TO FIND IT: NEW YORK'S BEST SERVICES

VI. WHERE TO BUY IT: NEW YORK'S BEST STORES

VII. WHERE TO "EXTRAS"

My Favorite Places

I. The World's Greatest City

New York City is far and away the largest city in the United States. According to the most recent census, 7.3 million people live in its five boroughs, 1.5 million of them in Manhattan. That means that roughly the combined populations of Alaska, Vermont, and Wyoming live on an island 12 miles long and only 2.3 miles across at its widest point!

Its detractors argue that Manhattan is the most crowded, dirtiest, and rudest place in the world. To some extent, they're right on all three points. It *is* crowded. More people live in a residential city block in Manhattan than in many small towns. On any given weekday, a quarter of a million people pass through the MetLife building in midtown, and there are enough people in the World Trade Center to make it the fourth largest city in my home state of Oregon! Manhattan *is* dirty: New York produces 13,000 tons of garbage a day. An estimated 12,000 cigarette butts are picked up every day in and around Times Square—that's something like 4.4 million a year! And who would argue that New Yorkers aren't rude—at least some of them, some of the time? (Although what they mostly are is blunt and very direct.) Everyone seems to be in a hurry, and chances are that anybody who smiles at you on the street isn't just being friendly.

So why visit? Because crowds, dirt, and rudeness aside, New York is the most interesting, exciting, and diverse city in the world. Although they sometimes don't act like it, most New Yorkers are proud of their city and can't imagine why anyone would want to live anywhere else. At the very least, anyone who lives in the United States or who visits this country ought to spend a week or two getting to know this incredible city. Things (safety, business conditions, crime, cleanliness) are indeed much better these days in New York City.

New York has something for everyone. Where else can you find a medieval garden with almost 250 different plants in it? A cafe with a kosher sushi bar and a computer terminal with access to the Internet at every table? Or several nesting pairs of peregrine falcons (which makes naturalists in other parts of the country crazy!)? Whether you love opera, jazz, or tribal drums; whether you're interested in history, architecture, or modern art; whether you like to shop, jog, or attend lectures; whether you live for Italian, Ethiopian, or Chinese food, New York has it all. This book is all about finding *your* New York—the little slice of this magnificent pie that's just right for your tastes and appetite.

1

GETTING THERE

So you're headed for New York! Whether you're traveling 90 miles from Philadelphia or 9,000 miles from Singapore, you're in for a wonderful treat. But first you need to get here.

AIRPORTS – New York City is served by three major airports. LaGuardia is most frequently used for domestic flights, while John F. Kennedy has flights going to and from just about every country on Earth. Both are in the borough of Queens. Newark, across the Hudson River in New Jersey, handles a large volume of both domestic and international flights. The most common ways of traveling between Manhattan and these airports are by taxicab, shuttle bus, and private car or limousine.

Taxi lines form in front of most terminals at all three airports, and the exits to them are usually well marked. These lines are legitimate and generally move quickly. Under *no* circumstances should you go with someone either inside or outside the terminal who asks if you want a taxi. It may seem tempting if the airport is crowded, but you'll end up paying far more than you should and will have no recourse. Assuming you don't run into bad traffic, the trip between LaGuardia and midtown will take about half an hour and cost roughly $25, plus bridge toll and tip. The trip between Kennedy (also called JFK) and anywhere in Manhattan can take as long as an hour and, under a new system that has tourists and locals alike cheering, costs a flat fee of $30 plus bridge or tunnel toll and tip. A trip between Newark and Manhattan also can take as long as an hour and costs roughly the same, although a $10 interstate charge is added to the fare. If you have a preference for which route to take into or out of Manhattan, tell the driver in advance. And be forewarned: although they are required by law to do so, cab drivers in Manhattan don't like taking people to the airport because it's sometimes hard to get quick fares back. In fact, they aren't even allowed to pick up passengers at Newark.

If a taxi seems a little steep, several companies run shuttle buses and vans between Manhattan and the airports. If you're alone and going to a major hotel in midtown, you can really save money by taking a shuttle bus. But it may not be worth it if there are three or four people in your party, if you're in a hurry, or if you're headed for a friend's apartment or an out-of-the-way hotel. Shuttle-bus tickets and schedules are available at the ground transportation desks at all three airports. The two largest shuttle companies are Carey and Gray Line. Carey has frequently scheduled bus service between LaGuardia and Kennedy, and to and from those airports and both its ticket office at 125 Park Avenue (between 41st and 42nd streets) and the Port Authority Bus Terminal's airport bus center (on the ground floor of the north terminal, right inside the entrance on West 42nd Street between Eighth and Ninth avenues). Tickets cost $13.50 to or from LaGuardia, $16.50 to or from Kennedy, and $14 to or from Newark per person. (Call 212/315-3006 for more information.) You can also take a New Jersey Transit bus between the Port Authority Bus Terminal's airport bus center and any airline terminal at Newark. A one-way ticket costs $7 or a round-trip ticket $12 per person. (Call 201/762-5100 for more information.) If you really want to save money and have all the time in the world, $1.50 will buy you a trip on the M60 bus between the corner of Broadway and West 116th Street (just outside the main gates to the Columbia University campus) and both the main terminal and the Marine Terminal at LaGuardia. The same $1.50 will get you a ride on the A train and then on a free shuttle bus from the Howard Beach subway stop through the long-term parking lots to Kennedy. Like everything else, these prices are subject to change, and it's worth asking about discounts for children and senior citizens. Moreover, these are by no means the only airport shuttle services. For a more complete list of options, call the Port Authority's Air-Ride recording (800/247-7433).

A third option is calling a private car or limousine service ahead of time and having a driver meet you at the gate or in the baggage claim area. The driver holds up a sign with your last name on it—which, depending on your personality, can make you feel important, embarrassed, or a little bit of both. Be forewarned that this can be pretty pricey, particularly if the driver has to wait because your flight is delayed. (They charge for waiting time.) Costs to and from LaGuardia run anywhere from around $25 plus tip if you just want a sedan and everything goes smoothly to well over $100 if there are delays or you request a limousine. Prices are higher to and from Kennedy and Newark. You can go to the ground transportation desks at any of the three airports to get a sedan or limousine after you've arrived. (For the names and phone numbers of several large, reputable companies, see the "Transportation" section in this chapter.)

Finally, if you're coming or going from LaGuardia, you can take the Delta Water Shuttle. It ferries passengers between LaGuardia's Marine Terminal and both Pier 11 near Wall Street and the 34th Street Pier on the East River. You don't need to be a Delta Airlines passenger and the shuttle often takes less time than a taxi, but it only runs hourly on weekday mornings and in the late afternoon. Tickets cost $20 one-way, $30 round-trip. Call Delta at 800/221-1212 for more information.

TRAINS—Dozens of Amtrak trains come in and out of New York City every day. The service is concentrated in what's called the Northeast Corridor, between Washington, D.C. and Boston, but you can catch a train between New York and Florida, Chicago, or even Seattle and many cities in Canada. Trains arrive and depart from Pennsylvania Station (usually called Penn Station), underneath Madison Square Garden between West 31st and West 33rd streets and Seventh and Eighth avenues. Penn Station is a major subway hub, but you also can find a legitimate and well-organized taxicab line immediately outside the doors once you've gone up the stairs at the far end of the main Amtrak concourse. (Under *no* circumstances should you go with someone who comes up to you either inside or outside Penn Station asking if you need a taxi or help with your bags.) You can choose between the Metroliner, sleeping cars, and other kinds of service. Multi-day excursion passes are also available. Although the station is no treat, a separate waiting area for ticketed Amtrak passengers in the middle of the main concourse makes it tolerable. If you need to stash your luggage for a couple hours and are willing to pay $1.50 per bag, you'll find an efficient and safe storage area near the far left end of the Amtrak ticket windows. (Call Amtrak at 800/872-7245 for fare and schedule information.) Train service to and from Connecticut and suburban New York is run by MetroNorth through Grand Central Station.

DRIVING—If you can avoid driving to or in New York, by all means do. You will end up paying exorbitant prices for tolls and parking (and your mental health will inevitably suffer, too). The fact that most New Yorkers don't own cars ought to tell you something! Indeed, the state of New York actually stopped giving driving tests in New York City a decade ago, and it's illegal for anyone under the age of 18 to drive here (which may explain the decidedly unreassuring fact that an estimated 15% of all New York drivers do not have valid licenses!). Once you're in New York, the only time you may possibly need a car is if you want to leave for a day or two—and then you can rent one, as a lot of New Yorkers do. The public transportation system in New York is extremely efficient and is used frequently by just about everyone.

If you still aren't convinced or have no alternative, get a map before setting out and study it carefully. The three major approaches to the city involve the New England Thruway (I-95), the New York State Thruway (I-87), and the New Jersey Turnpike (I-95). Expect long waits during rush hour at the bridges and tunnels leading in and out of Manhattan. Tune in AM radio stations 770, 880, or 1010 for area traffic reports if you're trying to decide which approach to take. Expect to pay around $3 or $4 for whichever bridge or tunnel you choose, although most charge only those cars entering Manhattan.

GETTING AROUND

In case you don't already know, I'll let you in on a secret: this book isn't really about New York. It isn't even about New York City. It's about Manhattan. Most people (including me) use New York, New York City, "the city," and Manhattan synonymously. But New York is one of the Northeast's largest states, and New York City actually includes five separate boroughs: Manhattan, Staten Island, the Bronx, Queens, and Brooklyn. Of those five boroughs, only the Bronx is attached to the mainland. Manhattan and the other three are all islands.

A LITTLE HISTORY—Now that you know we're talking only about the island of Manhattan, a little history may help you make sense of how the city is laid out. Native Americans were the first known residents of this area. Italian explorer Giovanni da Verrazano (for whom the Verrazano Narrows Bridge, between Brooklyn and Staten Island, is named) sailed into New York Harbor in 1524 and "discovered" Manhattan for his French patron, King Francis I. In 1609 Dutch East India Company trader Henry Hudson sailed into the harbor and up the river that now bears his name. The first permanent European settlement in Manhattan, a Dutch trading post called Nieuw Amsterdam, was established in 1625 at the very southern tip of the island, where Battery Park is today. The story you've probably already heard is true: the island was "bought" by the Dutch West India Company a year later from local Indians with beads, cloth, and other goods worth roughly $24. It was renamed New York in 1664 after the British—in the person of Charles II's brother, the Duke of York—gained control of the still tiny settlement.

It's hard to imagine today, but such areas as midtown and even Greenwich Village were way out in the country for another 150 years. Indeed, Wall Street is so named because a wall of logs was erected there in the middle of the 17th century to protect the farms in lower Manhattan from the wilderness beyond. New York's population—only 60,000 as late as 1800—remained concentrated on the southern tip of the island, while most of Manhattan was used for country estates and farmland or just left as forests and wilderness. When a commission headed by engineer John Randall, Jr., laid out a grid system for the largely undeveloped area from Houston Street north to 155th Street in 1807, the city's minute population laughed at the thought that it would ever be necessary.

THE RANDALL PLAN—For those of us trying to find our way around Manhattan, the so-called Randall Plan is a godsend. The streets below Houston (pronounced *House*-ton), particularly those below Canal Street, are laid out like the Dutch farm trails they once were. Even those that are relatively straight were not built for 20th-century traffic: the world-famous Wall Street, for example, is more narrow than the typical suburban driveway. Truth be told, not much about the city's layout makes sense south of about 14th Street. If you're ever at the corner of West 4th Street and West 10th Street in Greenwich Village, you'll know what I mean!

Thanks to the Randall Plan, however, everything north of 14th Street is as simple as a major city can be. Other than Broadway, originally an Indian path and now one of the country's longest streets (it extends from the southern tip of Manhattan to Albany as Route 9), and some of the streets in northern Manhattan, the streets and avenues are laid out in a north-south, east-west grid. All of the east-west streets are numbered, as are many of the north-south avenues. In general, most avenues are one-way and are alternately northbound and southbound. Most streets are one-way as well; the even-numbered ones tend to be eastbound, while the odd-numbered ones tend to be westbound. Exceptions include such major east-west thoroughfares as Canal, Houston, 14th, 23rd, 34th, 42nd, 57th, 72nd, 79th, 86th, and 96th streets. (See the "Key to Addresses" section following this one if you need help finding a specific address.)

EAST SIDE, WEST SIDE – Starting just north of Washington Square Park at about 8th Street in Greenwich Village, Fifth Avenue divides the city into East and West sides. Broadway acts as the east-west dividing line south of Washington Square, although it runs a little east of where Fifth Avenue would be. That east-west distinction is important, as most addresses in New York reflect it. For example, 125 East 52nd Street and 125 West 52nd Street are two distinct locations several blocks apart.

Let's start with the East Side of the city. Moving east from Fifth Avenue toward the East River, you'll find Madison Avenue, Park Avenue (Park Avenue South below East 34th Street and Fourth Avenue below that), Lexington Avenue (Irving Place between East 14th and East 20th streets), Third Avenue, Second Avenue, and First Avenue. Madison Avenue doesn't start until East 23rd Street, while Lexington Avenue begins as Irving Place at East 14th Street. Sutton Place starts at about East 51st Street between First Avenue and the river, turns into York Avenue at East 60th, and then stops at East 92nd Street. East End Avenue runs between York Avenue and the river from East 79th Street to East 90th Street. All of these avenues run north-south, parallel to Fifth Avenue. FDR Drive ("the FDR" to locals) runs between the easternmost avenue and the river, along the East Side of the island.

The West Side of Manhattan is a little more confusing. Moving west from Fifth Avenue toward the Hudson River, you'll find Avenue of the Americas (or Sixth Avenue, as everyone still calls it, despite the official name change in the 1950s), Seventh Avenue, Eighth Avenue (Central Park West north of West 59th Street), Ninth Avenue (Columbus Avenue north of West 59th Street), Tenth Avenue (Amsterdam Avenue north of West 59th Street), and Eleventh Avenue (West End Avenue north of West 59th Street until it ends at West 107th Street). You'll also find Broadway on the West Side above West 23rd Street. Avenue of the Americas and Seventh Avenue both end at the bottom of Central Park. Riverside Drive is between West End Avenue and the river running north from West 72nd Street. All of these avenues run north-south, parallel to Fifth Avenue (except Broadway, which meanders from time to time before more or less straightening out around West 79th Street). The Henry Hudson Parkway (also known as the West Side Highway and sometimes called Twelfth Avenue around midtown) runs along the entire West Side of the city.

Central Park occupies land between 59th and 110th streets, further dividing Manhattan's East and West sides. Fifth Avenue runs along the East Side of the park, and everything east of it is know as the Upper East Side. Central Park West runs along the West Side of the park, and everything west of it is known as the Upper West Side. Both the Upper East Side and the Upper West Side are largely residential, although most of the north-south avenues (as opposed to the east-west numbered streets) have plenty of shops and stores.

NORTHERN MANHATTAN – The avenues on the east side remain fairly consistent as they move north of Central Park into the area known as East (or Spanish) Harlem. East of Fifth Avenue, north of the park in Harlem itself, Lenox Avenue (which soon becomes Malcolm X Boulevard) picks up where Avenue of the Americas left off below the park; Adam Clayton Powell, Jr. Boulevard picks up where Seventh Avenue left off; and Central Park West becomes Frederick Douglass Boulevard. Amsterdam Avenue, Broadway, and Riverside Drive all remain relatively consistent as they move north, but such major roads as Convent Avenue, Saint Nicholas Avenue, Edgecombe Avenue, and Fort Washington Avenue also appear in Harlem and in the northern tip of Manhattan.

KEY TO ADDRESSES

So how do you find an address in Manhattan? I'm not sure who came up with the following systems, but I do know they work and aren't as complicated as they look.

AVENUES – If you know an address on one of the north-south avenues, you can determine the approximate cross street by canceling the last number, dividing the remainder by two, and adding or subtracting the relevant number listed below.

Avenue A, B, C, or D	Add 3
First Avenue	Add 3
Second Avenue	Add 3
Third Avenue	Add 10
Lexington Avenue	Add 22
Fourth Avenue/Park Avenue South	Add 8
Park Avenue	Add 35
Madison Avenue	Add 26
Fifth Avenue	
Address up to 200	Add 13
Between 201 and 400	Add 16
Between 401 and 600	Add 18
Between 601 and 774	Add 20
Between 775 and 1286	Subtract 18
Between 1289 and 1500	Add 45
Above 2000	Add 24
Sixth Avenue/Avenue of the Americas	Subtract 12
Lenox Avenue/Malcolm X Boulevard	Add 110
Seventh Avenue	Add 12
Adam Clayton Powell, Jr. Boulevard	Add 20
Broadway	
Up to 754 is below 8th Street	
755 to 846	Subtract 29
847 to 953	Subtract 25
Above 953	Subtract 31

Eighth Avenue	Add 10
Ninth Avenue	Add 13
Columbus Avenue	Add 60
Tenth Avenue	Add 14
Amsterdam Avenue	Add 60
Eleventh Avenue	Add 15
West End Avenue	Add 60
Convent Avenue	Add 127
St. Nicholas Avenue	Add 110
Manhattan Avenue	Add 100
Edgecombe Avenue	Add 134
Fort Washington Avenue	Add 158

Central Park West and Riverside Drive don't fit into this formula but have ones of their own. To find the cross street for a building on Central Park West, divide the address by 10 and add 60. To find the cross street for a building on Riverside Drive up to West 165th Street, divide the address by 10 and add 72.

A word of caution: because certain addresses, particularly those on Fifth, Madison, and Park avenues, are thought to be particularly prestigious, many buildings use them even though their entrance is on a side street. This is most common in midtown and on Fifth Avenue in the Upper East Side. If you can't find a building with such an address, look around the corner.

CROSS STREETS – The numbered cross streets run east-west. Addresses on them are easy to find. Allow for a little variation below East 23rd Street (because Madison, Eleventh, and Twelfth avenues have yet to begin) and throughout the city whenever Broadway is involved.

EAST SIDE

1 to 49	Between Fifth Avenue and Madison Avenue
50 to 99	Between Madison Avenue and Park Avenue
100 to 149	Between Park Avenue and Lexington Avenue
150 to 199	Between Lexington Avenue and Third Avenue
200 to 299	Between Third Avenue and Second Avenue
300 to 399	Between Second Avenue and First Avenue
400 to 499	Between First Avenue and York Avenue

WEST SIDE BELOW 59th STREET

1 to 99	Between Fifth Avenue and Avenue of the Americas
100 to 199	Between Avenue of the Americas and Seventh Avenue
200 to 299	Between Seventh Avenue and Eighth Avenue
300 to 399	Between Eighth Avenue and Ninth Avenue
400 to 499	Between Ninth Avenue and Tenth Avenue
500 to 599	Between Tenth Avenue and Eleventh Avenue
600 and up	Between Eleventh Avenue and Twelfth Avenue

WEST SIDE ABOVE 59th STREET

1 to 99	Between Central Park West and Columbus Avenue
100 to 199	Between Columbus Avenue and Amsterdam Avenue
200 to 299	Between Amsterdam Avenue and West End Avenue
Above 300	Between West End Avenue and Riverside Drive

Odd-numbered addresses on east-west streets are on the north (uptown) side of the street, while even-numbered ones are on the south (downtown) side.

NEIGHBORHOODS

It may be hard for visitors to think of it this way, but New York is really a collection of small neighborhoods. Some are more famous than others, but each has a history and flavor all its own. To get a full sense of this wonderful city, I encourage you to visit as many of these neighborhoods as possible. From north to south, they include:

INWOOD AND WASHINGTON HEIGHTS – Home to General George Washington's forces during the Revolutionary War, these neighborhoods cover all of Manhattan north of about West 151st Street. Racially and ethnically mixed, they have been home to generations of immigrants and now include both middle-class and quite poor areas. Several large and remarkably unspoiled parks, Yeshiva University, the Dyckman Farmhouse, the Cloisters, Columbia-Presbyterian Hospital, and Audubon Terrace are all in this area, as is the entrance to the George Washington Bridge. As the name implies, Washington Heights contains some surprisingly steep sections.

HARLEM – There are actually two Harlems: East Harlem (also called Spanish Harlem) and Harlem proper. East Harlem begins at about East 96th Street and runs on the east side of the island to its northern tip. The population of this area is almost entirely Latino, and Spanish is often spoken more frequently than English here. El Museo del Barrio is on the southwestern edge of East Harlem, while La Marqueta, the oldest public market still standing in New York and one of the best places in the city to buy fresh fruit and vegetables, is a little further north.

Harlem itself begins in a small corridor in the middle of the island at the top of Central Park (at West 110th Street) and then extends both north and west at the famous and always busy 125th Street. The population of Harlem is almost entirely African-American, and the historic neighborhood is known around the world as a center of African-American music, politics, and culture. As do Inwood and Washington Heights, Harlem includes both middle-class and very poor areas. You'll find the Schomburg Center for Research in Black Culture, Abyssinian Baptist Church, and the Studio Museum of Harlem here.

MORNINGSIDE HEIGHTS – This relatively small but vibrant area runs between Morningside Drive and the Hudson River from West 110th Street north to West 124th Street. The stretch of Broadway between those streets is the neighborhood's economic heart. The area is dominated by three large and well-known institutions: Columbia University, Riverside Church, and the Cathedral Church of St. John the Divine. Grant's Tomb is also here, across the street from Riverside Church at West 122nd Street in Riverside Park. The neighborhood is full of students and professors from all over the world.

UPPER WEST SIDE – A primarily residential area extending west of Central Park to the Hudson River from West 59th Street all the way north to West 110th Street, the Upper West Side is home to such famous apartment buildings as the Dakota and the Ansonia. The neighborhood is racially and ethnically mixed, and its residents pride themselves on their reputation for being politically progressive and tending toward the bohemian (although by downtown standards as I noted in the section on Chelsea, Upper West Siders are decidedly conventional). In the southern part of the neighborhood, ABC's studio (where soap operas are taped) and Lincoln Center dominate the low and high ends of cultural life. The fabulous food stores Fairway and Zabar's are landmarks a bit further north, as are the American Museum of Natural History and the New York Historical Society. The Barnes & Noble at Broadway and 82nd Street has become a major force in the neighborhood as well. Columbus Avenue, Amsterdam Avenue, and Broadway are lined with stores, while Central Park West, West End Avenue, and Riverside Drive are almost exclusively residential. The most elegant living sections of the Upper West Side are on Central Park West and the cross streets in the high 60s, the 70s, and the low 80s. Tourists probably won't want to spend time wandering north of West 96th Street, particularly on Columbus and Amsterdam avenues.

UPPER EAST SIDE – Although it's best known for its art museums, galleries, and upscale boutiques, the Upper East Side is also a prestigious residential neighborhood. Most of the city's elite private schools are here, too. It covers the area east of Central Park from Fifth Avenue to the East River between East 59th Street and East 96th Street. Fifth Avenue (also known as Museum Mile) is dominated by such famous institutions as the Metropolitan, Guggenheim, and Cooper-Hewitt museums, although it is also home to a large number of expensive apartment buildings, former mansions, and foreign consulates. You'll find the Whitney Museum and lots of galleries and upscale boutiques on Madison Avenue. Park Avenue and most of the cross streets are home to both residential buildings and such institutions as the Asia Society and the Americas Society. From Lexington Avenue east to the river above East 75th Street (an area known as Yorkville), rents go down a bit. You'll find Gracie Mansion, the mayor's residence, in Carl Schurz Park overlooking the river at about East 88th Street. Bloomingdale's is a major retail force in the southern end of the Upper East Side.

MIDTOWN – Squarely in the middle of the island south of Central Park, midtown Manhattan is one of the busiest places on earth on weekdays and almost deserted on Sundays (except during Christmas season). The area extends from 42nd to 59th streets between about Third and Seventh avenues. Fifth Avenue is the heart of midtown and one of the world's most famous shopping areas. The flagship stores of Tiffany's, FAO Schwarz, Lord & Taylor, Saks Fifth Avenue, Bergdorf Goodman, and all sorts of other upscale retailers are located here, as are a number of bookstores, Niketown, the Warner Brothers Studio Store, and other new "superstores." Many stately mansions once lined this part of Fifth Avenue, but only a few remain and none is actually used as a residence anymore.

St. Patrick's Cathedral and several other famous churches are also on Fifth Avenue in midtown, while St. Bartholomew's is on Park Avenue and the stately Central Synagogue is on Lexington Avenue. Landmark buildings like the Citicorp Center, Trump Tower, Rockefeller Center, and the Chrysler Building dominate the skyline here. Carnegie Hall, the Ed Sullivan Theater, and Radio City Music Hall sit on the western edge of midtown. Many of the city's tonier stores and galleries are on both sides of 57th Street in the northern part of midtown. Many of the hot "theme" restaurants, including Planet Hollywood, the Hard Rock Cafe, and the Motown Cafe, occupy the west side of 57th Street. Grand Central Station, the New York Public Library, and Bryant Park mark midtown's southern edge.

CLINTON – Home to the Hell's Kitchen Gang in the late 19th and early 20th centuries, this neighborhood was once among the most violent and dangerous in the nation. It stretches south from West 59th Street to about West 34th Street between Eighth Avenue and the Hudson River. Although the hype surrounding the ongoing rejuvenation of 42nd Street and the X-rated area around the Port Authority Bus Terminal sometimes outstrips the reality, the area is significantly cleaner and more family-friendly than it was even a year or two ago. In and around Times Square itself, a giant Disney store, the Virgin Records superstore, and several new theaters will soon be joined by another Warner Brothers Studio Store and an interactive arcade created in part by Steven Speilberg's Dream Works. Ninth Avenue, particularly in the high 30s and low 40s, is home to a lot of ethnic grocers, bakers, and butchers, and the west end of 42nd Street is home to a number of very good off-Broadway theaters. The Jacob K. Javits Convention Center and most of the city's passenger ship terminals are located here along the Hudson River.

MURRAY HILL — Covering the area between East 42nd Street south to East 34th Street, Murray Hill begins at Park Avenue and runs to the East River. This area is almost entirely residential; you'll find the nicest part around Park Avenue in the upper 30s. The only real visitor attractions are the Pierpont Morgan Library and the incredible new Science, Industry, and Business Library in the old B. Altman building at Madison and 34th Street.

CHELSEA — This is one of Manhattan's hottest areas. Another largely residential neighborhood, it extends from West 34th Street down to West 14th Street, and from Sixth Avenue west to the Hudson River. Madison Square Garden, Penn Station, and the city's main post office are all in the northeast corner of Chelsea, but it's the southern part of the neighborhood that has really taken off. Surprisingly quiet and relatively clean, the southwestern part of Chelsea has lots of turn-of-the-century townhouses and small apartment buildings. It's also home to the lovely grounds of the General Theological Seminary and the Chelsea Piers development, as well as the city's latest gallery craze (on and around the far west end of West 22nd Street). The southeastern edge of Chelsea, particularly where Chelsea and the Flatiron district overlap along Sixth Avenue in the high teens and low 20s, has become what it was a century ago: a retailing hub. Such superstores as Bed Bath and Beyond, Barnes & Noble, and Burlington Coat Factory occupy buildings that once housed famous department stores. The original Barney's, a clothing store New Yorkers swear by, is also in the southern part of Chelsea, as are a number of restaurants and nightspots.

FLATIRON DISTRICT — Named for the historic Flatiron Building, an architectural curiosity at the intersection of Broadway and Fifth Avenue at 23rd Street, this area was known in the late 19th Century as Ladies' Mile for its elegant department stores. (A famous jingle at the time was "From Eighth Street down, the men are earning it/From Eighth Street up, the women are spending it.") Those department stores went out of business at the beginning of this century, but the buildings and the neighborhood are again alive and well, thanks in large part to an influx of "superstores." The Flatiron District runs between Park Avenue South and Sixth Avenue and from 23rd Street south to 14th Street. Sixth Avenue is really thriving now, and parts of Fifth Avenue in this area also have undergone a resurgence lately. The Church of the Transfiguration (affectionately known as "the Little Church around the Corner"), the Marble Collegiate Church, and the Empire State Building are all just north of here.

GRAMERCY PARK — This aging but still pleasant neighborhood was once the city's most elegant residential area. It covers the area between Park Avenue South to Second Avenue and from East 34th Street South to East 14th Street. The nicest part of this area is around Gramercy Park itself. The city's only remaining private park, it is bounded by Park Avenue South and Third Avenue and by East 20th and East 21st streets. A stroll down Irving Place, which runs from the park south to East 14th Street, can be very pleasant indeed. The Flatiron District and the Gramercy Park area meet at Union Square, a lively area that serves to divide them from Greenwich Village and is home to the city's largest and most popular Greenmarket. The New York Police Academy and Theodore Roosevelt's birthplace are on the western edge of Gramercy Park, and Stuyvesant Park occupies both sides of Second Avenue between East 15th and East 17th streets. Two enormous residential areas, Stuyvesant Town and Peter Cooper Village, are just east of here abutting the East River, as is Bellevue Hospital.

MEATPACKING DISTRICT – This is one of the city's more bizarre and fascinating neighborhoods. Don't get me wrong: I'm not suggesting you wander around here. But the neighborhood west of Ninth Avenue from 15th Street south to Gansevoort Street between Chelsea and the West Village is being shaped by a collision of interesting forces. Traditionally this dirty, architecturally uninteresting area has been the home of New York's meatpacking industry, as well as a great deal of prostitution. But the number of meat businesses has been cut in half in recent years and community action has forced at least some of the prostitution elsewhere. Meanwhile, artists, bar owners, and even young families are being attracted by the neighborhood's cheap rents. Unfortunately, the sort of X-rated places that used to populate Times Square are being attracted by those rents and the neighborhood's unrestrictive zoning regulations. The result is a weird mix of trendy bars, wholesale meatpacking plants, studios, transvestites, and families with small children. Only in New York!

EAST VILLAGE – A hundred and fifty years ago the Astors, the Vanderbilts, and much of the rest of the city's elite lived here, but today the East Village is among the city's funkiest neighborhoods. It sits between Avenue B and Broadway from East 14th Street south to East Houston Street. Alphabet City (the avenues that begin in the eastern part of the East Village with alphabet names) and Tompkins Square are much tamer than they were in the 1980s, and some parts have become downright family friendly, but they're still home to a great many offbeat nightclubs. The area around East 6th Street between First and Second avenues is a thriving ethnic enclave known as Little India, while the area around East 7th Street and Third Avenue is home to a great many Ukrainian immigrants. The Ukrainian Museum, St. Mark's in the Bowery, and Grace Church are all in the northern part of the East Village. Old Merchant's House, the last remnant of the East Village of yesteryear, is on the neighborhood's western edge.

GREENWICH VILLAGE – Although Greenwich Village is best known today for the beatniks and jazz clubs of the 1950s, Edgar Allan Poe, Walt Whitman, Edna St. Vincent Millay, Frederic Church, and Edward Hopper all lived here at one time or another. In fact, this area has been among the city's most vibrant centers of culture since relatively affluent New Yorkers began moving here in the early part of the 19th century to avoid the epidemics of the increasingly crowded city to the south. Greenwich Village covers most of the area from Broadway west to the Hudson River and from West 14th Street south to West Houston. The section from Seventh Avenue west to the river is known to locals as the West Village, and the northern part of the section west of Ninth Avenue is the Meatpacking District (see above). The beautiful Jefferson Market Library, the Forbes Magazine Galleries, New York University, and lots of interesting shops and nightclubs are located here, as is the always lively Washington Square Park and its famed arch.

SOHO—Short for *South of Houston*, Soho went from being the center of New York in the middle of the last century to an almost entirely abandoned wasteland in the middle of this century. Discovered by artists looking for inexpensive space in the 1960s and by upscale retailers in the early 1990s, it's now a trendy and energetic neighborhood known for its galleries, lofts, performance spaces, and hip cafes. (In fact, it's so trendy—that is to say, crowded and overrun with tourists—that many of the galleries have begun to move to 57th Street in midtown and to the hot new gallery area at the western edge of Chelsea.) It begins several blocks south of Washington Square Park on West Houston and runs south to Canal Street between Broadway and Sixth Avenue. The neighborhood is most alive on weekends and in the evening. Almost everything down here stays open later than similar establishments in the rest of the city. You'll find the Alternative Museum, the Museum for African Art, the New Museum of Contemporary Art, and the Guggenheim Soho on the same block of Broadway between Houston and Prince streets. Many of the neighborhood's commercial galleries are concentrated on and around West Broadway (a separate street four blocks east of Broadway) between Houston and Broome streets.

TRIBECA—Shorthand for *Triangle Below Canal*, Tribeca used to be a rather dull and dirty commercial district but is becoming both residential and every bit as chic as Soho. It covers the area from Canal Street south to Chambers Street and from Broadway west to the Hudson River. Although it doesn't look as upscale as you might expect, Tribeca is home to emerging and established artists, commercial galleries, converted loft apartments, movie stars (Robert DeNiro's Tribeca Film Center has been a boon), and some good restaurants.

CHINATOWN—This neighborhood's 150,000 residents in roughly 40 square blocks make up the largest concentration of Chinese outside of Asia. Because it is always growing and increasingly overlaps such neighborhoods as Little Italy and the Lower East Side, Chinatown has boundaries nobody can quite agree how to define. I'll use the Chinatown Tourism Council's definition: from Grand Street south to Worth Street, between Broadway and Allen Street. Its busiest streets are Canal, Mott, and Pell. If you've ever been to Hong Kong or southern China, you'll be overwhelmed by the similarities between those places and this neighborhood. Look for all sorts of wonderful food stores down here, as well as the Museum of Chinese in the Americas and the marvelous Chinese New Year parade and celebration.

LITTLE ITALY—No longer home to many Italian immigrants and seemingly shrinking every year as Chinatown expands, this area nonetheless remains the emotional heart of the entire region's Italian-American population, many of whom return for weddings, funerals, holidays, and other special occasions. Mulberry Street (better known as Via San Gennaro) between Canal and Prince streets is the center of Little Italy and is known for its restaurants and festivals.

LOWER EAST SIDE—Many people use the Lower East Side as a geographic umbrella for Chinatown, Little Italy, and the Bowery, but I know it as a distinct neighborhood where generations of Eastern European and other immigrants first settled in overcrowded tenements and worked in sweatshops so their children could have better lives. (Many newer immigrants still live and work here in conditions that are not as much improved as you might think.) I also know it as the best place in Manhattan to shop for high-quality clothing, household goods, and accessories at a discount. Because many of the area's businesses are run by observant Jews, many stores are closed on Friday afternoon and Saturday. Sunday is *the* shopping day here. Canal and Orchard Streets are the area's heart, but it extends broadly from East Houston south to Canal and from the Sara D. Roosevelt Parkway east to Ludlow Street. The area is pretty run-down and some of the stores are really struggling these days, but it's still worth a visit. Make sure to stop by the Lower East Side Tenement Museum and the Eldridge Street Synagogue while you're here to get a sense of the area's rich history. A stop at the Lower East Side Visitors' Center (261 Broome Street, between Orchard and Allen streets) is also well worth your while. The even more run-down area known as the Bowery is just west of the Lower East Side.

DOWNTOWN – This area is a little hard to define except to say that it's centered around City Hall. Very roughly speaking, it runs between Chambers Street south to Fulton Street and from West Broadway east to Pearl Street. Lots of mom and pop stores as well as major chains are sited here, and its streets are always busy. However, the beautiful St. Paul's Chapel, the Woolworth Building, and the entrance to the Brooklyn Bridge's pedestrian walkway are virtually the only reasons for a tourist to come down here. It's not a dangerous area, but it always seems dirtier than the rest of the city. The South Street Seaport is located just east of here.

LOWER MANHATTAN – Extending from Battery Park in the south through Wall Street and other older parts of the Financial District in the north, this is the oldest part of New York City. Things are very compact and tall down here: the streets are as narrow as the buildings are big. The boat to the Statue of Liberty and Ellis Island leaves from near Castle Clinton National Monument in Battery Park, and the Staten Island Ferry's terminal is just east of the park. Look for the exceptional Museum of the American Indian, Trinity Church, the Federal Hall National Memorial, Fraunces Tavern Museum, and the New York Stock Exchange in lower Manhattan.

BATTERY PARK CITY – A relatively new residential area built entirely on landfill, this collection of high-rise apartment buildings sits on the western side of Manhattan's southern tip, starting a little bit north of Battery Park itself. The World Financial Center, where a lot of its residents work, is planted squarely in the middle of this neighborhood.

SHOPPING DISTRICTS

If you were going to open a specialty store, would you choose a location right between two existing stores that specialize in exactly the same thing? No? Then you're not a real New Yorker. Unlike other cities where the whole idea is to move into a neighborhood that doesn't have whatever you're selling, New York is full of areas like the four-block stretch of Canal Street in Chinatown that has virtually nothing but stores selling cheap gold jewelry. The city also has wonderful shopping districts for everything from diamonds to flowers to beads and trimming. The merchants seem to thrive on the competition.

   Two basic rules govern shopping in New York: you should never pay retail, and the best deals are often in "the districts." While there are not as many cohesive districts in New York as there once were, the ones that remain are well worth a visit.

ANTIQUES – Because rents are so expensive and the antique market is pretty soft, many dealers have either moved in together or moved out to the Bronx. If you're looking for really elegant pieces and money is not a concern, try some of the galleries in the somewhat fading two-story underground Place des Antiquaires (135 East 57th Street, between Park and Lexington avenues) and in the trilevel Manhattan Art & Antiques Center (Second Avenue at East 50th Street). You'll also find lots of individual stores of varying quality along Broadway just south of Union Square, in Soho, and sprinkled on and around East 60th Street and Madison Avenue on the Upper East Side. More adventurous shoppers ought to try Bruckner Boulevard in the Mott Haven section of the South Bronx.

DIAMONDS – This is the epitome of a New York shopping district and one of those places you have to see to believe. Concentrated on West 47th Street between Fifth and Sixth avenues, the Diamond District glitters with great deals on diamonds and other jewelry. Be careful, however. I've recommended a couple of places in the "Jewelry" section of Chapter VI, and I urge you to stick with them. Insist on seeing the Gemological Institute of America's report on any stone you're thinking about buying. All diamonds have one. Many of the businesses in the Diamond District are run by observant Jews, which means they're closed on Friday afternoons and Saturdays.

FABRIC, BEADS, AND TRIMMING – Part of the spillover from the garment district, this area is in the upper West 30s and lower West 40s, between Sixth and Seventh avenues. A lot of stores are up a flight or two of stairs, where rents are cheaper. In addition to every imaginable kind of fabric, bead, and trimming, you'll find hats, feathers, buckles, and bangles here. You can also find a couple of good fabric stores in the Lower East Side and on Broadway between Leonard and Broome streets. Look in the "Fabrics, Trimming" section of Chapter VI for particularly good ones.

FISH – Despite a major fire in 1995 and recent city intervention, the Fulton Fish Market continues to thrive as the city's source of fresh fish and seafood. Hard as it may be to believe, 125 million pounds of seafood are sold here annually. The market operates between midnight and 8 a.m. in the South Street Seaport at the eastern end of Fulton Street, just above the Financial District. They do sell to individuals and the prices are great, but 6 a.m. is considered late for a shopping expedition. If you want fresh fish but can't face those hours, look on Grand and Canal streets in Chinatown for significantly better prices than you'll find anywhere else in Manhattan.

FLOWERS – Roses are sold at deep discounts in specialty stores all over the city, and some of the biggest flower wholesalers have moved out to the South Bronx because of escalating rents in Manhattan. Still, the area between West 26th and West 30th streets and Sixth and Seventh avenues remains *the* place to get the best prices on flowers and plants. Business is done here very early in the morning, but wholesalers usually are willing to sell to individuals who show up by 7 a.m. Planters, soil, and other supplies also are sold in this area.

FUR – Go to the wholesale fur district between West 27th and 30th streets on and around Seventh Avenue if you want some great buys. As with diamonds, be careful. (I've listed some particularly good stores under "Furs" in the "Clothing and Accessories" section in Chapter VI.) While animal-rights advocates have made significant inroads into this market in recent years, many men and women still wear furs in New York in the winter. If you have questions, call the American Fur Industry at 212/564-5133.

FURNITURE—The wholesale furniture warehouses and showrooms are located on Lexington Avenue between East 29th and East 33rd streets, but the public is not welcome at most of them. It's worth going down there, however, as some showrooms have special sales when they change their displays, and a few will let you come in. Another good bet is the nearby North Carolina Furniture Showroom (Fifth Avenue at 21st Street), where the public is welcome. More specialized furniture stores have begun creating their own district in the area around Varick and Spring streets in Tribeca.

GALLERIES—Three areas in Manhattan are home to the vast majority of its art galleries: 57th Street in midtown, West Broadway and surrounding streets in Soho, and, most recently, the area between 26th and 20th streets west of Ninth Avenue in Chelsea. The 57th Street galleries tend to sell works by more established and conventional artists, while more innovative work is being shown these days in some of the Chelsea galleries. "Gallery hopping" is a favorite New York pastime. (See the "Galleries" section of Chapter III for more information about specific galleries.)

HANDBAGS—The area in the high 20s and 30s off Fifth Avenue has all sorts of good handbag stores. Look up, as most of them are on upper floors. The Lower East Side also has a couple stores with good discounts on fine leather and other handbags. (I've listed some of the stores in both areas under "Women's Accessories" in the "Clothing and Accessories" section of Chapter VI.)

INTERNATIONAL FOOD—A lot of people write off Ninth Avenue in the high 30s and low 40s as nothing more than the dull, dirty back door to Port Authority Bus Terminal. A closer look, however, reveals a startling concentration of ethnic grocery stores, butcher shops, restaurants, and bakeries. Whether you're looking for fresh Italian bread, West African cassavas, or West Indian spices, this is a great place. The Ninth Avenue International Food Festival is held here on the third weekend in May.

MEN'S DISCOUNT CLOTHING—Look in the Flatiron District on and around Fifth Avenue between 18th and 21st streets for some really good deals on men's clothing. This is another neighborhood where you need to look up to find most stores, although the people handing out flyers for them will be more than happy to give you directions. (I've listed some of the best stores in this area under "Men's, General" in the "Clothing and Accessories" section of Chapter VI.)

SUPERSTORES—Whether you love them or hate them, the invasion of the so-called superstores is now a part of Manhattan's history. Several national chains and corporations, including Nike, Coca-Cola, Warner Brothers, and, as of 1998, the Gap, have superstores along Fifth Avenue in the 50s. A great many high-end designers, including Armani, Prada, Valentino, and Vuitton, have superstores on East 57th Street near Madison Avenue. Some of the more suburban chains, including Burlington Coat Factory, Old Navy, Bed Bath and Beyond, and Today's Man, now dominate Sixth and Seventh avenues in Chelsea. And Virgin Records and Disney (to be joined by Warner Brothers) are just the most high-profile superstores in and around Times Square.

THRIFT SHOPS—You can find some offbeat thrift shops in the East Village, while the more upscale ones are in Gramercy Park, on Madison Avenue in the East 80s, and in the Yorkville section of the Upper East Side (First, Second, Third, and Lexington avenues in the upper East 70s, 80s, and lower 90s). We aren't talking Salvation Army here, but as a general rule the quality goes down the further north and east you go. (I've included a couple of good ones under "Thrift Shops" in the "Clothing and Accessories" section of Chapter VI.)

USED BOOKS – The area on and around West 18th and West 19th streets between Fifth and Sixth avenues has become a mecca for folks hunting for used and out-of-print books. While the Strand bookstore a little further south remains the grandfather of all used bookstores, this neighborhood now boasts scores of small and not-so-small shops and stores where you can find just about any book imaginable. Academy Book Store, Skyline Books, and the frequent book fairs at the Arts and Antiques Pavillion are just a few places to look.

WOMEN'S DISCOUNT CLOTHING – Probably the greatest concentration of decent discount women's clothing stores (and shoe stores) is on Orchard Street in the Lower East Side, from East Houston south to Grand Street. (Look under "Women's General" and "Shoes" in the "Clothing and Accessories" section of Chapter VI for some of my favorites.) Because many of these stores are run by observant Jews, they are closed on Friday afternoons and Saturdays. Sunday is definitely *the* shopping day in this area. West 8th Street between Fifth and Sixth avenues is also a good place to look for women's shoes.

I didn't include a couple of the districts in the list because they are not so easily defined and because I've covered them extensively in other parts of the book. If you're interested in art, look in the "Auctions" and "Galleries" sections of Chapter III. General-interest bookstores also are listed in Chapter VI under "Books" (although Fifth Avenue in midtown is a good place to start). If you want a more personal touch along with good discounts, try **Kaufman's Electronics** on the Lower East Side. Although many major toy companies have showrooms on and around Fifth Avenue and West 23rd Street, only one (**B. Shackman and Company,** at 85 Fifth Avenue) is open to the public. Finally, whatever you're looking for, make sure to check the exclusive shopping list at the beginning of Chapter VI.

OTHER DISTRICTS

FINANCIAL DISTRICT – Better known simply as Wall Street, the Financial District covers lots of other streets, too. The older part of the district sits between Broadway and Water Street from Maiden Lane south to Exchange Place. To get an idea of what I mean when I say "older," consider that Maiden Lane was named for the women who once gathered there to wash clothes! The New York Stock Exchange, the Federal Reserve Bank of New York, the Fraunces Tavern Museum, Trinity Church, Federal Hall National Memorial, and all sorts of financial institutions are located here. The newer part of the Financial District extends from Church Street east to the Hudson River, between Vesey and Albany streets. Adjacent to the northwest corner of the original district, it includes both the World Trade Center and the World Financial Center.

GARMENT DISTRICT – This district, also known as Seventh Avenue or Fashion Avenue, is dedicated to just one thing: the wholesale dressing of

American women. It runs between Broadway and Seventh Avenue from the southern end of Times Square at West 42nd Street to Herald Square at West 34th Street. Fashion models, clothing racks, and trucks filled with fabric jam the streets, especially in the summer. Make sure to look for stores selling such Garment District overflow as fabrics, beads, and trimmings throughout this area.

MUSEUM MILE – Beginning at East 70th Street and running north for almost 40 blocks along Fifth Avenue, Museum Mile is actually closer to two miles. Whatever you call it, this is the most stunning concentration of museums anywhere in the world. The highlights, from south to north, are the Frick, the Metropolitan, the Guggenheim, the National Academy of Design, the Cooper-Hewitt, the Jewish Museum, the International Center for Photography, the Museum of the City of New York, and El Museo del Barrio. In warm weather, you'll find all sorts of outdoor vendors selling books, crafts, T-shirts, and other items on the west side of Fifth Avenue, immediately south of the Metropolitan in the East 70s.

THEATER DISTRICT – Broadway is on Broadway. Right? Wrong, at least for the most part. And it's not on 42nd Street either, although some excellent off-Broadway theaters are clustered on West 42nd Street between Ninth and Tenth avenues and a lot of the rest of 42nd Street is in the midst of a real renaissance. The heart of the Theater District is between Broadway and Eighth Avenue from West 44th Street north to West 48th Street. While it has become much more of a daytime destination than it was even a couple years ago, the Theater District really comes alive at night with theatergoers, restaurant patrons, marvelous street performers, and lots and lots of lights.

TRANSPORTATION

New York is really very compact and easier to navigate than most of the world's other large cities. You have a whole range of choices for how to get around, listed here in order of my own preferences.

WALKING – Without question, this is my favorite way to get around New York. It may seem a little overwhelming at first (particularly in midtown at rush hour), and you'll stick out like a sore thumb if you wait on the curb for the "walk" signs, but walking is definitely the best way to see the city and get a sense of its neighborhoods. If you're walking north-south (uptown or downtown) in midtown, the Upper East Side, or the Upper West Side, 20 blocks are equivalent to one mile. Most east-west (crosstown) blocks, particularly those between Fifth and Sixth avenues and Sixth and Seventh avenues, are much longer. Unless you have small children or older folks who tire easily, or are trying to get from Columbia University (at West 116th Street) to New York University (at West 4th Street), walking is the least expensive and most interesting way to travel. Just be sure to bring along comfortable walking shoes!

SUBWAY – Some visitors and New Yorkers alike love to ride the subway, while others will do anything and everything to avoid it. For the 1.1 billion people who ride the subway each year, however, it's simply the fastest and most efficient way to travel. (As those numbers suggest, the subway can get very crowded. If you get claustrophobic, stay away from the subway around rush hour. And whatever time you travel, hold on tightly to the hands of any children who are with you.) Thanks to an ongoing anti-grafitti campaign, a beefed-up police presence, an increasingly well-enforced ban on panhandling, and lots of renovations in recent years, it also has become significantly more pleasant.

The subway system is the result of a merger of private lines like the BMT and the IRT that sprang up at the turn of the century. Most of the stations and some of the cars are quite old, so don't expect the relative luxury of BART in San Francisco or the Metro in Washington, D.C. Its 714 miles of track and 468 stations connect every borough except Staten Island. The system is concentrated in Manhattan south of 110th Street and particularly south of 59th Street. Maps of the system are available at token booths inside the stations and are posted in most cars and stations. If you need to study a map, I suggest doing so in your hotel room or some other private place so as not to advertise that you don't know where you're going. You'll also find a detailed map of the subway system in the front section of the Manhattan Yellow Pages.

The stairs leading down to most subway stations are marked by globes and signs with route numbers or letters. A red globe means the entrance is restricted or closed and no tokens are sold there. A green globe means that both the entrance and a token booth are open. In most of Manhattan, subway stations are underground. You'll find the token booths at the bottom of the stairs. Inside the station, signs point to the appropriate platform for the uptown (sometimes "Bronx-bound") or downtown (sometimes "Brooklyn-bound") train you want. Keep an eye out for "express" trains—they're great time-savers if you want to go where they're going, but they make a limited number of stops. The line number or letter, information about whether it's a local or an express, and the name of the last stop are written on the side of each subway car.

A subway ride costs $1.50 for adults. As this is being written, you can still use either a token or one of the relatively new Metrocards to get through the turnstiles. The Metropolitan Transit Authority wants to abolish the token, but the Metrocard still has lots of problems and has not met with a particularly warm welcome from New Yorkers. My guess is that the token will be around for years to come! Both tokens and Metrocards can be purchased at token booths, but be forewarned that the attendant will not take anything but cash and cannot accept bills larger than $20. As many as three children under 44 inches tall can ride free if they're accompanied by an adult. Once you've passed through the turnstiles and are inside the station, you can transfer between lines or ride as long as you like. And if you're using one of the new gold Metrocards, you can even transfer onto a bus within two hours! Stops usually are announced inside the cars over a public address system; a planned upgrade with fiber-optic technology hopefully will mean that those announcements are no longer garbled and hopelessly confusing. Look at the signs posted in the station as you pull in if you need to know where you are. Some lines stop running for a couple hours in the early morning, and many have less frequent or different service at night and on weekends, but the system itself runs 24 hours a day, seven days a week. If you have questions or a problem, call the Metropolitan Transit Authority any day between 6 a.m. and 9 p.m. at 718/330-1234 or pick up a copy of the MTA's extremely useful "Token Tips" at the New York Convention and Visitors' Bureau. (Non-English speakers can call 718/330-4847 between 7 a.m. and 7 p.m.)

Finally, a word about safety. Despite improvements in recent years and significantly fewer breakdowns than a decade ago, the subway stations and the cars themselves are often dirty and all sorts of strange people wander through them. Statistically, however, the system is no more dangerous than any other mode of transportation. Indeed, like crime in New York generally, crime in the subway has been cut in half in recent years. But do use common sense.

Don't ride late at night or very early in the morning, particularly if you're alone. *Don't* enter deserted stations. *Don't* ride in an otherwise empty car. *Don't* wear flashy jewelry. *Don't* wander around aimlessly. *Don't* stand too close to the tracks. *Don't* use the bathroom inside any station. Stick close to the designated off-hours waiting area if you're riding at an off-peak hour so that the token-booth attendant can keep an eye on you. And whatever else you do, watch your wallet or purse, particularly when riding in crowded cars.

TAXIS—All of the officially licensed medallion taxicabs in New York are yellow, have the words "NYC Taxi" and fare information written on their side doors, and have their medallion number in a box on the roof. Inside you'll see a meter and the driver's license (with his or her picture) and medallion number displayed on the dashboard, usually on the passenger's side. The city, particularly outside midtown, is full of unregulated "cars for hire" (a.k.a. "gypsy cabs") that are not legally allowed to pick up people south of 96th Street. Still, they sometimes try to do just that. I strongly encourage you to stick with the medallion cabs. The cost of a ride in a medallion cab is calculated per trip rather than per person, which means that a short trip for four adults in a cab can actually be cheaper than a bus or subway ride. That said, however, fares can add up quickly, particularly if you're stuck in heavy traffic. The charge begins at $2 the moment you get in and costs 30 cents for every one-fifth of a mile or 90 seconds stopped or slowed in traffic. In general, the meter should "click" every four blocks when you're going north-south and every block when you're going east-west. You pay for any tolls, and there's a 50 cent surcharge for rides made between 8 p.m. and 6 a.m. The meter in the front keeps a running total of your fare, and the driver is required to give you a receipt if you request one. (In fact, New York's cabs are now equipped with an annoying but effective recording reminding you to take your receipt and look around for anything you might have left behind.) A tip of between 15% and 20% of your fare is expected, and you probably will need to pay in cash. Drivers often cannot make change for bills larger than $20.

Drivers are required to take you anywhere within the five boroughs of New York City, to Westchester and Nassau counties, and to Newark Airport. That's the law, but the reality is that many cab drivers will make a fuss if you want to go to one of the airports, out to one of those suburban counties, or even to lower-income neighborhoods in Manhattan. If you have such a problem, jot down the driver's name and medallion number and write the New York City Taxi and Limousine Commission (221 West 41st Street, New York, NY 10036) or call 212/221-8294 to complain. These folks take their oversight responsibilities seriously.

So how do you go about hailing a cab? Stand on a curb or in the street right off it and stick your arm up and out. If the number (but not the "off-duty" sign) is lit in the rectangular box on a cab's roof, it's empty and on duty. Finding a cab in a snowstorm or in midtown on a rainy Friday afternoon is difficult, but you usually won't have trouble finding one in most parts of the city at most times of day. If you do have trouble, go to a major hotel or join the cab line at Penn Station, Grand Central Station, or Port Authority Bus Terminal. If you want the driver to take a particular route (it's a good idea to know exactly where you're going), say so when you get in. Assuming it isn't raining, I also suggest giving the driver the closest intersection rather than a street address as your destination. This is something locals do that will save you both time and money. Passengers ride in the back seat, although the driver will usually let one person ride in the front seat if there are four.

BUSES—In the first several editions of this book, I wrote that the only reason to take a city bus is if you have a lot of time and are afraid of the alternatives. A friend who lives in New York and rides the bus every day objected strongly. First of all, she pointed out, most buses are wheelchair-accessible (which the subway decidedly is not) and "elderly friendly" in that the driver can lower the stairs at the entrance for anyone who has trouble climbing high steps. Buses are also "stroller friendly" insofar as the doors don't close automatically and there are only a few steps to climb and descend. Precisely because the people who take the bus aren't in a hurry, they tend to be friendlier than the subway riders and often will give an older person or a harried parent their seat. The buses are very safe and usually don't attract the strange people who habituate subway cars and stations. Because there is a driver, you can ask questions or get directions. Finally, the bus stops frequently, and you can always see where you're going (a good and relatively cheap way to get a flavor of the city). I still find the bus system frustratingly slow and sometimes incomprehensible; roughly half of the city's aging fleet is due to be replaced. But buses do have some redeeming features, and many of the more than 450,000 people who ride the city's buses every year wouldn't think of traveling any other way.

Buses run up and down most avenues and on most major cross streets. Uptown buses stop at designated stops every two or three blocks, and crosstown buses stop on every block—assuming someone is waiting at a bus stop or a bus rider has pushed the tape or pulled the cord that alerts the driver that a stop is requested. Many bus lines have a limited "express" version that stops only every ten blocks or so; an orange "limited" sign is clearly visible in their front windshields. At a minimum, you can spot a bus stop by its blue sign with route numbers on it. The city is in the midst of renovating 3,000 bus shelters and adding 18,000 "Guide-a-Ride" signs with route maps. Most stops are used by more than one route, so check the screen on the front or side of each bus for its route number or simply ask the driver. Your fare entitles you to one transfer, and you should request the transfer ticket from the driver when you board. The transfer is good only for a continuous trip, but you actually have at least an hour to make a connection. You cannot, however, get off and then reboard another bus on the same route. And if you're using one of the new gold Metrocards, you can even transfer onto a subway within two hours.

The bus costs $1.50. You must use change, subway tokens, or a Metrocard. The fare box will not take pennies or bills, and the driver cannot make change. You can buy tokens or a Metrocard at any subway station token booth. If you're going to ride the bus with any frequency, I suggest buying several tokens at a time or a Metrocard good for several trips. Small children can ride for free when accompanied by an adult. Many buses run all night, although service is less frequent on weekends, late at night, and early in the morning.

You can get a map of Manhattan bus routes on most buses (ask the driver or look for boxes by the front and back doors), at most subway token booths, and from the New York Convention and Visitors' Bureau (2 Columbus Circle, near the southwest corner of Central Park at West 59th Street). You can also find a detailed map of the bus system in the Manhattan Yellow Pages. The map details where buses run, the frequency of service, and which bus to take to major museums and other attractions. If you have questions about how to get from one place to another on the bus, call the Metropolitan Transit Authority between 6 a.m. and 9 p.m. at 718/330-1234, or pick up a copy of the MTA's extremely useful "Token Tips" at the Convention and Visitors Bureau. (Non-English speakers can call 718/330-4847 between 7 a.m. and 7 p.m.)

If you're downtown south of Chambers Street, you also might look for the Alliance for Downtown New York's free bus service throughout the area. Started a couple of years ago to encourage shopping and tourism, it goes up West Street, across Liberty, and down Water Street. It runs from 7 a.m. to 10 p.m. on weekdays, from 10 a.m. to 9 p.m. on Saturdays, and from 10 a.m. to 7 p.m. on Sundays.

CAR SERVICES – If you notice a large number of Lincoln Town Cars and other black sedans in midtown and the Financial District, they are car services. Unlike taxicabs that cruise the streets looking for business, car services are available only by reservation and often exclusively for corporate clients. If you're in New York on business, your company may arrange to have you picked up from the airport and shuttled around town by one of these services. Chances are you will be given an account number and pay with a voucher provided either by your company or the driver. A client's name and car number will typically be posted in the window of the car and you'll be told in advance what to look for.

Some car services (limousine companies, too) take reservations from individuals. Carey Limousine (212/599-1122 or 800/336-4646) and Sabra (212/777-7171) are among the larger and more reputable companies. You can have a car meet you at the airport, be shuttled around town for a day, or simply arrive and depart from the opera in style. The cost is calculated by the hour or the trip rather than by mileage, so make sure you agree on a price before making a commitment. Reservations are required. Make them at least a day in advance and call to confirm several hours before you expect to leave. If you want a specific kind of car or limousine, say so when you're making reservations. These car services are on the high end of the business. You'll find lots of gypsy cabs and low-end car services in the outer boroughs and outside midtown, but I suggest avoiding them. Just so you know, licensed limousines are required to have a diamond-shaped decal on the right side of their windshield with an eight-digit number starting with T and ending with C.

DRIVING – If you read my comments earlier in this chapter, you already know that I strongly recommend against driving in New York. Leave the hassles and headaches to cab and bus drivers. The parking regulations alone ought to discourage you. There are alternate-side rules (call 212/442-7080 for specific information about these and other on-street parking regulations), special rules for several dozen official holidays, and weekend rules. And that's if you can find a space. Fines for illegal parking start at $40 and go up quickly. The penalty for parking in some zones is a $185 fine, plus towing fee! If you can't find a space on the street or want the security of a garage, you're going to pay big bucks. I once was charged $18 per half hour at a garage in midtown. On top of that, they cheated on the clock!

If that's not enough consider this: 750,000 cars come into Manhattan every day (and 80,000 more than that congest midtown during the Christmas season!). It's little wonder that the average speed of traffic going uptown or downtown is 8.2 miles an hour . . . and the average crosstown speed is 5.2 miles per hour! As I mentioned earlier, it's illegal for anyone under 18 to drive in New York City. If you must drive, I *highly* recommend becoming a member of AAA or some other major automobile club and getting all the information they have about traffic laws and driving in the city. Whatever else you do, make sure you know where you're going and be prepared for a lot of honking. Drivers in New York are not very patient people.

FERRIES – If all goes according to plan, some of the stress on the East Side's subway lines will be relieved by a new ferry service that takes passengers between the east end of 90th Street, the 34th Street pier, and Pier 17 at South Street Seaport. This service joins more than a dozen others, most of which have been started during the past two years, now taking passengers in and around New York Harbor. Most of the others take you to and from various points in New Jersey.

SAFETY

It makes sense that there are more crimes committed in New York than any other city, because more people live here than any other city. But New York is not nearly as dangerous as most people think. In fact, there are fewer crimes committed per capita in New York than in more than 20 other U.S. cities, and the violent crime rate has been going down for several years. Indeed, 1996 ended with fewer than 1,000 murders in New York for the first time since 1968. The decline continues as this goes to press.

The percentages definitely are with you, especially if you observe a few common-sense "don'ts":

- Don't display big wads of money or flashy watches and jewelry. In fact, don't even carry them with you. Leave most of your cash and all of your valuables at home or in the hotel safe.
- Don't open your wallet in public.
- Don't use automated teller machines (ATMs) when no one else is around.
- Don't leave those machines until you've put your money in your wallet and then put your wallet in your pocket or purse.
- Don't keep your wallet in your back pocket unless it's buttoned. Better yet, carry your wallet in your front pocket, along with keys and other important items.
- Don't wear your purse slung over one shoulder. Instead, put the strap over your head and keep your purse in front of you or to the side.
- Don't doze off on the subway or bus.
- Don't take the subway late at night or very early in the morning.
- Don't walk down empty streets or into empty subway stations.
- Don't go jogging in Central Park or anywhere else after dark.
- Don't let yourself believe that staying in "good" neighborhoods protects you from crime. The only time I was ever mugged was on Park Avenue at East 62nd Street, and you can't find a better neighborhood than that!
- Don't let anybody in your hotel room, even if they say they work for the hotel, unless you've specifically asked them to come or you've checked with the front desk.
- Don't talk to strangers who try to strike up a conversation unless you're very sure of their motivations.
- Don't leave any bags unattended. If you're going to put a bag or backpack on the floor, put your foot through the strap.
- Don't put your purse or anything else on the floor or on the back of the door in a public bathroom stall.
- Don't walk around with your mouth open, your camera slung over your shoulder, and your map out, while saying things like "Gee, honey, they sure don't have buildings like that back home." Don't resist. And don't ever be afraid to cross the street if a situation doesn't feel right or to shout for help if somebody is bothering you.

A common scam is for people to bump into you in a crowd, drop something that breaks, and then demand to be paid for its cost. A similar scam involves people squirting ketchup or mustard on you or simply pointing out a stain to create a distraction. The obvious solution in those situations is to just walk away (don't be intimidated if the person yells obscenities). Yet another scam involves shell games and other street gambling cons. The solution is simple: don't get involved. Then there are always pickpockets and purse-snatchers, so be on the lookout and guard your belongings carefully.

A final word of warning that has nothing to do with crime per se: watch where you walk. Manhattan has an incredible amount of traffic, and the struggle among cars, taxis, trucks, buses, and pedestrians is constant. Some particularly dangerous spots include Park Avenue at East 33rd Street, Sixth Avenue and Broadway as they cross West 33rd and 34th streets at Herald Square, and West 34th Street and Eighth Avenue around the Port Authority. It sounds silly to repeat a warning from childhood, but please look both ways before stepping into the street.

If there's an emergency, don't hesitate to call 911. If you need more general assistance, try the Travelers' Aid Society on the second floor of 1451 Broadway (at 42nd Street) or give them a call at 212/944-0013. These kind folks will help with medical referrals, emergency flight changes, and anything else you might need in a pinch.

SMOKING

Like many cities and states, New York has become increasingly hostile to smokers in recent years. Indeed, there has been a massive change in society's attitude toward smoking in the almost two decades since I started writing this book. Thanks to the city's 1995 Smoke-Free Air Act, New Yorkers and visitors alike now will find the number of places where they can smoke severely limited.

Even before the new city law was enacted, New York state banned smokers from airports, train stations, bus stops, and similar public areas. Now that ban extends to restaurants that seat more than 35 people, many bars where food is served, the seating areas of both indoor and outdoor sports arenas, and the public spaces of all buildings. Most hotels maintain rooms (and sometimes entire floors) for smokers and nonsmokers. (If you want to find establishments that welcome smokers, look in New York bookstores for *The Smoker's Guide to Dining in New York City* or *Lighten Up New York*. Both have lists of restaurants in Manhattan that allow smoking.)

While cigarette smoking is definitely on the outs these days, cigar smoking is very trendy in New York. Thanks at least in part to the high visibility of such cigar-smoking New Yorkers as David Letterman and Rush Limbaugh, several "cigar bars" have opened in recent years and sales of premium cigars are skyrocketing. One midtown steakhouse even has a special cigar night for women!

STROLLERS AND WHEELCHAIRS

New York is a walker's city. Walking in New York is not only the best way to see the city but also often the fastest way to get around. However, as anybody who has tried traversing the city with a baby stroller or in a wheelchair will tell you, New York is not a paradise for anybody who has trouble climbing steps or curbs and navigating through stopped or slowed traffic.

If you're coming to New York with a stroller in tow, make sure it's a durable one and be prepared for some obstacles. Because space is at a premium in New York, the aisles of grocery stores, boutiques, and even restaurants are often much narrower than they are in the suburbs. Despite the requirements of a variety of laws and significant improvements in recent years, many of New York's buildings are quite old and are not equipped with ramps or easily accessible elevators. While people use strollers on the subway system all the time, carting them up and down the stairs can be a pain, and wheeling children on them between platforms and subway cars is downright dangerous. Be forewarned that some places, including the United Nations and the Metropolitan Museum of Art (on Sundays), ban strollers altogether.

Obstacles for wheelchairs are even greater. Although most of the city's buses are equipped with special lifts and spaces for wheelchairs, the subway system is almost completely inaccessible. (Exceptions include some major stops, including Grand Central Station and the World Trade Center, where elevators are safe and functioning.) If you're coming to New York in a wheelchair, you ought to know about a couple of resources. First, make sure to get a copy of "Access for All," an exceptional guide to the city's cultural institutions that describes in detail what sorts of facilities those institutions have for people in wheelchairs (as well as the blind and deaf). This invaluable guide is available from Hospital Audiences, Inc. (220 West 42nd Street, New York, NY, 10036) for $5 a copy. This organization also runs a hotline (888/424-4685) on weekdays. Second, the Metropolitan Transit Authority has a special phone number (718/596-8585) for information about routes accessible to people in wheelchairs. Finally, the City of New York's Office for People with Disabilities publishes an access guide. Call 212/788-2830 to request that publication or for general information. One piece of good news: many Broadway theaters offer a few deeply discounted tickets for folks in wheelchairs and their companions. Call the individual theaters for more information.

TIPPING AND OTHER EXPENSES

Be forewarned: New York is expensive. *Really* expensive. Most nice hotel rooms in midtown run about $250 a night. The average meal can easily run upwards of $50 per person, and most theater and opera tickets are just plain outrageous. Everybody expects a tip. It's up to you, of course, but $1 per bag to the bellman, between 15% and 20% of your fare to the cab driver, and between 15% and 20% of your pre-tax restaurant bill (just double the tax—it's 8.25% on just about everything) to your waiter is expected (see page 28). Most people also tip wine stewards (10% of the wine bill), parking valets ($2), private tour guides (at least $5 a day), and doormen who hail cabs ($1), among others.

The good news is that prices have not risen much is recent years. The average cost of a meal, while still the highest in the nation, actually has gone down a bit. With a little effort, you *can* find cheaper hotels, less expensive restaurants, and even some free events and activities. (Make sure to check the "Manhattan for Free" section in Chapter VII, and look in the "Tickets" section of Chapter III for information about how to get bargains on theater tickets.) You don't always have to spend a lot to get what you want. After adding tax, an automatic gratuity, and a hotel surcharge to the cost of the item itself, a friend recently calculated the difference between buying a single bagel through room service in one midtown hotel and buying it in a deli a block away at more than $10! But in general my advice is be prepared to spend money and lots of it if you're here for a special visit. Don't nickel and dime yourself out of enjoying what could be a once-in-a-lifetime experience!

CHECKLISTS

If you're planning a trip to New York a couple months in advance, I suggest you think about what you want to do and read through the relevant sections of this book carefully. Pay special attention to the "Tours" and "Tickets" sections of Chapter III and the "Annual Events" and "Resources" sections of Chapter VII. Some things—tickets to certain events, television-show tapings, and tours, for example—require a bit of advance planning. Other things—special sales or events, for example—require that you visit at certain times of year. Weather is always a consideration. Average temperatures range from highs in the high 30s and low 40s in December, January, and February to highs in the 80s in June, July, and August. Whenever you come and whatever you plan to do, however, I recommend packing a couple of key items:

- Comfortable walking shoes
- An umbrella and raincoat
- A jacket and tie or nice dress
- Opera glasses
- An address book and postcard stamps
- Prescriptions and an extra pair of glasses
- Traveler's checks
- A fanny pack or money belt
- Tickets (airplane and otherwise)
- An AARP and/or Medicare card
- Student identification card

All the little things that you may want in your hotel room or when you're out and about cost a lot less at home than they do in New York. Most hotels will supply small sewing kits and tissue, and some will let you borrow an umbrella or hair dryer for free. But think of packing things like film, aspirin, instant coffee, snacks, and gum. Plan what you're going to need for the day before leaving your hotel room. A lot of people put a couple of credit cards, driver's license, and some money in a secure pocket, fanny pack, or money belt and then stash everything else in a shoulder bag so there's no worrying about a stolen purse or wallet. I suggest leaving your key at the front desk for the same reason. Depending on the time of year, here's a list of things I would take with me for a day of exploring:

- Addresses and phone numbers of places you plan to visit and details about how to get there
- Address and phone number of your hotel
- Bus and subway maps
- Tissues
- A list of public bathrooms in the areas you'll be going (see Chapter VII)
- An umbrella
- A coat or sweater
- Subway tokens or a Metrocard which work on buses, too
- Some loose change and small bills
- Finally, don't forget this book!

II. Where to Eat It: Manhattan a la Carte

Eating out is *in*. So are mashed potatoes, meat loaf, rich . . . *very* rich . . . desserts, hotel dining rooms, brew pubs, healthy salads, steaks, and real value for your money. Extravagance, cilantro, dressed-up dining, fussy plates, strange ethnic mixtures, watered-down drinks, and anything greasy are *out*. So the scene changes in a city that is without equal when it comes to a choice of restaurants, coffee shops, diners, bistros, theme palaces, grand dining rooms, and takeout. You know the saying: *If you can't find it here, it probably doesn't exist!*

What you will read in this section is the result of years of work, if you call trying out nearly 2,000 eating establishments work! When you combine the meals with visits (and sampling) at hundreds of food shops, from street soup vendors to the elegant halls of the finest gourmet shops, you are able to get a feel of what the food scene in Manhattan is all about. I pass along my comments, and they are mine alone, to help you find your way in this bewildering scene. I have tried to inform, entertain, and stimulate your taste buds.

Let me set the guidelines. I make no pretense of being a professional food critic. However, I am presenting information from my own informed perspective: that of someone who has spent over a quarter of a century in the food-service field, who owns and operates his own restaurant and gourmet cake shop in Oregon, and who has had the opportunity to make judgments based on dining experiences in over 140 nations.

The New York restaurant scene is in constant change. *Prix-fixe* meals have become very popular, and even the fanciest places have taken a second look at their out-of-sight tabs. A sizable number of newer restaurants are in the lower and moderate price ranges. This is because fewer New Yorkers and visitors are eating at home. Lack of time plus the trouble and expense of food preparation in one's own kitchen have contributed to this noticeable trend. Since they dine out so much, they want to do so affordably.

Expense accounts are being carefully monitored. Food has become simpler and healthier. Casual attire is now taken for granted; it is the rare establishment that sticks to a serious dress code. Trendiness rules; the mob hops from one new hot spot to another. In the restaurant biz, it is truly the survival of the fittest.

Many restaurant guides give stars or ratings. I have chosen not to go that route. Only those establishments that I feel are especially commendable (for food, ambience, service, and price) are included herein. The also-rans are not included, except in the "Don't Bother" section, where I think you should know my feelings about some of the better-known places.

These are things I look for: Good food, of course. A clean and inviting establishment. Value for money. Spotless kitchens and rest rooms. A tolerable noise level. Reservations that are promptly honored. Uncrowded conditions.

I also have some personal peeves: Paper tablecloths. Polyester napkins. Imperious maitre d's. Tiny plates overflowing with food. Items piled in an unappetizing manner. Dirty, greasy menus. Chatty servers. Lengthy recitations of "specials" by waiters. Bills with taxes added into the total, thereby inflating tip calculations. Cold bread. Tepid soups. Overseasoned entrees. Hypersophisticated food combinations. Day-old desserts. Ice cream and sherbets that have been re-frozen. Being seated by the restroom door. Haughty attitudes. You get the picture!

The first part of "Manhattan a la Carte" lists the outstanding places I have found. Each listing, organized by districts, includes the address, type of cuisine, and whether or not the establishment is open on Sunday. The next section features listings for different kinds of meals and occasions, such as breakfast, brunch, late evening, outdoor cafes, bistros, coffeehouses, personal favorites, burgers, seafood, and more. In the following section, I have compiled a listing of major food items and dishes, indicating where the best can be found. Rest assured, this is the cream of the crop, and the prices are right! Finally, I list and describe in detail several hundred places that deserve special attention. These reviews include important information (location, phone number, pricing, meals served) and a general feel for the ambience. In most cases I have purposely not been too specific on menu items, as they tend to change almost overnight. I have eliminated trendy establishments that will not survive, in my opinion, in this fast-changing environment.

The Smoke Free Air Act went into effect in New York City in 1995, and it has created much confusion for both operators and customers of local restaurants. The bottom line is that a number of restaurants have become creative in their rules and regulations, allowing those who want to light up to do so in designated areas. Arrangements change almost by the day, so the best strategy is simply to pick out your favorite restaurant, then call ahead (if you want to smoke) and find out their rules. In most cases, you will be accommodated, although you might have to sit at the bar or in a lounge, private dining room, or outdoor setting.

A few housekeeping details. "Inexpensive," to me, means under $15 for a meal, per person, without drinks. "Moderate" is roughly $16–$34. "Moderately expensive," $35-$45. "Expensive," $46 and up. Most establishments take all major credit cards, although a few accept American Express only. Sometimes the owners will take only cash. When applicable, this information is mentioned in the listings. These establishments will usually take a check, if proper identification is presented.

I am not a wine expert, therefore commentary on wine lists is not included.

If you have a question about dress codes, call the establishment. If a gentleman forgets his jacket and the dress code requires one, most places will provide a loaner.

In many cases, reservations are essential. An increasingly annoying habit is for the establishment to ask for a telephone contact or a reconfirmation. I strongly object to the latter. If you arrive on time, you should be seated immediately and not be shoved off to the bar so that your drink tab will grow heftier. You have every right to talk to the person in charge if the food, seating, or service is not to your liking. Do not make a scene, however. Check your bill carefully. Mistakes can happen. Figure your tip on the total amount of food and drink.

- If the service was appalling and the manager unresponsive, leave nothing.
- If service was poor to fair, tip 10% to 14%.
- If service was good, meaning prompt and accurate, tip 15%.
- If service was very good, meaning an attentive server with good knowledge of the menu, leave up to 18%.
- If service was excellent, above and beyond the expected, tip up to 20%.
- If service was extraordinary, meaning unforgettable, tip 21% to 25%.

A money-saving tip: more and more restaurants are offering off-menu daily specials. Be careful, because the pricing is usually considerably higher than printed menu items. Don't be afraid to ask for prices.

A few special hints! If things go particularly well, show it with an unexpected gift. Complain only to people who can do something about it. Don't be hesitant to ask for help with the wine list. *No shows* show no class. If you want really special service and attention, become a *regular*.

Again I must mention how volatile the eating scene is in Manhattan. Chefs and owners come and go. Restaurants change formats overnight. What is great one day can be not-so-great the next day. Because I self-publish, my information is more current than that provided by large publishers, but a few listings may become out-of-date before the next volume. If this happens, please accept my apologies. If you disagree with an evaluation, please remember that this is an informed but personal opinion. I would like to hear from you about a particularly good or bad dining experience.

Quick Reference Guide

CENTRAL PARK AREA

CHELSEA

CHINATOWN

EAST HARLEM

EAST SIDE/UPPER EAST SIDE

EAST VILLAGE

FLATIRON DISTRICT/GRAMERCY PARK/
LOWER BROADWAY/UNION SQUARE

GREENWICH VILLAGE/WEST VILLAGE

WEST SIDE/UPPER WEST SIDE

OUTSIDE MANHATTAN

An Exclusive List: Hundreds of the Best Taste Treats In New York City (Eat In and Takeout)

Antipasti, hot: Pasta Amore Trattoria (315 W 57th St)
Antipasto bar: Trattoria dell'Arte (900 Seventh Ave) and Da Umberto (107 W 17th St)
Appetizers, gourmet: Russ & Daughters (179 E Houston St)
Apple ring: Lafayette (298 Bleecker St)
Apple tart: Pitchoune (226 Third Ave)

Artichoke: La Lunchonette (18th St and Tenth Ave)
Babka: Gertel's (53 Hester St)
Baguettes: Flatiron Diner & Baking Co (18 W 18th St)
Baked Alaska: Flowers (21 W 17th St) and Rainbow Room (30 Rockefeller Plaza)
Banana parfait with macadamia nut brittle: La Métairie (189 W 10th St)
Baskets, gift and corporate: Basketfull (1133 Broadway), Manhattan Fruiter (105 E 29th St), and Petrossian (182 W 58th St)
Bass, striped: Cellini (65 E 54th St)
Beef, fillet of: Kings Carriage House (251 E 82nd St)
Beef Wellington: One If by Land, Two If by Sea (17 Barrow St)
Belgian nut squares: Duane Park Patisserie (179 Duane St)
Bialys: Kossar's (367 Grand St)
Bigoli (Venetian pasta): Remi (145 W 53rd St)
Biscuits, blueberry-peach: Taylor's Prepared Foods (523 Hudson St, 228 W 18th St, 175 Second Ave, and 156 Chambers St)
Biscuits, pepper: Vesuvio Bakery (160 Prince St)
Blini: Russian Express (306 E 86th St and 11 E 23rd St)
Blintzes: Blintz (81 Third Ave), Ratner's (138 Delancey St), and Kiev Restaurant (117 E 7th St)
Boeuf Bourguignon: Country Cafe (69 Thompson St)
Bomboloncini (fried doughnuts with fillings): Osteria del Circo (120 W 55th St)
Bouillabaisse (Sunday only): Wilkinson's Seafood Cafe (1573 York Ave)
Bratwurst: Schaller & Weber (1654 Second Ave)
Bread, chocolate: Amy's Bread (672 Ninth Ave) and Ecce Panis (1120 Third Ave and 1260 Madison Ave; Fri-Sat only)
Bread, corn: Moishe's Bakery (181 E Houston St and 115 Second Ave) and 107 West (2787 Broadway)
Bread, fruit: Anglers & Writers (420 Hudson St)
Bread, general: Hot & Crusty (various locations, including Third Ave at 17th St, Second Ave at 44th St, Second Ave at 63rd St, and Broadway at 87th St)
Bread, Indian: Akbar (475 Park Ave) and Dawat (210 E 58th St)
Bread, Irish soda: Zabar's (2245 Broadway)
Bread, Italian: D&G Bakery (45 Spring St) and Sullivan Street Bakery (73 Sullivan St)
Bread, pita: Turkish Cuisine (631 Ninth Ave)
Bread, raisin nut: E.A.T. (1064 Madison Ave)
Bread, Semolina raisin fennel: Amy's Bread (672 Ninth Ave and 75 Ninth Ave)
Bread, whole wheat: Bread Shop Cafe (3139 Broadway) and Dean & Deluca (560 Broadway)
Brie, baked: Pascalou (1308 Madison Ave)
Brioche: Chez Laurence Pâtisserie (245 Madison Ave) and Lipstick Cafe (885 Third Ave)
Brownies: Fat Witch Bakery (179 Duane St)
Brownies, zebra: Hudson Caterers Cafe (145 Hudson St)
B'stilla: Lotfi's Moroccan Restaurant (358 W 46th St)
Buns, sticky: William Greenberg (2187 Broadway, 1100 Madison Ave, 518 Third Ave, 60 8th St, and Macy's 34th St)
Burritos: Burritoville (1606 Third Ave and other locations), California Burrito Company (295 Park Ave S and other locations), Harry's Burrito Junction (241 Columbus Ave and other locations), Samalita's Tortilla Factory (1429 Third Ave), and Taqueria de Mexico (93 Greenwich Ave)

Burritos (to go): Benny's Burritos (113 Greenwich Ave and 93 Ave A)

Cabbage, pickled with pork and noddles: Ollie's Noodle Shop and Grill (200B W 44th St, 2315 Broadway, and 1991 Broadway)

Cacik: Turkish Kitchen (386 Third Ave)

Cake: Edgar's Cafe (255 W 84th St) and Ferrara (195 Grano St)

Cake, blackout: Gertel's (53 Hester St) and Serendipity 3 (225 E 60th St)

Cake, Bohemian (must order in advance): Cupcake Cafe (522 Ninth Ave)

Cake, butter cream and chocolate: Moishe's Bakery (181 E Houston St and 115 Second Ave)

Cake, carrot: Carrot Top Pastries (5025 Broadway and 3931 Broadway)

Cake, chocolate: Second Avenue Kosher Delicatessen and Restaurant (156 Second Ave), Hard Rock Cafe (221 W 57th St), and Jo Jo (160 E 64th St)

Cake, chocolate meringue with chocolate mousse: Soutine Bakery (104 W 70th St)

Cake, chocolate mousse: City Bakery (22 E 17th St)

Cake, chocolate raspberry: Caffe Roma (385 Broome St)

Cake, fruit, Milanese Italian: Bleecker Street Pastry (245 Bleecker St)

Cake, lemon poppy-seed pound: Island (1305 Madison Ave)

Calzone: Little Italy Gourmet Pizza (65 Vanderbilt Ave) and Piatti Pronti (1221 Sixth Ave and other locations)

Cannelloni: Piemonte Ravioli Company (190 Grand St) and Giambelli (46 E 50th St)

Cannoli: Caffe Vivaldi (32 Jones St) and De Robertis Pastry Shop and Caffé (176 First Ave)

Caviar: Petrossian (182 W 58th St)

Ceviche (marinated seafood)**:** Rosa Mexicano (1063 First Ave)

Champagne: Garnet Wines and Liquor (929 Lexington Ave) and Gotham Liquors (2519 Broadway)

Cheese cart: Parioli Romanissimo (24 E 81st St)

Cheese selection: Grace's Marketplace (1237 Third Ave) and Murray's Cheese Shop (257 Bleecker St)

Cheesecake, all flavors: Ruthy's Cheesecake & Rugelach Bakery (75 Ninth Ave)

Cheesecake, best: Mitchel London Foods (22A E 65th St)

Cheesecake, combination fruit: Eileen's Special Cheese Cake (17 Cleveland Pl)

Cheesecake, ricotta: Primavera (1578 First Ave) and Le Madri (168 W 18th St)

Chicken: El Pollo (1746 First Ave, 482 Broome St)

Chicken, beggar's: Shun Lee Palace (155 E 55th St) and Shun Lee West (43 W 65th St)

Chicken, Cajun: Susan Simon (32 E Second St)

Chicken, Dijon: Zabar's (2245 Broadway)

Chicken dishes: International Poultry (1133 Madison Ave and 983 First Ave)

Chicken, grilled: Da Nico (164 Mulberry St) and Rainbow Chicken (2801 Broadway, at 108th St)

Chicken hash: 21 (21 W 52nd St)

Chicken-in-the-pot: Fine & Schapiro (138 W 72nd St)

Chicken, parmesan: Il Mulino (86 W 3rd St)

Chicken, Peruvian style: El Pollo (482 Broome St and 1746 First Ave)

Chicken pot pie: Between the Bread (141 E 56th St and 145 W 55th St) and Jim McMullen's (1341 Third Ave)

Chicken, roasted: Montrachet (239 West Broadway)

Chicken salad: China Grill (52 W 53rd St)

Chicken salad, coriander: Petak's (1246 Madison Ave)

Chicken, Southern-Caribbean: Lola (30 W 22nd St)
Chili: Manhattan Chili Company (1500 Broadway)
Chinese vegetables: Kam Man (200 Canal St)
Chocolate: Maison du Chocolat (25 E 73rd St)
Chocolate desserts: Four Seasons Hotel (57 E 57th St)
Chocolate, fine: Richart (7 E 55th St)
Chocolate, gratin of: Daniel (20 E 76th St)
Chocolate, hot: City Bakery (22 E 17th St)
Cholent: Second Avenue Kosher Delicatessen and Restaurant (156 Second Ave)
Chops, mutton: Keens Steakhouse (72 W 36th St)
Choucroute garnie (on special holidays)**:** Maureen's Passion (1200 Lexington Ave)
Clams, baked: Frank's Trattoria (371 First Ave)
Cod, roast: Monkey Bar (60 E 54th St)
Cod, sperm (seasonal)**:** Katana (179 Prince St)
Coffee beans: Porto Rico Importing Company (201 Bleecker St, 107 Thompson St, and 40½ St Marks Pl) and Zabar's (80th St and Broadway)
Coffee, iced: Oren's Daily Roast (985 Lexington Ave, 33 E 58th St, Third Ave and 30th St, 1144 Lexington Ave, 31 Waverly Pl, and 1574 First Ave)
Coffeecake: Sticky Fingers (121 First Ave)
Congee: Lobster Club (24 E 80th St)
Cookies, butter: CBK of New York (226 E 83rd St and 366 Amsterdam Ave)
Cookies, chocolate chubbie: Sarabeth's Kitchen (423 Amsterdam Ave, 1295 Madison Ave, and 945 Madison Ave at the Whitney Museum)
Cookies, chocolate hazelnut meringue: De Robertis (176 1st St)
Cookies, decorated handmade: Baked Ideas (450 Broadway)
Cookies, gingerbread: Kathy's Kitchen (645 Hudson St)
Cookies, oatmeal: Cafe 112 (2885 Broadway)
Corn: Creative Corn Company (1275 Lexington Ave)
Corned beef: Katz's (205 E Houston St)
Corned beef hash: Broadway Diner (1726 Broadway and 590 Lexington Ave) and Carnegie Delicatessen and Restaurant (854 Seventh Ave)
Couscous: Provence (38 MacDougal St, on Sunday) and Cafe Crocodile (354 E 74th St)
Crab: Pisacane Midtown Corp (940 First Ave)
Crab cakes: Tropica (200 Park Ave) and Acme Bar and Grill (9 Great Jones St)
Crème brûlée: Tribeca Grill (375 Greenwich St), La Métairie (189 W 10th St), Polo (Westbury Hotel, 840 Madison Ave), Barbetta (321 W 46th St), and Man Ray (169 Eighth Ave)
Crème brûlée, coffee: Lumi (963 Lexington Ave)
Crème caramel, mocha: États-Unis (242 E 81st St)
Croissants: J.P. French Bakery (54 W 55th St) and Paris Croissant (303 Park Ave S, 1776 Broadway, and other locations)
Croissants, almond: Marquet Patisserie (15 E 12th St)
Cupcakes: Cupcake Cafe (522 Ninth Ave)
Curry: Baluchi's (193 Spring St and 1565 Second Ave)
Custard, frozen: Custard Beach (33 E 8th St)
Delicatessen assortment: Dean & Deluca (560 Broadway)
Dessert, all-natural frozen: PAX Gourmet Deli (109 E 59th St)
Dessert, frozen, low-calorie: Tasti D-Lite (Lexington Ave at 86th St and other locations)
Doughnuts: Krispy Kreme (265 W 23rd St and 280 W 125th St)

Doughnuts, jelly and glazed: Georgie's Pastry Shop (50 W 125th St)
Doughnuts, whole wheat: Cupcake Cafe (522 Ninth Ave)
Duck: Apple Restaurant (17 Waverly Pl)
Duck, Beijing: Shun Lee Palace (155 E 55th St)
Duck, braised: Quatorze Bis (323 E 79th St) and Tang Pavilion (65 W 55th St; order in advance)
Duck, Napoleon: Essex House (160 Central Park S)
Duck, Peking: Peking Duck House Restaurant (22 Mott St), Shun Lee Palace (155 E 55th St), and Shun Lee West (43 W 65th St)
Duck, roasted: La Boheme (24 Minetta Lane) and Four Seasons (99 E 52nd St)
Dumplings: Chef Ho Dumpling House (9 Pell St and 148 W 49th St), Chin Chin (216 E 49th St), Excellent Dumpling House (111 Lafayette St), Pig Heaven (1540 Second Ave), and Great Shanghai (27 Division St)
Egg cream: Gem Spa (131 Second Ave), Carnegie Delicatessen and Restaurant (854 Seventh Ave), EJ's Luncheonette (447 Amsterdam Ave and 1271 Third Ave), Mill's Korean Restaurant (2895 Broadway; in summer or special order), and Tom's Restaurant (782 Washington Ave, Brooklyn)
Eggs, fresh Jersey: (72 E 7th St, Thurs only: 7-5:30)
Eggs, Jersey (extra large): 1750 Second Ave
Eggs, Scotch: Myers of Keswick (634 Hudson St)
Empanadas: Ruben's (64 Fulton St, 77 Pearl St, and 15 Bridge St) and Empanada Oven (826 Seventh Ave)
Espresso: Chez Laurence Patisserie (245 Madison Ave) and Caffe Dante (79-81 MacDougal St)
Fada's capretto: San Domenico (240 Central Park S)
Fajitas: Zarela (953 Second Ave)
Falafel: Habib's Place (438 E 9th St), Sahara East (184 First Ave), and Pita Cuisine of Soho (65 Spring St)
Fish, fresh: Citarella (2135 Broadway) and Central Fish Company (527 Ninth Ave)
Fish, smoked: Russ & Daughters (179 E Houston St) and Barney Greengrass (541 Amsterdam Ave)
Foie gras: Gramercy Tavern (42 E 20th St), La Caravelle (33 W 55th St), Le Périgord (405 E 52nd St), and Raoul's (180 Prince St)
Fondue: Swiss Inn (311 W 48th St)
Food and kitchen extravaganza (best all-around in the world): Zabar's (2245 Broadway)
Frankfurters: Leo's Famous (100 W 32nd St)
French fries: Cafe de Paris (924 Second Ave), Pommes Frites (123 Second Ave), Tout Va Bien (311 W 51st St), Au Cafe de Bruxelles (118 Greenwich Ave), Steak Frites (9 E 16th St), and Michael's (24 W 55th St)
Fries, Tuscan: Coco Pazzo (23 E 74th St)
Frites (French fries with mayonnaise): Pommes Frites (123 Second Ave)
Fruits and vegetables, fresh: Fairway (2127 Broadway) and Balducci's (424 Sixth Ave)
Fruit dessert plate, fresh: Primavera (1578 First Ave)
Game: Ottomanelli's Meat Market (285 Bleecker St) and Da Umberto (107 W 17th St)
Gateau Charlene Blanche: Patisserie J. Lanciani (414 W 14th St)
Gelati: Caffe Dante (79-81 MacDougal St)
Gelato: Bussola (65 Fourth Ave)
Gift basket: Petrossian (182 W 58th St)

Gingerbread houses: Kathy's Kitchen (645 Hudson St)

Goat, roast baby: Primavera (1578 First Ave)

Groceries, discount: Gourmet Garage (453 Broome St and 301 E 64th St)

Grouse: Hudson River Club (250 Vesey St)

Guacamole: Manhattan Chili Company (1500 Broadway) and Rosa Mexicano (1063 First Ave)

Gumbo: Chantale's Cajun Kitchen (510 Ninth Ave)

Halibut, poached: Le Bernardin (155 W 51st St)

Ham, peach and bourbon-glazed: Word of Mouth (1012 Lexington Ave)

Hamburgers: Jackson Hole Burgers (232 E 64th St and other locations), Corner Bistro (331 W 4th St), and Hamburger Harry's (157 Chambers and 145 W 45th St)

Hen, Cornish: Lorenzo and Maria's Kitchen (1418 Third Ave)

Heros: Italian Food Center (186 Grand St) and Hero Boy (492 Ninth Ave)

Heros, sausage: Manganaro Grosseria Italiana (488 Ninth Ave)

Hominy grits: Cafe Beulah (39 E 19th St)

Hotcakes: Royal Canadian Pancake House (180 Third Ave, 2286 Broadway, and 1004 Second Ave)

Hot chocolate: City Bakery (22 E 17th St)

Hot dogs: Brooklyn Diner USA (212 W 57th St), Leo's Famous (861 Sixth Ave), Katz (205 E Houston St), Old Town Bar (45 E 18th St), Gray's Papaya (8th St at Sixth Ave, and 2090 Broadway), and Papaya King (86th St at Third Ave)

Huitlacoche (Mexican equivalent of a black truffle): Rosa Mexicano (1063 First Ave)

Ice cream: Serendipity 3 (225 E 60th St)

Ice cream, white pepper: Vong (200 E 54th St)

Ices, Italian: Custard Beach (33 E 8th St)

International foods: Soho Provisions (518 Broadway)

Jambalaya: 107 West (2787 Broadway)

Kebabs: Turkish Cuisine (631 Ninth Ave) and Turkish Kitchen (386 Third Ave)

Kielbasa: First Avenue Meat Products (140 First Ave)

Lamb, rack of: Gotham Bar and Grill (12 E 12th St)

Lamb shanks: Bolo (23 E 22nd St)

Lamb stew: Bouterin (420 E 59th St) and Pamir (1437 Second Ave)

Liver, chopped: Second Avenue Kosher Delicatessen and Restaurant (156 Second Ave)

Lobster: Docks (2427 Broadway and 633 Third Ave) and Wilkinson's (1573 York Ave)

Lobster, live: Blue Ribbon Sushi (119 Sullivan St)

Lobster thermidor: Rainbow Room (30 Rockefeller Plaza)

Macaroni and cheese: Fresco by Scotto (34 E 52nd St), Quilty's (177 Prince St), and the Screening Room (54 Varick St)

Marinara sauce: Patsy's (236 W 56th St)

Marzipan: Elk Candy Company (240 E 86th St)

Matzoh Brei: Lobster Club (24 E 80th St) and the Saloon (1920 Broadway)

Meat, grill-ready: Les Halles (411 Park Ave S)

Meat, kosher, grilled: Cafe Masada (1239 First Ave)

Meat loaf: Lobster Club (24 E 80th St) and Mortimer's (1057 Lexington Ave)

Meat, wholesale: Old Bohemian Meat (452 W 13th St)

Meats, prime: Jefferson Market (450 Ave of the Americas)

Moussaka: Periyali (35 W 20th St)

Mousse, chocolate (the very best): Bistro Margot (26 Prince St)

Mousse, white chocolate, in a bittersweet chocolate basket: Manhattan Ocean Club (57 W 58th St)

Mozzarella: Alleva Dairy (188 Grand St) and Melampo (105 Sullivan St)

Mozzarella and ricotta, homemade: Russo and Son (344 E 11th St)

Muffins: Between the Bread (145 W 55th St and 141 E 56th St), My Favorite Muffins (11 John St), Petak's (1246 Madison Ave), Lee & Elle (336 Madison Ave), Connecticut Muffin (206 Elizabeth St), and Muffin Shop (222 Columbus Ave)

Muffins, corn: 107 West (2787 Broadway)

Muffins, nonfat: Brooklyn Diner USA (212 W 57th St)

Mushrooms: Aux Delices des Bois (4 Leonard St)

Mushrooms, grilled portobello: Giovanni (Venti Cinque) (25 E 83rd St)

Mushrooms, wild: Grace's Marketplace (1237 Third Ave)

Mussels: Jubilee (347 E 54th St)

Nachos: Benny's Burritos (93 Ave A and 113 Greenwich Ave)

Napoleon: Ecco (124 Chambers St)

Natural foods: Whole Foods in Soho (117 Prince St)

Noodles: Sammy's Noodle Shop & Grill (53-61 Sixth Ave)

Noodles, Asian: Republic (37 Union Sq W)

Noodles, buckwheat: Honmura An (170 Mercer St)

Noodles, cold with hot sesame sauce: Sung Chu Mei (615 Hudson St)

Noodles, Shanghai-style: Shun Lee Palace (155 E 55th St)

Nuts: A. L. Bazzini Co. (339 Greenwich St)

Nuts and packaged dried fruits (great prices)**:** J. Wolsk and Company (81 Ludlow St)

Oatmeal: Sarabeth's Kitchen (1295 Madison Ave, 423 Amsterdam Ave, and other locations)

Octopus: Cascabel (218 Lafayette St)

Olives: International Grocery Store (529 Ninth Ave) and Istana (New York Palace Hotel, 455 Madison Ave)

Omelets: Romaine De Lyon (29 E 61st St) and Potbelly (94 Christopher St)

Onion rings: Palm (837 Second Ave), Lola (30 W 22nd St), and Sweet Ophelia's (430 Broome St)

Orange juice, fresh-squeezed: hole-in-the-wall stand at 1428 Sixth Ave, at Central Park S

Organic foods: Angelica's (147 First Ave)

Oyster pan roast: Grand Central Oyster Bar Restaurant (Grand Central Station)

Oyster stew: Grand Central Oyster Bar Restaurant (Grand Central Station)

Oysters, fried: Tramps Cafe (45 W 21st St)

Oysters, Louisiana: Cafe des Artistes (1 W 67th St)

Paella: Sevilla (62 Charles St)

Pancakes: Friend of a Farmer (77 Irving Pl; weekends) and Royal Canadian Restaurant (2286 Broadway, 1004 Second Ave, and 180 Third Ave)

Pancakes, blue corn: Mesa Grill (102 Fifth Ave; weekends)

Pancakes, kimchi: Dok Suni's (119 First Ave)

Pancakes, potato: Rolf's (281 Third Ave)

Panna cotta (dessert): Gramercy Dining Room (42 E 20th St)

Parfait, watermelon: Coco Pazzo Teatro (235 W 46th St)

Pasta: Caffe Buon Gusto (236 E 77th St), Col Legno (231 E 9th St), Cafe Pertutti (2888 Broadway), Arqua (281 Church St), Gabriel's (11 W 60th St), and Todaro Bros (555 Second Ave)

Pasta, angel hair: Contrapunto (200 E 60th St), Piemonte Homemade Ravioli Company (190 Grand St), and Nanni's (146 E 46th St)

Pasta, handmade egg: Balducci's (424 Sixth Ave)
Pasta (inexpensive): La Marca (161 E 22nd St)
Pasta, Venetian: Remi (145 W 53rd St)
Pastrami: Carnegie Delicatessen and Restaurant (854 Seventh Ave)
Pastrami, salmon: Park Avenue Cafe (100 E 63rd St)
Pastries: Bleecker Street Pastry (245 Bleecker St)
Pastries, Hungarian: Hungarian Pastry Shop (1030 Amsterdam Ave)
Pastries, Italian: LaBella Ferrara Pastry & Caffe (108-110 Mulberry St) and
   Rocco Pastry Shop (243 Bleecker St)
Paté: Les Trois Petite Cochons (453 Greenwich St)
Peanuts, candied: A. L. Bazzini Co. (339 Greenwich St)
Penne with prosciutto: Petak's (1246 Madison Ave)
Peppers, roasted: Rao's (455 E 114th St)
Pickles: Guss Pickles (35 Essex St) and Pickle-Licious (88th St and Amsterdam
   Ave)
Pie, apple: William Greenberg Jr. Desserts (2187 Broadway, 1100 Madison
   Ave, and 518 Third Ave)
Pie, black bottom: Toukie's (220 W Houston St)
Pie, caramel-nut crunch: Houlihan's (729 Seventh Ave and other loca-
   tions
Pie, cheddar-crust apple (seasonal): Little Pie Company (424 W 43rd St)
Pie, Key lime: Little Pie Company (424 W 43rd St)
Pie, pecan: Magnolia Bakery (401 Bleecker St)
Pie, shepherd's: Landmark Tavern (626 11th Ave)
Pie, walnut sour-cream apple: Little Pie Company (424 W 43rd St)
Pig sandwich (pulled pork): Hard Rock Cafe (221 W 57th St)
Pig's feet (special only): Daniel (20 E 76th St)
Pizza, deep-dish: PIZZAPIAZZA (785 Broadway)
Pizza, designer: Paper Moon Milano (39 E 58th St)
Pizza, Sicilian: Sal's and Carmine Pizza (2671 Broadway)
Popcorn: Creative Corn Co. (1275 Lexington Ave) and Pug Bros. (265
   Columbus Ave)
Popovers: Popover Cafe (551 Amsterdam Ave)
Pork: 69 Mott Street (69 Mott St)
Pork, braised breast (seasonal) Daniel (20 E 76th St)
Pork, European-style cured: Salumeria Biellese (376 Eighth Ave)
Pork shank: Maloney & Porcelli's (37 E 50th St)
Potato pancakes: Ideal Lunch and Bar (322 E 86th St)
Potatoes, huge stuffed baked: Citarella (2135 Broadway)
Potatoes, mashed: Lenox Room (1278 Third Ave) and Union Square Cafe (21
   E 16th St)
Pot-au-feu: Bouterin (420 E 59th St), Cafe des Artistes (1 W 67th St), and Le
   Bernardin (155 W 51st St; special only)
Pretzels: Pennsylvania Pretzel Company (295 Greenwich St)
Pretzels and cookies, hand-dipped chocolate: Evelyn's Chocolates (4 John St)
Prime rib: Fresco (34 E 52nd St), Two Two Two (222 W 79th St), and Smith &
   Wollensky (201 E 49th St)
Produce, fresh: Fairway Market (2127 Broadway)
Profiteroles: Chez Ma Tante (189 W 10th St)
Pudding, rice: Marti Restaurant (238 E 24th St and 1269 First Ave)
Pudding, Yorkshire: Popover Cafe (551 Amsterdam Ave)
Quiche: Chez Laurence (245 Madison Ave)

Raspberry Charlotte (summer months)**:** Dolci on Park Caffe (12 Park Ave)
Ravioli: Osteria del Circo (120 W 55th St), the Ravioli Store (75 Sullivan St).
   Piemonte Homemade Ravioli Company (190 Grand St), and Di Palo Fine
   Food (206 Grand St)
Ravioli, steamed Vietnamese: Indochine (430 Lafayette St)
Red snapper, roasted (seasonal)**:** Daniel (20 E 76th St)
Ribs: Sylvia's Restaurant (328 Lenox Ave), Wylie's Ribs and Company (891
   First Ave), and Brother Jimmy's Bar-B-Q (1461 First Ave)
Ribs, baby-back: Baby Buddha (753 Washington St), Emily's (1325 Fifth Ave),
   and Mesa Grill (102 Fifth Ave)
Ribs, barbecue: Dok Suni's (119 First Ave)
Ribs, braised, short beef: Daniel (20 E 76th St), Lespinasse (2 E 55th St),
   and Spartina (355 Greenwich St)
Rice: Rice (227 Mott St)
Risotto: Lespinasse (2 E 55th St) and Picholine (35 W 64th St)
Rogoleh: Royale Pastry Shop (237 W 72nd St)
Salad bar: City Bakery (22 E 17th St)
Salad, Caesar: Post House (28 E 63rd St)
Salad, lobster: Hurricane Island (1303 Third Ave)
Salad, potato, nicoise: Manny Wolf's (145 E 49th St)
Salad, seafood: Gotham Bar and Grill (12 E 12th St)
Salad, tuna: Todaro Bros. (555 Second Ave)
Salad, warm white bean: Caffe Grazie (26 E 84th St)
Salami: Zeppole (186 Franklin St)
Salmon: Jo Jo (160 E 64th St)
Salmon cakes: All State Cafe (250 W 72nd St)
Salmon, marinated: La Réserve (4 W 49th St)
Salmon, smoked: Aquavit (13 W 54th St) and Sable's (1489 Second Ave)
Salmon, truffle-crusted: Montrachet (239 West Broadway)
Sandwich, brisket: Second Avenue Kosher Delicatessen and Restaurant (156
   Second Ave)
Sandwich, club: Pierre Hotel (2 E 61st St)
Sandwich, gourmet: Columbus Bakery (957 First Ave)
Sandwich, grilled portobello: Zoë (90 Prince St)
Sandwich, grilled chicken breast: Island Burgers & Shakes (766 Ninth Ave)
   and Ranch 1 (684 Third Ave and other locations)
Sandwich, po'-boy: Two Boots (37 Ave A)
Sandwich, puff pastry: Dufour Pastry Kitchens (25 Ninth Ave)
Sandwich, tea (made to order)**:** Mortimer's (1057 Lexington Ave)
Sandwich, turkey: Viand Coffee Shop (1011 Madison Ave)
Sandwich wraps: Emerald Planet (2 Great Jones St)
Sardines, marinated: Oceana (55 E 54th St)
Satays: Typhoon Brewery (22 E 54th St)
Sauerbraten: Ideal Restaurant (322 E 86th St)
Sauerkraut: Katz's Delicatessen (205 E Houston St)
Sausage: Urban Hero (245 W 38th St)
Sausage, East European: Kurowycky Meat Products (124 First Ave)
Sausage, Hungarian: Tibor Meat Specialties (1508 Second Ave)
Sausage, Tuscan: Toscana (843 Lexington Ave)
Scallops: Le Bernardin (155 W 51st St)
Scallops in a chive nage: Lutece (249 E 50th St)
Schnecken: William Greenberg Jr. (518 Third Ave, 1100 Madison Ave, and
   2187 Broadway)

Scones: Tea and Sympathy (108 Greenwich Ave), Muffin Shop (Columbus Ave and 70th St), and Mangia (50 W 57th St and 16 E 48th St)
Seafood dinners: Pisces (95 Ave A), Wilkinson's (1573 York Ave), Le Bernardin (155 W 51st St), and Le Pescadou (18 King St)
Seafood platter: Mezzogiorno (195 Spring St)
Shabu-Shabu: Seryna (11 E 53rd St)
Sherbets: La Cigale (231 Mott St)
Shrimp Creole: Jezebel (630 Ninth Ave)
Singing waiters: Asti (13 E 12th St)
Sliders (mini burgers): Sassy's Sliders (163 First Ave)
Snacks, soups, sandwiches: Serendipity 3 (225 E 60th St)
Snails: Lutece (249 E 50th St)
Sole, Dover: Le Régence (37 E 64th St)
Sorbet: E&O (100 West Houston St) and La Boite En Bois (75 W 68th St)
Soufflés: Capsouto Frerès (451 Washington St), La Caravelle (33 W 55th St), and La Côte Basque (60 W 55th St)
Soufflé, chocolate: La Réserve (4 W 49th St)
Soup, black bean: Union Square Cafe (21 E 16th St)
Soup, chestnut & fennel: Picholine (35 W 64th St)
Soup, chicken: Brooklyn Diner (212 W 57th St) and Second Avenue Kosher Delicatessen and Restaurant (156 Second Ave)
Soup, Chinese: Chao Chow (111 Mott St)
Soup, duck: Kelley and Ping (127 Greene St)
Soup, French onion: La Bonne Soupe (48 W 55th St)
Soup, homemade: Kiev Restaurant (Second Ave at 7th St)
Soup, hot and sour: Shun Lee Cafe (43 W 65th St)
Soup, Mandalay fish: Road to Mandalay (380 Broome St)
Soup, matzoh ball: Second Avenue Kosher Delicatessen and Restaurant (156 Second Ave)
Soup, minestrone: Il Vagabondo (351 E 62nd St) and Trattoria Spaghetto (232 Bleecker St)
Soup, mushroom (occasionally): Flavors (8 W 18th St)
Soup, pumpkin: Mesa Grill (102 Fifth Ave)
Soup, raison d être: Shopsin's General Store (63 Bedford St)
Soup, tomato: Sarabeth's Kitchen (423 Amsterdam Ave, 1295 Madison Ave, and 945 Madison Ave at Whitney Museum)
Spaghetti: Paolucci (149 Mulberry St)
Spareribs, Chinese: Fu's (972 Second Ave)
Spices: Aphrodisia (264 Bleecker St)
Spinach pies, Greek: Poseidon Bakery (629 Ninth Ave)
Spring rolls: An American Place (2 Park Ave)
Spring rolls, crab: Vong (200 E 54th St)
Squid, grilled stuffed: I Trulli (122 E 27th St)
Steak, au poivre: Chez Josephine (414 W 42nd St)
Steak, Black Angus, and French fries: Steak Frites (9 E 16th St)
Steak, Cajun rib: Morton's of Chicago (551 Fifth Ave and 90 West St) and the Post House (28 E 63rd St)
Steak, Porterhouse: Manhattan Cafe (1161 First Ave) and Morton's of Chicago (551 Fifth Ave and 90 West St)
Steak, strip: Restaurant Charlotte (145 W 44th St)
Steak tartare: Voulez-Vous (1462 First Ave)
Strawberry shortcake: An American Place (2 Park Ave)

Strudel: Big Apple Strudel (1652 Second Ave), Cafe 112 (2885 Broadway), and Mocca Hungarian (1588 Second Ave)

Sushi: Kurumazushi (18 W 56th St), Sushi Hatsu (1143 First Ave), Avenue A Sushi (103 Ave A), Iso (175 Second Ave), TakeSushi (71 Vanderbilt Ave), Ten Kai (920 W 56th St), Hatsuhana (17 E 48th St), and Nippon (155 E 52nd St)

Swordfish, cured: Fifty-seven Fifty-seven (Four Seasons Hotel, 57 E 57th St)

Tabbouleh: Benny's (321½ Amsterdam Ave)

Tacos, soft: Fresco Tortilla Grill (36 Lexington Ave, 253 Eighth Ave, 125 W 42nd St, 766 Ninth Ave, and 769 Sixth Ave)

Tamales: Zarela (953 Second Ave)

Tapas, Spanish: Domingo (209 E 49th St), El Cid (322 W 15th St), La Paella (557 Hudson St), ñ (33 Crosby St), Solera (216 E 53rd St), Tapestry (575 Hudson St), and Xunta (174 First Ave)

Tartlet, warm bittersweet chocolate: Lespinasse (2 E 55th St)

Tarts and logs, stuffed puff pastry: Dufour Pastry Kitchen (25 Ninth Ave)

Tarts, apple: Quatorze Bis (323 E 79th St)

Tarts, fruit: Ceci-Cela (55 Spring St)

Tarts, fruit and vegetable: Once Upon a Tart (135 Sullivan St)

Tartufo: Erminia (250 E 83rd St) and Il Corallo (176 Prince St)

Tea: T Salon and T Emporium (11 E 20th St)

Tea and coffee, iced: Henri's (16 Maiden Ln)

Tempura: Inagiku (Waldorf-Astoria Hotel, 111 E 49th St)

Tiramisu: Mezzogiorno (195 Spring St), Caffe Dante (79-81 MacDougal St), and Biricchino (260 W 29th St)

Torte, chocolate mocha (seasonal): Ecce Panis (1120 Third Ave)

Torte, delizia: Sant Ambroeus (1000 Madison Ave)

Torte, sacher: Duane Park Patisserie (179 Duane St)

Torte, Viennese chocolate: Peacock Caffe (24 Greenwich Ave)

Tortillas: Azteca Deli Grocery (698 Amsterdam Ave)

Tripe: Les Halles (411 Park Ave S)

Truffles: Black Hound (149 First Ave)

Truffles, champagne: Teuscher (25 E 61st St and 620 Fifth Ave)

Tuna, seared: Two Two Two (222 W 79th St)

Tuna steak: Union Square Cafe (21 E 16th St)

Tuna tartare: Flowers (21 W 17th St)

Turnover, apple: La Boulangere (49 E 21st St)

Veal: Pierre au Tunnel (250 W 47th St)

Veal carpaccio: Gotham Bar & Grill (12 E 12th St)

Veal chops: Aperitivo (20 W 56th St), Daniel (20 E 76th St), and La Réserve (4 W 49th St)

Veal scaloppini: Zinno's (126 W 13th St)

Veal stew: Pierre au Tunnel (250 W 47th St)

Vegan baking: Whole Earth Bakery & Kitchen (70 Spring St)

Vegetable terrine: Montrachet (239 West Broadway)

Vegetarian combo: Hudson Falafel (516 Hudson St)

Vegetarian items: Vegetarian's Paradise (144 W 4th St)

Vegetarian meals: Natural Gourmet Cookery School (48 W 21st St)

Venison (seasonal): Chanterelle (2 Harrison St)

Waffles (Sunday brunch): Berry's (180 Spring St)

Waffles, Belgian (weekend brunch): Cafe de Bruxelles (118 Greenwich Ave)

Waffles, pumpkin: Sarabeth's Kitchen (1295 Madison Ave, 423 Amsterdam Ave, and 945 Madison Ave at Whitney Museum)

Watermelon parfait: Coco Opera (58 W 65th St)
Whiskeys, malt: Soho Wines & Spirits (461 W Broadway)
Wines: Crossroads Wines & Liquors (55 W 14th St)
Wines, European: Quality House (2 Park Ave)
Yogurt: Emack & Bolio's (389 Amsterdam Ave)
Yogurt, "Only 8" frozen: Peppermint Park Cafe (1225 First Ave)
Yogurt shake: TCBY (69 E 8th St and 2052 Broadway)
Zabaglione: Il Monello (1460 Second Ave)

Appetizers

Barney Greengrass (541 Amsterdam Ave): sturgeon king
Caviarteria (502 Park Ave): a small caviar heaven
Murray's Sturgeon (2429 Broadway): oldtime reliability
Russ & Daughters (179 E Houston St): the very best, with a personal touch
Zabar's (2245 Broadway): There's no place in the world like it!

Bagels

Absolute Bagels (2788 Broadway)
Bagel City (720 W 181st St)
Bagel Works (1229 First Ave)
Columbia Hot Bagels (2836 Broadway)
Daniel's Bagels (569 Third Ave)
Ess-A-Bagel (359 First Ave and 831 Third Ave)
H&H Bagels (2239 Broadway and 639 W 46th St)
H&H Bagels East (1551 Second Ave)
Hot Bagels (168 Madison Ave)
Lenny's (2601 Broadway)
Mom's Bagels (15 W 45th St)
Murray's Bagels (500 Sixth Ave)
Pick-a-Bagel (1083 Lexington Ave)

Barbecues

Big Wong (67 Mott St): Chinese style
Brother's Bar-B-Q (228 W Houston St): smoked ribs
Copeland's (547 W 145th St): Harlem setting
Dallas BBQ (1265 Third Ave, 27 W 72nd St, 21 University Place, and 132 Second Ave): big and busy, but only fair in quality
Rusty's (1271 Third Ave): all-American tasty baby-back ribs
Shun Lee Cafe (43 W Fifth St): classy Chinese
Stick to Your Ribs (433 Amsterdam Ave): consistently tasty
Sylvia's (328 Lenox Ave): reputation is better than the food
Virgil's Real Barbecue (152 W 44th St): big, brassy, mass-production
Wylie's Ribs (891 First Ave): consistently good
Zacki's Carolina Pit B.B.Q. (1752 Second Ave): nothing fancy except the taste

Breakfast

Breakfast is a big deal in New York. Some folks use it for a business setting. Others want just a social get-together. More and more look at their first meal of the day as something healthy before or after the morning workout. Still others want something tasty, in a hurry, at a good price.

For the real *power* scenes, hotels are the preferred locations. The biggest names are the **Regency** (540 Park Ave), the **Peninsula** (700 Fifth Ave), the **Plaza**

Edwardian Room (Fifth Ave at 59th St), **Fifty-seven Fifty-seven** at the **Four Seasons** (57 E 57th St), the **Paramount** (235 W 46th St), and the **Royalton** (44 W 44th St).

Some other recommended places with excellent day-starters include **Aggie's** (146 W Houston St), **Bubby's** (120 Hudson St), **Cafe Botanica** (Essex House, 160 Central Park S), **Cafe Word of Mouth** (1012 Lexington Ave), **Comfort Diner** (214 E 45th St), **E.J.'s Luncheonette** (447 Amsterdam Ave), **Ellen's Stardust Diner** (1377 Sixth Ave), **Good Enough to Eat** (483 Amsterdam Ave), **Jerry's** (101 Prince St), **Le Gamin** (50 MacDougal St), **Noho Star** (330 Lafayette St), **Popover Cafe** (551 Amsterdam Ave), **Sarabeth's Kitchen** (423 Amsterdam Ave, 1295 Madison Ave, and 945 Madison Ave at the Whitney Museum), **Tivoli** (515 Third Ave), and **Tramway Coffee Shop** (1143 Second Ave).

The breads are great (and expensive) at Eli Zabar's **E.A.T.** (1064 Madison Ave), the pancakes (53 varieties) at the **Royal Canadian** (2286 Broadway, 1004 Second Ave, and 180 Third Ave) and at **Fifty-seven Fifty-seven** (57 E 57th St) are excellent. **Aggie's** (146 W Houston St) home fries are hard to beat (so are her bacon and omelets), **Friend of a Farmer** (77 Irving Pl) has a late pancake feast, and the **Columbus Bakery** (474 Columbus Ave) offers sinful cheese danishes and yummy croissants.

Brunch

The classiest Manhattan Sunday brunch is offered at the **Palm Court** at the Plaza Hotel (Fifth Ave and 59th St). The entire Palm Court is opened up to showcase a dazzling array of hot and cold dishes, seafood, salads, and fresh fruit, along with a dessert selection that can only be equaled at Gerry Frank's Konditorei in Salem, Oregon! It is not inexpensive. **Cafe Botanica** at the Essex House (160 Central Park S) is excellent. A special brunch treat—along with a delicious assortment of dairy, butcher's market, seafood, pastry, and produce dishes—is the view from the 54th-floor setting atop the **RIHGA Royal Hotel** (151 W 54th St).

Also consider the following:

Amici Miei (475 W Broadway): outdoor garden in summer
Berry's (180 Spring St): for Nova Scotia salmon
Cafe Botanica (Essex House, 160 Central Park S)
Cafe des Artistes (1 W 67th St): Both the ambience and the food are classy.
Capsouto Fréres (451 Washington St)
Cendrillon (45 Mercer St): Filipino flavors
Chelsea Bistro & Bar (358 W 23rd St)
Crystal Fountain (Grand Hyatt Hotel, Park Ave at Grand Central)
Cub Room (131 Sullivan St)
Cupping Room Cafe (359 West Broadway)
Danal (90 E 10th St): luscious French toast
Emily's (1325 Fifth Ave, at 111th St): soul food
Flowers (21 W 17th St)
Friend of a Farmer (77 Irving Pl)
Good Enough to Eat (483 Madison Ave)
Iridium (44 W 63rd St): live gospel music
Julian's (802 Ninth Ave)
La Gallerie (1435 Second Ave): very romantic
Le Régence (Hotel Plaza Athenee, 37 E 64th St): very classy Sunday brunch
Lobster Club (24 E 80th St)
Lola (30 W 22nd St)
Mackinac Bar & Grill (384 Columbus Ave): creative brunch dishes

Mark's Restaurant (25 E 77th St): classy
Match Uptown (33 E 66th St and 160 Mercer St)
Mesa Grill (102 Fifth Ave)
Miracle Grill (112 First Ave)
Mortimer's (1057 Lexington Ave): for people-watching
Odeon (145 West Broadway)
Paris Commune (411 Bleecker St): Bohemian-looking West Village bistro
Park Avenue Cafe (100 E 63rd St): American dim sum, Saturday only
Peacock Alley at the Waldorf-Astoria Hotel (301 Park Ave)
Provence (38 MacDougal St)
Rainbow Room (30 Rockefeller Plaza): for nostalgia
Sarabeth's Kitchen (423 Amsterdam Ave, 1295 Madison Ave, and 945 Madison
    Ave at Whitney Museum): for dependably good food in a relaxed environment
Soho Steak (90 Thompson St): high-protein bistro fare
Tapika (950 Eighth Ave): Southwestern
Tartine (253 W 11th St)
Tavern on the Green (Central Park W at 67th St): for entertaining out-of-town
    guests
Vinegar Factory (431 E 91st St)
Voulez-Vous (1462 First Ave): for marvelous steak tartare
Water Club (500 E 30th St)

Here are some brunch bargains:

Arlo's (1394 York Ave)
Cottonwood Cafe (415 Bleecker St)
E.J's Luncheonette (433 Amsterdam Ave)
Landmark Tavern (626 Eleventh Ave)
9 (110 St. Mark's Pl)
Popover Cafe (551 Amsterdam Ave)

Burgers

Abby (254 Fifth Ave)
Aggie's (146 W Houston)
All-State Cafe (250 W 72nd St)
Bar 89 (89 Mercer St)
Big Nick's (2175 Broadway): You'll love it!
Billy's (948 First Ave)
Brew's (156 E 34th St)
Burger Heaven (20 E 49th St)
Cal's (55 W 21st St): excellent
Chelsea Grill (135 Eighth Ave)
Chumley's (86 Bedford)
Corner Bistro (331 W 4th St)
Diane's (249 Columbus Ave)
44 (Royalton Hotel, 44 W 44th St)
Hamburger Harry's (157 Chambers St and 145 W 45th St)
Hard Rock Cafe (221 W 57th St): where the action is as tasty as the burgers
Harper (1303 Third Ave)
Home (20 Cornelia St)
Island (1305 Madison Ave)
Jackson Hole Burgers 232 E 64th St, Third Ave at 35th St, and Second Ave
    at 84th St)
Keen's Steakhouse (72 W 36th St)

Knickerbocker Bar and Grill (33 University Pl)
McDonald's (160 Broadway at Liberty St): This one has class.
P.J. Clarke's (915 Third Ave)
Penguin Cafe (581 Hudson St)
Planet Hollywood (150 W 57th St)
Sassy's Sliders (163 First Ave): small and tasty burgers
Silverspurs (771 Broadway)
Smith & Wollensky (797 Third Ave)
Taste of the Apple (1016 Second Ave)
21 (21 W 52nd St)
Union Square Cafe (21 E 16th St)
World Cafe (201 Columbus Ave)
Zachary's (51 W 64th St)
Zoë (90 Prince St)

Cheap Eats

Some of the better deals in town:

Aggie's (146 W Houston St)
Alley's End (311 W 17th St)
B&H Dairy (127 Second Ave)
Baby Jake's (14 First Ave)
Bar Six (502 Sixth Ave)
Barking Dog Luncheonette (1678 Third Ave)
Bendix Diner (219 Eighth Ave)
Big Nick's (2175 Broadway)
Bistro Margot (26 Prince St)
Boca Chica (13 First Ave)
Bona Fides (60 Second Ave)
Bus Stop Cafe (597 Hudson St)
Cafe Lalo (201 W 83rd St)
Cafe Pertutti (2888 Broadway)
Cafe Riazor (245 W 16th St)
Caffe Buon Gusto (236 E 77th St)
Caffe Lure (169 Sullivan St)
Caffe Vivaldi (32 Jones St)
Carmine's (2450 Broadway)
Chantale's Cajun Kitchen (510 Ninth Ave)
Chelsea Grill (135 Eighth Ave)
Chez Brigette (77 Greenwich Ave)
Christine's (208 First Ave)
City Bakery (22 E 17th St)
Coffee Shop (29 Union Sq W)
Col Legno (231 E 9th St)
Comfort Diner (214 E 45th St)
Corner Bistro (331 W 4th St)
Cucina (256 Fifth Ave)
Cucina di Pesce (87 E 4th St)
Cucina Stagionale (275 Bleecker St)
Cupcake Cafe (522 Ninth Ave)
Dallas BBQ (1265 Third Ave, 27 W 72nd St, 21 University Pl, and 132 Second Ave)
Danal (90 E 10th St)

Da Nico (164 Mulberry St)
Dining Commons (City University of New York, 33 W 42nd St, 18th floor)
Edgar's Cafe (255 W 84th St)
Eighteenth & Eighth (159 Eighth Ave)
El Pollo (1746 First Ave)
Elvie's Turo-Turo (214 First Ave)
English Harbour Fish & Chips (246 E 14th St)
Film Center Cafe (635 Ninth Ave)
First (87 First Ave)
Flor de Mayo (2651 Broadway)
Frank's (85 Tenth Ave)
Fresco Tortilla Grill (36 Lexington Ave)
Gabriela's (685 Amsterdam Ave)
Golden Unicorn (18 East Broadway)
Good Enough to Eat (483 Amsterdam Ave)
Gray's Papaya (2090 Broadway)
Hallo Berlin (402 W 51st St)
Hamburger Harry's (157 Chambers St)
Home (20 Cornelia St)
Hot Tomato (676 Sixth Ave)
Hurley's (1240 Sixth Ave)
Hurricane Island (1303 Third Ave)
Il Bagatto (192E Second Ave)
Indigo (142 W 10th St)
Isola (485 Columbus Ave)
Jean-Claude (137 Sullivan St)
Jo-An Japanese (2707 Broadway)
Joe Jr's (482 Sixth Ave)
John's Pizzeria (several locations)
Katz's Delicatessen (205 E Houston St)
Key West Diner & Cafe (2532 Broadway)
Kitchen Club (30 Prince St)
L'Ardoise (1207 First Ave)
La Bonne Soupe (48 W 55th St)
La Cocina (217 W 85th St)
La Foccaceria (128 First Ave)
La Taza De Oro (96 Eighth Ave)
Lemon Tree Cafe (769 Ninth Ave)
Leo's Famous (100 W 32nd St)
Mama's Food Shop (200 E 3rd St)
Margon (136 W 46th St)
Marnie's Noodle Shop (466 Hudson St)
Mavalli Palace (46 E 29th St)
McDonald's (160 Broadway)
Mee Noodle Soup (795 Ninth Ave)
Mill, The (2895 Broadway)
Mingala West (325 Amsterdam Ave)
Monck's Corner Take Out (644 Ninth Ave)
Moondance Diner (80 Sixth Ave)
New York Noodletown (28½ Bowery St)
Nha Trang (87 Baxter St)
Ollie's Noodle Shop and Grill (190 W 44th St)

107 West Restaurant (2787 Broadway)
Orlin (60 E 42nd St)
Pad Thai (114 Eighth Ave)
Panna II (93 First Ave)
Papaya King (179 E 86th St)
Patsy's Pizza (2287 First Ave and 509 Third Ave)
Persepolis (1423 Second Ave)
Pintaile's Pizza (26 E 91st St)
Pisces (95 Ave A)
Pitchoune (226 Third Ave)
PIZZAPIAZZA (785 Broadway)
Pó (31 Cornelia St)
Popover Cafe (551 Amsterdam Ave)
Positively 104th (2725 Broadway)
Rainbow Chicken (2801 Broadway)
Rao's (455 E 114th St)
Royal Canadian Pancake House (2286 Broadway, 1004 Second Ave, and 180 Third Ave)
Royal Siam Thai (240 Eighth Ave)
Second Avenue Kosher Delicatessen and Restaurant (156 Second Ave)
Seventh Regiment Armory Mess Hall (643 Park Ave)
Sevilla (62 Charles St)
Shopsin's General Store (63 Bedford St, at Morton St): an original!
Siam Cuisine (1411 Second Ave)
Silverado Bar and Grill (99 E 19th St)
Soho Kitchen and Bar (103 Greene St)
Spring Street Natural Restaurant (62 Spring St)
Sweet Ophelia's (430 Broome St)
Sylvia's (328 Lenox Ave)
Symposium Greek Restaurant (544 W 113th St)
Tanti Baci Cafe (163 W 10th St)
Taqueria de Mexico (93 Greenwich Ave)
Teresa's (103 First Ave)
13 Barrow St (13 Barrow St)
Tibetan Kitchen (444 Third Ave)
Topaz Thai (127 W 56th St)
Tres Aztecas (66 Rivington St)
Turkish Cuisine (631 Ninth Ave)
Uncle Nick's (747 Ninth Ave)
Veronica (240 W 38th St)
Veselka (144 Second Ave)
Viand (1011 Madison Ave, 673 Madison Ave, and 300 E 86th St)
Wong Kee (113 Mott St)

Cigar Friendly

Alva (36 E 22nd St)
Ansonia (329 Columbus Ave)
Cafe des Artistes, the Parlour (1 W 67th St)
Cigar Room at Trumpets (Grand Hyatt Hotel, Park Ave and Grand Central)
City Wine & Cigar Company (62 Laight St)
Club Macanudo (26 E 63rd St)
Cub Room (131 Sullivan St)

Havana (265 E 78th St)
Hudson Bar and Books (636 Hudson St)
Lattanzi (361 W 46th St)
Monkey Bar (60 E 54th St)
Onieal's (174 Grand St)
Plaza Hotel Oak Room (768 Fifth Ave)
Pravda (281 Lafayette St)
Remi (145 W 53rd St)
St. Regis Hotel King Cole Bar (2 E 55th St)
Sullivan's (1697 Broadway)
Tatou Le Cigar (151 E 50th St)
Windows on the World Skybox (1 World Trade Center)

A *Manhattan Special* is not an express bus from Brooklyn, and it has nothing to do with the subways, but it's been part of New York City since 1885. Described as "the world's most delicious coffee soda," the *Manhattan Special* is a hand-brewed concoction of freshly roasted coffee beans and 100% granulated sugar (practically unheard of in the beverage industry today). The result is a lusty coffee soda. It also comes sugar- and caffeine-free, too!

Coffeehouses

They are very "in"! You can relax, enjoy good company, and drink various coffee beverages at the following:

Au Cafe (1700 Broadway)
Au Petit Beurre (2737 Broadway)
Basset Coffee & Tea Company (123 West Broadway)
Biblio's (317 Church St)
Big Cup (228 Eighth Ave)
Bleecker Street Pastry (245 Bleecker St)
Bodum (673 Madison Ave)
Broadway Bagels Deli (2658 Broadway)
Cafe La Fortuna (69 W 71st St)
Cafe Lalo (201 W 83rd St)
Cafe Orlin (41 St. Mark's Pl)
Caffe Biondo (141 Mulberry St)
Caffe Dante (79 MacDougal St)
Caffe del Corso (19 W 55th St)
Caffe Novocento (33 West Broadway)
Caffe Reggio (119 MacDougal St)
Caffe Roma (385 Broome St)
Caffe Vivaldi (32 Jones St)
Chez Laurence Patisserie (245 Madison Ave)
City Bakery (22 E 17th St)
Coffee Arts (5 World Trade Center)
Coffee Bar (2151 Broadway)
Cooper's Coffee and Espresso Bar (2151 Broadway)
Cupcake Cafe (522 Ninth Ave)
Cupping Room Cafe (359 W Broadway)

DT.UT (1626 Second Ave)
Daily Caffe (Rockefeller Center)
Dean & Deluca (560 Broadway)
Dolci on Park (12 Park Ave)
Espresso Madison (33 E 68th St)
Eureka Joe (168 Fifth Ave)
Ferrara's (195 Grand St)
French Roast (458 Sixth Ave)
Golden Frog Coffee Company (564 Third Ave)
Hungarian Pastry Shop (1030 Amsterdam Ave)
Jonathan Morr Espresso Bar (12394 Sixth Ave)
Kaffeehaus (131 Eighth Ave)
Le Gamin (50 MacDougal St)
Lipstick Cafe (885 Third Ave)
New World Coffee (449 Sixth Ave)
Newsbar (366 West Broadway)
9 (110 St Mark's Pl)
Oren's Daily Roast (many locations)
Pane & Cioccolato (10 Waverly Pl)
Peacock (24 Greenwich Ave)
Philip's Coffee (155 W 56th St)
Sant Ambroeus (1000 Madison Ave)
Sarabeth's Kitchen (1295 Madison Ave, 423 Amsterdam Ave, and 945 Madison Ave at the Whitney Museum)
Scharmann's (386 West Broadway)
Seattle Bean Company (1573 Second Ave)
Seattle Coffee Roasters (150 Fifth Ave)
Sensuous Bean (66 W 70th St)
Starbucks (many locations)
Timothy's (1285 Sixth Ave)
Uncommon Grounds (533 Third Ave)
Veniero Pasticceria (342 E 11th St)
Veselka Coffee Shop (144 Second Ave)
Xando Coffee and Bar (2160 Broadway)

Delis

Barney Greengrass (541 Amsterdam Ave)
Bernstein-on-Essex (135 Essex St)
Carnegie Delicatessen and Restaurant (854 Seventh Ave)
E.A.T. (1064 Madison Ave)
Fine & Schapiro (138 W 72nd St)
Katz's Delicatessen (205 E Houston St)
Second Avenue Kosher Delicatessen and Restaurant (156 Second Ave)
Stage Delicatessen (834 Seventh Ave)
Third Ave Delicatessen (276 Third Ave)
Wolf's Sixth Ave Delicatessen (101 W 57th St)

Desserts

Don't let anyone tell you desserts aren't popular! Most of the places also serve fine coffee, espresso, and cappuccino.

Cafe Lalo (201 W 83rd St): the best European-style cafe!
Caffe Biondo (141 Mulberry St): little Italy's star

Caffe Bondi (7 W 20th St): Italian tortes
Caffe Pertutti (2862 Broadway): a waist-expanding experience
Carnegie Delicatessen and Restaurant (854 Seventh Ave): Everything here is big.
Delices de France (289 Madison Ave): The name says it all.
Dolci on Park Caffe (12 Park Ave): undiscovered gem
Eclair Pastry Shops (Grand Central Terminal, Herald Square, 54th St at First Ave, and 141 W 72nd St): good selection
Ferrara (195 Mulberry St): Italian gelati
Gindi (935 Broadway): great pastries
Halcyon (151 W 54th St): spectacular!
Hard Rock Cafe (221 W 57th St): all-American treats
Le Cirque (Palace Hotel): world famous!
Les Delices West (370 Columbus Ave): fine French pastries
Les Friandises (972 Lexington Ave): fabulous chocolate mousse cake
Lo Spuntino (117 Mulberry St): ice cream specialties
Madeline's (117 Prince St): end of a great meal
Palm Court (Plaza Hotel, 59th St at Fifth Ave): vintage New York
Patisserie J. Lanciani (271 W 4th St): pastries plus
Peppermint Park (1225 First Ave): outrageous offerings
Sant Ambroeus (1000 Madison Ave): rich and classy
Serendipity 3 (225 E 60th St): an institution for the young-at-heart
Succes la Côte Basque (Henri Bendel, 1032 Lexington Ave): successful for curing hunger pangs!
Tavern on the Green (Central Park W at 67th St): There's nothing like it back home!
Velvet Room (209 E 76th St): pages of great desserts
Zabar's Cafe (80th St at Broadway): big treats, low prices

THE BEST PASTRY CHEFS IN TOWN . .. these are the people to ask to help you out at your next dinner party !

Amy's Bread: Amy Scherber
Bouley: Bill Yosses
Chanterelle: Michael Klug
Daniel: Francois Payard
Four Seasons Hotel: Bruno Feldeisen
La Côte Basque: Lincoln Carlson
Le Bernardin: Florian Bellanger
Le Cirque: Jacques Torres
Les Célébrités: André Rénard
Maxim's: D. Jemal Edwards
Mesa Grill: Wayne Brackman
Park Avenue Cafe: Richard Leach
Plaza Hotel: Eric Gouteyron
Rainbow: Anne McManus
Sarabeth's Kitchen: Sarabeth Levine
Windows on the World: Herve Poussot

Dim Sum

The serving of small tea pastries called dim sum originated in Hong Kong and has become a delicious Chinatown institution. Although dim sum is usually eaten for brunch, some restaurants will also serve it as an appetizer before dinner. The food is rolled over to your table on carts, and you simply point at whatever looks good. This eliminates the language barrier and encourages experimentation. When you're finished, the small plates you've accumulated are counted, and the bill is drawn up. Some of the most popular dim sum dishes include:

Cha Siu Bow (steamed barbecued pork buns)
Cha Siu So (flaky buns)
Chun Guen (spring rolls)
Dow Sah Bow (sweet bean-paste-filled buns)
Fancy Fans (meat-filled wonton skins)
Floweret Siu Mai (meat-filled dumplings)
Four-Color Shiu Mai (meat- and vegetable-filled dumplings)
Gee Cheung Fun (steamed rice-noodle rolls)
Gee Yoke Go (savory pork triangles)
Ha Gow (shrimp dumplings)
Jow Ha Gok (shrimp turnovers)
Pot Sticker Kou The (meat-filled dumplings)
Pot Sticker Triangles (meat-filled wonton skins)
Siu Mai (steamed pork dumplings)

For the most authentic and delicious dim sum in New York, I recommend:

China Royal (17 Division St)
Golden Unicorn (18 East Broadway): serves an especially fine selection
H.S.F. (46 Bowery and 578 Second Ave)
Jing Fong (20 Elizabeth St)
Mandarin Court (61 Mott St)
Nice Restaurant (35 East Broadway)
Oriental Pearl (103 Mott St)
Shun Lee Cafe (43 W 65th St)
Silver Palace (50 Bowery)
Sun Hop Shing Tea House (21 Mott St)
Tai-Hong-Lau (70 Mott St)
Triple 8 Palace (59 Division St)

Diners

There are not many classic diners left in Manhattan. The best survivors are:

Aggie's (146 W Houston St)
Broadway Diner (590 Lexington Ave)
Brooklyn Diner (212 W 57th St): outstanding
Buffa's (54 Prince St)
Ellen's Stardust (1650 Broadway)
Empire Diner (210 Tenth Ave)
Lost Diner (357 West St)
Market Diner (Eleventh Ave at 43rd St)
Moondance Diner (80 Sixth Ave)

Dining and Dancing

Cafe Pierre (Pierre Hotel, 2 E 61st St): refined

Decade (1117 First Ave at 61st St): modern food, 60s and 70s music
Delia's (197 E 3rd St): alphabet-land French-Caribbean dancing
Rainbow Room (30 Rockefeller Plaza, 65th floor): This is *the* place for refined romance.
Supper Club, The (240 W 47th St): vintage 40s with big bands
Tavern on the Green (Central Park W at 67th St): great setting
Well's (2247-49 Seventh Ave): Harlem soul food and jazz
World Yacht Cruises (Pier 81, W 41st St at the Hudson River): It's a constant party.

Dining Solo

Some of these restaurants have dining counters, others are tranquil and suitable for single diners:

Arizona 206 (206 E 60th St)
Between the Bread (141 E 56th St)
Brasserie (100 E 53rd St)
Broadway Diner (590 Lexington Ave and 1726 Broadway)
Cafe des Sports (329 W 51st St)
Cafe SFA (Saks Fifth Ave, 611 Fifth Ave)
Carnegie Delicatessen and Restaurant (854 Seventh Ave)
Chez Napoleon (365 W 50th St)
Coffee Shop (29 Union Sq W, at 16th St)
Elephant & Castle (68 Greenwich St and Seventh Ave at 11th St)
Grand Central Oyster Bar Restaurant (Grand Central Station, lower level)
Hosteria Fiorella (1081 Third Ave)
J. G. Melon (1291 Third Ave)
Jackson Hole Burgers (232 E 64th St, Third Ave at 35th St and Second Ave at 84th St)
Jour et Nuit (337 West Broadway, 498 Seventh Ave, and 152 W 36th St)
La Bonne Soupe (48 W 55th St)
Lexington Avenue Grill (Loews Summit Hotel, 569 Lexington Ave)
Lipstick Cafe (885 Third Ave)
Mme. Romaine de Lyon (132 E 61st St)
Raoul's (180 Prince St)
Sarabeth's Kitchen (1295 Madison Ave at Hotel Wales, 423 Amsterdam Ave, and 945 Madison Ave at Whitney Museum)
Second Avenue Kosher Delicatessen and Restaurant (156 Second Ave)
Stage Deli (834 Seventh Ave)
Trattoria dell'Arte (900 Seventh Ave)
Tropica (Met Life Bldg, 200 Park Ave)
Union Square Cafe (21 E 16th St)
Verbena (54 Irving Pl)
Viand Coffee Shop (300 E 86th St, 1011 Madison Ave, and 637 Madison Ave)
Yellowfingers di Nuovo (200 E 60th St)
Zoë (90 Prince St)

Don't Bothers

Too many restaurants spoil the real reason for coming: to get a good meal in a comfortable setting at a fair price. With so many great restaurant choices in Manhattan, why waste time and money on poor or mediocre ones? Many on the following list are well known and popular, but I feel you can get better value elsewhere.

Angelo of Mulberry Street: The portrait of former prez Reagan is their only claim to fame.

Bice: very "in," very noisy, very unimpressive

Black Sheep: once was fun, but that's history

Bowery Bar: The servers are as disinterested as you will be in the food.

Cafe de la Paix: The only things worth watching are other customers.

Cafe Lure: The smell is enough to take away your appetite.

Charley O's: the Benetton of the food scene

Chiam: charming in every way except the most important, the food

City Crab: The amateurish service and mediocre food is enough to make anybody crabby.

Cub Room: needs a lot of mothering, from the tasteless food to the hideous uniforms

Dava: An overpriced menu is all you will remember about this place.

Demarchelier: very ordinary

E.A.T.: exorbitant prices

Elaine's: You gotta be kidding.

El Teddy's: Only the desserts are worth the effort.

Ernie's: The pickup scene must be awfully good.

Fashion Cafe: few redeemable features, except the models

Gage & Tollner: great ambience, great reputation, but really not worth the trip to Brooklyn

Great American Health Bar: Ugh!

Harley Davidson Cafe: Let's stick to the cycles.

Houlihan's: places of the past

"21 Club" in its day was one of the finest and most popular places to eat in Manhattan. Regulars were treated like they were visiting their own private club. Alas, sadly, things have changed. And not for the better. Even though the surroundings have been spruced up a bit, the food (even their famous burger) is tired, and so are some of the waiters. You'll see some familiar faces here, but the caché is gone.

Island: There are better ones in the Caribbean.

Jekyll & Hyde: for ghoulish appetites

Le Bar Bat: Even the name turns me off.

Le Veau d'Or: Heaven help the stranger.

Lexington Avenue Grill: poor service

Mickey Mantle's: a strikeout

Mortimer's: for the eyes only

Nusantara: Indonesia is a long way away.

Official All Star Cafe: The score—Joe Montana 10, Diners 1

Old Homestead: "Old" is the best description.

Ottomanelli Cafe: Haven't they heard what happens to conglomerates?

Ratner's: Why pay to get insulted?

Rumpelmayer's: reborn, barely

Sardi's: once great; twice bad; thrice, coming back slowly

Savoy: uncomfortably "cute," unappealing plates

Sloppy Louie's: lives up to the name

Spirit Cruises: Take along your Dramamine.

Tennessee Mountain: not much at the top

Two Eleven: disinterested help serving interesting food
Wylie's Ribs: Pass the Pepto-Bismol.

Eating at the Bar

China Grill (52 W 53rd St)
Christer's (145 W 55th St)
44 (Royalton Hotel, 44 W 44th St)
Gramercy Tavern (42 E 20th St)
Lobster Club (24 E 80th St)
Mesa Grill (102 Fifth Ave)
Monkey Bar (60 E 54th St)
Palio (151 W 51st St)
Patroon (160 E 46th St)
Penang (109 Spring St)
Petrossian (182 W 58th St)
Pravda (281 Lafayette St)
Rain (100 W 82nd St)
Redeye Grill (890 Seventh Ave)
Tapika (238 W 56th St)
Union Square Cafe (21 E 16th St)
Vodka Bar & Cafe (260 West Broadway)
Zoë (90 Prince St)

Family-Style Dining

Carmine's (2450 Broadway)
Coco Pazzo (23 E 74th St; Fri, Sat, and Sun)
Drovers (9 Jones St)
Marchi's (251 E 31st St)
Sambuca (20 W 72nd St)
Szechuan Hunan (1588 York Ave)

Fireplaces

Avanti (700 Ninth Ave)
Barbetta (321 W 46th St)
Black Sheep (344 W 11th St)
Christer's (145 W 55th St)
Gramercy Tavern (42 E 20th St)
Hunter's (1397 Third Ave)
I Trulli (122 E 27th St)
Keens Steakhouse (72 W 36th St)
La Boheme (24 Minetta Lane)
March (405 E 58th St)
Marchi's (251 E 31st St)
Marylou's (21 W 9th St)
One If By Land, Two If By Sea (17 Barrow St)
René Pujol (321 W 55th St)
Savoy (70 Prince St)
Sign of the Dove (1110 Third Ave)
Water Club (500 E 30th St)
Ye Waverly Inn (16 Bank St)

Foreign Flavors

There are some unusual foreign-flavor establishments featured that do not have full write-ups in this book. Here are the best of the more exotic cuisines:

Afghan: Afghanistan Kebab House (764 Ninth Ave) and Pamir (1437 Second Ave)

African: La Baraka (153 Broadway) and Metisse (239 W 105th St)

Asian: Rain (100 W 82nd St)

Belgian: Cafe de Bruxelles (118 Greenwich Ave) and Petite Abeille (107 W 18th St)

Brazilian: Cabana Carioca (123 W 45th St), Churrascaria Plataforma (316 W 49th St), Circus (808 Lexington Ave), Emporium Brazil (15 W 46th St), Ipanema (13 W 46th St), Rice and Beans (744 Ninth Ave), and Riodizio (417 Lafayette St)

Burmese: Mingala West (325 Amsterdam Ave) and Road to Mandalay (380 Broome St)

Caribbean: Bambou (243 E 14th St), Caribe (117 Perry St), Caridad (4311 Broadway), and Tropica (200 Park Ave)

Chinese: Au Mandarin (250 Vesey St), Big Wong (67 Mott St), Chin Chin (216 E 49th St), China Fun West (246 Columbus Ave), First Taste (53 Bayard St), Fu's (1395 Second Ave), Golden Unicorn (18 East Broadway), H.S.F. (46 Bowery), Joe's Shanghai (9 Pell St), Kam Chueh (40 Bowery), New Hong Kong City (11 Division St), New York Noodletown (28½ Bowery), Oriental Garden (14 Elizabeth St), Oriental Pearl (103 Mott St), Pig Heaven (1540 Second Ave), Shanghai 1933 (209 E 49th St), Shun Lee Palace (155 E 55th St), Shun Lee West (43 W 65th St), Sunny East (21 W 39th St), Szechuan Kitchen (1460 First Ave), Tang Pavilion (65 W 55th St), 10 Pell St (10 Pell St), Wu Liang Ye (36 W 48th St), and Zen Palate (34 Union Sq E, 663 Ninth Ave, and 2170 Broadway)

Cuban: La Caridad (2199 Broadway) and Victor's Cafe (240 Columbus Ave)

Czech: Vasata (339 E 75th St)

Dominican: La Sarten (564 Amsterdam Ave)

Ethiopian: Zula (1260 Amsterdam Ave) and Meskerem (468 W 47th St)

Filipino: Elvie's Turo-Turo (214 First Ave)

French: see restaurant listings

German: Hallo Berlin (402 W 51st St), Heidelberg Restaurant (1648 Second Ave), Kleine Konditorei (234 E 86th St), and Rolf's (281 Third Ave)

Greek: Artos (307 E 53rd St), Ithaka (48 Barrow St), Meltemi (905 First Ave), Periyali (35 W 20th St), Uncle Nick's (747 Ninth Ave), Viand (1011 Madison Ave, 673 Madison Ave, and 300 E 86th St), and Molyvos (871 Seventh Ave)

Hungarian: Red Tulip (439 E 75th St) and Mocca Hungarian Restaurant (1588 Second Ave)

Indian: Akbar (475 Park Ave), Banjara (741 Ninth Ave), Bay Leaf (49 W 56th St), Bengal Express (789 Ninth Ave), Bombay Dining (320 E 6th St), Chutney Mary (40 E 20th St), Darbar (44 W 56th St), Dawat (210 E 58th St), Jewel of India (15 W 44th St), Rose of India (308 E 6th St), Salaam Bombay (317 Greenwich St), Shaan (57 W 48th St), and Taj Mahal (328 E 6th St)

Indonesian: Bali Nusa Indah (651 Ninth Ave)

Irish: Landmark Tavern (626 Eleventh Ave), Neary's (358 E 57th St), and Thady Con's (915 Second Ave)

Italian: see restaurant listings

Jamaican: Jamaican Hot Pot (2260 Adam Clayton Powell Jr. Blvd)

Japanese: Jo-An (2707 Broadway), Chikubu (12 E 44th St), Iso (175 Second Ave), Itcho (402 E 78th St), Japonica (100 University Pl), Katana (179 Prince St), Kiiroi Hana (23 W 56th St), Menchanko-Tei (39 W 55th St), Mitsukoshi (461 Park Ave), Nadaman Hakubai (Kitano Hotel, 66 Park Ave), Nobu (105 Hudson St), Seryna (11 E 53rd St), Shinwa (645 Fifth Ave), Sushisay (38 E 51st St), Toraya (17 E 71st St), Omen (113 Thompson St), Honmura An (170 Mercer St), Hatsuhana (17 E 48th St), and Benihana (120 E 56th St)

Korean: Dok Suni's (119 First Ave), Kang Suh (1250 Broadway), Mirezi (59 Fifth Ave), Oori House (302 W 51st St), Woo Chon (8-10 W 36th St), and Hangawi (12 E 32nd St; vegetarian)

Lebanese: Al Bustan (827 Third Ave)

Malaysian: Malaysia and Indonesia (18 Doyers St), Malaysia Restaurant (48 Bowery), Penang (109 Spring St), and Three Degrees North (210 Spring St)

Mediterranean: Gus' Place (149 Waverly Pl), Mezze (10 W 44th St), Provence (38 MacDougal St), and Spartina (355 Greenwich St)

Mexican: Cottonwood Cafe (415 Bleecker St), El Parador (325 E 34th St), El Teddy's (219 West Broadway), Ernesto Restaurant (2277 First Ave), Fresco Tortillas (766 Ninth Ave), La Hacienda (219 E 116th St), Mambo Grill (174 E 82nd St), Mi Cocina (57 Jane St), Pedro Paramo (430 E 14th St), Rinconcito Mexicano (307 W 39th St), Rosa Mexicano (1063 First Ave), Taqueria de Mexico (93 Greenwich Ave), Tortilla Flats (767 Washington St), and Zarela (953 Second Ave)

Middle Eastern: Al Bustan (827 Third Ave), Cleopatra's Needle (2485 Broadway), Layla (211 West Broadway, and Lemon Tree Cafe (769 Ninth Ave)

Moroccan: Anda-Lousia (28 Cornelia St), Cafe Fes (246 W 4th St), and Lofti's (358 W 46th St)

Persian: Persepolis (1423 Second Ave)

Peruvian: Felipe's Peruvian Restaurant (688 Tenth Ave)

Polish: Christine's (438 Second Ave and 208 First Ave), Teresa's (103 First Ave), and Veselka (144 Second Ave)

Portuguese: O Lavrador (138-40 101st Ave) and Pão (322 Spring St)

Puerto Rican: La Taza De Oro (96 Eighth Ave)

Russian: Cafe Andrusha (1742 Second Ave), Firebird (365 W 46th St), The Pie (340 E 86th St), Pravda (281 Lafayette St), Russian Samovar (256 W 52nd St), and Uncle Vanya (315 W 54th St)

Spanish: Bolo (23 E 22nd St), Cafe Riazor (245 W 16th St), Ballroom (253 W 28th St), El Cid (322 W 15th St), El Faro (823 Greenwich St), Solera (216 E 53rd St), and Toledo (6 E 36th St)

Sri Lanka: Lakruwana (358 W 44th St)

Swedish: Snaps (230 Park Ave), Aquavit (13 W 54th St), and Christer's (145 W 55th St)

Swiss: Roettele A.G. (126 E 7th St)

Thai: Kin Khao (171 Spring St), Rain (100 W 82nd St), Royal Siam Thai (240 Eighth Ave), Siam Grill (586 Ninth Ave), Thailand Restaurant (106 Bayard St), Topaz (127 W 56th St), Thai House Cafe (151 Hudson St), Siam Cuisine (1411 Second Ave), and Vong (200 E 54th St)

Tibetan: Tibetan Kitchen (444 Third Ave), Tibetan Shambala (488 Amsterdam Ave), and Tsampa (212 E 9th St)

Turkish: Deniz (400 E 57th St), Layla (211 West Broadway), Uskudar (1405 Second Ave), and Turkish Cuisine (631 Ninth Ave)

Ukrainian: Ukrainian East Village (1240 Second Ave)

Vietnamese: Hue (210 E 23rd St), Me Kong (44 Prince St), Miss Saigon (1425 Third Ave), Monsoon (435 Amsterdam Ave), Nam (222 Seventh Ave), Nam Phuong (19 Sixth Ave), New Viet Huong (77 Mulberry St), Nha Trang (87 Baxter St), Orienta (205 E 75th St), Le Colonial (149 E 57th St), River (345 Amsterdam Ave), and Vietnam (11 Doyers St).

Ordering a Chinese Meal

Get together a large party in order to sample a wide variety of dishes. While everyone's taste should be taken into account, it is advisable to let one person organize the order. A well-balanced meal comprises the five basic tastes of Chinese cuisine: acid, hot, bitter, sweet, and salty. Texture should vary between dry and sauced, crisp and tender. A good rule of thumb is to order one dish per diner, plus one soup. Your utensils will be chopsticks, which are ideal for the small pieces of food commonly found in Chinese cooking, but most restaurants will gladly supply chopstick novices with knives, forks, and spoons.

A Chinese meal usually starts with a cold meat dish and is then followed by fish or seafood, red or white meat, vegetables, and soup. Steamed white rice is a usual accompaniment, but you can also order a fried noodle or rice dish to be served at the end of the meal. In northern Chinese-style restaurants, bread or noodles often replace rice.

Asian food tips

- **Chinese:** The most popular Chinese cuisines are: Cantonese (heavy on fish, dim sum a specialty); Chiu Chow (thick shark's fin soup, sliced goose, the "Sicilians" of China); Hakka (salted, use of innards); Hunan (very spicy, try fried chicken with chili); Peking (Peking duck and beggar's chicken are the best known); Shanghai (freshwater hairy crab is very popular); and Szechuan (spiciest of all, simmering and smoking are common cooking methods).

- **Indian:** Not necessarily hot; north Indian food features wheat bread and curries. Fish or chicken is cooked in tandoor clay oven.

- **Indonesian:** Satay (skewered chicken or beef, barbecued, and served with peanut sauce) is the main dish.

- **Japanese:** Most popular is sashimi (fresh slices of raw fish), sushi (light, vinegary rice rolled around raw fish), tempura (deep-fried vegetables and fish), and teppanyaki (beef, seafood, garlic, and veggies cooked at a central griddle). And, of course, sake (rice wine).

- **Korean:** Table-top griddles are used for barbecuing beef slices for a dish called *bulgogi*.

- **Malaysian:** Best-known specialty is *laska,* a creamy-thick coconut-based soup with noodles, shrimp and chicken.

- **Singaporean:** A combination of cultures: fried *mee* (thick yellow noodles) and satay (skewered and barbecued meat). Coconut is featured in sweet rice cakes and *laska* noodle soup.

- **Taiwanese:** Full-flavored, heavy on fish and other seafoods cooked in hot pots and enhanced by chili and sesame-flavored oil condiments.

- **Thai:** Spicy! National dish is *tom yum gung* soup, made with chili, lemon grass and coriander and topped with shrimp, chicken or squid.

- **Vietnamese:** French-inspired dishes like fried frog legs, sausage and salami cold cuts platter. Spring rolls wrapped in lettuce leaves are traditional.

Game

Aquavit (13 W 54th St)
Barbetta (321 W 46th St)
Bouterin (420 E 59th St)
Chanterelle (2 Harrison St)
Hudson River Club (4 World Financial Ctr)
Jo Jo (160 E 64th St)
La Réserve (4 W 44th St)
Le Cirque (Palace Hotel)
Le Périgord (405 E 52nd St)
Les Halles (411 Park Ave S)
Mesa Grill (102 Fifth Ave)
Montrachet (239 West Broadway)
Park Bistro (414 Park Ave)
Primavera (1578 First Ave)
Terrace, The (400 W 119th St)
Union Square Cafe (21 E 16th St)

Healthy Fare

You can find healthy fare at the following restaurants, some of which have special menus:

Akbar (475 Park Ave): Indian
Angelica Kitchen (300 E 12th St)
Arcadia (21 E 62nd St)
Blanche's Organic Cafe (22 E 44th St and 972 Lexington Ave)
Buckwheat and Alfalfa (182 Eighth Ave)
Four Seasons (99 E 52nd St): expensive
Fraunces Tavern Restaurant (54 Pearl St): historic
Health Pub (371 Second Ave)
Healthy Candle (Lexington Ave at 71st St and 1307 Third Ave)
Marylou's (21 W 9th St)
Nosmo King (54 Varick St)
Popover Cafe (551 Amsterdam Ave)
Quantum Leap Natural Food (88 W 3rd St)
Salad Bowl (1516 Broadway)
Spring Street Natural Restaurant (62 Spring St): your best bet
Time Cafe (380 Lafayette St)
Zen Palate (663 Ninth Ave and others)

Hi-Tech Eateries

How about cyber cafes? Not surprising in the Internet world. Computer terminals make food seem secondary at these:

Alt.coffee (137 Avenue Ave)
@cafe (12 St. Mark's Pl)
Cyber Cafe (273-A Lafayette St)
Ditto Internet Cafe (48 W 20th St)
IDT Cafe & Pizza (19 W 45th St)
Internet Cafe (82 E 3rd St)

Hotel Dining

One of the biggest changes on the restaurant circuit in Manhattan has been the resurgence of hotel dining. No longer are on-premises eateries just for the convenience of guests. Now they are, indeed, destinations for those who desire a bit more atmosphere and a less trendy scene. Following are some of the best:

Algonquin (59 W 44th St): Rose Room, Oak Room (evening cabaret)
Carlyle (35 E 76th St): Cafe Carlyle (features Bobby Short, very expensive)
Elysee (60 E 54th St): Monkey Bar (great history, great American cuisine)
Essex House (160 Central Park S): Les Célébrités (very classy) and Cafe Botanica (more casual)
Four Seasons (57 E 57th St): Fifty-Seven Fifty-Seven (superb dining)
Grand Hyatt (Grand Central Station and Park Ave): Sun Garden (nice setting)
Inn at Irving Place (54 Irving Pl): Verbena (charming)
Kitano (66 Park Ave): Nadaman Hakubai (Japanese)
Lowell (28 E 63rd St): Post House (very good meat and potatoes)
Mark (25 E 77th St): Mark's Restaurant (one of the very best)
Marriott Marquis (1535 Broadway): four restaurants, including The View (top floor, revolving)
Millenium Hilton (55 Church St): Taliesin (classy)
New York Hilton (1335 Sixth Ave): Grill 53 (steaks, chops) and Cafe New York (snacks)
New York Palace (455 Madison Ave): Le Cirque 2000 (a New York one-and-only by Sirio Maccioni)
Omni Berkshire (21 E 52nd St): Kokachin (good seafood)
Pierre (2 E 61st St): Cafe Pierre (stately and beautiful)
Plaza (768 Fifth Ave): Edwardian Room (overlooks Central Park), Palm Court (vintage New York), Oak Room (serious), and Oyster Bar (seafood)
Plaza Athenee (37 E 64th St): Le Régence (elegant and excellent)
Regency (540 Park Ave): 540 Park Avenue Restaurant (power scene) and The Library (informal)
RIHGA Royal (151 W 54th St): Halcyon (beautiful appointments and fine food)
Ritz Carlton (112 Central Park S): Fantino (somewhat pretentious)
Royalton (44 W 44th St): 44 (chic, favorite of publishing moguls)
Sheraton Manhattan (790 Seventh Ave): Bistro 790 (very good midtown value)
Sheraton New York (811 Seventh Ave): Streeter's (café) and Hudson's Bar and Grill (casual dining)
Sheraton Russell (45 Park Ave): Russell's American Grill (solid and dependable)
St. Regis (2 E 55th St): Lespinasse (you can't do better)
Stanhope (995 Fifth Ave): Restaurant at the Stanhope (less formal)
Surrey Suite Hotel (20 E 76th St): Daniel (high society)
Trump International (1 Central Park W): Jean Georges (the Donald's personal gem)
Waldorf-Astoria (301 Park Ave): four restaurants, including Bull & Bear (British atmosphere), Inagiku (Japanese), Peacock Alley (has come back to life) and Oscar's (cafeteria)
Wales (1295 Madison Ave): Sarabeth's Kitchen (delightful)
Warwick (63 W 54th St): Ciao Europa (new look)
Westbury (840 Madison Ave): Polo (gracious)

Japanese Bars

Angel's Share (8 Stuyvesant St, 2nd floor)

Decibel (240 E 9th St)
J&A Pub (214 E 49th St)
New Tokyo 18 (113 E 18th St)
Riki (248 E 52nd St)
Sai Kai (141 E 45th St)
Tomi Jaz (216 E 10th St)

Kosher

There is a tremendous choice in kosher restaurants in New York, and all of their kitchens must meet the standards of experienced non-kosher diners as well. Kosher is no longer a captive market, and the spots that survive are offering excellent menus, fine preparation, and outstanding dishes. As always, the caveat to call before you go applies. Be sure to ask if the restaurant is still kosher.

Abigael's (9 E 37th St): one of the finest—class and elegance
Alexi 56 (25 W 56th St): the meat version of one of the most elegant choices in town—expensive
All-American Health Bar & Cafe (24 E 42nd St): quick lunch pick-up
American Cafe, Health Bar & Pizza (160 Broadway): Wall Street area
Blue Moon (325 Fifth Ave): everything from sushi to shwarma
Cafe 1-2-3 (2 Park Ave): great fish grill, salads and focaccia pizza
Cafe Classico (35 W 57th St): continental gourmet, from pasta to steak
Cafe 18 (8 E 18th St): The tables are minuscule, the decor spartan, the food nondescript.
Cafe Masada (1239 First Ave): menu is Israeli grill
China Shalom II (686 Columbus Ave): Chinese with a sidewalk cafe
Deli Kasbah (251 W 85th St): one of the best grills in the area
Dougie's BBQ & Grill (222 W 72nd St): Ribs are the one thing kosher does not do well.
Galil Restaurant (1252 Lexington Ave): Israeli Moroccan
Glatt Dynasty (1049 Second Ave): one of the better Chinese
Gourmet Garden (175 Madison Ave): dairy delicacies
Grand Deli (399 Grand St): one of the few remaining Lower East Side legends
Haikara Grill (1016 Second Ave): The newest rage in kosher dining is Japanese sushi and steakhouses.
Jasmine Restaurant (11 E 30th St): Persian Glatt kosher
Kosher Tea Room (193 Second Ave): Afghan *nouvelle* restaurant with Russian accents
Le Marais (150 W 46th St): The first and arguably best French kosher steakhouse.
Levana Restaurant (141 W 69th St): one of the best values in New York
Mom's Bagels (15 W 45th St): some of the tastiest bagels in town
My Most Favorite Dessert Company (120 W 45th St): The desserts are the stars.
Provi, Provi (228 W 72nd St): Locals consider this their neighborhood kitchen.
Ratner's Dairy Restaurant (138 Delancey St): Ratner's and its decrepit, ageless waiters remain exactly the same. The onion rolls are unequalled, you can still get sour milk (your choice of glass or bowl), and the blintzes are sold world-wide but never taste this good anywhere else.
Vegetarian Heaven (304 W 58th St): delicious, healthy, and remarkably light on the wallet (as well as the heart)
What's Cookin' (18 E 41st St): East African, Middle Eastern, and East Side homages

Late Hours (See also "Manhattan at Night")

The city that never sleeps . . .

24 hours:
Big Nick's (2175 Broadway)
Coffee Shop (29 Union Square W)
Empire Diner (210 Tenth Ave)
Gray's Papaya (2090 Broadway)
Moondance Diner (Sixth Ave at Grand St)
Odessa (119 Ave A)
Sarge's Deli (548 Third Ave)
Tivoli (515 Third Ave)
Viand Coffee Shop (1011 Madison Ave, 673 Madison Ave, and 300 E 86th St)
Woo Chon (8-10 W 36th St)

Open until about four a.m.:
@cafe (12 St. Mark's Pl)
Blue Ribbon (97 Sullivan St)
Cafe Noir (32 Grand St)
Corner Bistro (331 W 4th St)
Florent (69 Gansevoort St)
Jekyll & Hyde (91 Seventh Ave S)
Lucky Strike (59 Grand St)
Match (160 Mercer St)
P.J. Clarke's (915 Third Ave)
Sanzin (180 Spring St
Yorkville Brewery (1359 First Ave)

Open until about three a.m.:
First (87 First Ave)
Pravda (281 Lafayette St)
Tapas Lounge (1078 First Ave)
Merchants, N.Y. (1125 First Ave)
Screening Room (54 Varick St)

Open until about two a.m.:
Ansonia (329 Columbus Ave)
Big Cup (228 Eighth Ave)
Broome Street Bar (363 West Broadway)
Cafe Lalo (201 W 83rd St)
Caffe Vivaldi (32 Jones St)
Elaine's (1703 Second Ave)
Garage Cafe (99 Seventh Ave S)
I Tre Merli (463 West Broadway)
Match Uptown (33 E 60th St)
Odeon (145 West Broadway)
Opaline (85 Ave A)
Papaya King (179 E 86th St and 201 E 59th St)
Spy (101 Greene)
Stage Deli (834 Seventh Ave)
Tatou (151 E 50th St)
Tio Pepe (168 W 4th St)
White Horse Tavern (567 Hudson St)
Wollensky's Grill (205 E 49th St)

Open until about one a.m.:
America (9 E 18th St)
Brooklyn Diner (212 W 57th St)
Chez Josephine (414 W 42nd St)
Chumley's (86 Bedford St)
Halcyon (RIHGA Royal Hotel, 151 W 54th St)
Hard Rock Cafe (221 W 57th St)
Hunan Park (235 Columbus Ave and 721 Columbus Ave)
Il Cortile (125 Mulberry St)
Il Vagabondo (351 E 62nd St)
Jackson Hole Burgers (232 E 64th St, Third Ave at 35th St, and Second Ave at 84th St)
Metro Diner (2641 Broadway)
Mezzaluna (1295 Third Ave)
Motown Cafe (104 W 57th St)
Nirvana (30 Central Park S)
Planet Hollywood (140 W 57th St)
Rainbow Room (30 Rockefeller Plaza)
Windows on the World (1 World Trade Ctr, 107th floor)

Munching at the Museums

Some of the more appealing possibilities while you digest a bit of art and culture:

American Museum of Natural History (Central Park W at 79th St): Garden Cafe and the Whale's Lair (weekends only)
Guggenheim Museum (1071 Fifth Ave): Museum Cafe
Jewish Museum (1109 Fifth Ave): Cafe Weissman
Metropolitan Museum (Fifth Ave at 82nd St): Museum Restaurant, Great Hall Balcony Bar, Museum Bar and Cafe, and Roof Garden Espresso and Wine Bar (in warm weather only)
Museum of Modern Art (11 W 53rd St): Garden Cafe and Sette MoMA
Pierpont Morgan Library (29 E 36th St): Morgan Court Cafe
Whitney Museum (945 Madison Ave): Sarabeth's Kitchen

Offbeat

Looking for someplace a bit different? Here are some ideas:

Acme Bar & Grill (9 Great Jones St): swinging
Afghan Kebab House (764 Ninth Ave and 1345 Second Ave): kebabs
Barney Greengrass (541 Amsterdam Ave): You're in the 1940s.
Becco (355 W 46th St): family dining
Boathouse Cafe (Central Park Lake, Fifth Ave at 72nd St): overlooks water
Brother Jimmy's Bar-B-Q (1461 First Ave): great ribs
Coco Pazzo (23 E 74th St): crazy chef!
Frank's (85 Tenth Ave): meat and potatoes
Great Jones Cafe (54 Great Jones St): eclectic
Khyber Pass (34 St Mark's Pl): Afghan
Landmark Tavern (626 Eleventh Ave): historic
Nobu (105 Hudson St): Oriental delight
Noho Star (330 Lafayette St): diner
Nosmo King (54 Varick St): organic
Rao's (455 E 114th St): way uptown
Red Tulip (439 E 75th St): Hungarian

Ruby's River Road Cafe (1754 Second Ave): Cajun
Sammy's Roumanian (157 Chrystie St): Lower East Side
Seventh Regiment Mess (643 Park Ave): unusual setting
Sugar Reef (93 Second Ave): Caribbean
Sylvia's (328 Lenox Ave): soul food
Twins (1712 Second Ave): You'll see double.
Veselka Coffee Shop (144 Second Ave): Polish-Ukrainian

Old-timers

How far back do you want to go?

1763: Fraunces Tavern Restaurant (54 Pearl St)
1854: McSorley's Old Ale House (15 E 7th St)
1864: Pete's Tavern (129 E 18th St)
1865: Landmark Tavern (626 Eleventh Ave)
1868: Old Homestead (56 Ninth Ave)
1870: Billy's (948 First Ave): oldest family-run restaurant in Manhattan
1879: Gage & Tollner (372 Fulton St, Brooklyn)
1885: Keens Steakhouse (72 W 36th St)
1887: Peter Luger (178 Broadway, Brooklyn)
1888: Katz's Delicatessen (205 E Houston St)
1890: P.J. Clarke's (915 Third Ave)
1905: Ratner's (138 Delancey St)
1906: Barbetta (321 W 46th St)
1907: Plaza Hotel restaurants (768 Fifth Ave)
1912: Frank's (85 Tenth Ave)
1913: Grand Central Oyster Bar Restaurant (Grand Central Station)
1914: Cafe des Artistes (1 W 67th St)
1920: Waverly Inn (16 Bank St)
1926: Palm (837 Second Ave)
1927: Minetta Tavern (113 MacDougal St)

Outdoor Dining

A taste of the outdoors in a garden, patio, or on the sidewalk:

American Festival Cafe (Rockefeller Center)
Aureole (34 E 61st St)
Barbetta (321 W 46th St)
Barolo (398 W Broadway)
Boathouse Cafe (Central Park Lake, Fifth Ave at 72nd St)
Bouterin (420 E 59th St)
Bryant Park Grill (25 W 40th St)
Cafe la Fortuna (69 W 71st St)
Caffe Bondi (7 W 20th St)
Caffe Bianco (1486 Second Ave)
Caffe Dante (79 MacDougal St)
Cel Rouge (176 Seventh Ave)
Chelsea Commons (242 Tenth Ave)
Chez Ma Tante (189 W 10th St)
Cloister Cafe (238 E 9th St)
Courtyard at the Villard House (New York Palace Hotel, 455 Madison Ave)
Da Silvano (260 Sixth Ave)
Demi (1316 Madison Ave)
Dia Center for the Arts (548 W 22nd St)

Druids (736 Tenth Ave)
Empire Diner (210 Tenth Ave)
Fletcher Morgan Provisions (864 Lexington Ave)
Flowers (21 W 17th St)
Gascogne (158 Eighth Ave)
Grove (314 Bleecker St)
Hatsuhana (17 E 48th St)
Home (20 Cornelia St)
I Trulli (122 E 27th St)
Il Monello (1460 Second Ave)
Jackson Hole Burgers (232 E 64th St)
Jean Georges (Trump International Hotel, Columbus Circle)
John's Pizzeria (408 E 64th St)
La Boheme (24 Minetta Lane)
Le Jardin Bistro (25 Cleveland Pl)
Le Madri (168 W 18th St)
Le Relais (712 Madison Ave)
Luna Park (1 Union Sqare E)
March (405 E 58th St)
Mezzogiorno (195 Spring St)
Miracle Grill (112 First Ave)
Mortimer's (1057 Lexington Ave)
Moustache (405 Atlantic Ave)
Museum of Modern Art (11 W 53rd St)
One If By Land, Two If By Sea (17 Barrow St)
Orson's (175 Second Ave)
Pete's Tavern (129 E 18th St)
Pigalle (111 E 29th St)
Provence (38 MacDougal St)
Restaurant Raphael (33 W 54th St)
River Cafe (1 Water St, Brooklyn)
Saloon, the (1920 Broadway)
San Pietro (18 E 54th St)
Seagrill (19 W 49th St)
Sign of the Dove (1110 Third Ave)
Spring Street Natural Restaurant (62 Spring St)
Stanhope Hotel (995 Fifth Ave)
Sumptuary (400 Third Ave)
Tavern on the Green (Central Park W at 67th St)
Tavolo (1481 York Ave)
Time Cafe (380 Lafayette St)
Trattoria dell'Arte (900 Seventh Ave)
Verbena (54 Irving Pl)
Vince & Eddie's (70 W 68th St)
Vinegar Factory (431 E 91st St)
Voulez-Vous (1462 First Ave)
Water Club (East River at 30th St)
White Horse Tavern (567 Hudson St)
Yaffa (97 St Mark's Pl)

Oyster Bars

Blue Ribbon (97 Sullivan St)
Docks Oyster Bar and Seafood Grill (2427 Broadway and 633 Third Ave)
Fanny's Oyster Bar (765 Washington)

Grand Central Oyster Bar Restaurant (Grand Central Station, lower level)
Plaza Oyster Bar (768 Fifth Ave)

People Watching

Aureole (34 E 61st St)
Bice (7 E 54th St)
Bryant Park Cafe (25 W 40th St)
Cafe Centro (MetLife Bldg, 200 Park Ave)
Cascabel (218 Lafayette St)
Chanterelle (2 Harrison St)
Coco Pazzo (23 E 74th St)
Daniel (20 E 76th St)
Ecco (124 Chambers St, bet West Broadway and Church St)
Elaine's (1703 Second Ave)
Flowers (21 W 17th St)
44 (44 W 44th St)
Four Seasons (99 E 52nd St)
Gotham Bar & Grill (12 E 12th St)
Gramercy Tavern (42 E 20th St)
Harry Cipriani (Fifth Ave at E 59th St)
Il Mulino (86 W 3rd St)
Jean Georges (Trump International Hotel, Columbus Circle)
Jim McMullen (1341 Third Ave)
Jo Jo (160 E 64th St)
La Côte Basque (5 E 55th St)
La Grenouille (3 E 52nd St)
La Réserve (4 W 49th St)
Le Cirque (Palace Hotel, 58 E 65th St)
Le Madri (168 W 18th St)
Le Périgord (405 E 52nd St)
Le Rivage (340 W 46th St)
Mezze (10 E 44th St)
Mickey Mantle's (42 Central Park S)
Mortimer's (1057 Lexington Ave)
Osteria del Circo (120 W 55th St)
P.J. Clarke's (915 Third Ave)
Palio (151 W 51st St)
Palm (837 Second Ave)
Palm Court (Plaza Hotel, Fifth Ave at Central Park S)
Paper Moon Milano (39 E 58th St)
Park Avalon (225 Park Ave S)
Planet Hollywood (140 W 57th St)
Provence (38 MacDougal St)
Rainbow Room (Rockefeller Center, 65th fl)
Remi (145 W 53rd St)
San Domenico (240 Central Park S)
Sette Mezzo (969 Lexington Ave, on Sunday nights)
Tavern on the Green (Central Park W at 67th St)
Trattoria dell'Arte (900 Seventh Ave)
Tribeca Grill (375 Greenwich St, at Franklin St)
21 (21 W 52nd St)
Union Square Cafe (21 E 16th St)

Vong (200 E 54th St)
Windows on the World (2 World Trade Center)
Zoë (90 Prince St)

Personal Favorites

Everybody has a list of favorite places, and I am happy to share mine:

Adrienne (Peninsula Hotel, 700 Fifth Ave): elegance
Alison on Dominick Street (38 Dominick St): a hand-holding charmer
Blue Ribbon (97 Sullivan St): value for your buck
Cafe des Artistes (1 W 67th St): restful
Cafe des Sports (329 W 51st St): homey French
Cent Anni (50 Carmine St): consistent
Edwardian Room (Plaza Hotel, 59th and Central Park S): right on the park
États-Unis (242 E 81st St): homey
Gabriel's (11 W 60th St): sophisticated
Gotham Bar & Grill (12 E 12th St): Everything is good.
Gramercy Tavern (42 E 20th St): the "in" place
Il Mulino (86 W 3rd St): Italian heaven!
Jackson Hole Burgers (various locations): the best burgers
La Boheme (24 Minetta Ln): unpretentious
La Caravelle (33 W 55th St): Everything seems important.
La Grenouille (3 E 52nd St): beautiful
La Métairie (189 W 10th St): cozy
La Réserve (4 W 49th St): perfection!
Le Chantilly (106 E 57th St): civilized
Le Périgord (405 E 52nd St): impeccable
Lespinasse (St Regis Hotel, 2 E 55th St): grand
March (405 E 58th St): imaginative
Mark's (Mark Hotel, 25 E 77th St): as hotel dining should be
Montrachet (239 W Broadway): very professional
One If By Land, Two If By Sea (17 Barrow St): romantic
Parkside (107-01 Corona Ave, Queens): Come here to eat!
Piccolo Angolo (621 Hudson St): like family friends
Primavera (1578 First Ave): superb service
River Cafe (1 Water St, East River, Brooklyn): Oh, that view!
Rosemarie's (145 Duane St): intimate
Sonia Rose (132 Lexington Ave): The place to propose!
Terrace, The (Columbia University, 400 W 119th St): great outlook
Toscana (843 Lexington Ave): quality folks
Union Square Cafe (21 E 16th St): justly famous
Wong Kee (113 Mott St): basic Chinatown

Pizza

You can't go wrong with any of these:

Allegria (66 W 55th St)
Arturo's Pizzeria (106 Houston St)
Barocco (297 Church St)
Broadway Grill (Holiday Inn Crowne Plaza, 1605 Broadway)
California Pizza Kitchen (201 E 60th St)
Candido (1606 First Ave)
Coffee Shop (29 Union W Sq)

Court of the Three Sisters (157 E 55th St)
Da Nico (164 Mulberry St)
Don Giovanni's (210 Tenth Ave)
Figaro Pizza (1469 Second Ave)
Fisher & Levy (875 Third Ave)
Hosteria Fiorella Seafood Grill (1081 Third Ave)
Il Corallo (176 Prince St)
Isola (485 Columbus Ave)
John's Pizzeria (278 Bleecker St, 48-50 W 65th St, 260 W 46th St, and 408 E 64th St)
La Boheme (24 Minetta Lane)
La Traviota (461 W 23rd St)
Le Madri (168 W 8th St)
Lemon Tree Cafe (769 Ninth Ave)
Lento's (7003 Third Ave)
Lombardi's (32 Spring St)
Martini's (810 Seventh Ave)
Mezzogiorno (195 Spring St)
New Haven Pizza Co. (140 W 13th St)
Nick's Pizza (108-26 Ascan Ave, Forest Hills, Queens)
Orso (322 W 46th St)
Osteria al Doge (142 W 44th St)
Patsy's Pizza (61 W 74th St)
Pintaile's Pizza (26 E 91st St)
Pizza Joint Too (70 W 71st St)
Pizzeria Uno (432 Columbus Ave)
Pronto Pizza (6 E 42nd St)
Sal's & Carmine Pizza (2533 Broadway)
Sofia Fabulous Pizza (1022 Madison Ave)
Trattoria dell'Arte (900 Seventh Ave)
Trattoria Gubbio (1544 Second Ave)
Vinnie's Pizza (285 Amsterdam Ave)

Power Meals

Cafe des Artistes (1 W 67th St)
Cafe Pierre (Pierre Hotel, Fifth Ave and 61st St)
Campagna (24 E 21st St)
Carlyle Hotel (35 E 76th St)
Edwardian Room (Plaza Hotel, Fifth Ave at 59th St)
Elaine's (1703 Second Ave)
Four Seasons (99 E 52nd St)
Gabriel's Bar and Restaurant (11 W 60th St)
Il Mulino (86 W 3rd St)
Jean Georges (Trump International Hotel, Columbus Circle)
La Grenouille (3 E 52nd St)
La Réserve (4 W 49th St)
Le Bernardin (155 W 51st St)
Le Cirque (Palace Hotel, 58 W 65th St))
Lespinasse (St Regis Hotel, 2 E 55th St)
Maloney & Porcelli (37 E 50th St)
Michael's (24 W 55th St)

Monkey Bar (60 E 54th St)
Morton's of Chicago (551 Fifth Ave)
Nobu (105 Hudson St)
Palm (837 Second Ave)
Paramount Hotel (235 W 46th St)
Park Avenue Cafe (100 E 63rd St)
Peninsula Hotel (700 Fifth Ave)
Primavera (1578 First Ave)
Rainbow Room (30 Rockefeller Plaza, 65th floor)
Regency Hotel (540 Park Ave)
Sette Mezzo (969 Lexington Ave)
Smith & Wollensky (797 Third Ave)
21 (21 W 52nd St)
West 63rd Street Steakhouse (44 W 63rd St)

Pubs and Good Bars

To feel the real flavor of New York, visit a pub on St. Patrick's Day. However, these spots feature good brew, good times, and good company every day:

Billy's (948 First Ave)
Blind Tiger Ale (518 Hudson St): olde flavor
Brewsky's (43 E 7th St): top-quality beer
Burp Castle (41 E 7th St): small, waiters appear as monks
Chelsea Brewing Company (Pier 59, West St at 18th St): big place, big steaks
Chumley's (86 Bedford St)
Commonwealth Brewing Company (10 Rockefeller Plaza): German lagers
d.b.a. 41 First Ave (41 First Ave): relaxed, good drinking
Ear Inn (326 Spring St)
East Side Ale House (961 Second Ave): upstairs
Frank's (85 Tenth Ave)
Great Jones Street Cafe (54 Great Jones St)
Greenwich Pizza & Brewing Co (418 Sixth Ave)
Hansen's Times Square Brewery (160 W 42nd St): in the middle of it all
Heartland Brewery (35 Union Square W): try the charcoal (stout)
Highlander Brewery (190 Third Ave): Scottish fare
Jack Dempsey (61 Second Ave): books plus fireplace
Jimmy Armstrong's (875 Tenth Ave)
Jimmy Day's (186 W 4th St)
KGB (85 E 4th St): once a speakeasy
Kinsale Tavern (1672 Third Ave): Irish atmosphere, good food
Landmark Tavern (626 Eleventh Ave)
Manhattan Brewing Company (42 Thompson St)
McSorley's Old Ale House (15 E 7th St)
Monkey Bar (60 E 54th St)
Morgan's Bar (235 Madison Ave): great ambience
Nacho Mama's Brewery (40-42 Thompson St): English-style ales
Neptune Brewery (448 W 16th St): first microbrewery in Manhattan
North Star Pub (93 South St): authentic English style
Old Town Bar (45 E 18th St)
Pete's Tavern (66 Irving Pl): New York's oldest continuously operating pub
P.J. Clarke's (915 Third Ave)
Pugsley's Pub (Albany and Washington St)
Rao's (455 E 114th St)

Soho Kitchen and Bar (103 Greene St)
Telephone Bar & Grill (149 Second Ave)
Wall Street Kitchen & Bar (70 Broad St): 128 beers on tap
Westside Brewing Company (340 Amsterdam Ave)
White Horse Tavern (567 Hudson St)
Wollensky's Grill (205 E 49th St)
Yorkville Brewery and Tavern (1359 First Ave): wheat beer, pizzas

---

Bartenders . . . the better ones:

Hurley's (Sixth Ave at 49th St)
King Cole Bar (St Regis Hotel, 2 E 55th St)
Maguire's Cafe (42nd St at Second Ave)
Rainbow Promenade Bar (30 Rockefeller Plaza, 65th floor)
Ritz-Carlton Hotel (12 Central Park S)

Romantic

Some great places for hand-holding (or whatever):

Alison on Dominick Street (38 Dominick St)
Aureole (34 E 61st St)
Barbetta (321 W 46th St)
Boathouse Cafe (Central Park at 75th St)
Bouterin (420 E 59th St)
Cafe des Artistes (1 W 67th St)
Cafe Pierre (Pierre Hotel, 61st St at Fifth Ave)
Cafe Trevi (1570 First Ave)
Caffe Vivalédi (32 Jones St)
Capsouto Frères (451 Washington St)
Casa La Femme (150 Wooster St)
Chanterelle (2 Harrison St)
Chez Josephine (414 W 42nd St)
Flowers (21 W 17th St, rooftop)
Four Seasons (99 E 52nd St)
Hudson River Club (World Financial Center)
Il Cortile (125 Mulberry St)
La Boheme (24 Minetta Ln)
La Caravelle (33 W 55th St)
La Côte Basque (5 E 55th St)
La Grenouille (3 E 52nd St)
La Métairie (189 W 10th St)
La Réserve (4 W 49th St)
Le Chantilly (106 E 57th St)
Le Cirque (Palace Hotel, 455 Madison Ave)
Le Périgord (405 E 62nd St)
Les Célébrités (160 Central Park S)
Le Train Bleu (Bloomingdale's, 1000 Third Ave)
March (405 E 58th St)
Mark's (Mark Hotel, 25 E 77th St)
One If By Land, Two If By Sea (17 Barrow St)

Palm Court and Edwardian Room (Plaza Hotel, Fifth Ave and Central Park S)
Paola's (347 E 85th St)
Provence (38 MacDougal St)
Rainbow Room (Rockefeller Center, 65th floor)
River Cafe (1 Water St, Brooklyn)
Rosemarie's (145 Duane St)
Sign of the Dove (1110 Third Ave)
Sonia Rose (132 Lexington Ave): the most romantic!
Tavern on the Green, Crystal Room (Central Park W and 67th St)
Terrace, The (Columbia University, 400 W 119th St)
Village Atelier (436 Hudson St)
Windows on the World (1 World Trade Ctr)
Zoë (90 Prince St)

Sandwiches

There are thousands (yes, thousands) of places that serve sandwiches in Manhattan, and most of them are pretty ordinary. But the following turn out exceptionally good combinations for eating in or taking out:

America (9-13 E 18th St)
Barocco (301 Church St)
Bread Market & Cafe (485 Fifth Ave)
Burke and Burke (2 E 23rd St)
Carnegie Delicatessen and Restaurant (854 Seventh Ave)
Casanas & Sons (461 Columbus Ave)
Chez Bernard (323 West Broadway)
City Bakery (22 E 17th St)
Cleaver Company (229 West Broadway)
Cooper's Coffee (2151 Broadway)
Cosi Sandwich Bar (165 E 52nd St)
Cucina & Company (200 Park Ave)
Delices de France (289 Madison Ave)
Devon & Blakely (461 Fifth Ave)
Ecce Panis (1120 Third Ave and 1260 Madison Ave)
Hudson Caterers Cafe (145 Hudson St)
Kathy's Kitchen (645 Hudson St)
La Boulangère (49 E 21st St)
Lyn's Cafe (12 W 55th St)
Manganaro's Hero Boy (105 Sullivan St)
Melampo (105 Sullivan St)
Old Navy Coffee Shop (610 Sixth Ave): in the store
Olive's (120 Prince St)
Once Upon a Tart (135 Sullivan St)
Reality Sandwich (230 Thompson St)
Sullivan Street Bakery (73 Sullivan St)
Telephone Bar and Grill (149 Second Ave)
Union Square Cafe (21 E 16th St)
Yellowfingers di Nuovo (200 E 60th St)

Seafood

Aquagrill (210 Spring St)
Aquavit (13 W 54th St)

Bridge Cafe (279 Water St)
Blue Ribbon (97 Sullivan St)
Blue Water Grill (31 Union Square W, at 16th St)
Captain's Table (860 Second Ave)
Charlton's (922 Third Ave)
Docks Oyster Bar and Seafood Grill (2427 Broadway)
Fishin Eddie (73 W 71st St)
Grand Central Oyster Bar Restaurant (Grand Central Station)
Joe's Fish Shack (520 Columbus Ave)
King Crab (871 Eighth Ave)
Kokachin (21 E 52nd St)
Le Bernardin (155 W 51st St)
Manhattan Ocean Club (57 W 58th St)
Maryland Crab House (237 Third Ave)
Marylou's (21 W 9th St)
Oceana (55 E 54th St)
Oriental Town Seafood (14 Elizabeth St)
Primola (1226 Second Ave)
Remi (145 W 53rd St)
Sanzin (180 Spring St)
Seagrill (19 W 49th St)
Tropica (MetLife Building, 200 Park Ave)
Wilkinson's (1573 York Ave)

Shopping Breaks

To replenish your energy, here are some good places to eat in the major Manhattan stores:

ABC Carpet & Home (881 and 888 Broadway): Parlour Cafe (contemporary American)
Barney's Uptown (660 Madison Ave): Fred's (upscale)
Bergdorf Goodman (men's store, (745 Fifth Ave): Cafe 745
Bergdorf Goodman (women's store, (754 Fifth Ave): Cafe on 5
Bloomingdale's (1000 Third Ave): Le Train Bleu (fine dining) and Show Time (self-service)
Henri Bendel (712 Fifth Ave): Salon de The (tearoom; the Lalique windows are magnificent!)
Lord & Taylor (424 Fifth Ave): Cafe 424 (1st floor; coffee and pastries), Restaurant Cafe (American style), and Soup Bar
Macy's (151 W 34th St): Greenburg Cafe (7th floor, on Seventh Ave side), Le Cafe (balcony) Mangia (cellar), Restaurant California Fresh (4th floor), and 34th Street Diner (7th floor)
Old Navy (610 Sixth Ave): Old Navy Coffee Shop
Saks (611 Fifth Ave): Cafe SFA (tasty and classy; 8th floor) and Espresso Bar (3rd floor)
Takashimaya (693 Fifth Ave): Tea Box Cafe (Oriental flavor)

Soups

Al Yeganeh (259A W 55th St)
Chez Laurence (245 Madison Ave)
Daily Soup (17 E 17th St)
Hale and Hearty Soups (849 Lexington Ave)

Seaport Soup Company (76 Fulton St)
Second Avenue Kosher Delicatessen and Restaurant (156 Second Ave)
Soup Kitchen International (259-A W 55th St)
Soup Nutsy (148 E 46th St)
Soupcon (226 E 53rd St)
Soups Cafe (210 W 10th St)
Tea Den (940 Eighth Ave)
Urban Hero (245 W 38th St)
Veselka (144 Second Ave)

Southern Flavors/Soul Food

Acme Bar and Grill (9 Great Jones St)
Baby Jake's (14 First Ave)
Birdland (2745 Broadway)
Cafe Beulah (39 E 19th St)
Cafe Con Leche (424 Amsterdam Ave)
Cajun (129 Eighth Ave)
Chantale's Cajun Kitchen (510 Ninth Ave)
Copeland's (547 W 145th St)
Copeland's Country Kitchen (203-205 W 125th St)
Emily's (1325 Fifth Ave)
Great Jones Cafe (54 Great Jones St)
Harlem Cafe (2527 Frederick Douglass Blvd)
Jezebel (630 Ninth Ave)
Londel's (2620 Frederick Douglass Blvd)
Louisiana Community Bar & Grill (622 Broadway)
Mekka (14 Ave A)
107 West (2787 Broadway)
Orleans (1438 Third Ave)
Savannah Club (2420 Broadway)
Sister's Cuisine (1931 Madison Ave)
Sylvia's (328 Lenox Ave)
Toukie's (220 W Houston St)
Zacki's BBQ (1752 Second Ave)

Sports Bars

Jimmy Weston's (932 Second Ave)
Park Avenue Country Club (381 Park Ave S)
Play-by-Play (4 Penn Plaza)
Polo Grounds (1472 Third Ave)
Runyon's (932 Second Ave)
Rusty's on 5th (575 Fifth Ave)
Sporting Club (99 Hudson St)
Sports on Broadway (2182 Broadway)

Steaks

Steaks are in—big-time. For meat-and-potato lovers, here are the best steaks in town:

Angelo and Maxie's (233 Park Ave S): reasonable prices
Ben Benson's (123 W 52nd St)
Bistro le Steak (1309 Third Ave): inexpensive and good

Bull & Bear (Waldorf-Astoria, 301 Park Ave)
Cité (120 W 51st St)
Dan Maxwell's Steakhouse (1708 Second Ave): good value, good eating
Frank's (85 Tenth Ave)
Frankie & J Johnnie's (269 W 45th St)
Gage & Tollner (372 Fulton St, Brooklyn)
Gallagher's (228 W 52nd St)
Keens Steakhouse (72 W 36th St)
Le Marais (150 W 46th St): kosher
Le Steak (1089 Second Ave)
Les Halles (411 Park Ave S)
Maloney & Porcelli (37 E 50th St)
Manhattan Cafe (1161 First Ave)
Morton's of Chicago (551 Fifth Ave and 90 West St): the best of the new
  steakhouses
Old Homestead (56 Ninth Ave)
Oliver's (1442 Third Ave)
Palm and Palm Too (837 Second Ave and 840 Second Ave)
Patroon (160 E 46th St): outrageously expensive
Pen and Pencil (205 E 45th St)
Peter Luger (178 Broadway, Brooklyn): a tradition since 1887
Pietro's (232 E 43rd St)
Post House (28 E 63rd St)
Ruth's Chris Steak House (148 W 51st St)
Seryna (11 E 53rd St)
Smith & Wollensky (797 Third Ave)
Sparks (210 E 46th St)
Steak Frites (9 E 16th St)
West 63rd Street Steakhouse (44 W 63rd St): nice atmosphere but the food's
  only so-so

Sushi

During the boomtime of the 1980s, sushi bars were the fast-food joints of the
fashionable set. To this day, New Yorkers love to wrap their chopsticks around
succulent bits of raw fish on rice. Although many fans are content to order the
assortment plates concocted by the chef, true aficionados prefer to order by the
piece. To tailor your next sushi meal to your own specific tastes, here's what
you need to know:

Amaebi (sweet shrimp)
Anago (sea eel)
California roll (avocado and crab)
Hamachi (yellowtail)
Hirami (halibut)
Ika (squid)
Ikura (salmon roe)
Kappa maki (cucumber roll)
Maguro (tuna)
Nizasakana (cooked fish)
Saba (mackerel)
Sake (salmon)
Tekka maki (tuna roll)

Toro (fatty tuna)
Unagi (freshwater eel)
Umeshiso maki (plum roll)

Give any of these a try for sushi:

Avenue A Sushi (103 Ave A)
Blue Ribbon Sushi (119 Sullivan St)
Catch 21 (31 E 21st St)
Hatsuhana (17 E 48th St)
Iso (175 Second Ave)
Japonica (100 University Pl)
Jour et Nuit (337 West Broadway)
Kurumazushi (18 W 56th St)
Match (160 Mercer St)
Nippon (155 E 52nd St)
Nobu (105 Hudson St)
Otabe (68 E 56th St)
Sushi Bar (256 E 49th St)
Sushi Hana (1501 Second Ave)
Sushi Hatsu (1143 First Ave)
Sushi Zen (57 W 46th St)
Takahachi (85 Ave A)
TakeSushi (71 Vanderbilt Ave)
Takino Japanese (1026 Second Ave)
Ten Kai (920 W 56th St)
Tomoe Sushi (172 Thompson St)
Yama (122 E 17th St)

Teatime

Afternoon tea is usually served between 3 and 6 p.m. The common story is that the Duchess of Bedford started the practice in the 18th Century because it helped fortify her Ladysmith between lunch and dinner. It is common practice to serve tea sandwiches, scones and a sweet.

Some tips:
* Tea bags are definitely *out.*
* Weak tea is diluted with hot water from a separate pot.
* Sugar (never more than two cubes) and milk (not cream) can be added.
* Paper-thin tea sandwiches (two only) should be put on your tea plate, not on the saucer.
* Never butter an entire scone at once.

Now you're ready for an invitation to take tea with the Queen!

Anglers and Writers (420 Hudson St)
Barclay Restaurant at the Hotel Inter-Continental (111 E 48th St)
Cafe SFA at Saks Fifth Avenue (611 Fifth Ave)
Carlyle Hotel Gallery (35 E 76th St)
Cocktail Terrace at the Waldorf-Astoria (301 Park Ave)
Danal (90 E 10th St)
Felissimo Tea Room (10 W 56th St)
Fifty-seven Fifty-seven (Four Seasons Hotel, 57 E 57th St)

Gold Room at the New York Palace (455 Madison Ave)
Gotham Lounge at the Peninsula Hotel (700 Fifth Ave)
King's Carriage House (251 E 82nd St)
Lady Mendl's (56 Irving Pl)
Le Salon at the Stanhope (995 Fifth Ave)
Le Salon de Thé at Henri Bendel (712 Fifth Ave)
Le Train Bleu at Bloomingdale's (Third Ave at 59th St)
Mark, The (25 E 77th St)
Mayfair Regent Hotel (610 Park Ave)
Oak Room at the Algonquin Hotel (59 W 44th St)
Palm Court at the Plaza Hotel (Fifth Ave at 59th St)
Pembroke Room at the Lowell Hotel (28 E 63rd St)
Polo Lounge at the Westbury Hotel (Madison Ave at 69th St)
Regency Hotel (540 Park Ave)
Rotunda at the Hotel Pierre (2 E 61st St)
Sant Ambroeus (1000 Madison Ave)
Serendipity 3 (225 E 60th St)
Stanhope Hotel (995 Fifth Ave)
Stone Room at the National Academy of Design (1083 Fifth Ave)
Sweet Tea Room at Mackenzie-Childs (824 Madison Ave)
Tea & Sympathy (108 Greenwich Ave)
Tea Box Cafe Takashimaya, 693 Fifth Ave)
Toraya (17 E 71st St)
21 (21 W 52nd St)
Waldorf-Astoria Hotel (301 Park Ave)

Top-Rated Restaurants
(The following appear in most listings.)

Aureole (34 E 61st St)
Chanterelle (2 Harrison St)
Daniel (20 E 76th St)
Four Seasons (99 E 52nd St)
Gotham Bar & Grill (12 E 12th St)
Il Mulino (86 W 3rd St)
Jean Georges (Trump International Hotel, Columbus Circle)
La Caravelle (33 W 55th St)
La Grenouille (3 E 52nd St)
La Réserve (4 W 49th St)
Le Bernardin (155 W 51st St)
Le Chantilly (106 E 57th St)
Le Cirque (Palace Hotel)
Le Régence (Hotel Plaza Athenee, 37 E 64th St)
Les Célébrités (Essex House, 160 Central Park S)
Lespinasse (St Regis Hotel, Fifth Ave at E 55th St)
Lutèce (249 E 50th St)
March (405 E 58th St)
Montrachet (239 W Broadway)
Morton's of Chicago (551 Fifth Ave and 90 West St)
Nobu (105 Hudson St)
Oceana (55 E 54th St)
Primavera (1578 First Ave)

River Cafe (1 Water St, Brooklyn)
Sushisay (38 E 51st St)
Union Square Cafe (21 E 16th St)

Vegetarian

Angelica Kitchen (300 E 12th St)
B&H Dairy (127 Second Ave)
Bachué (36 W 21st St)
Benny's Burritos (113 Greenwich Ave and 93 Ave A)
Bertha's (2160 Broadway)
Candle Cafe (1307 Third Ave)
City Bakery (22 E 17th St)
Good Earth (167 Amsterdam Ave)
Good Food Cafe (401 Fifth Ave)
Good Health Cafe (324 E 86th St)
Health Pub (371 Second Ave)
Indian Delhi (392 Columbus Ave)
Integral Yoga (229 W 13th St)
Natural Food Bar (166 W 72nd St)
Nature Works (200-A W 44th St)
Planet One (76 E 7th St)
Quantum Leap (88 W 3rd St)
Ratner's Dairy Restaurant (138 Delancey St)
Scallions (48 Trinity Pl)
Souen (28 E 13th St and 210 Sixth Ave)
Spring Street Natural (62 Spring St)
Two Boots (37 Ave A)
Vegetable Garden (15 E 40th St)
Vege Vege II (544 Third Ave)
Village Natural (46 Greenwich Ave)
VP 2 (144 W 4th St)
Whole Earth Bakery and Kitchen (70 Spring St and 130 St. Marks Pl)
Zen Palate (663 Ninth Ave, 34 Union Sq, and 2170 Broadway)

View

Contrary to the axiom that good food does not come with a good view, the food at all of these "rooms with a view" is terrific.

American Festival Cafe (Rockefeller Plaza): From the sidelines of the skating rink, the art deco monuments of Rockefeller Plaza tower above you.
Crab House at Chelsea Piers
Delegates' Dining Room (United Nations, First Ave at 42nd St, visitors' entrance)
Hudson River Club (World Financial Center, 250 Vesey St)
Le Pactole (2 World Financial Center): Hudson River views
Museum of Modern Art (Fifth Ave and 82nd St)
Peninsula Hotel Bar (Fifth Ave and 55th St, 23rd floor)
Rainbow Room (30 Rockefeller Center, 65th fl): An elegant and romantic perch that provides a panoramic midtown view.
River Cafe (1 Water St, Brooklyn): A window seat affords that famous view of the downtown skyline you've seen on postcards and in movies.
Tavern on the Green (Central Park W at 67th St): Magical!
Terrace, The (400 W 119th St): The windows here show you what the city looks like from uptown.

Top of the Tower (3 Mitchell Pl): An art deco penthouse delight.
View, The (Marriott Marquis Hotel): You're high above Times Square and revolving.
Water Club, The (East River at E 30th St): Try the view with Sunday brunch.
Windows on the World (1 World Trade Center): You're on top of the world.
World Yacht Cruises (Pier 81, W 41st St at Hudson River): Manhattan from the water

Western

These places are a good distance from the Wild West, but they deliver a taste of cattle country!

Arizona 206 (206 E 60th St)
Canyon Road (1470 First Ave)
El Rio Grande (Third Ave bet 37th and 38th St)
Mesa Grill (102 Fifth Ave)

Wine Bars

Harry's at Hanover Square (1 Hanover Sq)
I Tre Merli (463 West Broadway)
Seagrill (19 W 49th St)
Soho Kitchen and Bar (103 Greene St)

New York Restaurants: Best of the Lot

ACROSS THE STREET
444 E 91st St (at York Ave)   212/722-4000
Dinner: Daily
Moderately expensive

There are three things you can say about Eli Zabar (the proprietor of Across the Street): (1) He makes just about the best bread in town (and does it right across the street from this restaurant). (2) The quality of his food is very good. (3) He sure knows how to charge for his goodies. Having said all of that, Across the Street, in appearance very much like an upscale coffee shop, fits the bill in all three catgeories. Every night the inventive chef offers four rather unique appetizers, four delicious entrees, a cheese selection, and three desserts. Of course, there is Eli's crusty bread on the table to start. The menu changes every day, so you are always in for a surpise when seated. The name of this novel eatery comes from the fact that the Vinegar Factory, another of Eli's enterprises that features more reasonably priced (for him) gourmet items, is a hop, skip, and jump away.

ADRIENNE
Peninsula Hotel
700 Fifth Ave (at 55th St)   212/903-3918
Breakfast: Daily; Lunch: Mon-Fri; Dinner: Tues-Sat;
Brunch: Sun
Moderately expensive

In keeping with the New York trend of a rebirth of fine dining in the better hotels, the Peninsula offers delicious food and professional service in a luxurious setting at their Adrienne restaurant. This is a dress-up type of room, whether you come for breakfast, lunch, dinner, Sunday brunch (which is very special), or afternoon tea. A business lunch is offered; come if you want to impress an important client with a pheasant and wild mushroom dish, for example. Other possibilites: classy sandwiches (like smoked salmon on sourdough), pastas, and grilled seafood dishes. Afternoon tea includes finger sandwiches, wonderful hot scones with Devonshire cream, and sinful cakes and tarts. All of this is reminiscent of the namesake hotel in Hong Kong! A pretheater dinner menu is available, as well as a full dinner selection of seafood, poultry, and meat specialties. Don't rush, but when you are ready, ask to be surprised with a special dessert. They all taste just as good as they look!

AKBAR
475 Park Ave (bet 57th and 58th St)   212/838-1717
Lunch: Mon-Sat; Dinner: Daily
Moderate

If you are interested in north Indian cuisine, you can't do better than Akbar. You'll get a real taste of the region in a distinguished atmosphere, where *muglai* cooking at its very best is featured. The nice part is that the food it is not too hot or oily. Wonderful tandoori breads, baked in a traditional clay oven, are real treats. There are other tandoori specials: several chicken dishes, minced lamb, cubes of fish, and large prawns. You can taste them all in a mixed-grill plate. At noontime there are set menus. In the evening, you can choose from delicious vegetarian dishes (very reasonably priced), traditional lamb entrees, and mildly spiced seafood specialties. Try a lassi with your meal; it is a yogurt drink that comes salted or sweet. Although most folks don't come to an Indian restaurant for desserts, the cottage cheese and milk flavored with rose water is surely different!

ALISON ON DOMINICK STREET
38 Dominick St   212/727-1188
Dinner: Daily
Expensive

Genteel is the appropriate word here. Nothing trendy. No hip waiters. No complicated multi-ethnic dishes. It is right for a special evening out, when you want to bring a bit of class back into your life. There have been constant rumors that Alison intends to move this tiny and romantic French bistro. This West Soho address is hard to find; most taxi drivers have never heard of the street. But insist! The menu changes often; you will probably find special delights like roast quail, roast sweetbread salad, and a number of special seafood dishes with out-of-this-world sauces. If their famous lamb shanks are on the menu, this choice is a must. Servers (and all personnel) are especially friendly and efficient. Pricey desserts are worth every buck. The trio of chocolate mousses (dark, white, and milk) is one of the most expensive but memorable treats in Manhattan.

ALVA
36 E 22nd St   212/228-4399
Lunch: Mon-Fri; Dinner: Daily
Moderate

I'd go back here anytime for one reason: their personnel are extremely friendly without being overbearing. Owners Ferando Saralegui and Charles Palmer set the upbeat mood. The room is small, manageable, and attractively done, but the emphasis is in the quality of the American bistro type food and the reasonable pricing. You'll find a continental menu, complete with delicious burgers, salads, and fish dishes at noon. In the evening there's chicken, lamb, steak, and everything else the American palate desires. Desserts? You bet. Try their banana ice cream sandwich or homemade cheesecakes.

AMERICA
9-13 E 18th St   212/505-2110
Lunch, Dinner: Daily; Brunch: Sat, Sun
Inexpensive to moderate

There is just one word to describe this place: BIG! The room is big, the menu is big, the portions are big, the noise level is big. The good news is that the tab is relatively small. The kids will love it: burgers, chili, pasta, pizza, great sandwiches. Mom and Dad have their items, too: omelets, Boston brown bread, Cincinnatis (shoestring french fries drenched in gravy), deep-fried crawfish tails, Buffalo chicken wings, New Mexican black-bean cakes, roast turkey, shrimp jambalaya, and South Carolina crab cakes. Super desserts: your choice of Toll House cookies, Death by Chocolate, key lime pie, ice cream, and more. This is not gourmet dining, but it's vintage America-at-the dinner-table—a big dinner table.

AMERICAN FESTIVAL CAFE
20 W 50th St   212/332-7620
Breakfast, Lunch: Mon-Sun; Dinner: Daily; Brunch: Sat, Sun
Moderate

You're in the heart of things at this restaurant! The ice-skating rink at Rockefeller Center is glamorous in summer or winter. There's always a lot going on at Rockefeller Center: entertainment, shopping, eating, and people-watching. I'd say it's a must for any visitor to the city. The cafe serves good salads, sandwiches, and items from the charcoal grill. The chef's salad (greens, veal bacon, corncob ham, smoked turkey, peppered beef, and cheese) is delightful, as are the crab cakes. For kids, the hamburgers are just right, and the desserts are unusually appetizing. Try the key lime pie, sundaes, or strawberry shortcake. A large number of domestic and imported beers are also available.

AN AMERICAN PLACE
2 Park Ave (at 32nd St)   212/684-2122
Lunch: Mon-Fri; Dinner: Mon-Sat
Moderately expensive to expensive

An American Place is the dream of Larry Forgione, a well-respected chef who has created a winning establishment that features classic regional-style dishes using only fresh American products. The ambience can best be described as adequate; it is the food and the service that excel. Be prepared for large portions of such delicious dishes as warm potato crisp Napoleon with Hudson Valley foie gras and forest mushrooms; terrine of three smoked fish with their respective caviars and champagne dressing; or cedar-planked Atlantic salmon with toasted corn sauce, winter squash, and an apple cider vinegar with toasted pumpkin seeds. Of course, the menu will vary by season. Being a red, white, and blue flag-waver myself, I almost want to sing "God Bless America" after a meal here. You will, too. Oh yes, the desserts are pure Yankee, like the fabulous strawberry shortcake, banana Betty, or your choice of puddings: bread or double chocolate.

ANGELS
1135 First Ave (bet 62nd and 63rd St)   212/980-3131,
212/371-8484 (delivery)
Daily: 11:30-11:30
Inexpensive

Wouldn't you expect two people named Angela and Angelo to open a place called Angels? Well they did, and it has heavenly food at heavenly prices. Angels is a non-fancy pastaria, with angels all over the place—on the plain tables and on the plain walls. The food is contemporary Italian, with a heavy emphasis on delicious pastas, salads, and chicken. You are treated here as a member of the family with informal service and loving care. It is no wonder that the place is busy all day and evening. Desserts include gelati, Oreo cheesecake, and a wonderfully rich Mississippi (in an Italian restaurant?) mud cake. The goodies don't stop here. Make sure you go around the corner to their takeout at 365 E 62nd St (212/371-8484), where you will find an absolutely fantastic assortment of bakery and prepared foods, pastas, sandwiches, and salads—all of which are made in the Angels' kitchen. The prices are extremely reasonable, the quality exceptional. Catering services are available, and so is delivery.

ANSONIA
329 Columbus Ave (bet 75th and 76th St)   212/579-0505
Dinner: Daily
Moderate

The double-decked premises (it used to be the very popular restaurant Memphis) are cold, bare and ugly. The uniforms are hideous. There is absolutely no atmosphere. But the delicious contemporary American cuisine presented by talented chef Bill Telepan is sensational. The dishes show great imagination. Consider the likes of halibut with a chanterelle sauce, lavender-glazed Muscovy duck, and free-range center-cut pork loin with walnut-savory crust. The appetizers are equally enticing: tuna tartare with cucumber radish salad or roasted quail with bacon and mustard vinaigrette. Late-night goodies include delicious spare ribs and sourdough onion rings. Desserts are equally imaginative, like raisin brioche waffles with armagnac ice cream or a parfait of roasted strawberries, nectarines, and lemon verbena ice cream.

ANTON'S
259 W 4th St (at Perry St)   212/675-5059
Dinner: Tues-Sun
Moderate

On a quiet corner in the West Village, Anton's provides a welcome change from the noise and frantic atmosphere of so many Manhattan restaurants. Outside, a white picket fence surrounds several spaces that appeal during nice weather (although the view is not the greatest). Inside, a dozen tables covered with paper cloths are the setting for casual dining at its home-style best. You'll find a nice selection of salads, different daily pastas, and several fresh fish dishes, all done with chef-owner Anton Linder's personal touch. There are several other choices: chicken breast, Viennese schnitzel, rack of lamb or perhaps New York shell steak. Homemade tarts and filling Viennese apple strudel will complete a pleasant and affordable meal.

AQUAVIT
13 W 54th St   212/307-7311
Lunch: Mon-Fri; Dinner: Mon-Sat; Smorgasboard: Sun (12-3)
Expensive

Aquavit presents an attractive, wholesome background for some very tasty (and expensive) Scandinavian dishes. The setting is a feast for the eyes, while the platters are a feast for the tummy. One has a choice of eating upstairs in the slightly less expensive cafe or in the several areas downstairs, including a covered patio with a waterfall. From here, the diner looks eight stories skyward in a dramatic atrium (the former John D. Rockefeller townhouse). Major alterations have been made to the menu, which is now prepared by chef Marcus Samuelsen. Cafe specialties include herring, gravlax, and delicious salmon (poached or pan-fried). Danish open-faced sandwiches are also available. Outstanding dishes in the dining room include smoked duck (as an appetizer), pan-roasted loin of beef, loin of Arctic venison, Arctic char (like salmon trout), and rack of lamb. For dessert, how about a warm chocolate ganache?

ARIZONA 206
206 E 60th St   212/838-0440
Lunch: Mon-Sat; Dinner: Daily
Moderate

The best way to describe this American Southwesterner would be uncomfortable, jumping, noisy — and delicious. Folks who know and like the Arizona/New Mexico type of cuisine swear by their Santa Fe veggie rolls or the traditional chicken tamale with sweet corn masa. Other luncheon favorites include New Mexican nicoise salad and lobster guacamole. For dinner, things get a bit heavier. Chef Miles Angelo offers novelties like seared ostrich tartare and chile-rubbed quail as appetizers; Peking duck tamales or salmon and truffle enchiladas are popular main course items. Dessert? How does a pear in a teepee (with cinnamon whipped cream and pear-anise jus) or molten Aztec chocolate truffle cake with blackberry caramel sound?

What Goes Around Comes Around . . .

What's hot? Mashed potatoes. Meat loaf. And now, believe it or not, macaroni and cheese! If that sends you, try the different styles at the **Lobster Club** (24 E 80th St), the **Screening Room** (54 Varick St), or **Quilty's** (177 Prince St).

ARQUA
281 Church St   212/334-1888
Lunch: Mon-Fri; Dinner: Mon-Sun
Moderate

There are Italian restaurants of every size, price range, and specialty in almost every neighborhood of Manhattan. I sometimes wonder if there aren't more Italian restaurants in Manhattan than in all of Italy. To be outstanding in New York, an Italian restaurant must have something special going for it. Arqua is special because the staff does things so plainly, simply, and well. This is not a fancy, pricey restaurant of the moment. Arqua (named for a small city near Venice) is situated in an old warehouse with high ceilings, which adds to the noisy atmosphere. The folks who run this place are not fancy, either. It shows in the TLC they give all the patrons, and the food is exceptional. You can have your choice of homemade pastas, Venetian dishes, marinated salmon, and ravioli with butternut squash. Squab and duck are specialties. There are also excellent veal dishes. The flourless espresso chocolate cake is exceptional.

A TAVOLA
1095 Lexington Ave (at 77th St)   212/744-1233
Breakfast, lunch, dinner: daily
Inexpensive to moderate

An inexpensive Italian diner in the midst of the high-rent Upper East Side? Yes sir, and they serve excellent food. An unbelievably small kitchen turns out dozens of hot and cold appetizers, soups, stews, seafood, sandwiches, poultry, steaks and chops, pastas, pizzas, and much more. There are complete Italian meals with very tasty Italian breads and just about anything else your heart desires. There's nothing fancy in the decor, the service is homey and informal, and the owners seem really happy to welcome you. The breakfast menu offers the whole gamut: juices, fresh fruit, omelets, lox and bagels, cereals, and griddle items. Don't ask me how they manage to do it all so well, but this is a real find . . . and the price is right. Their tartufo is as good as any I have tasted in Italy.

AUREOLE
34 E 61st St (bet Madison and Park Ave)   212/319-1660
Lunch: Mon-Fri; Dinner: Mon-Sat
Expensive

I grudgingly include Aureole in this volume. Not that it isn't a fine restaurant; at the prices they charge, it should be. Owner-chef Charlie Palmer usually does a fine job with the preparation of his dishes. They are beautifully served by personnel who are not a little bit impressed that they work for this establishment. If you can get the noses down far enough to seat you (without questionable waits at the bar) and are lucky enough to sit on the first floor, with its seasonal garden views, you are fortunate. Best bets are the game dishes, signature plates like smoked salmon with cucumber salad and sea scallop sandwiches in crisp potato crusts, and roast pheasant. Desserts look better than they taste. Personally, I can think of a lot of other ways to spend your hard-earned bucks, although the four-course *prix fixe* luncheon is a good value.

AU TROQUET
328 W 12th St   212/924-3413
Dinner: Daily
Moderate

Allow extra time if you're arriving here by taxi since most drivers will have trouble delivering you to the front door. And be sure to call for reservations. The place is small and very popular with neighbors as well as knowledgeable diners who have previously enjoyed Au Troquet's delights. This is a no-nonsense French country restaurant where food is prepared professionally. Your plate is flamboyant in presentation and exceptional in taste. Au Troquet deserves special mention for its seasonings; they know how it's done. The soups are all delicious, as is the *pate de foie de canard*. You can go on to fillet of sole, grilled salmon, lobster, or a fabulous rabbit dish. There is almost always a fine selection of lamb dishes available. Homemade desserts include a great mousse and sorbets. This is the kind of place to go to when you feel like having a relaxed, cozy dinner for two.

BARBETTA
321 W. 46th St (bet Eighth and Ninth Ave)   212/246-9171
Lunch, Dinner, Supper: Mon-Sat
Moderate to expensive

This is an elegant restaurant serving Piemontese cuisine. Piemonte is located in the northern part of Italy, and the cuisine reflects that charming part of the country. You can dine here in European elegance. One of New York's oldest restaurants, having celebrated its 90th anniversary, Barbetta is still owned by the family who founded it. One of the special attractions is dining alfresco in the garden during the summer. The main dining room and private party rooms are magnificent! There is an a la carte luncheon menu, as well as a six-course before-theater dinner menu, which offers fish specialties, swordfish, and a number of other selections served expeditiously so that you can make opening curtain. If you have more time and can enjoy a leisurely dinner, think about the minestrone (which is almost a meal in itself), ravioli that is made by hand, or the fabulous *finocchio e parmigiano* salad. Barbetta specializes in fish and game dishes that vary daily. Try the squab if you're lucky enough to find it on the menu. Other selections include rabbit, beef braised in red wine with polenta, and a delicious rack of venison. Desserts include several chocolate offerings and an assortment of cooked fruits, as well as *panna cotta*—one of the best in the city. An added attraction: a pianist during pre-theater dinner every night and lunchtime fashion show on Wednesday.

BAROCCO
301 Church St   212/431-1445
Lunch: Mon-Fri; Dinner: Daily
Moderate

If you are looking for simple and well-prepared food in the Tribeca area, this *trattoria* with a Tuscan flavor is your best bet. Barocco has a special way with seasonings that make their dishes light and easy to digest. This style of dining attracts many celebrities, who are so mindful of their figures! Specialties include wonderful homemade grilled bread with garlic and olive oil (*fettunta*), lasagna, spinach ravioli, grilled Norwegian salmon, grilled lamb chops, roast chicken, and prime New York strip steak. Top it all off with Tuscan almond cookies. Many items served in the restaurant are available for takeout next door.

BEN BENSON'S
123 W 52nd St   212/581-8888
Lunch: Mon-Fri; Dinner: Daily
Moderately expensive

With all the excitement of a number of new steakhouses in Manhattan, it is easy to overlook the old reliables. For years, Ben Benson's has been a favorite of the meat-and-potatoes set, and with justification. The atmosphere is very macho-clubby, the air is nicely tinged with cigar smoke from boys having an evening out on the town, and the food is uniformly good. Unlike some of the other steakhouses, the service here is courteous and efficient. The menu is what you would expect: sirloin steak, filet mignon, T-bone, prime rib, chops, and the like. But there is much more. Ben Benson's also offers seafood, chicken, calves liver, and chopped steak. Wonderful potatoes (your choice of kind), onion rings, or healthy spinach complete the stomach-filling experience. Lunchtime specials include lobster salad, grilled chicken breast, roast beef hash, and Louisiana bay shrimp. Don't come here looking for bargains. Ben treats you well, and you pay well for what you get!

BIG NICK'S
2175 Broadway (at 77th St)   212/362-9238
Open 24 hours
Inexpensive

For those readers who feel this volume deals only in pricy places, that is simply not true! Take Big Nick's, for example. This place is unfancy, unexpensive, untrendy, and practically unknown . . . except for those who want really good food at really low prices and don't care about atmosphere! The burgers are sensational. There is a special selection for diet-watchers. Meat pies, cheese pies, spinach pies, and filo pastries are all specialties. There are lots of pizzas, baked potatoes served any way you want, delicious cakes and pies, homemade baklava, and yogurt. The service is super-friendly, and they offer free delivery. Oh yes, breakfasts are super, too, and they serve lots of salads and sandwiches for lunch. They've been at it since 1962 with no publicity. Now the secret is out!

BILLY'S
948 First Ave   212/753-1870, 212/355-8920
Lunch, Dinner: Daily; Brunch: Sat, Sun
Moderate

This is New York's oldest family-owned restaurant! For those who like old-fashioned setups, complete with white-tiled floors, checkered tablecloths, and a busy bar right in the center of the dining area, Billy's is your kind of place. Established in 1870, this bustling pub/restaurant has been in the same family since opening day! It is a First Avenue institution where the food is as inviting as the atmosphere. Their weekend brunch is a must. No menus, just a blackboard listing steaks, scallops, chops, hamburgers, and the like. All are well prepared, with large portions accompanied by French fries, homemade mashed potatoes, or baked potatoes. Cole slaw is served when you are seated. The waiters are vintage New York. The ethnic mix of the Big Apple makes for exceptional talent in baking, and you can enjoy fine breads at restaurants like Billy's. Desserts include delicious ice cream, cheesecake, pies, and homemade rice pudding. Top it all off with Irish coffee. There is a *prix fixe* menu for early evening, and a late-evening menu is available as well.

BISTRO MARGOT
26 Prince St   212/274-1027
Dinner: Daily; Brunch: Sat, Sun
Moderate
Cash or checks only

You have heard of a sliver of a place . . . well, Bistro Margot fits the description very well! An open kitchen in the middle with a garden in the back and some cozy tables make up the entire establishment. Small though it is, Bistro Margot turns out excellent French bistro plates: fresh salads, patés, charcuterie, smoked salmon, and a nice assortment of cheese. A number of sandwiches and entrees are featured, with beef stew in red wine the big winner. What a dish for a chilly evening! Dress down, bring cash only (along with your appetite), and you'll have a superior meal. The chocolate mousse dessert is as good as I've ever tasted at any of Manhattan's pricier rooms.

BISTRO 790
Sheraton Manhattan Hotel (790 Seventh Ave, at 51st St)
212/621-8537
Lunch, Dinner: Daily
Moderate

Bistro 790, the Sheraton Manhattan's signature restaurant, is located in the lobby of the hotel. This American bistro offers cuisine of the Americas which combines ingredients, recipes, and foods indigenous to North and Central America. Low in calories, total fat, saturated fat, cholesterol, and sodium, the cuisine is tailor-made for those watching their waistline.

BLUE RIBBON
97 Sullivan St (bet Spring and Prince St)   212/274-0404
Tues-Sun: 4 p.m.-4 a.m.
Moderate

This place is aptly named. It deserves a blue ribbon in just about every respect . . . except for quiet, leisurely dining. Blue Ribbon is one of the most popular spots in Soho, with a bustling bar scene and a line waiting for its limited number of tables. The regulars know of the exceptional food served in this unpretentious restaurant. There is a raw bar to attract seafood lovers, along with clams, lobster, crab, boiled crawfish, and the house special, the "Blue Ribbon Royale." One can choose from two dozen appetizers, including barbequed ribs, smoked trout, caviar, and chicken wings. Entrees are just as wide-ranging: sweetbreads, sesame-glazed catfish, tofu ravioli, fried chicken and mashed potatoes, burgers, and much more. How the smallish kitchen can turn out so many different kinds of dishes is amazing, but they certainly do it well. Don't come here for a relaxed evening; this is strictly an all-American culinary experience. Note the hours for those who experience hunger pangs in the wee hours.

BOATHOUSE CAFE
Central Park   212/517-CAFE
Lunch: Daily (Mar 21–Nov 1);
Dinner: Daily (May 1–Oct 1)
Moderate

Central Park has come back to life, and the Boathouse Cafe is one of its best attractions. It's situated in a charming spot on the east side of the park, between the 72nd and 79th Street entrances. A free shuttle brings guests from the 72nd Street and Fifth Avenue park entrance from 7 p.m. onward. The dockside has been partially tented, and an authentic Venetian gondola is available for rent (by reservation), as are rowboats. The view is great, the setting couldn't be more romantic, and the food is tasty and well presented. The menu is contemporary American. There is a great private party area located in a landscaped English garden.

BOLO

23 E 22nd St   212/228-2200
Lunch: Mon-Fri; Dinner: Daily
Moderate to moderately expensive

The menu here is not a copy of the one at the Ritz Hotel in Madrid, but it does encompass contemporary Spanish flavors in an attractive and comfortable setting. The atmosphere and personnel are upbeat, and the folks want your meal to be both fun and tasty. The logistics are a miracle, with a tiny kitchen that is able to turn out a bevy of wonderful dishes. The best of the lot: steamed baby clams, crispy sweetbreads, oven roasted duck salad. I'd also recommend the grilled salmon or oven-roasted garlic lamb shank. The shellfish and chicken paella with rice and peas is another popular dish. For dessert, the apple cake is a winner.

BOULEY

The undisputed top innovator in the food world today is David Bouley. For years he ran a restaurant (with his name above the door) in such a professional manner that it was widely acclaimed as the pacesetter for the city. There is no compromise with perfection with this gentleman, and he now he is embarking on a series of exciting new ventures that will shake up the food world.

At **118 West Broadway** (at Duane St) his new bakery features the best of regional breads, baked right on the premises. Along with the baked items, a full-service cafe features light fare, rotisserie items, and healthy plates from lunchtime until the early morning hours.

Manhattan has been without a really good Viennese restaurant since Vienna 79 closed some years ago. Leave it to David to bring back serious Viennese dining at **162 Duane Street**. The house will be open for lunch and dinner, with European-trained masters providing dishes of the highest quality, including authentic local pastries. (Is there anything quite as good as real sacher torte?)

Bouley at Home, due to open in 1998 at 25 Hudson Street, will be housed in a huge (18,000 sq. ft.) store that takes as its model the fabulous food halls of Harrod's Department Store in London. A large array of healthy organic products will be featured, along with an area where you can enjoy goodies right on the spot. The store will forge a partnership with customers, educating them about eating and preparing healthy food.

Finally, at **36 Hudson Street**, this enterprising genius has put together two buildings that will house: an international cafe with an Asian influence on the first floor; the classic **Bouley,** elegant and cozy (with fireplace) on the second floor; private rooms on the third floor; a domestic and international-staffed cooking school on the fourth floor; and a novel research and testing food lab on the fifth floor. Talk about vision!

BOUTERIN

420 E 59th St   212/758-0323
Lunch: Mon-Fri; Dinner: Mon-Sat (Sun in winter)
Moderate to moderately expensive

This has to be one of the most charming rooms in Manhattan. Antoine Bouterin, for years the talented and highly respected chef at Le Périgord, has opened his dream restaurant, and it is a beauty. The *provençal* theme has been carried out with exquisite taste; the result is warm and enchanting. But the real attraction is the food, personalized by Antoine himself. He is assisted in the presentation by a low-key and helpful staff. The result: a wonderful experience for the diner. You can choose from artichoke mousse, smoked salmon, and eggplant caviar as cold appetizers. On the warm side, pistou soup or risotto of Mediterranean seafood. How does a dandelion omelet (with turkey bacon), red snapper filet, venison medallions, or lamb stew sound? The latter is cooked for seven hours and is meant to be eaten with a spoon! Look no further than the caramelized banana galette, with chocolate sorbet and caramel sauce, for dessert. For the health conscious, vegetarian diet dishes are available.

BRAVO GIANNI

230 E 63rd St   212/752-7272
Lunch: Mon-Fri; Dinner: Mon-Sun
Moderately expensive

Fans of Bravo Gianni — and there are many — may be upset that I'm mentioning it in this book. They want to keep it a secret. It's so comfortable and the food is so good that they don't want it to become overcrowded and spoiled. But it doesn't look like there's any real danger of that happening as long as Gianni himself is on the job. The not-too-large room is pleasantly appointed, with beautiful plants on every table. The intimate atmosphere makes it seem as though you're in your own private dining room. And what tastes await you! You can't go wrong with any of the antipasto selections or soups. But do save room for the *tortellini alla panna* or the *fettuccine con ricotta*; no one does them better. I can recommend every dish on the menu, with top billing going to the fish dishes and rack of lamb. Marvelous desserts, many of them made in-house, will surely tempt you. Legions of loyal customers come back again and again; it's easy to see why. But please, keep all this to yourself!

BROOKLYN DINER

212 W 57th St   212/977-1957
Breakfast, Lunch, Dinner, Late Supper: Daily
Moderate

The Brooklyn Diner (note: located in Manhattan) is *very* in! With an excellent location, all-day dining, expansive menu, pleasant personnel, better-than-average diner food, and reasonable prices, the place is a winner. You can find just about anything your heart desires: typical breakfast fare, sandwiches (the Reuben is a must), salads, hearty lunch and dinner plates, homemade desserts, and good drinks. Their muffins are moist, flavorful, and outrageously good. A tile floor, comfortable booths, and old-time movies add to the pleasant ambience.

BUTTERFIELD 81
168-170 E 81st St   212/BU8-2700
Dinner: Mon-Sun; Brunch: Sun
Moderately expensive

Only on Manhattan's Upper East Side would you find a restaurant like this — clubby, comfortable, classy. It might remind you of dining in London! The menu is somewhat limited, with some soups and salads to start, but my favorite is the barbecued shrimp dish with pineapple chutney. I could make a whole meal out of this winner. There are burgers, chicken, wood-grilled salmon, delicious honey mustard pork tenderloin, and more. Crispy onion rings and garlic mashed potatoes are exceptional. The final touch: a caramelized banana split with hot butterscotch or chocolate brownie with Tahitian vanilla bean ice cream. Again, Ken Aretsky shows that he can read the neighborhood where he operates.

CAFE BOTANICA
Essex House
160 Central Park S   212/247-0300, 212/484-5120 (direct)
Breakfast, Lunch, Dinner: Daily (Brunch on Sunday)
Moderate

Chalk up another winner for the increasing number of good dining spots in Manhattan hotels. The Essex House features two excellent top-quality restaurants, very much in keeping with the fine ambience of this Nikko property. Cafe Botanica overlooks Central Park, with the added pleasure of magnificent table settings to go along with the tasty fare. Villeroy and Boch's "Botanica" pattern is the theme for the serving pieces. Along with the colorfully backed chairs and the light and airy feel of the room, the china makes the terrace area of the restaurant one of Manhattan's most attractive dining rooms. Spicy crab cakes or a selection of cold appetizers will get you started well. There are great pizzas and pastas, and excellent grilled tuna and swordfish steaks. It's a wonderful spot for a very special lunch — the closest thing to a private dining room in Central Park!

CAFE CENTRO
MetLife Building
200 Park Ave (E 45th St and Vanderbilt Ave)   212/818-1222
Lunch: Mon-Fri; Dinner: Mon-Sat
Moderate

In a rather large room that's very attractively appointed and broken up into appealing spaces, Restaurant Associates (a major player in the city) has created a purely American restaurant. One is greeted by a gas-fired working rotisserie and a beautiful open kitchen that's spotlessly clean and very efficient. There are *prix fixe* dinners, if you so desire. The chicken pie *bisteeya* (with almonds, raisins, and orange-flower essence) is worth a trip to Cafe Centro in itself; it is not a normal chicken pot pie, but a very tasty and light dish. There is a raw bar, a hefty seafood platter, excellent steaks and French fries, and daily roasts. Crusty French bread is laid out right in front of you. Other specialties include *maftoul couscous*, penne pasta, and a moist and flavorful double breast of chicken. The pastry chef obviously has a chocolate bias (good for him): *la marquise au chocolat*, bittersweet chocolate mousse, *souffle chaud au chocolate*, *valrhona* bittersweet chocolate ice cream, and chocolate tarts with caramel sauce are just a sampling. If chocolate is not your bag, try macaroons filled with Kahlua and coffee parfait. Adjoining the dining room is a very busy beer bar that serves light sandwiches and appetizers.

CAFE DES ARTISTES
1 W 67th St   212/877-3500
Lunch: Mon-Fri; Dinner: Daily; Brunch: Sat, Sun
Moderate

George Lang has created an absolute masterpiece on the West Side, just off Central Park. It's truly a landmark. There are several dining levels and some hidden tables, giving each diner the impression of being in a small, cozy establishment. Beautiful murals by Christy complement the charming decor. The personnel are wonderfully accommodating, and the food is absolutely delicious. Try the unusual Sunday brunch. Some of the mouth-watering selections include smoked salmon Benedict, asparagus omelet, crisp salmon-scallop cakes, and delicious stuffed French toast. Dinner appetizers include salmon four ways: smoked, poached, dill-marinated, and tartare; assorted planked *cochonnailles;* foie gras de Canard; and an array of delightful salads. For the main course, there is swordfish, rack of lamb with basil crust, duck confit, a variety of pasta dishes, and much more. By all means don't overlook desserts. The selection changes but includes mouth-watering choices from cheesecake sorbet to Ilona torte. A great dessert plate features samples of their dessert varieties. Three-course, price-fixed lunches and dinners are offered, and the menu selection changes often. This is a lovely, romantic place at any time, but I especially recommend it for an after-theater supper.

Going to Hell to Eat . . . Hell's Kitchen, That Is:

Avanti (700 Ninth Ave, at 48th St)
Basilica (676 Ninth Ave, at 47th St)
Ralph's (862 Ninth Ave, at 56th St)
Vintage (753 Ninth Ave, at 51st St)

CAFE UN DEUX TROIS
123 W 44th St   212/354-4148
Lunch, Dinner: Daily; Brunch: Sat, Sun
Moderate

Want to see one of your favorite actors? This cafe could be his or her hangout! Paper tablecloths seem like a stingy way to dress a restaurant table, but at this bustling cafe, there's a reason. Two reasons, in fact. One is that it helps keep the tab down. The other is to provide drawing paper; crayons are furnished on every table. Doodling helps pass the time, and isn't it something you've always wanted to do since you were a kid? The surroundings (an old hotel lobby) are plain, but the location is handy if you're going to the theater. Service is prompt and cordial, and prices are moderate. Though the menu is limited, each item is handled with obvious attention to quality and taste. Begin with a hearty onion soup, salade nicoise, or paté de canard. Seafood *en papillote* is an excellent selection. The steak tartare is the best in the city. This spot is also popular with the recording industry and young people. Desserts are all made on premises and are excellent.

CAFFE BONDI
7 W 20th St (nr Fifth Ave)   212/691-8136
Lunch, Dinner: Mon-Sat; Brunch: Sat, Sun
Moderate

In the mood for Sicilian cuisine? Well, this is the place. Lunches and dinners are excellent, and desserts are superb. You can sit indoors or on the outside patio and savor every one of those delicious calories in the shape of marvelous tortes and cakes. It's a convenient place for meeting friends if you are working near Broadway or Fifth Avenue in the 20s. The baked goods are special. *Prix fixe* lunches and dinners are available, and historical menus are a unique treat.

CAMPAGNA
24 E 21st St   212/460-0900
Lunch: Mon-Fri; Dinner; Mon-Sun
Moderate

When the food is good, atmosphere is secondary. Such is the case at Campagna, an Italian knockout downtown. The surroundings are rather nondescript, but the dishes are anything but! There are daily pasta specials at lunchtime, including *lasagna alla nonna* (Grandma's lasagna), which is not to be missed. Daily fresh fish specials include salmon and tuna presentations. A fresh-market antipasto table is inviting. In the evening you can choose from an expanded list of pastas (spaghetti with baby clam sauce is special), couscous, spicy seafood stew (*cacciucco*), grilled baby chicken, squab, osso buco, and rabbit. A large dessert menu is offered; try the bittersweet chocolate mascarpone cake with chocolate espresso sauce. More conservative diners might try the warm apple tart with cinnamon gelato or one of their delicious tarts. Campagna is a friendly, professional, and satisfying place to dine.

CANTON
45 Division St   212/226-4441, 212/966-7492
Lunch, Dinner: Wed-Sun (closed five weeks during summer)
No credit cards
Moderate

For those in the know, Canton has been a favorite spot for over 40 years. Why? The place is clean, and the personnel are friendly and polite. But most of all, unlike so many Chinese restaurants, the cooking is done on an individual basis. It's almost like stepping into the kitchen of a Chinese family. Tell your waiter the kind of Cantonese delicacies you wish to have. You will be delighted with the results! I would suggest butterfly shrimp, diced chicken with vegetables and mushrooms, or fried young squab. All the seafood is fresh and tasty. So gather up a group of friends for a special Chinese treat. You'll be pleased with the quality of the food *and* the moderate bill.

CAPSOUTO FRÈRES
451 Washington St (one block south of Canal St)   212/966-4900
Lunch: Tues-Fri; Dinner: Daily; Brunch: Sat, Sun
Moderate

Capsouto Frères gets better and better. In 1891, when the building in which Capsouto Frères is located was constructed, this might have been an "in" area. But, alas, times (and neighborhoods) have changed. The Landmark Building is still a beauty; however, the rest of the surroundings aren't the greatest. Inside, it's another story. Three brothers and their mother team up to operate a classic establishment, complete with ceiling fans, wooden tables, good cheer, and tasty plates. At noon a special *prix fixe* lunch is offered, or you can order from an a la carte menu laden with salads, fish, meat, and pasta dishes. In the evening, they offer more of the same, along with quail, duckling, and first-rate sirloin steak. This bistro is a great setting for a casual, let-your-hair-down evening with good friends who like to live it up!

There is always the "hottest" restaurant of the moment, and at this writing, that accolade goes to **Balthazar** (80 Spring St, at Crosby St. (212/343-2252). A Keith McNally French brasserie that looks like it has been around for a long time, it has an experienced kitchen and wait staff to fit that description. For people watching, this high-energy charmer is a must; everyone who is anybody is fighting over the chairs. But hold on . . . tomorrow it may be someplace else.

CARMINE'S
2450 Broadway (bet 90th and 91st St)   212/362-2200
Dinner: Daily

200 W 44th St (bet Seventh and Eighth Ave)   212/221-3800
Lunch, Dinner: Daily

American Express
Moderate

Time to treat the whole gang? Or the whole family? The first thing you want to do is round up at least six of your heavy-eating friends, call Carmine's for reservations, and show up famished wearing loose clothing. You won't be disappointed! Carmine's presents Southern Italian family dining fare with *huge* portions and zesty seasonings that come with the territory. Not only are the platters full, they are delicious. If you go with fewer than a half-dozen friends, my advice is to go early. The wait can be as long as an hour, as they will not reserve tables for smaller parties. The menu choices run the gamut of pizzas, pastas, chicken, veal, seafood, and tasty Italian appetizers such as calamari. Oh, yes, there is no printed menu. Wall signs explain the offerings.

CARNEGIE DELICATESSEN AND RESTAURANT
854 Seventh Ave (at 55th St)   212/757-2245, 800/334-5606
Breakfast, Lunch, Dinner: Daily (6:40 a.m.-4 a.m.)
No credit cards
Moderate

There's no city on earth with delis like New York's, and the Carnegie is one of the best. Its location in the middle of the hotel district makes it perfect for midnight snacks. Everything is made on the premises, and Carnegie offers free delivery between 7 a.m. and 3 a.m. if you're within a five-block radius. Where to start? Your favorite Jewish mother didn't make chicken soup better than the Carnegie's homemade variety. It's practically worth getting sick for! It comes with matzo balls, garden noodles, and rice, homemade kreplach, or real homemade kasha. There's more: Great blintzes. Open sandwiches, hot and delicious. Ten different deli and egg sandwiches. A very juicy burger with all the trimmings. Lots of fish dishes. Corned beef, pastrami, and rare roast beef. A choice of egg dishes unequaled in New York. Salads. Side orders of everything from hot baked potatoes to potato pancakes. Outrageous cheesecake topped with strawberries, blueberries, pineapple, or cherries (or just served plain). Desserts from A to Z—even Jell-O.

CASCABEL
218 Lafayette St   212/431-7300
Dinner: Mon-Sat
Moderate

Although located in Soho, Cascabel feels more like an uptown dining room. Chef Sam Hazen (whose credentials include the Terrace and La Côte Basque) has put his imprint on this house featuring "global American cuisine." As a matter of interest, his uncle was the personal chef for President Dwight Eisenhower. You would have to call this place bipartisan, as owner John Zaccaro, Jr., is the son of politician Geraldine Ferraro! The offerings here likewise have a broad appeal: wonderful pan-roasted quail stuffed with figs, pan-roasted duck breast, seared venison medallions, potato crusted salmon. Two different tasting menus (one is vegetarian) offer five-course meals. Pastry chef Christine Del Lima smothers us dessert lovers with her espresso bombe, a chocolate shell surrounding espresso ice cream and stuffed with a dark chocolate kiss and a creamy chocolate sauce. Besides the good food, the people watching is pretty terrific, too.

CHANTERELLE
2 Harrison St (at Hudson St)   212/966-6960
Lunch: Tues-Sat; Dinner: Mon-Sat
Expensive

Mentioning Chanterelle to New Yorkers with well-honed taste buds will almost certainly raise a smile. It was only a matter of time before Karen and David Waltuck would have to move from their tiny Soho restaurant on Grand Street. The place simply wasn't big enough to handle the legion of loyal customers who feel that Chanterelle is one of New York's better restaurants. Well, the Waltucks moved to a space with a larger dining room (which seats about 60), a bigger kitchen, and a cute after-dinner area. The setting is formal and attractive, with interesting high, stamped-tin ceilings in the historic Mercantile Exchange Building in Tribeca. The menu changes periodically, but every dish is a masterful creation. With David in the kitchen preparing great fish and lobster dishes, and Karen out front pampering her guests, it is a good bet you won't even notice the size of the tab for the *prix fixe* dinner or tasting menu.

CHAT 'N CHEW
10 E 16th St   212/243-1616
Lunch, Dinner: Daily; Bruch: Sat-Sun
Inexpensive

I am always a bit leery of eating establishments that have a multitude of signs in their windows. Somehow it gives an aura of desperation. But in this case I proceeded anyway and am glad that I did. However, a word of warning, dear readers. This is definitely a place for twenty- and thirty-somethings, maybe even forty-somethings who are young at heart (and stomach). The decor is horrendous: a mish-mash of signs on the walls, uneven tables crowded together, a few old-time relics. The genial servers, all harried, look like they just got out of bed. Don't fret; the main reason you came is for a good, cheap meal and that is what you get, in spades. Delicious fresh salads, wonderful sandwiches, and huge entrees are the name of the game. The turkey dinner beats anything at your grandmother's on the big day. There is also honey-dipped fried chicken, grilled pork chops, and vegetarian chili. And those desserts! All homemade, all luscious, all displayed as you enter the dining room. Keep your blinders on and your palate fresh, and you'll have a great (and reasonable) meal.

CHELSEA BISTRO & BAR
358 W 23rd St   212/727-2026
Dinner: Daily
Moderate

Chelsea now offers a number of trendy eating establishments; this is one of the best. It used to be a cave, but now it is a bustling bistro! In a comfortable space that includes a front room as well as an attractive terrace, this well-run house has a menu that will please both adventurous and conservative diners. For appetizers, there is a cassolette of snails, sea scallops, a warm flan of wild mushrooms, or tartar of salmon. Seafood entrees are best: smoked-to-order salmon, roasted red snapper, Maine lobster, sea scallops. The nicoise salad is hard to beat; other specialties include hanger steak in red wine sauce, dry-aged ribeye steak for two, roasted duck, and braised lamb shank. It is in the tart department that his place really shines. Ask about daily specials.

CHEZ JACQUELINE
72 MacDougal St   212/505-0727
Dinner: Daily
Moderate

This modest French bistro in the Village is one of the undiscovered pleasures of Manhattan. The atmosphere is very relaxed. You'll see cozy couples eating at the bar or serene seniors holding hands at one of the small number of tables in this popular neighborhood restaurant. Fresh, large salads are a specialty, as well as country paté, duck liver mousse, and mussels with garlic. Among the dozen items that are regularly available as entrees, house favorites include broiled rack of lamb, chicken casserole, veal kidneys, veal sweetbreads, and a hearty beef stew in a red wine, tomato, and carrot sauce. The portions are generous and the prices fair. If you can manage a dessert, crème brûlée or white and dark chocolate mousse cake will convince you the kitchen knows what it's doing.

CHEZ JOSEPHINE
414 W 42nd St   212/594-1925
Dinner: Mon-Sat
Moderate

Those who follow the entertainment business will remember the late Josephine Baker, who was the toast of Paris in the first quarter of this century. Well, one of her adopted children, Jean-Claude, has kept the showbiz interest and added the food business to his accomplishments. He has created a first-class atmosphere with sexy, attractive decor, a background of live jazz music, and delicious food to match. Chez Josephine is a haven for those who have made it and those who wish they had—it is dining with theatrics. This is a great place, now over a decade old, for a late-night, after-theater rendezvous. If Jean-Claude settled down for a minute, you would find him fascinating company. The menu has French tones, as you would imagine. The warm apple and rhubarb cake is very special, as is the *bombe pralinee*. A private party room is available upstairs. The bistro is a charmer, and so is Jean-Claude!

Caviar

We aim to please all tastes and all pocketbooks in this volume, so it is only right that we devote a line or two to readers with expensive tastes:

Bubble Room (228 West Broadway): The real stuff, plus hundreds of champagnes and wines.

Caviarteria (502 Park Ave): I like everything about this place, especially the friendly attitude of boss Eric Sobol.

Firebird (3 65 W 46th St): Re-creation of a pre-revolutionary Russian mansion.

Petrossian (182 W 58th St): Stepping inside here provides caviar set ambience; it's a spectacular place to dine.

Zabar's (2245 Broadway): If price is important this should be your first stop.

CHEZ MA TANTE
189 W 10th St (bet W 4th and Bleecker St)   212/620-0223
Dinner: Daily; Brunch: Sun
Moderate

You don't have to be big and expensive to be good. Chez Ma Tante proves that. Friendly and cozy in the winter, the place is just as charming in the summer as the bistro opens onto the sidewalk. Manager Joseph Sutton and chef Denis Whittun handle the duties up front and in the kitchen; hordes of regular customers will attest to their capabilities. Appetizers like homemade duck paté and *tomate au Montrachet* and main dishes including the "favorite French dish" (steak, French fries, and green salad), and grilled snapper or tuna are specialties of the house. Dessert? Profiteroles topped with white and dark chocolate sauce (and served warm) are a delicious variation on the popular French dish.

CHEZ MICHALLET
90 Bedford St (at Grove St)   212/242-8309
Dinner: Daily; Brunch: Sun
Moderate

Imagine you are sitting in the window of a quaint little restaurant in a picturesque village in the French countryside. The place has 17 tables, the decor is eclectic, the kitchen tiny . . . but the food and service are wonderful. All this is true, except you are looking out on the corner of Bedford and Grove Streets in Greenwich Village! What a charming place this is. The friendly waiters couldn't be more helpful in explaining the varied menu: steak, salmon, duck, lamb, veal, chicken, fish . . . anything your heart desires. The desserts are good as well. Choose from tarts, a great chocolate truffle cake, crème brûlée, profiteroles, or fresh berries. For a perfectly satisfying and relaxing evening, this spot is hard to beat. There is also a special pre-theater menu.

CHEZ NAPOLEON
365 W 50th St   212/265-6980
Lunch: Mon-Fri; Dinner: Mon-Sat
Inexpensive to moderate

With all the problems of daily life, it's fun to go to a place where the atmosphere is cheerful. Chez Napoleon is that kind of place. The owner greets you like a long-lost friend and seats you in a small, clean dining area. It's an old house—warm, cozy, and a neighborhood favorite for many years. The cooking is dependable and hearty. My top recommendations from the large menu are coquille St. Jacques, bouillabaisse (served only on weekends), rabbit with mustard sauce, and sweetbreads. Many of the desserts are homemade. But the big plus is the freshness of the dishes and the gracious hospitality.

CHIN CHIN
216 E 49th St (bet Second and Third Ave)   212/888-4555
Lunch: Mon-Fri; Dinner: Daily
Moderate to moderately expensive

Chin Chin is a very classy Chinese restaurant whose ambience and price reflect a superior cooking style. There are two rooms and a garden in back. The soups and barbecued spareribs are wonderful for starters. The Szechuan jumbo prawns are sensational. As a matter of fact, I'd concentrate on the seafood dishes. But you might also try the wonderful Peking duck dinner, with choice of soup, crispy duck skin with pancakes, fried rice, poached spinach, and homemade sorbet and ice cream. The menu is much the same for lunch or dinner. A reasonable *prix fixe* lunch is available.

CHINA GRILL
52 W 53rd St (at Sixth Ave, in CBS Building)   212/333-7788
Lunch: Mon-Fri; Dinner: Daily
Moderate to moderately expensive

The cuisine here is described as contemporary Ameurasian, whatever that means. Simply put, the dishes here do have an Oriental look and flavor, and they are served family style in very large portions. Sometimes a bit of Italy sneaks in (like Oriental antipasto and string vegetables over angel hair pasta), sometimes it is strictly American (like T-bone lamb chops or sweet potato dumplings), but you can also feast on Shanghai lobster or a Confucious chicken salad. The room is spacious and high-ceilinged, the noise level intolerable, the atmosphere casual or business, according to your mood. Dessert possibilities include chocolate chip tiramisu, warm banana cake, and cream-cheese mousse served in a coconut with fruit and fruit coulis.

COCO PAZZO
235 W 46th St   212/827-4222
Lunch: Mon-Sat; Dinner: Mon-Sun
Moderate to moderately expensive

It is nice to know that there is a spot right in the center of the Theater District where you can get a really good meal in a pleasant atmosphere with beautiful dinnerware served quickly if you desire. Coco Pazzo meets all of these requirements—as well it should with highly experienced manager Pino Luongo behind the scenes. Lunch is mainly pastas, pizzas, salads, and light fish. The menu is essentially Italian, with a good selection of salads, seafoods, pastas, and pizzas. Signature dishes include a lobster presentation in two acts . . . delicious! The pizza bianca is a winner. To insure that you stay awake for the entire performance, you may want to skip the delicious desserts . . . but you'd be making a real mistake by passing up their baked Alaska or the chocolate-covered ginger tartufo. Just tell your server you have a curtain deadline, and you will be treated to very special service. A smoking section is available.

COL LEGNO
231 E 9th St (bet Second and Third Ave)   212/777-4650
Dinner: Tues-Sun
Inexpensive to moderate

The folks here take life easily and casually, and this attitude is reflected in the kind of dining experience you can anticipate at this East Village hangout. For honest value, Col Legno is hard to beat. The pizzas, uniformly delicious and bargain-priced, are made in the oven right inside the dining area. Wonderful lasagna, spaghetti, and *tagliatelle* dishes are as tasty as those served in fancier uptown Italian houses at twice the price. There is more: fresh fish, quail, and a tasty mixed grill done with herb-infused oils. In warmer weather there are tables out front, which are pleasant if you don't mind the neighborhood cat keeping you company. One thing you don't get here is inspiration from the rather bored waiters, but don't let that keep you from trying this little-known treasure.

CONTRAPUNTO
200 E 60th St (at Third Ave)   212/751-8616
Lunch, Dinner: Daily
Moderate

So you are famished after running from floor to floor at Bloomie's and feel that a great pasta dish, a salad, or a grilled veal chop with mashed potatoes would fortify you for the next round? Problem easily solved. Just step across the street to this upstairs charmer, where harried waiters mix with harried shoppers. While slow service is a drawback, portions are big, the views are vintage Manhattan, and the gelati and chocolate-banana créme brûlée are commendable. Quality abounds here, and the somewhat Italian ambience is appealing. I make a special trip just for the roasted artichoke!

CUCINA & CO.
MetLife Building Lobby
200 Park Ave   212/682-2700
Breakfast, Lunch, Dinner: Mon-Fri
(takeout open 7 a.m.-9 p.m.; Sat: 8-4)
Moderate

Hidden between two hyped restaurants (Tropica and Cafe Central) in the bowels of the huge MetLife Building, Cucina & Co. is an undiscovered treasure. The takeout is one of the best in mid-Manhattan: all sorts of prepared foods, sandwiches, salads, great cookies and cakes, breads, and whatever else you might want to take home or to the office. Adjoining is a bustling, crowded, noisy cafe that serves first-class food at very reasonable prices for such a prime location. Daily specials feature many items available for carryout. You will also find delicious burgers (served on a sesame brioche roll), baked pastas, quiches, seafood, health dishes, and a good selection of dessert items. The service is extremely fast, the quality of the food top-notch, and the personnel highly professional. They have to be in order to serve so many people in the rush hours. I'd heartily recommend this place, especially for lunch.

CUCINA STAGIONALE
275 Bleecker St   212/924-2707
Lunch, Dinner: Daily
No credit cards
Inexpensive

When you serve good food at a small price, word gets around. So it's no wonder there's a line in front of this small Village cafe almost any time of day. Its name translates as "seasonal kitchen," and the seasonal specialties are real values, indeed. It's a bare-bones setup, with seating for only several dozen hungry folks. Service is impersonal and nonprofessional, but who cares at these prices? Innovative Italian cuisine is served here—tasty, attractive, and filling—and you can do very well on a slim budget. Recommended appetizers include smoked salmon with endive and radiccio, and sauteed wild mushrooms. For a few pennies more, you can get a large dish of vegetarian lasagna, linguini, or ravioli. I'm constantly asked about inexpensive places that serve quality food, and I have no hesitation recommending this spot. One word of warning: don't go if it's raining, because you'll probably have to wait outside to get seated.

DANAL
90 E 10th St   212/982-6930
Breakfast, lunch, dinner: Wed-Sun (Sun noon is brunch);
Tea: Fri-Sat
Moderate

Here are Gerry Frank's guideposts to a good eating spot: Bread is fresh, crisp, and warm. Vegetables are not overcooked. Salads are cool, and the house salad is not just a bunch of lettuce. If homemade ice cream is served, it is rich and creamy and has no ice particles in it. Finally, the owner is on the job. Danal passes all of the above with flying colors. The location is the East Village, on a quiet and safe street. The atmosphere is what the owner calls "country French." I would call it homey mix-and-match. The service is understated and friendly, with no pretense. The dishes are uniformly delicious, served in right-sized portions. The menu varies every day but features something tasty for any appetite. No liquor, just wine. A special find.

DANIEL
20 E 76th St   212/288-0033
Lunch: Tues-Sat: Dinner: Mon-Sat
Expensive to very expensive

Some of Manhattan's lunchiest ladies thought that the world was coming to an end when former Le Cirque chef Daniel Boulud left Sirio Maccioni (the owner and eminent man-about-the-restaurant) to open his own eatery. *Eatery?* Not really. More like an institution. And that is exactly what Daniel (heavy on the first syllable) has turned out to be. Although some of Sirio's customers have returned to their native haunts, others have followed him to a new home here in a room that cost a cool two million bucks. Comfortable eating it is not:

too crowded and noisy. But when it comes to the main act, it is superb. Daniel is a French master of our time, and his exotic dishes are flavored with sauces that are nothing but *awesome*. Daniel searches the fresh markets daily. I would go here not knowing what I wanted to eat and be pleasantly surprised—if not downright amazed—at the daily offerings. The veal medallions are worth a special visit!

Shoppers know that your author is not a big fan of **Barney's,** the upscale uptown department store. But down in the bowels of the store at 30 E 61st St (212/833-2220) is a first-rate restaurant, market, and espresso bar, **Fred's.** For the hungry and tired shoppers there are delicious salads, soups, unusual pizzas, pastas, and heavier entrees (seafood, Tuscan pot roast, rack of baby lamb), and a great burger (it should be at $17). The real treat is the square Belgian *pomme frites,* served in a tall glass and wrapped in paper . . . delicious. And the desserts are rich and interesting too. Lunch starts at 11:30 daily; dinner begins at 5:30; Sunday hours are 12-6 p.m.

DARBAR
44 W 56th St   212/432-7227
Lunch, Dinner: Daily
Moderate

It's a joy to walk into an appealing and well-designed restaurant where tables are separated by partitions and one can really have a private conversation. Darbar is such a spot, and all of the staff wait on you in a quick and respectful manner while providing informed, efficient service and presenting fresh, attractive Indian dishes. A wonderful start for your meal would be the *murgh pakoras* (tender pieces of chicken sauteed in yogurt and Indian spices and batter-fried). Specialties from the charcoal clay oven are sizable in selection: chicken, prawns, and lamb. The tandoori prawns are my favorite. By all means try some of the Indian breads. A real taste treat is the vegetarian *paratha*—unleavened whole wheat bread filled with vegetables and baked in the tandoor with butter. Rice dishes are excellent, and desserts are exceptional. The chocolate cinnamon ice cream is worth the visit in itself. There is a buffet lunch daily.

DA SILVANO
260 Sixth Ave (bet Houston and Bleecker St)   212/982-2343
Lunch: Mon-Sat; Dinner: Daily
Moderate

Long a favorite for those who like food inspired by the chefs of Florence, this small Tuscan restaurant housed in a Village storefront presents dishes handled with taste and talent. With a large list of daily specials, you may want to try the roasted rabbit or the lamb shank braised in white wine with carrots, celery and onions on a bed of beans. In the seafood column, roasted pompano filled with fresh herbs and lemon is a house favorite. There are nearly 30 specials a day, including fish, game, and pasta. For dessert, try the *pannacotta* (baked cream topped with melted chocolate). Excellent service, cozy brick-wall ambience, and outside dining in nice weather all add up to make this a very pleasant place to dine.

DA UMBERTO
107 W 17th St (off Sixth Ave)   212/989-0303
Lunch: Mon-Fri; Dinner: Mon-Sat
Moderate to moderately expensive

Da Umberto is for serious Italian diners! This Florentine bistro is a feast for the eyes as well as the palate. A groaning table of inviting antipasto dishes greets guests; one could easily make an entire meal just from this selection. The appealing part of the presentation is that all of the platters look so fresh and healthy. Umberto Assante himself is around much of the time, insuring that the service is as good as the food. One can look into the glass-framed kitchen at the rear to see how real professionals work. What to have? Lasagne. Gnocchi. Linguine. Risotto. The three-color salad is a house specialty. On to well-prepared fish, veal, or chicken. Your waiter will have many specials to detail. If you have room, the chocolate truffle cake and the tiramisu are the best of the dessert selections.

DAWAT
210 E 58th St   212/355-7555
Lunch: Mon-Sat; Dinner: Daily
Moderate

Dawat is a quality operation. It serves tasty, reasonably priced Indian food in a refined atmosphere with superior service. There are a number of wonderful seafood choices, including a sensational shrimp entree cooked with herbs and spices. You'll also find chicken dishes, goat and lamb offerings, and such vegetarian selections as homemade cheese cubes with delicious vegetables, eggplant with sweet-and-sour tamarind sauce, and stir-fried cauliflower with ginger and cumin seeds. One of the trademarks of an Indian restaurant is its bread, and at Dawat they do it to perfection. Different varieties are offered, and no meal is complete without trying a couple. The desserts here are vastly improved.

DEGREZIA
231 E 50th St   212/750-5353
Lunch: Mon-Fri; Dinner: Mon-Sat
Moderate to moderately expensive

For sure this hidden treasure has only been discovered by the natives; as you look around the two packed dining areas, there is not a touristy type in sight. Maybe mention herewith will change all that, for everything about DeGrezia is absolutely first-class. From the minute you are cordially greeted as you make your way down a little stairway off of East 50th Street to the moment you finish your homemade dessert, the service and plates are without peer. The professional waiters seem to want you to have a good time, and that is exactly what will happen. Lots of different pastas are offered, but the real treats are the Northern Italian specialties, like whole chicken breast topped with eggplant prosciutto or double-cut veal chops sauteed with fresh sage and white wine. For either lunch or dinner, this charmer rates high with your author. Private party rooms are available.

For inside names and numbers for top New York restaurants, get "NY KEN Kitchen Employers' Network" ($34.95; 800/576-5658).

DINING COMMONS
City University of New York Graduate Center
33 W 42nd St (18th floor)   212/642-2013
Mon-Fri: 10-6:30
Inexpensive

This is definitely a find for those who don't mind cafeteria dining. Right in the center of town, on the top floor of City University Graduate Center, is a first-class cafeteria that offers excellent food all day long in nice surroundings at reasonable prices. Continental breakfasts, featuring muffins, danishes, croissants, bagels, and fruit, are available from 8 a.m. to 11:30 a.m. Lunch and dinner—deli sandwiches, salads, hot entrees with vegetables and potatoes, desserts, and beverages—are available until 8 p.m. You can eat heartily for under $10. If a sandwich is all you want, the tab will be half that. Seating is available, but all items may be taken out. A full-service bar is adjacent to the Commons, which offers a special catering menu with rock-bottom prices. The cafeteria is open to faculty, students, and the general public, with students getting a special discount upon presentation of CUNY identification cards. This is not your run-of-the-mill fast-food operation. Restaurant Associates does a particularly good job of offering tasty, adequate portions without fancy touches that cost extra bucks. A great midtown spot for groups, young people, singles, and folks in a hurry.

DOCKS OYSTER BAR AND SEAFOOD GRILL
2427 Broadway (bet 89th and 90th St)   212/724-5588
Lunch: Mon-Sat; Dinner: Daily; Brunch: Sat, Sun

633 Third Ave (at 40th St)   212/986-8080
Lunch: Mon-Fri; Dinner: Daily; Brunch: Sun

Moderate

For those who appreciate a great raw bar, Dock's is the place to anchor! Sail right up Broadway or to Docks' larger location on Third Avenue. At both lunch and dinner, you'll find fresh swordfish, lobster, tuna, Norwegian salmon, red snapper, and other seafood specials of the day. The crab cakes are outstanding. In the evening, you can enjoy a raw bar with four oyster varieties and two selections of clams. All this comes with Docks cole slaw and choice of potatoes. Vegetables are a la carte. For a lighter meal, try the steamers in beer broth or the mussels in tomato and garlic. Delicious smoked fish, like sturgeon and whitefish, is available. Docks has a special New England clambake on Sunday and Monday nights. For dessert, the chocolate mud fudge is a fitting way to finish your culinary cruise. The atmosphere is congenial, and so are the professional waiters.

DUANE PARK CAFE
157 Duane St (bet West Broadway and Hudson St)   212/732-5555
Lunch: Mon-Fri; Dinner: Mon-Sat
Moderate

If you find yourself in Tribeca, take advantage of some of the interesting places to eat in the area. Many are located on or near Duane Street. Duane Park Cafe is one of them. The menu is eclectic, as you might expect from chef-owner Seiji Maeda. There is a touch of Italian, a heavy emphasis on seafood, and a nod to Cajun and Japanese influences. The dishes sparkle, especially because of the tasty manner in which herbs are used. Even some of the delicious homemade breads have herbal flavors. A selection of pasta is offered at all times. The desserts are done on the premises, showing off the vivid imagination of pastry chef John Dudek. Seasonal wine-tasting dinners are featured.

EDGAR'S CAFE
255 W 84th St (bet Broadway and West End Ave)   212/496-6126
Lunch, Dinner: Daily (open late)
No credit cards
Moderate

The folks on the Upper West Side claim this place as their private secret. One can understand why. The place isn't very big, but the selection, value, and quality certainly are. They offer great coffees and hot drinks, an unusually large selection of iced drinks, and a fine assortment of salads and sandwiches. Super wonderful cakes and pies are sinfully rich. All are available for takeout (or eat-in). Gelati and sorbetti fans will also be in seventh heaven.

EDWARDIAN ROOM
Plaza Hotel (Fifth Ave and Central Park S)   212/759-3000
Breakfast, Lunch: Daily; Dinner: Tues-Sat
Expensive

Eloise will tell you that there are some New York experiences that one never forgets. I remember a magical evening in the Edwardian Room at the Plaza Hotel, overlooking the heart of New York at Fifth Avenue and Central Park. Outside, the streets and sidewalks were being dusted by a snowfall; inside, the tables sparkled with the finest silver, china, and glassware. The candles flickered, and the piano music provided the final romantic ingredient. This was years ago. Alas, the room underwent many changes by a series of uncaring owners. But in keeping with the current popularity of hotel dining, this distinguished room glows anew. There just isn't another spot like it anywhere in New York. Hansom cabs sit outside the windows, and the kitchen is once again turning out superb cuisine, in keeping with the room's history. This is the place to take your guests to celebrate an engagement or important occasion. With gorgeous flowers and old-time waiters, along with an extensive menu of continental favorites, who could ask for anything more?

EL PARADOR
325 E 34th St (nr First Ave)   212/679-6812
Lunch, Dinner: Daily
Moderate

When you have been in the restaurant business for over three decades in New York, you are obviously doing something customers like. El Parador is doing just that: serving delicious Mexican food in a fun atmosphere at down-to-earth prices. Besides all that, they are some of the nicest folks in the city. Warm nachos are put on the table the minute you arrive; from here you have a choice of specialties. There are quesadillas, Spanish sausages, and black-bean soup to start. Delicious shrimp and chicken dishes follow. Create your own tacos and tostaditas if you like. How about stuffed jalapenos? You'll probably want some tequila to make the evening complete. El Parador has over 30 brands of premium tequilas and what many consider the best margaritas in New York. It is really the granddaddy of Mexican restaurants.

ERMINIA
250 E 83rd St (bet Second and Third Ave)   212/879-4284
Dinner: Mon-Sat
American Express
Moderate

The Lattanzi family now has five branches, and Erminia, the smallest, is the jewel in the crown. It has about a dozen tables in a pleasant and rustic atmosphere just right for a leisurely, intimate dinner. I've found it an absolutely charming spot with helpful personnel and outstanding food. To start, try the artichokes cooked in olive oil. In the pasta category, you can't go wrong ordering tender dumplings with potatoes and tomatoes or large noodles with ricotta cheese. The number of entrees is limited. Some are grilled and served with delicious vegetables. There is grilled chicken, seafood items on skewers (great shrimp), a special fish dish, and lamb or veal chops. Dessert selections vary daily. Jackets are required!

ÉTATS-UNIS
242 E 81st St (bet Second and Third Ave)   212/517-8826
Dinner: Mon-Sat
Moderate to moderately expensive

États-Unis is more like a large family dining room, with just a dozen tables and a busy kitchen where the Rapp family produce some of the best food this side of your grandmother's! The family is represented by father and son in the kitchen and an attractive daughter out in front (what a charmer she is). There is no point in talking about the individual items on the menu, as the appetizers, entrees, and desserts (usually about five of each) change every evening. They are uniformly delicious. It's very wholesome food, not cute or fancy but served in a professional manner and in portions that are substantial but not overwhelming. Fresh homemade bread is an additional attraction. The tab is not cheap, but in order to support this type of operation—with limited hours and few tables—the Rapps have to make every meal count. The entire room is available for private parties on Saturdays. One hint: when calling for reservations (they are very busy), ask if the cool mocha crème caramel is on the menu. It is absolutely one of the best desserts I have ever tasted.

The Cheese Course

One of the nicest traditions in Europe is the serving of cheese after the main course. It has become fashionable in some of Manhattan's finer restaurants to offer an interesting cheese plate as a first course, just before dessert, or as a substitute for dessert. Here are some locations for this treat:

Chanterelle (2 Harrison St, at Hudson St)
Gramercy Tavern (42 E 20th St)
Le Bernardin (155 W 51st St)
Les Célébrités (155 W 58th St)
Parioli Romanissimo (24 E 81st St)
Picholine (35 W 64th St): the best!

FERRIER
29 E 65th St   212/772-9000
Lunch, Dinner: Daily
Moderate

Convenient location. Great people-gazing, especially for the gentlemen. Cozy atmosphere. Pleasant personnel. Moderate prices. Oh yes, good food, too! This is exactly what Alain Chevreux has put together at his busy bistro. He got his start with Chez Ma Tante in the Village and brought the best aspects of that operation to the Upper East Side. There is a wide choice of hot and cold hors d'oeuvres, pastas, chicken dishes, seafood, salads, paté, and goodies you can munch on at any time of the day or evening. Homemade sorbets, caramelized apple tarts, and sinful profiteroles look good by sunlight or starlight. A good place to remember when hunger pangs strike at inconvenient hours!

FIFTY-SEVEN FIFTY-SEVEN
57 E 57th St (Four Seasons Hotel, lobby level)   212/758-5757
Breakfast, Lunch, Dinner: Daily; Brunch: Sun
Moderate to moderately expensive

One can always be assured when the name Four Seasons is on the door that the service on the inside is going to be something special. And so it is at Fifty-Seven Fifty Seven, one of Manhattan's stars in the continuing trend toward excellence in hotel dining rooms. The room is highlighted by handsome cherry floors with mahogany inlays, ceilings of Danish beechwood paneling, and bronze chandeliers. The table tops match the floor in both material and design. In an informal yet elegant atmosphere, the food presentation has the authority of classic American cooking. The menu changes by season, featuring big-time flavors, such as some exceptionally well-thought-out pasta entrees. Cured swordfish is a winner! This is a room where taste and personal attention, not the ego of a famous chef, are the name of the game. A thoughtful touch is the offer of rapid service for breakfast guests.

44
44 W 44th St (Royalton Hotel, bet Fifth and Sixth Ave)   212/944-8844
Breakfast, Lunch, Dinner: Daily; Brunch: Sat, Sun
Moderately expensive

Forget about the fact there's no name on the door (it is the Royalton Hotel) and ignore the stark lobby (filled with noisy yuppies), the outrageously uncomfortable seating, and the ugly black uniforms of the servers. Just concentrate solely on the food. You will not be disappointed. The food is as magnificent as the ambience is unappealing. Every dish is a work of art, from the spit-roasted sweetbreads and *duck l'orange* appetizers to the dozen fish, poultry, and meat entrees. The roasted guinea hen comes in two courses (one would be plenty for anyone), the grilled ribeye steak melts in your mouth, and the whole Maine lobster is a picture. Those crisp *roesti* potatoes with bacon and shallots are addictive. To top it off: profiteroles (with three ice creams and two chocolate sauces), black-pepper canoli (with caramel mascarpone and fresh berries), or chocolate crepes with roasted bananas and milk chocolate malt ice cream.

FOUR SEASONS
99 E 52nd St (bet Park and Lexington Ave)   212/754-9494
Lunch: Mon-Fri; Dinner: Mon-Sat
Expensive

If you were entertaining someone who had just arrived from overseas, a person of style and substance who had never before tasted an American meal, the magnificent Four Seasons restaurant would be the obvious choice. The place is very big, cool, and comfortable—elegant and awe-inspiring in its simplicity and charm. There are two separate dining areas—the Grill Room and the Pool Room—and they are different in both menu and appeal. You will find the dark suits (translation, the business and media heavy hitters) at noon in the Grill Room, where the waiters know each of them and what they like (baked potatoes, great salads, steak tartare, burgers). The Pool Room, set beside an actual marble pool, is romantic and more feminine. Here the ladies who lunch or the couple who wants to dine with the stars are right at home with superb service, wonderful duck, and a dessert menu that only can be described as obscene, with individual souffles in coffee cups a splendid treat.

FRANK'S
85 Tenth Ave   212/243-1349
Lunch: Mon-Fri; Dinner: Daily
Moderate

The Molinari family—the third generation in a business that started in 1912—has kept up the quality and appeal of this popular spot. Customers are usually large folks with large appetites! Reservations are suggested, as the place is very popular. There are great pastas, huge steaks, superb prime ribs, fresh fish, veal, lamb, and really good French fries. New York cheesecake is the best dessert choice.

FRANK'S TRATTORIA
371 First Ave (at 22nd St)   212/677-2991
Lunch, Dinner: Daily
Inexpensive

It's true in New York, just as it is anywhere else in the country: no one knows the best inexpensive places to eat better than the boys in blue. Manhattan's finest are some of the best customers of this modest *trattoria,* and it is easy to see why. The menu runs the gamut of Florentine dishes, each one prepared to order and served piping hot. And so is the bread, which is always a good sign. There is a large seafood selection, and all the fish are first quality and very fresh. You can choose from over 20 pizzas, served whole or in individual pieces. Everyone here is very informal and friendly, and Frank, the boss, is delighted that the good word about his place has spread beyond the neighborhood regulars.

FRAUNCES TAVERN RESTAURANT
54 Pearl St   212/269-0144
Breakfast, Lunch, Dinner: Mon-Fri
Moderate

General George Washington is supposed to have said goodbye to his officers at a reception at Fraunces Tavern in 1783. George obviously had good taste if the tavern was as top-notch then as it is now. It's an inviting, historic spot serving authentic American fare in a charming part of lower Manhattan. It has been in the same family since 1937. The dining areas are spacious and comfortable, the service is professional, prices are reasonable, and the menu (with daily specials) is sizable. One of the more outstanding appetizers is the seafood sampler, consisting of fresh lump crab and Maine lobster meat, shrimp, oysters, and clams—a feast in itself. A specialty of the house is the baked chicken a la Washington (cubes of tender chicken and mushrooms baked *en casserole* au gratin). Absolutely delicious! I'd suggest making a beeline here on Wednesdays for the Yankee pot roast with red cabbage and potato pancakes. On Tuesdays you can sample ales from around the world. And don't overlook dessert! The cheesecake, Georgia pecan pie, and chocolate mousse are well worth investigating. After your meal, go upstairs and visit the Fraunces Tavern Museum. It is one of the oldest museums in the city and a historic landmark. There you'll find exhibits focusing on 18th- and 19th-century life in America. By the way, the breakfast menu offers a fine selection of omelets, eggs, fruit, and muffins. It's one of the best buys in New York.

Horn and Hardart opened its first automated cafeteria at Broadway and 13th Street in 1902. Branches of this popular institution sprang up all over the city until they numbered several dozen. Their popularity waned, and the last automat, on 42nd Street and Third Avenue, closed in 1991. The novelty here was to look at the varied food items that were placed in boxes, not unlike what you see these days in some old-fashioned post offices. Diners would insert coins, then reach in to take out their goodies. I can well remember, as a youngster, this was one of the most intriguing places to eat in Manhattan. My parents did not share this view!

FRESCO
34 E 52nd St   212/935-3434
Lunch: Mon-Fri; Dinner: Mon-Sat
Moderate to moderately expensive

In a setting that could only be described as singularly unattractive, Fresco manages to serve some of the most attractive dishes in midtown Manhattan. Admittedly, you don't necessarily go out dining to enjoy the scenery (although in my opinion, it is important). You really are looking for a good place to eat—and this is one of them. From the grilled, roasted, and marinated veggies to the grilled pizzas to the wonderful marinated Louisiana shrimp to the homemade potato ravioli, each dish is superbly done. And what portions! They are big enough for two hearty appetites. The grilled entrees are especially inviting: whole boneless bass, veal chops, fillet mignon of tuna, T-bone steak—all are worth a try. Even the desserts are something special. I went for the almond toffee chocolate cake with bitter chocolate sauce, but the pumpkin mascarpone tart with pecan crust and the panna cotta with caramel sauce and toasted coconut looked equally sinful. So put on your dark glasses and concentrate on what is put in front of you, as mother would say!

GABRIEL'S BAR & RESTAURANT
11 W 60th St (bet Broadway and Ninth Ave)   212/956-4600
Lunch: Mon-Fri; Dinner: Mon-Sat
Moderate

There is something special when you walk into a restaurant, are greeted by an extremely friendly host (who happens to be Gabriel, a co-owner with chef Ralph Perroti), and the background music is "Gabriel . . . Gabriel"! But there is much more. Wonderful homemade pepper biscuits and delicious bread. Fresh melon and blood orange juice. A bowl of fresh fruit on the bar. A fine assortment of Italian appetizers. Then on to really first-class pastas (like *tagliatelle* with pesto), chicken, steaks, and grilled seafood dishes. The in-house gelati creations are among New York's best, as is the chocolate espresso torte. To cap it all off, Gabriel offers a selection of nine unusual teas (like peach melba, raspberry, and French vanilla). Gabriel doesn't have to blow his own horn here; the satisfied customers do it for him!

GASCOGNE
158 Eighth Ave (at 18th St)   212/675-6564
Lunch: Mon-Fri; Dinner: Daily; Brunch: Sun
Moderate

Hearty appetites and southern French cooking spell happiness with a capital *H* at this intimate Chelsea bistro. No fuss or fancy affectations by the capable and friendly waiters, all of whom are only too happy to explain the fine points of the rather limited menu. The salads are mainly warm: roquefort with warm duck tenderloins, warm goat cheese and puree of shallots, warm scallops and garlic confit. *Foie gras* lovers will be in heaven. The main-course menu features duck, cassoulet, quail, and roasted rabbit. Seafood dishes are especially tasty. All desserts are made in-house, and they do show imagination. There are sorbets, fruit tarts, souffles, and some unusual ice cream flavors (prune, Armagnac, and chocolate mint). A small dining area is available downstairs, but it is rather claustrophobic. The garden is charming. If you are really longing for an extensive French dining experience, take a look at the *prix fixe* menu. By the way, Gascony is the only region in the world where Armagnac is produced, and chef-owner Pascal Coudouy's family has been making the drink since 1504!

GINO
780 Lexington Ave (at 61st St)   212/758-4466
Lunch, Dinner: Daily
Cash only (checks accepted if known on premises.)
Moderate

As you look around the crowded dining room of this famous New York institution, you can tell immediately that the food is great. Why? Because this Italian restaurant is filled with native New Yorkers. You'll see no tourist buses stopping out front. The menu has been the same for years: a large selection of popular dishes (over 30 entrees), from antipasto to soup, pasta to fish. There are daily specials, of course, but you only have to taste such regulars as the chicken a la Capri, the Italian sausages with peppers, or scampis a la Gino, and you are hooked. Gino's staff has been here forever, taking care of patrons in an informed, fatherly manner. The best part comes when the tab is presented. East Side rents, as you know, are always climbing, but Gino has resisted the price bulges by taking cash only and serving delicious food that keeps the tables full. No reservations, so come early.

GOLDEN UNICORN
18 East Broadway (at Catherine St)   212/941-0911
Lunch, Dinner, Dim Sum: Daily
Inexpensive

Golden Unicorn serves the best dim sum outside of Peking! This bustling, two-floor Hong Kong-style Chinese restaurant serves delicious dim sum every day of the week. Besides the delicacies from the rolling carts, diners may choose from a wide variety of Cantonese dishes from the regular menu. Pan-fried noodle dishes, rice noodles, and noodles in soup are house specialties. Despite the size of the establishment (they can take care of over 400 diners at one time), you will be amazed at the fast service, the cleanliness, and (most of all) the price tag. This has to be one of the best values in Chinatown.

GOTHAM BAR & GRILL
12 E 12th St   212/620-4020
Lunch: Mon-Fri; Dinner: Daily
Moderately expensive

There are some restaurants worth getting excited about revisiting. The Gotham is one of them. It has not always been that way. This place has painstakingly worked itself up into the ranks of New York's best. It is not inexpensive, but every meal I have had here has been worth the tab. However, there is a really good *prix fixe* lunch deal. The talented chef, Alfred Portale, is one of the best in the city. The modern, spacious, high-ceilinged space is broken by direct spot lighting on the tables. Fresh plants give a bit of color. There are great salads (try the seafood one), excellent free-range chicken, and superior grilled salmon. Each entree is well seasoned, attractively presented, and uniformly delicious. The rack of lamb is one of the tastiest served in the area. Desserts are all made in-house; try the vanilla crème brûlée or the Gotham chocolate cake. Dining here can be summed up in one word: exciting!

GRAMERCY TAVERN
42 E 20th St (bet Park Ave S and Broadway)   212/477-0777
Lunch: Mon-Fri; Dinner: Mon-Sun
Moderately expensive

When a restaurant opens up with all the hype that this one did, it is impossible to live up to expectations. Owner Danny Meyer and his crew have done their level best under exceedingly difficult conditions. They have created an unusually attractive space. Every detail is in superb taste, and the ambience is so appealing that the food almost becomes secondary. The ceilings are a work of art, the view from every single table is compelling, and the private party room is magnificent. Singles are in heaven; the drinks and the accompanying light menu (including a fabulous selection of cheeses) add strength to possible conquests. In the dining room, a constantly changing menu that's heavy on the seafood side offers quality dishes. They're all beautifully presented. Top choices: breast of chicken, sea scallops, lobster. I can't think of a more appealing place to take out-of-town visitors for a taste of what only New York can offer: seductive surroundings, a palate-pleasing meal, and an opportunity to star-gaze where the telescope offers nothing but high-intensity sights.

GRAND CENTRAL OYSTER BAR RESTAURANT
Grand Central Station (lower level)   212/490-6650
Mon-Fri: 11:30-9:30
Moderate

If you are a native New Yorker, you know about the 80-year-old institution that is the Oyster Bar at Grand Central. It was once quite popular with commuters and residents. A midtown institution that was neglected for years, it has been restored and is doing quite nicely again, thank you. (They serve over 2,000 folks a day!) Located in the caverns of Grand Central, it is attractive. The young help are most accommodating, and the drain on the pocketbook is minimal. The menu boasts more than 90 seafood items (with fresh new entrees daily), a dozen kinds of oysters, a super oyster stew, clam chowder (Manhattan and New England), oyster pan roast, bouillabaisse, coquille St. Jacques, Maryland crab cakes, broiled Maine lobster, 60 wines by the glass, and marvelous homemade desserts. (Note: Recent fire damage is being repaired.)

GRANGE HALL
50 Commerce St (at Barrow St)   212/924-5246
Lunch: Mon-Fri; Dinner: Daily; Brunch: Sat, Sun
Moderate
American Express

Hidden away on a picturesque corner in the West Village is this charmer, an ex-speakeasy! Inside you will find peace and relaxation in addition to excellent "comfort" food! The menu changes by season, but you can count on homemade soups, a large selection of small dishes (as appetizers or in addition to your main dish), fresh salads, and ample, delicious entrees. The latter can be ordered simple (entree and accompaniment as listed on the menu) or complete (with soup or salad). Things start off right with a loaf of warm homemade bread with all other items served either piping hot (all entrees cooked to order) or chilly cold, as they should be. I was particularly taken with the appetizer selection: unusual items like spicy string beans, hand-cut yam fried potatoes, freshly made sausage, wild rice and wheat berry medley, and baked eggplant steaks. Your choices may not be the same, but will no doubt be equally inventive! Desserts are also made in house, and the accommodating help makes the experience almost like eating at home. You'll love the ambience.

GUIDO'S
511 Ninth Ave (at 39th St)   212/502-4842
Lunch: Mon-Fri; Dinner: Mon-Sat
No credit cards
Inexpensive

You might ask yourself what a nice person would be doing in the middle of Ninth Avenue, having lunch in the back room of a macaroni factory? Well, this is no usual back room and no ordinary macaroni factory! Up front, as you walk in, you'll see a display of 23 brands of macaroni. That was the original business (they have been open over a half century), but now it's just a sideline. The real draw is the smallish restaurant in the back, which is as busy as Times Square. Tom Scarola is the third-generation family member who runs this unusual operation. Whether you're coming for lunch or dinner, make sure you have a reservation. You might rub shoulders with some celebrities. Even if they're not here in person, their pictures (along with the blue-checkered tablecloths and wine bottles on the ceiling) help create a special atmosphere at Guido's. You don't want to miss the lobster, rigatoni with vodka sauce, shrimp *francese,* veal sorrentino, or the house specialty, chicken *alla* Guido. The pasta is freshly made, authentic, inexpensive, and delicious. Finish with an assortment of mixed pastries and fresh cakes, along with a special espresso, and you will have had a marvelous meal. Lunch specials include four different chicken, veal, and shrimp entrees, as well as linguini or spaghetti with all the trimmings.

HALCYON
RIHGA Royal Hotel (151 W 54th St)   212/468-8888
Breakfast, Lunch, Dinner: Daily
Moderately expensive

This is an oasis of civility for dining. The restaurant has a dual life: a free-standing room of its own that also serves as the dining area for the adjoining hotel. The room is spacious and elegant, quiet and calming. Table settings are enhanced by beautiful Villeroy and Boch French Garden plates, and fresh flowers adorn each table. The menu is continental: salads, soups, pastas, seafoods, and grilled items. There is a pre-theater dinner, a popular late light supper (10:30 p.m.– 1 a.m.), and a Sunday brunch served in the 53rd floor Gershwin Penthouse, with its fabulous view of Manhattan. The kitchen will accommodate deviations from the set menu—a nice touch in these days of restricted ordering. It is in the dessert area, however, that the operation really shines. Each plate is an absolute work of art, with the signature name drizzled on the presentation dish. Ask to see the daily selection, as well as the set dessert menu, which changes by season. Nightly entertainment is an additional feature.

Tips For Steak Lovers

Ribeye: Has the most flavor but is a little bit fatty.
Hangar: Named for the muscle that supports the diaphragm, this has a rich, organlike taste, is salty, and should be served rare.
Filet Mignon: The Mercedes of the steak family, is low on fat and the six-ounce size is about right for one person.
Porterhouse: Thicker T-bones, tough on the waistline.
Sirloin: Rear cut, chateaubriand, very flavorful, needs little preparation, the healthiest for you.
Shell Steak: T-bone without filet, very tender.

HARRY'S
Woolworth Building
233 Broadway   212/513-0455
Lunch, Dinner: Mon-Fri
Moderate

Never mind that you're not a member of the Harvard or Yale Club or that you don't have a gold pass to the private dining room of Citicorp or Chase Manhattan. Just head for the lower level of the Woolworth Building, and you'll find a remarkable eating spot called Harry's. You would probably never know about it unless you worked in a nearby office—or read this book! What with all the wood and leather (a very masculine atmosphere), good food, and reasonable prices, it's a real find. Although dinner is served until 10:30 p.m., this is basically a luncheon spot. Ladies are certainly welcome, but the clientele is predominantly males of the important-looking, three-piece-suit variety. While big deals are being made at the surrounding tables, you can feast on clams, smoked trout, marinated herring, and smoked sturgeon. Omelets and homemade pastas are available, as well as selections from the cold buffet, including chicken salad, sliced turkey, and tuna salad platters. There are also grilled items, cold sandwiches, seafood, and several specials each day. If you drop by on Tuesday, try the braised sauerbrauten, and if you visit on Friday, the boiled brisket of beef is outstanding. This is an ideal place to take business associates; they will, no doubt, be pleasantly surprised to learn about it. Harry's is open on weekends only for private events.

Falafel

This is a staple and popular food of the Middle East. You'd never guess how tasty it truly is by the unpleasant odors coming from some of the push cart purveyors on the city streets. What's in it? Chick peas, coriander, green onions, jalapeno peppers, garlic black pepper and other ingredients. The treat is cheap, always served on pita bread, often with a heavy dose of green peppers. Where to find the best? Try **Omar Cafe** (143 First Ave, nr St Mark's Pl), **Habib's Place** (438 E 9th St), **Falafel House** (1752 Second Ave, nr 91st St), and **Mar Yum's** (411 E 70th St).

HATSUHANA
17 E 48th St   212/355-3345
Lunch: Mon-Fri; Dinner: Mon-Sat
Moderate

Hatsuhana has deservedly become known as the best sushi house in Manhattan. One can sit at a table or at the bar and get equal attention from the informed help. There are several dozen appetizers, including broiled eel in cucumber wrap; steamed egg custard with shrimp, fish, and vegetables; squid mixed with Japanese apricots; and chopped fatty tuna with aged soybeans. Next, try the salmon teriyaki (fresh salmon grilled with teriyaki sauce) or any number of tuna or sushi dishes best described by the personnel. Forget about the desserts and concentrate on the exotic appetizer and main-dish offerings.

HUDSON RIVER CLUB
4 World Financial Center, lobby level   212/786-1500
Lunch: Mon-Fri; Dinner: Mon-Sat
Moderate to moderately expensive

How often have you dined in sight of the Statue of Liberty? The setting for the Hudson River Club is magnificent: spacious, with high ceilings and a view of the river and yacht harbor. Nothing has been spared to make the difficult-to-find destination worth the trouble. Don't be put off by the word *Club*. Though it serves as a special place for residents of Battery Park City, it is open to everyone. The menu is strictly American, with an emphasis on food from the Hudson Valley. A five-course dinner offers specialties from the area for every course. Luncheons feature excellent soups, several salads (like smoked venison and Maine lobster), and such marvelous lighter dishes as daily farmer's vegetables and herbed, free-range chicken. In the evening they serve a large selection of seafood and house specialties like roast wild-shot pheasant, Catskill Mountain trout, grouse, shank of veal, and Hudson Valley venison chop and loin. Desserts are a feast for the eye and the palate. The orange milk chocolate crème brûlée will knock your eyes out. This is a delightful place to entertain someone who thinks he or she has been "everywhere" in the Big Apple.

HUDSON'S SPORTS BAR & GRILL
Sheraton New York Hotel & Towers (811 Seventh Ave, at 53rd St)
212/581-1000
Breakfast, Lunch, Dinner: Daily
Moderate

The quintessential sports bar and grill, Hudson's offers continuous entertainment for the sporting enthusiast, including satellite coverage of local, national, and worldwide sporting events on 30 monitors (including three wide-screens), autographed memorabilia, and interactive programming. Complementing bar-food favorites like chicken wings, nachos, burgers, and steaks, Hudson's offers over 25 varieties of beer from around the world, as well as a full bar.

HUNTERS
1387 Third Ave (bet 78th and 79th St)   212/734-6008
Lunch: Mon-Fri, Dinner: Daily; Brunch: Sat, Sun
Inexpensive

For an Upper East Side dining spot to serve really good food with some entrees listed as low as $7.95 is rare; when you combine this with a pleasant atmosphere and friendly service, it is time to take notice. Hunters is just such a place. In casual surroundings, where walls are covered with hunting scenes and a cozy fireplace sits near the dining-room entrance, this American bar and grill is a natural for a family meal. Nothing fancy on the menu: salads, sandwiches, pastas, omelets (a wide selection), steaks, burgers, seafood, and several veal dishes. Real bargains are the side dishes, like homemade mashed potatoes and old-fashioned creamed spinach. You have probably heard that meat loaf is very "in" these days; Hunters' home-style offering is delicious. The dessert selection is pretty basic—like chocolate mousse cake, the ever-present tiramisu, warm bread pudding—but the real winner is a delicious pecan pie *a la mode*. Yum-yum!

IL BAGATTO
192 E 2nd St (bet Ave A and B)   212/228-0977
Dinner: Tues-Sun
Inexpensive
Cash only

One of Manhattan's best bargains, Il Bagatto is the place to come if you're feeling adventurous. Housed in tiny digs in an area you would hardly call compelling, the doors open on this extremely popular Italian *trattoria*. The owners have discovered the rule of success: being on the job, insuring that every dish tastes just like it came out of mama's kitchen. About a dozen tables upstairs (and one downstairs) are always filled, so it's best to call ahead for reservations. There's delicious spaghetti, homemade gnocchi with spinach, tortellini (meat sauce made with their own secret recipe), and wonderful *tagliolini* with seafood in a light tomato sauce. But there's more: chicken, thin slices of beef, salads and always a few specials. Offerred for dessert: delicious spongecake with *zabaione* sauce and fresh berries.

IL CORTILE
125 Mulberry St (bet Canal St and Hester St)   212/226-6060
Lunch, Dinner: Daily
Moderate

Little Italy is more for tourists than serious diners, but still there are some exceptions. Il Cortile is an oasis of tasty Italian fare in an attractive and romantic setting. A bright and airy garden area in the rear is the most pleasant part of the restaurant. The menu is typical Italian, with just about anything you want. Entree listings are heavy on the chicken and veal dishes, plus excellent spaghetti, fettuccine, and ravioli. Sauteed vegetables, like bitter broccoli, hot peppers, mushrooms, spinach, and green beans, are specialties of the house. One thing is for certain here: the waiters act like they are on roller skates. No wasted time; service is excellent. If you can fight your way through the gawking visitors, you will find Il Cortile is worth the effort!

IL GIGLIO
81 Warren St (bet West Broadway and Greenwich St)   212/571-5555
Lunch, Dinner: Mon-Fri
Moderate

Il Mulino's "little brother" is doing well. So well, in fact, he might be even more handsome than his father! If you can find the place (the neighborhood is drab and dull, to say the least), you will be delighted to discover a bright, clean, classy operation that serves absolutely great northern Italian food. Smallness is a virtue here, as the two dozen tables are looked after by a crew of highly trained, tuxedo-clad waiters, most of whom have been on the premises since its opening. The specials are almost as numerous as the menu items (be sure to ask for prices), and by all means look over the display of fresh fruits, desserts, and other goodies by the entrance. The scampi and veal dishes are superb, and few places in Tribeca (or elsewhere in Manhattan) do pasta any better. Moreover, all desserts are made in-house.

Il MULINO
86 W 3rd St (bet Sullivan and Thompson St)   212/673-3783
Lunch: Mon-Fri; Dinner: Mon-Sat
Moderately expensive

Those who live to eat will want to pay attention to this entry. Never mind that reservations usually must be made a week or so in advance. Never mind that it's always crowded, the noise level is intolerable, and the waiters nearly knock you down as you wait to be seated. It's all part of the ambience at Il Mulino, one of New York's best Italian restaurants. Your greeting is usually "Hi, boss," which gives you the distinct impression that the staff are accustomed to catering to members of the, uh, "family." When your waiter finally comes around, he reels off a lengthy list of evening specials with glazed-over eyes. On the other hand, a beautiful, mouth-watering display of daily specials is arrayed on a huge table at the entrance. Once you're seated, the waiter delivers one antipasto after another while he talks you into ordering one of the fabulous veal dishes with portions bountiful enough to feed King Kong. Osso buco is a favorite dish. By the time you finish one of the luscious desserts, you'll know why every seat in the small, simple dining room is kept warm all evening.

IL TOSCANACCIO
7 E 59th St   212/935-3535
Lunch: Mon-Fri; Dinner: Mon-Sun
Moderate to moderately expensive

In a location that has seen its share of comings and goings, Il Toscanaccio has all the attributes that come with longevity. The savvy operators of Coco Pazzo and Le Madri are in charge here, so you know there is professional management. And it shows. The room is light, colorful, and appealing, the atmosphere is friendly and informal, and the servers are particularly polite. The area probably needs another Italian restaurant like a hole in the head, but it seems that New Yorkers can't get enough Italian fare. The pasta dishes are uniformly delicious; main course offerings include stewed veal chunks, fresh fish, and an unusual dish called "overcooked lamb served in a bread crust shell." In keeping with our fascination with desserts, the crowning plate might be an individual warm chocolate cake filled with soft chocolate hazelnut ganache or a Tuscan-style poundcake with raisins, pine nuts, and mascarpone sauce. This is a great place to refresh in the middle of a shopping spree along Fifth and Madison avenues.

IL VAGABONDO
351 E 62nd St   212/832-9221
Lunch: Mon-Fri; Dinner: Daily
Inexpensive

This bustling restaurant has been a favorite with knowledgeable New Yorkers for more than 30 years. The atmosphere is strictly old-time, complete with checkered tablecloths, four busy rooms, and an even busier bar. No menus are offered; the pleasant but harried waiters reel off the regular items and daily specials. You may have spaghetti or ravioli, an absolutely marvelous mine-strone, chicken parmesan, or sliced beef. I can also heartily recommend the Friday scampi or pasta *pescatore*. There is no pretense in this place. It is a great spot for office parties and folks with slim pocketbooks. You will see happy faces, compliments of a delicious meal and the extremely reasonable bill. Save room for the great "bocce-ball dessert" (*tartufo*). Il Vagabondo, you see, is the only restaurant in New York with an indoor bocce court!

INDIGO
142 W 10th St   212/691-7757
Dinner: Daily
American Express
Moderate

The clientele and the menu go together at this eclectic Village hideaway. You will see three-piece suits and fashionable ladies, and at the next table will be tank tops, green hair, and earrings. Everyone seems to feel comfortable, and that is one of the charms of the place. The menu is also a mixed bag, with an international flavor leaning heavily to the healthy dishes. There is grilled Thai beef salad and Indian-style curried sauteed shrimp. There are unusual pastas like roasted duck noodles a spaghettini with clams and lots of garlic. Chef de cuisine Scott Bryan features spiced pork, roast leg of lamb, and several seafood dishes (like roast Maine cod or grilled salmon) for main courses. Healthy diners will want to try the apple crisp. As for me, I opted for the decadent chocolate torte with mocha sauce and coffee ice cream. For those who want to dawdle over their meals, a huge selection of after-dinner drinks is available. Smokers may puff away in the front bar area.

Egg Cream

A New York invention, the egg cream is generally credited to Louis Auster, a Jewish immigrant who owned a candy store at Stanton and Cannon streets during the early part of the century. Mostly to amuse himself, he started mixing carbonated water, sugar, and cocoa together until he got a drink he liked. It was such a hit that Schrafft's reportedly offered him $20,000 for the recipe. Auster wouldn't sell and secretly continued making his own syrup in the back room of his store. When he died, his recipe went with him. Some years later, Herman Fox created another chocolate syrup, which he called Fox's U-Bet. Fox's brand is regarded as the definitive egg cream syrup to this day.

JACKSON HOLE BURGERS

232 E 64th St	Third Ave at 35th St	Second Ave at 84th St
212/371-7187	212/679-3264	212/737-8788

1270 Madison Ave (at 91st St)   517 Columbus Ave (at 85th St)
212/427-2820   212/362-5177

No credit cards   69-35 Astoria Blvd, Flushing
Inexpensive   718/204-7070

You might think that a burger is a burger is a burger. But having done hamburger taste tests all over the city, I've chosen Jackson's as one of the best. Each one weighs in at seven juicy, delicious ounces. You can get all types of hamburgers, along with great coffee and French fries. You can have a pizza burger, an alpine burger, an English burger, or a Baldouney burger (mushrooms, fried onions, and American cheese). Or try an omelet, if you prefer. A Mexican menu has been added. The atmosphere isn't fancy, but once you sink your teeth into a Jackson Hole burger, accompanied by great onion rings and a homemade dessert, you'll see why I'm so enthusiastic.

JEAN GEORGES

1 Central Park West (Trump International Hotel and Tower)
212/299-3900
Lunch, Dinner: Mon-Sat (cafe open daily also for breakfast)
Very expensive

Jean Georges Vongerichten is a New York legend (Lafayette, Jo Jo, Vong) so it was no surprise that the opening of his lastest venture created much excitement. The main dining room is very attractive, with limited seating and enough help to run a place twice the size (I counted 15 waiters and officious managers on the floor at one time). In addition to the 64-seat big show, there is an adjacent 30-seat cafe, and when the sun shines, you'll be able to eat outdoors. The novelty here is bringing wonderful food aromas to the table; most main courses (continental) are given final touches in front of your eyes. The appointments are magnificent, as they should be for the prices charged. When calling for reservations, you'll hear how booked they are, but don't give up. Walk in and you might get seated, but not at the table always reserved for Donald Trump for whenever he might show up. Despite a number of nice touches like delicious small rolls, a refreshing complimentary between-course fruit drink, and dessert goodies, the food can best be classified as very good but not always exceptional. At $10-$14, dessert plates are underwhelming.

JIMMY SUNG'S
219 E 44th St (bet Second and Third Ave)   212/682-5678
Lunch, Dinner: Daily
Moderate

For over two decades Jimmy Sung has been a talented player in the highly competitive world of Chinese restaurants in Manhattan. Now he has fulfilled his career goal: a large new house, seating over 250 customers in the main area and in seven exceptionally attractive private dining rooms that can accommodate groups of all sizes. The cuisine includes Hunan, Canton, Shanghai, and Manchurian dishes that range from mild to very spicy. Some of Jimmy's favorites: vegetarian pie with house pancake, spicy golden chrysanthemum chicken, sauteed frog legs with garlic sauce, and a seafood combination in a bird's nest. Jimmy is always on the job himself, providing a personal touch to this busy spot. The next time the office gang plans a get-together, put Jimmy Sung's at the top of the list. On top of everything, the prices are very affordable.

JOHN'S PIZZERIA
278 Bleecker St   212/243-1680
408 E 64th St (bet First and York Ave)   212/935-2895
48-50 W 65th St (bet Broadway and Central Park)   212/721-7001
260 W 46th St (bet 8th St and Broadway)
Daily: Noon-11:30 p.m. (Fri, Sat until 12:30 a.m.)
Moderate

Pete Castelotti (there is no John) is known as the "Baron of Bleecker Street." However, he has expanded to the Upper West Side and the Upper East Side so that more New Yorkers can taste some of the best brick-oven pizza in the city. Pete offers 55 (count 'em) varieties, from cheese and tomatoes to a gourmet extravaganza of cheese, tomatoes, anchovies, sausage, peppers, meatballs, onions, and mushrooms. If homemade spaghetti, cheese ravioli, or manicotti is your preference, John's is also the place for you. The surroundings on Bleecker Street are a bit shabby; things are higher-class uptown.

JO JO
160 E 64th St   212/223-5656
Lunch: Mon-Fri: Dinner: Mon-Sat
Moderate to moderately expensive

It is satisfying and fun to share in a real American success story. For years Jean-Georges Vongerichten presided over the outstanding kitchen at Lafayette, a grand four-star French dining establishment. Although only in his mid-30s, he decided if he were to work that hard, he'd rather do so for himself. Jo Jo is the result. It is a happy establishment with those extra touches that make dining a memorable experience: unusual napkin rings; wonderful warm bread; pleasant and helpful waiters; a very classy lady maitre d'. There are only a half-dozen appetizers, entrees, and desserts; every one is unique, tasty, and beautifully presented. Foie gras, 27 vegetables, rabbit, soup, and salad are among the choices to start. Then move on to salmon, lobster, chicken, lamb, or duck. Superb warm chocolate cake or apple confit is the way to finish. Upstairs is a charming room with fireplace for private entertaining or after-dinner drinks and conversation. Don't miss Jo Jo! (He has two other winners: Vong, with a Thai accent, and Jean Georges, a new restaurant in the Trump International Hotel and Tower.)

JUBILEE
347 E 54th St (bet First and Second Ave)   212/888-3569
Lunch, Dinner: Daily; Brunch: Sun
Moderate

Jubilee is a pleasant, satisfying, and unique French bistro, serving well-prepared food in a refined atmosphere. On Thursday evenings a jazz trio adds to the fun. Authentic French plates include lamb shanks, grilled steak with marvelous French fries, duck cassoulet, and ravioli stuffed with portabello, shitake, and oyster mushrooms. Mussels are a specialty of the house, served several ways: curried, with chicken-mushroom sauce, *mariniare,* vinaigrette, or *farcies a la Provencale.* Try the cozy and romantic table in the rear for tasty desserts like a lemon tart with meringue topping or Cointreau crème brûlée.

KATZ'S DELICATESSEN
205 E Houston St (at Ludlow St)   212/254-2246
Sun-Wed: 8 a.m.-10 p.m.; Thurs: 8 a.m.-11 p.m.;
Fri, Sat: 8 a.m.-12 p.m.
No credit cards
Inexpensive

Lower East Side hunger pangs? Try Katz's Delicatessen. It is a super place with some of the biggest and best sandwiches in town, hand-carved and overstuffed. The atmosphere goes along with the great food, and the prices are reasonable. Go right up to the counter and order—it is fun watching the no-nonsense operators slicing and fixing—or sit at a table where a seasoned waiter will take care of you. Try dill pickles and sauerkraut with your sandwich. Incidentally, Katz's is a perfect way to sample the unique "charm" of the Lower East Side. While you wait for a table or discover that the salt and pepper containers are empty and the ketchup is missing, you'll know what I mean. Catering (at attractive rates) and private party facilities are available.

KEENS STEAKHOUSE
72 W 36th St   212/947-3636
Lunch: Mon-Fri; Dinner: Mon-Sat
Moderate

Some of the best old restaurants in New York tend to get lost in the shuffle. With glamorous new places opening every week and people always wanting to know which places are "in," we sometimes forget about dependable restaurants that consistently do a good job. One of them is Keens Steakhouse, a unique New York institution. I can remember going there decades ago when those in the garment trade made Keens their lunch headquarters. This has not changed.

Keens still has the same attractions: the bar reeks of atmosphere, and there are great party facilities and fine food to match. Keens opened in 1885, and it has been a fixture in the Herald Square area ever since. For some time it was a "gentlemen only" place, and although it still has a masculine atmosphere, ladies now feel comfortable and welcome. The famous mutton chop with mint is the house specialty, but other delicious dishes include veal, steaks, lamb, and fish. For the light eater, especially at lunch, there are some great salads. There's a hearty, robust atmosphere about the place, and the waiters are no-nonsense. They do monthly single Scotch tastings from fall to spring, and they possess one of the largest single Scotch collections in New York. If you have a meat-and-potatoes lover in your party, this is the place. Make sure you save a little room for the deep-dish apple pie.

KIN KHAO
171 Spring St (nr Thompson St)   212/966-3939
Dinner: Daily
Moderate

There are a lot of hole-in-the-wall Thai restaurants all over Manhattan. They are increasingly popular because the food is light and the price is right. Kin Khao, in Soho, is one of the best. It is clean, attractive, and professional. Best of all, the regional Thai and Bangkok dishes are authentic and uniformly delicious. The spring rolls are a special treat, healthy and tasty. You may choose from a number of meat, seafood, and chicken dishes, some rather hot and others sweet and mild. Their sticky rice is a special feature of the restaurant. You'd have to travel several thousand miles to find any better!

KING'S CARRIAGE HOUSE
251 E 82nd St   212/734-5490
Lunch: Mon-Sat; Dinner: Daily
Moderately expensive

Even folks in the immediate neighborhood don't know about this sleeper! It is indeed an old carriage house, remade into a charming two-story dining salon that your mother-in-law will love. The mood is Irish, with the menu changing every evening. In this quaint setting, with real wooden floors, one dines by candlelight in a very civilized atmosphere. The luncheon menu stays the same: salads, sandwiches, and lighter fare. Afternoon tea is a treat. The continental menu in the evening may feature grilled items (like loin of lamb or red snapper); on Sundays, it is a roast dinner (leg of lamb, loin of pork, chicken, or tenderloin of beef). The menu is *prix fixe,* and it is really a good value. Personally, I found the Stilton cheese (with a nightcap of ruby port) absolutely perfect for dessert, but you may prefer chocolate truffle cake or rhubarb tart. For a fleeting dinner hour, you can be taken back a century or so, with nary a thought of computers, answering machines, or the dismaying nightly news.

KIOSK
1007 Lexington Ave (bet 72nd and 73rd St)   212/535-6000
Lunch, Dinner: Daily; Brunch: Sat and Sun
Moderate

Kiosk is well-named! The place is not much bigger than a couple of telephone booths, but don't let that deter you from a very pleasurable meal. In a skinny room with a two-stool bar in the center, diners sit at copper-topped tables. They are served by some of the more pleasant personalities on the Manhattan food scene and have the added advantage of a fascinating people-watching experience. Lunchtime offerings include burgers, grilled chicken and organic salad, several seafood dishes, a quiche and a pasta item, and a special soup everyday. Grilled chicken, steak, and varying specials are added for the evening diner. Mashed potatoes are very "in" these days, and those at the Kiosk are excellent. Rich desserts (like double chocolate gelato) are available in the afternoon, as well as at mealtime.

LA BOHEME
24 Minetta Lane (Sixth Ave bet 3rd and Bleecker St)   212/473-6447
Dinner: Tues-Sun; Brunch (and full menu): Sun
Moderate

Pari Dulac likes people and food, and it shows. The part-Iranian, part-French hostess is right on the job in her cozy, informal Bohemian bistro, dispensing delicious edibles at moderate prices. The setting is a quiet, charming street in the Village. When the front doors are open in warmer weather, you get the impression of being in a quaint European town. Inside, soothing music puts you in the mood to enjoy some of the best pizza you have ever tasted. In the back, an open kitchen puts out pasta, salads, and French dishes done to perfection. On Sundays, you can't beat the Country French brunch or the unique omelet selection. Dessert specialties include tarts made in-house, as well as first-class chocolate mousse cake and lemon soufflé with raspberry sauce. Pari has been wise to use only the best ingredients in her dishes, and she has resisted the temptation to raise prices to a point where value is questionable.

LA BOITE EN BOIS
75 W 68th St   212/874-2705
Dinner: Daily
No credit cards
Moderate

You don't have to be able to pronounce the name of this restaurant properly to have a good time! It packs them in every evening for obvious reasons. Owner Alain Brossard, an ex-chef, has hit upon that winning combination: delicious food, personal service, and moderate prices. The salads are unusual; the country paté is a great beginner. For an entree, I recommend filet of snapper, roast chicken with herbs, or the *pot-au-feu*, La Boite en Bois style. The atmosphere is intimate, and all the niceties of service are operative from start to finish. The desserts are made in-house; I suggest one of their sorbets. Call for reservations, since La Boite en Bois is very small and popular.

L'ABSINTHE
227 E 67th St   212/794-4950
Lunch, Dinner: Daily; Brunch: Sun
Moderately expensive

Don't ask me why Jean-Michel Bergougnoux (of Lutèce and Raphael fame) chose such a difficult-to-pronounce name! This is an extremely high-energy hangout for Upper East Siders who (1) don't wear earrings . . . the males, that is; (2) want to show off their latest acquisitions; and (3) want to see and be seen by anyone under 45 who has a corner office in a major Wall Street, Madison

Avenue, or Manhattan law firm. The atmosphere is convivial to say the least, the personnel super-friendly, the table tops covered with paper to make it easier to outline big deals for your guests, and most importantly, the food is very good. There are expensive appetizers like pan-seared jumbo sea scallops and escargots broiled with shitake mushrooms. Main-course specialties include beef tartare, roasted red snapper, and hangar steak. How about *baba au rhum* or cold rhubarb soup for dessert? Why not order the warm chocolate cake at the start of your meal? A special Bourgeoise French-cuisine menu of past years with items like slow-braised lean beef or Beaujolais-style warm poached sausage is available. A *prix fixe* Sunday brunch includes such specialties as poached hen in a truffle broth and roasted Moroccan-style salmon. Late evening, after ten, a la carte offerings include roasted beef ribs, French baguette sandwich, shellfish, salads, and lots of other goodies that will help you sleep well. In the warmer months, doors open to the sidewalk.

LA CARAVELLE
33 W 55th St (bet Fifth and Sixth Ave)   212/586-4252
Lunch: Mon-Fri; Dinner: Mon-Sat
Expensive

Utterly refined. Thoroughly classy. Totally delicious. Those words best describe this Manhattan institution, one of the most celebrated of the New York French restaurants. Chef Cyril Renaud uses fresh natural ingredients in dishes whose lightness is in keeping with the desires of modern diners. The selection of appetizers is so appealing that one could almost make a meal from these choices. But there is much more to follow: crispy salmon, marvelous Dover sole, tender rack and loin of lamb, and roasted lobster with curry sauce. The dishes are presented by service personnel from the old school. Warm lemon gratin or warm banana tart will satisfy light dessert eaters. I prefer the peanut crunch with white chocolate mousse. The chef presents a *menu d'inspiration,* which will undoubtedly inspire you to go on a diet the first thing tomorrow.

LA COLOMBE D'OR
134 E 26th St   212/689-0666
Dinner: Daily
Moderate

When you serve well-prepared meals at reasonable prices, word gets around. That's why La Colombe d'Or is always busy. Besides, the place has an intimate French *provençal* atmosphere, the service is prompt and efficient, and when the founders are back on the job, you know things are going well. Wonderful salads are featured here, like the famous salad nicoise (tuna fish, tomatoes, roasted red pepper, onions, hard-boiled eggs, *haricots verts,* boiled potatoes, and *mesclun*). Then there are a variety of pastas, your choice of a half-dozen fresh seafood dishes excellent couscous, plus legs of preserved duck (with Turkish figs), roast leg of lamb, and superb steaks. But the real treat here is the cassoulet: a simmered French white bean stew from Languedoc, made from white beans cooked in duck stock, with tomato, onion, and bacon layered in an individual crock with confits of pork, lamb sausage, and braised duck. Oh yes: on top is a crust of duck cracklings and sourdough bread crumbs. If you can still manage a dessert, their chocolate cake, *gateau Victoire,* will keep you humming!

LA CÔTE BASQUE
60 W 55th St   212/688-6525
Lunch: Mon-Sat; Dinner: Mon-Sun
Expensive

Yes, it's expensive. Quite expensive *(prix fixe)*. But dining at La Côte Basque is an experience worth every dollar. I doubt whether there is any room, anywhere in the world, more attractive and comfortable than this one. With gorgeous murals, superb lighting, and a magnificent open setting (no high banquettes), La Côte Basque is a feast for the eyes as well as the stomach! The service is ultra-professional, as one would expect. Of course there are marvelous appetizers like Petrossian caviar, sauteed wild mushrooms, seared duck liver, and oak-smoked salmon. For entrees, on to a magnificent black bass filet, roasted duckling with honey, or a special cassoulet by chef-owner Jean-Jacques Rachou. The desserts belong in a museum of beauty and good taste. Lemon-grass ice cream with lemon sorbet is mighty refreshing, but the chocolate cube with espresso sherbet is out-of-this-world. As if this weren't enough, a box of dessert goodies is placed temptingly in front of you. What an evening!

There is never a shortage of fads when it comes to food! Now one of the popular crazes is wraps—simply described as multicultural cuisines wrapped up in tortillas. Personally, I wouldn't walk up the block for them, but if you must, here are a few joints to try: **Wrap Factory** (62 University Pl, bet 10th and 11th St); **Cafe Bari** (529 Broadway, at Spring St); **Au Bon Pain** (various locations). Don't say I didn't warn you. Yuck!

LA GRENOUILLE
3 E 52nd St (at Fifth Ave)   212/752-1495
Lunch, Dinner: Tues-Sat
Expensive

After charming Manhattan for over 35 years, La Grenouille remains one of those special places that one really has to see to believe. It's impossible to describe. The beautiful fresh flowers are but a clue to a unique, not-to-be-forgotten dining experience. The food is as great as the atmosphere, and although prices are high, it's worth every penny. Celebrity-watching adds to the fun. You'll see most of the famous faces in the front of the room; also-rans are delegated to rear tables. The French menu is complete, the staff professional. Be sure to try their cold hors d'oeuvres; they're a specialty of the house, as are the lobster dishes, sea bass, and poached chicken. Nowhere in New York are sauces any better. Don't miss the superb dessert soufflés. The tables are very close together, but what difference does it make when the people at your elbows are so interesting?

LA LUNCHONETTE
130 Tenth Ave (at 18th St)   212/675-0342
Lunch: Mon-Fri; Dinner: Daily: Brunch: Sun
Inexpensive to moderate

The folks at La Lunchonette took exception to my contention in the last edition that this place is situated in a rather rundown and unattractice area. I stand by my description. This is hardly a place to please the eyes. But much more important, it does please the stomach and pocketbook. In a small and very modestly equipped kitchen, the personnel turn out really delicious food that can be as sophisticated as that of much fancier places uptown. At lunch there are salads and omelets, even *escargot au cognac* and sweetbreads from time to time. The dinner menu, which changes frequently, usually offers free-range chicken, steak, swordfish, and pan-seared trout.

LA MÉTAIRIE
189 W 10th St (bet W 4th and Bleecker St)   212/989-0343
Lunch: Sat-Sun; Dinner: Daily
Moderate

Once just a tiny hole in the wall, La Métairie ("a small communal farm") has expanded into a delightful place to dine in the Village. The atmosphere is still cozy, the food exceptional, the service prompt and accommodating – and the price is right! The kitchen offers a wide choice of French dishes. Specialties of the house include couscous, wild boar stew with fresh noodles, bouillabaisse, and rack of lamb.

LANDMARK TAVERN
626 Eleventh Ave (at 46th St)   212/757-8595
Daily: 11:45 a.m.-midnight; Brunch: Sun
Inexpensive

How about a cozy meal by a fireplace or potbellied stove? Landmark Tavern is open friendly hours for sandwich platters, a variety of salads, fresh seafood, steaks, and roast prime rib of beef. The real treat here is Sunday brunch. A tradition in the city since 1868, the Landmark is not content to copy everyone else's fare. Indeed, normal brunch items are available, but so is shepherd's pie (ground lamb sauteed with herbs), delicious lamb steaks, and English-style fish and chips. There is the added pleasure of sampling their famous soda bread, made fresh every hour and served with imported jams and marmalade. Corned beef hash is a favorite. And those great homemade desserts like Irish soda bread pudding and Jack Daniel's cake will make you want to come back every Sunday. The bar is friendly, the help is harried, and the atmosphere reeks of nostalgia. More important, the food is delicious, and prices are a bargain.

LA RÉSERVE
4 W 49th St   212/247-2993
Lunch, Dinner: Mon-Sat
Expensive

When I am asked if there is one restaurant in New York I would choose for a "last meal," my unqualified answer is La Réserve. There are all sorts of reasons for this top billing: the food, the ambience, the consistency. But the main plus is the host and owner, Jean-Louis Missud, one of the most charming and talented hosts in the business. New York has no shortage of fine rooms, but this one shines with appealing lighting, gracious and informed service, and the feeling that you are an honored guest. What to eat? Whatever your heart desires! I would suggest letting Jean-Louis or one of his talented captains order for you. Then sit back and enjoy your journey to culinary heaven. If romance is the name of the game, you can't do better than this French charmer. A pre-theater dinner is available, and private party facilities are yours for the asking.

LA RIPAILLE
605 Hudson St (at W 12th St)   212/255-4406
Dinner: Mon-Sat
Moderate

This small, bright, romantic Parisian-style bistro makes a cozy spot for an informal dinner. The tables are rickety, but the chef puts his heart into every dish. Most entrees are done to perfection; the seafood is always fresh (seafood in puff pastry is a specialty), and they do an excellent job with sweetbreads and rabbit. White chocolate is a house favorite—at least half of the dessert offerings use it as an ingredient. Proudly displayed at the front of the room are rave notices from a number of New York gourmets. They can add my enthusiastic endorsement, too!

LAYLA
211 West Broadway (at Franklin St)   212/431-0700
Lunch: Mon-Fri; Dinner: Daily
Moderate to moderately expensive

Drew Nieporent has done it again . . . this time with a Turkish flair! Layla is a unique, colorful, and fun destination for those who enjoy the charm of this mysterious part of the world. Traditional and specialty *mezzes* (appetizers) like hummus, *tadziki,* tabbouleh and lamb rissoli are featured, along with hot starters like crabmeat fillo and falafel. Unusual entrees include cinnamon-braised lamb shank, spiced chicken, pomegranate-glazed lamb kebob, and a vegetarian flatbread dish with grilled veggies. For dessert, try the warm chocolate torte with pistachio halvah ice cream. Patient servers will guide you through a truly delicious and memorable meal. A complete family-style dinner is available.

LE BERNARDIN
155 W 51st St   212/489-1515
Lunch: Mon-Fri; Dinner: Mon-Sat
Expensive

If your pocketbook is fat and you're craving seafood, you can't do better! The ambience is tasteful and classy, with colorful fishing scenes adorning the walls. As you would expect (and deserve, at these prices), the service is informed and professional. Oyster lovers will be in heaven; an assortment of oysters or Little Neck clams is offered at both lunch and dinner. The pizza Bernardin (topped with minute broiled shrimp) is exceptional and different. There is a selection of what they call "simply raw" with a number of tuna dishes or lightly smoked gravlax. Another section of the menu offers lightly cooked seafood dishes; my favorite is the fricassee of mussels, clams, and oysters. For the main course, just about any seafood you desire is available. Veal or lamb chops may be requested (but *why* at this place?). Extravagant desserts cap off a feast: chestnut frozen soufflé or a selection of caramel items or heaven by chocolate layers.

LE BIARRITZ
325 W 57th St (bet Eighth and Ninth Ave)   212/245-9467
Lunch: Mon-Fri; Dinner: Mon-Sat
Moderate

New York is full of neighborhood restaurants, and Le Biarritz is one of the best. It seems like home every evening as the regulars claim most of the seats in this warm, smallish eatery. The place has been at the same location and in the same hands for three decades. Gleaming copper makes any eating establishment look inviting, and here you can see a first-rate collection of beautiful French copper cooking and serving pieces. If you're in the mood for *escargots* to start, the chef knows how to prepare them well. You might also try French onion soup or crepes a la Biarritz (stuffed with crab meat). You can't go wrong with either. Entrees include frog's legs *provençale,* duck in cherry sauce with wild rice, and roast goose with chestnuts. The menu includes all kinds of chicken, lamb, beef, veal, and fish dishes, each served with fresh vegetables. Although there are no unusual desserts, all are homemade and very good. The reasonably priced dinners include soup, salad, and choice of dessert. I recommend Le Biarritz if you are going to a Broadway show or an event in the Lincoln Center area.

Dining in Central Village/Noho

Great Jones Street Cafe (54 Great Jones St): noisy; okay food
Indochine (430 Lafayette St): Vietnamese; once a star. now trying comeback
Noho Star (330 Lafayette St): comfort food
Riodizio (422 West Broadway): Brazilian
Temple Bar (Lafayette and Bleecker St): pickup bar/not food
Time Cafe (380 Lafayette St): healthy

LE BILBOQUET
25 E 63rd St   212/751-3036
Lunch, Dinner: Daily
Moderate

Philippe Delgrange presides over this cozy Upper East Side Parisian sidewalk cafe as if it were his own backyard. He seems to know everyone; indeed, most of the loyal clientele live in the neighborhood. Nonetheless, hungry visitors looking for good, informal dining all day long will feel just as welcome. It's amazing that so small a kitchen can turn out such good food. The paté and *terrine de saumon* are delicious appetizers. Le Bilbouquet is best known for its salads; the nicoise and duck salad with mangoes are the best bets. All of the assorted tarts are excellent, but my favorite is lemon. The chocolate *gateau* is definitely waist-expanding! Philippe's constant presence is surely the secret of Le Bilboquet's success.

LE CHANTILLY
106 E 57th St (near Park Ave)   212/751-2931
Lunch: Mon-Sat; Dinner: Daily
Expensive

New Yorkers know the name Joan Hamburg very well. Dealing mainly with consumer issues, she is among the most informed, respected, and popular personalities on radio in Manhattan. She is also a restaurant connoisseur. After the two of us had lunch at Le Chantilly, she exclaimed (and I ageed) that it was one of the most pleasant dining experiences we had ever had. The room is gracious and romantic, the personnel extremely well-informed and professional, and owner-chef David Ruggerio is one of the towering figures on the local restaurant scene. There are so many good things to choose from. For starters, non-traditional onion soup, Maine lobster salad, and seared foie gras with pistachio. Move on to wonderful grilled fish dishes, braised veal shanks, or mushroom-encrusted rack of lamb. Let your captain choose an outstanding and different menu for you. Special Sunday dinners, a chef's tasting menu, and a reasonably-priced pre-theater menu (5:30-6:30 pm) are features. Finish it all off with a soufflé or the banana caramel tart with chocolate sauce and crème Chantilly.

LE CIRQUE 2000
New York Palace Hotel
(Villard House, 455 Madison Ave, bet E 50th and 51st St)
212/303-7788
Lunch, Dinner: Daily; Brunch: Sun
Expensive

When an average Manhattan restaurant changes locations, the reaction is ho-hum. But when Le Cirque closed doors at the Mayfair Hotel and moved to the New York Palace Hotel, it was a major event in the city that loves celebrities. Owner Sirio Maccioni is just such a person, and his personality, combined with a reputation for outstanding food and beautiful people as guests, was sure to produce a winner. It is that, and then some. This man is pure genius: showman, culinary master, superb host. The theme is circus: colorful blue and red decor, magnificent china, fun touches in the two dining rooms, outdoor cafe, bar, and banquet facilities (for 250). Chef Sottha Khunn presides over a superb kitchen staff of 55 (including 9 pastry chefs), $250,000 stoves, and a private area for special guests to eat in the midst of it all. The Sultan of Brunei (you know, the wealthiest guy in the world) footed most of the bill for the $3 million kitchen and furnishings. The food can only be described in one word: superb. Even the souffles, which usually take extra time to prepare, appear at a moment's notice. Don't miss a chance to have a memorable meal at this legendary palace!

L'ÉCOLE
462 Broadway (at Grand St)   212/219-3300
Lunch: Mon-Fri; Dinner: Mon-Sat
Moderate

Class is in session at the kitchen of L'École, the dining room of the French Culinary Institute. The students, eager and excited, are preparing daily meals under the watchful eyes of the dean of culinary studies, their head chef, and his team. They are learning their lessons well. Out front, the neighborhood is hardly inviting, and the maitre d' adds little to the effort inside. The room itself is attractive enough, if you can keep your eyes at table height and forget about the tall, unbecoming ceiling. But meals here are a real bargain! Dinner consists of a *prix fixe* four- or five-course gourmet presentation. It is obvious that the instructors are watching very carefully, for each dish is delicious and beautifully presented. Because there is a limited menu, the would-be chefs are able to concentrate on a few dishes. But the price is right, and the school cafeteria you remember from years back was never this good! There is also a three-course *prix fixe* and an a la carte menu at noon.

LE GRENADIN

13 E 37th St   212/725-0560
Lunch: Mon-Fri; Dinner: Mon-Sat
Moderate

Hidden in the clutter of awnings and tawdry storefronts on this midtown street, Le Grenadin is a private retreat for those who work in the neighborhood. Lunchtime is busy as savvy office workers know where one of the most underrated Manhattan eateries serves some of the tastiest dishes around. This is not a formal establishment; you are treated more like a member of the family by Chef Jean Claude Trulade and his crew. The noon menu includes pastas, seafood, calves liver, chicken breast, and lamb chops for the heavier eaters. There are a dozen innovative appetiters (like fricassee of escargots or homemade duck terrine with walnuts), soups, salads, and a fair selection of desserts. If you have a yearning for a particular dish, they will try to satisfy you . . . just like at home! There's no sticker shock when the check arrives, and the friendly thank-yous will remind you to visit Le Grenadin again. The dinner menu is much the same, and the place is considerably quieter in the evening.

LENOX ROOM

1278 Third Ave (at 73rd St)   212/772-0404
Lunch: Sat, Sun; Dinner: Daily
Moderate to moderately expensive

Partly due to the high profile of the individuals involved in the operation, Charles Palmer and front man Tony, this cozy retreat took off as one of Manhattan's hottest spots to see and be seen. The raw bar features tasty oysters, clams, prawns, lobster and even Petrossian caviar. The appetizer selection varies from the usual fare: yellowfin tuna tartare, crab and avocado salad, foie gras, chicken liver parfait, and excellent spring rolls. The roasted guinea hen and citrus-tarragon-basted chicken from the rotisserie are highlights. There is excellent roasted lobster for seafood lovers and wonderful shoestring potatoes. In keeping with current trends, each dessert is a feast for the eyes as well as the tummy. The lemon-custard tart is especially intriguing after the hefty portions served in this friendly and professional establishment.

LE PÉRIGORD

405 E 52nd St   212/755-6244
Lunch: Mon-Fri; Dinner: Mon-Sun
Expensive

Style and then some! Le Périgord should be reserved for special occasions, because this is, indeed, a very special restaurant. At the start, you are cordially greeted at the door by the charming owner, Swiss-born Georges Briguet. By the time you reluctantly leave the warm, cozy premises completely satisfied, you will have experienced a brief interlude with a level of class that is rapidly disappearing from our world. The French menu features a *prix fixe* tab ($32 at lunch, $52 at dinner), with certain specialty items a slight bit more. But it is worth the cost in every way. The room is appealing, the service highly professional, the quality of the food unbeatable. The cold appetizer display is mouthwatering. This is one of the few places in Manhattan that adheres strictly to a proper dress code: jackets and ties are a must. (And why not, once in a while, when you want to do something special?) What to eat? Whatever you have always longed for at a superb French restaurant. Don't overlook the soufflés!

Theme Restaurants

Kids love them. Their elders should wear earplugs, take a hefty dose of Pepto-Bismol, and remember that they were young once. The first, and still the best, is the **Hard Rock Cafe** (221 W 57th St). Here the food is really quite good, especially the burgers, and the line for Hard Rock T-shirts and other memorabilia never seems to end. **The Brooklyn Diner** (212 W 57th St) could be considered a theme restaurant, although more in the diner category. The oldies will feel they are back in the mid-50s, while the kids will love their hot dogs, burgers, and other sizable plates. There is even a soda fountain!

The **Fashion Cafe** (51 Rockefeller Plaza) is without doubt one of the saddest excuses for a dining establishment in the city. The only possible reason to come here would be the off chance of seeing some of the model owners. I can't imagine that they eat their own food. For sheer noise level, it's hard to beat the **Harley Davidson Cafe** (1370 Sixth Ave, at W 56th St). If the family is into bikes, it's worth taking a look, but that's all. **Television City** (64 W 50th St, at Sixth Ave) has 130 television sets and over $1 million in production equipment. Besides the food. **The Jekyll & Hyde Club** (1409 Sixth Ave, at W 57th St) always seems to have a line out front, even with those eerie creeps all over the place. I thought haunted houses were just for Halloween, but some tourists think that the costuming should last all year long. At least the creepies and crawlies make you forget the forgettable food.

A former automat that calls itself **Motown Cafe** (104 W 57th St), combines soul music with soul food that does little for the soul. Some of the Motown songs done live aren't bad, but it's not for the kids. **Planet Hollywood** (140 W 57th St) with all the big-name hype, appeals to lovers of action-adventure flicks. It is second best (next to the **Hard Rock**) in the food category, and memorabilia collectors love to show off that logo. **The All-Star Cafe** (151 W 46th St) will appeal to those who get turned on by viewing past sports events. Most get so excited they don't remember what they are eating, which is just as well. If you can tear the kids away from some of these places, try the vastly more appealing **Serendipity 3** (225 E 60th St), where you and your brood will find great food in a fun atmosphere at affordable prices.

LE RÉFUGE

166 E 82nd St (bet Third and Lexington Ave)   212/861-4505
Lunch, Dinner: Daily; Brunch: Sat, Sun
Moderate

In any city other than New York this would be one of the hottest restaurants in town. But aside from folks in the neighborhood, few seem to have heard of Le Réfuge, a charming, three-room French country inn that offers excellent food, professional service, and delightful surroundings. The front room is cozy and comfortable, and the rear two sections provide nice views and pleasant accommodations. A back garden is open in the summer. This is another house where the owner is the chef, and as usual, it shows in the professionalism of the presentations. Specialties of the house: duck with fresh fruit, *bouillabaisse de crustaces,* and couscous Mediterranean with shrimp. Finish off the meal with the flourless *gateau soufflé au chocolate.* A delightful *prix fixe* brunch is served on weekends.

LE RÉGENCE
Hotel Plaza Athenee (37 E 64th St)   212/606-4647
Lunch, Dinner: Daily; Brunch: Sun
Expensive

The setting of Le Régence is understated and immensely attractive, and the tables are far enough apart to allow private conversation. The presentation is outstanding, and the French food is superb! One impressive point is that the personnel are not smitten with self-importance. The waiters and maitre d' are pleasantly accommodating, hard working, and well informed. You can't go wrong with any of the selections, but a few favorites stand out. I strongly recommend the Dover sole, grilled red snapper, and paillard of chicken with mushrooms. The luncheon salads are magnificent. Even something as mundane as French fries are done to perfection. And don't overlook the desserts: like *Rôve des Iles* (warm caramelized bananas and tangy pineapple fritters alongside luscious coconut ice cream drizzled with gingered chocolate sauce). Wow! The Sunday brunch is superb.

LES CÉLÉBRITÉS
Essex House
155 W 58th St (bet Sixth and Seventh Ave)   212/484-5113
Dinner: Tues-Sat
Expensive

You, too, can be a celebrity! That is, a food celebrity. Close your eyes for a moment and forget you are in a hotel dining room on Central Park in the midst of teeming Manhattan. Imagine yourself in the grand dining room of a luxurious estate in the early part of the century. This is as fine and magnificent a room as there is in New York. Decorated in superb taste, it is small enough to be intimate and large enough to give the feeling that dining here is a grand occasion. The name comes from the selection of artwork that adorns the walls. All are paintings created by American celebrities, including Phyllis Diller, Van Johnson, Peggy Lee, and Elke Sommer. The works are for sale; proceeds go to local charities. The menu matches the decor in splendor. A six-course menu degustation is available, as well as seasonal specialty *prix fixe* dinners. The a la carte menu changes but usually offers the kind of dishes you wouldn't prepare at home: burger of duck foie gras, squab with cabbage in a white truffle oil, and lobster with asparagus, snow peas, and grated truffles. What else but a chocolate soufflé with praline ice cream or a black currant and vodka cake on a chocolate and peanut biscuit for dessert? You won't want to wake up after this sumptuous culinary dream.

LES HALLES
411 Park Ave S (bet 28th and 29th St)   212/679-4111
Daily: noon to midnight
Moderate

Les Halles has struck a responsive note on the New York restaurant stage. Perhaps it is because France remains the most romantic scene to many gourmets or that bistros have become the "in" thing in Manhattan. But most probably it is because this establishment provides the necessary ingredients in today's restaurant sweepstakes: tasty food in an appealing atmosphere at reasonable prices. Specialties like blood sausage with apples, lamb stew, or fillet of beef are served in hefty portions with a fresh salad and delicious French fries on the side. Harried waiters try their best to be polite and helpful, but they are not always successful, as tables turn over more rapidly than at most fast-food outlets. If a week in Paris is more of a dream than a reality, you might settle for snails, onion soup, and classic cassoulet at this busy establishment. Unless you are big in the tart department, the dessert selection is a disappointment. (P.S. An attractive butcher shop is at your service right by the front door. It is open Monday through Saturday.)

LESPINASSE
St. Regis Hotel (Fifth Ave at 55th St)   212/339-6719
Breakfast, Lunch, Dinner: Daily Mon-Sat; Sun: Breakfast only
Expensive

The Old World comes to life in Manhattan! To dine here is an event and an experience. In a setting that befits the magnificent $100 million renovation of this historic hotel property, Lespinasse is a crown jewel in hotel dining in Manhattan. (Ask to see the kitchen!) The room, with high ceilings and magnificent floral arrangements, is comfortable and sophisticated. The tables are far enough apart to allow for the kind of intimate conversation one feels is in keeping with the atmosphere. (What a place to propose!) Waiters are there when you need them but disappear into the background while you enjoy your food and drink. And what food chef Gray Kunz presents! The marinated beef short ribs are the best I have ever tasted. There are seafood selections, venison, duckling, and everything else you would expect from a classy establishment. Heavenly desserts include such classics as crème brûlée, baked apples, and chocolate banana soufflé, plus three other chocolate choices and more. Of course, you pay the price, but it is worth it. The classy crowning touch: the coat-check lady doesn't give you a check. She remembers everyone's garment! *You'll* remember Lespinasse.

LES ROUTIERS
568 Amsterdam Ave (bet 87th and 88th St)   212/874-2742
Dinner: Mon-Sun
Moderate

This charming small French bistro set amid scruffy-looking storefronts is a happy find on the Upper West Side. This is no carbon-copy French establishment; it is the real thing, with a French menu and genuine ambience. There are snails and mussels with wine, skewered sea scallops, patés, duck, breast of chicken, veal stewed in white wine sauce—all those things you might find in the heartland of France. Wonderful salads are almost a meal in themselves. An enticing selection of sweet things is available; take a look at the dessert table as you come in. By the way, Les Routiers features specials on the menu every evening. Call ahead and see if your favorite dish is is among them!

Three-fourths of New York City's restaurants change hands or close before they are five years old.

LIBRARY AT THE REGENCY HOTEL
540 Park Ave (at 61st St) 212/759-4100
Breakfast, Lunch, Tea, Dinner, Dessert Daily, 7 a.m.-1 a.m.
Moderate

If you want to take your family or guests (or yourself) to a class place but are worried about the check, then the Library is for you! The Regency Hotel brings visions of big tabs and big deals . . . probably true in the regular dining room, but not in the adjoining Library. Here you will find a la carte breakfasts, a delightful tea service, and an entree menu ranging from salads (warm chicken, beefsteak tomato and mozarella) to tarts, omelets, sandwiches, grilled ahi tuna, and steak. The atmosphere is cordial and clubby, with magazines and papers for you to scan. Amazingly, the service is not a bit haughty. A full caloric dessert menu is offered: double chocolate pudding, old-fashioned chocolate layer cake, and an outrageous Library sundae. This is a unique spot, and people-watching is an added treat

LOBSTER CLUB
24 E 80th St 212/249-6500
Moderately expensive

Talented chef Anne Rosenzweig has created her own club for the Upper East Side! But non-East Siders are certainly welcome in this warm and inviting charmer, complete with a nautical flair and magnificent marble bar. Diners are served on two levels, as well as in the bar. Lots of seafood appetizers are offered. Among them: crab and couscous cake, baked snails in garlic butter, and roasted clams. There are soups, salads (like smoked trout with endive), pastas, and mashed potatoes with wild mushroom gravy and truffled bourbon. Of course, there's no shortage of lobster dishes, including lobster congee soup and the entree-sized lobster club. I was particularly intrigued with the grilled short ribs and the different daily mom's meatloaf entrees – delicious! Anne has outdone herself with unusual desserts, like warm chocolate bread pudding, caramel and chocolate tart in a pecan shortbread crust, and cool apple soup with carmelized apple. The downstairs room is the most inviting. Visit with the gregarious bartender, who sets the tone for this delightful newcomer.

LUTÈCE
249 E 50th St (bet Second and Third Ave) 212/752-2225
Lunch: Tues-Fri; Dinner: Mon-Sat
Expensive

The image of Lutèce was embodied in the person of Andre Soltner. He created not just a restaurant but an institution. How does anyone follow a legend? Well, Eberhard Müller is doing just that, and doing it very well. Housed in an old brownstone, this place reeks of class, composure, and comfort. The garden room is not super-attractive: the upstairs dining rooms have more appeal. The classics are still there: rack of lamb, duck, roasted lobster, grilled squab. A signature dish is a rich triple-decker "club sandwich" of sauteed fresh foie gras with an apple compote. (Don't even think about a cholesterol test!) The menu changes seasonally, as Eberhard is keen on fresh products (especially in the seafood category, from his background at Le Bernardin). Warm chocolate cake or one of their signature soufflés will top off a grand meal.

MALONEY & PORCELLI
37 E 50th St (bet Park and Madison Ave)   212/750-2233
Lunch, Dinner: Daily
Expensive

The lawyers whose names appear on the masthead should first insist that these folks get reasonable with their prices. No argument that the food is very good, but the tab is simply outrageous. Maybe that is because their bread basket is so exceptional. Pizzas and crabcakes with ratatouille or pastrami salmon are delicious appetizers. I have seldom tasted a better sirloin steak. (It *should* be at that price!) Lobster, equally tasty, is even more expensive. Don't pass up the "angry lobster"! If this is a business meal, go for it. And include some cowboy onion rings or a portabello potato pie. Don't leave without the profiteroles with caramel ice cream and hot fudge sauce or the chocolate brownout cake. The supervisory staff here could lower their noses a notch or two, but the floor staff is pleasant and try to be accommodating (though they're not very well trained). I hope these talented foodies don't go the way of one of their former tenants (Gloucester House), who found out that pockets do indeed have a bottom!

MANGIA È BEVI
800 Ninth Ave (at 53rd St)   212/956-3976
Lunch, Dinner: Daily
Inexpensive to moderate

This is definitely not the spot for a relaxing, intimate, refined meal. But it is definitely a top choice for delicious food at unbelievably low Manhattan prices. The noise level is almost unbearable, the tables allow you to instantly become friendly with some new folks, and the waiters are all very casual and surprisingly helpful. The abundant antipasto platter, overflowing with nearly a dozen choices, is a house specialty. This rustic trattoria also features a large selection of pastas, fish, many meat dishes, salads and a bevy of in-season veggies. Brick-oven pizza lovers will be in seventh heaven with pleasing combinations and equally pleasing prices. There's nothing special about desserts, except that the overexposed tiramisu served here is homemade. It is easy to see why colorful Mangia è Bevi is one of the most popular destinations along Ninth Avenue.

MANHATTAN CAFE
1161 First Ave (at 64th St)   212/888-6556
Lunch: Mon-Fri; Dinner: Daily; Brunch: Sun
Moderate to expensive

Steakhouses are "in"—and the classy, continental Manhattan Cafe has been in for quite some time. It is indeed an attractive, pleasant place to dine. But it is more than that! The steaks are large and delicious, as are the lamb chops and prime rib. Even the seafood, especially the filet of sole, is worth trying. A number of veal dishes are available, with veal piccata being particularly good. Accompany your choice with the excellent cottage-fried potatoes. For dessert, the *tartufo* equals any I've tasted in Italy (except Tre Scalini's in Rome), and the cheesecake melts in your mouth. A pre-theater menu is available daily before 6:15 p.m. Manhattan Cafe is a cigar-friendly restaurant with a separate smoking and cigar room featuring a built-in humidor.

MARCH
405 E 58th St (bet First Ave and Sutton Pl)   212/754-6272
Dinner: Mon-Sat
Expensive

If you want to be spoiled, start here. In this attractive and romantic townhouse, with high ceilings and teak floors, you will dine in one of three rooms in absolutely regal style. Executive chef Wayne Nish and partner Joseph Scalice (who oversees the front house) have raised the art of dining to perfection. I would like to come back here eight nights, for only in that way could one try all eight of the unusual appetizers, eight of the fabulous entrees, and eight of the gourmet desserts. The *prix fixe* menu ($50) is well worth the tab, for the sky is the limit when it comes to service and quality. The fact that it is so busy is a tribute to the format. An attractive, glass-enclosed back porch overlooks a small garden in this Sutton Place neighborhood.

MARCHI'S
251 E 31st St   212/679-2494
Dinner: Mon-Sat
Moderate

This must be one of the best-kept secrets in New York. Though there's no sign out front, Marchi's has been a New York fixture since 1930, when it was established by the Marchi family in an attractive brownstone townhouse. The Marchis, joined by their three sons, are still on hand, giving a homey flavor to the restaurant's three dining rooms and garden patio (a great spot for a private dinner). It's almost like going to dinner at your favorite Italian family's house, especially since there are no menus. Be sure to bring a hearty appetite so you can take full advantage of a superb feast. The first course is a platter of antipasto, including radishes, *finocchio,* and Genoa salami, plus a salad of tuna, olives, and red cabbage. The second is an absolutely delicious homemade lasagna. The third is a crispy deep-fried fish. The side orders of cold beets and string beans are light and tempting. The entree is delicious roast chicken and veal served with fresh mushrooms and a tossed salad. For dessert, there is a healthy bowl of fresh fruit, cheese, a lemon fritter, and sensational *crostoli* (crisp fried twists sprinkled with powdered sugar). The price tag is overwhelmingly reasonable. Come to Marchi's for a unique, leisurely meal and an evening you will long remember.

MARGUERY GRILL
133 E 65th St   212/744-2533
Lunch: Mon-Fri. Dinner: Daily
Moderately expensive

Chef Robert Weland has done what so few others do: concentrate on a few items and do them all well. This intimate Upper East Side retreat offers congenial dining for those who want their plates done with a bit of class and expertise. Hot and chilled starters include oysters, salads, and exotic items like grilled quail and an unusual spicy South Shore clam soup. From the wood grill, one can have a Moroccan mixed plate, marinated rare yellowfin tuna, garlic rubbed ribeye of lamb, or a delicious Black Angus sirloin. There are also several seafood dishes, a pan-seared smoked squab or moist and crisp Wellington Farm chicken. A *prix fixe* menu is available, and daily specials are featured. (Come on Friday for an excellent bouillabaise.) Top desserts: the glazed berry tart and the trilevel parfait of chocolates (dark chocolate custard, milk chocolate mousse, bittersweet glaze). My only complaint concerns the price of the entrees.

MARK'S RESTAURANT
Mark Hotel (25 E 77th St)   212/879-1864
Breakfast, Lunch, Dinner: Daily; Brunch, Sun
Moderately expensive

One of the best! You can enjoy a fine meal here in a sedate atmosphere reminiscent of an English club. Adding to the pleasure of delicious food is the refined, professional service, solid wood tables, beautiful flowers, gorgeous china, and a feeling of being particularly welcome. How do these sound? For appetizers: Louisiana prawn and truffle ravioli or seared tuna with Asian slaw. For entrees: cedar-plank-roasted striped bass or pan-seared Maine lobster. For desserts: cinnamon soufflé or white chocolate macadamia cheesecake. Many Upper East Siders who are not guests of the hotel make this dining room a frequent stop. It is not difficult to understand why.

MAZZEI
1564 Second Ave (at 81st St)   212/628-3131
Dinner: Daily
Moderate

This small Upper East Side hideaway (it has had several previous lives under different names) now takes its cue from Philip Mazzei, an Italian-American diplomat of the 18th century who was active in furthering relations between this country and Italy. Now Restaurant Mazzei certainly keeps on that track, cementing the love affair between New Yorkers and good, hearty Italian fare. The brisk, professional service, the energy created by full tables of neighborhood diners (out-of-towners would have a hard time finding this jewel), and the vast assortment of daily specials make a visit here memorable. There are different appetizers from the wood-burning oven each evening. Recommended dishes include an excellent veal chop, baked prawns, and boneless breast of chicken. Be sure to ask for some of the small specialty potatoes, which are as tender and tasty as you'll ever encounter. In the sea of Italian eateries that now has Manhattan rivaling the native country, this one will have a good shelf life as long as chef Mario Deruda sticks to the basics he does so well.

MESA CITY
1059 Third Ave (bet 62nd and 63rd St)   212/207-1919
Lunch: Mon-Sat; Dinner: Daily; Brunch: Sun
Moderate

Mesa Grill has an offspring, and it's doing very well. If you can stand the noise, Mesa City is the next best place to dining in Santa Fe! (By the way, most of the folks who eat here look like they haven't been much further west than Manhattan's West Side.) Anyway, the place is jumping, the young staff is exceptionally friendly, and the plates are big and tasty. What to eat with a Southwestern flavor? Black bean and roasted jalapeno soup. Smoked shrimp cake with tomatillo sauce. Grilled blue-corn sweet-potato tacos. Wonderful quesadillas. Grilled pork chops *adobo* with a spicy apple chutney. Molasses BBQ ribs. By all means, don't leave without an order of Southwestern fries; they're absolutely the best I've ever tasted. I couldn't stop, though their portions are huge! Best dessert bet: the ice-cream sandwich.

METISSE
239 W 105th St (bet Amsterdam Ave and Broadway)   212/666-8825
Dinner: Mon-Sun
Moderate

In the neighborhood surrounding Columbia University, good dining is not easy to find. So it is with pleasure that I can heartily recommend Metisse, a small French bistro. Metisse will be a comfortable destination for your palate and your pocketbook. The place is quiet and restful, the waiters unobtrusive, and the cuisine light and satisfying. A number of salads are available as appetizers, but I'd suggest the corn-breaded shrimp with spicy dipping sauce. Delicious! Entrees are slanted on the seafood side (grilled tuna, sauteed cod, black bass, or red snapper), along with steak and chops. And the French fries are first rate! Their warm chocolate cake with vanilla ice cream is the most popular dessert, although less filling fruit specialties are available. It's a delightful spot for a casual meal if business or pleasure brings you to this part of the Upper West Side.

MEZZOGIORNO
195 Spring St   212/334-2112
Lunch, Dinner: Daily
Moderate

One of the most charming cities in the world is Florence, Italy, not only for its abundance of great art but also for the wonderful small restaurants on every street corner. At Mezzogiorno, a Florence-style *trattoria* in New York, the food is just as good (though some of the art is questionable). The place is busy and noisy, and tables are so close together that conversation is impossible. The decor is best described as "modern Florence"; check out the unusual writing on the ceiling done by master fresco artist Pontormo. Better yet, keep your eyes on the food. The salad selection is outstanding, as are all the meat carpaccios. If you like lasagna, theirs is one of the best. Mezzogiorno is also famous for the pizzas it serves. You'll find all the ingredients for a wonderful make-believe evening in Florence.

MINETTA TAVERN
113 MacDougal St   212/475-3850
Lunch, Dinner: Daily
Moderate

Do you want to take your guests to a Village restaurant where the coat-and-tie, meat-and-potatoes set feel comfortable? Well, Minetta Tavern—established in 1937 and serving excellent food for generations—is the place to go. Located on the spot where Minetta Brook wandered through Manhattan in the early days, this tavern was made famous by Eddie "Minetta" Sieveri, a friend of many sports and stage stars of yesteryear. Dozens of old pictures adorn the walls of this intimate, scrupulously clean tavern, where professional personnel serve no-nonsense Italian food at attractive prices. Grilled mushrooms, steamed clams, or *pasta e fagioli* are good ways to get the juices flowing. Follow that up with homemade pastas like penne *alla* vodka. If you'd like something a bit heftier, veal is available. Chocolate mousse cake, profiteroles, and other pastries make a wonderful cap to a satisfying meal. By the way, if you have to wait, the bar stools are among the most comfortable in New York.

MME. ROMAINE DE LYON
132 E 61st St   212/758-2422
Lunch: Daily; Dinner: Mon-Sat
Moderate

The best omelets in New York are served at Mme. Romaine's. If you can't find what you want from their 545 varieties, it probably doesn't exist. How about a lobster, spinach, or chicken omelet? They will make any combination you want. When you're in the mood for a light lunch or dinner, this is the place to go. If omelets are not your preference, try the chef salad or smoked salmon. At dinnertime, a full menu of continental cuisine is available, plus piano music each evening.

Of course, the first place to look for suggestions about where to eat is in the volume you now have in your hands. The **Zagat Survey** is another source; the reviews contained in that volume are pithy comments from hundreds of diners. Another source is **Foodphone** (212/777-FOOD). You will be able to hear information about hundreds of Manhattan restaurants by type of cuisine, location, and price range.

MONKEY BAR
60 E 54th St   212/838-2600
Lunch: Mon-Fri; Dinner: Mon-Sun
Moderate to moderately expensive

Ask any old-time New Yorker about the famous Monkey Bar at the Elysee Hotel, and they will regale you with stories. The reincarnation of the landmark is now packed with the "beautiful people," and they are all enjoying the "beautiful food"! (Note that jackets are required for men.) Great old-time pictures adorn the walls; the whimsical monkey paintings look like new. Chef John Schenk provides very special dishes like grilled salmon, roast Amish chicken, and rack of lamb. I love shoestring potatoes, and theirs are delicious and difficult to eat politely! Leave room for the superb baked Alaska (with caramel ice cream) for dessert, or how about the coconut parfait (coconut ice cream, chocolate sorbet, and macaroons)? Don't monkey around; relive the past in grand style!

MONTRACHET
239 West Broadway (bet White and Walker St)   212/219-2777
Lunch: Fri; Dinner: Mon-Sat
American Express
Moderately expensive

Thriving and exciting places like Montrachet make Tribeca a very appealing place to visit. Once inside Montrachet, the feeling of drabness dissipates. You can concentrate undistracted on fine modern French dishes such as seafood, game, and meat prepared to perfection by the restaurant's superchef, Chris Gesualdi. The menu changes regularly; exciting things are done with fresh produce. If you are lucky enough to find bouillabaisse on the menu, go for it. Roast squab, roast chicken, and roast duck are outstanding choices. Salmon and tuna dishes are done to perfection. The three simply decorated rooms do not detract from the main reason you are there: good eating. Having tasted many crème brûlées, I can say with authority that Montrachet's is top-notch.

MORTON'S OF CHICAGO
551 Fifth Ave (entrance on 45th St)   212/972-3315
90 West St   212/732-5665
Lunch: Mon-Fri; Dinner: Mon-Sun
Moderately expensive to expensive

Now this is a real steakhouse. Forget about the "of Chicago"—this is New York at its best! These folks are experts, as well they should be: they have units all over the country. Every member of the highly efficient staff has been trained in the Morton's manner. At the start you are shown a cart with samples of entree items, fresh vegetables, lobster, and whatever else they happen to be featuring. Every dish is fully explained by your waiter. Appetizers are heavy in the seafood department: shrimp, oysters, smoked salmon, sea scallops. Attractive and appetizing salads include one with sliced beefsteak tomatoes and purple onions. The steaks and chops are so tender you can cut them with a fork. Best of all, they arrive promptly, unlike so many steakhouses. Potatoes come in several styles, including wonderful hash browns. Sauteed spinach and mushrooms or steamed broccoli and asparagus are fresh and tasty. Top it all off with a delicious soufflé—chocolate, Grand Marnier, lemon, or raspberry—that is big enough for two hefty diners.

NICOLA'S
146 E 84th St (bet Lexington and Third Ave)   212/249-9850
Dinner: Daily
Moderately expensive

Upper-crust New Yorkers who like a clubby atmosphere and good food (which are not often found together) love this place! In a setting of rich wood and familiar faces on the walls, and a noise level that sometimes reaches that of a Broadway opening, no-nonsense waiters serve delicious platters of pasta, veal, chicken, fish, and steak. There are daily specials in every category, and each is inviting. It is difficult to come up with really good home fries in a busy restaurant, but Nicola's has the secret . . . theirs are sensational! Concentrate on the early part of your meal, as the desserts show little imagination.

NOBU
105 Hudson St   212/219-0500
Lunch: Mon-Fri; Dinner: Daily
Moderately expensive

When you combine the culinary talents of chef Nobu Matsuhisa, the restaurant management expertise of Drew Nieporent, and a sensational setting done by the David Rockwell group, you have a winning combination. So it is at this Japanese beauty in Tribeca. A loud Oriental shout greets diners as they enter, a comfortable and appealing sushi bar awaits those so inclined, and airy seating completes the scene. There is a full menu that will please the traditional Japanese food lover, while those with less adventurous tastes will find items they can enjoy. Besides the sushi and sashimi, there are sushi rolls, tempura, kushiyaki (beef, chicken, veggies, and seafood on skewers), and a large selection of daily specialties that run heavy on the seafood side. Service has been refined to perfection. The ambience is unique—surely not that of a typical Tokyo establishment. And the pastry chef has created some trans-Pacific specialties: orange tart with bitter chocolate sorbet, yellow plum and sake sorbet, green tea crème caramel, and cherry walnut and red bean spring roll. Nobu is not a bargain, but the experience of dining in a truly professional ethnic restaurant is worth the extra bucks.

OCEANA
55 E 54th St (bet Park and Madison Ave)   212/759-5941
Lunch: Mon-Fri; Dinner: Mon-Sat
Moderately expensive

Oceana proves that you don't have to be located on the water to be a superb seafood house. On several floors of a midtown townhouse that used to be Le Cygne, chef Rick Moonen (who was on the water at the Water Club) presents an unusually tasty selection of the freshest fish dishes. Everything he prepares uses spices and herbs in the best possible manner. A three-course *prix fixe* lunch includes a chilled oyster selection (theirs are the best), lobster ravioli, or house cured salmon gravlax, and steamed mussels or Oceana seafood gumbo. A memorable three-course *prix fixe* dinner might have this menu: warm house-smoked trout to start, grilled filet of Florida mahi-mahi (this has a garlic crust), and poached pear with muscoot cheese or Oceana's chocolate sampler for dessert. For those who are into this type of dining, there is a six-course tasting menu. You'll need a boat to carry you out!

ONE IF BY LAND, TWO IF BY SEA
17 Barrow St (bet Seventh Ave and 4th St)   212/228-0822
Dinner: Daily
Expensive

Most everyone I've sent to this restaurant has been enchanted. Finding it is a bit of a challenge, but what a reward when you do! The building, once Aaron Burr's carriage house, is unique, and the atmosphere is warm (with working fireplaces) and friendly. One If By Land is especially popular with young people, who appreciate the romantic ambience and the extraordinary food. Make reservations before coming, and allow yourself time to find Barrow Street (one of the Village's most charming yet hard-to-find side streets) and the restaurant (there's no sign out front). Be sure to spend a few minutes enjoying the live piano music while having a drink at the spacious bar by the fireplace. Try to get a table on the balcony level; it's especially romantic. As for dinner, the roast rack of lamb, Norwegian salmon, grilled filet mignon, and beef Wellington are all excellent. Dessert is an ever-changing selection of delicious homemade goodies. Late night Friday and Saturday entertainment (until 3 a.m.) is available.

ONIEAL'S
174 Grand St   212/941-9119
Dinner: Daily
Moderate

Now here is a charmer, and talk about atmosphere! From magnificent wood ceilings with carved devil's heads to the storybook tunnel that connects the building to an old police station (the tunnel is now used to store wine), this small establishment is just the spot for a special New York evening. There are only 35 seats in the dining room, cigar and cigarette smoking is allowed, so be prepared if smoke bothers you. An attractive bar area is full of smokers, too! But on to the food: caviar, oysters, or smoked salmon to start. Barbecued venison pot pie or roasted quail as appetizers. Lamb shanks, grilled vegetable roulade or striped sea bass for entrees. If pot roast is on the menu, go for it! The soufflé chocolate cake with fresh berries and ice cream is a dessert winner, as is the espresso float, a sinful ice cream dish with chocolate, caramel, and citrus dust. The folks here are as friendly as the ambience is inviting. Forget about the grungy buildings nearby and steep yourself in an establishment whose home has been a New York institution for over 125 years.

OPALINE
85 Avenue A (bet 5th and 6th St)   212/475-5050
Dinner: Daily
Moderate

Opaline is an only-in-New-York experience from start to finish. The location is in what is known as Alphabet Land, for years a haven for druggies and undesirable elements. Fortunately, the region has been cleaned up, but there remains an air of mystery and intrigue. Opaline is reached down a flight of stairs; you almost feel like someone behind the doors is checking you out for a visit to a speakeasy. But no, you enter a restaurant that is unique: a lounge that looks like it belongs in a bawdy house, a large dining room with ceiling fans, and a raised area for entertainment. You came for good food, too, and you won't be disappointed. There are mussels steamed in tomato garlic broth and braised lamb shanks with roasted garlic whipped potatoes and chocolate souffle cake with *crème fraiche* ice cream. Prices are so low they will astound you. The image of the old Absinthe House (from which Opaline gets its name) is that of intimate and slightly sinister meeting place where elegant people gathered. Tonight it is your dining room. The scene has been transferred to the bowels of this great city, and you will have an evening you'll never forget.

OPUS II
242 E 58th St   212/753-2200
Lunch: Mon-Fri; Dinner: Mon-Sat
Moderate

Attention, ladies. At last a non-macho steakhouse. Bruno (he also owns the restaurant next door, with his name prominent at the door) has come up with a different twist for a steakhouse. There is no printed menu, no blackboard, just a recitation by the captain of the steak, chop, chicken, and fish dishes. Each day the appetizers, salads, veggies, and desserts are different. And it is one reasonable fixed price. The atmosphere is not overpowering, and neither are the waiters. I found everything done to perfection. If Bruno keeps up the quality of this establishment, he will have a winner.

ORSO
322 W 46th St   212/489-7212
Mon, Tues, Thurs, Fri, Sun: noon–11:45;
Wed, Sat: 11:30 a.m.–11:45 p.m.
Moderate

This restaurant features the same menu all day, which is great for those with unusual dining hours and handy for those going to the theater. Orso is one of the most popular places on midtown's "restaurant row," so if you're thinking about a six o'clock dinner, be sure to make reservations. The smallish room is cozy and comfortable and watched over by a portrait of Orso, a Venetian dog who is the mascot for this Italian bistro. The kitchen is open in the back and visible to diners. You can see for yourself just how experienced the staff is. The changing menu includes many good appetizers, like cold roast veal and fried artichokes. A variety of pizzas and some excellent pasta dishes are also offered. For an entree, you can't go wrong with the lamb sausage or veal shank. The chocolate devil cake, one of many homemade desserts, will finish off a great meal.

OSTERIA DEL CIRCO
120 W 55th St   212/265-3636
Lunch: Mon-Sat, Dinner: Mon-Sun
Moderately expensive

If it were not for the fact that the owners here are the sons of leqendary Sirio Maccioni (of Le Cirque) fame, this establishment might just be written off as another Manhattan Italian restaurant. But here we have three brothers: Mario, Marco, and Mauro (and mother Egidiana) operating a classy establishment with a very friendly ambience, and, incidentally, not the usual Italian menu. There is a circus theme to the decor that it is well done but given the idea could be far more dramatic. The three very pleasant young men had a tough time getting their act together at the start, with amateurish service all too obvious. The tastiest items include great pizzas, satisfying soups, unusual pastas (the ravioli is superb), and a wonderful flash-seared beef carpaccio. A unique dessert is an Italian favorite called *bomboloncini:* very small vanilla, chocolate and raspberry filled doughnuts.

PALM
837 Second Ave (at 44th St)
212/687-2953

PALM TOO
840 Second Ave (at 44th St)
212/697-5198

Lunch: Mon-Fri; Dinner: Mon-Sat
Expensive

Even with all the excellent new Manhattan steakhouses, steak and lobster lovers in Manhattan still have a special place in their hearts for the Palm and Palm Too. These restaurants are located across the street from each other, and both have much the same atmosphere. They're noted for huge, delicious steaks, chops, and lobsters, but don't miss the terrific Palm fries—homemade potato chips—or try a combination order of fries and onion rings. It's an earthy spot, so don't get too dressed up. Indolent waiters are part of the scene.

PAMIR
1437 Second Ave (bet 74th and 75th St)   212/734-3791
Dinner: Tues-Sun
Moderate

One of Manhattan's best ethnic restaurants! Turnovers are an Afghan specialty, and Pamir offers several. If you like extra-spicy food (like that served in the native country), they will gladly oblige. The Afghan bread is great, and it comes with each entree. Lamb is the order of the day: seasoned lamb with rice, almonds, and pistachios; chunks of lamb in an onion-and-garlic-flavored spinach sauce; lamb and eggplant cooked with tomatoes, onions, and spices; lamb on a skewer, marinated in spices; lamb chops broiled on a skewer. All are worth a try. Several vegetarian dishes are also available. Eat heartily from the start, because the desserts are zilch. The folks here are unpretentious, the desire to please is sincere, and the prices are modest.

PAOLA'S
343 E 85th St   212/794-1890
Dinner: Daily
Moderate

Paola's is a prime spot for a romantic evening. The only problem might be that you'll have an audience for the proposal, since the room has just 20 tables, and it gets crowded. But no matter. The Italian home cooking is first-class. Paola is in the kitchen taking care of the food. Great homemade filled pasta, superb veal dishes, and tasty, hot vegetables (like baby artichoke hearts) are house specialties. Take along a breath mint if romance is in the air, because they don't spare on the garlic. Mirrors reflect the warmth and flicker of the candles, and the lady of the house will charm any guest. To top off the reasonably priced dinner, try a dish of rich chocolate mousse.

PAPER MOON MILANO
39 E 58th St   212/758-8600
Lunch, Dinner: Mon-Sat
Moderate

This offshoot of the well-known Milan House bills itself as a "restaurant-pizzeria." It does a good job in both departments. In a high-rent area, the atmosphere is friendly and casual; patrons in jeans and sportswear will feel perfectly comfortable. Decor is simple and appealing. The harried help tries its best to be accommodating. A fine selection of salads and pastas is offered, each presented with finesse that comes from years of experience in Italy. The full menu includes fish, meat, and poultry dishes, as well as several carpaccio dishes (thin slices of raw beef with various toppings). But you will be missing something special if you don't try the pizzas. A talented young Italian pizza chef turns out some of the lightest, tastiest combinations you will ever savor. Each is a meal in itself. A refreshing dish of gelati will top off a wonderful lunch or dinner.

PARIS COMMUNE
411 Bleecker St   212/929-0509
Dinner: Daily; Brunch: Sat, Sun
Moderate

Mayo Roe, the previous owner, has bought back this popular spot, and it is better than ever! The dining room has been brightened up, and the menu now changes frequently. The Paris Commune is a popular Village gathering spot, where regulars outnumber visitors every night. There are only a dozen tables, and the staff is prompt and efficient. Dining by candlelight with an adjoining fireplace is the attraction! The weekend brunch features spectacular French toast, along with the other usual fare. Delicious omelets include cheddar cheese and bacon, apples and Jarlsberg cheese, and marinated artichoke hearts and mozzarella. Their cheesecakes are good and rich.

PARK AVENUE CAFE
100 E 63rd St (at Park Ave)   212/644-1900
Lunch: Mon-Fri; Dinner: Daily; Brunch: Sun
Moderately expensive

A beautiful room that once housed Le Périgord Park and later Hubert's is now a showpiece for Alan Stillman (who has his tasty fingers in the Post House,

Cité, Manhattan Ocean Club, and Smith & Wollensky). He obviously is a man of eclectic interests. Here Chef David Burke does unusual things that please most diners while puzzling some with less sophisticated tastes. The basically American menu is served by very professional waiters who look like they might have been influenced sartorially by Larry King. The signature dish is a swordfish chop served with a tart lemon sauce. The people watching is great, and the conversations at the next table can be fascinating. Desserts are sensational!

PARK BISTRO
414 Park Ave S (bet 28th and 29th St)   212/689-1360
Lunch: Mon-Fri; Dinner: Mon-Sun
Moderate

These days it is special fun to go to a place with smiles, and the Park Bistro is that! This is a small, homey dining room that specializes in cuisine from the Provence region of France. It's a jewel. From the start, when warm and tasty bread is placed before you, to the finishing touch of rich and luscious homemade desserts (like crème brûlée, tortes, and a sinful chocolate gateau), you are surrounded by attentive service and magnificent food. Don't miss the hanger steak or braised lamb shank. A professional team runs this place, and it shows.

PARKSIDE
107-01 Corona Ave (at 51st Ave and 108th St, Corona, Queens)
718/271-9274
Lunch, Dinner: Daily
Moderate

Do you want to show that person who claims to know everything about New York something he or she doesn't know? Do you want to eat on your way to or from La Guardia or Kennedy airport? Do you want a special meal in an unusual setting? Well, all of the above are excellent reasons to visit Parkside, in Queens. I make an exception in including a restaurant not in Manhattan because it *is* exceptional. Richard D'Angelo runs a first-class, spotlessly clean restaurant that serves wonderful Italian food at prices that make most New York restaurateurs look like highway robbers. Start with garlic bread and then choose from two dozen kinds of pasta and an opulent array of fish, steak, veal, and poultry dishes. The meat is all prime cut—nothing frozen here. You'll also find polite, knowledgeable waiters in an informal atmosphere. Get a table in the garden room or the Marilyn Monroe room upstairs. Eat until your heart's content, and be amazed at the tab.

PATSY'S
236 W 56th St (bet Broadway and Eighth Ave)   212/247-3491
Lunch, Dinner: Daily
Moderate

For over half a century, the Scognamillo family has operated this popular eatery, specializing in Neapolitan cuisine. At the moment the son is taking care of the front of the house, while the grandson is following the family tradition in the kitchen. "Patsy" was an immigrant gentleman chef whose nickname was soon attached to a New York tradition that has now grown into a two-level restaurant. Each floor has its own cozy atmosphere and convenient kitchen. The family makes sure that every guest is treated as if they are in a private home; courtesy and concern are the name of the game. A full Italian menu is available, with numerous specials that include a different soup and seafood entree each day. If you can't find what you like among the two dozen pasta choices, you are in deep trouble!

PEACOCK ALLEY
Waldorf-Astoria Hotel
301 Park Ave (at 50th St)   212/872-4895
Breakfast: Daily; Lunch: Mon-Fri; Dinner: Tues-Sat;
Brunch: Sun
Moderate to moderately expensive

The old Waldorf-Astoria Hotel stood on the site of the present Empire State Building. There were really two hotels—the Waldorf on the 33rd Street corner, and the Astoria on the 34th Street corner. An alley connected the two; it became . known as Peacock Alley because the beautiful people of that day paraded like peacocks in the connecting corridor. Now the newly restored grand hotel has a magnificent lobby area, where one can still enjoy the passing parade and feast in the adjoining Peacock Alley restaurant. The food matches the setting, certainly steps above the usual hotel fare that one thought of years ago. But it is on Sunday that this place is the real treat. A magnificent brunch is laid out in a portion of the main lobby around the famous Waldorf-Astoria clock. Here you will find fresh fruits, baskets of delicious pastries, salads, cheeses, patés, seafood, breakfast items, main courses with seasonal vegetables, assorted omelets, and a scrumptious dessert buffet. The pasta dishes prepared right before your eyes are a special treat. A meal here cannot help but bring to mind memories of what it used to be in those much-talked-about "good old days"!

From time to time we all look for a small, rather off-the-beaten path type of place that we can go for a meal without getting dressed up, making reservations, or whatever. I've found that kind of place, and the food is very good. Try **Jacques' Bistro**, serving French cuisine, at 204 E 85th St (bet Second and Third Ave), 212/327-2272. They are open for lunch, dinner, and weekend brunch. The price is right, and atmosphere is extra friendly.

PEPPERMINT PARK CAFE & BAKERY
1225 First Ave (bet 66th and 67th St)
212/288-5054 (cafe); 212/288-5415 (bakery)
Breakfast, Lunch, Dinner: Daily (open late)
Moderate

There are five excellent reasons to visit Peppermint Park: (1) you want a light meal; (2) you're a dessert lover; (3) you want to eat after a show; (4) you've got kids with you; or (5) you simply prefer informal restaurants with a carnival-like atmosphere. For sustenance, there are fantastic crepes, like the Crepe Train Robbery (creamed spinach with your choice of sharp cheddar or Roquefort cheese) or Crepe Canaveral—they say it blasts your spirits into orbit. Another good combination: fresh mushrooms, sauteed onions, melted Gruyere, and blended herbs. Several dessert crepes are also available, such as one with maple syrup, melted butter, and powdered sugar. There are all kinds of Belgian waffle concoctions and a few quiches. The big news, though, is the fantastic selection of homemade ice creams (from mocha chip—Number One for me—to rum raisin and black raspberry), several sherbets and sorbets, big banana splits, really thick shakes, yogurt, a selection of ten toppings (among them walnuts in syrup, crushed cherries, and hot butterscotch), and an array of pastries, cakes, and cookies you won't believe. There is also a great selection of low-fat lunch specials for more timid souls!

PICHOLINE
35 W 64th St   212/724-8585
Lunch: Tues-Sat; Dinner: Daily
Moderate

Terrance Brennan is a workhorse, and it shows in his attractive restaurant. The rustic atmosphere is a perfect backdrop for the Mediterranean-inspired plates. The many pluses here include delicious homemade breads, perfectly done fish dishes, superbly prepared game, and one of the best cassoulets in the city. If you're having a party at Lincoln Center, the small private party room is a fabulous setting for a memorable evening. There are daily classic cuisine specials. (How does *civet* of duck on Sunday sound?) If you really want to splurge, try the *daube* of oxtail and *foie gras tortelloni* . . . and follow up with sauteed black sea bass with black truffles. I look forward to the magnificent cheeses for dessert, but the warm rhubarb tart (with vanilla ice cream) will more than satisfy as well.

PIETRO'S
232 E 43rd St (bet Second and Third Ave)   212/682-9760
Lunch: Mon-Fri; Dinner: Mon-Sat
Expensive

Pietro's is a steakhouse with Northern Italian cuisine; everything is cooked to order. The menu features great salads (they claim New York's best Caesar salad), steaks, chops, seafood, chicken, and an enormous selection of veal. Tell your companion not to bother getting dressed up. Bring your appetite, though, because the portions are huge. Although steaks are the best known of Pietro's dishes, you will also find ten chicken dishes and ten veal selections (marsala, cacciatore, scaloppine, piccata, *francaise*, etc.). For meat-and-potatoes lovers, there are nine different potato dishes. Prices border on expensive and the service is boisterous, but you'll certainly get your money's worth. By the way, Pietro's is very child-friendly.

PIG HEAVEN
1540 Second Ave (bet 80th and 81st St)   212/744-4333
Lunch, Dinner: Daily
Moderate

The look is French country, the food is Chinese, and pigs are everywhere. You'd never know you were in a Chinese restaurant, judging from the wood-covered walls and fresh flowers. The menu offers many hot and cold pork dishes, the best of which are spring rolls and steamed dumplings in a basket. The barbecued spare ribs are super. Other winners include beef with snow peas and flattened shrimp in shells with hot pepper sauce. A number of dishes are spicy, so be forewarned. You can look through a glass window at the kitchen and see the various items being prepared for both house consumption and takeout. Finally, someone got smart about desserts in a Chinese restaurant. Instead of the limited selection offered in most, here you can enjoy American apple pie, Peking snow balls, and a sensational frozen praline mousse.

PLAZA HOTEL PALM COURT
Plaza Hotel (59th St at Fifth Ave)   212/759-3000
Breakfast, Lunch: Mon-Sat; Tea, Supper: Daily; Brunch: Sun
Moderate

Some rooms, like some people, just get better with age, and happily this is one of them. If just one place in the city could be singled out as the embodiment of all that folks dream of as the New York of yesteryear—romantic and carefree, delicious and proper—it would have to be the Palm Court at the Plaza Hotel. The great and near-great have laughed and loved here with the likes of Eloise and Auntie and Uncle, creating thousands of memories of special times. You can enjoy breakfast, luncheon quiches, salads, wonderful teas with tea sandwiches, and caloric goodies, all to the accompaniment of classic piano and violin music. There are also super snacks, seafood salads, assorted smoked fish, and some unusual sandwiches and pastries. The fabulous Sunday buffet—the largest and most glamorous in the city—is a popular New York tradition. Many three-generation families show the young ones where they used to go in the "good old days." A real treat, day or night, and a must for visitors.

PÓ
31 Cornelia St (bet Bleecker and 4th St)   212/645-2189
Lunch: Wed-Sun; Dinner: Tues-Sun
Moderate

Mario Batali and Steve Crane have found the formula for a successful eating establishment. The space is crowded, but tables are not on top of each other. The service is family-friendly, informed, and quick. The food is hearty, imaginative and unusually tasty. The portions are king-size. The prices are right. No wonder the place is always busy. As I have noted before, if the bread is good, chances are what follows will be also; Pó has hearty, crunchy, fresh Italian bread. The pastas are huge: tagliatelle, tortellini, linguine, and always a special or two. Best dish: the braised beef, like a pot roast with chianti and balsamic glazed cipolline. Great values on tasting menus: five course pastas for $25; six-course meal for $29. Pastas and some heavier entrees (like grilled salmon) are available for lunch, along with inventive sandwiches like braised veal with garlic or marinated portabello with roasted peppers. An unusual and satisfying dessert is called *affogato* (coffee gelato in chilled cappuccino with chocolate sauce).

POLO
Westbury Hotel (Madison Ave at 69th St)   212/439-4835
Breakfast, Lunch, Dinner: Daily
Moderately expensive

This is not to be confused with Ralph Lauren's Rhinelander mansion clothing and home furnishings store just up the avenue. The only thing the two of them have in common is style and class! Polo is a distinguished, provocative, American dining room with an upper-crust clientele who appreciate consistently good food served with aplomb in a refined atmosphere. Tuna lovers will especially savor their menu: sashimi of yellowfin tuna with caperberries, olives, and panzanella as an appetizer, and seared, spice-crusted tuna with Swiss chard, haricots verts, and lemon coulis for a main course. Of course, there is much more—just as one would expect from a major hotel dining room.

PORTICO
1431 Second Ave (bet 74th and 75th St)   212/794-1032
Dinner: Daily
Moderate

There's nothing glitzy about this cozy Upper East Side retreat . . . just good honest Northern Italian family cooking! Your pastas, salads, fish and meat are all cooked individually to order. For a special treat, try the Sicilian ricotta: sticks of moist ricotta wrapped in grilled eggplant and zucchini with chopped tomato and garlic. Delicious home-made desserts will finish off a satisfying evening.

POST HOUSE
28 E 63rd St   212/935-2888
Lunch: Mon-Fri; Dinner: Daily
Moderate to expensive

The Post House is an "in" social and political hangout on East 63rd Street that serves excellent food in comfortable surroundings. The guest list usually includes many well-known names and easily recognizable faces. They are attracted, of course, by the good food and warm ambience. Hors d'oeuvres like crabmeat cocktail, lobster cocktail, and stone crabs are available in season, but the major draws are steak and lobster. Prices for the latter two entrees are definitely not in the moderate category; ditto for lamb chops. However, the quality is excellent, and the cottage fries, fried zucchini, hash browns, and onion rings are superb. Save room for the Post House chocolate box (white and dark chocolate mousse with raspberry sauce). If you can walk out under your own steam after all this, you're doing well!

PRIMAVERA
1578 First Ave (at 82nd St)   212/861-8608
Dinner: Daily
Expensive

So many times an establishment reflects a proprietor's personality and talent; nowhere is this more apparent than at Primavera. Nicola Civetta, the owner, is the epitome of class. He knows how to make you feel at home and how to present a superb Italian meal. Don't go if you're in a hurry, though. This place is for relaxed dining. I could wax eloquently with descriptions of the dishes, but you can't go wrong no matter what you order. Let Nicola choose for you, as there are specials every day. To top it all off, they have one of the most beautiful desserts anywhere: a gorgeous platter of seasonal fruit that looks too good to eat. Primavera is always busy, so reservations are a must. Before- and after-theater dinners are offered.

PROVENCE
38 MacDougal St (at Prince and Houston St)   212/475-7500
Lunch, Dinner: Daily
American Express
Moderate

You won't quickly forget a visit to Provence! This bustling region of France has been transported, in a charming manner, to Greenwich Village, where tasty and wholesome food is professionally served at sensible prices. Garlic is another reason you won't forget this bistro. If you like this taste, you'll love Provence!

The French country menu is served in several spaces: one noisy room by the bar, overlooking the Village streets; another more romantic area in the back; and a comfortable outside patio. You'll find dishes typical of the region (fish and steamed vegetables) on the menu. If you like some of the signature dishes (*pot-au-feu,* cassoulet, bouillabaisse, couscous), I'd suggest calling to find out what item is being featured that evening. Wonderful French fries come with some dishes. Top it all off with a Provence tart.

QUATORZE BIS
323 E 79th St (bet First and Second Ave)   212/535-1414
Lunch: Tues-Sun; Dinner: Daily
Moderate

The genius of Quatorze Bis is its simplicity: a limited menu, with quality food and professional service. The portions are enormous; for friends with large appetites, this is a safe bet. Lunch features a great offering of soups and sandwiches. For dinner, the *choucroute garnie* is a specialty. Other choices include grilled Black Angus sirloin, roast chicken, braised duck, fresh oysters, grilled salmon, cassoulet, and sauteed brook trout. Their specialty dessert, the chocolate regal, is superb.

QUILTY'S
177 Prince St (bet Sullivan and Thompson St)   212/254-1260
Lunch: Tues-Sat; Brunch: Sun; Dinner: Daily
Moderate

If this Soho establishment keeps up the quality evidenced at the start of its career, I predict a long life. In stark white surroundings and a relatively tiny space, all attention is on what is called new contemporary American cooking, with menu changes every season. This means appetizers like gulf shrimp steamed in parchment and country salad with fennel and blood oranges. My favorite is char-grilled baby artichokes on a skewer. Even spinach, one of my least favorite dishes, is done so well that a non-admirer like myself would have to call it a winner! The presentation of the main courses—grilled pork tenderloin, braised rabbit, rack of Colorado lamb—is first rate. Chef Katy Sparks has a taste for superb sauces, and it shows. From the warm bread basket to the tasty apple tart (for two) or the chocolate banana empanada with a caramel-rum sauce, you won't be disappointed. Crowds make reservations a must.

RAFAELLA
381 Bleecker St   212/229-9885
Dinner: Daily; Brunch: Sat, Sun
Moderate

One gets a bit nervous looking at a huge menu in a small establishment. How can they do well with all of those dishes? Well, have no worry here, though the menu is indeed all-encompassing. Takeout is available. There are a dozen appetizers, from baked oysters to stuffed mushrooms, four different soups, and over two dozen pasta dishes. Their risotto is especially delicious. There are also a dozen entrees, many from the grill. A half-dozen tasty dessert dishes complete your opportunity for a great meal at a reasonable price. This Village find is very popular with locals, so reservations are highly recommended. The youngish staff seem pleased to be of service and are particularly helpful in guiding you through the maze of goodies.

RAIN
100 W 82nd St (at Columbus Ave)   212/501-0776
Lunch, Dinner: Daily
Moderate

There's no need to travel across the Pacific; a culinary visit to Rain will do the trick—if it is only food you are concerned with, that is! Under one attractive roof, you will be treated to Vietnamese, Malaysian and Thai fare . . . some of it quite spicy, be forewarned! Spring (and summer) rolls are a personal favorite, and the ones here are superb. Of course, there is more to start with: soups, broths, noodles, steamed ravioli, and Thai crab cakes. Lots of seafood on the entree menu: popular crispy snapper, stir-fried spicy jumbo shrimp, stir-fried prawns, cracked lobster, and shrimp. Forget about the desserts, however.

RAINBOW
30 Rockefeller Plaza (General Electric Building, 65th floor)
212/632-5000
Dinner: Tues-Sun; Brunch: Sun
Expensive

On October 3rd, 1934, the Rainbow Room opened atop Rockefeller Center, giving New Yorkers and visitors a thrill found nowhere else. The lights of the city below were vibrant and visible from the opulent room, where celebrated chefs and famous bands worked to make the evening a special event. On December 29th, 1987, that scene was re-created when a spectacular two-floor facility, redone by the Rockefellers at a cost of $20 million, opened on the same site. Joe Baum has turned the 64th and 65th floors into a magnificent private club during the day and a great dining and dancing spot in the evening. The Rainbow Room, a two-story, glass-enclosed jewel, is the showpiece of the new layout. Smartly uniformed personnel serve gourmet food to the accompaniment of a ten-piece dance band. The Rainbow Promenade Bar is a smaller room, with cozy tables and light meals. Rainbow & Stars is the dining and supper club, featuring live cabaret entertainment Tuesday through Saturday. Views from all rooms are spectacular, but the one facing directly north to Central Park is breathtaking. The sights inside the rooms aren't so bad either; a million-dollar collection of modern American art adorn the walls. An evening of being pampered and spoiled is certain to be quite an occasion for even the most jaded diner. Just having their lobster thermidor is worth a visit! The Rainbow also offers party and banquet facilities. An added treat: the fabulous Sunday brunch is back!

RAO'S
455 E 114th St   212/722-6709
Dinner: Mon-Fri
No credit cards
Inexpensive

After a devastating fire, all ten tables at Rao's are back in business! And, don't be put off by rumors about Rao's, such as two-month waits for reservations. If you want to go to Rao's—an intimate old-time (1896) Italian restaurant—you should plan a bit in advance, however. The place is crowded all the time for two good reasons: the food is great, and prices are ridiculously low. Don't walk or take a car; hail a taxi and get out in front of the restaurant. When you're ready to leave, have Frankie call a local taxi service to pick you up. Frankie is a gregarious and charming host who makes you feel right at home; he'll even sit at your table while you order. Be prepared for leisurely dining. While you're waiting, enjoy the excellent bread and warm atmosphere. I've enjoyed such especially tasty offerings as the pasta and *piselli*. Veal marsala and piccata are excellent choices, as are any number of shrimp dishes. Believe it or not, the Southern fried chicken is absolutely superb; it would be my number-one choice. Don't miss this spot in Spanish Harlem. (Hint: Try appearing unannounced at the door or call the same day. Tables are often available on the spur of the moment.)

RAOUL'S
180 Prince St (bet Sullivan and Thompson St)   212/966-3518
Dinner: Daily
Moderate

There are dozens of good places to eat in Soho, and Raoul's is one of the best. The long, narrow restaurant used to be an old saloon. There are paper tablecloths and funky walls covered with a mishmash of posters, pictures, and calendars of every description. The bistro atmosphere is neighborly, friendly, and intimate, the prices moderate, and the service attentive. The trendy clientele runs the gamut from jeans to mink. The house specialties are steak au poivre and paté *maison*. Raoul's is a natural for those whose days begin when the rest of us are ready to hit the sack.

RAYMOND'S CAFE
88 Seventh Ave (bet 15th and 16th St)   212/929-1778
Lunch, Dinner: Daily; Brunch: Sat, Sun
Moderate

If some of the old haunts in the Chelsea area have lost their appeal, here is a new one with a lot going for it. Chef Raymond is obviously a perfectionist. The place is spotlessly clean with an up-to-date look, the food well presented and very tasty. Choices run the gamut from pastas and sandwiches at noon to delicious hot and cold appetizers and fresh seafood items at dinner. The weekend brunch features omelets, various linguini dishes, and warm chicken salad. A renovated private dining room is available, and there is free delivery within eight blocks. The early-bird dinner is a three-course bargain!

(THE FAMOUS) RAY'S PIZZA OF GREENWICH VILLAGE
465 Sixth Ave (at 11th St)   212/243-2253
Sun-Thurs: 11 a.m.-2 a.m.; Fri, Sat: 11 a.m.-3 a.m.
No credit cards
Inexpensive

You must be named "Ray" to be in the pizza biz in Manhattan—or so it seems. None of the pizzerias in the Big Apple are any better than this one, supposedly featuring the *real* Ray. The pizza is gourmet at its best, and you can create your own from the many toppings offered. You can have a fresh slice, a whole pizza, or a Sicilian square, all fresh. Kids love the baby pizzas. You won't leave hungry, as pizzas are a generous 18 inches. A new product has been added: take-and-bake personal pizzas (ten-inch personal pies that are all natural and handmade, with 100% real cheese). They bake in your oven in 12 minutes and are sold only at this location! Free delivery is available.

REDEYE GRILL
890 Seventh Ave (at 56th St)   212/541-9000
Lunch: Mon-Fri; Dinner: Daily; Brunch: Sat, Sun
Moderately expensive

From the day it opened, this "home of the dancing shrimp bar" has been a busy place! The name attracted my attention, because I am a frequent coast-to-coast redeye flyer; when I first entered the place, I could see I had a lot of company. The room is huge, with an attractive shrimp and seafood bar (where you can eat if you desire) near the entrance. Owner Sheldon Fireman knows how to appeal to the eye, taking a cue from his very successful nearby Trattoria dell'Arte antipasto bar. Specialties include shrimp done in all shapes and sizes, smoked salmon, a huge seafood appetizer platter (at a huge price), a smoked maki and sashimi bar, grilled fish and pastas. You can even find weiner schnitzel, burgers, smoked fish, and egg dishes. A most unattractive showing of model (non-edible) desserts detracts from what is otherwise rather decent food. The personnel are hip and helpful, but the scene is the major attraction here.

REMI
145 W 53rd St (bet Sixth and Seventh Ave)   212/581-4242
Lunch: Mon-Fri; Dinner: Daily
Moderate

Remi operates in a spectacular space in midtown, handy to hotels and theaters. In an unusually long room dominated by a dramatic 120-foot Venetian wall painting by Paulin Paris, the food soars as high as the setting. In warm weather, the doors open up and diners can enjoy sitting at tables in the adjoining atrium. Waiters, chairs, and wall fabrics all match in attractive stripes. Antipasto, like shrimp and crab cakes or roasted quail wrapped in bacon, will get you off to a delicious start. Main dishes are not of the usual variety; the spaghetti, linguine, and ravioli (stuffed with ginger and tuna) can match any house in Venice. Of course, there are fish and meat dishes for more mainstream appetites. The caramelized banana tart, served with toasted almond ice cream with caramel sauce, is enough to make anyone feel guilty. Being a gelati lover myself, I found the homemade cappuccino flavor sensational. Paddle on down (Remi means "oar") for a first-class experience!

RENÉ PUJOL
321 W 51st St   212/246-3023
Lunch, Dinner: Mon-Sat
Moderate

First things first: order a chocolate soufflé right away for dessert! René Pujol is a very attractive French restaurant that makes an ideal spot for a pre-theater dinner. It's always busy, and it's obvious that a large number of customers are regular patrons, which always speaks well of a restaurant. One reason René Pujol is so successful is that it's a family enterprise. The owner is on the job, and the waiters are superb. Housed in an old brownstone, the restaurant has two warmly decorated, cozy, and comfortable dining rooms, complete with a working fireplace in winter. There are private party rooms upstairs, and they are attractive, too. The menu is vintage French, with filet mignon, grilled Atlantic salmon, couscous, and tasty tarts being specialties of the house. They boast an award-winning wine list, too!

RESTAURANT RAPHAEL
33 W 54th St   212/582-8993
Lunch: Mon-Fri; Dinner: Mon-Sat
Expensive

You don't have to worry about quality when you take guests here. Restaurant Raphael is expensive but worth it! This elegant, intimate French restaurant, which does a few things very well, is for the serious diner. Tasty smoked salmon, gnocchi, or onion tart get you off to a great start. Main courses of lamb, veal, duck, and house-smoked red snapper are served imaginatively, with superb seasonings and sauces. There is no on-the-job training for the servers; they all know what is expected in a first-class operation. Take your time, savor the taste of contemporary French cooking, and finish with a warm, crusty chocolate cake that is as rich and delicious as any you have tasted.

RISTORANTE GRIFONE
244 E 46th St (bet Second and Third Ave)   212/490-7275
Lunch: Mon-Fri; Dinner: Mon-Sat
Moderate

It's sad but true: New Yorkers get so hyped up about trendy new places that they tend to forget about some of the old-timers that have quietly been around for awhile. Grifone is one of those. If you are looking for an attractive, comfortable, and cozy place to dine — one with impeccable service and great food — then try this place. Seemingly only neighborhood regulars have heard of it. The menu is Northern Italian; there are so many daily specials that you probably won't even look at the printed sheet. Quality never goes out of style.

RIVER CAFE
1 Water St, Brooklyn   718/522-5200
Lunch, Dinner: Daily
Moderately expensive

The River Cafe isn't in Manhattan, but it *overlooks* Manhattan. And that's the main reason to come here. The view from the window tables is fantastic, awesome, romantic — you name it. There's no other skyline like it in the world. And so, just across the East River in the shadow of the Brooklyn Bridge, the River Cafe remains an extremely popular place. Call at least a week in advance to make reservations, and be sure to ask for a window table. This is a true Yankee, flag-waving restaurant, proud of its American cuisine. There's no point in describing the dishes in detail, since you'll be looking out the window more than down at your plate. However, the seafood, lamb, and game entrees are particularly good, and desserts are rich and fresh. The Brooklyn Bridge, done in dark chocolate, is a dessert you will never forget . . . take along your camera.

ROLF'S
281 Third Ave (at 22nd St)   212/477-4750
Lunch, Dinner: Daily; Brunch: Sun
Moderate

Rolf's is a German restaurant worth remembering. A colorful spot, its several dozen tables and wooden benches fit in perfectly with the eclectic decor. Fake Tiffany lampshades, old pictures, tiny lights, strings of beads, and what-have-you add up to a charming and cozy spot for tasty German dishes. The schnitzels, goulash, sauerbraten, boiled beef, veal shanks, and bratwurst are served in ample portions with delicious potato pancakes and sauerkraut. For pancake lovers there are German, apple, and potato varieties, with applesauce on the side. For dessert, save room for the homemade apple strudel or the Black Forest cake. Rolf's is plenty good.

ROSA MEXICANO
1063 First Ave (at 58th St)   212/753-7407
Dinner: Daily (open late)
Moderate to moderately expensive

No touristy Mexican dive, this is the real thing. If you are lusting for classic Mexican cuisine, an evening here will be something special. Start with the guacamole *en molcajete;* prepared fresh at the table, it is the best around. There are also great appetizers like small tortillas filled with sauteed shredded pork, small shrimp marinated in a mustard and chili vinaigrette, and raviolis filled with sauteed chicken and served with tomato and onion. Main-course entrees include tasty (and huge) crepes filled with shrimp, and a multi-layered tortilla pie with all manner of goodies. Grilled specialties like beef short ribs and whole red snapper are tempting possibilities. Even the desserts are first-class. Choose from a traditional flan, cornmeal custard smothered with chocolate sauce, or a layered chocolate mousse cake with a taste of chili in a coffee sauce. The atmosphere is friendly, the energy level high, and the dining top-drawer.

ROSEMARIE'S
145 Duane St (bet West Broadway and Church St)
212/285-2610
Lunch: Mon-Fri; Dinner: Mon-Sat
Moderate

This is one of those hidden treasures that regulars don't talk about. Rosemarie's is indeed hidden in the junky atmosphere of a Tribeca street. Leaving the real world behind, you enter a smallish establishment that seems more like a private dining room than a restaurant. Both the lunch and dinner menus provide an excellent choice of Italian dishes, all done with the tender care of a loving kitchen. The risotto with wild mushrooms is first-class; so are the seared salmon and grilled red snapper. A *prix fixe* menu is offered at noon. Indulge yourself with homemade gelati for dessert.

SANZIN
180 Spring St (at Thompson St)   212/965-0710
Dinner: Daily; Brunch: Sun
Moderate

They call Manhattan the city that never sleeps, and that is quite obvious if you are out and about in the wee small hours for whatever reason. And if you are, and you seem to have hunger pangs, then Sanzin is a good destination (they are open until 4 a.m.). I would not call this one of the more attractive spaces in the city, but the very good food makes up for the uncomfortable atmosphere. Jonathan Sanzin has acquired superb experience at some of the city's top houses, so quality is in his veins. It shows in the food, the service, a well-trained kitchen staff, the little touches (like great bread), the flavors, the sauces. If you want some of the best scallops, tuna, grilled shrimp, or warm lobster salads in the city, come on down. The reasonable prices extend to the delicious desserts: white chocolate mousse, a molten Vahlrona chocolate soufflé cake, and an outstanding cheese plate. Sometimes it does pay to be an insomniac!

SARABETH'S KITCHEN

423 Amsterdam Ave (at 80th St)   212/496-6280
Breakfast, Lunch, Dinner: Daily

1295 Madison Ave (at 92nd St)   212/410-7335
Breakfast, Lunch, Dinner: Daily
Moderate

SARABETH'S AT THE WHITNEY

(in the Whitney Museum of American Art)
945 Madison Ave (bet 74th and 75th St)   212/570-3670
Lunch: Tues-Fri; Brunch: Sat, Sun
Moderate

You can now partake of outstanding visual and culinary art at the same time! Swinging, it is not. Reliable, it is. One is reminded of the better English tearooms when visiting one of Sarabeth's locations. The big draw is the homemade quality of all the dishes, including the baked items and the excellent desserts. They also make gourmet preserves and sell them nationally. Menu choices include excellent omelets for breakfast, a fine assortment of light items for lunch, and fish, game, or meat dishes for dinner. The chocolate truffle cake, lemon souffle, and cinnamon apple ice cream with macadamia nuts are outrageous desserts. Service is rapid and courteous. This would be an ideal place to take your mother-in-law.

SECOND AVENUE KOSHER DELICATESSEN AND RESTAURANT

156 Second Ave (at 10th St)   212/677-0606
Sun-Thurs 7 a.m.-midnight (Fri, Sat till 2 a.m.)
American Express
Inexpensive

You've heard all about the great New York delicatessens; now try one of the really authentic ones, located in the historic East Village. From the traditional *k*'s—knishes, kasha varnishkes (buckwheat groats with pasta), and kugel—to boiled beef or chicken in the pot (with noodles, carrots, and matzo balls), no one does it quite like the Lebewohl family. Portions are enormous. Homemade soups, three-decker sandwiches (tongue and hot corned beef are sensational), deli platters, complete dinners—you name it, they've got it. The smell is overwhelmingly appetizing, the atmosphere is "caring Jewish mother," and they don't mind if you take out your meal instead of dining in the colorful back room. Don't leave without trying the chopped liver or warm apple strudel.

SERENDIPITY 3

225 E 60th St   212/838-3531
Sun-Thurs: 11:30 a.m.-12:30 a.m.;
Fri: 11:30 a.m.-1 a.m.; Sat: 11:30 a.m.-2 a.m.
Moderate

The young and young-at-heart rate Serendipity 3 *numero uno* on their list of "in" places, as it has been for over 40 years. In an atmosphere of nostalgia set in a quaint, two-floor brownstone, this full-service restaurant offers a complete selection of delicious entrees, sandwiches, salads, and pastas. The real treats are the fabulous desserts, including favorites like hot fudge sundaes and frozen hot chocolate. An added pleasure is the opportunity to browse a shop loaded with gifts, books, clothing, and accessories, all very trendy. If you are planning a special gathering for the teen members of your clan, this should be the destination!

SETTE MEZZO
969 Lexington Ave (at 70th St)   212/472-0400
Lunch, Dinner: Daily
Cash only
Moderate

It's small, professional, very busy, and a great spot for people on Sunday evenings! There are no affectations at Sette Mezzo in decor, service, or food preparation. This is strictly a business operation, with the emphasis where it should be: on serving good food at reasonable prices. Don't worry about wearing your best gown or a suit and tie; many diners are informally dressed, enjoying a variety of Italian dishes done to perfection. At noon the menu is tilted toward lighter pastas and salads. In the evening, all of the grilled items are excellent. Fresh seafood is a specialty. Ask about the special pasta dishes; some of the combinations are marvelous. For more traditional Italian plates, try the breaded rack of veal, stuffed baked chicken, grilled boneless quail, or fried calamari and shrimp. All desserts are made in-house. They include several caloric cakes, tasty lemon tarts, sherbet and ice cream, and (take it from an expert) one of the best *tartufos* you've ever sinned over.

JAMES BEARD HOUSE
167 W 12th St   212/675-4984

The legendary James Beard had his roots in Oregon, so anything to do with his life is of special interest to this author. He was a familiar personality on the Oregon coast, where he delighted in serving the superb seafood for which the region is famous. When Beard died in 1985, his Greenwich Village brownstone was put on the market and purchased by a group headed by Julia Child. Now the home is run by the nonprofit James Beard Foundation as a food and wine archive, research facility, and gathering place. It is the nation's only such culinary center. There are nightly dinners anyone can attend where some of our country's best regional chefs show off their talents. For foodies, this is a great opportunity to have a one-on-one with some really interesting folks.

SHUN LEE CAFE and SHUN LEE WEST
43 W 65th St   212/769-3888
Lunch: Sat, Sun; Dinner: Daily
Moderate

Dim sum and street-food combinations are served in an informal setting adjoining Shun Lee West, an excellent old West Side Chinese restaurant. A large selection of special items is offered by a waiter who comes to your table with a rolling cart and describes the various goodies. The offerings vary from time to time, but don't miss the stuffed crab claws, if they are available. Go on to the street-food items: delicious roast pork, barbecued spare ribs, a large selection of soups and noodle and rice dishes, and a menu full of both mild and spicy entrees. Sauteed prawns with ginger and boneless duckling with walnut sauce are great choices. A vegetarian dish of shredded Chinese vegetables is cooked with rice noodles and served with a pancake (like moo shu pork, but without the meat). It's a fun place where you can try some unusual and delicious Chinese dishes. For heartier appetites, the adjoining Shun Lee West restaurant is equally good. Some of the best Chinese food in Manhattan is served here. If you come with a crowd, family-style dining is available. Prices are a bit higher in the restaurant than in the cafe.

SHUN LEE PALACE
155 E 55th St (bet Lexington and Third Ave)   212/371-8844
Lunch, Dinner: Daily
Moderate to moderately expensive

There are all manner of Chinese restaurants. The colorful Chinatown variety. The mom-and-pop corner operations. The over-Americanized establishments. The grand Chinese dining rooms. Shun Lee Palace belongs in the latter category, possessing a very classy (and refined) look. Here you are offered a delicious journey into the best of this historic cuisine. You can dine rather reasonably at lunch; a four-course *prix fixe* experience is available. Ordering from the menu (or from your captain) can be a bit pricier, but the platters are worth it. How does beggar's chicken (24 hours advance notice required), South Sea turtle in rock candy (48 hours required), crispy prawns with passion fruit, or Kung Po frog legs with hot pepper (24 hours required) sound? There's much more, including casserole specials and spa cuisine. Yes, this is dining in just about the nearest thing Manhattan has to a real Chinese palace.

SIGN OF THE DOVE
1110 Third Ave (at 65th St)   212/861-8080
Lunch: Tues-Fri; Dinner: Daily; Brunch: Sat, Sun
Moderately expensive

Although Sign of the Dove occupies a beautiful space, for a time there was a lingering question about the quality of the food and service in this up-and-down favorite of Big Apple romantics. No more. The Santos family (who also operate Yellowfingers di Nuovo, Contrapunto, Arizona 206, and the Arizona Cafe) has polished the image of this charming spot. Their bakery (Ecce Panis, next door at 1120 Third Ave) supplies the house with a great breadbasket full of goodies. The menu with specialties like seared Hudson foie gras, *oestra* caviar, grilled tuna, and rack of lamb changes seasonally. Desserts are superb: banana and mascarpone *semifredo,* chocolate soufflé cake, gingerbread with orange Bavarian cream, and much more.

SISTINA
1555 Second Ave (at 80th St)   212/861-7660
Lunch, Dinner: Daily
Moderate

Don't come here expecting beautiful decorations and extravagant surroundings. One comes to Sistina for the food, and it can't be beat. Four brothers run this outstanding Italian restaurant; one is in the kitchen, the others are out front. The only decoration is a picture of its namesake Sistine Chapel on the wall. The specialty of the house is seafood; both Mediterranean red snapper and salmon are excellent dishes. There are also the usual choices of pasta, veal, and chicken, as well as daily specials. The philosophy of this family operation is that the joy is in the eating, not the surroundings, and for that they get top marks.

SOHO KITCHEN & BAR
103 Greene St   212/925-1866
Lunch, Dinner: Daily
Inexpensive to moderate

With over 100 wines by the glass and 21 cold draft beers, this is one of the busiest bar and restaurant scenes in the lower canyons of Manhattan. They offer wine "flights," which are servings of from four to eight glasses of wine from a particular group (French, Spanish, chardonnays, and the like). Beer tastings are offered, too. The Soho Kitchen shines also in food. Besides soups, salads, and pastas, there are great hamburgers, steaks, and omelets. A delicious fruit and cheese plate is a welcome change from heavy eating. The real treat here is the pizza, made with homemade dough. You can choose from wild mushroom, pesto, vegetarian, or a fantastic Italian combination of sausage, roasted peppers, grilled eggplant, mozzarella, and provolone. Prices are very reasonable. A good place for a casual encounter.

SONIA ROSE RESTAURANT
132 Lexington Ave (bet 28th and 29th St)   212/545-1777
Lunch: Tues-Fri; Dinner: Daily
Moderate

This is one of my favorite places! Tucked away in the middle of the Indian section of Manhattan with a locked door that opens only after you are buzzed in, this is one of the most charming and delicious restaurants in the city. Named after a coral peach-color rose, it has only about a dozen tables, each with a single rose and a flickering candle. The menu is *prix fixe* for both lunch and dinner, with supplemental charges for several special items. Alison is in the front, always charming and helpful; her business partner is in the kitchen, dishing up some of the most attractive and delectable continental-style dishes you could imagine. The charm is in the exceptional attention to detail in both service and food. There is plenty of well-trained help. And the food plates are a sight for the eyes, as if an artist had arranged each bite. From the time you start with a refreshing hot towel to the ending selection of a half-dozen dessert samples, this is perfection.

SPARKS STEAKHOUSE
210 E 46th St   212/687-4855
Lunch: Mon-Fri; Dinner: Mon-Sat
Moderately expensive

You come here to eat, period. This is a well-seasoned and popular beef restaurant with little ambience. For years, businessmen have made an evening at Sparks a must, and the house has not let time erode its reputation. In the meat category, you can choose from veal and lamb chops, beef scaloppine, and medallions of beef, as well as a half-dozen steak items, like steak *fromage* (with Roquefort cheese), prime sirloin, sliced steak with sauteed onions and peppers, and top-of-the-line filet mignon. Seafood dishes are another specialty; the rainbow trout, filet of tuna, and halibut steak are as good as you'll find in most seafood houses. The lobsters are enormous, delicious, and expensive. Skip the appetizers and dessert, and concentrate on the main dish.

SPRING STREET NATURAL RESTAURANT
62 Spring St (corner Lafayette St)   212/966-0290
Daily; 11:30 a.m.-midnight; Fri-Sat until 1 a.m.
Inexpensive

Even before eating "naturally" was a big thing, the Spring Street Natural Restaurant was a leader in the field. That tradition continues today. In attractive surroundings, their kitchen provides meals prepared with fresh, unprocessed foods, with most everything cooked to order. Neighborhood residents are regular customers here, so you know the food is top-quality. Specials are offered every day, with a wide variety of organically grown salads, pastas, vegetarian meals, free-range poultry, and fresh farm-fed and line-caught fish and seafood. Brown rice and steamed veggies have been served here since 1973. The best is saved for last: Spring Street believes in great desserts, like chocolate walnut pie, honey raspberry blueberry pie, and honey pear pie. The latter two have no sugar and no dairy products.

TAPIKA
950 Eighth Ave (at 56th St)   212/397-3737
Lunch: Mon-Fri; Dinner: Daily; Brunch: Sun
Moderate

Food fads come and go; today one of the hottest trends is Southwestern cuisine. Tapika is one of the better practitioners of these tasty treats. There are such novel dishes as blackened chicken and cabbage soup or spicy bean puree, with ground chorizo, crumbled goat cheese and roasted garlic flatbread. The grilled vegetable pizza is popular; I particularly enjoyed the hot turkey sandwich with melted *caciotta* cheese, smoked bacon, corn salad and some of the best (and greaseless) French fries in town. Executive chef David Walzog has put together an interesting menu (including seafood dishes like roasted red snapper, coriander-crusted tuna, and chile-rubbed salmon) and is supported by one of the youngest and friendliest staffs in town. Accompaniments include mashed potatoes, plus wild mushroom barley for the health conscious. Being a dessert lover, I have to mention one of the best I've tried in a long time: Southwestern profiteroles *churros* with coffee ice cream and warm *ibarra* chocolate sauce. Santa Fe, here I come! An appealing three-course pre-theater dinner is available at a reasonable price.

TARTINE
253 W 11th St (at 4th St)   212/229-2611
Lunch: Tues-Fri; Dinner: Tues-Sun; Brunch: Sat, Sun
Cash only
Moderate

Tartine is your type of place if you don't mind: (1) waiting outside in the rain, cold, or heat; (2) bringing your own drinks; (3) paying cash; and (4) having your fork set back down in front of you for the next course. All of this, of course, is secondary to the fact that this tiny spot (about 30 chairs) serves some of the tastiest dishes in the Village. There are soups, salads, quiches, and omelets plus chicken, meat, and fish entrees at pleasing prices. The French fries are a treat. Desserts, Danish, and all pastries are baked on the premises. For about half the price of what you would pay uptown, you can finish your meal with splendid custard-filled tarts, a fabulous hazelnut-covered chocolate ganache, strawberry shortcake, or thinly sliced warm apples with cinnamon on puff pastry with ice cream. There is always a wait at dinner. That is a good sign, as neighbors know what is best!

TAVERN ON THE GREEN
Central Park W (at 67th St)   212/873-3200
Lunch, Dinner: Daily
Moderate to moderately expensive

Can you imagine a restaurant with over $30 million in revenue? Well, I doubt if there are any other operations in the world that can match that figure! Tavern on the Green is not just another place to eat; proprietor Warner LeRoy has created a destination attraction. The setting in Central Park, with the twinkling lights on the nearby trees and the glamour of the inside fixturing, makes for an occasion residents and visitors alike will never forget. Even though the place is big and busy, the food and the service are usually first-rate. Chef Patrick Clark is doing some innovative things with the menu. If you are planning an evening that has to be extra special, make reservations in the Crystal Room. Your relatives will love it!

THE TERRACE
400 W 119th St   212/666-9490
Lunch: Tues-Fri; Dinner: Tues-Sat
Moderate to moderately expensive

You'll have to go a bit out of the way to visit the Terrace restaurant, but it's well worth the time. The Terrace is located on the roof of a Columbia University building, providing a superb view of Manhattan. A table by the window is absolutely enchanting. An outdoor roof garden is a special feature! You'll be impressed by the classy atmosphere, beautiful table settings (attractive china, candlelight, and a single red rose), and soft dinner music. The tables are spaced nicely apart, giving one a chance to talk confidentially. Indeed, if there's one word that describes this operation, it's *style*. The food is as good as the atmosphere. The menu is classical French with some touches of Mediterranean cuisine. Special services include free valet parking and a glass-enclosed greenhouse for private parties.

13 BARROW ST
13 Barrow St (bet Seventh Ave and 4th St)   212/727-1300
Dinner: Mon-Sat
Moderate

Probably because 13 Barrow St. is not the easiest place to find, the clientele here are mainly native New Yorkers, particularly Village residents. They know, by word of mouth, that this establishment serves some of the tastiest food in the area, with good value for the dollar. The menu is interesting and different: appetizers like lobster and veggie spring rolls, steamed shrimp and chicken dumplings "in a puddle of Asian dipping sauce" or a *crepinette* of polenta with cheese, mushrooms, and tomatoes. There is a popular raw bar, good pizzas, a selection of pastas, salads, and meat (like seared filet mignon), seafood (tuna mignon), and poultry (grilled breast of organic chicken) for entrees. All are delicious, served by busy "hip" waiters in a room with a very high noise level. You must have the peanut caramel fudge brownie for dessert, along with a huge coffee cup that will allow you to linger and enjoy the passing parade.

THOMAS SCOTT'S ON BEDFORD
72 Bedford St   212/627-4011
Dinner: Tues-Sun; Brunch: Sun
Moderate

In a room that is small and quietly elegant, you will find very tasty meals served with tender loving care. The menu features American regional cuisine in a relaxed and pleasant atmosphere. Villeroy & Boch china and sparkling silver add to the graciousness of this establishment. You'll find such treats as vegetable strudel, roasted breast of duck, steaks, rack of lamb, and a daily pasta. The Sunday brunch menu features old-fashioned chicken pot pie, marinated and grilled chicken served on French bread with mozzarella, waffles, and superb omelets. Come as you are and be assured this will be one of your more pleasant dining experiences.

TOSCANA
843 Lexington Ave (bet 64th and 65th St)   212/517-2288
Lunch, Dinner: Mon-Sat
Moderate

Cozy and comfortable, Toscana does just what it has been doing for over two decades: serving delicious Tuscan food. Great dishes like *pappardelle* with duck—a signature Tuscan pasta dish made fresh daily at Toscana—brings loyal customers back no matter what the restaurant location may be. But the thing that really impresses me about this house is the friendly family feeling exhibited by all the personnel. It comes right from the top! Assisting Sergio Bitici in providing that TLC are two of Bitici's daughters. Besides providing care to diners, Bitici and his staff present some pasta dishes you won't find on most Italian restaurant menus. What else to order? Calamari in ink sauce, sweetbreads with capers, Tuscan sausage. Dessert is also a special happening, with ricotta cheese cake or *zabaglione* being my choices. Takeout and delivery is available.

TRATTORIA DELL'ARTE
900 Seventh Ave (at 57th St)   212/245-9800
Lunch: Mon-Fri; Dinner: Daily; Brunch: Sat, Sun
Moderate

Just because you don't hear a lot about a restaurant doesn't mean that it isn't of star quality. This is the case with Trattoria dell'Arte, a bustling spot across the street from Carnegie Hall. The natives surely know about it, as the place is bursting at the seams every evening. A casual cafe is at the front, seats are available at the antipasto bar in the center, and the dining room is in the rear. One would be hard-pressed to name a place at any price with tastier Italian food than is served here. The antipasto selection is large, fresh, and inviting; you can choose a platter with various accompaniments. There are daily specials, superb pasta dishes, grilled fish and meats, *focaccia* sandwiches, and salads. Wonderful pizzas are available every day. Delicious cannoli will finish off a very special meal. The atmosphere and personnel are warm and pleasant. I recommend this place without reservation—although you'd better have one if you want to sit in the dining room.

I'm not in the book-writing business to tear things down. We have enough of that all around us every day in the media. But it is my duty, as an observer and participant in the New York scene, to report accurately for my readers. You may have been reading all the hype about a Manhattan restaurant opened by three top models. Lots of glitz, lots of TV coverage. But the **Fashion Cafe** (51 Rockefeller Plaza) is an example of trendy New York taken to the ultimate. What is promoted as a place to dine turns out to be a gawker's paradise. People line up in front for some of the poorest service and the most incredibly mediocre (I'm being polite) food that I have ever encountered in the city.

TRIBECA GRILL
375 Greenwich St (at Franklin St)   212/941-3900
Lunch: Mon-Fri; Dinner: Daily; Brunch: Sun
Moderate

First, please note the address is Greenwich *Street,* not Avenue! The setting is a Tribeca warehouse. The inspiration is Robert De Niro. The bar comes from the old Maxwell's Plum restaurant. The kitchen is first-class. The genius is Drew Nieporent (of Montrachet fame). Put it all together, and you have a winner. A huge old coffee-roasting house in a decidedly unglamorous neighborhood now plays host to a very glamorous clientele who enjoy a spacious bar and dining area with new lighting, fabulous private movie-screening room upstairs, an expanded collection of paintings by Robert De Niro, Sr., and banquet facilities for private parties. The food is stylish and wholesome. Excellent salads, seafood, veal, steak, and first-rate pastas are house favorites. So are the potato pancakes! The tarts, tortes, and mousses rate with the best.

TROPICA
200 Park Ave (MetLife Building)   212/876-6767
Lunch, Dinner: Mon-Fri
Moderate

Realizing that most New Yorkers have limited time to spend over lunch, Tropica provides speedy and efficient service in addition to very tasty food. Dinner hours are a bit more relaxed in this bright, charming, tropical seafood house, which is hidden away on the concourse of the MetLife building in midtown. Featured entrees include excellent tuna (in the sushi and sashimi assortment), jumbo shrimp, and seafood salads. The bittersweet chocolate soufflé cake easily wins best dessert honors. Stick to the fish and shellfish, and you'll be more than satisfied here.

TURKISH KITCHEN
386 Third Ave (bet 27th and 28th St)   212/679-1810
Lunch: Mon-Fri; Dinner: Daily
Moderate

This is a Turkish delight that has great ethnic food, is absolutely spotless, with a staff that literally exudes TLC! There are all kinds of Turkish specialties, like zucchini pancakes, *istim kebab* (baked lamb shanks wrapped with eggplant slices, hummus, and a number of tasty baked and grilled fish dishes. You can wash it all down with sour cherry juice from Turkey or *cacik,* a homemade yogurt. (Turkish music is the Tuesday feature.) This family-run Gramercy-area operation is one of the best.

TWO TWO TWO
222 W 79th St (bet Broadway and Amsterdam Ave)   212/799-0400
Dinner: Daily
Moderate

This one is a surprise for several reasons. First, the location, which is hardly the center of great Manhattan dining. Second, the size: a smallish townhouse, with one crowded and very noisy room and several dozen tables. Oh yes, there is also a miniature cubicle (if you really want togetherness) that takes care of four persons . . . just barely. But put all that aside. Dinners are great, and service is of the same caliber. Grilled dishes are featured: tuna steak, sirloin steak, breast of chicken. By now you might have guessed that rack of lamb is one of my favorite dishes, and they do it very well at Two Two Two. The crème brûlée is superb. An early-bird *prix fixe* dinner is a good value. All in all, this is a good choice if you want to rub shoulders with Manhattan's "dining out" crowd and leave the tourists behind.

TYPHOON BREWERY
22 E 54th St   212/754-9006
Lunch, Dinner: Mon-Sat
Moderate

If you thought the streets of Bangkok were noisy, they can't compare with the din at this booming Thai eatery and brewery in midtown. The ground floor houses a huge bar with a vast selection of handcrafted American beers on draught and others (domestic and imported) in bottles. There must be several dozen of them, and they even serve a "flight" of three. Chef James Chew provides quite a culinary selection upstairs, with tasty satays like beef with Penang curry glaze and wonderful shrimp with spicy tamarind glaze. A raw bar offers oysters from both coasts, as well as Littleneck clams. All five Thai flavors—salty, sweet, sour, bitter and spicy—are featured on the menu. Take your choice of five selections in each category. Family-style platters add to the fun: great squid with garlic, delicious lemon-grass chicken, superb seared monkfish in sour tamarind broth, tasty soft-shell crab. Desserts? Not bad, for a Thai house. Banana Nana Na (warm boxes of surprises with banana ice cream) and Typhoon brûlées (Thai coffee crème, coconut jelly, apple tofu) head the list. It's crowded and fun but no place for those wearing hearing aids.

UNION SQUARE CAFE
21 E 16th St   212/243-4020
Lunch: Mon-Sat; Dinner: Mon-Sun
Moderate

Put this one down in your "must visit" list! The Stars and Stripes fly high here; Union Square Cafe is very much an American restaurant. The clientele is as varied as the food, with conversations often oriented toward the publishing world, as well-known authors and editors are in attendance at lunch. The menu is creative, the staff unusually down-to-earth, and the prices are very much within reason. Owner Danny Meyer offers such specialties as oysters Union Square, hot garlic potato chips, and wonderful black bean soup. For lunch, try the tuna club or hamburger served on a homemade poppy seed roll. Dinner entrees from the grill are always delicious (tuna, shell steak, or veal). I go here just for the homemade caramel and mocha ice cream *tartufo* or warm banana tart with honey-vanilla ice cream and macadamia-nut brittle. A Yankee winner!

UNITED NATIONS DELEGATES' DINING ROOM
United Nations Headquarters
First Ave and 46th St   212/963-7626, 212/963-7099 (banquets)
Lunch: Mon-Fri (open nights and weekends for special functions)
Moderate

Don't let the name put you off! The public can eat here and enjoy the special international atmosphere. Conversations at adjoining tables are conducted in almost every language. The setting is charming, overlooking a patio and the river. The room is large and airy, the service polite and informed. Although there is a large selection of appetizers, soups, salads, entrees, and desserts on the regular menu, the best deal is the Delegates' Buffet. A huge table of salads, baked specialties, seafoods, roasts, vegetables, cheeses, desserts, and fruits await the hungry noontime diner. (The room is used for private gatherings in the evening.) There isn't a more appetizing complete daily buffet available in New York than this one. All of the dishes are attractively presented and very tasty. After a tour of the United Nations building, this is a great place to relax, dine, and discuss world affairs!

VERBENA
54 Irving Pl (bet 17th and 18th St)   212/260-5454
Lunch: Tues-Fri (May-Sept); Dinner: Tues-Sun; Brunch: Sun
Moderately expensive

Chef-owner Diane Forley, bearing excellent credentials from the Gotham and Petrossian, now has her own charming retreat in the Gramercy Park area. Take your glasses along, as it is not an easy place to find. Once there, concentrate on the changing seasonal menu, which is heavy with herbs and all manner of healthy things in unusual combinations. For lunch there is a hefty club sandwich, pastas, omelets, and more substantial entrees. At dinner, the beer-braised ribs of beef are magnificent. The atmosphere is rather nondescript, but the sophisticated diner will be in heaven. How does roasted Black Mission figs stuffed with fig ice cream and armagnac syrup sound for dessert?

VERONICA RISTORANTE
240 W 38th St   212/764-4770
Breakfast, Lunch: Mon-Fri
Inexpensive to moderate

A friend who works in the Garment District told me about a fantastic Italian restaurant in the area but wouldn't give me the name or location because he was afraid I'd put it in my book. This piqued my interest, so I did some investigating. The restaurant turned out to be Veronica, a tiny place in the heart of the Garment District that's open only for breakfast and lunch. Run by Andrew Frisari and his wife, Ceil Hermes, this marvelous cafeteria-style restaurant serves sensational home-cooked food. What wonders they serve up! There is veal piccata, mouth-watering homemade lasagna, delicious tortellini, and chicken salad. Other favorites are pasta primavera and chicken *florentina* (breast of chicken with creamed spinach, prosciutto, mozzarella, and mushrooms in cream sauce). Low-fat and cholesterol-free items are featured. The clientele is sophisticated, the atmosphere informal and homey. Try the homemade cheesecakes or other great homemade desserts. Most items are available for takeout, individual orders, parties, and special occasions.

VESPA
1625 Second Ave (bet 84th and 85th St)   212/472-2050
Dinner: Daily
Moderate

As soon as the words *"buona sera"* greet you at the door, you're in a place where the romantic country of Italy lives! Vespa has expanded its dozen or so tables to include a bar, fireplace, and backyard garden. Some of Vespa's signature dishes are the marinated grilled baby calamari, homemade pastas, osso buco, and veal chops. Not forgotten are the superb chicken dishes and smooth risotti. Innovative specials are created daily, reflecting a variety of European classics and fresh fish. Once your entree is finished, anticipate a glorious ending. Try the chocolate pecan *crostata,* the cappuccino cheesecake, or the *sorbetti.*

VILLAGE ATELIER
436 Hudson St (corner of Morton St)   212/989-1363
Lunch: Mon-Fri; Dinner: Mon-Sat
American Express
Moderate

Romance abounds! We all know of friends whose cooking is so good that we are excited when a dinner invitation arrives. The Village Atelier is like a good neighbor whose kitchen produces some of the best dishes around. Just 12 eclectic tables make up this establishment, many showing off handsome wooden tops. Take a look at the cozy bar at the back of the room; it is just like one you would like to have in your own home! Each dish tastes like it was cooked just for you—fresh and cool when it should be, well seasoned and warm when called for. Each day a special soup is offered, along with a wide selection of salads, fish, and unusual appetizers. The roast stuffed *poussin* (baby chicken) is the best I have ever tasted. It is smothered with Montmorency cherry and maple glaze. The desserts, like fruit pies and cobblers, are all made in-house. (The owner's mom makes them.) After dinner, visit "Be-speckled Trout," a charming, old-fashioned general store down the street.

VINCE & EDDIE'S
70 W 68th St   212/721-0068
Lunch: Mon-Sat; Dinner: Daily; Brunch: Sun
Moderate

Eddie and Vince have taken rooms that housed several now-defunct operations and created a homey, well-priced bistro that is at once charming and professional. I have a problem with the long, narrow quarters, as you must pass by the rest rooms and kitchen to reach the rear dining room and garden. But never mind. The cozy fireplace near the entrance will make you feel wanted, even if the help seem a little overpowered by their attentive customers. The menu selections will please most any taste; it's nothing fancy, just good home cooking. Let's hope that 70 W 68th does not go through any more reincarnations. I like this one just the way it is!

VIVOLO
140 E 74th St   212/737-3533
Lunch: Mon-Fri; Dinner: Mon-Sat
Moderate

Angelo Vivolo has created a neighborhood classic in an old townhouse that has been converted into a charming two-story restaurant with cozy fireplaces and professional service. Now he has expanded his empire to include a specialty food shop (Cucina Vivolo) next door at 138 East 74th Street. There are great things to eat in both places. You can sit down and be pampered, have your goodies ready for takeout, or delivered to your front door free of charge (from 66th to 80th streets, York to Fifth Avenue). The Cucina menu offers wonderful Italian specialty sandwiches, made with all kinds of breads, as well as soups, cheeses, sweets, espresso, and cappuccino. In the restaurant proper there are daily specials, wonderful pastas, stuffed veal chops, and much more. The capellini primavera pasta is the house favorite. At Vivolo, there are over 60 different scaloppine preparations. Their secret is simple: they use vegetable oil when sauteing the scaloppine and add butter later when finishing the sauce. (Butter alone burns at the high temperatures required.) To romance your taste buds, this is a great choice. Save room for the cannoli alla Vivolo, a pastry filled with ricotta cream. A special *prix fixe* menu is available after 9 p.m.

VONG
200 E 54th St (bet Second and Third Ave)   212/486-9592
Lunch: Mon-Fri; Dinner: Daily
Moderate to moderately expensive

If one word could describe Jean-Georges Vongerichten, it is *inventive,* and this showplace of his is just that. The atmosphere is Thai-inspired, with romantic and appetizing overtones. The ladies will love the colors and the sexy lighting, and the gentlemen will remember the great things he does with peanut and coconut sauces. I could make a meal on just the appetizers, like chicken and coconut milk soup, the prawn satay with oyster sauce, and the raw tuna wrapped in rice paper. If the crispy squab or venison medallions are available, stop right there! Of course, there is rice for dessert: sticky rice with mango and coconut milk or crispy rice crepes with raspberries and coconut cream. I also recommend the apple crumble with spiced ice cream and green apple sorbet. Dining here is a lot cheaper than a week at Bangkok's Oriental Hotel, and honestly just as delicious!

VOULEZ-VOUS
1462 First Ave (at 76th St)   212/249-1776
Lunch: Mon-Sat; Dinner: Mon-Sun; Brunch: Sun
Moderate

You can't help but enjoy this friendly bistro, no matter what day of the week you come to savor their special dishes. A rotating menu features a different region of France every week. You can enjoy French specialties like *choucroute* Alsacienne, cassoulet Toulousain, *pot-au-feu,* bouillabaisse, and *poulet aux 40 gousses d'ail.* Jacques Rameckers makes sure that his guests are well taken care of from the time they enter until they leave, stuffed and satisfied. The Sunday brunch menu is outstanding, as is the dessert selection. The cappuccino frozen soufflé is sensational.

WALKER'S
16 N Moore St (at Varick St)   212/941-0142
Lunch, Dinner: Daily
Inexpensive

If you are looking for atmosphere and a glimpse of what old Manhattan was like, you'll love Walker's. In three crowded rooms, at tables covered with plain white paper so that diners can doodle with crayons, you will be served hearty food at agreeable prices. The regular menu includes homemade soup, salads, omelets (create your own), sandwiches, and quiches. Their burgers are big and satisfying. A dozen or so daily specials include fish and pasta dishes, as well as full entree meals. Homemade desserts (ask what's been freshly made) are unusually tasty and easy on the palate and the pocketbook. For those coming from uptown, it is a bit of a project to get here. For those in the neighborhood, it is easy to see why Walker's is a community favorite, especially on Sunday jazz nights.

Really Cheap . . . Really Funky . . . And Really Good Food!

Sound impossible? The place is **Mama's Food Shop** (200 E 3rd St, bet Ave A and B, 212/777-4425). The location is pretty unattractive, there is no table service, but those are about the only negatives. Step up to the counter and choose from a selection of already prepared dishes (fried, grilled, or roasted chicken, meat loaf, grilled salmon, veggie plate). Add some sides (smashed potatoes, macaroni and cheese, sweet potatoes, broccoli, green beans, salads, pastas, roasted carrots and beets, daily specials), and then pick a dessert (banana cream pie, cobblers, bread pudding, homemade cakes). You can either sit at one of the six tables or take out your goodies. You'll have to eat big to make the check reach $10! The best part is that all of the dishes are truly delicious, just like Mama used to make. (Hours: Mon-Sat: 11-11.)

WATER CLUB
East River at 30th St   212/683-3333
Lunch: Mon-Sat; Dinner: Daily; Buffet Brunch: Sun
Moderately expensive

Warning! Do not fill yourselves with the marvelous small scones that are made fresh in the Water Club's kitchen and served warm. They are absolutely the best things you have ever tasted, but they can be devastating to your appetite for what will be an excellent meal to follow. The Water Club presents a magnificent setting right on the river. The place is large and noisy but has a fun atmosphere that is ideal for special occasions. (They also have excellent private party facilities.) There is nightly entertainment, as well as accommodations for a drink or meal on the roof if weather permits. A large selection of seafood appetizers is available, including a great seafood gumbo served in a cast-iron crock. Entrees include numerous fish dishes, but you can also find meat and poultry items, as well as a special pasta dish. Homemade ice cream and sorbet, along with dessert soufflés and a fresh-baked apple tart, will round off a special meal. The Water Club's flourless chocolate cake, served with devil's-food ice cream and mango sauce, competes favorably with the famous one originally served at the Coach House. Be advised that getting here from the north can be confusing. (Get off FDR Drive at 23rd Street and make two left turns.)

WEST 63RD ST STEAKHOUSE
44 W 63rd St (at Broadway)   212/246-6363
Dinner: Mon-Sat
Moderately expensive to expensive

The West 63rd Street Steakhouse is where to go when the man in the family likes meat and potatoes but the lady doesn't appreciate the cigar smoke and rude waiters at the average steakhouse. This place joins the ranks of new Manhattan beef houses with an ambience all its own. In a wood-paneled atmosphere that could pass for an English manor house, it has attractive table settings far enough apart to allow privacy and a simple menu devoted to the very best in every category. The menu is much as you would expect: seafood appetizers, several soups (including a delicious lobster bisque), fresh salads, a variety of veggies and potatoes, and a dozen main courses (steaks, grilled rack of lamb, veal chops, lobster, chicken, and several seafood plates). All are fresh and of high quality. You'll pay for all of this. You don't come to a steakhouse for dessert, so forget that part!

Under the new law, smoking is permitted at the bar of a restaurant if the dining tables are at least six feet away, or if the bar area is separated from the dining area by a solid floor-to-ceiling partition. Some restaurants are able to accommodate a small number of smokers because smoking is permitted in 15% of seating as long as that seating is in the same area as the bar. But if the bar is in the same area where patrons wait for their tables, then smoking is prohibited at the bar. Stand-alone bars are also exempt from the measure.

The following restaurants do allow cigar smoking in their bar areas: **Campagna, Gallagher's, Keen's Steakhouse, La Caravelle, Mark's, Morton's of Chicago, Post House,** and the **21 Club.** The following also have areas where you can enjoy a puff: **Cafe Tabac** (232 East 9th St), **Lucky Strike** (59 Grand St), **Match** (160 Mercer St), and **Viceroy** (160 Eighth Ave). They are all aptly named, eh?

WILKINSON'S SEAFOOD RESTAURANT
1573 York Ave (bet 83rd and 84th St)   212/535-5454
Dinner: Daily; Brunch: Sun
Moderate to expensive

Everything looks good at Wilkinson's! The people look good because the lighting is flattering. The pink tones make diners look as though they've just returned from a holiday in the sun. The food looks good, because it really is. This is a delightful, intimate seafood house. It does not pretend to be everything to everybody, but it does particularly well with a somewhat limited menu. The appetizers are unique. My favorite is cured Norwegian salmon. For an entree, grilled yellow-fin tuna, grilled swordfish with mango orange chutney, and pan-roasted lobster with zucchini and tarragon sauce are good choices. You can also enjoy such delicious desserts as chocolate mousse cake or espresso and praline sandwich with caramel ice cream.

WINDOWS ON THE WORLD
One World Trade Center (107th Floor)
212/524-7000 or 212/524-7011 (reservations)

Restaurant: Lunch: Mon-Fri; Dinner: Daily; Brunch: Sun

The Greatest Bar on Earth: *Bar/Food:* Mon-Thurs: 4 p.m.-1 a.m.;
Fri: 4 p.m.-2 a.m.; Sat: Noon-2 a.m.; Sun: 11 a.m.-11 p.m.;
Sun brunch: 11 a.m.-4 p.m.; *The Skybox:* Mon-Thurs: 7 p.m.-1 a.m.;
Fri: 7 p.m.-2 a.m.; Sat: Noon-2 a.m.; Sun: 11 a.m.-11 p.m.

Cellar in the Sky: Dinner: Tues-Sat from 7 p.m.

Expensive

Windows is an "occasion" destination. And what a destination! The elevator ride up is an experience in itself. The views from the top of the city are magnificent, and the furnishings and appointments show a great deal of thought. The Greatest Bar on Earth features three separate bars (oysters, shabu-shabu, sushi) with live piano music and a full restaurant menu. Adjoining is the Skybox, a smoker-friendly place that cigar smokers will appreciate. Windows on the World is lavish, with highly attentive service and attractively presented dishes that sometimes look better than they taste. However, the menu is innovative: foie gras French toast, fillet of buffalo, roasted rabbit, and more commonplace items like filet mignon, double chicken breast, and short ribs of beef. Portions are huge, as well they might be at this price. What a dessert selection! Cheese platters, several frozen desserts, gooey pastries, fruit, custards, and ice creams. Cellar in the Sky, a separate room, is magnificent. For a private dinner, when the tab is of no consequence, this would be a superb choice. Everything here is first class: the wine, the ambience, the multicourse platters, the attention. But there is more: private dining rooms and the exclusive World Trade Center Club. Joe Baum has done it again. If you have guests in the city, they'll love a memorable visit here! Just don't forget to wear a jacket, and no jeans in the restaurant.

WOO CHON
8 W 36th St (off Fifth Ave)   212/695-0676
Daily: 24 hours
Moderate

Sparkling clean, friendly, and inviting describe this Korean restaurant, which never closes. For a group dinner, order a variety of beef, pork, or shrimp dishes and have fun broiling them right at your table. The sizzling seafood pancake is a winner! All of the accompanied dishes add a special touch to your meal. Besides the marinated barbecue items, there are such tasty delights as Oriental noodles and veggies, traditional Korean herbs and rice served in beef broth, a variety of noodle dishes, and dozens of other Far East treats. If you are unfamiliar with Korean food, the helpful personnel will do their best to explain what you are eating and how to eat it. Woo Chon is a different style of dining that is fun to experience.

You might get a kick out of the comments of some restaurant operators about us, their customers. These were printed in *Town and Country* magazine. Their main beefs: intoxicated customers; diners who race through meals (I accept this criticism personally.); those who demand menu substitutions; diners with unruly children; and customers who table-hop, use cellular phones, and don't follow smoking policies. However, the real problems are no-shows, who are very costly people; those among us who haggle about tables (the food really tastes the same no matter where you sit); the discourtesy shown by those who appear in inappropriate dress; staff abuse; complaints made to friends, rather than to management; and finally, the press (like me) who think they know it all. I assure you we don't, and I agree we can be unfair at times. Sorry about that.

YE WAVERLY INN
16 Bank St   212/929-4377
Dinner: Daily; Brunch: Sat, Sun
Moderate

Ye Waverly Inn, a picturesque Village restaurant in confined quarters, dates from the early part of the century. There are four rooms with three working fireplaces and an outside eating area with adequate though uncomfortable furnishings, but the atmosphere is truly delightful. It's a given that the food is good, because the place is always crowded and a number of famous folks often dine here. If all this is not reason enough to come to Ye Waverly, their chicken pot pie is absolutely one of the best I have ever tasted. Other possibilities include sauteed calf's liver, barbecued rack of ribs, boiled beef and horseradish sauce, and boneless chicken breast. Try the fresh fruit and cheese, corn pudding, or baked brie with sour cherry preserves. The dessert selection is excellent, especially the tasty pecan pie. I can see why legions of Village regulars flock here, and you will, too.

ZARELA
953 Second Ave (bet 50th and 51st St)   212/644-6740
Lunch: Mon-Fri; Dinner: Daily
Moderate

If you want the very best Mexican meal in New York, get yourself invited to the home of Zarela Martinez. Failing that, head for her charming and busy restaurant, a two-story building on Second Avenue. Don't let them seat you downstairs, because the second-floor dining room, complete with fireplace, is much more quaint and colorful. You'll understand how Zarela has earned her reputation for some of the best south-of-the-border cuisine when you taste her *antojitos*, which include a wonderful poblano chile stuffed with chicken and dried fruit, rolled fried-chicken tacos, and fried calamari in a spicy sauce. And there is much more: Seafood dishes such as shrimp sauteed in a spicy jalapeno sauce. Grill-smoked salmon. Several chicken dishes. Grilled duck breast with peanut-and-pumpkin-seed sauce. Delicious meat entrees, like the *jalisco*-style pork and hominy stew. There's also a great selection of Mexican side dishes like refried black beans, golden-fried cauliflower, and fried plantain slices with mole sauce. Even the desserts are special. The chocolate crepes are heaven-sent. But if you're going Mexican all the way, try the Mexican fruit-bread pudding with applejack brandy butter sauce or maple walnut cheesecake.

ZEPPOLE
186 Franklin St (bet Hudson and Greenwich St)   212/431-1114
Lunch, Dinner: Mon-Sat
Moderate

Leave it to Drew Nieporent! This master of new ideas and concepts has come up with another winner. Zeppole, named after a Southern Italian dessert of deep-fried dumplings, features attractively priced lunches of salads and sandwiches, and a full dinner menu. In addition, tasty items from the Tribakery, along with pastas, are available for carryout at the front of the restaurant. The space is airy and compelling, with brick walls and marble-top tables. You will encounter some of the most pleasant and helpful personnel around. A magnificent antipasto bar greets diners, and what a selection it is! All sandwiches are served on homemade breads. Pizza is also offered at noon. In the evening, well-presented pasta, meat and fish dishes are served. I especially recommend the grilled shrimp *spiedini* with artichokes. The signature dessert is unusual and fattening . . . but then, what dessert isn't? I suggested covering these beauties with chocolate or berries for some needed flavor. Perhaps by the time you read this they will have. The blood orange sorbet is tops.

ZOË
90 Prince St   212/966-6722
Lunch: Tues-Fri; Dinner: Mon-Sun; Brunch: Sat, Sun
Moderate

In an area that has shown more signs of life and a bit more class, Zoë operates in an old building with the original tiles and columns still visible. A wood-burning grill, wood-fueled pizza oven, and rotisserie, all in open view, add to the pleasant ambience. If you like, sit at the counter and take in all the kitchen action. The contemporary American menu features crispy calamari with Vietnamese dipping sauce, rotisserie pork loin with herbed polenta and smoked ham hocks, and magret duck breast with spaetzle and cider sauce. A great dessert: chocolate crème brûlée crunch cake. The menu changes seasonally. Pizza, pasta, and sandwiches are offered at noon.

III. Where to Find It: Museums, Tours, and Other Experiences

For some people, New York means eating out. For others, it means shopping. But you can't eat constantly and eventually even the most die-hard shoppers need a break. What's more, some people who come to New York never even set foot inside a restaurant or store. They've come for everything else: the museums, the sights, the parks, the shows . . . even the birdwatching in Central Park (one of the best places in the whole country to do it!).

Want to see the *Rocky Horror Picture Show*? Go down to Movieland Eighth Street. Interested in the Revolutionary War? Visit the Dyckman Farmhouse and the Morris-Jumel Mansion, where George Washington set up headquarters in 1776. Gothic architecture? Try the Cathedral Church of St. John the Divine and Riverside Church. Sports? Head for the Chelsea Piers sports complex. What about a game of Scrabble? Look for that and other games to rent in Bryant Park. Want tickets to see *Late Nite with David Letterman*? I've got the address.

I said it at the outset and I'll say it again: there is something for everyone in New York. Whoever you are and whatever you like, take a look through the following pages. I defy you to sit back and turn on the television instead of getting out and enjoying the wonderful diversity of this great city.

Auction Houses

Whether you're in the market for rare antiques or just looking for a fun experience, New York's auction houses can be a real treat. Look in the Weekend section of the Friday *New York Times* or the Arts and Leisure section of the Sunday *Times* for advertisements about auctions and previews at the auction houses listed below and others. The classified section of the *New York Times* also has an auction section, and all of Manhattan's auction houses are listed in the Manhattan Yellow Pages under "Auctioneers."

Before you go, think carefully about what it is that you're doing. If you just want to learn a little about the art world, simply show up, hang back, and take it all in. If you're even remotely serious about making a purchase, however, make sure you know the rules of the game before it starts. I strongly encourage you to get your hands on the auction's illustrated catalog and to take full advantage of auction previews. Attend some of the lectures and courses offered at the auction houses listed below to learn about a particular period or medium.

Finally, a word of warning: the people you will find at most auctions in New

York are professionals. They know what they are looking for, they know what they want to pay, and sometimes they know each other. Auctions in New York are a one-of-a-kind experience and can be lots of fun. Just don't go expecting to beat the professionals.

The fine art and antiques market in New York and indeed throughout the world is dominated by two houses: Christie's and Sotheby's. I've added William Doyle Galleries, a third quite reputable one, to that list.

Christie's—Located at 502 Park Avenue (at 59th Street), this British auction house specializes in fine arts and antiques. For information about upcoming auctions and previews, look for the Christie's advertisement in the *New York Times,* call its 24-hour Auctionline at 212/371-5438, or talk to a representative at 212/546-1000 during business hours. For information about lectures and courses, call 212/546-1092.

Christie's East—Located at 219 East 67th Street (between Second and Third avenues), this is the junior version of Christie's and sells what a lady at the reception desk once described to me as anything of value that "would not pass the clientele at the big Christie's." Christie's East also advertises its upcoming previews and auctions in the *New York Times.* Call 212/606-0400 during business hours for more information.

Sotheby Parke Bernet—Located at 1334 York Avenue (at 72nd Street), Sotheby's is arguably the most elite auction house in the world. Like Christie's, it's British and specializes in fine arts and antiques. Sotheby's also has a junior version, Sotheby's Arcade, where the more affordable pieces are sold. For information about upcoming previews, auctions, and exhibitions at both places, look for Sotheby's advertisement in the *New York Times.* For information about Sotheby's, call its 24-hour recording at 212/606-7245 or talk to a representative at 212/606-7000 during business hours. Out-of-towners can call 800/444-3709 to order catalogs or register for special courses and events. For information about Sotheby's Arcade, call 212/606-7409.

William Doyle Galleries—Located at 175 East 87th Street (between Lexington and Third avenues), this American-owned auction house specializes in American and British estates. For information about upcoming previews and auctions at a variety of price levels, look for its advertisement in the *New York Times* or call 212/427-2730. Make sure to ask for a copy of their newsletter. Also make time to poke around the Tag Sale next door for estate pieces not sold at the auctions. The prices in this crowded place and its "treasure auctions" are terrific. The Tag Sale's phone number is 212/410-9285.

Customs Service and Internal Revenue Service—Edison, New Jersey, is just one of a number of sites around the country where the Customs Service and Internal Revenue Service hold auctions of confiscated and abandoned merchandise. Anything and everything you can imagine is auctioned here: cars, houses, manhole covers, jukeboxes, and clothing that can only be sold for export. There's even a grab-bag section of abandoned personal property, like a suitcase that may contain the crown jewels or someone's dirty laundry. The hitch is that you won't know what's inside until you've bought it. For information about upcoming auctions, call 703/351-7887.

Films

Like any city, New York has lots of theaters for first-run movies. Indeed, many movies open in New York and Los Angeles before they open anywhere else (and, depending on the size of the crowds they draw, some never do open anywhere else). The *New Yorker, Time Out New York, New York Magazine,* and the *New York Times'* Friday Weekend section and its Sunday Arts and Leisure section are all good places to look for what is playing where at any given time. You can also call 212/777-FILM (3456) for information about what movies are showing at virtually every theater in Manhattan and, if you have a credit card, to purchase tickets in advance at many of those theaters.

If you want to combine an excellent dinner with a first-run movie for a surprisingly reasonable price, head for the **Screening Room,** at 54 Varick Street in Tribeca (212/334-2100). If you're looking for an old movie, a foreign film, an unusual documentary, a 3-D movie (in the Sony IMAX Theater), or something out of the ordinary, try calling one of the following theaters. Most of the phone numbers connect you with a recording that tells what is playing, how much tickets cost, and how to get there.

American Museum of Natural History's IMAX Theater: Central Park West bet 77th and 81st St (212/769-5034)
Angelika Film Center: 18 West Houston St, at Mercer St (212/995-2000)
Angelika 57: 225 W 57th St (212/586-1900)
Anthology Film Archives: Second Ave and 2nd St (212/505-5181)
Carnegie Hall Cinema: Seventh Ave near 57th St (212/265-2520)
Cinema Village: 12th St bet University Pl and Fifth Ave (212/924-3363)
Film Forum, Film Forum 2, and **Film Forum 3:** 209 W Houston St, near Sixth Ave (212/727-8110)
Florence Gould Hall at the French Institute: 55 E 59th St (212/355-6160)
Lincoln Center Plaza Cinemas: Broadway bet 62nd and 63rd St (212/757-2280)
Millenium Film Workshop: 66 E 4th St (212/673-0090)
Movieland Eighth Street: 36 E 8th St (212/477-6600)
Museum of Modern Art: 11 W 53rd St (212/708-9480)
Museum of Television and Radio: 25 W 52nd St (212/621-6800)
Quad Cinema: 13th St bet Fifth and Sixth Ave (212/255-8800)
Sony IMAX Theater: Broadway and 68th St (212/336-5000)
Sony Paris Theater: 4 W 58th St (212/980-5656)
Symphony Space: 2537 Broadway, at 95th St (212/864-5400)
Walter Reade Theater at Lincoln Center: 165 W 66th St (212/875-5600)
Whitney Museum of Modern Art: 945 Madison Ave, at 75th St (212/570-3676)

Like everything else, the price of movie tickets in New York tends to be higher than anywhere else in the country. (If, like 50,000 other people in New York every week, you purchase tickets over the phone and thus incur a $1.25 per ticket surcharge, you'll spend $20 for two adults!) The second-run theaters, film societies, and museums usually charge at least a little less than the first-run theaters, however. It's also worth finding out what's playing in the seven theaters at **Cineplex Odeon's Worldwide Plaza** (50th Street between Eighth and Ninth avenues). Every seat in the house is $3 and the movies, while not brand new, are surprisingly recent releases. Call 212/504-0960 for more information and showtimes.

Finally, New York is home to several popular film festivals. The best known is the Film Society of Lincoln Center's **New York Film Festival,** held in late September and early October. This annual event showcases 20 films and gets more popular every year. Call 212/875-5600 for more information. The Society also cosponsors a **New Directors/New Films** series (212/708-9480) with the Museum of Modern Art in late March. The American Museum of Natural

History showcases documentaries at the **Margaret Meade Film Festival** (212/769-5650) in early November. Those who want to see the work of famous-directors-in-the-making should check out the work of New York University's film school students at their **First-Run Film Festival** (212/924-3363) in early April. Both the **Lesbian and Gay Film Festival** at the Public Theater (212/598-7171) and the **Human Rights Watch Film Festival** at the Walter Reade Theater in Lincoln Center (212/875-5620) are held in June.

Flea Markets

Craft and street fairs pop up all over New York on the weekends in spring, summer, and fall. If you hear about or just stumble onto one, by all means go. Real New Yorkers go to these, so you'll get a very different sense of the city and the people who live here than you would walking around midtown on a weekday. You'll also find everything from woven baskets made by somebody's relatives in Nigeria to socks and underwear sold at steep discounts. You'll also find some great food. That said, however, many street fairs have begun to look alike in recent years and some neighborhoods have grown weary of them. Moreover, I suggest watching your pockets in a crowd.

In addition to these craft and street fairs, New York also has several regularly scheduled **flea markets** as well as **Greenmarkets**. (See the "Fruits, Vegetables" section of Chapter IV for more information on these wonderful markets.) Take cash, don't be embarrassed to haggle a bit, and look around before you buy anything—sometimes you'll see the same thing at more than one place. Collectors and treasure hunters often go at the beginning of the day when selections are best, while bargain hunters usually wait until the end of the day when dealers may lower prices. Remember that there are no guarantees and no refunds.

The flea markets in the following list all are relatively well-established. Be forewarned that virtually all of them shrink a bit in the colder months and some may disappear without notice. In addition, zoning changes, including one planned for the area now inhabited by the largest flea market in Manhattan, may push some of these markets into new areas or out of business entirely. You might look under "Flea Markets" in the special "Antiques" classified listing in the Friday *New York Times'* Weekend section before setting out.

Annex Antiques Fair and Flea Market—You'll find this sprawling market in parking lots on Sixth Avenue from 24th to 26th streets. The antiques section is closer to 26th Street and is open from 9 a.m. to 5 p.m. on both Saturdays and Sundays, while the flea market is closer to 24th Street and is open from 9 a.m. to 5 p.m. on Sunday only. Admission to the antiques section is $1, but the flea market is free.

The Garage—Run by the same folks who run the Annex Antiques Fair and Flea Market, this indoor space is home to all sorts of dealers. Located at 112 West 25th Street, near Sixth Avenue, it's open weekends from 9 a.m. to 5 p.m.

Intermediate School 44 Flea Market—Inside and outside Public School 44 on Columbus Avenue between 76th and 77th streets, this very popular market is held on Sundays from 10 a.m. to 5:30 p.m. Look for one of the city's Greenmarkets here, too.

Malcolm Shabazz Harlem Market—On Malcolm X Boulevard between 116th and 117th streets, this lively market is home to many African and African-American vendors who used to camp out along 125th Street in Harlem. It's open all week.

Public School 183 Flea Market—Open Saturdays from 9 a.m. to 5:30 p.m., this decidedly upscale flea market is known for its antiques. It's held at Public School 183, on East 67th Street between First and York avenues.

Soho/Canal Street Flea Market—Held at the intersection of Broadway and Grand Street, this market is open Saturdays and Sundays from 9 a.m. to 5 p.m.

Union Square Farmers Market—This is the grandfather of all Greenmarkets. Held all year on Wednesdays, Fridays, and Saturdays at the north end of Union Square (between Broadway and Park Avenue South on 17th Street), this popular market offers all sorts of fresh goodies: seasonal produce, baked goods, jams, jellies, and flowers.

Galleries

When people think of art, they sometimes think only of museums. While the art museums in New York are exceptional, anybody interested in art ought to think about visiting commercial galleries, too. Galleries are places where potential buyers and admirers alike can look at the work of what are usually contemporary and other 20th-century artists (a few galleries specialize in older work) at their own pace and without charge. Let me stress "admirers alike." A lot of people are afraid to go into galleries because they think they'll be expected to buy something or be treated poorly if they don't know everything there is to know about art. That just isn't true, and an afternoon of "gallery hopping" can be lots of fun.

First decide what kind of art you want to see. New York has long been considered the center of the contemporary art world, and it follows that the city is home to literally hundreds of galleries of all sizes and styles. In general, the more formal and conventional galleries are on or close to Madison Avenue on the Upper East Side and on both East and West 57th Street. (You need to look up to find a lot of them, particularly on 57th Street.) Some of the less formal, avant-garde galleries tend to be in Soho on West Broadway between Broome and Houston streets, on Greene Street between Prince and Houston streets, and on Prince Street between Greene Street and West Broadway. Some of the latter are also in Tribeca. Lately, the west end of Chelsea, around the Dia Center for the Arts on and around West 22nd Street and Tenth Avenue, has become the city's hottest gallery spot.

If you want to get a sense of the diversity of the New York gallery scene, sample a couple galleries in each neighborhood. In Soho, you can try **Leo Castelli** and **Sonnebend** (both at 420 West Broadway), **Pace Wildenstein** (142 Greene Street), and **Holly Solomon** (172 Mercer Street). In midtown, try **Mary Boone** (745 Fifth Avenue), **Marlborough** (40 West 57th Street), **Galerie St. Etienne** (24 West 57th Street), and **Andre Emmerich** (41 East 57th Street). In Chelsea, check out **Matthew Marks** (522 West 22nd Street), **Barbara Gladstone** (513-523 West 24th Street), and **Greene/Naftali** (526 West 26th Street). Of course you can just wander the neighborhoods and enter whichever galleries appeal to you!

For a free directory of galleries that belong to the Art Dealers Association of America (not all of them do) and their specialties, write the association at 575 Madison Avenue, New York, NY, 10022 or call 212/940-8590. You can also ask at any gallery for a free copy of the *Art Now Gallery Guide,* a monthly listing of exhibits at several hundred Manhattan galleries.

Galleries are typically known for the artists they showcase. If you are interested in the work of just one artist, both the *New Yorker* and *New York*

Magazine contain listings of gallery shows by artists' names. Be sure to look at the dates, as shows sometimes change quickly. *Time Out New York* has a geographical list of galleries in its "Arts" section complete with descriptions of current shows. *New York Magazine* also lists the names of galleries displaying the work of several artists, and the Sunday *New York Times'* Arts and Leisure section devotes several pages of advertisements from various galleries and reviews of new shows. The *Times'* Friday Weekend section also contains reviews, as do *Art in America* and *Arts* magazines.

Most galleries are open Tuesday through Saturday from 10 or 11 a.m. to 5 or 6 p.m. Some close for a couple of weeks during the summer.

Museums

New York is home to some of the most famous, most interesting, and most unusual museums in the world. With one exception, I've limited the following list to museums in Manhattan, but that does not mean that museums in the other boroughs aren't worth exploring. The **Brooklyn Museum** (718/638-5000), for example, is among the oldest and largest art museums in the country and has one of the best Egyptian collections in the world. The **New York Hall of Science** in Queens (718/699-0005), the **Museum of the Moving Image** in Queens (718/784-0077), the **Staten Island Children's Museum** (718/273-2060), the **Bronx Zoo** (718/367-1010), and the **New York Botanical Garden** (718/817-8700) also have lots of fans.

Even if you aren't a museum person, take a look through the following list. I can't imagine that you won't find at least one place that strikes a chord. Most of them have gift shops, the larger and more interesting of which I've described in the "Museum and Library Shops" section in Chapter VI. For a list of the best museums for children, see the "Manhattan for Children" section in Chapter VII. And for a complete list of museums offering free admission or special free hours, see the "Manhattan for Free" section in Chapter VII. For museums off the beaten tourist path, I've provided suggestions about how to get there.

As a general rule, I suggest calling ahead. Some of the smaller museums and galleries close for a couple days or even a couple weeks when exhibits are being changed, and all sometimes change their hours. If you want to know about current exhibits, look in the front of the *New Yorker,* the back of *New York Magazine,* the "Arts" section of *Time Out New York,* or *Museums New York.* The latter is devoted entirely to the goings-on at all the various museums in the five boroughs and beyond.

ABIGAIL ADAMS SMITH MUSEUM
421 E 61st St (bet First and York Ave)   212/838-6878

This little (and little-known) gem will transport you back to the days when midtown Manhattan was a country escape for New Yorkers living at the southern end of the island. Constructed in 1799 as a carriage house for a 23-acre estate and converted into the Mount Vernon Hotel in 1826, this stone building sits on land originally owned by Colonel William Smith and his wife, Abigail Adams Smith, daughter of President John Adams. The house is run by the Colonial Dames of America, the oldest women's genealogical society in the United States, and preserved in its hotel incarnation. Because both staff and volunteers are as enthusiastic as they are knowledgeable, part of the pleasure of a visit is that someone walks around the house with guests to answer any questions about the hotel or the period. Anyone interested in social history or antiques ought to put this well-run and interesting museum at the top of the itinerary. The tour lasts about half an hour. **Hours:** Tuesday through Sunday from 11 to 4 (Tuesday evenings in July until 9). The museum is closed in August. **Admission:** $3 for adults, $2 for senior citizens and students, free for children under 12.

ALTERNATIVE MUSEUM
594 Broadway (bet Houston and Prince St)   212/966-4444

Located in Suite 402 of a building largely occupied by commercial galleries, this small, artist-run museum definitely merits a visit if you're spending time in Soho and are interested in contemporary art. (Also check out the New Museum of Contemporary Art across the street.) The Alternative Museum was founded in 1975 and is dedicated to exhibiting "the work of emerging and mid-career artists who have been under-recognized or disenfranchised because of ideology, race, gender, or economic inequality." In addition to its changing exhibits, the museum sponsors a variety of lectures, concerts, and other events. **Hours:** Tuesday through Saturday from noon to 6. **Admission:** free (although a contribution to this nonprofit museum is encouraged).

AMERICAN BIBLE SOCIETY
1865 Broadway (at 61st St)   212/408-1200

The American Bible Society is an organization dedicated to making the Christian Bible readily available to people in this country and around the world. Founded in 1816, ABS has distributed more than 6.9 billion Bibles and other portions of Scripture. If you're interested in religious history, the small gallery on the second floor of its headquarters is well worth the trip. In addition to Bibles and other material printed in Amharic, Chiyo, Quichua, and other exotic languages, the gallery displays a portion of a Torah scroll that was found after the flooding of Kai Feng Fu in China in 1643. The second floor also houses a research library. **Hours:** Monday through Friday from 9:30 to 4:30. **Admission:** free.

AMERICAN CRAFT MUSEUM
40 W 53rd St (bet Fifth and Sixth Ave)   212/956-3535

This is one of those museums that you'll either love or wonder why you came. Its modern galleries are wide open and well lit, and the atmosphere is decidedly unhurried. Both its changing displays and permanent collection are dedicated to crafts of the 20th century—quilts, baskets, pottery, clay sculpture, and other media that fit under that umbrella. If your definition of art is limited to the great masters, stick to Museum Mile along Fifth Avenue or go out on a limb at the Museum of Modern Art across the street. But if your definition of art includes innovative crafts, or if you just want to expand your horizons, by all means make time for a visit here. Call before coming and ask for the Information Department if you're interested in taking a tour. The helpful folks in that department or at the front desk can also give you information about upcoming lectures, films, and family workshops. **Hours:** Tuesday through Sunday from 10 to 6 (Thursday until 8). **Admission:** $5 for adults, $2.50 for senior citizens and students with ID cards, free for children under 12.

AMERICAN MUSEUM OF NATURAL HISTORY
Central Park West bet 77th and 81st St   212/769-5100

If ever there was a perfect answer for what to do with children on a rainy day, this sprawling collection of 30 million (yes, *million*!) artifacts and specimens is it. You could spend an entire day on any one of the museum's four floors. (The main entrance puts you on the second floor.) I suggest getting a floor plan at the information desk and planning what you want to see if time is limited. I also suggest going during the week to avoid what are often overwhelming weekend crowds. The exhibits include recently restored and expanded dinosaur and fossil halls; a hall of ocean life, complete with a whale suspended from the ceiling; one devoted to African mammals, complete with elephants; gems and minerals (keep an eye out for the Star of India sapphire); and fascinating displays about different cultures and people from all over the globe. On top of all that, construction of a new planetarium and the Center for the Planet Earth is underway. (The scheduled opening is the turn of the century.) Guided tours of the museum's highlights leave from the African Mammals Hall at 10:15, 11:15, 1:15, 2:15, and 3:15 (Saturdays and Sundays at 12:15 as well). If you would rather go it alone and don't have small children in tow, spend a little extra for an "audio expedition" of 50 of the museum's greatest treasures. If you're a member who's contributed at least $100, look into the "Walk on the Wild Side" exercise program in the museum on weekday mornings! You'll find a decidedly downscale cafeteria and the more pleasant Garden Cafe on the lower level, and the Whale's Lair for drinks and snacks under the whale (where else?) on weekends and holidays. Request information about the IMAX Theater (212/769-5034) at the information desk. It costs extra, but whatever is showing is bound to be excellent. **Hours:** Sunday through Thursday from 10 to 5:45, Friday and Saturday from 10 to 8:45. **Admission:** $6 for adults, $4 for students and senior citizens, and $3 for children between 2 and 12 are "suggested" and indeed presented as if they're required, but you can pay whatever you feel is appropriate.

AMERICAN NUMISMATIC SOCIETY
Audubon Terrace (Broadway bet 155th and 156th St)   212/234-3130

Audubon Terrace in Washington Heights isn't exactly on most New York tourist maps, particularly since the National Museum of the American Indian moved into its new location on the other end of Manhattan. Besides, a place with a name like the American Numismatic Society certainly isn't going to attract great crowds. But if you're interested in the history of money or just like unusual museums, put this fascinating place on your list of places to visit. Founded in 1858, the Society is dedicated to the study of money and maintains an unusually large and diverse collection of more than half a million coins and medallions. Call ahead to express an interest in a particular period or region, and one of the museum's curators will personally arrange to show you certain pieces. You can take either the M4 bus up Madison Avenue or the M5 bus up Sixth Avenue to get to the museum and then take either back down to Fifth Avenue in midtown. **Hours:** Tuesday through Saturday from 9 to 4:30, Sunday from 1 to 4. **Admission:** free.

AMERICAS SOCIETY ART GALLERY
680 Park Ave (at 68th St)   212/249-8950

This classy operation is housed in a beautiful neoclassical townhouse that once served as home to the Soviet Union's delegation to the United Nations. Its relatively small gallery showcases a variety of changing exhibits of art from Latin America, the Caribbean, and Canada. The Americas Society has no permanent collection of its own, so the work in the exhibitions is all on loan from museums and other collections. Call for information on its various series and programs. **Hours:** Tuesday through Sunday from noon to 6. **Admission:** free.

ASIA SOCIETY GALLERY
725 Park Ave (bet 70th and 71st St)   212/288-6400

The Asia Society is a nonprofit organization founded in 1956 to foster mutual understanding between Asian nations and the United States. One of the many ways it reaches out to the public is through changing art exhibitions in its marvelous gallery. Gallery talks are held Tuesday through Saturday at 12:30, Thursdays at 6:30, and Sunday at 2:30. Call ahead to be sure an exhibition is showing when you plan to visit. For information about concerts, lectures, and other special programs, drop by the information desk in the lobby or call the event line at 212/517-6397. The Asia Society also runs a shuttle service on Saturday to and from the impressive Isamu Noguchi Garden Museum in Long Island City. (Call that museum from the beginning of April through the end of October at 718/721-1932 for details.) **Hours:** Monday through Friday from 10 to 6:30, Saturday from 11 to 6, and Sunday from noon to 5. **Admission:** $3 for adults, $1 for students and senior citizens, and free for children under 12 accompanied by an adult.

BARD GRADUATE CENTER FOR STUDIES IN THE DECORATIVE ARTS
18 West 86th Street (bet Central Park West and Columbus Ave)
212/501-3000

A welcome newcomer to the New York art world, the Bard Graduate Center devotes the first two floors of its elegant *beaux-arts* townhouse to changing exhibitions of home furnishings and other decorative arts. As is the case in many smaller museums and galleries in New York, half the pleasure of a visit here is simply being inside the building itself. Call ahead to learn about tours and public lectures. **Hours:** Tuesday through Sunday from 11 to 5 (Thursday until 8). **Admission:** $2 for adults, $1 for senior citizens, free for children under 12 accompanied by an adult.

CHILDREN'S MUSEUM OF MANHATTAN
212 W 83rd St (bet Broadway and Amsterdam Ave)   212/721-1234

I really want to love this place. It sounds wonderful on paper and it *has* improved in recent years. There are buttons to push, ladders to climb, all sorts of things to sort, touch, and examine, an early childhood center and play space, and even a media center with audiovisual equipment and other communication technologies for children six and older. The changing exhibits are often creative and well designed — a recent one devoted to Dr. Seuss was particularly fun. You'll also find storytelling, workshops, and other events going on through the day. But the museum's space is lousy, its layout can be confusing, and some of the staff people seem as bored as the legions of nannies who bring their charges here during the week. Also be forewarned that the museum gets very crowded and unpleasantly warm on weekends and rainy days. Strollers must be parked at the entrance and food is not allowed in the museum. Look for a monthly calendar of events by the front door or the daily schedule posted by the elevator. **Hours:** Wednesday through Sunday from 10 to 5. **Admission:** $5 for adults and children, $2.50 for senior citizens, free for children under one. (Many workshops and performances cost an additional dollar or two.)

CHINA INSTITUTE GALLERY

125 E 65th St (bet Lexington and Park Ave)   212/744-8181

The extremely small but interesting gallery is run by the non-partisan China Institute in America and housed on the first floor of the Institute's lovely brownstone. In addition to the changing exhibits of Chinese art and artifacts, the gallery has a tiny gift shop specializing in books about China and Chinese art. The China Institute itself offers a wide array of educational programs, lectures, tours, performances, and language courses. **Hours:** Monday, Wednesday, Thursday, Friday, and Saturday from 10 to 5; Tuesday from 10 to 8; Sunday from 1 to 5. **Admission:** $5 is suggested.

THE CLOISTERS

Fort Tryon Park   212/923-3700

Perhaps the finest medieval art museum in the world, the Cloisters is also one of the quietest and most beautiful places in all of Manhattan. Built on land donated by John D. Rockefeller, Jr., in the late 1930s, the museum incorporates large sections of cloisters and other pieces of buildings brought to the United States from southern France by sculptor George Grey Barnard. His collection was purchased by the Metropolitan Museum of Art with money donated for that purpose by Rockefeller in 1925, and The Cloisters is still part of the Metropolitan. The truly spectacular collection also includes carved wood and ivory, tapestries, and sculptures. The museum is rarely crowded, and its outdoor terrace offers a great view of the Hudson River. Though it takes about an hour each way, the M4 bus brings you right to the front entrance from Madison Avenue in midtown and back again via Fifth Avenue. **Hours:** Tuesday through Sunday from 9:30 to 5:30 (5 from November through February). **Admission:** $8 for adults, $4 for students and senior citizens, free for children under 12 when accompanied by an adult. The fee entitles you to same-day admission to the Metropolitan Museum of Art.

CON ED ENERGY MUSEUM

145 E 14th St (bet Irving Pl and Third Ave)   212/460-6244

If you're interested in New York's history or in learning a little bit about what makes the city work, this relatively small but fascinating museum is a real treat. It's run by Consolidated Edison, the folks whose electricity lines power New York, and briefly but thoughtfully tells the story of how Thomas Edison changed the world forever when he introduced his new invention to New York a little more than a century ago. The various displays offer a glimpse into a time when some of the city's few elevators were actually powered by live horses housed in the basements of buildings! Those displays also let you see what factories and kitchens looked like before and after electricity was introduced. The last part of the museum is devoted to the future of energy and covers such topics as solar power and conservation. **Hours:** Tuesday through Saturday from 9 to 5. **Admission:** free.

COOPER-HEWITT NATIONAL MUSEUM OF DESIGN

2 E 91st St (bet Fifth and Madison Ave)   212/860-6868

Founded by three granddaughters of Peter Cooper (their last name was Hewitt) as the Cooper Union Museum for the Arts of Decoration just before the turn of the century, this exceptional museum became part of the Smithsonian Institution in 1967 and moved into Andrew Carnegie's Fifth Avenue mansion in 1976.

Drawing from a permanent collection of almost a quarter million pieces involving every imaginable aspect of design, the museum's exhibitions change frequently. Outstanding lectures, workshops, tours, and special gallery talks are developed around the exhibitions. They often are free but usually require advance reservations (call 212/860-6321 for more information). Of course, part of the pleasure of a visit to the recently renovated Cooper-Hewitt is seeing the Carnegie Mansion itself, including the spectacularly beautiful Great Hall (where an organ was once played at 8 a.m. every morning to wake up the household!). **Hours:** Tuesday from 10 to 9, Wednesday through Saturday from 10 to 5, and Sunday from noon to 5. **Admission:** $3 for adults, $1.50 for senior citizens and students over 12, free for children under 12 accompanied by an adult and associate members of the Smithsonian. It's also free to everybody on Tuesday evening between 5 and 9.

DAHESH MUSEUM
601 Fifth Ave (Bet 48th and 49th St, 2nd floor)   212/759-0606

A new museum in New York? On Fifth Avenue in midtown? Thanks to the late Lebanese writer and philosopher after whom the museum is named, this tiny space is a showcase for popular French and other European artists of the 19th and early 20th centuries. Dr. Dahesh, who died in 1984, was an art collector extraordinaire who dreamed of opening a public museum for European art in Beirut. Sadly, that never came to pass, but his wondrous collection found its way to New York and the result is this museum. The changing exhibits, most of them drawn from the Dahesh collection, are consistently interesting, and the gallery space itself offers a quiet respite from the hustle of midtown. If you're interested in gallery talks, lectures on related subjects, or the museum's programs for families, be sure to ask for a copy of the latest *Dahesh Muse*. **Hours:** Tuesday through Saturday from 11 to 6. **Admission:** free.

DIA CENTER FOR THE ARTS
548 W 22nd St   212/989-5912

This renovated warehouse is the anchor of the growing art scene in Chelsea and an exhibition space for large-scale projects designed specifically for it. Those interested in Minimalism, Conceptualism, and Earth Art know that the Dia Center—and the Dia Art Foundation before it—has been a major force in supporting the careers of many of the world's most innovative contemporary artists. If those schools are your thing, the four floors of this museum and its rooftop will be a real treat. If they aren't, you'll wonder why in heaven's name you made the trip all the way over to the edge of the Hudson River! The Dia Center also sponsors lectures, poetry readings, and conferences, as well as several long-term installations. These include the Dan Flavin Art Institute in Bridgehampton, the Cy Twombly Gallery in Houston, and the Andy Warhol Museum in Pittsburgh. **Hours:** Thursday through Sunday from noon to 6. **Admission:** $4 for adults, $2 for students and senior citizens.

DYCKMAN FARMHOUSE
4881 Broadway (at 204th St)   212/304-9422

This is the last surviving example of the sort of farmhouse built all over New York well into the 19th century. It is a real treat for anybody interested in the city's history or the Revolutionary War period. The Dyckman family emigrated to what were then the American colonies from the Netherlands in the 17th century and had a thriving orchard in this area before the Revolutionary War. They were forced to flee during the war, however, and both their home and orchard were occupied and ultimately destroyed by British troops. When they returned to the area in 1784, the Dyckmans built this home and later used the surrounding area for grazing cattle on their way to market downtown. The adjoining buildings housing the slave quarters and outdoor kitchen no longer exist, but the house itself has been preserved much as it was then. You'll find several rooms with period furniture (some of which actually belonged to the Dyckmans) on the first and second floors and a kitchen in the basement. Probably the most interesting room in the house is the Relic Room, which houses a display of such Revolutionary War artifacts as a general's uniform, a tattered American flag with 13 stars, cannonballs, and bayonets. All of the items on display in this room were excavated from around the house at the beginning of this century. The cherry tree and flowers on the lovely grounds surrounding the house come alive during the spring and early summer. You can get to Dyckman House from midtown by taking the M1 bus up Madison Avenue to East 125th Street and transfering to the M100. The M100 will drop you off right in front of Dyckman House and pick you up again on the corner of 204th Street and Broadway for a return trip down Fifth Avenue). You can also get there by taking the A subway to 207th Street and walking south to 204th Street on Broadway. It's actually only a block, as there are no 205th and 206th Streets. **Hours:** Tuesday through Sunday from 11 to 4. **Admission:** free.

EL MUSEO DEL BARRIO
1230 Fifth Ave (near 105th St)   212/831-7272

El Museo del Barrio—Spanish for "Museum of the Neighborhood"—is the only museum New York and one of only four in the United States devoted exclusively to the art and culture of Latin America. Located at the southern end of Spanish Harlem and the northern tip of Museum Mile, El Museo is in the northern part of an old and rather odd building that runs the length of the block between East 104th and 105th streets. El Museo, a special place clearly devoted to the people and cultures of the surrounding community, has undergone a lot of welcome renovation in recent years and is currently in the process of expanding. It features both permanent and changing exhibitions of contemporary and traditional art, and sponsors all sorts of film festivals, lectures, workshops, and other outreach programs. **Hours:** Wednesday through Sunday from 11 to 5. Call for extended summer hours from May through September. **Admission:** $4 for adults, $2 for students with identification and senior citizens. $1 for children under 12.

ELLIS ISLAND MUSEUM OF AMERICAN IMMIGRATION
Ellis Island   212/363-3200

Think of immigration to the United States and Ellis Island comes to mind. At least one in every four Americans today can trace one or more relatives who came through the immigration processing center on the island between 1892 and 1954. Whether or not you're one of them, this is one of New York's "must see" museums. Located in the shadow of the Statue of Liberty in New York Harbor, Ellis Island was all but abandoned until it was restored and opened to the public in 1990. Walk through the moving display of photographs and artifacts brought to this country by immigrants, and you'll inevitably come across someone telling his children or grandchildren about what his family brought when they came to this country. Other displays include one that retraces the steps the immigrants took once they arrived on the island and another discussing immigration in the U.S. through the present. An Academy Award-winning film by Charles Guggenheim—*Island of Hope, Island of Tears*—is shown frequently and is well worth watching. To get to Ellis Island, take a Circle Line ferry from Battery Park. (The ticket booth is in Castle Clinton, and the ferry makes stops at both Ellis Island and the Statue of Liberty.) The best time to go is early in the morning on a weekday, as lines can get pretty long in the afternoon and on Saturday and Sunday. The least expensive and most efficient way to get to Battery Park is by taking the 1 or the 9 subway to the South Ferry stop. (Be sure to get in one of the front cars, as only a few doors open at this stop.) **Hours:** 9:30 to 5 in the winter and 9:30 to 5:30 in the summer, although the last ferry leaves at about 3 or 3:30. **Admission:** A price hike is in the works as this is going to the publisher, so I suggest calling the ferry service (212/269-5755) for fare and schedule information. Admission to both Ellis Island and the Statue of Liberty is included in the price of a ferry ticket.

EQUITABLE GALLERY
787 Seventh Ave (bet 51st and 52nd St)   212/554-4818

Perhaps the nicest of several gallery spaces in the lobbies of midtown office buildings, this one is located in the right-hand corner of the Equitable Center's soaring atrium. It consists of four interconnected rooms that play host to a variety of consistently well-conceived exhibitions. While you're here, make sure to rest your feet in the unusually pleasant and peaceful sitting area in the building's atrium while looking at Roy Lichtenstein's five-story *Mural with Blue Brushstroke*. The Brooklyn Museum runs a small shop to the right of the gallery entrance. **Hours:** Monday through Friday from 11 to 6, Saturday from noon to 5. **Admission:** free.

FORBES MAGAZINE GALLERIES
62 Fifth Ave (bet 12th and 13th St)   212/206-5548

What do 10,000 toy soldiers, 12 Faberge eggs, documents written by Abraham Lincoln and other American presidents, and an Imperial Russian diadem have in common? They're in the Forbes Magazine Galleries (on the first floor of the *Forbes* magazine building). Assuming you're among the 900 people allowed in on a first-come, first-served basis every day, you can view them for free. These small galleries can get a little cramped on Saturday, but the collections assembled over the years by the late Malcolm Forbes and his sons definitely have something for everyone. Children under 16 are not allowed in without an adult, and no more than four children can accompany one adult. Call ahead to make a reservation if you want to take one of the guided tours offered on Thursdays. **Hours:** Tuesday through Saturday from 10 to 4. **Admission:** free.

FRAUNCES TAVERN MUSEUM
54 Pearl St (at Broad St)   212/425-1778

If you're interested in Colonial and early U.S. history and culture, you'll really enjoy this often overlooked museum. The site of General George Washington's farewell address to his officers in 1783 and an anti-British meeting place before and during the Revolutionary War, this tavern has seen many generations and a lot of history come and go through its doors. If you open the front door of the Fraunces Tavern only to find yourself in a restaurant, don't think you've gone to the wrong place! The first floor of the building is home to one of Wall Street's more pleasant places to eat. Just proceed straight ahead and up the stairs.

On the second and third floors, you'll find period rooms (including the room in which General Washington gave his address) with marvelous antique furniture and excellent explanations; a fascinating collection including newspapers, glasses, a cider mill, and a wine press from the late 18th and early 19th centuries; and changing exhibitions. Make sure to ask about movies, special events, and walking tours. **Hours:** Monday through Friday from 10 to 4:45, Saturday and Sunday from noon to 4. **Admission:** $2.50 for adults, $1 for students, senior citizens, and children under 12.

THE FRICK COLLECTION
1 E 70th St (bet Fifth and Madison Ave)   212/288-0700

The home of the late Henry Clay Frick, this exceptionally elegant and peaceful mansion displays Frick's collection of paintings, sculpture, rugs, furniture, porcelain, and other artwork. Take time to wander around and look at the mansion itself — the moldings, the floors, the ceilings, the light fixtures, and the stairs — as well as the art. Built in 1914, this is one of the last great mansions on Fifth Avenue. Unlike the guards at a lot of other museums, the sentinels here are very knowledgeable and obviously proud of the building and the collection. If you ask, they'll even tell you about the giant heat lamps that are brought out every night for the plants and flowers in the carriage court turned inner garden! Because the museum's temperature is kept at a constant 70 degrees, you'll be glad they require you to check your coat (at no charge). A special exhibition is held downstairs two or three months out of each year, so be sure to ask about it. Although not a place to take children (those under 10 are not allowed), this exceptionally beautiful and uncrowded museum is a real treat for art buffs and oglers alike. **Hours:** Tuesday through Saturday from 10 to 6, Sunday from 1 to 6. **Admission:** $5 for adults, $3 for students with identification and senior citizens.

THE GROLIER CLUB
47 E 60th St (bet Fifth and Madison Ave)   212/838-6690

You won't find any bells or whistles here, and it's definitely not for the kids. Dedicated to the study and preservation of books, the Grolier Club is an old, reserved, and elegant institution. It mounts a variety of exhibits on such esoteric topics as the history of Greek translation in a small gallery on the first floor of its townhouse for its members and anybody else who happens to be interested. Check in with the receptionist immediately inside the front hall before heading back to the gallery. **Hours:** Monday through Saturday from 10 to 5. **Admission:** free.

THE GUGGENHEIM MUSEUMS
1071 Fifth Ave (bet 88th and 89th St)   212/423-3500
575 Broadway (at Prince St)

Housed in an enormous white spiral designed by Frank Lloyd Wright, the Solomon R. Guggenheim Museum is as famous for its building as for its collection. That is saying a lot, given a collection of 20th-century art that is arguably the best in the world. A second Guggenheim location in Soho opened in 1992 to showcase parts of the museum's permanent collection as well as special exhibitions designed to complement those at the Fifth Avenue location. A third Guggenheim museum, the Peggy Guggenheim Collection, is located in Venice — but that's another trip! The works displayed at these museums offer a who's who of 20th-century art: Chagall, Miro, Calder, Kandinsky, Picasso, and

Gauguhin are just a few of the artists whose work you'll come across. The Guggenheim Museum Soho was recently renovated, expanded, and "wired," putting an emphasis on high-tech art and electronic media. Both museums mount special exhibits featuring world-renowned collections and artists. They also offer gallery talks and other special events. **Hours:** The Fifth Avenue location is open Sunday through Wednesday from 10 to 6, Friday and Saturday from 10 to 8. The Soho location is open Sunday, Wednesday, Thursday, and Friday from 11 to 6, Saturday 11 to 8. **Admission:** $10 for adults, $7 for senior citizens over 65 and students with ID at the Fifth Avenue location; $7 for adults, $5 for senior citizens over 65 and students with ID at the Soho location. Children under 12 are admitted free at both places. For $15 ($10 for senior citizens and students), you can get a seven-day pass to both museums.

HISPANIC SOCIETY OF AMERICA
Audubon Terrace (Broadway bet 155th and 156th St)   212/926-2234

Founded as a public museum and research library in 1904, this little-known place is home to a diverse and impressive collection of art and artifacts from the Iberian Peninsula (Spain and Portugal). The building itself, located directly across from the dramatic El Cid statue in the middle of Audubon Terrace, is beautiful, but the lighting in the galleries is awful and descriptions of most things are less than complete. That said, however, the Hispanic Society is well worth a visit. You'll find seals from the Roman Empire, a 15th-century silver processional cross from Barcelona, and paintings by such masters as Goya, Valazquez, and El Greco. Make sure to look at the beautiful tiles and mosaics in the walls on your way up the stairs between floors. A small sales desk selling reproductions of the society's holdings in postcard and print form is located in the Sorolla Room (named for Joaquin Sorolla y Bastida's dramatic murals on the walls) at the far right end of the first floor. You can take either the M4 bus up Madison Avenue or the M5 bus up Sixth Avenue to get to the museum and then take either back to Fifth Avenue in midtown. **Hours:** The museum is open Tuesday through Saturday from 9 to 5, Sunday from 1 to 4. The Library Reading Room is open Tuesday through Friday from 1 to 4:15, Saturday from 10 to 4:15. **Admission:** free.

INTERNATIONAL CENTER OF PHOTOGRAPHY
1130 Fifth Ave (at 94th St)   212/860-1777
1133 Sixth Ave (at 43rd St)   212/768-4680

If you're interested in photography, put the International Center of Photography (ICP) galleries at the top of your list of places to visit. Devoted to displaying photography as both art and historical record, these galleries have changing exhibits of work by photographers from all over the world, as well as ones drawn from the center's permanent collection. The main ICP gallery on Fifth Avenue is in a relatively small townhouse, but its unhurried, quiet atmosphere allows you to take in exhibits at your own pace. The newer gallery in midtown is almost twice the size, but the atmosphere is every bit as pleasant. **Hours:** Tuesday from 11 to 8, Wednesday through Sunday from 11 to 6. **Admission:** $4 for adults, $2.50 for senior citizens and students, $1 for children under 12, and free for everyone from 6 to 8 on Tuesday.

INTREPID SEA-AIR-SPACE MUSEUM
Pier 86 (at 46th St and the Hudson River)   212/245-0072

The water in the Hudson River is not particularly inviting and you'll find few pedestrians in this area, but a trip down here can be lots of fun if you're interested in aircraft carriers, submarines, space exploration, and the like. The centerpiece of this museum is the giant *U.S.S. Intrepid,* an aircraft carrier that served in both World War II and the Vietnam War. The *U.S.S. Edison* (a destroyer used in Vietnam), the Coast Guard cutter *Tamoroa,* and the *U.S.S. Growler* (a guided-missile submarine), are also here. You must take a guided tour to see the *Growler,* but for everything else you can choose between a tour or wandering around by yourself. Galleries, display halls, and theaters are scattered throughout the complex. You won't have much trouble finding the museum, as the *Intrepid* dominates everything else along this part of the river. The ticket booth and gift store are right inside the main entrance past the tanks. The best way to get to the museum from midtown is either by taxi or the M42 bus (make sure it says "Piers" on the front) all the way to the end of West 42nd Street. **Hours:** Monday through Saturday from 10 to 5 and Sunday from 10 to 6 between May 1 and September 30, Wednesday through Sunday from 10 to 5 during the rest of the year. The ticket booth closes at 4 (5 on Sundays in summer), and the last tours finish at 6. **Admission:** $10 for adults; $7.50 for veterans, students between 12 and 17 with ID cards, and senior citizens; $5 for children between 6 and 11; free for the first child under six and $1 for each one after that.

THE JEWISH MUSEUM
1109 Fifth Ave (at 92nd St)   212/423-3200

Operated by the Jewish Theological Seminary of America and housed in yet another elegant Fifth Avenue mansion, the Jewish Museum displays the largest collection of Jewish art and Judaica in the United States. Much of the museum's collection was rescued from European synagogues before World War II, and all of it is extremely well displayed. Renovated in the early 1990s, the museum has a large permanent exhibit tracing the Jewish experience that's entitled "Culture and Continuity: the Jewish Journey," as well as a variety of changing exhibits. Families will also want to visit the children's gallery and ask about special family programs and workshops. Cafe Weissman in the museum's basement is a pleasant place for a light lunch or snack. **Hours:** Sunday, Monday, Wednesday, and Thursday from 11 to 5:45 and Tuesday from 11 to 8. The museum is closed on most Jewish holidays. **Admission:** $7 for adults, $5 for students and senior citizens, free for children under 12 (and for everyone between 5 and 8 on Tuesday).

LOWER EAST SIDE TENEMENT MUSEUM
90 Orchard St (at Broome St)   212/431-0233

Founded in 1988, this unique museum is making an enormous contribution to the preservation of American social history and the urban immigrant experience. In the gallery itself are permanent and changing exhibits, an oral-history video, and a slide show tracing the history of the tenement building across the street at 97 Orchard Street. The really exciting part of this museum, however, is that tenement building. Home to as many as 10,000 people from more than two dozen nations between 1863 and 1935, four of its apartments have been restored to different periods in their history. Together, they offer a glimpse of what life in one of these incredibly crowded places must have been like (or what it still is like for hundreds of thousands of people who still live this way). The museum's volunteers—who lead tours of the tenement Tuesday through Friday at 1, 2, and 3 and on Sundays every 45 minutes between

11 a.m. and 4:15 p.m.—are enormously interesting, well informed, and dedicated. Reservations are stongly encouraged. **Hours:** Tuesday through Friday from noon to 5, Saturday and Sunday from 11 to 6. **Admission:** $7 for adults, $6 for senior citizens, $5 for students, free for children under five. That fee includes entrance to both the gallery and the half-hour tour of the tenement building. Exceptionally well-conceived and educational walking tours are offered on weekends for an additional charge.

METROPOLITAN MUSEUM OF ART
Fifth Ave bet 80th and 84th St   212/535-7710

The Met, as it is known to New Yorkers (not to be confused with the Metropolitan Opera), is one of those places you can visit a hundred times and never see the same thing twice. Whether you're interested in Egyptian tombs, Greek and Roman coins, paintings by the great Renaissance masters, African masks, Chinese and Asian art, Tiffany windows, or arms and armor from the Crusades, the Met has a lot you'll want to see. Start by picking up a floor plan at one of the information desks in the main hall and mapping out your visit. Make sure to ask for a "Dining Guide" of the museum's five restaurants, bars, and cafes. Although the Met often has extremely popular special exhibits, I sometimes head for places with fewer people so I can wander and gaze at my own pace. If you want to avoid the crowds (almost five million people come through the Met every year), the best time to visit is on a weekday morning. Self-guided audio tours in English and other languages are available at an extra charge. The Met also sponsors an incredible number of films, lectures, gallery talks, concerts, and other special programs. Call 212/879-5500 for information on gallery and museum tours, as well as upcoming schedules and programs, or pick up a seasonal program at one of the information desks. If you come to New York frequently and like to visit the Met and its gift shops, consider becoming a National Associate. For a $40 annual fee, people who live outside a 200-mile radius of New York City can get free admission to both the Met and The Cloisters, a 10% discount at the Met's many gift shops, seasonal schedules, and a subscription to the museum's magazine. **Hours:** Sunday, Tuesday, Wednesday, and Thursday from 9:30 to 5:15; Friday and Saturday from 9:30 to 8:45. **Admission:** $8 for adults, $4 for senior citizens and students, free for children under 12. The fee entitles you to same-day admission to The Cloisters.

MORRIS-JUMEL MANSION
160th St (bet Edgecombe Ave and Jumel Terrace)   212/923-8008

Built in 1765 as a summer house for Colonel Roger Morris and his wife, this graceful Georgian country house sits atop a hill overlooking the East River. It briefly served as General George Washington's headquarters in 1776 and later was home to Madame Eliza Jumel and her second husband, Aaron Burr. (Rumor has it that Madame Jumel's ghost has been spotted yelling at neighborhood children to be quiet from the second floor balcony!) Throughout the house you'll find exceptional period furniture, including a 19th-century French mahogany *directoire* sleigh bed said to have belonged to Napoleon Bonaparte when he was First Consul of France. The surrounding neighborhood has definitely seen better days, but the mansion itself has recently been renovated. The grounds are particularly pretty in the spring and early summer. Take the M2 bus up Madison Avenue to the front of the mansion on Edgecombe Avenue. Getting back to midtown is a little more complicated. I recommend taking a taxi or going on a tour (look under Harlem in the "Tours" section of this chapter).

Hours: Wednesday through Sunday from 10 to 4. **Admission:** $3 for adults, $2 for senior citizens over 60 and students with ID, free for children under 10.

MUSEUM FOR AFRICAN ART
593 Broadway (bet Houston and Prince St)   212/966-1313

Although both the Metropolitan Museum of Art and the American Museum of Natural History have African collections, this is the only museum in New York and one of only a few in North America devoted exclusively to African art. In a renovated space designed by Vietnam War Memorial architect Maya Lin, the museum's two floors house changing exhibits from all over the continent. You walk in through part of the eclectic gift shop and bookstore. (Check out the magnificent coffee-table books and the children's books to the right of the reception desk.) The museum also sponsors gallery talks, special events, and trips to Africa and other places abroad. **Hours:** Tuesday through Friday from 10:30 to 5:30, Saturday and Sunday from noon to 6. **Admission:** $5 for adults, $2.50 for children, senior citizens, and students.

MUSEUM OF AMERICAN FOLK ART
2 Lincoln Square (Columbus Ave bet 65th and 66th St)   212/595-9533

You'll find a lot of what I call Americana here: weather vanes, quilts, whirligigs, wooden carousel horses, and some marvelous paintings. The gallery is quite small but has lots of benches and can be a very pleasant place just to sit and think. Best of all, it's free. The museum also sponsors lectures, educational programs, and demonstrations. **Hours:** Tuesday through Sunday from 11:30 to 7:30 **Admission:** free.

MUSEUM OF AMERICAN ILLUSTRATION
128 E 63rd St (bet Park and Lexington Ave)   212/838-2560

On the first floor of the Society of Illustrators' townhouse offices, this gallery houses changing exhibits of advertising, artistic, and other work by professional illustrators. Most of the exhibits center around the Society's annual juried competitions for illustrators in a variety of categories. A small museum shop offers books by and for illustrators, exhibition catalogs, and other items. **Hours:** Tuesday 10 to 8, Wednesday through Friday from 10 to 5, Saturday noon to 4. **Admission:** free.

MUSEUM OF CHINESE IN THE AMERICAS
70 Mulberry St (at Bayard St, 2nd floor)   212/619-4785

Designed in the shape of a 15-sided traditional Chinese lantern, this recently opened successor to the Chinatown History Museum is a small but wonderfully interesting place in the heart of Chinatown. Its stated mission is to reclaim, preserve, and broaden the understanding of the incredibly diverse story of Chinese people in North, South, and Central America. The museum's fascinating permanent exhibit—"Where Is Home? Chinese in the Americas"—combines the extraordinary with the ordinary to give visitors a glimpse into that story. If you're visiting Chinatown, this museum offers some perspective on the world bustling around you on the streets below. **Hours:** Tuesday through Sunday from 10:30 to 5. **Admission:** $3 for adults. $1 for senior citizens and students, free for children under 12.

MUSEUM OF THE CITY OF NEW YORK
1220 Fifth Ave (bet 103rd and 104th St)   212/534-1672

This treasure is often overlooked by tourists and New Yorkers alike because of its location at the far north end of Fifth Avenue's Museum Mile. It's dedicated to the history of the city from the earliest European settlement through the present, and it offers something for just about everyone. Permanent exhibits include period rooms, an exquisite silver collection, toys and dollhouses, a fire-fighting gallery, and an enormous number of model ships. Thanks to popular demand, what was a temporary exhibit on Broadway now seems to have become a permanent one. The actual bedroom and dressing room from the home of John D. Rockefeller, Sr., on the museum's fifth floor are a truly breathtaking pleasure for anyone who likes antiques. Changing exhibits cover everything from the history of theater in New York to the city's different ethnic groups. A 22-minute film, *The Big Apple*, is shown frequently in the basement theater and gives a good overview of New York's history. The museum also offers an exceptionally diverse array of walking tours, children's programs, lectures, classes, and other events. Call the Education Department (ext. 206) for more information, or pick up a seasonal schedule at the information desk right inside the entrance. **Hours:** Wednesday through Saturday from 10 to 5 and Sunday from 1 to 5. Call before going, however, as the museum plans to upgrade and expand in the near future and may temporarily move out of its current home altogether. **Admission:** free, but contributions of $5 for adults, $4 for senior citizens, students, and children, and $10 for families are strongly encouraged.

MUSEUM OF MODERN ART
11 W 53rd St (bet Fifth and Sixth Ave)   212/708-9480

Affectionately known as "MoMA" to New Yorkers, the Museum of Modern Art is among the most important museums in the world devoted to modern art. If a major contemporary work is not at one of the two Guggenheims, chances are it's at MoMA. This is a big museum, and wandering through its many galleries takes time. MoMA does host some traveling exhibits, but its permanent collection is as enormous as it is impressive. If you need to rest, spend some time in the sculpture garden behind the front entrance on the ground floor or head for the very pleasant and not terribly expensive (although sometimes quite crowded) Garden Cafe at the far northeastern corner of the ground floor. Sette MoMA, an Italian restaurant overlooking the sculpture garden, is a popular place for lunch and dinner (call 212/708-9710 for reservations). MoMA also offers lectures, workshops, films, and a weekly "Conversations with Contemporary Artists" series on Friday evenings as well as jazz in the Garden Cafe. Information and schedules are available at the information desk in the main lobby. **Hours:** Saturday through Tuesday from 11 to 6, Thursday and Friday from noon to 8:30. **Admission:** $8.50 for adults, $5.50 for students with identification and senior citizens, free for children under 16 accompanied by an adult, and "pay-as-you-wish" for everybody on Thursday and Friday evenings between 5:30 and 8:30.

MUSEUM OF TELEVISION AND RADIO
25 W 52nd St (bet Fifth and Sixth Ave)   212/621-6800

Television fans, young and old alike, will definitely not want to miss this terrific place (or its new branch, opened in 1996 in Beverly Hills!). Its extensive collection includes thousands of radio and television programs and commercials, many of which are periodically shown to the public and all of which are available for individual viewing. Indeed, the museum's computerized catalog makes six decades worth of television immediately accessible. Several galleries display changing exhibits on every imaginable aspect of television and radio, but most people come to watch their favorite shows. Check the schedule in the lobby or give the museum a call to find out what is going on at any given time. The International Children's Television Festival, held every spring, is particularly fun. I suggest going on a weekday, as the museum gets crowded on weekends. **Hours:** Tuesday through Sunday from noon to 6 (Thursday until 8). The theater stays open on Friday until 9. **Admission:** $6 for adults, $4 for students with identification and senior citizens, $3 for children under 13.

NATIONAL ACADEMY OF DESIGN
1083 Fifth Ave (bet 89th and 90th St)   212/369-4880

Founded in 1825, this museum, fine-arts school, and artists association was modeled after the Royal Academy in London. In addition to workshops and classes for artists, the Academy has changing exhibits of American and European paintings and other art. During the Academy's "Annual Exhibition," some of the work is actually for sale. The museum is in a surprisingly large townhouse, and wandering through its three floors of galleries is a real pleasure. Winslow Homer, Thomas Eakins, and John Singer Sargent are just a few of the artists who have been members of the academy and whose work is part of its permanent collection. A small book and card shop is inside the museum's lobby. For information on lectures and other programs, call 212/369-4880 or pick up a seasonal schedule at the museum's information desk in the lobby. For information about the school itself, call 212/996-1908. **Hours:** Wednesday, Thursday, Saturday, and Sunday from noon to 5, Friday from noon to 8. **Admission:** $5 for adults, $3.50 for students, children under 16, and senior citizens, "pay-as-you-wish" for everyone on Friday from 5 to 8, and free to art students with identification on Wednesday.

NATIONAL MUSEUM OF THE AMERICAN INDIAN
1 Bowling Green (at the foot of Broadway)   212/668-6624

I can't say enough good things about this exceptionally well-conceived museum and its thoughtful, well-displayed exhibits. Opened in late 1994, it replaces the old Museum of the American Indian on Audubon Terrace and is the first of three planned museums showcasing the Smithsonian's enormous collection of North, Central, and South American Indian art and artifacts. (Assuming budget cuts don't scuttle the plan, the other two will be in Washington, D.C.) The museum's permanent exhibit—"Creation's Journey: Masterwork of Native American Identity and Belief"—offers insight into the histories and cultures of the incredibly diverse Native American community. A second exhibit—"All Roads Are Good: Native Voices on Life and Culture"—is the result of 23 Native American artists, scholars, elders, storytellers, and others from throughout the Western Hemisphere getting together to choose artifacts for display, and to talk about why they chose them and what those artifacts mean to them. As if the exhibits weren't enough, the building—the former U.S. Customs House—is spectacular and worth visiting in and of itself. Take time to look up at the intricate detail in the ceilings, and make sure to go down the exquisite staircase to the gift shop. **Hours:** daily (except Christmas) from 10 to 5 (Thursday until 8). **Admission:** free.

NEW MUSEUM OF CONTEMPORARY ART

583 Broadway (bet Houston and Prince St)   212/219-1222

This showcase for contemporary artists is definitely worth a visit if you're in Soho. Its changing exhibits feature individual artists and thematic collections, which tend to be unusually well displayed and conceived. The museum is known for its multidisciplinary approach to art, focusing on group and solo shows accompanied by educational public programs. The museum, which recently doubled its size, offers gallery talks and group tours tailored to the age and interest of the participants. Call 212/219-1355 for recorded program information. **Hours:** Wednesday, Thursday, Friday, and Sunday from noon to 6, Saturday from noon to 8. **Admission:** $4 for adults; $3 for artists, students, and senior citizens; free for children under 12 and for everyone from 6 to 8 on Saturday.

NEW YORK CITY FIRE MUSEUM

278 Spring St (between Hudson and Varick St)   212/691-1303

This museum, located in a turn-of-the-century firehouse, is dedicated to the history of fire-fighting and fire prevention. In addition to a relatively modern fire engine, a quite old ladder truck, a hand-pulled hand pump from 1820, and many other fire apparatuses, the museum displays pictures from fire stations all over New York, a collection of 19th-century leather fire buckets, and an assortment of badges. You'll also find collections of presentation shields, trumpets, and Currier and Ives prints. Kids will love looking at the equipment, and most things are quite well displayed. Still, I wish they had an engine, which children could climb around. The museum is a bit out of the way, although less so since Soho has become a major tourist destination. Call ahead to make sure your visit isn't going to coincide with that of a large school group. **Hours:** Tuesday through Sunday from 10 to 4. **Admission:** $4 for adults, $2 for students and senior citizens, and $1 for children under 12.

NEW YORK HISTORICAL SOCIETY

Central Park West bet 76th and 77th St   212/873-3400

For almost two centuries, the New York Historical Society has been what the *New York Times* recently described as "New York City's archive and attic." The grand old institution is a real treasure trove, with almost a million books; 3 million maps, manuscripts, and other documents; thousands of pieces of art; and even John James Audubon's watercolor "Birds of America" series. Unfortunately, however, the Historical Society fell on hard times and was forced to close its doors in 1993. Thanks to an innovative director and some rather unorthodox fundraising, those doors and the galleries inside were reopened recently. While I certainly recommend a brief stop at this lovely old building, particularly to visit the Luman Reed Gallery (and the library on the second floor, if you're interested in New York history), I'm sorry to say that it's a bit of a disappointment given the tremendous archives and reputation. (If you're really interested in the city's history, the Museum of the City of New York is a real treat!) **Hours:** Wednesday through Sunday from noon to 5 (the library is open only Wednesday through Friday). **Admission:** a "suggested donation" of $5 for adults and $3 for senior citizens and children.

NEW YORK TRANSIT MUSEUM
Boerum Pl and Schermerhorn St in Brooklyn   718/243-3060

Anybody interested in New York's amazing subway system will understand why I've made an exception to my "only in Manhattan" rule to include this wonderful museum. It is run by the Metropolitan Transit Authority and is technically devoted to both buses and subways. Old subway cars and exhibits detailing the system's history are the real draws here. Kids will love getting on and off the cars, while history buffs will get a kick out of the old signs and ads like those publicizing the Miss Subways competition. The entire museum is housed in an abandoned station a couple of blocks from Brooklyn's Borough Hall. Take the 2, 3, 4, or 5 subway line to the Borough Hall Station, and then look at the neighborhood map by the token booth to get your bearings. On weekends and in summer, the museum offers a wide range of popular workshops and other programs for adults, children, and families. If you're going on a weekday during the school year, call ahead to make sure your visit doesn't coincide with that of a large school group. **Hours:** Tuesday, Thursday and Friday from 10 to 4 (Wednesday till 6), and Saturday and Sunday from noon to 5. **Admission:** $3 for adults, $1.50 for children under 17 and senior citizens.

NEW YORK UNEARTHED
17 State St (bet Pearl and Whitehall St)   212/748-8628

This hard-to-find little museum actually is run by folks at South Street Seaport but is housed just off Battery Park. It seems to be run on a shoestring but is definitely worth a stop if you're in the area and are interested in urban archeology. You'll find displays of artifacts from various periods and places in the life of New York on the first floor, and (assuming the basement isn't being used for a lecture or workshop) exhibits and discussions of archeology in the city downstairs. **Hours:** Monday through Saturday from noon to 6 (closed Saturday in winter). **Admission:** free.

NICHOLAS ROERICH MUSEUM
319 West 107th St (just off Riverside Dr)   212/864-7752

Located in an aged but still elegant townhouse on an unusually pleasant block between Riverside Drive and Broadway, this museum is dedicated to the life and work of Russian-born artist-philosopher-author-educator Nicholas Roerich. History buffs may remember him as author of the Roerich Pact, an agreement signed by President Franklin Roosevelt and the leaders of 20 Latin American countries in 1935 stipulating that a banner be flown over museums, monuments, and other cultural institutions in times of war and peace alike. You'll find a number of books written by and about Roerich in several languages, but the real reason to come to this museum is the large collection of unusual paintings of the Himalayas, various religious scenes, and other subjects by Roerich. Very little is labeled and the displays are quite informal, but it's a pleasant place off the beaten track. Seasonal schedules of poetry readings, concerts, and other events are available in the front hall, as are postcards with reproductions of some of Roerich's paintings. **Hours:** Tuesday through Sunday from 2 to 5. **Admission:** free.

OLD MERCHANT'S HOUSE
29 E 4th St (between Broadway and Lafayette St)   212/777-1089

Once home to a hardware merchant and his family, this 1832 rowhouse now offers its visitors a glimpse of life in an age when Greenwich Village was considered the suburbs. The house is filled with much original furniture and fixtures (including pipes for gas lighting, which was then cutting-edge technology). A self-guided tour is available inside the front door, and you can wander around at your own pace. The house is often used for readings, concerts, and other programs, so call ahead before coming. **Hours:** Sunday through Thursday from 1 to 4. **Admission:** $3 for adults, $2 for students and senior citizens, free for children under 12.

PAINE-WEBBER GALLERY
1285 Ave of the Americas (bet 51st and 52nd St)   212/713-2885
The folks at Paine-Webber have set aside the east end of their wood-paneled lobby for a variety of changing exhibits. Much like those at the gallery in the Equitable Center's lobby, the exhibits here are often high quality. Look for printed exhibit information on either side of the lobby immediately inside the entrance. **Hours:** Monday through Friday from 8 to 6. **Admission:** free.

PIERPONT MORGAN LIBRARY
29 E 36th St (at Madison Ave)   212/685-0610
Have you ever wondered where to find a copy of the Guttenberg Bible? Wonder no more. You'll find one of the few original Guttenberg Bibles, as well as a remarkable collections of medieval and Renaissance manuscripts, books, drawings and art here in the Pierpont Morgan Library. Built at the turn of the century by financier J. Pierpont Morgan to house his personal collection, the library was open to the public by his son in 1924. It's now a scholarly research center and museum with changing and permanent exhibitions. By far the most exciting thing here for even the casual art fan is "Mr. Morgan's Library," a study and private three-story library connected by a rotunda. Free tours are offered of these rooms, which contain an unbelievable collection of mostly Italian Renaissance carvings, furniture, paintings, tapestries, mosaics, and other marvels. Call 212/685-0610 for recorded information about guided tours, current exhibitions, and special events. **Hours:** Tuesday through Friday from 10:30 to 5, Saturday from 10:30 to 6, Sunday from noon to 6. **Admission:** $5 for adults, $3 for students and senior citizens.

POLICE ACADEMY MUSEUM
235 E 20th St (bet Second and Third Ave)   212/477-9753
This unusual little museum is on the second floor of the New York City Police Academy. If you're interested in antique firearms or the history of the police in New York City, you'll really enjoy this place. Collections of badges, shields, nightsticks, handcuffs, and trophies are also on display, as are exhibits on fingerprinting, mug shots, drugs, and youth gangs. Bring identification and call at least a day in advance to talk with the friendly staff to make sure the museum will be open. **Hours:** Monday through Friday from 9 to 3. **Admission:** free.

ROSE MUSEUM
Carnegie Hall (Seventh Ave and 57th St)   212/903-9600
Actually just a handsome, wood-paneled room with well-lit display cases, this small museum is home to changing exhibits relating to the history of Carnegie Hall and the people who have made their careers there. The museum, on the second floor of Carnegie Hall, is open during intermissions of perfor-

mances, but it's also accessible to the general public during the day. The entrance is off West 57th Street between the main Carnegie Hall lobby and the Carnegie Hall Tower. **Hours:** daily except Wednesday from 11 to 4:30. **Admission:** free.

SOUTH STREET SEAPORT MUSEUM
east end of Fulton Street   212/748-8600

This is not a museum in the traditional sense but rather a collection of exhibits, ships, stores, and restaurants spread throughout 11 square blocks of what was once the city's bustling port and economic center. You can walk around the South Street Seaport complex and look at everything from a distance without paying a dime, a fact that has spelled financial trouble for the museum in recent years. That museum includes the four-masted *Peking,* a light ship called the *Ambrose,* a tall ship called the *Wavertree* (which is now being restored), several galleries with changing exhibitions, a printer's shop, and a children's center with all sorts of hands-on workshops and displays. Paying admission to visit these places is worth it, particularly since your money goes to support educational outreach, historical research and preservation, and urban archaeological programs. Stop by the visitors center a block and a half down Fulton Street from the main entrance on your right or the ticket booth on Pier 16 to get a map and more information. On any given day (particularly in the warmer months), you'll find all sorts of special tours and activities throughout this fascinating complex. **Hours:** daily from 10 to 6 (Thursday until 8) between April 1 and September 30; daily except Tuesday from 10 to 5 from October 1 to March 31. Restaurants and some stores stay open longer in the summer. **Admission:** $6 for adults, $5 for senior citizens over 65, $4 for students with identification, $3 for children under 12.

THE STUDIO MUSEUM IN HARLEM
144 W 125th St (bet Malcolm X and Adam Clayton Powell, Jr. Blvd)
212/864-4500

This light and modern space is a real jewel. The name reflects its original mission to be a studio for working artists. Since inception more than two decades ago, it has evolved into a premier museum of contemporary and traditional African, Caribbean, and African-American art. The museum mounts exhibits from the permanent collection and plays host to traveling ones. It also offers lectures, gallery talks, performances, and other programs throughout the year. (To get to the museum from midtown, take the M101 bus up Third Avenue to the corner of West 125th Street and Malcolm X Boulevard. To return, board the M101 bus downtown from the opposite corner of what becomes Lexington Avenue.) **Hours:** Wednesday, Thursday, and Friday from 10 to 5, Saturday and Sunday from 1 to 6. **Admission:** $5 for adults, $3 for students and senior citizens, $1 for children under 12.

THEODORE ROOSEVELT BIRTHPLACE
28 E 20th St (bet Broadway and Park Ave)   212/260-1616

Tucked on a side street in a neighborhood often overlooked by New Yorkers and visitors alike (although the street was once among the city's most elegant), this wonderful brownstone is a reconstruction of Theodore Roosevelt's childhood home. The building here was torn down in 1916 but rebuilt by the president's sisters and wife using original blueprints and the house next door as a model. The rooms were then furnished and decorated largely as they had been in Teddy's childhood. You come in at what was once the servants entrance on the ground floor and browse through a collection of pictures, clothing, and other items that belonged to the Roosevelt family in a wonderful wood-paneled room. Then you are taken through the living quarters on the second and third floors by a National Park Service guide. (This is a National Historic Site run by the U.S. Park Service.) If you're interested in presidential history and the late 19th and early 20th centuries or just want to see how the wealthy lived in the 1850s and 1860s, put this museum on your itinerary. Tours are given on the hour. **Hours:** Wednesday through Sunday from 9 to 5 (the final tour begins at 4). **Admission:** $2 for adults, free for senior citizens and children under 17.

UKRAINIAN MUSEUM
203 Second Ave (bet 12th and 13th St)   212/228-0110

Founded by the Ukrainian National Women's League of America in 1976 and housed in the top two floors of a townhouse owned by the League and the Ukrainian Congress Committee on the northern edge of the East Village, this out-of-the-way place is a real find for anybody interested in the Ukraine and the heritage of its people. The best time to visit is the roughly two-month period around Easter, when the museum displays its extraordinary collection of *pysanky,* the elaborately decorated Ukrainian Easter eggs that were once used as talismans to ward off evil spirits. The museum also sponsors demonstrations and classes during this period and around Christmas. You'll find Ukrainian costumes and crafts on display all year round and a small gift shop on the fifth floor. The museum is very much a part of New York's Ukrainian immigrant community. **Hours:** Wednesday through Sunday from 1 to 5. **Admission:** $1 for adults, 50 cents for senior citizens and students, free for children under 12.

URBAN CENTER GALLERY
457 Madison Ave (bet 50th and 51st St)   212/935-3960

The Municipal Art Society (MAS) is a very active nonprofit organization dedicated to urban planning and historic preservation. In addition to sponsoring some of the city's best walking tours, lectures, and other public programs, the society maintains Urban Center Books and the Urban Center Gallery at its headquarters on the north side of McKim, Mead & White's elegant Villard Homes. You can learn a great deal about New York from the gallery's changing exhibits on the city and its people and architecture. You can also pick up tour schedules and other MAS information in the lobby. **Hours:** Monday, Tuesday, Wednesday, Friday, and Saturday from 11 to 5. **Admission:** free.

WHITNEY MUSEUM OF AMERICAN ART
945 Madison Ave (at 75th St)   212/570-3676

This museum has a decidedly modern focus, although the Whitney's collection includes works by American artists from throughout this country's history. Several exhibits run concurrently, some focusing on one artist and others built around a theme. The Whitney's Biennial Exhibit, which opens in March of odd years and runs for several months, is a much-discussed tradition in the New York art world and is eagerly awaited by the museum's many fans. If you're interested in gallery talks, special events, or what's on display at any given time, pick up a "This Week at the Whitney" schedule outside the museum's main entrance or drop by the information desk just inside the front door. A branch of Sarabeth's Kitchen, long a popular East Side restaurant, is located on the museum's lower level. **Hours:** Wednesday, Friday, Saturday, and Sunday from 11 to 6, Thursday from 1 to 8. **Admission:** $8 for adults, $6 for students with identification and senior citizens over 62, free for children under 12 and for everybody on Thursday evening from 6 to 8.

The small **Whitney Gallery and Sculpture Court** is located in the lobby of the Philip Morris Building (120 Park Avenue, at 42nd Street). The gallery is open weekdays from 11 to 6 (until 7:30 on Thursday evening), and admission is free. The sculpture court, which doubles as a pleasant sitting area, is open Monday through Saturday from 7:30 a.m. until 9:30 p.m., and Sunday from 11 to 7. Call 212/878-2550 for more information.

YESHIVA UNIVERSITY MUSEUM
2520 Amsterdam Ave (at 185th St)   212/960-5390

Located on the main campus of Yeshiva University, this often overlooked museum has an exceptional collection of paintings, books, religious artifacts, and other things related to Jewish life and culture. It mounts one major exhibit each year, in addition to smaller exhibits that change throughout the year. Ask about special holiday events and workshops for adults and children. Before heading up here, you ought to know that the university campus is safe but the surrounding neighborhood can get rough after dark. It's also full of steep hills, in case you're thinking about walking around. The M101 bus will take you to the museum up Third Avenue from midtown and back again down via Lexington Avenue. **Hours:** Tuesday, Wednesday, and Thursday from 10:30 to 5, Sunday from noon to 6. The museum is closed on Jewish holidays. **Admission:** $3 for adults, $2 for senior citizens and children, free for children under 4.

Parks

As hard as it may be to believe when you're standing amidst the skyscrapers of midtown, Manhattan has almost 2,600 acres of parkland. That means 17% of the city is grass, rocks, lakes, playgrounds, and walking trails. Central Park, spanning 843 acres in the middle of the island, is the biggest and certainly the most famous. Smaller ones like Carl Schurz Park and Lighthouse Park on Roosevelt Island can sometimes be more peaceful, however, because fewer people know about them. Inwood Hill Park and Fort Tryon Park on Manhattan's northern tip are so wooded and hilly you won't believe you're in New York.

Unless you are going to a scheduled event such as a play or concert, you probably don't want to walk around in any park at night. (It is worth noting, however, that the Central Park police precinct is the safest in all of Manhattan.) If you are by yourself, stay away from isolated areas and dense shrubs even during the day. Unfortunately, funds for park upkeep have been cut and some areas of the larger parks are looking a bit shabby these days. All that said, however, the parks are real treasures to explore and enjoy—and they offer a wonderful respite from the concrete and chaos.

The following is a short list of some of the city's biggest parks, as well as some personal favorites among the lesser known:

Battery Park—Named for the gun battery built along its old shoreline during the War of 1812, this 23-acre park sits at the very southern tip of Manhattan, below State Street and Battery Place. Castle Clinton, a National Monument (and the place to buy tickets for trips to the Statue of Liberty and Ellis Island), is in Battery Park, as is one of the last remaining kiosks for the original subway system. The Staten Island Ferry Terminal is adjacent to the park's eastern edge, and the marvelous new National Museum of the American Indian is just north of the park. You'll find lots of benches and pathways here, as well as an excellent view of New York Harbor.

Bryant Park — Behind the New York Public Library (between 40th and 42nd streets and Fifth and Sixth avenues), this was the site of the 1853 World's Fair, where Isaac Singer unveiled his sewing machine and Elisha Otis introduced his elevator. After years of neglect, the park underwent a multimillion-dollar renovation in the early 1990s and is now a real gem. The benches are great resting spots, and you'll find lots of vendors and a fine garden in the spring and summer. You'll also find games like checkers and Scrabble for rent, toy boats to rent and sail in the fountain, and free movies on Monday nights in summer. Bryant Park even has clean and safe public bathrooms (just off West 42nd Street, directly behind the library), complete with security guards, attendants, and fresh flowers in the ladies' room.

Carl Schurz Park — Between East End Avenue and the East River from 84th to 90th streets, this is probably the safest public park in the city. Named for a German immigrant-turned-U.S. Senator and Secretary of the Interior, the park includes Gracie Mansion, the official residence of New York's mayor. In addition to a great view of barge traffic along the East River, the park offers plenty of benches and playgrounds.

Central Park — Designed in 1858 by Frederick Law Olmsted, the same landscape architect who designed the U.S. Capitol Grounds in Washington, D.C., this is the ultimate urban park. Its 843 acres are bounded by 59th and 110th streets and Fifth Avenue and Central Park West. The park has two ice-skating rinks (in winter), lakes, ponds, a marvelous wildlife conservation center, theaters, jogging tracks, a reservoir, baseball diamonds and other playing fields, playgrounds, tennis courts, a miniature golf course (in summer), and a castle. There's lots of open space and 58 miles of paths. For maps and a current schedule of events, stop by the Visitor Information Center at the Dairy, just behind Wollman Rink at about what would be 65th Street and Sixth Avenue (if those roads went into the park), the Henry Luce Nature Observatory in Belvedere Castle at mid-park near 79th Street, or at the Charles A. Dana Discovery Center. in the park's northeast corner, near 110th Street and Fifth Avenue. You can also call 212/794-6564 for current information. If you ever get lost in the park, it might help to know that the first digits of the number plate on the lampposts in the park correspond to the nearest cross street. Particularly in warmer months and on weekends, the park is a paradise for walkers, joggers, bike riders, and rollerbladers. In summer, Central Park is home to a wide variety of cultural events, including Shakespeare in the Park, various concerts on the "Summer Stage," and free concerts by the New York Philharmonic and the Metropolitan Opera.

Fishers Park — One of what are commonly called "vest-pocket parks" because of their small size, this pleasant surprise is tucked between Sixth and Seventh avenues off 54th and 55th streets. It has a fountain, trees, greenery, tables, seats, and working pay phones.

Fort Tryon Park — This 66-acre gift from John D. Rockefeller, Jr. extends from Riverside Drive to Broadway and from West 192nd Street to Dyckman Street. Home to The Cloisters, this hilly and wooded park offers magnificent views of the Hudson River. Take a friend along if you plan on walking here.

Greenacre Park—Another vest-pocket park, this was a gift from the daughter of John D. Rockefeller, Jr. It's located on 51st Street between Second and Third avenues. On a nice day during the work week, follow the lunchtime crowds.

Hudson River Park—In Battery Park City, near the World Financial Center, this delightful riverside park opened in 1992. You'll find great playgrounds, walkways, and wide open spaces. Particularly in warmer months, the park's spectacular views of the Hudson River, New York Harbor, and the Statue of Liberty make a trip here well worth the effort.

Inwood Hill Park—The second largest park in Manhattan, Inwood Hill Park is at the northwest tip of Manhattan. Bordered by the Harlem River to the north and the Hudson River on the west, this rugged park of nearly 200 acres is home to a saltwater marsh, caves once used by Algonquin Indians, a new urban ecology center, and the island's last remaining stands of virgin timber. Hiking and climbing enthusiasts will love its relatively unspoiled wilderness, but I suggest going in groups.

Lighthouse Park on Roosevelt Island—If you really want to get away but only have a little time, go to Lighthouse Park. Located on the northern tip of Roosevelt Island in the middle of the East River, this park has picnic facilities and clean open space, as well as the lighthouse for which it is named. The view of the Manhattan skyline from the west side of the park is among the best in the city. A tram to Roosevelt Island leaves frequently from its own station on Second Avenue between 59th and 60th streets. It costs $1.50 each way, and the bus that takes you from the tram station to the northern end of the island costs another 10 cents.

Riverside Park—Running between Riverside Drive and the Hudson River from 72nd to 159th streets, this is another one of Frederick Law Olmsted's creations. In addition to playgrounds, great paths for walking, jogging, and bicycling, popular clay tennis courts at 92nd Street, and a terrific view of the Hudson River, the park is home to the new Eleanor Roosevelt statue (at 72nd Street), the 79th Street Boat Basin, the Soldiers and Sailors Monument (at 89th Street), and Grant's Tomb (at 122nd Street). People used to complain about erosion and vandalism in the park, but those who live around it now take adoptive responsibility for its upkeep (including Bette Midler, who has hired ten people to make sure its more remote reaches are kept clean!).

Stuyvesant Square Park—This park was given to the city by Peter Stuyvesant, the last Dutch governor of "Nieuw Amsterdam" in the mid-17th century. Once among the most elegant places in the city, it still has a little charm and a lot of benches. You'll find it on both sides of Second Avenue at the southern end of the Gramercy Park neighborhood, between 15th and 17th streets.

Union Square Park—Known for its drug scene a decade ago, this old park has really come back to life in recent years. It stretches from 14th and 17th streets between Broadway (called Union Square West through here) and Park Avenue South (Union Square East). It is home to the city's most popular Greenmarket, and you'll also find playgrounds, picnic benches, and, in warmer months, an outdoor bar and cafe near the Abraham Lincoln statue in the park's north end. The George Washington statue at the park's southern end was erected in 1856 to commemorate the 80th anniversary of the signing of the Declaration of Independence.

Washington Square Park—Long considered the emotional if not geographic center of Greenwich Village, this park sits at the foot of Fifth Avenue and is best known for the Washington Memorial Arch. The park was constructed in 1827, while the marble arch was not dedicated until 1895. (It replaced a wooden one.) The park is near New York University, and its chess tables, playgrounds, and other features are much used by students and other neighborhood residents.

For recorded information on what's happening on any given day in the parks around Manhattan and the other boroughs, call 212/360-3456.

Places of Worship

Manhattan is home to some of the oldest, largest, and most famous churches and synagogues in the United States. These places, many of which are Episcopal churches (a relic of the city's life under British colonial rule) are integral to the social and architectural history of the city. Many of them allow people to come in and look around, but you should always behave respectfully and remember that you are in a place of worship rather than a museum or gallery. Here are some of my favorites.

Abyssinian Baptist Church—Located at 132 West 138th Street (between Frederick Douglass and Adam Clayton Powell, Jr. boulevards), this church is one of the oldest in Harlem, and it boasts one of the city's largest congregations. Made famous by the late U.S. Congressman, the Reverend Adam Clayton Powell, Jr., the church contains a display of pictures of Powell and memorabilia from his career. Call 212/862-7474 for information about services and programs.

Cathedral Church of St. John the Divine—Facing Amsterdam Avenue at 112th Street near Columbia University, this magnificent Episcopal cathedral has been under construction for more than a century and will be among the largest Christian houses of worship in the world when (and if) it is completed sometime in the next century. The stonework, art, and stained glass are exceptional, as is the combination of Gothic, Romanesque, and Byzantine architectural styles. Even if you are not particularly interested in cathedrals, architecture, or religion, this somewhat out-of-the-way marvel is nonetheless a must-see. To give you some sense of its scale: the Statue of Liberty could fit comfortably inside the main sanctuary. The rose window over the entrance is 40 feet in diameter! The Cathedral Shop, in what will one day be the cathedral's north transcept, has an eclectic assortment of books and gifts (see the "Museum and Library Shops" section in Chapter VI for more information). Call 212/316-7490 for information about services and other programs, including the much anticipated annual blessing of the animals. (For information about tours, see the "Tours" section later in this chapter, or call 212/932-7314.)

Central Synagogue—On the southwest corner of Lexington Avenue and 55th Street, this reform synagogue is the oldest continuously used synagogue in the city. Completed in 1872, it was designed by Henry Fernbach and is a rare example of early Victorian religious architecture. The beautiful Moorish Revival exterior, complete with magnificent carved wooden doors, is well worth a look. The red, gold, and blue stenciling inside the synagogue is breathtaking. Call 212/838-5122 for information about services and programs.

Church of the Holy Trinity—Near Gracie Mansion at 316 East 88th Street (between First and Second avenues), this Episcopal church is a French Gothic marvel that dates back a hundred years. It's a favorite of classical music lovers because of its frequent winter concerts. Call 212/289-4100 for information about services, concerts, and programs.

Church of the Transfiguration—On the north side of East 29th Street between Fifth and Madison avenues, this Episcopal church is known to older generations as "the little church around the corner." It's known to younger generations for its marvelous programs of Vivaldi and other music throughout the year. You'll find a lovely garden in front of this low-lying brick church and beautiful stained-glass windows inside. Call 212/684-6770 for information about services, concerts, and programs.

First Presbyterian Church—On the west side of Fifth Avenue between 11th and 12th streets, this church is the direct decendent of the First Presbyterian congregation in the United States. The building itself was built in 1846 (the original church was on Wall Street). The sanctuary has wooden pews with doors, a beautifully carved wooden pulpit that towers over the congregation, and a glorious blue rose window. Call 212/675-6150 for more information about services and programs.

Grace Church—On Broadway between 10th and 11th streets, this exquisite Episcopal church was built in 1846 and is one of several in New York designed by James Renwick, Jr. It is an elegant Gothic presence in the neighborhood and one of the most important examples of early Gothic Revival architecture in the country. The church is best known for its daily prayer services, carved pulpit, and outstanding music. Call 212/254-2000 for information about services and programs.

Holy Trinity Greek Orthodox Cathedral—Located on the north side of 74th Street between First and Second avenues, this magnificent brick cathedral actually doesn't look like much from the outside. Once inside the lovely wooden doors, however, you'll think you're in ancient Greece. Call 212/288-3215 for information about services and programs.

Islamic Center of New York—Opened in 1991, this sleek mosque and its grounds are hard to miss as they dominate Third Avenue between 96th and 97th streets. The mosque, a gift to New York's Muslim community from several Islamic countries, was built at an angle so that it faces Mecca. Call 212/722-5234 for information about services and programs or to arrange a visit.

Marble Collegiate Church—At the northwest corner of Fifth Avenue and 29th Street, this stately church was designed by Samuel Warner in 1854 and made famous by Dr. Norman Vincent Peale. It is an example of Early Romanesque Revival and draws its name from the Tuckahoe marble used in its construction. Its congregation is quite large and socially active. Call 212/686-2770 for information about services and programs.

Riverside Church—A gift of John D. Rockefeller, Jr., this interdenominational church was inspired by the famous Chartres cathedral in France and can seat up to 2,500 people. Its 22-story bell tower dominates the northern end of Morningside Heights, and the 74-bell carillon can be heard throughout the area. (For $2 and a lot of energy, you can climb to the top!) Known for its beauty as well as its social activism, the church is located at 490 Riverside Drive, between

120th and 122nd streets. Call 212/222-5900 for information about services and programs.

St. Bartholemew's Church—Complete with a carved triple-arched portico (designed by architect Sanford White) and a mosaic dome, this brick and stone Episcopal church sits between 50th and 51st streets on Park Avenue. It has fallen on hard financial times in recent years and has been forced to close its once-popular fitness facility and thrift shop. However, it remains one of the most dramatic and beautiful sights in midtown. Call 212/751-1616 for information about services and programs.

St. Mark's in the Bowery—Constructed on the site of Peter Stuyvesant's personal chapel in 1799, this understated but elegant Episcopal church has lovely yards on either side. This Episcopal church is located on the northwest corner of 10th Street and Second Avenue in what is now the East Village but what was once Stuyvesant's farm. ("Bouwerie" is *farm* in Dutch.) Call 212/674-6377 for information about services.

St. Patrick's Cathedral—Designed by James Renwick, Jr., more than a century ago, this astonishing building is the largest Roman Catholic church in the United States and the seat of the archdiocese of New York. It takes up the entire block between 50th and 51st streets and Fifth and Madison avenues. The main organ alone has 9,000 pipes! Its steps along Fifth Avenue are a great place to rest your feet and watch the world go by. Call 212/753-2261 for information about services.

St. Paul's Chapel—On Broadway between Fulton and Vessey streets, this Episcopal parish is housed in the oldest church building in the city. Construction began in 1764 when New York was New Amsterdam and America was a British colony, as the dates on the gravestones in the surrounding cemetery suggest. The interior is surprisingly plain but exceptionally elegant and lit by Waterford crystal chandeliers. (Look for George Washington's pew in the north aisle.) This is yet another church known for its music programs, often held on weekdays at lunchtime. Call 212/602-0874 for information about services, concerts, and programs.

St. Peter's Lutheran Church—The only really modern church on this list, St. Peter's is nestled under the towering Citicorp Center at the southeast corner of 54th Street and Lexington Avenue. The church has an extensive program of jazz, opera, and other music on Sunday and during the week. Look for a posted schedule outside the main entrance or call 212/935-2200 for information about services, concerts, and programs.

St. Thomas Episcopal Church—On the northwest corner of Fifth Avenue and 53rd Street, this beautiful church is best known for its magnificent music programs. The incredibly ornate stone carvings on the church's exterior, its lovely doors, and its stately bell tower make it a real presence on Fifth Avenue. Call 212/757-7013 for information about services, concerts, and programs.

Spanish and Portuguese Synagogue—Home of the orthodox Congregation Shearith Israel, founded in 1654 by descendents of Jews who fled the Spanish Inquisition, this synagogue was built in 1897 but contains remnants from its congregation's original synagogue, built on the Lower East Side in 1730. The Tiffany stained-glass windows are particularly impressive. The synagogue is located at 8 West 70th Street, near Central Park West. Call 212/873-0300 for information about services and programs.

Temple Emanu-El – Built in 1929 and capable of seating 2,500 people, this is the largest Reform synagogue in the world. Stained-glass windows and mosaics grace the interior, while the limestone facade is a beautifully carved combination of Eastern and Western architectural styles. While the entrance is at 1 East 65th Street, be sure to look at the doors on Fifth Avenue. Call 212/744-1400 for information about services and programs.

Trinity Church – At the intersection of Broadway and Wall streets at the heart of the financial district, this is the third building of an Episcopal church founded in 1698 on land donated by King William III of England. This building was completed in 1846, although the oldest headstones in its 2.5-acre graveyard date back to 1681. Alexander Hamilton is among the many famous people buried here. Believe it or not, Trinty Church was the tallest building in Manhattan for much of the 19th century. The church offers a small museum, guided tours (see "Tours" later in this chapter), and concerts, in addition to daily services. Call 212/602-0800 for information.

If you want to find out when services are held at churches, synagogues, and other places of worship, the first section of the Saturday *New York Times* includes advertisements for Catholic, Protestant, Ethical Culture, Hindu, and a few Jewish services under the heading "Religious Services." The Manhattan Yellow Pages also include extensive listings under the headings "Churches," "Synagogues," and "Religious Organizations."

Recreation

Visitors sometimes see Manhattan as nothing but concrete and can't imagine what those who live here do for exercise other than walking. The people who live here, however, know that you can do just about everything in New York that can be done anywhere else – and then some! Whether it's miniature golf, riding horses, or scuba diving, chances are that New York has got it if you know where to look. Unless otherwise noted, call the Manhattan Department of Parks and Recreation (212/360-8133) for information.

Baseball – There are seven public baseball diamonds in Central Park and at least a dozen more in other parts of Manhattan.

Basketball – Between schoolyards and city parks, you'll find more than a thousand public basketball courts in Manhattan. You can also try Basketball City, down by the Chelsea Piers Complex at Pier 63 (212/924-4040).

Bicycling – You can go bike riding in Central Park, Riverside Park, and even on the city's streets if you have the nerve. Bicycles are available for rent at Loeb Boathouse (212/517-2233) in Central Park for $6 an hour and at most bicycle shops in the city. If you're looking for company or suggestions about where to ride, call the New York Cycle Club (212/242-3900).

Billiards – Manhattan has several dozen pool and billiard halls. Chelsea Billiards (212/989-0096) at 54 West 21st Street is the largest. You can also try The Billiard Club (212/206-7665), at 220 West 19th Street; Julian Billiard Academy (212/475-9338) at 138 East 14th Street; Jack's Billiards (212/315-5225) at 614 Ninth Avenue; or the Amsterdam Billiard Club (212/496-8180) at 344 Amsterdam Avenue.

Birdwatching—Believe it or not, Central Park is a tremendous spot for bird-watching. Of the roughly 800 species of birds in North America, nearly 300 have been spotted here. There's even a hotline reporting rare and interesting sightings (212/979-3070). Call the New York Audubon Society (212/691-7483) for information about outings, or check in at the Charles A. Dana Discovery Center (212/860-1370) or the Henry Luce Nature Observatory in Belvedere Castle (212/772-0210) in Central Park.

Boating and Sailing—Rowboats are rented at Loeb Boathouse (212/517-2233) in Central Park between May and early October. Believe it or not, you can also find a Venetian gondola, complete with gondolier, here on summer evenings. Other on-the-water alternatives include kayaking in New York Harbor with Atlantic Kayak Tours (914/246-2187); taking sailing lessons at North Cove Sailing School in Battery Park City (800/532-5552), Great Hudson Sailing Center at Chelsea Piers (212/741-7245), or the Chelsea Sailing School (212/627-7245); or, for $2, using one of the Park and Recreation Department's three launch sites in Manhattan (212/360-8131). (For information about bigger boats, see the "Manhattan on the Water" section of Chapter VII.)

Bowling—Try Bowlmor Bowling (212/255-8188) at 110 University Place (between 12th and 13th streets) or Leisure Time Bowling (212/268-6909) on the second floor of Port Authority Bus Terminal.

Boxing—Try Geraldo Rivera's Broadcast Boxing (212/319-4142) at 41 West 57th Street or the Equinox Fitness Club (212/780-9300) at 897 Broadway.

Bridge—Try the Beverly Bridge Club (212/486-9477) at 130 East 57th Street or the Manhattan Bridge Club (212/799-4242) at 27 West 72nd Street.

Carriage Rentals—Horse-drawn carriages line up across the street from the Plaza Hotel at the southeast corner of Central Park, on Central Park South. A ride costs $34 for 30 minutes. Other prices are printed on the carriages.

Chess, Checkers, and Backgammon—For $2 an hour, you can play to your heart's content at the Backgammon Chess Club (212/787-4629) at 212 West 72nd Street. You can often find a game of chess at the Chess Shop (212/475-9580) at 230 Thompson Street. In warm weather, there's usually games of checkers going at Washington Square Park, in the Chess and Checkers House in Central Park, or in Bryant Park.

Climbing—Central Park Outward Bound (212/348-4867) teaches climbing courses on the walls in the middle of Central Park at about 97th Street. The city also maintains an indoor climbing wall at the West 59th Street Recreation Center (212/397-3166) at 533 West 59th Street. Finally, Sports Center at the Chelsea Piers has a 10,000-square-foot rock-climbing wall.

Fencing—If you're looking for company, try the New York Fencers Club (212/874-9800) at 154 West 71st Street after 5 p.m. If you're looking for lessons, give the folks at Metropolis Fencing a call (212/463-8044). They can be found on the second floor at 45 West 21st Street.

Fishing—To fish on the Hudson, Harlem, or East rivers, or anywhere else with fresh water, you'll need to purchase a New York State fishing license for a minimal fee. Call 914/985-2275 for more information. If you want to do saltwater fishing and are willing to spend a couple hundred dollars, call New York Harbor Sportfishing (201/941-1988). The company is based in New Jersey but will pick you up for a day of fishing in the shadow of the Statue of Liberty at South Street Seaport or by the pier at East 23rd Street. If you want to borrow poles and fish with the kids in the well-stocked Harlem Meer in Central Park in spring, summer, and fall, bring picture identification to the Charles A. Dana Discovery Center (212/860-1370), near Fifth Avenue and 110th Street. Children under 16 do not need a fishing license in New York.

Gardening—If you want to garden and do volunteer work at the same time, call the Parks and Recreation Department (212/360-1390) or Operation Green Thumb (212/788-8059).

Golf—Manhattan has neither a 9- nor an 18-hole course. However, duffers can play at some of the nation's great courses, thanks to video technology, or you can go down to Chelsea Piers and hit a bucket of balls at the four-tiered driving range on Pier 59. If miniature golf is more your speed, try Donald Trump's 9-hole Gotham Golf in Central Park's Wollman Rink during the summer. If you have your heart set on a real golf course, call the Metropolitan Golfer's Club (800/463-8465). They have access to more than 20 public and semi-private courses throughout the area and will arrange for you to play and even rent clubs. You can also call 718/255-4653 for information on public golf courses in New York's four other boroughs.

Handball—Try La Raquette (212/245-1144) in the Parker Meridien Hotel at 119 West 56th Street. For outdoor courts, try the ones in Central Park near 97th Street and Transverse Road or in St. Vartan's Park at Second Avenue and 35th Street.

Horseback Riding—If you know how to ride, you can rent a horse at Claremont Riding Academy (212/724-5101) for $30 an hour and ride in either Central Park or the academy's ring. Located at 175 West 89th Street, the academy also offers lessons. You can also check out membership at the new Chelsea Equestrian Center on Pier 63, next to the Chelsea Piers complex at the west end of 23rd Street (212/367-9090).

Ice Hockey—On weekend mornings in season, you can join the free-for-all game going at Lasker Rink (212/996-1184) in Central Park near West 110th Street and Lenox Avenue. Check the city's other rinks for seasonal hockey leagues and schedules.

Ice Skating—The most famous rink in New York and probably the world is the one in front of Rockefeller Plaza (212/757-5730), just off Fifth Avenue between 49th and 50th streets. Central Park also has rinks at its south and north ends: Lasker Rink (212/996-1184), near 110th Street and Lenox Avenue, and Wollman Rink (212/517-4800), near what would be 62nd Street and Sixth Avenue. For a small, uncrowded rink, try Rivergate Rink (212/689-0035) at 401 East 34th Street. You can also try the clean, spacious rink in Riverbank State Park (212/694-3642) at 145th Street and Riverside Drive. The World Trade Center has a new rink, the Recreation World Ice Chalet, in the plaza at 4 World Trade Center (212/524-4386). The once appropriately named Sky Rink (212/336-6100) used to be on the 16th floor of a building but has moved to Chelsea Piers. Sky Rink is open all year but the others have limited seasons, so call ahead to make sure they're open. All of them rent skates.

Model Boats—Model boats can be sailed at the Kerbs Model Boathouse in

Central Park, near Fifth Avenue and 74th Street. Regattas are held on Saturday during the summer. Model boats can also be found at the fountain at Bryant Park.

Pinball—Time Out Family Amusement Center in Penn Station and Broadway Arcade (212/247-3725) at 1659 Broadway have lots of machines.

Racquetball—Try the Manhattan Plaza Racquet Club (212/594-0554) at 450 West 43rd Street or Club La Raquette (212/245-1144) in the Parker Meridien Hotel at 119 West 56th Street.

Rollerblading—The proper name for this sport is "in-line skating," as Rollerblade is actually a brand name. Whatever you call it, it's all the rage in Manhattan. You can rent skates by the hour or day from Blades West (212/787-3911) at 105 West 72nd Street; Blades East (212/996-1644) at 160 East 86th Street; Manhattan Sports (212/580-4753) at 2188 Broadway; and at a variety of other skating stores. NYC Skate (212/964-1944), at 128 Chambers Street, even offers free one-hour lessons with its rentals.

Roller Skating—Try the Lezly Dance and Skate School (212/777-3232) at 622 Broadway, or the new rinks at the Chelsea Piers complex (212/336-6100).

Running—Two of Manhattan's most popular places to run are Riverside Park and the one-and-a-half-mile trail around the reservoir in Central Park. If you want some other ideas or company (the latter is always a good idea), call the New York Road Runners Club (212/860-4455). The Road Runners can also tell you about upcoming races.

Scuba Diving—Pan Aqua Diving (212/496-2267) at 166 West 75th Street runs certification courses at various sites throughout the city.

Shooting—Try the Downtown Rifle and Pistol Club (212/233-5420) at 24 Murray Street or the Seventh Regiment Rifle Club (212/772-7219) at 643 Park Avenue.

Soccer—Central Park has four public soccer fields. One is on the Great Lawn, behind the Metropolitan Museum of Art, and three are in the North Meadow, near the park's northern end.

Squash—Try the Park Avenue Athletic Complex (212/686-1085) at 3 Park Avenue; City Hall Squash Club (212/964-2677) at 25 Park Place; or Club La Raquette (212/245-1144) in the Parker Meridien Hotel at 119 West 56th Street.

Swimming—You can find public beaches in the other boroughs and out on Long Island, but swimming in Manhattan is limited to pools. Inexpensive indoor options include the Asser Levy Pool (212/447-2020) at 23rd Street and Avenue A; the pool at the 59th Street Recreation Center (212/397-3166) at 533 West 59th Street; the pool at the John Jay College of Criminal Justice; and the pool in Riverbank State Park (212/694-3665) at 145th Street and Riverside Drive.

Table Tennis—Try the West Side Table Tennis Club at Eleventh Avenue and 50th Street (212/246-1060).

Tennis—Manhattan has more than a hundred public tennis courts. Permits cost $50 and can be purchased at the Arsenal (Fifth Avenue and 64th Street). For more information, call 212/360-8131. To find out about lessons at the Central Park Tennis Center, call 212/280-0201.

Volleyball—Call the New York Urban Professional League (212/877-3614) for the time and location of its games.

Yoga—Try the Integral Yoga Institute in Greenwich Village (212/929-0586) at 227 West 13th Street or on the Upper West Side (212/721-4000) at 200 West 72nd Street.

You can find a little bit of just about everything at the Ys in Manhattan. They include the **92nd Street YMHA** (212/427-6000) at 1395 Lexington Avenue; the **West Side YMCA** (212/787-4400) at 5 West 63rd Street; the **YWCA** (212/735-9755) at 610 Lexington Avenue; the **Vanderbilt YMCA** (212/755-2410) at 224 East 47th Street; and the **McBurney YMCA** (212/741-9216) at 215 West 23rd Street.

Another good option are the 13 recreation centers in Manhattan run by the Department of Parks and Recreation. For $25 a year, you can find all sorts of facilities and classes. The **Asser Levy Recreation Center** (212/447-2020) at Avenue A and 23rd Street; the **59th Street Recreation Center** (212/397-3166) at 533 West 59th Street; and the **Carmine Recreation Center** (212/242-5228) at 1 Clarkson Street, are among the best. Seasonal passes to **Riverbank State Park** on Riverside Drive at 145th Street (212/694-3600) are inexpensive, and the facilities are excellent.

For information about gyms and fitness centers, see the "Health and Fitness" section of Chapter IV.

Sights and Other Pleasant Places

Some of the places that make New York unique don't fit neatly into "Museums," "Places of Worship," or any of the other categories included in this book. Many can be visited without a guide or a formal agenda—indeed, simply walking around and gazing is pleasurable. A diverse lot, the following list includes some of the most famous, interesting, and unusual sights and places in Manhattan. Unless otherwise noted, admission is free.

Alwyn Court Apartments—Of all the magnificent apartment buildings in New York, this is my favorite one to look at from outside. Built between 1907 and 1909, it's a block from Carnegie Hall on the corner of 58th Street and Seventh Avenue. You could spend hours looking at the elaborate carved terra-cotta exterior. Its features include a crowned salamander, the symbol of Renaissance art patron Frances I, in whose style the building was built. For the best view, cross the street.

Brooklyn Bridge—Spanning the East River between Manhattan and Brooklyn, this was the world's longest suspension bridge when built, and it remains one of the most spectacular. The 5,989-foot bridge took 15 years (1868-1883) and two generations of Roeblings to construct. After John Roebling, the engineer who designed the bridge, died from injuries sustained in an accident, his son Washington and wife Emily finished the project. You can get an incredible view of New York Harbor and the city's skyline by taking a stroll on the bridge's historic promenade. To reach it, go through the Municipal Building, just off Park Row on the southeast side of City Hall, and follow signs in the subway tunnel. Better yet, ask one of the policemen patroling the area for directions.

Carnegie Hall—On the corner of Seventh Avenue and 57th Street, this magnificent concert hall opened in 1891 with the American conducting debut of Peter

Ilyich Tchaikovsky. Named for steel magnate Andrew Carnegie, it recently underwent a $60 million renovation that has improved its acoustics dramatically (actually, it *restored* the acoustics of old by taking out a piece of concrete that was added during an earlier renovation!) and expanded its seating capacity to more than 2,800. If you want to visit during the day, take a tour or stop by the new Rose Museum at Carnegie Hall. (See the "Tours" and "Museums" sections of this chapter for more information.) For box-office information, call 212/247-7800 or drop by the lobby. **Hours:** weekdays and Saturdays between 11 and 6, Sunday between noon and 6.

Castle Clinton National Monument—Probably the best known of Manhattan's seven National Parks—it's the gateway to two others and headquarters for them all—Castle Clinton is a red circular building in Battery Park, at the southern tip of Manhattan. Built on what was then an island as part of a series of forts defending New York Harbor at the beginning of the 19th century, Castle Clinton has been different things through the years: an entertainment center, an immigrant receiving station (8 million came through between 1855 and 1890), and home to the New York Aquarium. Castle Clinton is best known to most as the place to buy tickets for the short boat rides to Ellis Island and the Statue of Liberty, but take a few minutes to visit the small museum detailing the site's history inside the door to your right as you come through the gate. **Hours:** daily from 9 to 5.

Central Park Wildlife Conservation Center—When people in New York hear the word *zoo*, they tend to think of the big one in the Bronx. But the Central Park Wildlife Conservation Center—the animal-friendly replacement for the dilapidated and depressing Central Park Zoo—is well worth a visit for kids and grownups alike. Divided into three sections by climate, the center includes an indoor rain forest, an outdoor temperate zone, and an indoor "Edge of the Icepack" exhibit. You'll find everything from a bat cave and a colony of leaf-cutter ants to Japanese snow monkeys and chinstrap penguins in this well-designed and manageably sized place. There are even a couple of polar bears! The center is located in Central Park at Fifth Avenue and 64th Street behind a big building called the Arsenal. It sponsors lots of classes, workshops, and other events for children and families on weekends and in warmer months, although a visit on a winter weekday can be enjoyable, too. Call 212/861-6030 for general information or 212/439-6538 for information on classes and workshops. The gift shop is nothing special, but the hot-dog-and-French-fries crowd will love the small cafe. **Hours:** weekdays from 10 to 5 and weekends from 10:30 to 5:30 (till 4:30 from November through March). The last tickets are sold half an hour before closing. **Admission:** $2.50 for adults, $1.25 for senior citizens, 50 cents for children between 3 and 12, free for children under 3.

Chelsea Piers—When they were built at the beginning of the 20th century, Piers 59, 60, 61, and 62 on the Hudson River in Chelsea quickly became the destination for such elegant passenger ships as the *Lusitania* and the *Ile de France*. Indeed, the *Titanic* was headed for the Chelsea Piers when she sank in 1912. But when the length of ships increased in the 1930s and 1940s, new piers were built near West 44th Street, and the ones in Chelsea were largely abandoned. Thanks to a visionary developer, the Chelsea Piers have sprung back to life. Running between the far west ends of 17th and 23rd streets, the Chelsea Piers Sports & Entertainment Complex encompasses 1.7 million square feet of golf (yes, there's a year-round, outdoor driving range in Manhattan!), ice skating, rock climbing, gymnastics, and other activities in the gym and sports center.

There's more: two restaurants, a 1.2-mile esplanade, a maritime center, and Silver Screen Studios (home to NBC's *Law and Order*). It's really an amazing place. Whether you're interested in classes for all ages and skill levels in just about every sport, membership at the sports center, or a one-time visit, call 212/336-6000. For more information about specific facilities at the Chelsea Piers, look in the "Recreation" section of this chapter.

Chrysler Building—One of New York's most recognized sights, this art deco building on Lexington Avenue between 42nd and 43rd streets was built as the home of the Chrysler Corporation between 1928 and 1930 at the dawn of the automobile age. Its stainless-steel spire is easy to spot, but take a closer look at the radiator-cap gargoyles, based on the 1929 Chrysler, and the racing cars built into the relief. The Chrysler Corporation no longer maintains offices here and the interior isn't particularly interesting, but the lobby is open to the public.

Citicorp Center—A relative newcomer to the New York skyline, this 59-story building between Lexington and Third Avenue and 53rd and 54th streets opened in 1977. Its slanted roof and modern design allow the Citicorp building to stand out among its more traditional neighbors, and its diverse shops, restaurants, and food court have made it a favorite with the midtown lunch crowd. Its large and pleasant atrium is often used for concerts, workshops, and other events on weeknights and weekends.

Eldridge Street Synagogue—New York is full of time capsules, but this one must be seen to be believed. Located at 12 Eldridge Street in what was the largely Jewish Lower East Side but is now the edge of Chinatown, this magnificently elaborate synagogue was home to more than a thousand worshipers at the turn of the century. Although the orthodox Congregation K'hal Adath Jeshurun hasn't missed a Sabbath since the synagogue opened in 1887, its numbers steadily shrank in the middle of this century, and the building fell into such disrepair that pigeons were living in the sanctuary. Thanks to a few visionary and committed people, the sanctuary has been saved, and an $8.5 million capital campaign is now underway. Call 212/219-0888 for more information or to schedule a tour of this very special place. **Hours:** Sunday from 11 to 4, plus Tuesday and Thursday tours at 11:30 and 2:30. **Admission:** $4 for adults, $2.50 for students, senior citizens, and children. All money goes to the synagogue's restoration.

Empire State Building—When people think of New York, this 102-story building is often the first image that comes to mind. Conceived as a great office building but almost bankrupted when it opened in 1931 because of the Great Depression, the Empire State Building soars above its neighbors on Fifth Avenue between 33rd and 34th streets. The neighborhood and the building itself are a bit grimy these days, most of the staff is alternately bored and rude, and the deadly gunfire that erupted here in early 1997 still weighs heavily on everyone's mind. All that said, however, this New York landmark still draws almost 3 million visitors a year, and the views from the top live up to every expectation (assuming it's a relatively clear day or night). For more information about the outdoor terrace on the 86th floor and the indoor observation deck on the 102nd floor, call 212/736-3100, ext. 347. Although many people beg off, I urge you to make the trip to the 102nd floor—the views are spectacular. **Hours:** daily from 9:30 to midnight (the last tickets are sold at 11:25 p.m.). **Admission:** Tickets to the terrace and observation deck cost $4.50 for adults, $2.50 for children under 12, military personnel, and senior citizens.

Federal Hall National Memorial — Here's a history test for the kids: where was the nation's first capital? Not Washington, D.C., or even Philadelphia. It was New York City. And the building that housed it (yes, one building housed the entire federal government!) occupied this site. General George Washington took his first oath of office and Congress debated the Bill of Rights here. Before that, this site was home to New York's first city hall (dating back to 1703). Federal Hall — a grand structure at the corner of Wall and Nassau streets that was built in 1842 as the U.S. Customs House — is now a National Monument run by the National Park Service with exhibits on the site's incredible history. (It's also the starting point for wonderful walking tours of the area run by Heritage Trails New York. See the "Tours" section of this chapter for more information.) Call 212/825-6888 for more information. **Hours:** weekdays from 9 to 5.

Flatiron Building — This 22-story architectural oddity was built at the intersection of Fifth Avenue and Broadway (at 23rd Street) in the early years of this century. The prow of the building is said to sit on the windiest street corner in all of Manhattan. Its triangular shape and terra cotta exterior have made it a familiar landmark, and the thriving neighborhood around it — the Flatiron District — carries its name.

Ford Foundation Gardens — The warm, multilevel garden in the Ford Foundation's glorious atrium is one of New York's great escapes, especially in the winter. The plants are watered with rain and steam condensation gathered in a cistern on the building's roof, and any coins thrown into the little pool are donated to UNICEF. The building is at 320 East 43rd Street (between First and Second avenues). You also can enter the atrium from 42nd Street. **Hours:** weekdays from 9 to 5.

Grand Central Terminal — This stunningly beautiful *beaux-arts* station was built at the turn of the century during the great age of railroads. It replaced a station built on the spot by Cornelius Vanderbilt after steam engines were banned south of 42nd Street in 1854. Scores of commuter trains to Westchester County and Connecticut arrive and depart here. A wonderful gift shop run by the New York Transit Museum and the famous Oyster Bar are just two of the many shops and restaurants on the multilevel concourses, but the real pleasure of a visit to Grand Central is gazing out over the main lobby. A two-year, $175 million cleaning and renovation of this grand old place was in its final stages when this book went to the publisher. To say that the project was long overdue is an understatement — the ceiling hadn't been cleaned since 1944! The Municipal Art Society offers a fascinating free tour of the station at 12:30 on Wednesdays. (See the "Tours" section of this chapter for more information.) The most dramatic entrance to Grand Central Station is through the driveway off Vanderbilt Avenue (a small street just east of Madison Avenue) at 43rd Street. Incidentally, the original waiting room off Park Avenue was recently cleaned and renovated and is well worth a visit. While you're at it, spend a couple minutes at the Whisper Gallery outside the Oyster Bar. Stand in opposite corners facing the wall, and try to hear each other whisper! **Hours:** daily, except from 1:30 to 5:30 a.m.

Grant's Tomb — If you're a Civil War or American history buff, you'll want to venture to the far reaches of the Upper West Side to visit this not-so-subtle final resting place of President (and General) Ulysses S. Grant and his wife, Julia. When you're up at this lonely place in Riverside Park at 122nd Street, inspired by Napoleon's tomb in Paris and run today by the National Park Service, it's hard to imagine that a quarter million people filed through City Hall in the 48 hours Grant lay in state there and that a million more lined Broadway to watch as his coffin was taken here. For anyone who remembers Grant's Tomb as being a bit seedy, I've got good news. As part of the centennial marking the dedication of this monument in 1897, the interior and exterior have been cleaned and restored.

Haughwout Building — Considered by many architectural historians to be the finest example of cast-iron construction in the country, this building at the corner of Broadway and Broome Street was built in 1857 and contained one of Elisha Otis' first elevators. Originally home to E. V. Haughwout (how-it) & Company — a silver, china, and porcelain manufacturer and retailer — the building fell on hard times around the turn of the century and was almost demolished in the 1960s. Thanks to the Landmarks Preservation Commission and its current owners, however, the Haughwout Building not only remains standing but also is being cleaned and restored to at least some of its original grandeur.

Jefferson Market Library — I've included this courthouse-turned-public library because it looks just like a castle in a fairy tale and people are always wondering what it is. Built in 1877 and modeled after Mad King Ludwig's *Neuschwanstein* in Bavaria, it was saved from years of neglect and abuse by community activists and is now one of the city's nicest (and most used) public libraries. A wonderful community garden grows on its south side during warmer months. A bit of trivia: the library's bell, thought to be the second largest in New York, was rung in 1995 for the first time in 97 years. The last time it was rung? To commemorate Admiral George Dewey's triumph in Manila Bay during the Spanish-American War. Thus the graffiti on the bell, which reads: "To hell with Spain — Remember the Maine — 1898"! It's now rung every day on the hour. You'll find the library at 425 Sixth Avenue (at 10th Street) in Greenwich Village. Call 212/243-4334 for more information.

Lincoln Center — This amazing but sometimes overwhelming complex sits along Columbus Avenue near Broadway between 62nd and 65th streets. Constructed between 1959 and 1969, Lincoln Center includes Avery Fisher Hall, the New York State Theater, Alice Tully Hall, a wonderful public library and museum devoted to the performing arts, the Juilliard School of Music, the Guggenheim Bandshell, the Vivian Beaumont Theater, and the Metropolitan Opera House. An open plaza, complete with a fountain, sits in the center of the complex, and small parks and open spaces flank the opera houses. The entire complex is a pleasant place to wander or sit for awhile, and craft fairs and free concerts are often held in the outdoor spaces in warmer months. (For information about backstage tours, see the "Tours" section in this chapter.) Make sure to visit the specialty stores inside the Opera House and eat in the delightful Panevino Ristorante (212/874-7000) at Avery Fisher Hall. Call 212/546-2656 for the Lincoln Center information hotline.

Madison Square Garden — The only real sporting arena in Manhattan, Madison Square Garden plays host to everything from the International Cat Show and the circus to professional basketball's New York Knicks. There have been three Madison Square Gardens; the one at this location opened in 1968. It covers most of the blocks between Seventh and Eighth avenues from 31st to 33rd streets. Oddly enough, Penn Station — the terminal for Amtrak and New Jersey Transit, through which 750 trains pass every day — sits directly underneath "the Garden." You'll also find the Paramount Theater inside the complex. (For information about tours, see the "Tours" section of this chapter.) To find out what's going on at any given time, call 212/465-6741.

National Debt Clock—You'll find this unnerving clock by looking up on the west side of Sixth Avenue right before 43rd Street. It keeps a running total of the total national debt and the amount of that debt owed by a family of four. That total, by the way, is increasing by $10,000 a second!

New York Public Library—The main branch of the extraordinary New York Public Library system is a treasure trove for researchers and architecture fans alike. This beautiful building sits on Fifth Avenue between 40th and 42nd streets, adjacent to Bryant Park. The marble stairs and open areas outside—a favorite brown-bag lunch spot for people who work in the area—are dominated by statues of two lions, Patience and Fortitude. You'll find a gallery with changing exhibits and a terrific gift shop on the first floor. A nonprofit group, Friends of the New York Public Library, offers frequent tours of exhibits and the library itself. (For more information, stop by its desk in the lobby or see the "Tours" section of this chapter.) Call 212/869-8089 for recorded information about the library, current exhibits, and special events. **Hours:** Tuesday and Wednesday from 11 to 6; Monday, Thursday, Friday, and Saturday from 10 to 6.

New York Public Library for the Performing Arts—If you're interested in the performing arts, put this amazing place at the top of your list. While it's not a museum, you'll always find something interesting in its four galleries. An exhibit of material from the New York Philharmonic may be in one gallery, the history of ballet in another. Not just a book library, its collection includes tens of thousands of recordings, videos, and printed materials from dance, theater, classical music, and other media. You can listen or watch whatever you choose without leaving the library! The library's Bruno Walter Auditorium is frequently used for concerts, dramatic readings, and other performances. The library is located in Lincoln Center between the Metropolitan Opera House and the Vivian Beaumont Theater. Call 212/870-1600 for event information or drop by the information desk inside the main entrance. **Hours:** Monday and Thursday from noon to 8; Wednesday, Friday, and Saturday from noon to 6. **Admission:** free.

New York Stock Exchange—Although the elegant home of the New York Stock Exchange is on the corner of Broad and Wall streets, the visitors' entrance is at 20 Broad Street, between Wall and Exchange streets. Tickets are distributed outside or immediately inside the door for entrance to the two-tiered visitors' gallery on the third floor overlooking the trading floor. You will be turned away at the elevators if you do not have one. When the place gets crowded, they stagger the tickets, so there may be a short wait to get in. Once inside you can move around at your own pace. The visitors gallery and its new interactive learning center sometimes close for renovations and other reasons, so call (212/656-5167) before coming. **Hours:** weekdays (except federal holidays) between 9:15 and 2:45.

Plaza Hotel—On the south side of Central Park South, just west of Fifth Avenue, this elegant old hotel is a sentimental and architectural favorite. A stroll through the lobby is a stroll through pure class. You might even catch a glimpse of Eloise (or at least her portrait)!

Radio City Music Hall—This 6,200-seat art deco wonder was the largest theater in the world when it was built in the early 1930s as part of the Rockefeller

Center complex. Its murals and art alone are worth a visit, but Radio City is best known for its long-running Christmas and Easter shows, featuring the Rockettes. Call 212/247-4777 or drop by its lobby at the corner of Sixth Avenue and 50th Street to find out what's scheduled. (If you're interested in taking a tour, see the "Tours" section of this chapter for more information.) **Hours:** weekdays and Saturday from 10 to 8, Sunday from 11 to 8.

Rockefeller Center—The 19 buildings in Rockefeller Center stretch from 47th to 52nd streets between Fifth and Seventh avenues, but the heart of it all is off Fifth Avenue, between 49th and 50th streets. All sorts of interesting shops, the famed statue of Prometheus, the ice-skating rink, the *Today Show*'s studios, and the beautiful Channel Gardens (the future of which is uncertain because of the recent departure of its marvelously talented director) are all here in the shadow of 30 Rockefeller Plaza. "30 Rock" is the home of NBC's network studios. (For information about the NBC Studio Tour, see the "Tours" section of this chapter.) In December, it's also the home of one of the nation's most photographed Christmas trees. Call 212/632-3975 for more information about the complex and special events.

Roosevelt Island—If you want an experience that even most New Yorkers haven't had, along with some of the best views of the city's skyline, take the tram to Roosevelt Island in the middle of the East River. It leaves regularly from its station on Second Avenue between 59th and 60th streets and costs $1.50 per person each way. Although they are only minutes away from midtown Manhattan, the 7,500 people who live over here might as well be on another planet. Their island—which was at various times home to a hog pasture, a debtor's prison, and an insane asylum—is quiet, unhurried, and almost crime-free. For 10 cents you can take one of the rather elderly red buses that traverse the island from the tram station through the small shopping area to Lighthouse Park on the island's northern end. Buy a map at the tram station and see the sights or just wander around. Whatever else you do, however, make sure to walk along the sidewalk on the island's west side to get a view of the Manhattan skyline that's not to be believed.

Schomburg Center for Research in Black Culture—This branch of the New York Public Library is a stunningly comprehensive resource for scholars and others interested in the Harlem Renaissance, enduring African traditions, the civil rights movement, and a wide variety of topics associated with the African-American experience in this country. It's also home to some 300,000 prints and photographs, 10,000 pieces of art and artifacts, and 5,000 hours of oral histories. While its two galleries are small and not in the best shape, you'll often find unique exhibits here. The Center's Langston Hughes Theater is used for performances and special programs. Call 212/491-2200 for more information or 212/491-2265 to schedule a tour. The Center is located at the corner of Malcolm X Boulevard and 135th Street, across from Harlem Hospital. To get there from midtown, take the M102 bus up Third Avenue to the corner of Malcolm X Boulevard and 135th Street. To return, catch the M102 bus from the opposite corner down to what becomes Lexington Avenue. **Hours:** Monday through Thursday from noon to 8, Friday and Saturday from 10 to 6, Sunday from 1 to 4. (Hours for the galleries and collections vary, so call to confirm that what you want to see is open before coming.)

Science, Industry, and Business Library—Known around town as SIBL (as in the woman's name), this amazing library—in the old B. Altman department store—is among the most technologically advanced and user-friendly libraries in the world. Intended for use by the general public and business people, the library unites the New York Public Library system's enormous collections of scientific, technological, mathematical, and business-related materials. (What's enormous? How about 1.2 million books, along with microfilm, microfiche, magazines, and journals!) Whether you're interested in patents and trademarks, labor history, advertising practices, or how the Small Business Administration works, this is the place to look for information. But don't expect to browse through the stacks. With the exception of a circulating collection of 40,000 books on the first floor, everything is housed in electrically operated moving stacks at the core of the building. Each of the library's 500 seats is wired for laptop computer use, and 100 computer stations are available if you want to search electronic databases or go online. If you're interested in learning how to "surf the Net," sign up for one of the library's free classes, offered through its Electronic Training Center. Call 212/340-0887 for more information. The library is located at the corner of Madison Avenue and 34th Street. **Hours:** Monday, Friday, and Saturday from 10 to 6; Tuesday, Wednesday, and Thursday from 11 to 7.

Sony Wonder Technology Lab—A brilliant public-relations and merchandising ploy, and a huge favorite among preteens and teenagers, this four-story interactive wonderland is inside the Sony Corporation's building on Madison Avenue and 56th Street. After checking in on the ground floor and getting a personal access card, you'll be whisked by elevator to the fourth floor, where you "log in" your voice, name, and photograph. You then wind through a good exhibit on the history of communication technologies before reaching a variety of interactive laboratories and stations. Whether you want to try your hand at surgery or making a music video, you'll definitely find something to do and explore. The lab is often very crowded, especially on weekends and in summer. Call 212/833-8100 for more information. **Hours:** Wednesday through Saturday from 10 to 6, Sunday from noon to 6.

South Street Seaport—This is the only place I've included in both the "Museums" section and this one, because it's a little of both. The main entrance to this popular area is on Water Street at Fulton, but the area stretches for several blocks between Water Street and the East River. If you've ever been to Boston's Quincy Market or Baltimore's Inner Harbor, you'll recognize the concept here immediately: upscale shops, food courts, restaurants, and history all wrapped into one. South Street was one of the city's most important ports for many years, and this district was created more than two decades ago to preserve that history. You can stroll through the cobblestone streets, look at the early 19th-century buildings along Schermerhorn Row and gaze at the tall ships, or buy a ticket that entitles you to tour the ships and visit the seaport's galleries and children's center. (For a few extra dollars in warmer months, you also can take a cruise of New York Harbor.) Start your trek at the visitors center, a block and a half inside the main entrance on Fulton Street. Call 212/748-8600 for information about South Street Seaport and special events. **Hours:** South Street Seaport Museum itself is open daily from 10 to 6 (Thursday until 8) in the summer and daily except Tuesday from 10 to 5 in the winter, although many shops and restaurants in the area stay open much later.

Statue of Liberty—This 151-foot gift from France was built on Liberty Island in New York Harbor in 1886 and has been among New York's most recognized sights ever since. (Before the statue was erected, the island was used for hanging pirates and later as a fort!) Generations of immigrants remember seeing Lady Liberty and her raised torch when they arrived at nearby Ellis Island, and the Emma Lazarus poem ("Give me your tired . . .") still expresses the most noble instincts of our country. It's more than a little touristy these days, but a climb up to her crown or a stroll around the grounds can be fun for children and adults alike. A small exhibit tells you about the statue's construction. To reach the Statue of Liberty, you must take a ferry from Castle Clinton in Battery Park. For more information about the ferry (which also goes to Ellis Island), call 212/269-5755. For recorded information about the Statue of Liberty, call 212/363-3200. **Hours:** 9:30 to 5 in winter, 9:30 to 5:30 in summer (although the last boat leaves Castle Clinton at about 3). **Admission:** A price hike is in the works, so I suggest calling the ferry service (212/269-5755) for fare and schedule information. Admission to both Ellis Island and the Statue of Liberty is included in the price of a ferry ticket.

Times Square — When I first began writing this book, Times Square was among the most unpleasant places in Manhattan. It was synonymous with petty crime, pornography, and filth. Not anymore. While the area around the triangle created by Seventh Avenue, Broadway, and 42nd Street still has a ways to go, crime is way down, the peep shows are closing, and the streets are actually clean (or at least cleaner). Indeed, Disney has opened up shop here, Warner Brothers is about to move in, Virgin Records has a superstore, and Steven Speilberg's Dreamworks is working on an interactive arcade. Who would have believed it? The Times Square Business Improvement District runs a well-supplied and friendly tourist information center at 229 West 42nd Street, between Seventh and Eighth avenues.

Trump Tower — This 66-floor building, named for flamboyant financier Donald Trump, sits on Fifth Avenue between 56th and 57th streets. Its six-story pink marble atrium — complete with galleries, shops, restaurants, outdoor gardens (on levels 4 and 5), and a dramatic waterfall — is open to the public and almost always crowded. Apartments begin on the 30th floor; tenants come through a separate entrance to avoid the perpetual crowds. **Hours:** daily between 8 a.m. and 10 p.m.

United Nations — The United Nations runs along First Avenue (called United Nations Plaza) between 42nd and 47th streets. The flags of all member nations fly along the entire length of the complex, and you'll hear all sorts of languages spoken inside the UN and on surrounding streets. The main visitors' entrance, between 45th and 46th streets, is well marked and manned by UN guards. The park and plaza inside the gate offer wonderful views of the East River and comfortable benches. Once you've passed through a security checkpoint inside the main building, you can wander through the enormous lobby, eat in the Delegates' Dining Room, go on a tour, or head downstairs to visit the wonderful UN post office and a great assortment of shops. An information desk located in the middle of the main lobby provides daily schedules of meetings and events. Remember that the people who work here are involved in some pretty important projects. Look around and ask questions, but be quiet and respectful. For information about tours and other programs at the UN, call 212/963-7713. **Hours:** weekdays from 9 to 5; Saturday, Sunday, and holidays from 9:15 to 5.

Vietnam Veterans Memorial — While certainly moving, this is somewhat of a disappointment if you've been to the unforgettable Vietnam Veterans Memorial in Washington, D.C. It's made of green glass etched with excerpts from speeches given during the war and letters written by soldiers during their tours. The plaza surrounding it is full of places to sit and offers terrific views of downtown Brooklyn and New York Harbor. You'll find the memorial and the plaza between two enormous office buildings on Water Street, just north of Broad Street. (The actual cross street is named Coenties Slip, but I defy you to find that on any map!)

Washington Arch – Thanks to scenes in movies like *When Harry Met Sally,* you probably know what this marble triumphal arch looks like. It was erected at the end of the 19th century at the foot of Fifth Avenue, just south of 8th Street in Washington Square Park. The marble arch replaced a wooden structure commemorating the inauguration of George Washington, who was sworn in as president in New York.

Woolworth Building – Constructed of 17 million bricks, 28,000 tons of tile, and 53,000 pounds of bronze and iron hardware, this national landmark is among the city's most impressive office buildings. The cathedral-like lobby has extraordinary mosaics on its vaulted ceilings and is a definite "don't miss" if you're in the area. Dime-store king F.W. Woolworth paid $13.5 million in cash to have his namesake building erected in 1913, and it reigned as the world's tallest building for more than a decade. You'll find the Woolworth Building near City Hall at 233 Broadway (between Barclay Street and Park Place). **Hours:** The lobby is open to the public 24 hours a day.

World Trade Center – This complex of office buildings is dominated by the towering twin stories of 1 and 2 World Trade Center. (Believe it or not, thanks to a recent boom in the construction of tall buildings in Asia, they are no longer even close to being the world's tallest building!) You'll find eight acres of stores and restaurants on the lower levels, all sorts of outdoor markets and events around the complex during the spring and summer, and stunning views and lots of touristy entertainment on the recently renovated observation deck on the 107th floor of 2 World Trade Center. The complex sits between West, Vesey, Liberty, and Church streets. A TKTS outlet, tourist information desk, and ticket desk for the observation deck are on the mezzanine of 2 World Trade Center. For more information about the observation deck, call 212/435-7377. For information about the World Trade Center itself, call 212/435-4170. **Hours:** The observation deck is open daily from 9:30 to 9:30 (11:30 in summer). **Admission:** $10 for adults, $8 for senior citizens, and $5 for children 6 to 12.

World Financial Center – In the heart of Battery Park City between Vesey and Albany streets at the Hudson River, the World Financial Center is in the newer part of an area known as home to many of the nation's leading brokerage and financial firms. Often confused with its bigger neighbor, the World Trade Center, this complex of four buildings surrounding the exquisite Winter Garden does indeed have a life and character of its own. In general, the World Financial Center complex tends to be significantly cleaner and quieter than the World Trade Center complex. You'll find several dozen upscale stores, and restaurants in the World Financial Center, as well as some pleasant sitting areas both indoors and out. Call 212/945-0505 for information about events and programs.

Sports

Some people associate New York with fine food and expensive stores, while others link the city with the Yankees, the Knicks, or one of the city's other professional sports teams. In fact, the New York area is home to more than half a dozen professional sports teams—although only two, basketball's Knicks and hockey's Rangers, actually play in Manhattan. (Home field for the city's two pro football teams is across the river in New Jersey!) Diagrams of all the various stadiums appear near the front of the Manhattan Yellow Pages.

Tickets for most regular-season baseball games often can be purchased as late as game day. Tickets for football's Giants and Jets, however, are almost impossible to find unless you have a generous friend who's a season-ticket holder. Even Knicks tickets are increasingly hard to come by. If you're planning a trip to New York, it's worth finding out which team is in town and who they're playing.

A word of warning: New York sports fans are like no others. They are loud, rude, and typically very knowledgeable about their teams and the sport they're watching. I'm not sure which would be worse: being a referee or a fan of an opposing team at a New York sporting event. A friend from Oregon who goes to see the Knicks play the Portland Trail Blazers when they come to Madison Square Garden would argue the latter!

Belmont Park—Home to the Triple Crown's Belmont Stakes and some of this country's best thoroughbred racing in the late spring, summer, and early fall, this famous racetrack is out on Long Island. At other times of year, try Aqueduct in Jamaica, Queens. Both are run by the New York Racing Association. Call 718/641-4700 or write the New York Racing Association, P.O. Box 90, Queens, NY 11417 for more information about either track.

New York Giants—The 1991 Super Bowl champion Giants play in the National Football Conference of the National Football League. To give you some idea of how unlikely it is that you will get tickets for a Giants game: if you put your name on the waiting list for season tickets today, you would have a wait of roughly three decades! Individual tickets are sold at least a season in advance. If you're really planning ahead, write the Giants (The Meadowlands, East Rutherford, NJ 07073) or call their box office (201/935-8222). If you happen to get tickets, buses go to the Meadowlands from Port Authority Bus Terminal.

New York Jets—The team made famous by quarterback Joe Namath, the Jets play in the American Football Conference of the National Football League. Tickets for Jets games are easier to score than those for Giants games, but you still ought to plan well in advance. They also play at the Meadowlands. For information, write the Jets (1000 Fulton Avenue, Hempstead, Long Island, NY 11553) or call them (516/560-8200). Buses run between Port Authority Bus Terminal and the Meadowlands.

New York Knickerbockers—The Knicks, who dominated the National Basketball Association in the 1970s with such outstanding players as Bill Bradley and Willis Reed, play at Madison Square Garden. The better the Knicks are doing (and they've been doing quite well), the harder it is to get tickets. For information, call Ticketmaster at 212/307-7171 or Madison Square Garden at 212/465-6741. You might also try writing the Knicks (Madison Square Garden, 4 Penn Plaza, New York, NY 10001). Unlike the Meadowlands, Madison Square Garden is easily accessible by public transportation—it sits right on top of Penn Station!

New York Mets—The Mets play in Major League Baseball's National League.

Their home is Shea Stadium in Queens, an easy subway ride from Manhattan. (Take the 7 line from 42nd Street to the Willets Point/Shea Stadium stop.) Tickets for their games are usually easy to get and, relative to their football and basketball counterparts, are not very expensive. Call Ticketmaster (212/307-7171) or the Shea Stadium box office (718/507-8499) for tickets and schedule information, or write the Mets (Shea Stadium, 126th Street and Roosevelt Avenue, Flushing, NY 11368).

New York Rangers—Like the Knicks, the National Hockey League's Rangers play at Madison Square Garden. Also like the Knicks, the Rangers have been doing quite well in recent years (they won the Stanley Cup in 1994), and tickets are often hard to get. Call Ticketmaster (212/307-7171) or the Garden (212/465-6741) to find out if tickets are available.

New York Yankees—The Yankees, the team America loves to hate—and winners of the 1996 World Series—play in Major League Baseball's American League. Although there often is talk of moving to a new stadium (and it may happen when their lease expires in 2002), for now they play at Yankee Stadium in the Bronx. Known to many as the House that Ruth Built, because Babe Ruth played here in the early part of this century, it's a real sports landmark. It's also an easy subway ride from Manhattan. (Take the 4 line from the East Side or the C or D line from the West Side to the 161st Street/Yankee Stadium stop.) Call the Yankees (718/293-6000) or write them (Yankee Stadium, 800 Rupert Place, The Bronx, NY 10451) for ticket and schedule information.

U.S. Open—The U.S. Open, one of professional tennis' four Grand Slam tournaments, is held in late August and early September at the United States Tennis Center in Queens. The finals are held over Labor Day weekend. Tickets to the semifinals and finals sell out immediately, but tickets for earlier rounds can usually be purchased before the tournament. Call Ticketmaster (212/307-7171) for ticket information. For tournament information, write the U.S. Tennis Center (Flushing Park, Queens, NY 11365) or call 718/760-6200.

WTA Tennis Championship—This popular women's tournament is held at Madison Square Garden every November. Tickets for the next year go on sale in December. Call Ticketmaster at 212/307-7171 for tickets and 212/465-6500 for tournament information.

> College basketball and boxing fans should call Madison Square Garden (212/465-6741) to find out about schedules and tickets. College basketball's **National Invitational Tournament** is played at the Garden every March, and boxing's **Golden Glove** series is held there in January and February.

Tickets

In one recent survey, 40% of all visitors to New York said the primary reason for their trip was to see a Broadway play or musical. (Plays are getting harder and harder to find, as musicals now account for at least 80% of Broadway's revenue!) Another 13% cited some other cultural event as their primary reason for coming. It's little wonder: nowhere else in the world will you find such a wealth of performing arts. No trip to New York would be complete without going to see at least one play, musical, ballet, concert, or opera.

The trick, of course, is getting tickets. People have written entire books about how and where to get tickets, and others have made lucrative careers out of procuring them for out-of-towners. What I've tried to do here is give you a variety of approaches for getting theater tickets and to help you find out about other performances. (If you want tickets to sporting events, see the first part of the "Sports and Recreation" section in this chapter.) Keep your eye out for student and other discounts, but be forewarned that good deals for the best shows and performances are few and far between.

For reliable service and superb ticket availability (at a price, naturally), call Manhattan Entertainment (212/382-0633 or 212/582-3600). This outfit can provide reserved tickets for theater, sports, cinema, and music events.

BROADWAY

Different people may have different things in mind when they say they want to see a show. Some have their hearts set on great seats at a Saturday night performance of the hottest show on Broadway, while others are willing to sit anywhere to see anything. A lot of people fall somewhere between those extremes. In addition, some are willing to pay whatever it takes to see the show they want, while others just won't go if they can't pay less than full price. If the whole reason for your trip is to see a particular show (or shows), call 800/334-8457 to find a travel agent near you who can put together a tour package that includes theater tickets. Other approaches:

Hottest Shows in Town—Look in the Sunday Arts and Leisure section or the Friday Weekend section of the *New York Times,* the front of a current *New Yorker,* the "Theater" section of *Time Out New York,* or the back of a current *New York Magazine* to find out where the play or musical you want to see is being performed. The front section of the Manhattan Yellow Pages has a list of Broadway and off-Broadway theaters and a map of the theater district; *Stubs* magazine contains detailed diagrams of seating in most theaters. The Theater Development Fund's NYC/Onstage line (212/768-1818) tells you what is playing and where and also gives a plot summary.

If you want to save a little money and pick your seat, go directly to the theater's box office with cash or a major credit card. Ask to see a diagram of the theater if it isn't posted, although most theaters are small enough that everybody has a pretty good view. The best time to try is midweek.

If you're willing to spend a little extra and let random chance (in theory, it's "best available") pick your seat, call the number listed for phone orders and have your credit card ready. Most numbers will be for Telecharge (212/239-6200) or Ticketmaster's Broadway performance line (212/307-4100). Both services charge a per-ticket handling fee in addition to the ticket price. Tickets can be purchased directly from Ticketmaster's site on the World Wide Web at www.ticketmaster.com. You can also try calling the Broadway Show Line at 212/563-2929.

Be forewarned: full-price tickets to Broadway shows typically cost between $50 and $70 each. Moreover, if the play or musical you want to see is really hot, it may be sold out the entire time you're in New York. If it is, but you still have your heart set on seeing it, ask the hotel concierge for help or look under "Ticket Sales—Entertainment & Sports" in the Manhattan Yellow Pages for the name and phone number of a ticket broker. Either way, this approach will cost extra.

If You're Flexible – If you want to see a Broadway show but are willing to be a little flexible and have some free time, go to one of the TKTS outlets in Manhattan. Operated by the Theater Development Fund, these outlets sell whatever tickets happen to be left for various shows on the day of performance for half price or less (plus a $2.50 per-ticket charge). The most popular TKTS outlet is in Duffy Square, at 47th Street and Broadway. It's open from 3 p.m. to 8 p.m. daily, although matinee tickets are sold from 10 a.m. to 2 p.m. on Wednesday and Saturday and from 11 to 7 on Sunday. You can't miss the line. A less crowded TKTS outlet with better hours is on the mezzanine level of 2 World Trade Center, diagonally across from the ticket booth for the World Trade Center's Observation Deck. It's open from 11 a.m. to 5:30 p.m. on weekdays and from 11 a.m. to 3:30 p.m. on Saturday. They don't sell day-of tickets for evening performances past 1 p.m., but matinee and Sunday tickets go on sale here the day *before* a performance. You must pay with cash or traveler's checks at both places.

The Theater Development Fund also offers extremely good deals on tickets to theater and other performances to its members. If you're a student, member of the clergy, on active duty in the armed forces, teacher, union member, retired, or a performing artist and are planning well in advance, send a stamped, self-addressed envelope for an application to Theater Development Fund, Attention: Application, 1501 Broadway, New York, NY 10036. From time to time, the Ticketmaster outlet on the third floor of Bloomingdale's offers Broadway tickets at a discount of between 25% and 50%. The outlet's phone number is a very closely guarded secret, so I suggest you stop by to see what's available. All Broadway theaters offer a small number of deeply discounted tickets to people in wheelchairs and their companion or attendant. Call the theater box office directly for more information. Finally, standing room only tickets are sometimes available for sold-out performances on the day of the performance for between $10 and $20. Again, call the theater box office for more information.

Twofers – If you just want to see *something* on Broadway and save money too, keep your eye open for twofers. This is one way theaters sell tickets to less-than-hot shows and those old standbys that have been running for years. By exchanging them at the given theater's box office, you can get two tickets for the price of one. (Actually, discounts run anywhere between 15% and 50%.) Twofers look like actual tickets and can be found in hotel lobbies, restaurants, and at the New York Convention and Visitors' Bureau (2 Columbus Circle at the southwest corner of Central Park). You can also get twofers by sending a self-addressed, stamped envelope to Hit Show Club, 630 Ninth Avenue, Room 808, New York, NY 10036. Call 212/581-4211 for more information.

Off-Broadway and Off-Off Broadway – In part because staging a Broadway production has become almost prohibitively expensive in recent years, off-Broadway and off-off-Broadway theater have really taken *off*. Thanks to a glut of talented actors and actresses in New York, such theater is typically excellent and often quite innovative. The front section of the Manhattan Yellow Pages has a list of off-Broadway theaters, and descriptions of what's playing both off-Broadway and off-off-Broadway are published every Sunday in the *New York Times* Arts and Leisure section, in the back of *New York Magazine,* and in *Time Out New York.* Tickets for off-Broadway and off-off-Broadway productions tend to be significantly less expensive in the first place, and TKTS outlets and twofers sometimes offer discounts.

OPERA AND CLASSICAL MUSIC

I think it's safe to say that no other city in the world has as much music from which to choose as New York. Look in the "Annual Events" section of Chapter VII for information about some of the free concerts offered here or in the "Dancing and Other Clubs" section of Chapter VII for information about rock, big band, and jazz clubs. I also urge you to call the 92nd Street YMHA (212/996-1100) if you're interested in chamber music or recitals by top performers. The front section of the Manhattan Yellow Pages contains diagrams of the city's major music halls. If you're willing to pay for the service, ask the hotel concierge for help if you have a particular opera or concert in mind and tickets are sold out. *Time Out New York* has an excellent listing of classical and opera performances, including information on locations, times, and ticket prices. Otherwise, here's how to find schedule and ticket information:

Carnegie Hall—You'll find individual musicians, out-of-town orchestras, and chamber music ensembles performing in Carnegie Hall all year. If you're planning well in advance, write Carnegie Hall (57th Street and Seventh Avenue, New York, NY 10019) for a schedule and ticket information. You can also drop by the lobby or call CarnegieCharge (212/247-7800) between 11 and 6.

Lincoln Center Chamber Music Society—To get schedule and ticket information about the Lincoln Center Chamber Music Society and other performances, write Alice Tully Hall (Lincoln Center, New York, NY 10023), call CenterCharge (212/721-6500), or call the box office (212/875-5030).

Metropolitan Opera—This internationally renowned opera's season runs from fall through spring, but ticket sales are broken into three different periods. Write the Metropolitan Opera House (Lincoln Center, New York, NY 10023) for schedule and ticket information, drop by the Opera House lobby or call the box office (212/362-6000).

New York City Opera—This exceptional but often overlooked opera's season runs through the summer and early fall. Write the New York City Opera (New York State Theater, Lincoln Center, New York, NY 10023) for schedule and ticket information or call the box office (212/870-5570). You can also try Ticketmaster (212/307-4100).

New York Philharmonic—The Philharmonic's season runs from September through June. Write the New York Philharmonic (Avery Fisher Hall, Lincoln Center, New York, NY 10023) for schedule and ticket information or call CenterCharge (212/721-6500), the box office (212/721-6500), or the New York Philharmonic information line (212/875-5656).

DANCE AND BALLET

Ballet and dance companies have been having a tough time financially in recent years, but New York still is home to several world-class companies. Many of them (the American Ballet Theater and the New York City Ballet are exceptions) spend at least part of their season performing at the marvelous Moorish emporium known as the City Center of Music and Drama (212/581-1212). It's located at 131 West 55th Street (between Sixth and Seventh avenues). Each has a slightly different season. Look for a diagram of the City Center Theater in the front section of the Manhattan Yellow Pages. *Time Out New York* has a particularly good section on dance, including reviews and a day-by-day calendar of large and small performances by local and visiting companies. No matter which company you want to see, I suggest writing or calling the specific companies to get schedule and ticket information:

Alvin Alley—211 West 61st Street, New York, NY 10023 (212/767-0590)

American Ballet Theater—Metropolitan Opera House, Lincoln Center, New York, NY 10023 (212/362-6000)

Dance Theater of Harlem—466 West 152nd Street, New York, NY 10031 (212/690-2800)

New York City Ballet—New York State Theater, Lincoln Center, New York, NY 10023 (212/870-5570)

Paul Taylor Dance Company—522 Broadway, New York, NY 10012 (212/431-5562)

TELEVISION SHOW TAPINGS

Fine arts aside, there is one other kind of ticket everybody wants to get in New York: those that allow you to become part of the television studio audience for one of the many talk shows filmed here. I've listed some of the most popular shows (in alphabetical order) and rules for getting tickets. In general, tickets are free and children under 16 (18 in some cases) are not welcome.

Geraldo—Send a self-addressed, stamped envelope to Geraldo Tickets, CBS Television, 524 West 57th Street, New York, NY 10019. Include your name, address, phone number, and how many tickets you want. Expect to wait about a month. For more information, call 212/265-1283.

Late Nite with Conan O'Brien—Tickets are distributed in the NBC Lobby at 50th Street between Fifth and Sixth avenues at 9 a.m. on the day of show tapings (usually Tuesday through Friday) on a first-come, first-serve basis. Standby tickets are distributed in the NBC Lobby at 4:45 p.m. as well. You can also reserve tickets by phone as much as three months in advance. Call 212/664-3056 or 212/664-3057 for more information.

Late Show with David Letterman—These are among the hottest tickets in town. Send a postcard to The Late Show Tickets, 1697 Broadway, New York, NY 10019. Include your name, address, and phone number. Two tickets are allotted per postcard. (Don't try sending more than one postcard, as duplicates are discarded.) Expect to wait at least six to eight months. And bring a jacket: Dave insists that the theater be kept at 52° all year! A hundred standby tickets are distributed on weekdays at noon at the Ed Sullivan Theater, on Broadway between 53rd and 54th streets. They do not guarantee admission, and only one standby ticket is distributed per person. Call 212/975-1003 for more information.

Live with Regis and Kathie Lee—These tickets are pretty hot, too. Send a postcard to Live Tickets, P.O. Box 777, Ansonia Station, New York, NY 10023-0777. Include your name, address, phone number, and how many tickets you want (up to four). Expect to wait at least a year. A standby ticket line forms at the ABC Studio at 67th Street and Columbus Avenue early in the morning, and one standby ticket is distributed per person after regular ticket holders have been seated at about 8 a.m. Be forwarned that the studio where the show is taped is pretty chilly. Call 212/456-3537 for more information.

Rosie O'Donnell Show—Another hot ticket, this show has a ten-month wait for tickets. If you're interested, send a postcard to The Rosie O'Donnell Show, NBC Tickets, 30 Rockefeller Plaza, New York, NY 10019. Two tickets are distributed per postcard. Standby tickets are available at 7 a.m. the show day of taping in the NBC Lobby (on 50th Street between Fifth and Sixth avenues). They do not guarantee admission and are not available for children under five.

Saturday Night Live—Despite the precipitous decline in this legendary show's quality, these are still the hardest tickets of all to get. A lottery is held every August from postcards collected during the preceding 12 months, and every winner gets only two tickets. If you want to be included in the lottery, send a postcard to Saturday Night Live, NBC Tickets, 30 Rockefeller Plaza, New York, NY 10112. Standby tickets are available at 9:15 a.m. on the day of the show at the 49th Street entrance to 30 Rockefeller Plaza. They do not guarantee entrance and only one ticket is distributed per person over 16.

Today Show—As anybody who watches this popular morning show knows, its broadcast studio has windows in front of which crowds gather to watch hosts Matt Lauer and Katie Couric. You don't need tickets to be part of that crowd. Just show up on the sidewalk on 49th Street and Rockefeller Plaza (between Fifth and Sixth avenues) around 7 a.m. on any weekday.

Tours

No matter what your interest, price range, or schedule, chances are that New York has a tour for you. I've divided "Tours" into four categories: tour organizers, tours of New York, tours of specific sights and neighborhoods, and individuals and organizations that put together walking tours of various areas. In general, the first category is for groups and corporate clients rather than individuals who want to tag along. Some of the tours in the other three categories simply require you to show up and pay a couple of dollars, while others require reservations in advance and can be costly. Some are well established and reliable, while others are either new or eccentric and may not be around by the time you read this. As with just about everything else, my advice is to call in advance. Speaking of calling, you can always get in touch with the Guides Association of New York for advice about the kind of tour or guide you're looking for as well as a list of its members and their specialties. The Association's number is 212/969-0666.

TOUR ORGANIZERS

Art Horizons International—If your group of eight or more is serious about art and would like to meet some gallery owners or museum curators, give Art Horizons International a call and they'll help arrange it. This well-regarded organization also puts together tours of the fashion industry and Broadway. Call 212/969-9410 for more information or a brochure.

Cover New York—This is a specialty tour operator that does "insider" visits for groups of eight or more. They specialize in shopping, fashion, theater, art, architecture, and interior design visits. Corporations, school groups, and tourist organizations make use of their specialized service, and find their multilingual guides to be a real advantage. Call 212/737-1726 for more information.

Daily-Thorp Cultural Tours—In addition to organizing tours for opera and music lovers around the world, Daily-Thorp teams up with the Metropolitan Opera Guild in New York to arrange spectacular "deluxe" and "Opera Express" tours to New York involving the Metropolitan Opera, the New York Philharmonic, and the New York City Opera, as well as Broadway shows. Guests on the deluxe tours usually stay at the Peninsula or the Plaza hotels and have just about every need and want taken care of by a staff of real professionals. The Opera Express tours are a bit more downscale (and cheaper) but are run just as well. Call 212/307-1555 for more information or a brochure.

Doorway to Design – Sheila Sperber offers a personalized approach to educational and fun events in the Big Apple. For over 20 years, she has created exclusively tailored itineraries for individuals and groups with an emphasis on entree to private homes and clubs, plus shopping and behind-the-scenes visits to Manhattan's creative community. You can tour auction houses, Soho studios, wholesale fashion outlets, private kitchens of top chefs, interior design showrooms closed to the general public, and even landmark townhouses and Victorian mansions! Call 212/221-1111 for more information.

Manhattan Passport – Run by Ina Lee Selden, this terrific company organizes customized trips and tours to New York and other places in the region for corporate clients and special-interest groups from the U.S. and other countries. Whether you're thinking ultimately elegant or more than a little offbeat, chances are Ina and her staff can make it happen. Call 212/861-2746 for a brochure and information.

New York Inside/Out, Inc. – Groups interested in interior design, the fashion world, or arts and antiques ought to call these folks. New York Inside/Out, Inc., is staffed by professionals who can organize day-long tours or week-long trips. Call 212/861-4114 for more information or a brochure.

Unique New York – Chris Richie is a terrific resource for anyone who plans to visit New York but feels a little intimidated by it. For reasonable rates, he and his partner Gina Burton will work with you to find a little slice of the Big Apple that's right for your tastes and appetites. They can show how New Yorkers really live or take you on a trip through your family's history, a shopping tour, or Central Park. Unique New York handles individuals, families, and groups. Call 212/267-8374 for more information, and give some advance notice so they can design a unique itinerary.

Viewpoint International – Whether you're organizing a gala event for thousands or just want a first-class customized tour put together for a couple of people, these folks can help. Their extraordinary client list speaks volumes about the professional, reliable, and creative service you'll get here. While they're best known for corporate-event work, Viewpoint International offers lots of interesting tours, too. Call 212/355-1055 for more information or a brochure.

TOURS OF NEW YORK

Big Apple Greeters – A volunteer service, this outfit will hook you up with a personal guide to New York. If you're looking for a personalized introduction to this sometimes overwhelming city, Big Apple Greeters may be for you. Best of all, it's free! Just give a couple days notice and tell them what part of New York you would like to see. Call 212/669-8159 for more information.

Circle Line – Particularly on warm days, the three-hour boat trip around the entire island of Manhattan on one of Circle Line's boats is a real treat. In addition to some nice breezes, you'll get a good sense of how Manhattan is laid out and what neighborhoods are where. A guide offers commentary as the boat makes its way down the Hudson River, into New York Harbor, up the East

River, across the top of the island in the Harlem River, and back down the Hudson. Trips depart Pier 83 (at 43rd Street and the Hudson River) at least several times a day (almost a dozen at the height of the season) between mid-March and December. Tickets cost $20 for adults and $10 for children under 12. Shorter tours, a Saturday night dance cruise, and even a family cruise complete with a magician are also available. Call 212/563-3200 for more information or a brochure.

Gray Line—If you're feeling overwhelmed by New York and want to be completely anonymous as someone shows you the highlights, try a Gray Line tour. The company offers a wide range of partial and full-day bus tours to different parts of Manhattan, including a marathon nine-and-a-half-hour "Manhattan Comprehensive" that goes from Harlem to Wall Street and even out to the Statue of Liberty and Ellis Island. Most tours run at least once a day, and some are offered in French, German, Italian, Portuguese, and Spanish, as well as English. Gray Line also offers package tours to places like West Point, factory outlets north of the city, Niagara Falls, and even Washington, D.C. Show up at Gray Line's headquarters at 900 Eighth Avenue, between 53rd and 54th streets, from 7:45 a.m. and 7 p.m.to purchase tickets. Call 212/397-2600 for more information or a brochure.

Gray Line Double-Decker Loop—This is a terrific way to see many of the city's major sights without having to pay for taxis or brave the public transportation system. Somewhat like the Tour Mobile in Washington, D.C., Gray Line's open-air double-decker buses and trolleys run every half hour between Battery Park, South Street Seaport, the Empire State Building, and three dozen other places. Tickets cost $29 for adults and $19 for kids, and are good for two days and as many different stops as you want to make. Tickets for less extensive routes are less expensive. Schedules change by season. Call 212/397-2600 for more information.

Island Helicopter—One of several outfits in Manhattan offering helicopter tours, this one is based at the heliport at the eastern end of 34th Street. Prices range from $49 to $129, depending on the flight pattern you choose. (Save $5 on tickets by purchasing them from the hotel concierge rather than at the heliport.) Island Helicopters operates from 9 a.m. to 9 p.m. seven days a week but requires at least two passengers per flight. Call 212/683-4575 for more information.

Liberty Helicopter Tours—This company's helicopters take off from the heliport at the western end of 30th Street and from the Wall Street Heliport on Pier 6 near the end of Whitehall Street. Prices begin at $44 and go up to $150, depending on the flight pattern you choose. Liberty Helicopter Tours also operates daily but requires at least three passengers per flight. Call 212/967-6464 for more information or a brochure.

TOURS OF SPECIFIC PLACES AND AREAS

ARTime—A relative newcomer to the tour scene, this outfit puts together "Saturday in the Galleries" tours of various Soho and Chelsea galleries. Tours are centered around particular themes and geared to elementary school children and their families. It's run by two art historians whose background includes working with children at the Brooklyn Museum. Ninety-minute tours cost $20 for each child-adult pair and $5 for each additional child (additional adults are free). Call 718/797-1573 for more information.

Carnegie Hall—Lincoln Center may have the Metropolitan Opera and the New York Philharmonic, but Carnegie Hall remains synonymous with classical music. If you want to take a look around during the day, 75-minute tours are offered on Monday, Tuesday, Thursday, and Friday at 11:30, 2 and, 3. The tour costs $6 for adults, $5 for students and senior citizens, and $3 for children under 12. Call 212/903-9790 for more information or drop by the house manager's window inside Carnegie Hall's lobby at 153 West 57th Street, just off Seventh Avenue. Tours meet inside the lobby.

Cathedral Church of St. John the Divine—If you're even remotely interested in Gothic architecture or just want to see one of the most amazing and beautiful places in all of New York, I urge you to take a tour of this cathedral-in-progress. Located on Amsterdam Avenue at 112th Street, this Episcopal church makes a real effort to welcome people of all faiths. Regular tours cost $2 and meet at a table in the back of the narthex, inside the main doors. They begin at 11 a.m. Tuesday through Saturday and after morning services at 1 p.m. on Sunday. The so-called "vertical tour" takes place every other Saturday and costs $10. Although definitely not something for small children, people with disabilities, or those afraid of heights (you must sign a waiver at the outset), this tour affords participants an absolutely fascinating view of the cathedral's spectacular stained-glass windows, architecture, and many hidden spaces. Space is limited and reservations are required at least one week in advance. Also, if you can get ten people together, the folks here will organize a tour tailored to your particular interests. Call 212/316-7540 for general information and 212/932-7347 on weekday afternoons to make reservations.

Central Park—This incredible park is so extensive that you may want to get the lay of the land by taking a 90-minute guided trolley tour run by Gray Line and the Central Park Conservancy. It leaves at 10:30 a.m., 1 p.m., and 3 p.m. from the information kiosk at 59th Street and Fifth Avenue on weekdays in late April through October. The price is $15 for adults, $12 for senior citizens and students, and $7.50 for children under 11. Call 212/397-3807 for more information or to make reservations. Another possibility is Tom Ahern's Central Park Bicycle Tour, a two-hour romp through "New York's front yard." For $25 per adult and $20 for children, you get a tour and a bicycle. For reservations or more information, call Bite of the Apple Tours at 212/541-8759. You might also check with the city's Urban Park Rangers (212/427-4040) to see if they have any free walking tours scheduled.

Downtown and Wall Street—With four well-marked trails to guide you throughout the areas now known as downtown and Wall Street, Heritage Trails New York will escort you on a wonderfully educational walking trip through early American history. Stop by the Heritage Trails Hub & Visitors Information Center in the Federal Hall National Memorial (built on the site of the country's first capital and the place George Washington took his oath of office) before setting out to get a copy of their fascinating and well-written guide (which costs $5). If you would rather join a guide for a morning or afternoon walk, prices are $14 for adults, $7 for children 7-12 (accompanied by an adult), and free for children 6 and under. Reservations are required. Federal Hall National Memorial is on the corner of Broad and Wall streets. Call 888/487-2457 for more information.

Eldridge Street Synagogue—This stunning synagogue was built by Eastern European immigrants at 12 Eldridge Street (between Canal and Division streets) on the Lower East Side in 1887. Although the same congregation that built it still worships here, the building fell into disrepair in the middle of this century and is now being renovated. Fascinating tours are offered every Sunday on the hour between 11 and 4 and on Tuesday and Thursday at 11:30 and 2:30. Admission, which helps pay for the renovation, is $4 for adults, and $2.50 for students, senior citizens, and children. They also have all sorts of specially designed tours and talks for student groups and children. Call 212/219-0888 for more information.

Federal Reserve Bank — Free tours of the gold vaults (which contain almost 11,000 tons of monetary gold) and other parts of this incredible institution are given twice in the morning and twice in the afternoon on weekdays (except major holidays). You must make reservations at least a day or two in advance. Write the Public Information Department, 33 Liberty Street, New York, NY 10045 or call 212/720-7839 to find out whether they have space on a day that works for you. You'll find the Federal Reserve on Liberty Street between Nassau and Williams streets.

Fulton Fish Market — This amazing operation on Pier 17 in the South Street Seaport complex supplies the city's restaurants with tons of fish every month. Business hours are from midnight to 8 a.m., and tours are offered at 6 a. m. on the first and third Thursday of every month between April and October. Reservations are required. The Fish Market seems to be in a constant state of upheaval, so call 212/669-9424 to be sure it's open and the tour is being offered.

Gracie Mansion — Thanks to Fiorello LaGuardia, New York is the only city in the U.S. with an official mayoral residence. This historic mansion, built in 1799 and one of the oldest continuously occupied homes in New York, is located in Carl Schurz Park, overlooking the East River (at about 88th Street and East End Avenue). Two morning and two afternoon tours are offered on Wednesday by appointment. Call 212/570-4751 for more information or a reservation. A contribution of $4 for adults and $3 for senior citizens is suggested.

Grand Central Station — In addition to excellent walking tours, the Municipal Art Society conducts a 90-minute free tour of this beautiful building every Wednesday at 12:30 p.m. I highly recommend this popular tour. Grand Central Station is one of the city's real landmarks, and the society's tour will give you a sense of its grandeur and history, while allowing you to see a lot of features that most commuters don't even know exist. The tour meets at the Chemical Bank branch on the main concourse directly across from the grand staircase. Call 212/935-3960 for more information. The Grand Central Partnership also offers a free tour of the neighborhood on Friday at 12:30 p.m. It meets at the Whitney Museum's gallery inside the Philip Morris Building, across 42nd Street from the station. Call 212/818-1777 for more information.

Harlem — Whether you want to visit a jazz club, stop by historic buildings like the Morris-Jumel Mansion and the Apollo Theater, or go to church on Sunday morning to hear a gospel choir, Harlem Spirituals probably has a tour that's right for you. In addition to English, they offer tours in Italian, German, Spanish, French, and Portuguese when there's a demand. All tours are by bus and prices depend on your itinerary. Stop by their offices at 690 Eighth Avenue (between 44th and 43rd streets) between 8:30 a.m. and 6 p.m. or call 212/757-0425 for more information. You can also try Harlem Your Way! (212/690-1687), a tour group specializing in customized tours for individuals and groups, family reunions, and other events.

Lincoln Center—If the Lincoln Center complex seems a little overwhelming but you are interested in seeing its magnificent auditoriums and concert halls, a minumum of four one-hour tours are given every day between 10 a.m. and 5 p.m. Because the center's schedule is put together only a day in advance, you must call on the day you want to take a tour to find out exactly when they will be offered. The tour costs $8.50 for adults, $7.75 for students and senior citizens, and $4.50 for children 6 to 12. (If that seems a little steep, check out the prices of opera and concert tickets!) Lincoln Center stretches between 62nd and 65th streets along Columbus Avenue. The tour office is on the lower level of the Metropolitan Opera House, directly in back of the main square. Call 212/875-5350 for more information or a brochure.

Lower East Side—This is really a shopper's tour, put on by the Historic Orchard Street Shopping District (an association of its merchants). If you're interested in learning about this wonderful area's shops and its retailing history, the tour meets on Sunday at 11 a.m. at Katz's Delicatessen (on the corner of East Houston and Ludlow streets) from April through December. It lasts about an hour and is free. Call 212/226-9010 for more information.

Lower East Side Tenement Museum—I can't say enough good things about this wonderful museum and its volunteers. In addition to tours of the restored apartments in the tenement at 97 Orchard Street, the museum offers fascinating tours exploring the surrounding area's rich and diverse ethnic heritage on weekends in the warmer months. They aren't cheap but are well worth the price. Tours leave from the museum's offices at the corner of Orchard and Broome streets. Call 212/431-0233 for more information.

Madison Square Garden—If you've always wanted to go into the Knicks' locker room, this is the tour for you! It's offered every hour between 10 a.m. and 3 p.m. Monday through Saturday, and between 11 a.m. and 3 p.m. on Sunday (although schedules are frequently abbreviated because of events at the Garden). Tickets cost $10 for adults and $9 for children under 12 and are available at the Garden's box office. Call 212/465-5800 for more information.

Metropolitan Opera—The Metropolitan Opera Guild offers 90-minute tours of this extraordinary place between the start of the opera season around the end of September and the end of the ballet season in or around June on weekday afternoons and Saturday mornings. You should make reservations well in advance, but you can always call at the last minute to see if space is available or to go on a standby basis. Tickets cost $8 for adults and $4 for full-time students. Call 212/769-7020 between 10 and 4 weekdays for more information or a brochure.

NBC Studios—Children under six are not admitted, but anybody else can take an hour-long tour of the NBC's television studios for $10 per person. The quality of the tour varies dramatically, depending on both chance (what famous person happens to be getting off the elevator when you're getting on) and whether some big news event is breaking. The tour leaves every 15 minutes between 9:30 a.m. and 4:30 p.m. on Monday through Saturday from NBC's lobby on 50th Street between Fifth and Sixth avenues. Call 212/664-7174 for more information.

New York Harbor—Kayaking tours of New York Harbor and even a 30-mile circumnavigation of the island of Manhattan are available through Atlantic Kayak Tours. The company also offers lessons for students at all skill levels. Call 914/246-2187 for more information.

New York Public Library—An informative tour of the grand New York Public Library is offered free of charge Monday through Saturday at 11 a.m. and again at 2 p.m. It leaves from the Friends of the Library desk to the right of the library's main entrance on Fifth Avenue at 41st Street. Tours of the changing exhibit in the library's Gottesman Hall are also offered free of charge on Tuesday through Saturday at 12:30 p.m. and 2:30 p.m. Call the library's volunteer office at 212/930-0911 for more information.

New York Public Library for the Performing Arts—Free hour-long tours of this exceptional facility in Lincoln Center are offered every Wednesday at 2 p.m. Talk to the unusually helpful folks at the information desk inside the library's main entrance or call 212/870-1670 for more information.

Police Academy—You can take a free tour of the New York City Police Academy on weekdays, but you must schedule it in advance and arrive with identification. The Police Academy is located at 235 East 20th Street, between Second and Third avenues. Make a point of visiting the Police Academy's museum while you're here (see the "Museums" section of this chapter for more information). Call 212/477-9753 for more information.

Police Department—If you're interested in seeing the real NYPD Blue in action, this tour of headquarters takes you to the firing range, central booking, and inside the 911 system. Police headquarters are between Chambers and Centre streets in downtown Manhattan. The tour lasts roughly 40 minutes. Call 212/374-3804 for more information.

Radio City Music Hall—If you want to get inside this art deco treasure but don't want to go to a concert or other event, try one of the daily tours. Schedules vary depending on activities going on and tours run about an hour and costs $13.75 for adults and $9 for children 12 and under. Call 212/632-4041 for more information. Radio City Music Hall is on the corner of Sixth Avenue and 50th Street, and tours meet inside the main lobby.

Schomburg Center for Research in Black Culture—Tours of the collection and galleries in this rich cultural resource on the corner of Malcolm X Boulevard and 135th Street are offered by appointment on Tuesdays and Wednesdays between 10 a.m. and noon. Call 212/491-2214 for more information or reservations.

Times Square—The Times Square Business Improvement District offers a free tour of this famous area on Fridays at noon. It meets at the Times Square tourist information center on 42nd Street between Seventh and Eighth avenues.

34th Street—The 34th Street Partnership sponsors a free 90-minute tour of the neighborhood around the Empire State Building on Thursdays at 12:30 p.m. The tour meets at the Fifth Avenue entrance of the Empire State Building, between 33rd and 34th streets.

Trinity Church—A guided tour of this historic church at Broadway and Wall streets leaves from the pulpit inside the sanctuary at 2 p.m. daily. It's free, although donations are accepted. Call 212/602-0800 for more information.

United Nations—If you want to peek inside the chambers of the United Nations General Assembly and learn a little about this incredible organization, tours begin about every half hour between 9:15 a.m. and 4:45 p.m. seven days a week (Monday through Friday only in January and February). The tour costs

$7.50 for adults, $5.50 for senior citizens and students from high school age on up, and $4.50 for children between 5 and 14. Children under 5 are not allowed on the tours, which last between 45 minutes and an hour and are offered in languages other than English upon request. The visitors' entrance to the United Nations is on First Avenue, between 45th and 46th streets, and the tour desk is directly across from the entrance, past the main lobby and down the hall. Call 212/963-7713 for more information.

Upper East Side – If you're interested in architectural history and want to take your own walking tour, get a copy of the New York Landmarks Conservancy's *Touring the Upper East Side: Walks in Five Historic Districts.* Written by Andrew Dolkart, an architectural historian at Columbia University, it's full of interesting stories about well-known and not so well-known parts of New York's most prestigious neighborhood. The $9.95 book is available from the Conservancy (141 Fifth Avenue at 21st Street). Call 212/995-5260 for more information.

Yankee Stadium – Groups of 12 or more can tour the dugout, press box, and other parts of "the House that Ruth Built" (which is, by the way, in the Bronx) on weekdays, but advance reservations are required and tours are not given on game days. The regular cost is $6 per adult and $3 per child, but special rates are available for senior citizens and student groups. Call 718/293-4300 for more information or a brochure.

Most museums offer tours of specific galleries, special shows, or their entire collection. Look under specific entries in the section on "Museums" in this chapter, or call specific museums for more information.

WALKING TOURS

Adventure on a Shoestring – The name pretty much sums up this marvelous organization. For a $40 annual membership fee, plus a $3 attendance fee for each event, you can go on any and all of the scores of interesting and often offbeat tours of the city and surrounding areas they put together. Call 212/265-2663 for more information, or send a check for $40 to Adventure on a Shoestring (300 West 53rd Street, New York, NY 10019) to join and get on their quarterly mailing list.

Big Onion Walking Tours – Seth Kamil, an enterprising Ph.D. candidate from Columbia University, and his band of guides with graduate degrees in American history from Columbia and New York University share their vast knowledge of New York through a wide array of walking tours in different parts of the city. Governor's Island, George Washington's New York, Historic Catholic New York, and the Civil War and Draft Riots are just a few of their many topics. Most tours cost $9 for adults and $7 for senior citizens and students; some are a bit more expensive. All last between two and two-and-a-half hours. Call 212/439-1090 for more information or to get on their mailing list.

Citywalks – For $12 a person, you can take one of John Wilson's guided walking tours of the Lower East Side, Greenwich Village, or one of lower Manhattan's other neighborhoods. Most tours are on the weekend and last for two hours. Call 212/989-2456 for more information or to get on his mailing list.

Cooper-Hewitt National Design Museum – One of New York's two branches of the Smithsonian, this museum offers unusual and sometimes rather expensive educational walking tours of areas in and around New York. The museum also offers periodic trips abroad. Reservations are required. Call 212/860-6321 for more information.

Municipal Art Society – This terrific advocacy group offers a wide array of thematic and area-specific walking tours for people interested in the city's architecture and history. Most tours are led by historians. The diverse topics include architectural oddities, immigrant New York, downtown skyscrapers, and subway art and design. Tours are offered on different days and meet at different places, but most last about 90 minutes and cost between $10 and $15 for adults (less for students and senior citizens). If you have your heart set on one of the more expensive and off-the-beaten track tours, be forewarned that such tours are sometimes cancelled because there isn't enough interest. If you want a private tour, call 212/935-3960. Call 212/439-1049 for general information or to get on the Society's mailing list.

Museum of the City of New York – This museum makes a real effort to be part of the city rather than an aloof observer, and its walking tours are very much in keeping with that spirit. Typically held every other Sunday from April to October, tours are led by experts and cost $15. Registration is required. Call the museum's education department at 212/534-1672, ext. 206, for more information or to get on the museum's mailing list.

92nd Street YMHA – This amazing institution often offers walking tours to complement its frequent lectures and other programs, as well as open houses in historic areas. Prices vary, but the guides are always knowledgeable and the tours are well run. They fill up quickly, and reservations are required. Call 212/415-5628 for more information or to get on the mailing list.

River-to-River Downtown Walking Tours – I don't know of a better guide for a "river to river" walk through lower Manhattan than Ruth Alscher-Green, a retired high-school teacher and lifelong New Yorker. A two-hour tour costs $35 for one person and $50 for two, and special rates are offered for groups and senior citizens. Call 212/321-2823 for more information or to get on her mailing list.

Urban Explorations – Landscape designer Patricia Olmstead offers thoughtful and informative walking tours of Battery Park City, Soho, Chinatown, the Flower District, the area around the 96th Street Mosque, and just about any other neighborhood or district you want to see. She specializes in garden tours throughout the city and will happily design an itinerary or private tour if nothing in her current repertoire suits you or your group. Most tours are held on weekends (but generally not in the summer) and cost $12 for adults and $10 for students, senior citizens, and repeat customers. Call 718/721-5254 for more information or to get on her mailing list.

Urban Park Rangers – No, you didn't misread that. The city's Department of Parks and Recreation employs Urban Park Rangers, and they give wonderful weekend walking tours and talks in Central Park and other parks throughout Manhattan and the city's four other boroughs. These tours are free, and many are designed for children or families. Call 212/427-4040 for more information or to get on their mailing list.

A Week in New York

You could spend an entire lifetime in New York and still never have time to see and do and eat everything this fabulous city has to offer. If you're here for a week or two, you obviously have a lot of choices to make.

The first thing you need to know when planning an itinerary is that some areas are best on certain days—Soho on Saturday and the Lower East Side on Sunday, for example. Others shut down on the weekend (the Financial District), Saturday (the Lower East Side), Sunday (Soho and most of midtown), or Monday (many major museums and theaters). If time is limited, I suggest picking a couple of things you really want to do or places you really want to see and build your days around them. Check the hours of the places you're planning to visit and plan your days accordingly so you can make the most of whatever time you have here.

If you're at a loss—you want to see everything but don't know where to start—I've sketched an outline of possible itineraries for seven days in New York that will give some ideas. In so doing, however, I do not mean to imply that the places I've included are necessarily better than others. Moreover, I do not recommend trying to do everything on every day. Part of the pleasure of New York is wandering and lingering and taking your time, and I don't want you to collapse from exhaustion.

MONDAY (Upper West Side)

- Breakfast to go from Fairway (2127 Broadway, at 74th St) or Zabar's (2245 Broadway, at 80th St)
- Cathedral Church of St. John the Divine (Amsterdam Ave, at 112th St)
- Columbia University, main campus (entrance off 116th St, at Broadway and Amsterdam Ave)
- Riverside Church's bell tower (Riverside Drive, bet 120th and 122nd St)
- American Museum of Natural History (Central Park West, bet 77th and 81st St)
- Late lunch at Tavern on the Green (inside the park at 67th St just off Central Park West)
- Stroll through Central Park
- Lincoln Center (Columbus Ave, bet 62nd and 65th St)
- Museum of American Folk Art (Columbus Ave, bet 65th and 66th St)
- Dinner at Gabriel's (11 West 60th St)

TUESDAY (Midtown)

- Macy's (151 West 34th St, bet Broadway and Seventh Ave)
- Pierpoint Morgan Library (29 East 36th St, at Madison Ave)
- New York Public Library (Fifth Ave, bet 40th and 42nd St and Bryant Park)
- International Center for Photography (1133 Sixth Ave, at 43rd St)
- Saks Fifth Avenue (611 Fifth Ave, bet 49th and 50th St)
- Lunch at the American Festival Cafe (Rockefeller Plaza, near Fifth Ave and 50th St)
- Rockefeller Center (bet Fifth and Sixth Ave and 49th and 51st St)
- Museum of Modern Art (11 West 53rd St, bet Fifth and Sixth Ave)
- Carnegie Hall (153 West 57th St, just off Seventh Ave)
- Dinner at Docks (633 Third Ave, at 40th St)
- Empire State Building observation deck (Fifth Ave, bet 33rd and 34th St)

WEDNESDAY

- United Nations (First Ave, bet 45th and 46th St)
- Ford Foundation Gardens (320 East 43rd St, bet First and Second Ave)
- Early lunch at Tropica (in the MetLife Building, at 200 Park Ave)
- 12:30 tour of Grand Central Station (offered by the Metropolitan Art Society)
- The Cloisters (Fort Tryon Park)
- Dyckman Farmhouse (4881 Broadway, at 204th St)
- Dinner at Carnegie Deli (Seventh Ave and 55th St)

THURSDAY (Museum Mile)

- Museum of the City of New York (1220 Fifth Ave, bet 103rd and 104th St)
- Jewish Museum (1109 Fifth Ave, at 92nd St)
- Cooper-Hewitt National Museum of Design (2 East 91st St, off Fifth Ave)
- Solomon R. Guggenheim Museum (1071 Fifth Ave, bet 88th and 89th St)
- Lunch at the Museum Cafe in the Guggenheim
- Metropolitan Museum of Art (Fifth Ave, bet 80th and 84th St)
- The Whitney Museum of American Art (945 Madison Ave, at 75th St)
- Frick Collection (1 East 70th St, bet Fifth and Madison Ave)
- Bloomingdale's (1000 Third Ave, bet 59th and 60th St)
- Dinner at Sette Mezzo (969 Lexington Ave, at 70th St)

FRIDAY (Financial District)

- Battery Park to Statue of Liberty and Ellis Island
- Museum of the American Indian (1 Bowling Green)
- Pick up half-price tickets for the theater (TKTS booth on the mezzanine of 2 World Trade Center)
- Lunch at Nobu (105 Hudson St)
- New York Stock Exchange (20 Broad St, bet Wall and Exchange St)
- Federal Hall National Monument (Wall and Nassau St)
- Trinity Church (Broadway at Wall St)
- Fraunces Tavern Museum (54 Pearl St, at Broad St)
- Pre-theater dinner at La Réserve (4 West 49th St, bet Fifth and Sixth Ave)
- Theater

SATURDAY (Soho)

- Gallery hopping on and around West Broadway
- Alternative Museum (594 Broadway, bet Houston and Prince St)
- Museum for African Art (593 Broadway, bet Houston and Prince St)
- Contemporary Museum (583 Broadway, bet Houston and Prince St)
- Guggenheim Museum Soho (575 Broadway, at Prince St)
- Dinner at Blue Ribbon (97 Sullivan St)

SUNDAY (Lower East Side)

- Lower East Side shopping
- Brunch at Katz's Delicatessen (205 East Houston St, at Ludlow St)
- Lower East Side Tenement Museum (97 Orchard St, bet Delancey and Broome St)
- Eldridge Street Synagogue (12 Eldridge St)
- Museum of Chinese in the Americas (70 Mulberry St, at Bayard St)
- Dinner in Chinatown at the Golden Unicorn (18 East Broadway, at Catherine St)

IV. Where to Find It: New York's Best Food Shops

Scratch what I said at the beginning of the last chapter: you *can* eat constantly. And in New York, it's very tempting to do just that! The bakeries alone (almost three dozen of which are listed in the following pages) could keep you going for weeks. Then there are such incredible New York institutions as Zabar's and Fairway on the Upper West Side, Grace's Marketplace on the Upper East Side, Balducci's in the West Village, and Dean & Deluca in Soho. And the city's amazing Greenmarkets. And, of course, the Italian food shops, the Indian ones, the butchers . . . the list goes on and on and on.

Most New Yorkers don't do all their food shopping in one big grocery store. They get bread at one place, meat somewhere else, fruits and vegetables at another store, pasta at yet another. The quality and freshness of food bought this way in New York can't be beat. And everybody has their favorite stores.

What I've tried to do here is give you "the best of the best." Whether you're eating constantly ("grazing" is the term for this art, by the way) or looking for a place to get the right food for a special occasion, the following pages are filled with mouth-watering choices.

Asian Foodstuffs (the best)

Chinese, Thai, Malasian, Philippine, Vietnamese

Asia Market (71-1/2 Mulberry St)
Bangkok Center Market (104 Mosco St, at Mott St)
Chinese American Trading Company* (91 Mulberry St, at Canal St)
East Broadway Meat Market (36 East Broadway)
Fong Inn Too (46 Mott St)
Fung Wong Bakery* (30 Mott St)
Hong Keung Seafood & Meat Market (75 Mulberry St)
Kam Kuo Foods (7 Mott St)
Kam Man Food Products* (200 Canal St)
Thuan-Nguyen Market (84 Mulberry St)

Indian:

Foods of India (121 Lexington Ave, bet 28th and 29th St)
K Kalustyan* (123 Lexington Ave, bet 28th and 29th St)

Japanese:

Katagiri* (224 E 59th St)

Korean:

Han Arum (25 W 32nd St)

*Descriptions in this chapter

Bakery Goods

> Some hints for keeping bread fresh and tasty: If you will be keeping it for several days, wrap the bread in airtight plastic or foil and store at room temperature. Heat uncovered at 350 degrees for five minutes or so to refresh the crust (preheat the oven). If you freeze bread (and it can be done for up to three months), be sure to refresh crust after defrosting at room temperature.

A. ORWASHER BAKERY
308 E 78th St (nr Second Ave)   212/288-6569
Mon-Sat: 7-7

Orwasher has been in existence for over three quarters of a century at the same location, operated by the same famiy. Many of its breads are from recipes handed down from father to son. You'll find Old World breads that once existed in the local immigrant bakeries and have now become extremely rare. Over 30 varieties are always available. Hearth-baked in brick ovens and made with natural ingredients, the breads come in a marvelous array of shapes and sizes—triple twists, cornucopias, and hearts, just to name a few. Be sure to sample the onion boards, rye, cinnamon raisin bread, and challah, available on Fridays. It's almost as good as the home-baked variety. Best of all is raisin pumpernickel, which comes in small rolls or loaves. When warm, it's moist, delicious, and sensational.

A. ZITO AND SON'S BAKERY
259 Bleecker St (bet Sixth and Seventh Ave)   212/929-6139
Mon-Sat: 6-7; Sun: 6-3

Those in the know, know Zito's. They flock here at sunrise to buy bread straight from the oven. Greenwich Village residents love Zito's because the bread crust is crunchy perfection—a sharp contrast to the soft, delicate inside. Two best sellers are the whole-wheat loaf and the Sicilian loaf. Anthony John Zito is proudest of the house specialties: Italian, whole-wheat, and white breads. The latter two come in sizes of 4, 7, and 13 ounces.

BONTE PATISSERIE
1316 Third Ave (bet 75th and 76th St)   212/535-2360
Mon-Sat: 9-6:30; closed August

Mrs. Bonte serves a delicious line of pastries and cakes. The style is decidedly French, but the taste has earned universal appreciation. The pastry is flaky smooth, the chocolates creamy satin, and the croissants and eclairs—well, they're perfection. Mrs. Bonte personally supervises the operation, and everything sold here bears the hallmark of a tremendously accomplished pastry chef. (Her husband is just as talented.)

BOW-WOW BAKERY
336 E 54th St (bet First and Second Ave)   212/230-1988
Mon-Fri 11-7; Sat: 11-6; Sun: 12-5

Now even Fido has a place in the rarefied world of unique New York bakeries. Bow-Wow is the first (and only) doggie dream house in the city, home-baking treats for your pet without salt, sugar, preservatives, or byproducts. In addition, this outlet offers unique gifts for dogs and dog lovers, and customizes baskets for a special birthday party when your four-legged friend reaches a milestone. There are peanut-butter bones, graham-cracker Scotty cookies, canine corn muffins, and even tuna muffins that are the cat's meow. Only in Manhattan!

BREAD MARKET & CAFE
485 Fifth Ave (bet 41st and 42nd St)   212/370-7356
Mon-Fri: 7-7; Sat: 7-5

Freshness is the key here! The bread is baked fresh daily in their rotating oven; if any is left over, it is donated to the Grand Central Partnership. You'll find very good San Francisco sourdough, cinnamon raisin, Italian braid, Jewish rye, European corn rye, German pumpernickel, and much more. Their sandwiches are excellent and come in a wide variety. Free delivery is offered.

BREAD SHOP
3139 Broadway (at LaSalle St)   212/666-4343
Daily: 8 a.m.-9 p.m.

The Bread Shop is a tiny, out-of-the-way bakery under the tracks at 123rd Street. It supplies some of the best handmade, untainted-by-preservatives bread in the city. Its customers are mostly local stores and New York's better food shops, but if you arrive between 10 a.m. and 3 p.m., one of the house specialties will be available fresh from the oven. Jenny Buchanan and Jim Fitzer, who run the shop, are big on healthy, natural ingredients, so the bread is not just delicious but good for you.

CAFE LALO
201 W 83rd St (at Amsterdam Ave)   212/496-6031
Mon-Thurs: 9 a.m.-2 a.m.; Fri, Sat: 9 a.m.-4 a.m.;
Sun: 9 a.m-2 a.m.

This is the best dessert shop in town, in my opinion. You will think you are in a fine European pastry shop as you enjoy fine cappuccino, espresso, cordials, and a large selection of delicious desserts. I know good cakes and pastries, as I judge them at the Oregon State Fair every year. Cafe Lalo offers 38 kinds of cake, 12 cheesecakes, and 18 pies! Yogurt and ice cream are also available, and soothing music makes every calorie go down sweetly. Breakfasts and brunches are all a treat.

COLUMBUS BAKERY
474 Columbus Ave (at 83rd St)   212/724-6880
Mon-Fri: 8-8; Sat, Sun: 9-8

The Upper West Side has a quality bakery that it can call its own. Columbus

Bakery sells great rosemary rolls, delicious onion rolls for burgers, multigrain breads, really crusty sourdoughs, wonderful cakes and pastries, and more. You can eat in or take out, but what a pleasure just to sit there and smell those fresh loaves. Gift baskets and catering are available.

CREATIVE CAKES
400 E 74th St (at First Ave)   212/794-9811
Tues-Fri: 8-4:30; Sat: 9-11

Being in the "creative cake" business myself, I know about the fun involved in making all kinds of unusual concoctions. Creative Cakes knows how to have fun, using fine ingredients and ingenious patterns. Cake lovers are fans of the fudgy chocolate with frosted buttercream icing and the sensational designs. Bill Schutz, the boss, has designed Bella Abzug's hat on a platter and even made a replica of the U.S. Customs House for a Fourth of July celebration. Prices are reasonable, and the results are sure to be a conversation piece at any party.

DUFOUR PASTRY KITCHENS
25 Ninth Ave (at 13th St)   212/929-2800
Mon-Fri: 8-5; call for Sat hours

The location is not the handiest. The air is full of pastry dough, so don't wear your best black outfit. And all items are frozen, so you'll have to bake them yourself (instructions included). But these are the only drawbacks! You'll find delicious and creative pastry items of high quality at sensible prices at Dufour, which counts many fancy uptown restaurants among its regular customers. Chocolate and regular puff-pastry dough are available in sheets and in bulk. Try the slice-and-bake savory puff pastry logs, like artichoke, black olive and tomato, asparagus fontina, or three-cheese spinach *rustica*. Wonderful hors d'oeuvres can be ordered in quantity: bite-size, hand-filled "party lites" in flavors like fresh-mushroom paté, Swiss and spinach, Southwestern black bean, smoked salmon, Caribbean paté, Indian curry, and ratatouille. Enchilada corn cups are a delicious melt of green chilies, tomatoes, and cheeses in a tasty corn shell. The apple and spice turnovers are great desserts. Lunch puffs—chili with fresh vegetables, tuna melt, smoked salmon, broccoli-spinach gratin, and more— provide a satisfying light meal. Holiday strudels are also available. All ingredients are natural.

ECCE PANIS
1120 Third Ave (bet 65th and 66th St)   212/535-2099
Mon-Fri: 9-8; Sat, Sun: 9-6

1260 Madison Ave (off 90th St)   212/348-0040
Mon-Fri: 9-7; Sat, Sun: 9-6

282 Columbus Ave (at 73rd St)   212/362-7189
Mon-Fri: 8-8; Sat, Sun: 8-6

This is one of Manhattan's better bakeries. Their offerings are unique and of high quality. Breads include dark and light sourdough, neo-Tuscan, whole-wheat currant, double walnut, dried fruit focaccia, Sunday raisin, baguettes, olive bread, and more. The chocolate *biscotti* is superb! Unusual gift baskets are a specialty.

THE EROTIC BAKER
212/721-3217
Tues-Fri: 10-6
Telephone orders only

According to their people, cake tops can be erotic, non-erotic, or just a bit erotic. Everything is made to order, so they can do all manner of variations. Courier service is used for deliveries in Manhattan.

FERRARA PASTRIES
195 Grand St (bet Mulberry and Mott St)   212/226-6150
108 Mulberry St   212/966-7867
Daily: 8 a.m.-midnight

This store in Little Italy is one of the largest little *pasticcerias* in the world. The business deals in wholesale imports and several other ventures, but the sheer perfection of their confections could support the whole business. Certainly, the atmosphere would never suggest that this is anything but a very efficiently run Italian bakery. Its Old World Caffe is famous for numerous varieties of pastry, gelati, and coffee.

GERTELS
53 Hester St   212/982-3250
Sun-Thurs: 7-5:30; Fri: 7-2

Customers who come here are almost evenly divided between those who call this place Ger*tels* (accent on the last syllable) and those who call it *Ger*tels (as in girdles), but all agree that the cakes and breads here are among the best in New York. Locals prefer the traditional babkas, strudels, and kuchens, but I find the chocolate rolls and chiffon blackout cake to be outstanding. For those who want to sample the wares, tables are available for customers to enjoy baked goods, coffee, or a light lunch. From the regulars at these tables, one can glean the choicest shopping tidbits on the Lower East Side. A final tip: every Thursday and Friday, Gertels makes potato kugels. People claim to have come all the way from California for a Thursday kugel! During a slow week, you can occasionally find one left over on a Sunday. (Note: They will ship anywhere in the United States.)

GLASER'S BAKE SHOP
1670 First Ave (bet 87th and 88th St)   212/289-2562
Tues-Fri: 7-7; Sat: 8-7; Sun: 8-3
Closed July and half of Aug

If it's Sunday, it won't be hard to find Glaser's. The line frequently spills outside as people queue up to buy the Glaser family's fresh cakes and baked goods. One isn't enough of anything here. Customers always walk out with arms bulging. The Glasers run their shop as a family business (since 1902 at this same location) and pride themselves on their breads, cakes, cookies, and wedding cakes. Try their chocolate-chip cookie!

GROSSINGER'S UPTOWN
570 Columbus Ave (at 88th St)   212/874-6996, 800/479-6996
Mon-Fri: 7-7; Sun: 7-5

Grossinger's was once known as Grossinger's Home Bakery, back when Columbus Avenue was plain and drab—a far cry from today's trendy boulevard. Since 1935, Grossinger's has been known for top-quality cheesecakes, European and Hungarian specialties (like *pogacsa*), ice-cream cakes—and a great homey aroma. This is the only kosher bake shop on Columbus Avenue.

H&H BAGEL
2239 Broadway (at 80th St)   212/595-8000
Daily: 24 hours

H&H is baking fresh bagels at 2 a.m., an hour at which you can get a piping hot bagel without having to wait on H&H's long daytime line. But you can satisfy your hot bagel craving at any hour of the day or night at H&H. Another only-in-New-York special, they are the best bagels in Manhattan.

KOSSAR'S BIALYSTOKER KUCHEN BAKERY
367 Grand St   212/473-4810
Daily: 24 hours

Tradition has it that the bialy derives its name from Bialystoker, where they were first made. Kossar's brought the recipe over from Europe almost a century ago, and the bialys, bagels, horns, and onion boards are fresh from the oven. The taste is Old World, and those who have never had one should try these authentic versions.

LET THEM EAT CAKE
287 Hudson St (at Spring St)   212/989-4970
Mon-Fri: 7:30-5

Just talking to Gloria Tarigo, who runs Let Them Eat Cake, makes one hungry. She will describe to you the great desserts of the house: carrot cake, chocolate velvet cake, bourbon pecan pie, triple chocolate layer cake, raspberry nut torte, and many more. All are made on-premises and are of top quality. The retail shop is open to the public, and it serves sandwiches, soups, a few hot dishes, and the house specialty desserts, which can be eaten in or taken out. Catering for corporate events or parties is available.

LITTLE PIE COMPANY
424 W 43rd St (at Ninth Ave)   212/736-4780
Mon-Fri: 8-8; Sat: 10-6; Sun: 12-6

Former actor Arnold Wilkerson started baking apple pastries for private orders in his own kitchen. Now he and Michael Deraney operate a unique attraction—a shop that makes handmade pies and cakes using fresh seasonal fruits. Although they specialize in apple pie (available every season), they also make fresh peach, cherry, blueberry, and other all-American fruit-pie favorites. Stop by for a hot slice of pie a la mode and a cup of cider. Also available are delicious brownies, bars, and muffins, applesauce carrot cake, white coconut cakes, chocolate cream pies, and cheescakes (with wild blueberry, cherry, or orange toppings).

MOISHE'S HOME MADE KOSHER BAKERY
181 E Houston St (bet Orchard and Allen St)   212/475-9624
Sun-Thurs: 7 a.m.-6 p.m.; Fri: 7-4

115 Second Ave   212/505-8555
Sun-Thurs: 7 a.m.-8:45 p.m.; Fri: 7-5

Jewish bakery specialties are legendary, and they are done to perfection at

Moishe's. The cornbread is prepared exactly as it was in the old country (and as it should be now). The pumpernickel is dark and moist, and the ryes are simply scrumptious. The house specialty is the black Russian pumpernickel, which probably cannot be bested in an old-fashioned bakery in Russia. But by no means should you ignore the cakes and pies. The owners, Mordechai and Hymie, are charming and eager to please, and they run one of the best bakeries in the city, with the usual complement of bagels, bialys, cakes, and pastries. Most of all, try the challah; Moishe's produces the best. The chocolate layer cakes are also superb.

PATISSERIE LANCIANI
271 W 4th St (bet Perry and 11th St)   212/929-0739
Mon-Sat: 8-8; Sun: 9-8

For those who haven't yet observed the delicacies at Patisserie Lanciani, a quick review of Joseph Lanciani's extensive credentials is in order. For starters, you may have seen Joseph's work. While chief pastry chef at the Plaza (a major recommendation in itself), he was the creator of Julie Nixon's wedding cake. He is also a certified expert in spun-sugar creations and is one of the best pastry chefs in the city. Lanciani's wares can be sampled at his own shop. The cakes, cookies, pastries, tortes, and mousses defy description.

PATISSERIE LES FRIANDISES
972 Lexington Ave (bet 70th and 71st St)   212/988-1616
Mon-Sat: 8-7: Sun: 10-6 (closed Sun in July and Aug)

The person you want to know to start your day off right is owner Jean Kahn; for breakfast she offers goodies like really sticky buns and pear- and apple-tart tatins. Also available are excellent soups, salads, quiches, and sandwiches at noon to eat in or takeout. Their double chocolate truffle log cake is a winner!

POSEIDON GREEK BAKERY
629 Ninth Ave (bet 44th and 45th St)   212/757-6173
Tues-Sat: 9-7; Sun: 10-4

Poseidon is a family-run bakery that endlessly and seemingly effortlessly produces Greek specialties. Tremendous pride is evident here. When a customer peers over the counter and asks, "What is that?," the response is usually a long description and sometimes an invitation to taste. There is homemade baklava, strudel, *kataif, trigona, tiropita* (cheese pie), spanakopita, *saragli,* and phyllo. They have cocktail-size frozen spinach, cheese, vegetable, and meat pies for use at home or for parties. Poseidon was founded in 1922 by Greek baker Demetrios Anagnostou. Today it is run by grandsons John and Anthony Fable to the same exacting standards. Poseidon's specialty is handmade phyllo pastry, which is world-renowned.

At the **New York Cake And Baking Center** (56 W 22nd St), you'll find everything you could imagine for decorating, making chocolate forms or whatever. It's a treasure house!

ST. FAMOUS BREAD
796 Ninth Ave (at 53rd St) 212/245-6695
Daily: 7-8

You can tell from the minute you walk in this shop that everything is baked fresh; their kitchen is busy all night. Customers get to choose from a real international selection: sourdough breads, homemade mini-muffins, cornbread (including jalapeno-cheese-onion), cookies, focaccia, banana-walnut bread, Irish soda bread, croissants, and many daily specials. The folks here seem genuinely happy to see you, and I guarantee you will not leave empty-handed!

STICKY FINGERS
121 First Ave (at 7th St) 212/529-2554
Mon-Sat: 6 a.m.-9 p.m.; Sun: 7 a.m.-8 p.m.

This is an old-fashioned bakery with one of the best reputations in town. The diverse ethnic makeup of the neighborhood is reflected in the variety of breads made here. The quality is endorsed by the local natives from Italy, Poland, the Ukraine, and Russia, who claim the peasant bread tastes as good as grandma's, if not great-grandma's! There is so much to recommend. The pumpernickel is dark and moist, and it tastes nothing like the commercial variety. The Italian breads are authentic. The Jewish contingent is represented by bagels and bialys. Each group thinks Sticky Fingers is their bakery. Could there be a higher compliment? There are also cakes, muffins, scones, and cookies.

STREIT MATZOTH COMPANY
150 Rivington St 212/475-7000
Sun-Thurs: 9-5

Matzoth, for the uninitiated, is a thin, waferlike square cracker. According to tradition, it came out of Egypt with Moses and the children of Israel when they had to flee so swiftly that there was no time to let the bread rise. Through the years, matzoth was restricted to the time around Passover, and even when matzoth production became automated, business shut down for a good deal of the year. But not today and not in New York. In a small building with a Puerto Rican mural stretching the length of one side, Streit's matzoth factory pours forth matzoth throughout the year, pausing only on Saturday, Jewish holidays, and to clean the machines. Streit's factory allows a peek at the actual production, which is both mechanized and extremely primitive. It also sells matzoth to the general public. Matzoth is baked in enormous thin sheets that are later broken up. If you ask for a batch that happens to be baking, they might break it right off the production line for you.

SULLIVAN STREET BAKERY
73 Sullivan St (bet Spring and Broome St) 212/334-9435
Mon-Sat: 8-8; Sun: 10 a.m.-dusk

If you savor really fresh authentic Italian country bread, this is the place to go. Their sourdough is used by a number of restaurants, so you know it is first-rate. Sullivan carries the only Pizza Bianca Romania (six feet long) in Manhattan. Raisin-walnut bread is one of their specialties.

VESUVIO BAKERY
160 Prince St (bet West Broadway and Thompson St)   212/925-8248
Mon-Sat: 7-7

Tony Dapolito was born and bred (no pun intended) in his family's store in Soho. Since that time, the family's expertise in baking has grown along with the bakery's claim to fame as Soho's common green. When he's not manning the ovens, Tony serves on the community planning board and disperses Soho lore to customers. Visitors unaware of Dapolito's status (it doesn't remain a secret long) come for the bread, biscuits, and rolls. They all have a reputation that reaches far beyond Soho. After all, it isn't every commercial bakery that eschews sugar, shortening, and preservatives and still manages to produce the tastiest Italian bread around. Try the biscotti, the pepper biscuits, or the whole-wheat brick oven-baked bread.

WHOLE EARTH BAKERY & KITCHEN
70 Spring St (bet Broadway and Lafayette St)   212/226-8280
Mon-Sat: 8 a.m.-9 p.m.; Sun: 9-7
130 St Mark's Pl (bet First Ave and Ave A)   212/677-7597
Daily: 9 a.m.-10:30 p.m.

This is the only bakery in Manhattan that makes baked goods using exclusively organic flours. No animal products, honey, or egg whites are used here, and all of their products are sugar-free. For the health-conscious, this is a good bet.

YONAH SCHIMMEL
137 E Houston St   212/477-2858
Daily: 8-6

Yonah Schimmel has been selling perfect knishes for so long that his name is legendary. National magazines have written articles about him. Schimmel started out dispensing knishes among the pushcarts of the Lower East Side, and a Yonah Schimmel knish is still a unique experience. It doesn't, incidentally, look or taste anything like the mass-produced things sold in supermarkets, at lunch stands, or at New York ballgames. A Yonah Schimmel knish has a very thin, flaky crust—almost like strudel dough—surrounding hot, moist filling. The best-selling filling is potato, but there is also kasha (buckwheat), spinach, and a half-dozen others. No two knishes come out exactly alike, since each is handmade.

ZEPPOLE AT THE TRIBAKERY
186 Franklin St (at Greenwich St)   212/431-1114
Daily: 7:30 a.m.-10:30 p.m.

This is a triple-header: three businesses under one roof. First there is a full-service restaurant (Zeppole), then a retail store with takeout and delivery, and finally a wholesale and retail bakery that produces some of the best eats around.

Their baguettes, Danishes, and rustic olive breads are tops. It is easy to see why this outfit provides bakery items to some of the best stores and restaurants in the city. Don't miss the salads and sandwiches for lunch!

Cakes

If you need a decorated cake, a number of places do an especially good job. Call ahead or go in and plan directly with the baker.

Baked Ideas (450 Broadway, 212/925-9097)
Creative Cakes (400 E 74th St, 212/794-9811)
Cupcake Cafe (522 Ninth Ave, 212/465-1530)
Patisserie Lanciani (271 W 4th St, 212/929-0739)
Sant Ambroeus (1000 Madison Ave, 212/570-2211)
Sylvia Weinstock Cakes (273 Church St, 212/925-6698)

Beverages

B&E QUALITY
511 W 23rd Ave   212/243-6559
Mon-Thurs: 9-6:30; Fri, Sat: 9-7

If you are planning a party and want to make a quantity purchase of beer and soda, this is a good place to go. They are a wholesale distributor but will also pass along savings to retail customers. Some 450 beers from around the world are available, as well as kegs in over 30 brands.

NEW YORK BEVERAGE WHOLESALERS
428 E 91st St (at York Ave)   212/831-4000
Mon-Sat: 10-9; Sun: Noon-8

The *buy*-words here: tremendous variety, great prices. This outfit claims to have the largest retail beer selection in Manhattan, with over 500 brands available. Prices are good for beer, soda, mineral and natural waters, iced teas, and seltzers. They will deliver to your door, supply specialty imports, and work with you on any quantities you might want.

RIVERSIDE BEER AND SODA DISTRIBUTORS
2331 Twelfth Ave (at 133rd St)   212/234-3884
Mon-Sat: 9-6

Run by Hector Borrero, this place mainly supplies wholesalers and large retail orders, but he's not averse to serving retail customers. Once you've shopped up there, might as well take advantage of the discount and buy in quantity.

If you're having a party with a crew of non-drinkers, give **Bevex** (230 W 55th St, at Broadway, 212/541-7171) a call. They will deliver all kinds of nonalcoholic beverages, like colas, sparkling waters, Gatorade, etc.

IT'S ALL IN THE WATER . . . CONFUSED?

Artesian water: underground well water
Distilled water: no minerals
Mineral water: between 250-1500 milligrams per liter of dissolved solids
Natural water: no processing
Sparkling water: carbonated naturally
Spring water: underground water that surfaces at springs
Still water: no natural or added effervescence

British

MYERS OF KESWICK
634 Hudson St (bet Horatio and Jane St)   212/691-4194
Mon-Fri: 10-7; Sat: 10-6; Sun: noon-5

Peter and Irene Myers are now doing with English food what Burberry, Church, and Laura Ashley have done with English clothing. They've made it possible for you to visit "the village grocer" for imported staples and fresh, home-baked items you'd swear came from a kitchen in Soho—the London neighborhood, that is. Among the tins, a shopper can find Heinz treacle sponge pudding, trifle mix, ribena, mushy peas, steak and kidney pie, Smarties, Quality Street toffee, lemon barley water, chutneys, jams and preserves, and all the major English teas. The fresh goods include sausage rolls, kidney pie, Scotch eggs, and Aberdeen kippers. There are also cheeses (the double Gloucester is outstanding) and chocolates. For Anglophiles and expatriates alike, Myers of Keswick is a *luverly* treat.

Candy

ECONOMY CANDY
108 Rivington St   212/254-1531, 800/352-4544 (outside New York)
Sun-Fri: 8-6; Sat: 10-5

The same family of owners has been selling everything from penny candies to beautiful gourmet gift baskets since 1937. What a selection of dried fruits, nuts, candies, coffees, teas, jams, spices, cookies, crackers, and chocolates! The best part is the price. You can get gourmet items like caviar and paté without exceeding your party budget. Mail orders are filled efficiently and promptly; a free catalog is available.

LEONIDAS
485 Madison Ave (bet 51st and 52nd St)   212/980-2608
Mon-Fri: 9-7; Sat: 10-7; Sun: 12-6 (closed Sun in summer)

This is the only U.S. franchise of the famous Belgian confectionary company, and it is a haven for those who appreciate good things. Over 60 varieties of confections—milk, white, and bittersweet pieces, chocolate orange peels, solid chocolate medallions, fabulous fresh cream fillings, truffle fillings, and marzipan—are flown in fresh every week. I guarantee that Leondias' pralines are sumptuous. Jacques Bergier, the genial owner, makes one hungry just describing his treasure trove. Best of all, prices are affordable.

LI-LAC CANDY SHOP
120 Christopher St (bet Bleecker and Hudson St)   212/242-7374
Mon-Sat: 10-8; Sun: 12-5;
Tues-Sat: 12-8; Sun: 12-5 (summer hours)

Since 1923, Li-Lac has been the source for fine chocolate in Greenwich Village. The most delicious creation is Li-Lac's own chocolate fudge, which is made fresh every day. If you tire of the chocolate, maple walnut fudge is every bit as good. Then there are pralines, mousses, French rolls, nuts, dried fruits, hand-dipped chocolates, and more, all made on the premises.

MONDEL CHOCOLATES
2913 Broadway (at 114th St)   212/864-2111
Mon-Sat: 11-7; Sun: 12-5

Mondel has been a tasty gem in the neighborhood for about a half-century. It was founded by the father of its present owner, Florence Mondel. The aroma here is fantastic! The chocolate-covered ginger, orange peel, nut barks, and turtles are special winners. They also offer a dietetic chocolate line.

NEUCHATEL CHOCOLATES
Plaza Hotel	212/751-7742	60 Wall St	212/480-3766
Fifth Ave and Central Park		Mon-Fri: 9-6	
Mon-Sat: 9 a.m.-10 p.m.;			
Sun: 10-9			

Neuchatel Chocolates is a class act—and you pay for it. Neuchatel offers a discount for orders of over $1,000, and it's not difficult to earn that discount. To create the finest Swiss chocolate from family recipes, chocolates are prepared by hand with natural ingredients. The taste has been likened to velvety silk. There are 70 varieties of chocolate, with the house specialty being handmade truffles. But that shouldn't keep anyone from trying the marzipan or pralines with fruit or nuts. Neuchatel's origins are Swiss, but perhaps its greatest virtue is that the chocolates are not flown in but created fresh in New York.

NEUHAUS CHOCOLATES
Saks Fifth Avenue (8th floor)
611 Fifth Ave (at 50th St)   212/940-2891
Mon-Wed, Fri, Sat: 10-6; Thurs: 10-8; Sun: 12-6

In 1857, the same year my great-grandfather started his one-man store on the riverfront in Portland, Jean Neuhaus settled in Belgium and established a pharmacy and confectionery shop. Succeeding generations have produced some of the finest handcrafted, enrobed, and molded-design bittersweet and milk chocolates in the world. They are still imported from Belgium. The showpiece is the Astrid Praline, named after the beloved late queen of Belgium; it is a sugar-glazed delight! Candy is sold in bulk, bars, and pre-packs.

TEUSCHER CHOCOLATES OF SWITZERLAND
25 E 61st St (at Madison Ave)   212/751-8482
Mon-Sat: 10-6

620 Fifth Ave (Rockefeller Center)   212/246-4416
Mon-Sat: 10-6; Thurs: 10-7:30

If there was an award for the most elegant chocolate shop, it would have to go to Teuscher. Theirs are not just chocolates; they're imported works of art. Bernard Bloom, who owns these Teuscher stores, imports chocolates once a week from Switzerland. The chocolates are packed into handmade boxes so stunning that they add to the decor of many a customer's home. The truffles are almost obscenely good. The superb champagne truffle has a tiny dot of champagne cream in the center. The cocoa, nougat, butter-crunch, muscat, orange, and almond truffles each have their own little surprise. Truffles are the stars here, but Teuscher's marzipan, praline chocolates, and mints (shaped like sea creatures) are of similar high quality.

For some of the tastiest and freshest candy, nuts, and dried fruit at very best prices, you can't beat **Sweet Life** (63 Hester St, cor Ludlow St, 212/598-0092). Hours: Sun-Fri 9-6.

Cheese

ALLEVA DAIRY
188 Grand St (at Mulberry St)   212/226-7990
Mon-Sat: 8:30-6; Sun: 8:30-3

Alleva, founded in 1892, is the oldest Italian cheese store in America. The Alleva family has operated the business since the start, always maintaining meticulous high standards. Robert Alleva is the current boss, overseeing the production of over 4,000 pounds of fresh cheese a week: *parmigiano, fraschi, manteche, scamoize,* and *provole affumicale.* The ricotta is superb, and the mozzarella tastes like it was made on some little side street in Florence.

BEN'S CHEESE SHOP
181 E Houston St (bet Allen and Orchard St)   212/254-8290
Sun-Thurs: 8:15-5:30; Fri: 8:15-3:30

About half the varieties of cheese sold here are made in the back of the shop. The locals swear by the farmer's cheese in any of its forms. Favorites include homemade farmer's cheese embedded with such tasty ingredients as strawberries, scallions, raisins, pineapple, and (my personal favorites) almonds and pistachios. Don't miss the baked farmer's cheese or the homemade cream cheese.

EAST VILLAGE CHEESE
40 Third Ave (bet 9th and 10th St)   212/477-2601
Mon-Fri: 8:30-6:30; Sat, Sun: 8:30-6

Value is the name of the game here. For years this store has prided itself on selling cheese at just about the lowest prices in town. Now relocated to larger quarters, they claim the same for bean coffee, fresh pasta, extra virgin olive oil, quiche, paté, and a wide selection of fresh bread. An added reason to shop here: this is not a self-service operation.

IDEAL CHEESE SHOP
1205 Second Ave (bet 63rd and 64th St)   212/688-7579
Mon-Fri: 9-6:30; Sat: 9-6 (summer: Mon-Fri: 9-6; Sat: 9-5)

Hundreds of cheeses from all over the world are sold here. As a matter of fact, the owners are constantly looking around for new items, just like in the fashion business. This store has been in operation since 1954, and many Upper

East Siders swear by its quality and service. Members of the founding family are on hand to answer your questions or to prepare special platters and baskets.

JOE'S DAIRY
156 Sullivan (bet Houston and Prince St)   212/677-8780
Tues-Sat: 9-6

Hands down, this is the best spot in town for fresh mozzarella. Joe Campanelli makes it all ways: smoked, with prosciutto, and more.

MURRAY'S CHEESE SHOP
257 Bleecker St (at Cornelia St)   212/243-3289
Mon-Sat: 8:30-7:30; Sun: 9-5

This is one of the very best cheese shops in Manhattan, and has been so rated by any number of polls. Murray's was founded in 1940; they offer both wholesale and retail international and domestic cheeses of every description. Boy, does the place smell good! But that isn't all. There is also a fine selection of cold cuts, pasta, antipasto, bread, sandwiches, and specialty grocery items. Rob Kaufelt has built on the traditions of the city's oldest cheese shop. Special attractions include great cheese platters, gift baskets, and wholesale charge accounts for locals.

Chinese

CHINESE AMERICAN TRADING COMPANY
91 Mulberry St (at Canal St)   212/267-5224
Daily: 9-8

If a homecooked authentic Chinese dinner is on your itinerary, there may be no better source than this store in Chinatown. Chinese American Trading boasts that 95% of its business is conducted with the Chinese community. In any case, they have an open and friendly attitude here, and great care is taken to introduce customers to the wide variety of imported Oriental foodstuffs, including Japanese, Thai, and Filipino products.

FUNG WONG BAKERY
30 Mott St   212/267-4037
Daily: 7 a.m.-9 p.m.

Fung Wong is the real thing. Everyone from local Chinatown residents to the city's gourmands extol its virtues. The pastries, cookies, and baked goods are traditional, authentic, and downright delicious. Flavor is not compromised to appeal to Western taste. The bakery features a tremendous variety, and it has the distinction of being New York's oldest and largest "real" Chinese bakery. Fung Wong is rated number one, and a visit is the surest way to see why.

KAM MAN FOOD PRODUCTS
200 Canal St (bet Mott and Mulberry St)   212/571-0330
Daily: 9-9

Kam Man is the largest Oriental grocery store on the East Coast. They also carry Japanese, Vietnamese, Philippine, Thai, and Singapore products. Even native Chinese will feel at home in this shop, where you can find every possible ingredient for a Chinese meal. Speaking Chinese is not a requirement for shopping at Kam Man. Some of the best English in Chinatown is spoken by the people who work here, and the amenities will be totally familiar to those who patronize the city's other gourmet delis and supermarkets. The difference is that at Kam Man the shopping carts wheel past produce displays of water chestnuts, bok choy, winter melon, and tofu; 50 types of Oriental delicacies (like shark's fin); and butcher and fish counters offering duck, sausages, pork dumplings, and shrimp. Desserts and teas round out the selection, and the prices—even for American tangerines and oranges—are very inexpensive.

Coffee, Tea

BELL-BATES HEALTH FOOD CENTER
97 Reade St (bet Church St and West Broadway)   212/267-4300
Mon-Wed: 9:30-6; Thurs, Fri: 9:30-6:30; Sat: 11-5

Bell-Bates is a hot-beverage emporium, specializing in all manner of teas and coffees for the retail customer. Their selection is extensive and prices are competitive. Bell-Bates considers itself a complete food center, stocking health food, vitamins, nuts, dried fruit, spices, herbs, and gourmet food, along with freshly ground coffees and teas. Ask for Mrs. Sayage; she's marvelous.

COFFEE GRINDER
348 E 66th St (bet First and Second Ave)   212/737-3490
Mon, Fri: 9:30-7; Sat: 9:30-6

All you have to do is smell the aroma when you walk into this tiny spot. The coffee appeal is overwhelming! For honest-to-goodness fine coffees and teas, look no farther.

EMPIRE COFFEE AND TEA COMPANY
592 Ninth Ave   212/586-1717
Mon-Fri: 8-7; Sat: 9-6:30; Sun: 11-5

Midtown java lovers have all wandered in here at one time or another. There is an enormous selection of coffee (75 different types of beans), decaf, tea, and herbs. Because of the aroma and array of the bins, making a choice is almost impossible. Empire's personnel are very helpful, but perhaps most helpful of all is a perusal of their free mail-order catalog before entering the shop. Fresh coffee beans and tea leaves are available in bulk, along with gourmet gift baskets. Everything is sold loose and can be ground. Empire also carries a selection of appliances.

McNULTY'S TEA AND COFFEE COMPANY
109 Christopher St (bet Bleecker and Hudson St)   212/242-5351
Mon-Sat: 10-9; Sun: 1-7

McNulty's has been supplying choosy New Yorkers with coffee and tea since 1895. Over the years they have developed a complete line that includes spice and herb teas, coffee blends ground to order, and coffee and tea accessories. They have a reputation for personalized, gourmet coffee blends, and they work hard to maintain it. That reputation will take its toll on the pocketbook, but their blends are unique and the personal service is highly valued. McNulty's maintains an extensive file on customers' special blends.

M. ROHRS
1692 Second Ave (bet 87th and 88th St)   212/427-8319
Mon-Sat: 9-7

Dennis Smith owned a candy store in Manhattan before he bought M. Rohrs, which was established in 1896. The tradeoff of candy for coffee beans was primarily for better working hours, but Smith is always on the premises long before the store opens and long after it closes. He is willing to expound on the various types of beans and teas the store stocks. His guidance is needed, because there are hundreds of varieties of tea, coffee, and honey in the store, as well as accessories. While M. Rohr is not a coffee shop, it is possible to get a cup of coffee and sample the wares. Incidentally, Smith is one of the most relaxed proprietors in the city. Either he doesn't drink coffee or he's right when he says that all the studies on caffeine don't amount to a hill of beans.

Types of Coffee Drinks:

Espresso: A coffee beverage produced by using pressure to rapidly infuse ground coffee beans with boiling water. A "tall" is any 12-ounce espresso drink, while a "grande" is any 16-ounce espresso drink. A "double" is any espresso drink with a second shot added. Finally, a "skinny" is any drink that uses nonfat milk. Here are some additional variations:

Americano: A two-ounce shot of espresso with hot water. This drink substitutes for drip coffee.

Caffe Latte: A popular version of espresso, combining a two-ounce shot of espresso with steamed milk and a spoonful of milk froth on top.

Caffe Mocha: A latte with an ounce of chocolate flavoring (either powder or syrup).

Cappuccino: A two-ounce shot of espresso with equal parts steamed milk and milk froth.

Flavored Caffe: A latte with an ounce of Italian syrup. Almond, hazelnut, and vanilla are a few of the more common flavors. Some like their espresso flavored with liqueurs.

Granita: Made with a granita machine, or *granitore,* these frozen Italian drinks can be made with espresso and milk, or with fresh fruits and juices.

PORTO RICO IMPORTING COMPANY

201 Bleecker St (main store)   212/477-5421
Mon-Sat: 9-9; Sun: 12-7

40½ St. Marks Pl (coffee bar)   212/533-1982
Mon-Fri: 8-8; Sat: 9-8; Sun: 12-7

107 Thompson St (coffee bar)   212/966-5758
Mon-Thurs: 8-6; Fri: 8-7; Sat: 10-7; Sun:10-6

In 1907, Peter Longo's family started a small coffee business in the Village. Primarily importers and wholesalers, they were soon pressured to serve the local community, so they opened a small storefront as well. That storefront gained a reputation for having the best and freshest coffee available and developed a loyal corps of customers. Since much of the surrounding neighborhood consisted of Italians, the Longo family reciprocated their loyalty by specializing in Italian espressos and cappuccinos, as well as "health" and medicinal teas. Dispensed along with such teas are folk remedies and advice to mend whatever ails you. Today, the store remains true to its tradition. Peter has added coffee bars, so now it is possible to sit and sip from a selection of 120 coffees and 150 loose teas while listening to the folklore or trying to select the best from the bins. All coffees are roasted daily. (Hint: The inexpensive house blends are every bit as good as some of the more expensive coffees.)

SENSUOUS BEAN OF COLUMBUS AVENUE
66 W 70th St (at Columbus Ave)   212/724-7725
Mon, Thurs, Fri: 8:30 a.m.-9 p.m.; Tues, Wed: 8:30-7;
Sat: 8:30-6; Sun: 9:30-6

In business long before the coffee craze started, this legendary coffee and tea house shows 72 varieties of coffee and 52 teas. A coffee-of-the-month club is offered, and after customers purchase ten lbs of coffee they receive one pound free! The bulk bean coffees and loose teas come from all around the world. Teas from England, France, Germany, Ireland, and Taiwan are featured.

Dairy Products

HARRY WILS & COMPANY
182 Duane St   212/431-9731
Mon-Fri: 6-3

For three-quarters of a century and through three generations, this venerable outfit has been supplying the food needs of New York's better restaurants. Butter, cheese, and eggs are the mainstays of the business, and they are sold in quantity to commercial buyers. They are also purveyors of European and American specialty products, including olive oil, vinegar, sun-dried tomatoes from Italy, baking and cooking chocolates (valrhona and cocoa berry), and a variety of pastry products (yeast, gelatin sheets, and extracts). The individual customer will probably not be turned away for orders of a reasonable amount of cheese or butter. For eggs, you would have to purchase at least 15 dozen. But the quality and prices can't be beat!

Delis, Catering, Food to Go

AGATA & VALENTINA
1505 First Ave (at 79th St)   212/452-0690
Daily: 8 a.m-9 p.m.

This is a very classy, expanded gourmet shop with an ambience that will make you think you're in Sicily. There are all kinds of good things to eat, with one counter more tempting than the next. In summer they have a sidewalk cafe. A great selection of gourmet dishes, bakery items, magnificent fresh vegetables, meats, candies, gelati, and everything in between is available. One specialty of the house is extra virgin olive oil. Don't expect bargain prices; come instead for quality!

AZURE
830 Third Ave (at 51st St)   212/486-8080
Daily: 24 hours

Wow! What a salad bar! Azure's 125 feet of hot and cold offerings is a sight. Of course there is more here: homemade soups, stuffed baked potatoes, pizzas, sushi, and great muffins. This place is eye- and stomach-tempting!

BALDUCCI'S
424 Sixth Ave (at 9th St)   212/673-2600
Daily: 7 a.m.-8:30 p.m.

Most everyone who visits Greenwich Village wants to stop at Balducci's, one of the premier food emporiums in the city. When Balducci's opened as a greengrocer in 1946, Mom and Pop tended a single cast-iron register, answered questions, serviced customers, and kept pencil accounts for their neighbors. To this day, you will see members of the family in the store helping customers. Under one roof they sell nearly everything: coffee, pastries, fine cheese, smoked salmon, fresh pasta, aged beef, hearth-baked breads, prepared entrees, and the largest selection of quality produce in the city. They produce many traditional specialties like focaccia, fresh-cut pasta and ravioli, sauces, *taralli,* country breads, and fresh-fruit tarts. Special services include personal shopping, catering, gift baskets, and seasonal catalogs from which you can mail-order many Italian home-cooked specials. Free delivery is available between Broadway, Houston, 15th, and West streets. Half the fun of shopping here is the crowded aisles and family atmosphere. Village residents and city-wide fans jostle for space in this yummy emporium.

BARNEY GREENGRASS
541 Amsterdam Ave (bet 86th and 87th St)   212/724-4707
Tues-Sun: 8-6 (takeout)
Tues-Fri: 8:45-4; Sat, Sun: 8:45-5 (restaurant)
closed first two weeks in Aug

Sportscaster Dick Schaap says: "Without my order from Barney Greengrass, I'd never survive Sundays!" Barney Greengrass is synonymous with sturgeon to New Yorkers. This family business has been located at the same place since 1929. Barney has been succeeded by his son Moe and grandson Gary, but the same quality gourmet smoked fish is still sold over the counter, just as it was in Barney's day. The Greengrasses lay claim to the title of "Sturgeon King," and there are few who would dispute it. While sturgeon is king here, Barney Greengrass also has schools of other smoked-fish delicacies. There is Nova Scotia salmon, belly lox, white fish, caviar, and pickled herring in the fish lines. The dairy-deli line — including vegetable cream cheese, homemade salads and borscht, and a smashing Nova Scotia salmon with scrambled eggs and onions — is world-renowned. In fact, because so many customers couldn't wait to get home to unwrap their packages, Greengrass started a restaurant next door.

BROADWAY FARM
2339 Broadway (at 85th St)   212/787-8585
Open 24 hours

Upper West Side shoppers enjoy this quality food outlet, which features a full deli, fruits, vegetables, seafood, pasta, excellent coffee and cheese selections, smoked fish, specialty beers, and unusual imported items. Delivery is free from 75th to 95th streets, between Central Park West and Riverside Drive.

CANARD AND COMPANY
1292 Madison Ave (at 92nd St)   212/722-1046
Daily: 7 a.m-9 p.m.

It seems as though you are in a rural country store when you step inside Canard and Company. The atmosphere is homey, and the personnel are eager to show the fabulous selection of prepared gourmet foods, specialty jams and jellies, rich desserts, custom gift baskets, fine candies, and some of the best sandwiches in Manhattan. Also available are the finest beluga and ossetra caviars and smoked salmon. Catering is a specialty here. No big-time hustle-and-bustle, but a truly enjoyable shopping experience awaits you here.

CAVIARTERIA
29 E 60th St   212/759-7410, 800/4-CAVIAR
Mon-Sat: 9-6

Caviarteria, the largest distributor of caviar in the U.S., operates out of a small store. That is sufficient, since most of the business is done by phone or mail. Because of the wholesale business, prices are as reasonable as they can be for caviar, and the quality is top-notch. The staff is friendly and helpful, and they assure safe delivery by shipping on ice. Caviarteria also stocks paté de foie gras, Scotch and Swedish smoked salmon, homemade biscotti, and New Zealand smoked eels. There is a caviar and champagne tasting bar, and food service is available.

CHARLOTTE'S
146 Chambers St (bet Greenwich St and West Broadway)   212/732-7939
Mon-Fri: 10-6

Quality is Number One here! Charlotte's has developed an outstanding reputation for catering, with no detail too small for their careful attention. Their client list reads like a who's who, including Citibank, Asprey, and Smith-Barney. Charlotte's is a full-service catering establishment, from menus and music to flowers and waiters' outfits. This is the place to come when you want real experts to do the work for wedding receptions, dinner dances, teas, luncheons, business meetings or dinners, and so forth. Specialties include wonderful tapas, a spa buffet menu, and outrageous desserts.

CHELSEA MARKET
75 Ninth Ave (bet 15th and 16th St)   212/243-6005
24 hours

Once again, there is no place like New York City! In a complex of 18 former industrial buildings, including the old Nabisco Cookie Factory of the late 1800s (where Oreo cookies first captured the stomachs of hungry kids), an 800-foot-long concourse now houses one of the most unique marketplaces in the city. The space is innovative, including a waterfall supplied by an underground spring. You'll find, among the nearly two dozen shops, **Amy's Bread** (big choice, plus a cafe), **Bowery Kitchen Supplies** (kitchen buffs will go wild!), **Chelsea Wholesale Flower Market** (cut flowers that look really fresh), **Chelsea Wine Vault** (climate-controlled), **Hale & Hearty Soups** (dozens of varieties), the **Lobster Place** (takeout seafood), **Manhattan Fruit Exchange** (big displays), plus bagels, ice creams, rugelach, meats, hospitality products, and more. **Ruthy's Cheesecakes** (212/463-8800) is outstanding!.

DEAN & DELUCA
560 Broadway (at Prince St)   212/431-1691
Mon-Sat: 10-8; Sun: 9-7

This is one of the great gourmet stores in the country. Long a tradition for smart food buyers, Dean & Deluca is now housed in a store four times as large as the original location. The temptations here are extraordinary: wonderfully fresh produce; a huge selection of cheeses; fresh bakery items; takeout dishes; all kinds of meat, poultry, and fish products; coffees; magnificent pastries and desserts; housewares; books; and much more. A very popular espresso and cappuccino bar greets customers at the door. This part of the operation has been expanded into small, convenient locations at 75 University Place, the Paramount Hotel in midtown, 121 Prince Street (the store's old location), and 50 Rockefeller Center. Professional kitchen equipment is available to both wholesale and retail customers, and a catering kitchen is located on-premises.

FAIRWAY
2127 Broadway (at 74th St)　　　212/595-1888
Daily: 7 a.m.-midnight

132nd St and Hudson River　　　212/234-3883
Sun-Wed: 8 a.m.-10 p.m.; Thurs: 8 a.m.-11 p.m.;
Fri, Sat: 8 a.m.-midnight

Fairway has been an institution on the Upper West Side for years, and now another store has been established way uptown. The specialties here are fruits and vegetables in huge quantities and assortments and at great prices. In the new and larger facility on the Hudson River, there is a veritable cornucopia of food, from cheeses and meats to bakery and more. Prices attract folks from a broad area who appreciate the fact that Fairway operates its own farm on Long Island and has developed money-saving relationships with produce dealers throughout the state. Between Zabar's and Fairway, Upper West Side shoppers have the best of two worlds.

FINE & SCHAPIRO
138 W 72nd St　　　212/877-2874
Daily: 9 a.m.-10 p.m.

Ostensibly a kosher delicatessen and restaurant, Fine & Schapiro offers some of the best dinners for at-home consumption in the city. Perhaps because of their uptown location, but more likely as homage to the quality of their foods, they term themselves "the Rolls-Royce of delicatessens." That description is cited here only because it is very apt. Fine & Schapiro dispenses a complete line of cold cuts, hot and cold hors d'oeuvres, Chinese delicacies, catering platters, and magnificent sandwiches. Everything that issues from Fine & Schapiro is perfectly cooked and artistically arranged. The sandwiches are masterpieces; the aroma and taste are irresistible. Chicken in the pot and stuffed cabbage are two of their best items.

FISHER & LEVY
875 Third Ave (at 53rd St, concourse level)　　　212/832-3880
Mon-Fri: 7:30-3:30 (call before 3 p.m. for dinner delivery)

Chip Fisher and his partner Thom Hamill have served the corporate catering needs of Manhattan with style and high-quality service for nearly two decades. They take care of big parties and solitary diners alike. Fisher & Levy begins the day with delicious breakfast items. How does a slice of coffee crumb cake sound? Or a fresh-baked blueberry scone? For lunch, dive into a juicy filet mignon sandwich with grilled red peppers or a roasted turkey breast with honey glaze. In addition to delicious pizza, their small retail store in the food court at 875 Third Avenue offers daily sandwiches, soups, interesting pastas and vegetable salads, Cobb salad, and desserts like homemade bread pudding. Desserts are all made in-house and include gooey brownies, raspberry ruggelah, and fabulous all-butter cookies.

FLAVORS CATERING & CARRYOUT
8 W 18th St (at Fifth Ave)   212/647-1234
Mon-Fri: 8-6:30; Sat: 10-5 (closed Sat in summer)

Flavors' specialties range from "High French" custom catering to modern, healthy to-go (or eat-in) from their retail shop to home and office delivery. They will do it all: special vegetarian dishes, custom gift baskets, picnic outings, catered cruises, and even a full-scale wedding in a historic New York City mansion. The client list includes ABC, Condé Nast, Nike, Martha Stewart Living, Revlon, and Tiffany. The price is right!

However good they taste, the following are all synonyms for *fat:* Alfredo, á la king, au beurre, au gratin, batter-dipped, bérnaise, carbonara, creamed, crispy, croquettes, fritto, fritters, hollandaise, meuniere, Newburg, parmigiana, and tempura. Don't say we didn't warn you!

FRASER MORRIS FINE FOODS
102 President St (at Hicks St, Brooklyn)   718/802-9771
Mon-Fri: 9-6; Sat: 9-5

Fraser Morris was a gourmet-to-go source eons before the neighborhood knew there was such a thing and certainly long before the Upper East Side became the center of all such operations. The result was a carriage-trade store offering gourmet delicacies at not-inconsiderable prices. With a virtual monopoly on the idea, Fraser Morris was the definitive shop and set the standard for the breed. These days the gourmet shop still stocks the finest fruit, cheese, candy, caviar, chocolate, delicatessen items (e.g., imported sliced ham and paté de foie gras), quiche, canned gourmet items, ice cream, cheesecake, caviar, and coffee beans. Some fine European names are stocked, such as Fauchon products and Dallmayr coffees. A catering department offers such delicacies as ,almon and crown roast of lamb. A bakery department features fruit tarts, Hungarian pastry, scones, and an international variety of goodies. Food baskets are a specialty. Finally, for the true gourmet-to-go, there's a sandwich department. This old spot has gracefully and successfully entered the modern age.

GARDEN OF EDEN
162 W 23rd St   212/675-6300
310 Third Ave (bet 23rd and 24th St)   212/228-4681
Mon-Sun: 7 a.m.-10 p.m.

These stores are a real farmer's market! Not only are all the food items appetizing and priced to please the pocketbook, the stores are immaculate and well-organized. To complete the pleasant shopping experience, the personnel are exceptionally helpful. You'll find everything: breads and bakery items, cheeses, fresh veggies, meat, seafood, pastas, desserts and whatever else your hungry tummy yearns for. All manner of catering services are available, including suggestions for locations, rentals, service, and music.

GLORIOUS FOOD
504 E 74th St   212/628-2320
Mon-Fri: 9-5

Glorious Food is at the top of just about everyone's list when it comes to catering. They are a full-service outfit, expertly taking care of every small detail of your event. Having been in business for over a quarter of a century, they have met most every challenge. Give 'em a try!

GOURMET GARAGE
451 Broome St (at Mercer St)   212/941-5850
301 E. 64th St   212/535-6271
2567 Broadway (at 96th St)   212/663-4927
Daily: 7:30 a.m.-8:30 p.m.

A working-class gourmet food shop is the best way to describe Gourmet Garage. These stores carry a good selection of in-demand items, like fruits and veggies, cheeses, breads, pastries, coffees, meats, and olive oils, all at low prices. Organic foods are a specialty.

GRACE'S MARKETPLACE
1237 Third Ave (at 71st St)   212/737-0600
Mon-Sat: 7 a.m.-8:30 p.m.; Sun: 8-7

Only the best of everything is here. You'll find smoked meats and fish, cheeses, fresh pastas and sauces, produce, a full range of baked goods, candy, coffee, tea, dried fruits, nuts, oils, vinegars, pastries, packaged items, and prepared foods. They are also well known for quality gift baskets and catering. Get a taste of puglia at their new cafe **Grace's Trattoria** located at 201 E 71st Street. No visit to New York is complete without an excursion to Grace's. For New Yorkers, this is one of the city's most popular food emporiums.

GREAT PERFORMANCES CATERERS
287 Spring St   212/727-2424
Daily: 9-5 (phone orders only)

Liz Neumark, the owner of Great Performances, should know the business from the bottom up. She is a former photographer who supported herself by working as a waitress in a help-for-hire agency. She soon realized there were quite a number of moonlighting artists in the city, so she decided to organize her own agency. Great Performances supplies New Yorkers with party help from the city's artistic community. Her company is a full-service caterer handling all kinds of affairs, from small dinner parties to gala dinners for thousands. They have added picnic catering and a drop-off dining program to their services. The folks at Great Performances are the kind you want to have around. Good show!

H&H BAGELS EAST
1551 Second Ave (bet 80th and 81st St)   212/734-7441
Daily: 24 hours

The initials H&H have long been synonymous with the best bagels on New York's Upper West Side. Now Upper East Siders can feast upon this fresh, delicious New York specialty, along with a choice of homemade croissants, pastries, super sandwiches, tasty salads, salmon, lox, sturgeon, and pickled herring. Although this is mainly a takeout operation, there are a few tables for those who can't wait to start noshing. H&H bagels are so good they're served at some of New York's classiest hotels: the Pierre, the Plaza, the Four Seasons, the Drake, and Essex House.

INDIANA MARKET & CATERING
80 Second Ave (at 5th St)   212/505-7290
Mon-Sat: 8-6

Indiana Market offers a full-service catering and corporate food-service operation. They will take care of staffing, rentals, insurance, unique party sites, music, photography, flowers, and all the incidentals necessary for a successful event. Their fax menu is sent out on a daily basis to clients who want to know the specials of the day. Menu items include a wide choice of soups, salads, entrees (poultry, meat, seafood, and vegetarian), side dishes (like corn casserole and wild-rice pancakes), and great desserts. Call and ask to be put on their newsletter mailing list.

INTERNATIONAL GROCERIES AND MEAT MARKET
529 Ninth Ave (bet 39th and 40th St)   212/279-5514
Mon-Sat: 8-6

Ninth Avenue is one great wholesale market of international cookery, resplendent with exotic spices. So what would an international market on Ninth Avenue be if not a retailer of exotic spices at wholesale prices? International Groceries and Meat Market is that, but it is also an excellent source for rudiments on which to sprinkle the spices. Food is displayed in huge, open burlap bags, and while this may be disconcerting to some, you will sacrifice the frills for some of the best prices and freshest foodstuffs in town. The meat market is a gourmet locale for afficionados of baby lamb and kid. It comes seasoned, prepared, and sliced.

KELLEY & PING
127 Greene St (bet Houston and Prince St)   212/228-1212
Daily: 11:30-11

One of the fastest growing categories in foreign flavors is in the exotic cuisine of Southeastern Asia. Thai, Chinese, Vietnamese, Japanese, Malaysian, and Korean foods are popular not only in restaurants, but also on home dining-room tables. Kelley & Ping specializes in groceries and housewares from this appealing part of the world. A restaurant is part of the operation, and they do catering. If you have questions about how to prepare special dishes from this region, these are the folks to ask.

LEE & ELLE
336 Madison Ave (bet 43rd and 44th St)   212/867-5322
Mon-Fri: 6 a.m.-7 p.m.; Sat: 8-7

Located almost in the center of midtown activity, this is a must-see for the hungry shopper or office worker. Seldom have I seen a more appetizing display of prepared foods: salads, meats, veggies, fresh turkey, and a great variety of freshly made sandwiches (which you may customize). But there is much more: burgers, light lunches, homemade soups, breakfasts (until 11 a.m.), cakes, bagels, homemade muffins, croissants, cookies . . . 150 items in all to choose from! Patrons can select from a raw bar with foods cooked on a hibachi grill during the noon hour, Monday through Friday. You can eat in or take out, and free delivery is available. What a place!

LUCKY DELI
138 Fifth Ave (bet 18th and 19th St)   212/675-0640
Daily: Open 24 hours

Manhattan has plenty of great delis and markets, and many of them offer a good sandwich and salad selection. But I doubt if you will find a place that does any better than the Lucky Deli. Fancy it is not. For quality, selection, and reasonable prices, it is just about the best. Here you will find over two dozen classic sandwiches, a dozen grilled and hot sandwiches, seven different triple-decker jobs (with French fries) and 43 (yes, 43) specialty combination sandwiches, all served on your choice of bread. In addition, there are a dozen salad platters, a sushi bar, and even homemade soup. For a quick bite on the run or a meal at your desk, the Lucky Deli should be your destination. Free delivery is available, and corporate catering is a specialty.

MANGIA
50 W 57th St (bet Fifth and Sixth Ave)   212/582-5882
Mon-Fri: 7:30-7; Sat: 9-5
(closed Sat in summer)

16 E 48th St (bet Fifth and Madison Ave)   212/754-7600
Mon-Fri: 7-6

At Mangia, the old European reverence for ripe tomatoes and brick-oven bread endures. This outfit offers four distinct services: corporate catering, with anything needed for an office breakfast or luncheon; a juice bar; a carryout shop with an antipasto bar, sandwiches, entrees, and cappuccino; and a restaurant with a full menu and pastas made to order. Prices are competitive, and delivery service is offered.

PEOPLE'S GOURMET
198 Eighth Ave (at 20th St)   212/691-3948
Daily: 8:30-8:30

With a top chef (Georges Masraff) in the kitchen here, you can be assured of top-quality pastries, pizzas, breads, low-calorie prepared foods and a large selection of organic produce. Cheeses are a specialty: over a hundred kinds are shown. People's provides free delivery for orders over $25.

BARGAIN HUNTERS ALERT!

What happens to left-over items in food stores at the end of the day? I'll tell you. You can get them at reduced prices. Here is where to try . . .

Agata & Valentina (1505 First Ave at 79th St): lunchbox specials
Balducci's (424 Sixth Ave at 9th St): roast chicken
Dean & Deluca (560 Broadway at Prince St): produce
Flavors (8 W 18th St): baked goods and more
Joseph Burke (100 Fifth Ave at 15th St): sandwiches, salads
J.P.'s French Bakery (54 W 55th St): sandwiches, pastries
Union Square Greenmarket (17th St at Broadway): veggies, fruit
Zaro's Bread Basket (Penn Station, lower level): breads

PETAK'S
1244 Madison Ave (bet 89th and 90th St)   212/722-7711
Daily: 7:30 a.m.-8 p.m.; Sun: 9-8

Richard Petak, third-generation member of a family that has owned appetizing businesses in the South Bronx and New Jersey, has made the leap to Manhattan, offering the first "appy shop" the Carnegie Hill neighborhood had seen in a long time. (As housing has gotten scarcer, Carnegie Hill emerged as a prime neighborhood. Not too many years ago, it was on the outskirts of Spanish Harlem.) No neighborhood has truly *arrived* without having a gourmet shop, and Petak's fills that need. There are all the appy standbys, such as salads (60 of them!), corned beef, pastrami, smoked fish, and all sorts of takeout foods. The store offers full corporate catering, a sushi chef on premises, gift baskets, picnic hampers, box lunches, and a full-service cafe/restaurant.

PRANZO
1500 Second Ave (at 78th St)   212/439-7777
Mon-Fri: 7 a.m-10 p.m.; Sat, Sun: 7:30 a.m.-9 p.m.

In addition to delicious food, there are two special reasons to shop at Pranzo: the extended hours and the free delivery service (from 60th to 96th streets, between the East River and Fifth Avenue). Prices are not inexpensive, but the quality is apparent in the wide selection of appetizers and entrees. Their custom-made sandwiches, served on a variety of specialty breads, are excellent. Table service in the retail store and a very good catering service are available.

REX DUVAL CATERERS
500 Hudson St   212/924-0711
Mon-Fri: 8:30-6 (special hours on request)

Rex Duval, long a favorite in the food and catering business in Manhattan, and Guy Pascal, who operates the Tea Salon at Henri Bendel, have teamed up to offer top-notch service to a highly selective clientele. They are able to handle social and corporate events like private lunches and dinner, big galas, cocktail receptions, family celebrations, and weddings. You are assured of great attention to detail with these proven experts.

RUSS & DAUGHTERS
179 E Houston St   212/475-4880, 800/RUSS-229
Sun-Wed: 9-6; Thurs-Sat: 9-7

A family business in its third generation, Russ & Daughters has been a renowned New York shop since it first opened its doors. There are nuts, dried fruits, lake sturgeon, pickled herring, sliced Gaspé salmon, and a number of fancy fish dishes, including caviar, smoked fish, sable, and herring. Russ & Daughters has a reputation for serving only the very best. Five varieties of caviar are sold at low prices. They sell both wholesale and over the counter, and many a Lower East Side shopping trip ends with a stop at Russ & Daughters. Their chocolates are premium quality. They also ship anywhere. If I were to give a five-star rating, this shop would qualify. It is clean, first-rate, friendly— what more could you ask?

SABLE'S SMOKED FISH
1489 Second Ave (bet 77th and 78th St)   212/249-6177
Mon-Fri: 8:30-7:30; Sat: 8-7:30; Sun: 8-5

Kenny Sze was the appetizers manager at Zabar's for 11 years, and he learned the trade well at that famous gourmet store. Now on his own, he has brought his knowledge to the Upper East Side, where he offers wonderful smoked salmon, sturgeon, caviar (good prices), cold cuts, cheeses, salads, fresh breads, and prepared foods. Sable's catering service can provide smoked fish platters, cold-cut platters, cheese platters, jumbo sandwiches, whole hams, cured meat, and more. Free delivery is offered in the immediate area. Cold cuts and chicken dishes are specialties. Tables are available.

SALUMERIA BIELLESE
376-378 Eighth Ave (at 29th St)   212/736-7376
Mon-Sat: 7-6

This Italian-owned grocery store (with restaurant in the back) is the best and the only French *charcuterie* in the city. If that isn't contradiction enough, ponder that the loyal lunchtime crowd thinks it's dining at a hero shop when it's really enjoying the fruits of a kitchen that serves many good restaurants in the city. To understand how all this came about, a lesson in New York City geography is necessary. In 1945, when Ugo Buzzio and Joseph Nello came to this country from the Piedmontese city of Biella, they opened a shop a block away from the current one in the immigrant neighborhood called Hell's Kitchen. (Today, it's gentrified and known as Clinton.) The two partners almost immediately began producing French charcuterie. Word spread rapidly among the chefs of the city's restaurants that Salumeria Biellese was producing a quality product that could not be duplicated anywhere. Buzzio's son Marc is one of four partners who run the business today.

SARGE'S
548 Third Ave (bet 36th and 37th St)   212/679-0442
Daily: 24 hours

It isn't fancy, but Sarge's could feed an army, and there's much to be said for the taste, quality, and price. Sarge's will cater everything from hot dogs to a hot or cold buffet for almost any size crowd. Prices are gauged by the number of people and type of food, but there are several package deals, and all are remarkably reasonable. Even one of the more expensive buffets—the deluxe smoked-fish version—runs about $15 per person, and that includes cream cheese and bagels, as well as sturgeon, sable, and stuffed smoked whitefish. Sarge's also caters deli items and has an excellent selection of cold hors d'oeuvre platters, offering everything from canapes of caviar, sturgeon, and Nova Scotia salmon to shrimp cocktail. To make the party complete, Sarge's can supply serving pieces, condiments, and staff. A carver, cutting board, knife, pastrami, warming oven, and table can all be obtained from Sarge's.

TODARO BROTHERS
555 Second Ave (bet 30th and 31st St)   212/532-0633
Mon-Sat: 7:30 a.m.–9 p.m.; Sun: 8–8

This is food heaven! Great lunch sandwiches, fresh homemade mozzarella, and authentic *panettone* are offered daily. Todaro carries the very best in imported and domestic gourmet food. Just about everything here is irresistible and will wreak havoc on pocketbook and diet alike. There is imported stuffed pasta, fresh fish, rare cheeses, olive oils, patés, jams, coffees, homemade sausages, and a half-dozen gourmet items, all top quality. Todaro even stocks fresh truffles, a delicacy seldom seen this side of a haughty restaurant. To top it off, Lucian Todaro imports the very best chocolates from Europe.

URBAN MARKET
119 W 26th St (bet Sixth and Seventh Ave)   212/691-0234
Mon-Fri: 8-6; Sat, Sun: 9-5 (in summer only)

Urban Market fills an unusual niche in the food business: a fully stocked international specialty food store that features Columbian, Italian, and West Indian food items at discounted prices. There are prepackaged takeout items; freshly prepared soups, salads and sandwiches; and baked goods. As it is a family business, many of the tasty recipes come from several generations' worth of the ownership families. There is a catering facility called Beauty and the Feast that services private and corporate customers. A small counter takes care of those who want to sample the goodies on the premises.

Craving some marinated artichoke hearts at 3:21 a.m.? No sweat. **Gourmet Heaven,** a one-stop gourmet shop at 1407 Second Ave (bet 73rd and 74th St, 212/439-9356) is open 24 hours a day.

Or you might try **Global** (93 Second Ave, 212/477-8427) for tapas; **Cafe Noir** (32 Grand St, 212/431-7910) for crab cakes; or **Florent** (69 Gansevoort St, 212/989-5779) for cheeseburgers and fries.

VINEGAR FACTORY
431 E 91st St (near York Ave)   212/987-0885
Daily: 7 a.m.-9 p.m.

It's not exactly in a great location (you can almost hear the FDR Drive traffic), and the name is really not very descriptive (vinegar is really not featured, although this shop did used to be a working vinegar factory). The fact that Eli Zabar is involved doesn't mean that the prices are sky high. To the contrary, this place has livable prices on fresh produce, pizzas, fish, flowers, meats, wines, liquors, desserts, seafood, cheeses, baked goods (including Eli's great bread), coffee, deli items, and housewares. Breakfast and brunch (on weekends) are available on the balcony. Now if only Eli would tone down the outrageous prices at his Madison Avenue establishment, he would emerge as an East Side hero. But don't let that keep you away from the Vinegar Factory, which is one of the most intriguing food factories around!

WORD OF MOUTH
1012 Lexington Ave (bet 72nd and 73rd St)
212/734-9483 (store); 212/249-5351 (cafe)
Store: Mon-Fri: 10-7; Sat: 10-6; Sun: 11:30-5:30
Cafe: Mon-Fri: 8-6; Tues-Fri: 8 a.m.-9 p.m. (*prix fixe* dinner);
Sat, Sun: 8-5; closed Sun in Aug

The history of Word of Mouth is actually the gastronomic history of Manhattan—or at least the Upper East Side. When Christi Finch (an Oregonian—they pop up everywhere!) opened her tiny shop in 1976, hers was one of the first establishments to offer home-style prepared foods for home or picnic use. Success was almost instantaneous, and by 1979 the shop had incorporated and moved around the corner. Today she enjoys a reputation as one of the finest sources for pasta, soups, vegetable and chicken salads, quiches, baked goods, and specialty meat dishes. The aim is still the same, however. Full-service home catering is offered. There is no ethnic orientation, though there are worldwide influences. The philosophy is basically home-style cooking that makes use of the finest ingredients. A wonderful brunch menu is offered on weekends.

ZABAR'S
2245 Broadway (at 80th St)   212/787-2000
Mon-Fri: 8-7:30; Sat: 8 a.m.-midnight; Sun: 9-6
Mezzanine: 9-6 daily

If you have time to visit only one New York landmark, make it this one! This is America's most unique gourmet, appetizer, and housewares shop. Zabar's is not just another food emporium; it is a New York institution. Don't expect neat aisles and fancy fixtures. The genius of the place is that it is like a permanent carnival. However, this carnival features top-quality food items in every category, with broad selections and enormous quantities at what are arguably the best prices in the city. You can find a huge selection of bakery goods, candy bargains you won't believe (they buy in large lots), every kind of cheese you could ask for, an appetizer section that has to be the busiest in the city, and a coffee department that sells more than any other store in the country. They sell more caviar at bargain prices than any other New York retailer. There are also staple grocery items, pots and pans hanging from the ceiling, and aisles stacked high with daily specials and demonstrations. Upstairs you will find the city's best bargains on housewares—everything from toasters to ice-cream machines and carving knives. Next door is an informal cafe where weary shoppers can be refreshed with orange juice, coffee, yogurt, and baked delicacies. For native New Yorkers, a visit to Zabar's is a normal routine. Visitors shouldn't leave the Big Apple without a look! A mail-order catalog is available.

Catering to the beautiful people . . .

If bucks are no object, and you're in the mood to throw a really big affair, you might consider the following: **Feast & Fêtes** (20 E 76th St, 212/737-2224), presided over by Daniel Boulud of Le Cirque and Daniel restaurant fame, or **Tentation Catering** (47 E 19th St, 212/353-0070), a partnership that includes Jean Georges Vongerichten of Jean George, Vong, and Jo-Jo. Along with **Glorious Food** (reviewed in this chapter), these are the very 'in' (read pricey) outfits.

Additional Caterers

Creative Edge Parties (410 E 13th St, 212/473-2700)
Fletcher Morgan (864 Lexington Ave, 212/288-6764)
Food in Motion (309 W 17th St, 212/807-8935)
Herban Kitchen (290 Hudson St, 212/627-2257)
Manna Catering (24 Harrison St, 212/966-3449)
Robbins Wolfe (521 West St, 212/924-6500)
Spoonbread (333 E 75th St, 212/734-3204)
Taste (113 Horatio St, 212/255-8571)

Fruits, Vegetables

GREENMARKET
130 E 16th St (office)   212/477-3220

Bowling Green (bet Broadway and Battery Pl)
City Hall (bet Centre and Chambers St)
Federal Plaza (bet Broadway and Thomas St)
World Trade Center (bet Church and Fulton St)
Washington Market Park (bet Greenwich and Reade St)
Harrison Street (bet Greenwich and N Moore St)
St. Mark's (bet 10th St and Second Ave)
Lt. Petrisino Park (bet Spring and Lafayette)
Tompkins Square (E 7th St at Ave A)
Abingdon Square (bet 12th St and Eighth Ave)
Union Square (bet 17th St and Broadway)
West 57th St (at Ninth Ave)
West 70th St (at Amsterdam Ave)
West 77th St (at Columbus Ave)
West 97th St (at Amsterdam Ave)
Harlem (bet 143rd St and Lenox Ave)
West 175th St (at Broadway)

Starting in 1976 with just one location, these unique open-air markets have been springing up in various neighborhoods. They are sponsored and overseen by a nonprofit organization. No middle man means prices are significantly less than at supermarkets. Another great advantage is that all produce (over 600 varieties), baked goods, flowers, and fish are straight from the farm or fisherman. When the supply is gone, the stand closes for the day. Come early. Call the above number to find out the nearest address and the day and time when that particular market will be open. Most are seasonal, operating from 8 a.m. to 3 p.m., although some stay open all year.

LA MARQUETA
Park Ave (under the tracks from 110th to 116th St)   212/534-4900

Tucked under the train tracks in Harlem, this is one of the most fabulous shopping places in the city. La Marqueta (established by Maya Fiorello LaGuardia in 1936) is famous, and the early-morning babble of voices here is proof that its customers are not only the local residents of Spanish Harlem. Although the accent is definitely Latin American, there is nothing that isn't sold here. Each building contains several individual businesses that hawk whatever is fresh that day. It's a friendly, informal place to get bargains.

Calories be damned! Full speed ahead! Wonderful doughnuts at **Krispy Kreme** (265 W 23rd St, 141 W 72nd St, Penn Station, and 280 W 125th St) and at legendary **Georgie's Pastry Shop** (50 W 125th St). They don't come any better.

Gift and Picnic Baskets

How does a day in the park sound? Make it complete, fun, and easy with a tasty basket from the following:

Balducci's (424 Sixth Ave, at 9th St)
Canard & Company (1292 Madison Ave, at 92nd St)
Dean & Deluca (560 Broadway, at Prince St)
Fraser Morris Fine Foods (102 President St, Brooklyn)
Grace's Marketplace (1237 Third Ave, at 71st St)
Petrossian (182 W 58th St)
Whole Foods Uptown (2421 Broadway, at 89th St)
Word of Mouth (1012 Lexington Ave, at 72nd St)

MANHATTAN FRUITIER
210 E 6th St (at Third Ave)   212/686-0404
Mon-Fri: 9-5:30

Most fruit baskets are pretty bad, but this outfit makes some great-looking and great-tasting masterpieces using fresh seasonal and exotic fruits. You can add such comestibles as hand-rolled cheddar-cheese sticks, biscotti, and individually wrapped chocolates. Locally handmade truffles and flowers are also available. Delivery charges in Manhattan are very reasonable.

SANDLER'S
212/279-9779, 800/75-FRUIT
Daily: 9-6

Sandler's is a key source for scumptious candies, delicacies, and some of the best chocolate-chip cookies in New York. Yet Sandler's is best known for gift baskets filled with fancy fresh fruit, natural cheeses, and gourmet delicacies. No one does it better!

WEST SIDE FRUITIER
145 W 20th St (bet Sixth and Seventh Ave)
212/727-2045, 888/BASKET8, 800/289-2106
Mon-Fri: 10-6

If you are looking for an upscale fresh-fruit gift basket, this is the place. West Side Fruitier uses both domestic and exotic fruits (like passion fruit, star fruit, papaya and persimmons), and mixes them with a fine selection of cheese, crackers, truffles, coffee, and the like. The baskets all have great eye appeal; they are custom-designed with attractive flowers, ferns, and wrappings. Deliveries (no charge in Manhattan below 96th Street) can be made to homes, hotels, hospitals, or offices. Ask for Dylan Wallace, the manager, who puts his seal of approval on every basket.

Greek

LIKITSAKOS
1174 Lexington Ave (bet 80th and 81st St)   212/535-4300
Mon-Fri: 8 a.m.-9 p.m.; Sat, Sun: 8-8

Likitsakos is one of the better places in New York to find all kinds of Greek and international specialties, including salads, fruits, vegetables, grains, dips, and appetizers.

> ## Caviar
>
> We aim to please all tastes and all pocketbooks in this volume, so I guess it is only right that we devote a line or two to readers with sophisticated tastes:
>
> **Bubble Room** (228 West Broadway): the real stuff, plus hundreds of champagnes and wines
> **Caviar Russe** (538 Madison Ave): a new luxury spot
> **Caviarteria** (502 Park Ave): I like everything about this place, especially the friendly attitudes of Eric and Bruce Sobol.
> **Firebird** (365 W 46th St): re-creation of a prerevolutionary Russian mansion
> **Petrossian** (182 W 58th St): Stepping inside here provides *caviar set* ambience; it's a spectacular place to dine.
> **Zabar's** (2245 Broadway): If price is important, this should be your first stop.

Health Foods

BENNIE'S
321-1/2 Amsterdam Ave (at 75th St)   212/874-3032
Daily: 11-10:30

Bennie's specializes in vegetarian foods, and they're among the best anywhere. Homage is paid to their Lebanese roots with the best *tabbouleh* in the city and a plate that speaks with a definite Middle Eastern and European accent. The health aspect is not ignored, either. In addition to three sensational chicken salads, Bennie's boasts the biggest selection of health foods in the neighborhood. A prime example is the *muda-data* (a salad of rice, onions, and lentils). It, too, is reasonably priced and excellent. English is not spoken fluently here, but with all these goodies, who cares?

COMMODITIES
117 Hudson St (at N Moore St)   212/334-8330
Daily: 10-8

Commodities is the largest natural-food store within a 100-mile radius, according to the store's staff. Their produce is of excellent quality, and prices are comparable to those of local supermarkets. They've earned that "largest" reputation with a well-rounded stock of canned and processed health foods, including vegetable and meat substitutes and a full line of health-food products. They are able to serve everyone from macrobiotics to those who are only marginally interested in chemically free food. A cafe serves organic prepared foods, sandwiches, veggies, and juices. The staff is helpful, and the store is large.

DOWN TO EARTH
33 Seventh Ave (bet 12th and 13th St)   212/924-2711
Mon-Fri: 10-9; Sat, Sun: 12-7

This is the Village's most complete, best-run, and most appealing health-food store. Look over the vitamins, packaged health foods, vegetables, frozen meats, bulk nuts, cereals, fruits, cheeses, and sprouts. All are top quality. The takeout sandwiches are filling and wholesome. They have made their prices competitive.

GOOD EARTH FOODS
1334 First Ave (bet 71st and 72nd St)   212/472-9055
Mon-Fri: 9-7:30; Sat: 9-6; Sun: 12-6

167 Amsterdam Ave (at 68th St)   212/496-1616
Mon-Fri: 9:30-7:30; Sat: 9:30-6:30; Sun: 12-6

Good Earth has the reputation of being best-stocked health-food store in New York—and one of the most expensive. The helpful and knowledgeable sales personnel will vehemently deny they are overpriced, but a quick comparison of prices shows otherwise. Just as surely, a quick visit will confirm their reputation for having one of the largest and freshest stocks. In addition to their enormous selection, Good Earth offers delivery anywhere within the city.

GRASSROOTS NATURAL MARKET
520 Broadway (at Spring St)   212/334-2444
Mon-Fri: 8 a.m.-10 p.m.; Sat: 10-10; Sun: 10-9

How can you beat good food items presented in an attractive atmosphere? When you add good service, you have an unbeatable combination. Grassroots Natural Market features organic produce, a tasty salad bar, gourmet prepared foods, and a great selection of vitamins, minerals, and herbs. Specialty health items and over 5,000 books can be found downstairs.

HEALTHY PLEASURES
93 University Pl (bet 11th and 12th St)   212/353-FOOD
Daily: 7 a.m.-10:30 p.m.

You feel healthy just walking in this place—and what a selection! Healthy Pleasures is a full-scale deli/health-products emporium and then some, with entree items (like roasted chicken, lasagna, and fish) for takeout, healthy platters (like organic steamed vegetables, salads, and soups), and delicious sandwiches. The soups have no added fat or dairy products and are full of organic veggies. Pies and cakes are baked on the premises. There is free delivery on all menu items, an all-natural catering service is available, and a daily breakfast-to-go menu features fresh juice, all-natural muffins and bagels, organic and decaf coffees, and herbal teas.

INTEGRAL YOGA NATURAL FOODS
229 W 13th St (bet Seventh and Eighth Ave)   212/243-2642
Mon-Fri: 10-9:30; Sat: 10-8:30; Sun: 12-6:30

Selection, quality, and health are the order of the day in this clean, attractive shop, which features a complete assortment of natural foods. Vegetarian items, packaged groceries, organic produce, bulk foods, juice bar, salad bar, deli, and baked items are all available at reasonable prices for the health-conscious shopper. They are located in the same building as a yoga center that offers classes in yoga, meditation, and philosophy. A vitamin and health-food store is located across the street.

LIFETHYME NATURAL MARKET
408-410 Sixth Ave (bet 8th and 9th St)   212/420-9099
Mon-Fri: 8 a.m.-10 p.m.; Sat, Sun: 9 a.m.-10 p.m.

You'll find one of the largest selections of organic produce in the area at this complete natural supermarket. In addition there is an organic salad table, a good variety of health-related books, a natural deli, and an organic juice bar. Located in two renovated 1839 brownstones in the heart of the Village, this busy shop also does catering, discounts vitamins, offers custom-baked goods for dietary needs, and will custom-cook foods.

WHOLE FOOD MARKETS
117 Prince St (bet Greene and Wooster St)   212/982-1000
Mon-Fri: 8 a.m.-10 p.m.; Sat: 9 a.m.-10 p.m.; Sun: 9 a.m.-9 p.m.

2421 Broadway (at 89th St)   212/874-4000
Daily: 8 a.m.-11 p.m.

These are Manhattan's premier health-food supermarkets. Featured are organic produce, fresh juices, vitamins at up to 25% discount, and a full line of healthy supermarket products. They will deliver anywhere in the metro area or ship anywhere in the world. The deli and salad bar at the uptown location are both organic and kosher.

Ice Cream
CHELSEA BAKING AND ICE COMPANY
259-263 W 19th St (bet Seventh and Eighth Ave)   212/989-9800
Open 24 hours

Imagine 600 different desserts! There are 100 flavors of ice cream, 80 sorbets, and 20 gelati flavors, plus cakes, tarts, pies, and all kinds of frozen desserts. Wedding and special-occasion cakes are a specialty. Quality is top-notch, and all the goodies are on display in the showroom.

Indian
K. KALUSTYAN
123 Lexington Ave (bet 28th and 29th St)   212/685-3451
Mon-Sat: 10-8; Sun: 11-

In 1944, Kalustyan opened as an Indian spice store at its present location. After all this time, Kalustyan is still a great spot. Everything is sold in bins or bales rather than prepackaged containers and is available in bulk or wholesale sizes for retail customers. The difference in cost, flavor, and freshness compared to that of regular grocery stores is extraordinary. The best indication of freshness and flavor is a simple whiff of the store's aroma! Kalustyan is not strictly an Indian store, but also an Orient export trading corporation with a specialty in Middle Eastern and Indian items.

Italian
MELAMPO
105 Sullivan St (bet Spring and Prince St)   212/334-9530
Mon-Sat: 11:30-5

In a tiny store not much larger than an oversized closet, Melampo manages to display a sizable variety of the best in Italian food items. The specialty, however, is their sandwiches. This is the place to go for super combinations like Marina (salami, provolone), Cristina (mozzarella, artichoke), and Alessandro (tuna, peppers, bel paese). All sandwiches are served on individual-sized white or whole-wheat bread loaves. For a treat you'll never forget in the summer, try the Bombolo Tricolore, consisting of fresh mozzarella, Jersey tomato, basil, and special dressing served on focaccia.

RAFFETTO'S CORPORATION
144 W Houston St (bet Sullivan and MacDougal St)   212/777-1261
Tues-Fri: 9-6:30; Sat: 8-6

You could go to a gourmet place for pasta, or you could go straight to the source. Raffetto's is *the* source for pasta, and has been since 1906. Since that time they have made all kinds of pasta and stuffing. Though most of the business is wholesale, Raffetto's will sell anyone 12 flavors of noodles, ravioli, mini-ravioli, tortellini, manicotti, gnocchi, and fettuccine with no minimum order. Variations on the theme include Genoa-style ravioli with meat and spinach and Naples-style ravioli with cheese. Over ten kinds of homemade sauces prepared by Mrs. Raffetto, daily bread, dry pasta, and bargain-priced olive oils and vinegars are featured.

RAVIOLI STORE
75 Sullivan St (bet Spring and Broome St)   212/925-1737
Mon-Fri: 10-7; Sat, Sun: 11-5

Custom pasta? Yes sir. The Ravioli Store was the first to launch the pasta craze, stuffing gourmet fillings inside ravioli. Their products are all natural. Custom shapes and fillings are available, and healthy (cholesterol- and wheat-free) items are in their product line.

Japanese

KATAGIRI & COMPANY
224 E 59th St (bet Second and Third Ave)   212/755-3566
Mon-Sat: 10-7; Sun: 11-6

Are you planning a Japanese dinner? Do you have some important clients from across the Pacific that you would like to impress with a sushi party? Katagiri features all kinds of Japanese food, sushi ingredients, and utensils. They also provide wholesale items for major hotels and restaurants. You can get some great party ideas from the helpful personnel here, and the prices are far more reasonable than in Tokyo.

Kosher

LEIBEL'S KOSHER SPECIALTIES
39 Essex St   212/254-0335
Sun-Thurs: 9:30-6:30; Fri: 9:30-3

Here's a handy place to buy all of your kosher food items, including cheese, fish, jams, and frozen goods. Almost every kosher specialty is available at this personable, family-operated store on the Lower East Side. Prices reflect the neighborhood, which means there are bargains by the dozen.

SIEGEL'S KOSHER DELI AND RESTAURANT
1646 Second Ave (bet 85th and 86th St)   212/288-3632, 212/288-2094
Mon-Thurs: 11-10; Fri-Sun: 10-10

If you are looking for a top kosher deli and gourmet appetizer store on the Upper East Side, you can't do better than Siegel's. Not only do they keep long hours (Sundays, too), but they also deliver from 10 a.m. to 9 p.m. Featured are fresh, decorated turkey dishes; overstuffed sandwich platters; barbecue, roasted, and fried chicken platters; hors d'oeuvre selections; smoked fish platters; fresh baked breads and salad trays; and a large selection of cakes, cookies, and fruit platters. The number of selections is awesome, with nearly two dozen sandwiches on the menu, ten kinds of soups, dozens of salads, and side dishes ranging from potato and meat knishes to kugel and kishka.

Liquor, Wine

ACKER, MERRALL & CONDIT
160 W 72nd St (bet Broadway and Columbus Ave)   212/787-1700
Mon-Sat: 8:30 a.m.-10 p.m.

AMC is the oldest operating wine and liquor store in America, first opening its doors in 1820. And what a place it continues to be! There are wine tastings every Saturday afternoon. Wine seminars are offered to companies. Wine parties can be arranged in homes for special occasions. Free delivery is available in Manhattan. This service-oriented firm carries an especially good inventory of American wines and specializes in purchases from Bordeaux and the Rhine.

BURGUNDY WINE COMPANY
323 W 11th St   212/691-9092
Tues-Sat: 10-7

One of the great pleasures of shopping in New York is that there is a store that specializes in just about everything. The customer is the winner, because the selection is huge and the price range broad enough to appeal to just about everybody. Such is the case with the Burgundy Wine Company, a compact and attractive store in the Village. These folks are specialists in fine Burgundies and Rhones, with over 1,500 labels to choose from. There are some great treasures in their cellars; ask the knowledgeable personnel.

CROSSROADS WINES AND LIQUORS
55 W 14th St (at Sixth Ave)   212/924-3060
Mon-Sat: 9-9

'Crossroads may have the best selection of wine in the city; 3,000 kinds from all the great wine-producing countries. There are rare, unique, and exotic liquors as well. Crossroads will special-order items, deliver, and help with party and menu planning. Finally, they are not in a snobby neighborhood, and their prices are as low as their attitude is low-key.

GARNET LIQUORS
929 Lexington Ave (bet 68th and 69th St)
212/772-3211, 800/USA-VINO (out of state)
Mon-Sat: 9-9

Don't you love that "800" number? You'll love Garnet's prices even more. This may be the most inexpensive place in the city for specialty wines. If you're in the market for champagne, Bordeaux, Burgundy, or other imported wine, check out the prices here first. They're good on other wines and liquors, too.

K&D FINE WINES AND SPIRITS
1366 Madison Ave (bet 95th and 96th St)   212/289-1818
Mon-Sat: 9 a.m.-10 p.m.

K&D is an excellent wine and spirits market on the Upper East Side. Hundreds of top brands and top wines are sold at more than competitive prices. Major ads in local newspapers occasionally highlight K&D's special bargains, but even on a regular basis the values here are outstanding.

MORRELL & COMPANY
535 Madison Ave (bet 54th and 55th St)   212/688-9370
Mon-Fri: 9-6:45; Sat: 9:30-6:30

Charming and well informed, Peter Morrell is the wine adviser at this small, jam-packed store, which carries all kinds of wine and liquor. The stock is overwhelming; since there isn't room for displaying everything, a good portion is kept in the wine cellar. All of it is easily accessible, however, and the Morrell staff is amenable to helping you find the right bottle. The stock consists of spirits, including brandy liqueurs, and many vintages of wine, ranging from rare and old to young and inexpensive.

QUALITY HOUSE
2 Park Ave (bet 32nd and 33rd St)   212/532-2944
Mon-Fri: 9-6:30; Sat: 9-5; closed Sat in July, August

Quality House boasts one of the most extensive assortments of French wine in the city; an equally fine offering of domestic and Italian wines; and selections from Germany, Spain, and Portugal. Oenologist Willie Gluckstern claims that Bernie Fradin (Quality House's owner) and his son Gary have the best wine palates in the city. This is a quality house, not a bargain spot. Delivery is available and almost always free.

SOHO WINES AND SPIRITS
461 West Broadway (bet Prince and Houston St)   212/777-4332
Mon-Sat: 10-8

Stephen Masullo's father ran a neighborhood liquor store on Spring Street for over 25 years. When his local neighborhood evolved into the Soho of today, his sons expanded the business and opened a stylish Soho establishment for wine. The shop is lofty. In fact, it looks more like an art gallery than a wine shop. The various bottles are tastefully displayed, with classical music playing in the background. Every advantage is made of the enormous floor space, and Stephen boasts that Soho Wines also has one of the largest selections of single malt Scotch whiskeys in New York. Again, in keeping with the neighborhood, Soho Wines and Spirits offers several unique services. Among them are party planning, wine-cellar advice, and specialty items of interest to the neighborhood.

WANT TO SEND THE BEST OF NEW YORK?
Great for gifts, or for you if you're house-bound .

Beef from **Lobel's** (800/5-LOBELS)
Country bread from **Ecce Panis** (212/517-4219)
Appetizers from **Russ & Daughters** (212/475-4880)
Bagels from **H&H** (800/NYBAGEL)
Cheesecake from **Junior's** (800/9-JUNIORS)
Sturgeon from **Barney Greengrass** (212/724-4707)
Knishes from **Yonah Schimmel** (212/477-2858)
Ricotta from **Alleva Dairy** (800/4-ALLEVA)
Coffee from **Porto Rico Importing Company** (800/453-5908)

Meat, Poultry

Everything you wanted to know about **SALAMI**:

Genoa: made from extra lean pork, plus garlic
Milano: fine ground, made with beef and pork
Sicilian: more robust, more garlic
Sopressata: coarsely ground, lightly seasoned, black peppercorns
Toscano: lean pork and coarsely ground fat
Abruzzese: coarse ground pork and spicy red pepper
Calabrese: slowly air dried, coarsely ground
Love & Garlic: a San Francisco favorite, with beef and pork
 (the San Francisco fog helps out in the drying process)
Kosher: all beef, cooked with spices
Hungarian: pork with added spices, air-dried for 90 days

FAICCO'S PORK STORE
260 Bleecker St (at Sixth Ave)   212/243-1974
Tues-Sat: 8-6; Fri: 8-7; Sun: 9-2

An Italian institution, Faicco's carries delectable dried sausage, cuts of pork, and sweet and hot sausage. They also sell an equally good cut for barbecue and an oven-ready rolled leg of stuffed pork. The latter, a house specialty, is locally famous. Note Faicco's full name: the shop really specializes in sausage and cold cuts rather than meats. There is no veal or lamb. But if you're into Italian-style deli, try Faicco's first. And if you're a lazy cook, take home some ready-to-heat chicken rollettes: breasts of chicken rolled around cheese and then dipped in a crunchy coating. It's the perfect introduction to Faicco's specialties. Prepared hot foods to take home, like eggplant parmesan, are also available.

JEFFERSON MARKET
450 Sixth Ave (at 10th St)   212/533-3377
Mon-Sat: 8 a.m-9 p.m.; Sun: 9-8

Quality and personal service are the bywords here. Originally a prime-meat and poultry market, Jefferson has grown into an outstanding full-line store. Second-generation family management insures hands-on attention to service. Prime meats, fresh seafood, select produce, fancy groceries, Bell and Evans chicken, and fresh salads are all tempting. There are expanded deli, cheese, produce, and fish sections. Delivery service is available. If you don't feel like cooking dinner, come by Jefferson and let Louis Montuori send you home with some delicious hot or cold prepared foods.

KUROWYCKY MEAT PRODUCTS
124 First Ave (bet 7th and 8th St)   212/477-0344
Mon-Sat: 8-6; closed Mon in July, Aug

Erast Kurowycky came to New York from Ukraine in 1954. He opened this tiny shop the same year, and almost immediately it became a mecca and bargain spot for the city's Poles, Germans, Hungarians, Russians, Lithuanians, and Ukrainians. Many of these nationalities still harbor centuries-old grudges, but they all come to Kurowycky's, where they agree on at least two things: the meats are the finest and the prices are the best available. A third-generation family member, Jaroslaw, Jr., now runs the shop. Hams, sausages, meat loaves, and breads are sold ready to eat, as well as in various stages of preparation. There are also condiments, including a homemade Polish mustard, honey imported from Poland, sauerkraut, and a half-dozen other Ukrainian specialties imported or reproduced from the area.

M. LOBEL AND SONS
1096 Madison Ave (bet 82nd and 83rd St)   212/737-1373
Mon-Sat: 9-6: closed Sat in summer

Lobel's runs periodic sales on some of the best cuts of meat in town (poultry and veal, too). Because of Lobel's excellent service and reasonable prices, there are few carnivores in Manhattan who haven't heard of the shop. The staff has published four meat cookbooks, and they are always willing to explain the best use for each cut. It's hard to go wrong, since Lobel carries only the best. They will ship all over the country. Great hamburgers, too!

OPPENHEIMER PRIME MEATS
2606 Broadway (bet 98th and 99th St)   212/662-0246, 212/662-0690
Mon-Fri: 9-6:55; Sat: 8-6

Reliable and trustworthy Oppenheimer is one of the first names mentioned for prime meats in New York. Under the new ownership of Robert Pence, an experienced chef, the traditions of Harry Oppenheimer are continued. It's an old-fashioned butcher shop offering the kind of service that used to be expected —and that supermarkets have never had. Supermarkets have never had this quality, either. There's milk-fed veal, free-range poultry, and game, all sold at competitive prices.

OTTOMANELLI'S MEAT MARKET
285 Bleecker St (bet Seventh Ave and Jones St)
212/675-4217
Mon-Fri: 8-6:30; Sat: 7-6

With renewed attention to federally inspected meats, Ottomanelli's now has an on-site inspector. The stock-in-trade here is rare gourmet fare. Among the regular weekly offerings are such meats as boar's head, whole baby lambs, game rabbits, and pheasant. This is not a place to act naive. Quality is good, but being served by the right person can make the difference between a good cut and an excellent cut. Other family members run similar operations in other sections of town, but this is the original store, and it's noteworthy. They gained their reputation by offering full butcher services and a top-notch selection of prime meats, game, prime-aged steaks, and milk-fed veal. The latter is available as prepared Italian roast, chops, and steaks, and its preparation by Ottomanelli's is unique. Best of all, they will sell it by the piece for a quick meal at home.

PREMIER VEAL
555 West St (off West Side Hwy, two blocks south of 14th St)
212/243-3170
Mon-Fri: 4 a.m.-1 p.m.

Mark Hirschorn worked various business jobs from Albany to Aspen before deciding to join the family wholesale veal distribution center. As he says, he's been on both sides of the counter. This translates as a wholesaler who has a good eye for what sells in restaurants and institutions while running a business that is friendlier than most to small, individual customers. Premier Veal offers veal and lamb stew, Italian cutlets, shoulder or leg roasts, and veal pockets for stuffing, all at wholesale prices with no minimum order. Of course, if you're trekking to West Street, it might be economical to make the order as large as possible. Hirschorn suggests that three or four customers get together and order a few loins. Less than that leaves too much waste and is not profitable for him or the customer. A loin weighing 26 pounds breaks down to 16 or 24 steaks and chops, and the price is a fraction of that at a butcher shop.

ROYALE PRIME MEATS
833 Washington St (near Little W 12th St)   212/243-3161
Mon-Fri: 4 a.m.-1 p.m.

If you are enjoying some delicious meat entree at your favorite Manhattan restaurant, it probably came from Royale Prime Meats. Although they have operated for years as a wholesaler, now the public can enjoy the same quality meats at excellent prices. They deliver and ship all over the world. Royale Prime is located in the oldest meat market in the United States; ask Eddie or Michael to fill you in on the history of the area. In addition to steaks, this firm offers other beef cuts, veal, lamb, pork, poultry, and game (including rabbit, squab, poussin, duck, goose, and guinea hens).

SCHALLER & WEBER
1654 Second Ave (bet 85th and 86th St)   212/879-3047
Mon-Fri: 9-6; Sat: 8:30-6

Once you've been in this store, the image will stay with you for a long time because of the sheer magnitude of cold cuts on display. Schaller & Weber is simply incredible. It is a *Babes in Toyland* for delicatessen lovers, and there is not a wall or nook that is not covered with deli meats. Besides offering a complete line of delicatessen items, Schaller & Weber also occasionally stocks game and poultry, and they claim to be a butcher shop as well. Try the sausage and pork. They will bake, prepare, smoke, or roll it for you, and that's just the beginning.

YORKVILLE PACKING HOUSE
1560 Second Ave (at 81st St)   212/628-5147
Mon-Fri: 8:30-6:30; Sat: 8-7; Sun: 11-5:30

Yorkville used to be a bastion of Eastern European ethnicity and culture before it became the Upper East Side's swinging singles playground. Here and there, remnants of Old World society remain. Yorkville Packing House is patronized by Hungarian-speaking little old ladies in black, as well as some of the city's greatest gourmands. And the reason is simple: except for its neighbors, these prepared meats are available nowhere else in the city and possibly nowhere else on the continent. The shop offers a vast variety of sausages and salami. Smoked meats include pork shoulder and tenderloin. Goose is a mainstay of Hungarian cuisine, so there is goose liverwurst, smoked goose, and goose liver. Fried bacon bits and bacon fried with paprika (another Hungarian staple) are other offerings. Ready for on-the-spot consumption is a selection of preserves, jams, spices, utensils, ground nuts, jellies, prepared delicacies, head cheese, and breads, as well as takeout meals. All of it is authentic.

Nuts

KADOURI IMPORT
51 Hester St (at Essex St)   212/677-5441
Sun-Thurs: 8-6; Fri: 8-3

Kadouri is a wholesale-retail store operating out of burlap bags. Everything here is natural and healthful. The main staples are nuts and dried fruits. The almonds and their derivatives are especially good. Kadouri carries candies, beans, canned items, and spices as well. Prices are wholesale, no matter how small the purchase. Specialty items from Israel—like pickles, jams, and soups—are available.

Pickles

GUSS PICKLES
35 Essex St (bet Grand and Hester St)   212/254-4477, 800/252-GUSS
Sun-Thurs: 9-6; Fri: 9-3

Two legendary rival businesses started decades ago, with Guss and Hollander each dispensing pickles, tomatoes, sauerkraut, pickled peppers, and watermelon rinds from barrels on the sidewalk. They have since merged into one business that operates at Hollander's store. Pickles still come sour or half sour, with a half-dozen gradations in between, and the business is still conducted out on the street, with the stock taking up the interior of the store. Customers can actually glimpse a semblance of order and even a refrigerator inside. That refrigerator is stocked with such items as watermelon rind (in season), hot peppers, freshly ground horseradish, sauerkraut, and whole pickled melons. But what's really important to remember is that this enterprise is still the best place in the world for fresh-from-the-barrel pickles. Pickled celery and carrots are a new and welcome addition.

Seafood

CATALANO'S FRESH FISH MARKET
Vinegar Factory
431 E 91st St (bet York and First Ave)   212/987-0885
Fish Market: Mon-Sun: 8-8; Vinegar Factory: Mon-Sun: 7 a.m.-9 p.m.

Joe Catalano is a rare blend of concern and knowledge. His customers, including many local restaurants, rely on him to select the best items for their dinner menus. This he does with a careful eye toward health, price, and cookery. He feels that a fish store should not be intimidating and that the only way to attract new customers is to educate them. Catalano's at the Vinegar Factory also has a good selection of poached fish and fish cakes, plus crawfish and soft-shell crab in season. On cold, wintry days, don't miss the Manhattan clam chowder.

CENTRAL FISH COMPANY
527 Ninth Ave (bet 39th and 40th St)   212/279-2317
Mon-Fri: 7:30-6:30; Sat: 7:30-5:30

Central doesn't look like much from the outside, but the stock is so vast that it's easier to list what is *not* available than what is. They have 35 fish species in stock at any given time, including fresh imported sardines from Portugal and live carp. Conducting customers through this whale of a selection are some of the friendliest and most knowledgeable salespeople I've encountered. Louis and Anthony Riccoborno and Calogero Olivri are skillful guides who stock all manner of fresh and frozen fish and seafood products. There are fish that even the most devoted seafood lover would have trouble identifying, and the prices are among the most reasonable in town.

CITARELLA
2135 Broadway (at 75th St)
1313 Third Ave (at 75th St)   212/874-0383
Mon-Sat: 8 a.m.-9 p.m.; Sun: 9-7

Citarella now has both the Upper West Side and the Upper East Side covered . . . and with expanded offerings! Originally a place for all kinds of fish (fresh and smoked), selections have increased to include prepared foods, prime meats, appetizers, cheeses, pastries, bread, and pastas. Delivery service and house accounts are offered.

JAKE'S FISH MARKET
2425 Broadway (bet 89th and 90th St)   212/580-5253
Daily: 8-8

The menu at Jake's: catering (including raw bar) and delivery; fresh fish, cut kosher upon request; prepared foods, including a seven-course weekend dinner with a menu that changes weekly; steamed lobsters; and clams and oysters on the half shell. The owner also operates first-class restaurants (Docks, Carmine's, EJ's Luncheonette). Phone customers get special attention.

LEONARD'S FISH MARKET
1241 Third Ave (bet 71st and 72nd St)   212/744-2600
Mon-Fri: 8-7; Sat: 8-6; Sun: 12-6

Leonard's, a family-owned business since 1910, is operated by five family members who display the same exacting standards maintained throughout the years. It's a neighborhood store that gears its selection to the locals' menus. There are sea trout, oysters, crabs, haddock, scampi, striped bass, halibut, salmon, live lobster, and squid. They also run specials on whatever happens to have been a good buy that day at the Fulton Fish Market. This is not to say that Leonard's is a bargain establishment. Leonard's is class all the way. Their takeout seafood department includes codfish cakes, deviled crabs and lobsters, and a super Manhattan clam chowder. Leonard's also carries a full range of imported appetizers. Yes, there is caviar, and you can also find filet mignon, smoked meats and fish, and canned delicacies. Barbecued poultry, cooked and prepared foods, and prime meats round out Leonard's extensive selection. Beware: their phone manners need much improvement.

When wine snobs are coming for dinner, pay a visit to **Best Cellars** (1291 Lexington Ave, at 87th St). This shop carries over 100 different wines, all priced under $10, and offers free delivery in Manhattan for cases of 12. See if the experts can tell the difference between these and more expensive wines. **Nancy's** (313 Columbus Ave) will help select an inexpensive wine that's right for every dish you are serving! They offer nearly 200 different wines under $10 a bottle.

MURRAY'S STURGEON SHOP
2429 Broadway (bet 89th and 90th St)   212/724-2650
Sun-Fri; 8-7; Sat: 8-8

Murray's is the definitive place to buy fancy and smoked fish, dispensing the finest in appetizing products. There is sturgeon, Eastern and Norwegian salmon, whitefish, kippered salmon, sable butterfish, pickled herring, schmaltz herring, and caviar. The quality is magnificent, and prices are fair.

ROSEDALE FISH AND OYSTER MARKET
1129 Lexington Ave (at 79th St)   212/861-4323
Mon-Fri: 8-6:30; Sat: 8-6

Rosedale has quality seafood in good supply at all times, plus a selection of takeout fish dishes and salads that are tasty, unusual, and noteworthy. All are individually prepared. They are not inexpensive; their high quality is accompanied by equally high prices. But according to many of the city's restaurants and caterers, they are the best fish source in New York. Free delivery is offered.

Spices

ANGELICA'S TRADITIONAL HERBS & FOODS
147 First Ave (at 9th St)   212/529-4335
Mon-Sat: 10-7:45; Sun: 11-6:45

The scent of Anglica's is heavily organic and home-remedy medicinal. This East Village shop caters to folks who want fresh, high-grade spices, essential oils, teas, and coffees. But the bulk of the business is in medicinal herbs, dried fruits and nuts, and related books. They claim to be the largest and best-stocked herb retailer in the country.

APHRODISIA
264 Bleecker St (bet Sixth and Seventh Ave)   212/989-6440
Mon-Fri: 11-7; Sat: 11:30-6:30; Sun: 12-5

Aphrodisia is stocked from floor to ceiling with nearly every herb and spice that exists. Seven hundred of them are neatly displayed in glass jars. Some of the teas, potpourri, dried flowers, and oils are really not what one might expect. The general accent is on folk remedies, but most every ingredient for ethnic cooking can be found here as well. Prices depend upon scarcity. Aphrodisia also conducts a mail-order business.

MEADOWSWEET HERBAL APOTHECARY
77 E 4th St (bet Second and Third Ave)   212/254-2870
Wed-Sun: 12-7; closed Aug

Bernadette and Kathleen believe in the power of herbs and herbal medicine. They offer a complete assortment of their own mixtures, pure essential oils, ointments, medicines, and formulas to aid a variety of ailments, from allergies to insomnia. In addition to herbal remedies, they have expanded their gift department to include potpourri, unusual incense, incense burners, candles, dream pillows, smudge sticks, stained-glass hanging pieces, musical tapes, massage oils, crystals, and crystal jewelry. The folks here share their experiences, which makes your visit particularly interesting.

V. Where to Find It: New York's Best Services

One of the great pleasures of New York is that finding the right service is almost never a question of *whether* but rather of *where*. Do you need an expert bookbinder? Does your cat need grooming? Are you looking for a homeopathic veterinarian? A horse-drawn carriage? Want to rent a fur? Do your dance shoes need fixing? Is an appliance in need of repair? Where to find an all-night locksmith? Need your barber shears sharpened? Where can you stay in New York with a fireplace in the room? And what should you do if you need a secretary . . . who speaks French? You've come to the right place.

Air Conditioning

AIR-WAVE AIR CONDITIONING COMPANY
212/545-1122
Mon-Fri: 7:30-5:30; (Sat in summer)

Is there anything more miserable than a humid, sticky, muggy, pollen-filled summer day in Manhattan? Well, if such a day is getting you down, or if you want to prepare so it won't trouble you, give these folks a call. Air-Wave has been in business for half a century and comes highly recommended. They have sold tens of thousands of units over the years—top brands like Friedrich, Chrysler Air Temp, Carrier, and Teknika. They will deliver and install the same day!

Animal Adoptions

AMERICAN SOCIETY FOR THE PREVENTION OF CRUELTY TO ANIMALS
424 E 92nd St   212/876-7700
Mon-Sat: 11-7; Sun: 11-5

This is one of the oldest animal protection organizations in the world, and the folks here take pet adoptions very seriously. You'll need to fill out an application, go through an interview, bring two pieces of identification (at least one with a photograph), a reference the ASPCA folks can call, and a utility bill to show that you do indeed live where you say you do. As you can imagine, the whole process sometimes takes longer than you think it should—but then *they're* sure you're serious and *you* can go home with a good pet who needs a home. Dogs and puppies cost $55; cats and kittens cost $45. The fee includes a veterinarian's exam, vaccinations, and spaying or neutering.

BIDE-A-WEE HOME ASSOCIATION
410 E 38th St   212/532-4455
Mon-Sat: 10-5; Sun: 11-5

Bide-a-wee means "stay awhile" in Gaelic. This is a warm, friendly place complete with volunteers who will match you up with the perfect pet. Puppies and kittens under six months require a $55 donation, while dogs and cats over that age will set you back $30. The fee includes a veterinarian's exam, vaccinations, and spaying or neutering.

Animal Services

ANIMAL MEDICAL CENTER
510 E 62nd St (bet FDR Dr and York Ave)   212/838-8100
Daily: 24 hours

If your pet becomes ill in New York, try the Animal Medical Center first. This nonprofit organization handles all kinds of veterinary work reasonably and competently with board-certified specialists. The care here is among the best offered anywhere in the city. They suggest calling for an appointment. Emergency care costs more.

CAROLE WILBOURN
299 W 12th St   212/741-0397
Mon-Sat: 9-6

Want to talk to the author of *Cats on the Couch*? and *Cat Talk*? Carole Wilbourn is an internationally known cat therapist who has the answer to most of your cat problems. She writes a monthly column for *Cat Fancy* magazine and has a special way with her furry patients. Carole makes house calls from coast to coast and can take care of many cat problems with just one session and a follow-up phone call. She also does international consultations and sees appointments at Westside Vet Center and the Animal Clinic of New York.

CAT GROOMING IN YOUR HOME BY HOWARD
240 E 35th St, #5A   212/889-1449
Daily: 8 a.m.—whenever!

Grooming can be a traumatic experience for your cat, so why not do it where your cat is happiest—in his or her own home. If your cat wants regal treatment, give professional Howard Bedor (the official groomer for the NYC Cat Show) a call. He gets the job done with patience and understanding. The familiar surroundings of home are less stressful for cats and more convenient for owners. No tranquilizers are used—just tender loving care.

DOGGIE DO AND PUSSYCATS, TOO!
567 Third Ave (bet 37th and 38th St)   212/661-9111
Mon-Fri: 8-7; Sat: 9-7

How to describe this place? Someone has called it "the Georgette Klinger for dogs and cats." In any case, you will find top-notch grooming facilities, an exclusive collection of custom-tailored coats and sweaters, European-designed collars, and much more. Doggie measurements are kept on file, of course, and your companion could even sport a Burberry's of London label. But there is more: a great day-care facility, exercise room, and party room for special celebrations. Hand-painted food and water dishes are sold here as well.

EAST VILLAGE VETERINARIAN
241 Eldridge St (at Houston St)   212/674-8640

This is the only practicing homeopathic veterinary in New York City. It features one of the most complete homeopathic dispensaries in New York, with over a thousand remedies in stock. It is also a full-service hospital with emphasis on prevention.

FIELDSTON PETS   718/796-4541
Mon-Sat: 9-7

Bash Dibra is a warm, friendly man who speaks dog language. Known as the "dog trainer to the stars" (clients include Mariah Carey, Martin Scorsese, Henry Kissinger, and Matthew Broderick), Bash is an animal behaviorist. If your dog has bad manners, Bash will teach it to behave. He believes in "tandem training"—training owners to train their dogs—because it's the owner who'll be in charge. Bash's experience in training a pet wolf gave him unique insight into the mind of dogs (the wolf's direct descendants), and his success in bringing the most difficult pets to heel has made him a regular on the talk-show circuit. In addition to training sessions, dog and cat grooming are available.

LE CHIEN
Trump Plaza
1044 Third Ave (bet 61st and 62nd St)   212/861-8100
Mon-Fri: 8:30-7; Sat: 9-7

Le Chien is known for their tiny AKC puppies, all bearing very distinguished credentials! All dogs and cats at this establishment drink and are bathed in chlorine- and bacteria-free water. It is a vertiable Saks and finishing school for the canine set rolled into one. Le Chien carries doggie dresses, coats, sweaters, collars and leashes, 14-karat gold identification tags, cultured pearls, and special fragrances in French crystal bottles. Lisa Gilford runs this establishment as an elegant spa for small and large breeds. A separate business grooms and trains cats and dogs. Day care, pickup, and delivery are offered, and boarding is provided for some breeds.

PET CARE NETWORK
Daily: 9-6 and by appointment   212/580-6004

Evelyn McCabe and her crew of 52 pet sitters and trainers will take care of your companions while you are away, and you can be sure they are in expert hands. Established in 1985, this is the oldest pet-care firm in New York. They have 45 locations around the city and will also come to your residence for service. All personnel are bonded. These folks will walk, groom, feed, pick up, clothe, and deliver your pet. Cat visits and boarding are specialties. Transportation and vet care are available, and service is around the clock.

Sometimes it is very handy to have a vet make a house call. One of the best is **Dr. Amy Attas** (212/581-7387).

Antique Repair

MICHAEL J. DOTZEL AND SON
402 E 63rd St (at York Ave)   212/838-2890
Mon-Fri: 8-4:30

Do you want a chandelier wired or assembled? Dotzel specializes in the repair and maintenance of antiques and precious heirlooms. Dotzel won't touch modern pieces or inferior antiques, but if your antique is made out of metal and needs repair, this is the place for the job. They pay close attention to detail and will hand-forge or personally hammer metal work, including brass. If an item has lost a part or if you want a duplication of an antique, it can be re-created. Dotzel also does stripping and replating, but since it isn't always good for an antique, they may try talking you out of it.

SANO STUDIO
767 Lexington Ave (at 60th St), Room 403   212/759-6131
Mon-Fri: 10-5; closed Aug

Mrs. J. Baran presides over this fourth-floor antique repair shop, and she has an eye for excellence. That eye is focused on the quality of the workmanship and of the goods brought here to be repaired. Both must be the best. Baran is a specialist who limits herself to repairing porcelain, pottery, ivory, and tortoise-shell works and antiques. She has many loyal adherents.

Appraisals

ABIGAIL HARTMANN ASSOCIATES
415 Central Park W (at 101st St)   212/316-5406
Mon-Fri: 9-6 (by appointment); weekends also available

This firm specializes in personal property (fine and decorative art) appraisals for insurance, donation, or other reasons. Theirs is a highly principled and experienced staff that does not buy, sell, or receive kickbacks. (This can be a common practice with some auction houses, insurance companies, and galleries.) Fees are by the hour, consultations are available, and the friendly personnel can provide restoration, framing, shipping, and storage contacts.

Art Services

A. I. FRIEDMAN
44 W 18th St   212/243-9000
Mon-Fri: 9-6:30; Sat: 10-5; Sun: 11-5

Those who want to frame it themselves can take advantage of one of the largest stocks of ready-made frames in the city at A.I. Friedman. Nearly all are sold at discount. In addition to fully assembled frames, they sell ones that can be put together and come equipped with glass and/or mats. Custom framing is also available.

ELI WILNER & COMPANY
1525 York Ave (bet 80th and 81st St)   212/744-6521
Mon-Fri: 9:30-5:30; Sat: by appointment

Eli Wilner's primary business is period frames and mirrors. He keeps over 2,000 19th- and early 20th-century American and European frames in stock and can locate any size or style. Wilner will even create an exact replica of a frame in his inventory to your unique specifications. With a staff of over 18 skilled craftsmen, Wilner also does expert restoration of frames. With such clients as the Metropolitan and the White House, Wilner's expertise speaks for itself.

GUTTMANN PICTURE FRAME ASSOCIATES
180 E 73rd St (bet Lexington and Third Ave)   212/744-8600
Mon-Thurs: 9-5

Though the Guttmanns have worked on frames for some of the nation's finest museums, including the Metropolitan, they stand apart from other first-class artisans in that they are not snobby or picky about what work they will take. They will restore, regild, or replace any type of picture frame. While they are masters at working with masterpieces, they are equally at home restoring or framing a Polaroid snapshot. Even better, they are among the few experts who don't price themselves out of the market. Bring a worn-out frame to them, and they will graciously tell you exactly what it will cost to fix it.

J. POCKER & SON
135 E 63rd St (bet Park and Lexington Ave)   212/838-5488
Mon-Fri: 9-5:30; Sat: 10-5:30

Three generations of this famiiy have been in the custom framing business since 1926, so you can rest assured they know what they are doing. Pickup and delivery are offered, plus expert advice from a superbly trained staff. As a sidelight, Pocker offers a gallery specializing in English sporting and botanical prints.

JULIUS LOWY FRAME AND RESTORING COMPANY
223 E 80th St (bet Second and Third Ave)   212/861-8585
Mon-Fri: 9-5:30

Serving New York City since 1907, Lowy is the definitive firm for the conservation and framing of fine works of art. Being the oldest and largest such firm in the nation, Lowy's comprehensive services include painting and paper conservation, professional photography, conservation framing, and curatorial services. Lowy's framing services include the sale of antique frames (Lowy has the largest inventory in the U.S.), the sale of authentic reproduction frames (the broadest selection anywhere), and complete conservation mat-making and -fitting services. Lowy's client base includes art dealers, private collectors, auction houses, corporate collections, institutions, and museums.

LEITH RUTHERFURD TALAMO
212/535-8293 (by appointment only)

Does your treasured painting have a dent? Did your movers handle a painting like a ping-pong table? Has the masterpiece that hung over the fireplace darkened with age? Do you need help hanging or lighting your collection? All of these services—plus cleaning, relining, and polishing of paintings and frames —are done here with class.

Babysitters

BABYSITTERS GUILD
60 E 42nd St, Suite 912   212/682-0227
Daily: 9-9

Established in 1940, the Babysitters Guild charges high rates, but their professional reputation commends them. All of their sitters have passed rigorous scrutiny, and only the most capable are sent out on jobs. There is a four-hour minimum, but as members of the New York Convention and Visitors Bureau, they will sometimes relax the rule for tourists. Among their sitters, 16 languages are spoken.

> Your youngster(s) will love their babysitter and you will relax, appreciating this firm's reliability: call Kathleen Lewis at **Pinch Sitters** (212/260-6005).

BARNARD COLLEGE BABYSITTING SERVICE
3009 Broadway (Milbank Hall), Room 11   212/854-2035
Mon, Wed, Fri: 10-4; Tues: 11-7:30; Thurs: 11-4

Barnard College Babysitting Service is a nonprofit organization run entirely by students of Barnard College, the undergraduate women's college of Columbia University. The service provides affordable child care for parents in the New York metropolitan area. At the same time, it allows students to seek convenient employment. One-time, regular basis, and live-in help are available. A minimum registration fee is required.

> **Nannies** (all highly recommended):
>
> **Basic Trust** (212/222-6602): day care
> **Fox** (212/753-2686): good record
> **Innovative Learning Center** (212/523-7461): day care
> **Pavillion** (212/889-6609): very reliable

Beauty Services

Day Spas

Anushka Institute (241 E 60th St, 212/355-6404)
Bliss Spa (568 Broadway, 212/219-8970)
Carapan (5 W 16th St, 212/633-6220)
Catharine Atzen Day Spa (856 Lexington Ave, 212/517-2400)
Christiana & Carmen Beauty Center (128 Central Park S, Suite 1A, 212/757-5811)
Dorit Baxter Skin Care, Beauty & Health Spa (47 W 57th St, 212/371-4542)
Elizabeth Arden Red Door Salon (691 Fifth Ave, 212/546-0200)
Estée Lauder Spa/Lancome's Institut de Beauté (Bloomingdale's, 1000 Third Ave, 212/705-2318)
Origins (Sports Center, Chelsea Pier, 60 Twelfth Ave, at 23rd St, 2nd floor, 212/336-6780)
Paul Labrecque Salon (150 Columbus Ave, 212/362-6800)
Peninsula New York Spa (700 Fifth Ave, 212/247-2200)
Soho Sanctuary (19 Mercer St, 212/334-5550)
Spa 227 (227 E 56th St, 212/754-0227)
Susan Ciminelli Day Spa (601 Madison Ave, 3rd floor, 212/688-5500)
Yi Pak (10 W 32nd St, 2nd floor, 212/594-1025)

Hair Care (best in Manhattan)

A.K.S. Salon (694 Madison Ave, 212/888-0707): big-time defectors from Frederic Fekkai

Frederic Fekkai (15 E 57th St, 212/753-9500): staff of 150, elegant

Garren New York (Henri Bendel, 712 Fifth Ave, 3rd floor atrium, 212/841-9400): personally customized services

John Barrett Salon (Bergdorf Goodman, 754 Fifth Ave, 212/872-2700): top cut

John Frieda (30 E 76th St, 2nd floor, 212/879-1000): very "in"

La Beauté (142 E 49th St, 212/754-0048): reasonably priced

La Coupe (22 E 66th St, 212/371-9230): popular

Nardi Salon (143 E 57th St, 212/421-4810): long-hair specialists

Oribe (Elizabeth Arden, 691 Fifth Ave, 212/546-0200): world-renowned

Ouidad Hair Salon (846 Seventh Ave, 212/333-7577): curly- and frizzy-hair specialists

Peter Coppola (746 Madison Ave, 212/988-9404): reliable

Private World of Leslie Blanchard (680 Fifth Ave, 2nd floor, 212/421-4564): excellent value

Saks Fifth Avenue Beauty Salon (Saks Fifth Ave, 611 Fifth Ave, 9th floor, 212/940-4000): top grade, full service

Stephen Knoll (625 Madison Ave, 212/421-0100): highly recommended

Vidal Sassoon (767 Fifth Ave, 212/535-9200): popular with both men and women

Hair Coloring

Brad Johns (693 Fifth Ave, 212/583-0034): If it's good enough for Carolyn Bessette-Kennedy . . .

Linda Tam Beauty Salon (680 Fifth Ave, 2nd floor, 212/757-2555)

Warren Tricomi (16 W 57th St, 212/262-8899)

Hair Removal

Allana of New York (160 E 56th St, 212/980-0216)

Home Services

Eastside Massage Therapy Center (212/249-2927)

John Sahag Workshop (212/750-7772): styling

Joseph Martin (212/838-3150): hair coloring, nails, pedicure, makeup

Lia Schorr Skin Care (212/486-9670): haircuts, makeup, massage

Lori Klein (212/996-9390): makeup

Makeup Shop (212/807-0447)

Trish McEvoy and Skin Care (212/758-7790): makeup

Makeup

Makeup Center (150 W 55th St, 212/977-9494): good value

Makeup Shop (131 W 21st St, 212/807-0447)

Nails

Cornelia's Nail Design (151 E 71st St, 212/535-5333): nail-wrapping (also facials, massage, body-waxing, eyelash-tinting)

Skin Care

Anushka (241 E 60th St, 212/355-6404)
Bloomingdale's (1000 Third Ave): Check the Chanel and Estée Lauder counters.
Georgette Kilinger (501 Madison Ave, 212/838-3200; 978 Madison Ave, 212/744-6900)
Lia Schorr (686 Lexington Ave, 212/486-9670)

Toupees

Bob Kelly (151 W 46th St, 212/819-0030)
Ira Senz (13 E 47th St, 212/752-6800)

Did you know that blondes have the most hairs per head and redheads the least?

Bookbinding

TALAS
568 Broadway (at Prince St)   212/219-0770
Mon-Fri: 9-5; call for Saturday hours

Jake and Marjorie Salik preside over this outlet which offers tools, supplies, and books for artists, restorers, collectors, bookbinders, museums, archives, libraries, calligraphers, and retail customers. Expanded inventories feature custom boxes and portfolios, a wide variety of photo-storage and display items, and archival papers.

WEITZ, WEITZ & COLEMAN
1377 Lexington Ave (bet 90th and 91st St)   212/831-2213
Mon-Thurs: 9-7; Fri: 9-5; Sat: 12-5

Weitz is a highly respected name in the rare-book field. Leo Weitz began a rare-book business in New York in 1909, becoming so well known that he did work for the Rockefellers, DuPonts, Firestones, and other famous families. Today, Herbert Weitz (his son) and partner Elspeth Coleman continue the tradition of fine bookbinding. Weitz and Coleman restore and rebind books and family heirlooms. They also design and create leather photo albums, guest books, archival boxes, presentation folders, and special gift books. Coleman's specialty is custom-designing to clients' specifications. Weitz and Coleman also buy and sell rare books.

Cabinetry

WOODSMITH'S STUDIO
220 E 67th St   212/879-4300
Daily: by appointment

Jerry Gerber ran a cabinetry business-cum-woodworking school until he was forced to move when his old location was demolished. Instead of merely relocating, Gerber reassessed the entire operation. When he went back into business, he stressed aspects of the craft that most appealed to him. Nowadays Gerber spends his time on custom cabinetry, particularly bookcases, wall units, tables, turnings, and carvings.

Calligraphy

CALLIGRAPHY STUDIOS, INC
100 Reade St (bet Church St and West Broadway)   212/964-6007
By appointment

Nothing sets off a card or a letter like calligraphy. Many claim to be experts, but if you really want first-class work, let Linda Stein and her crew customize your order. They are able to do work in any language you desire. Moreover, they carry 3-D memory boxes, leatherbound books, and party accessories. This studio is considered *the* expert in protocol.

Camping Equipment

DOWN EAST
50 Spring St   212/925-2632
Mon-Fri: 11-6

Owner Leon Greenman provides a phenomenal range of services to outdoor people. He started Down East as a service center for hiking, camping, and outdoor equipment. He has excellent credentials, having owned another camping equipment store and is a veteran hiker, camper, and trailblazer. From his own experience he came to recognize the lack of service centers for camping equipment, and when he was ready to run a store again, Down East was the result. This store is a godsend for campers. It offers guidebooks, hiking maps, and USGS topographic maps. Messenger bags by Manhattan Portage can be modified or customized. Outdoor gear can be modified, repaired, and customized.

Carriages

CHATEAU STABLES/CHATEAU THEATRICAL ANIMALS
608 W 48th St   212/246-0520
Daily: 9-5

How would you like to arrive at your next dinner party in a horse-drawn carriage? Chateau is the place to call. They have the largest working collection of horse-drawn vehicles in the United States. Although they prefer advance notice, they can take care of requests at any time for weddings, group rides, tours, movies, and overseas visitors. There is nothing quite as romantic as a ride in an authentic hansom cab.

Cars for Hire

CAREY LIMOUSINE NY
212/599-1122 (reservations)   718/898-1000 (office)   800/336-4646
24 hours

Carey is considered by many to be the grandfather of car-for-hire services. They provide chauffeur-driven limousines and sedans at any time and will take clients anywhere in almost any kind of weather. Last-minute reservations are accepted on an as-available basis. Discuss rates before making a commitment.

COMPANY II LIMOUSINE SERVICE
24 hours   718/430-6482

Steve Betancourt provides a responsible, efficient, and confidential service at reasonable prices. His reputation for reliability is well earned.

ROSA'S INTERNATIONAL LIMOUSINE
11-01 43rd Ave   212/989-5400
24 hours

Rosa's claim they can get a car to you within minutes of your call. Their garage includes every model, from 12-passenger super stretch limos to luxury sedans and 14-passenger executive transports. Ask for a Bentley, Rolls-Royce, Mercedes, Jaguar, or BMW, and they will probably be able to fill the order. For those who want super service, they also have executive jets!

VIP AIRPORT SERVICE
516/431-6938   emergency beeper: 800/225-0256 (PIN 80053)
24 hours, 7 days a week

This outfit is a traveler's best friend. It is a professional, personalized service providing airport representatives who will assist clients upon arrival or departure. They are also facilitators and troubleshooters, and they belong to the airline clubs, allowing clients to be escorted in as their guests. This makes check-in easy and waiting for departure time a pleasure. They will handle all the tedious chores (lost luggage, delayed flights, etc.) and can even assist with language barriers if given prior notice.

Casting

SCULPTURE HOUSE CASTING
155 W 26th St (bet Sixth and Seventh Ave)   212/645-9430
Mon-Fri: 8-6; Sat: 10-4

Sculpture House has been a family-owned business since 1918, thus making it one of the city's oldest casting firms. It is a full-service casting foundry, specializing in classical plaster reproductions, mold making, and casting in all mediums and sizes. Sculpting tools and supplies and ornamental plastering are also available.

Chair Caning

VETERAN'S CHAIR CANING AND REPAIR SHOP
442 Tenth Ave   212/564-4560
Mon-Fri: 8-4:30; Sat: 9:30-12:30
closed Sat in summer

John Bausert, a third-generation chair caner, has written a book about his craft. Certainly, the prices and craftsmanship are among the best in town, and Bausert believes in passing along his knowledge. His wife, Nancy, is store owner and sales manager. Customers are encouraged to repair their own chairs. The procedure is outlined in his book, and necessary materials are sold in the shop. If you don't want to try or have had disastrous results on your own, the shop will repair the chair. For a slight charge, they'll even pick it up from your home. In addition to caning, Veteran's also stocks materials for chair and furniture repair, does wicker repair, and repairs and reglues wooden chairs.

WESTSIDE CHAIR CANING AND REPAIR
371 Amsterdam Ave (bet 77th and 78th St, 2nd floor)   212/724-4408
Wed-Sat: 11-7; Sun: 1-5

Jeffrey Weiss has assembled a talented crew who do hand- and machine-caning, rush- and splint-seating, wicker restoration, and the regluing and repairing of furniture. They also have a substantial stock of unclaimed chairs for sale.

China and Glassware Repair

CENTER ART STUDIO
250 W 54th St, Room 901   212/247-3550
Mon-Fri: by appointment

"Fine art restoration and display since 1919" is the motto here. The word *fine* should be emphasized, for owners of really good crystal, porcelain, china, or bronze art should make Center Art Studio *the* place to go for repairs. The house specialty is antiques restoration. They will restore or repair scagliola, lacquer, porcelain, terra cotta, shells, and precious stones. They will also restore antique furniture and decorative objects, using original materials whenever possible. They'll even design and install display bases and cases. Finally, they will pack and crate articles for shipment. Among the oldest and most diverse art restoration studios in the city, Center Art offers a multitude of special services, like designs and sketches by fax and multilingual personnel for overseas shoppers. The owner, Lansing Moore, has a superbly talented staff who have worked on the likes of furniture designed by Frank Lloyd Wright.

EARTHWORKS POTTERY
1705 First Ave (bet 88th and 89th St)   212/876-6945
Tues-Thurs: 12-8; Fri-Sun: 12-5:30

Moye Thompson, a former teacher with Margaret Simonds, has expanded the space and operations here, moving the retail shop into a new area. This has given the potters more room in the wheel studio. There is a paint-a-pot studio, a separate room for parties, and classes for kids. This comprehensive establishment caters to stoneware, pottery, and porcelain pieces from the kiln to the "beyond hope" stages.

GLASS RESTORATIONS
1597 York Ave (bet 84th and 85th St)   212/517-3287
Mon-Fri: 9:30-5

Oops . . . you chipped your prize Lalique glass treasure. No worry! Glass Restorations restores all manner of crystal, including names like Steuben, Baccarat, Daum, and Waterford, as well as antique art glass. This place is a find, as there aren't too many quality restorers left in the country. Ask for Gus!

HESS RESTORATIONS
200 Park Ave S (at 17th St)   212/260-2255, 212/979-1143
Mon-Fri: 10:30-4; by appointment for later times

Hess has been in business since 1945, providing a restoration service so professional that previous damage is usually unnoticeable. Their emphasis is on restoration of fine European porcelains, ivory, tortoise shell, sculptures, and *objets d'art*. They are recommended by leading museums, auction houses, and galleries in Manhattan. The replacement of blue glass liners for antique silver salt dishes is unique. Hess accepts parcel post-insured shipments of items to be repaired and will send an estimate for restoration work.

Clock and Watch Repair

FANELLI ANTIQUE TIME
790 Madison Ave (bet 66th and 67th St), Suite 202   212/517-2300
Mon-Fri: 10-6; Sat: 11-5

In a beautiful clock gallery, Cindy Fanelli specializes in the care of high-quality "investment-type" timepieces, especially carriage clocks. They have one of the nation's largest collections of rare and unusual early-American grandfather clocks and vintage wristwatches. They do both sales and restorations, will make house calls, give free estimates, rent out timepieces for special assignments, and purchase single pieces or entire collections. Granddad would be happy to see his prize in the hands of these exceptionally able folks.

FOSSNER TIMEPIECES CLOCK SHOP
1057 Second Ave (at 56th St)   212/980-1099
Mon-Fri: 10-6; Sat: 11-4

In Europe, fine-watch repairing is a family tradition, but this craft is being slowly forgotten in our country. Fortunately, Manhattan has a four-generation family, the Fossners, who pass along this talent from father to son. You can have complete confidence in their work on any kind of watch. They guarantee repairs for six months and in most cases will get a job done within a week.

TIME PIECES
115 Greenwich Ave (at W 13th St)   212/929-8011
Tues-Fri: 11-6:30; Sat: 9-5

Grace Szuwala services, restores, repairs, and sells antique timepieces. Her European training makes her an expert on antique watches and clocks. She has a strong sensitivity for pieces that have more sentimental than real value. This amazing Grace can really do wonders with keepsakes from another time.

Clothing Repair

FRENCH-AMERICAN REWEAVING COMPANY
119 W 57th St (bet Sixth and Seventh Ave), Room 1406   212/765-4670
Mon-Fri: 10:30-5:30; Sat: 11-2

Is there a tear, burn, or other catastrophe in your favorite outfit? These folks can be a godsend. They will work on most any garment for men or women in nearly every fabric. In most cases, things will look just like new!

Computer Service/Instruction

For **kids** – Youngsters from age two and up (they are learning even younger these days) can be helped at 1264 Lexington Ave, at 85th St (212/427-2502).

For **rentals** – Try **Business Equipment Rental** (250 W 49th St, at Broadway, 212/582-2020). Prices are reasonable; pickup and delivery are available.

For **repair** – these are the best:

Datavision (445 Fifth Ave, 212/689-1111)
Machattan (381 Park Ave S, 212/545-7171): Macintosh only
RCS Computer Service (261 Madison Ave, 212/949-6935)
Rockwell Computer (261 Madison Ave, 212/949-6935)
Tekserve (163 W 23rd St, 212/929-3645): Macintosh only

Craft Instruction

CRAFT STUDENTS LEAGUE
YWCA of the City of New York
610 Lexington Ave   212/735-9731

For over 65 years, the Craft Students League has offered programs in crafts and fine arts. The curriculum is wide ranging and includes bookbinding, jewelry, pottery, woodworking, drawing, painting, and decorative finishes. For anyone yearning for a creative outlet, this school's convenient midtown location and excellent professional teaching staff are winners.

Delivery, Courier, Messenger Services
AIRLINE DELIVERY SERVICES
60 E 42nd St (bet Park and Madison Ave)   212/687-5145
24-hour service, 7 days a week

Before the big guys got in the business, this outfit was doing round-the-clock local and long-distance deliveries. If you have some time-sensitive material, give them a call. Not only will they promptly pick up your item (whether it is in the middle of the night or a snowstorm), they will also try to beat an amazing 97% on-time delivery rate for the more than 60 years they have been operating.

JIMINY SPLIT DELIVERY SERVICES
147 W 46th St   212/354-7373
Mon-Fri: 7-7

Jiminy Split can hand-deliver a package from New York to Washington, D.C., in less than five hours. Federal Express can't match that, and the U.S. mail is not even in the running. If you want fast, reliable, and personal service, call Jiminy Split. They can deliver anywhere within the continental U.S. as fast as a plane or train can deliver the messenger. Rates include travel fare, plus delivery expense. Within the city, rates depend upon distance traveled (the city is divided into zones) and how long delivery takes. There are several Jiminy Split branches.

KANGAROO COURIER
120 E 32nd St   212/684-2233
Mon-Fri: 8-6 (scheduled services all the time)

Messenger services range from bicycle couriers to international shipping firms. Some are fly-by-night operations (and I am not referring to the hours they travel). If you are used to sending envelopes crosstown, then you are at sea on warehouse distribution cross-country. And so are companies you deal with. Kangaroo's idea is that *all* shipping is in-house, and the same company oversees the entire job. Kangaroo boasts that they can do everything from a cross-town rush letter (delivery completed within an hour) to a 10,000-pound shipment, while tracking the entire job.

NOW VOYAGER
74 Varick St, Suite 307   212/431-1616
Mon-Fri: 12-5; Sat: 12-4:30

Now Voyager runs an international courier service, and you can be a part of it. The firm has a schedule of flights to various areas, mostly Europe, South America, and the Far East, and you can go at a fraction of the regular fare if you have only carry-on luggage. Also, they now have great deals on domestic flights and are starting to get into cruise discounts. Usually the flights are booked some weeks ahead, and it is a good idea to call or write as early as possible to see what might be available. Who knows—you might be able to take an exciting trip for next to nothing!

Detectives

DECISION STRATEGIES INTERNATIONAL
801 Second Ave (at 43rd St)   212/599-9400
Mon-Fri: 9-7

Need a corporate investigation? Someone cheating on you? Want some help with fraud prevention? Bart Schwartz and his staff of more than a dozen top-notch investigators are the ones to call. Their experience in nearly every field can save you not only a lot of headaches, but possibly a lot of cash.

Doll Repair

NEW YORK DOLL HOSPITAL
787 Lexington Ave (bet 61st and 62nd St, 2nd floor)   212/838-7527
Mon-Sat: 10-6

New York Doll Hospital has been fixing, mending, and restoring dolls to health since 1900. Owner Irving Chais has been operating in this cramped two-room "hospital" since 1947. That was the year he took over from his father, who had begun fixing the dolls of his clients' children in his hair salon. Chais came into the business one Christmas season when his father was ailing and needed help. Several flipped wigs later, Chais was the latest family member in the business. He has replaced antique fingers, reconstructed china heads and German rag dolls, and authentically restored antique dolls. Additional services include appraisals, made-to-order dolls, and buying and selling antique dolls and toys. He will also work on teddy bears, other stuffed animals, and talking dolls with computer chips.

Dry Cleaners, Laundries

CLEANTEX
2335 Twelfth Ave (at 133rd St)   212/283-1200
Mon-Fri: 8-4

Cleantex specializes in cleaning draperies, furniture, balloon and Roman shades, vertical blinds, and Oriental and area rugs. They provide free pickup and delivery service. Top museums, churches, and rug dealers use their facilities, underscoring the fact that they offer top-grade work.

HALLAK CLEANERS
1232 Second Ave (at 65th St)   212/879-4694
Mon-Fri: 7-6:30; Sat: 8-3; closed Sat in July, August

Hallak has been a family-run business for four decades. This probably accounts for the exceptional pride Joe Hallak and his sons, John-Claude and Joseph, Jr., take in personal service. Much of their work comes from referrals by designers of delicate fabrics and patterns. In addition, they now have a shirt laundry, fine linen service, fur storage, fire- and water-damage restoration, and wet cleaning. Their specialty is working with wedding gowns. For those (like your author) who have trouble with salad dressing landing in the middle of a beautiful necktie, Hallak is the place to go for help. Their skilled work takes time, though they will provide 48-hour emergency service when necessary.

LEATHERCRAFT PROCESS OF AMERICA
Call for locations   212/564-8980, 800/845-6155
Mon-Fri: 7:30-6:30

Leathercraft is all things to all suedes, sheepskins, and leathers. They will clean, re-dye, re-line, repair, and lengthen or shorten any suede or leather garment brought in. That includes boots, gloves, clothing, and handbags, as well as odd leather items. Because leather is extremely difficult to clean, the process can be painfully expensive. However, Leathercraft has a reputation dating back to 1938, and their prices have remained competitive.

MEURICE GARMENT CARE
31 University Pl (bet 8th and 9th St)   212/475-2778
Mon-Fri: 7:30-7; Sat: 7:30-5

245 E 57th St (bet Second and Third Ave)   212/759-9057
Mon-Fri: 8-6; Sat: 7:30-5

Meurice specializes in the cleaning and restoration of fine garments. They handle each piece individually, taking care of details like loose buttons and tears. Special services: exquisite hand-finishing, expert stain removal and dyeing, museum-quality preservation, cleaning and restoration of wedding gowns, and on-site leather cleaning and repairs. Delivery and shipping are available worldwide.

Does a favorite garment have a really stubborn spot? Try **Young's Cleaners and Launderers** (188 Third St, at 18th St, 212/473-6154). They are miracle workers!

MIDNIGHT EXPRESS CLEANERS
212/921-0111, 800/7MIDNITE
Mon-Fri: 9 a.m-11 p.m.; Sat: 9-3

What a handy place to know about! It is 10 p.m. and you want some dry cleaning picked up? No problem. Midnight does dry cleaning, shirt laundry, luggage repair, leather and suede cleaning and repair, shoe and boot repair, and bulk laundry. Best of all, they will pick up and deliver, day or night, for a small minimum charge. Prompt return is assured. They specialize in dry-cleaning restoration for smoke, fire, and water-damaged goods. This is Manhattan's only OSHA-compliant laundry service. Be sure to put their number in a prominent spot near your phone!

MME. PAULETTE DRY CLEANERS
1255 Second Ave (bet 65th and 66th St)   212/838-6827
Mon-Fri: 7:30-6:30; Sat: 8-5

160 Columbus Ave   212/501-1408
Mon-Fri: 5 a.m.-11 p.m.; Sat: 8 a.m.-9 p.m.

What a clientele: Versace, Christian Dior, Romeo Gigli, Geoffrey Beene, Saks, Bloomingdale's, and Henri Bendel. This full-service establishment has been in business for over 35 years. They do dry cleaning (including knits, suedes, and leathers), tailoring (including reweaving and alterations), laundry, and household and rug cleaning. They provide fur and box storage. Taking care of wedding dresses is a specialty. In addition, they will correct water- and fire-damaged garments, bleach-stained materials, do wet cleaning, and clean upholstery and tapestry by hand. Mme. Paulette offers free pickup and delivery service throughout the city, has charge accounts, and will provide one-day service upon request. If only they offered service on Sundays, they would do it all!

NEW YORK'S FINEST FRENCH CLEANERS
16 Hudson St (bet Duane and Reade St)   212/791-3859
Mon-Thurs: 7:30-6:30; Fri: 7:30-7; Sat: 8:30-6

Three generations of the same family have operated this quality business, featuring pickup and delivery and one-day service. Tailoring and storage are available, as is care for fine silks and leathers.

TIECRAFTERS
252 W 29th St   212/629-5800
Mon-Fri: 9-5

Old ties never die or even fade away here; instead, they're dyed, widened, straightened, and cleaned. Tiecrafters is dedicated to the philosophy that a tie can live forever, and they provide services to make that possible. In addition to converting tie widths, they will restore soiled or spotted ties and clean and repair all kinds of neckwear. Perhaps most impressive is Andy Tarshis' willingness to discuss tie maintenance so that frequent visits to the shop won't be necessary. (Hint: If you roll your tie at night, wrinkles will be gone by morning.) Tiecrafters offers several pamphlets on the subject, including one that tells how to take out spots at home. Tiecrafters accepts business via any carrier, and their charge for cleaning a tie is reasonable. They also make custom neckwear.

Best Upholstery Cleaners:

Clean Bright (212/283-6400)
Cohen Carpet, Upholstery and Drapery Cleaning (212/663-6902)
Buff-Away of Manhattan (212/477-7100)
Designer Upholstery and Furniture Service (718/461-0906)

Electricians
ALTMAN ELECTRIC
80 Fifth Ave (at 14th St)   212/741-7372, 800/287-7774
Daily: 24 hours

There is hardly anything as upsetting as an electrical emergency at the wrong time—like the middle of the night or just before a party. Don't fret. The licensed crew at this reliable outfit (all 18 of them) are available day and night, every day of the year. They will do small and large jobs at home or office, for reasonable rates. They must be first-rate, since they have been in business for over half a century.

Exterminators
ACME EXTERMINATING
460 Ninth Ave (bet 35th and 36th St)   212/594-9230
Mon-Fri: 7-5

Are you bugged? I'm referring to the type that crawls around. Acme is expert at debugging private homes, offices, stores, museums, and hospitals. Acme is state of the art in pest control, employing integrated pest management.

Eyeglass Repair

DELL AND DELL
19 W 44th St (at Fifth Ave)   212/575-1686
Mon-Fri: 9-6; Sat: 9-1
July, August: Mon-Fri: 9-5:30; closed Sat

If you desperately need Dell and Dell, you probably can't read this. No need to worry, as they do on-the-spot emergency repair on glasses. This is *the* place to go for eyeglass emergencies in the city. They also repair binoculars. Of course, Dell and Dell won't mind if you stop by for regular optical needs, too.

Fashion Schools

FASHION INSTITUTE OF TECHNOLOGY
Seventh Ave at 27th St
212/217-7759 (admission), 212/217-7654 (placement)

The Fashion Institute of Technology (FIT), part of the State University of New York, is the world's premier institute serving the fashion industry. The school was founded more than 50 years ago. It includes a graduate roster that reads like a "who's who" of the fashion world. Jhane Barnes, Calvin Klein, and Norma Kamali are just a few. The school offers a multitude of majors like accessories, advertising, display and exhibit, toy, jewelry, interior, textile and fashion design, illustration, photography, fine arts, fashion buying and merchandising, apparel production management, pattern-making, and marketing. FIT also maintains a student-placement service. All students are top-caliber. The Edward C. Blum Design Laboratory is the world's largest repository of the history of fashion, with over a million articles of clothing. It is open to the public, as are the galleries at FIT. Call 212/217-5851 for information about exhibits and shows.

WOOD TOBE-COBURN SCHOOL FOR BUSINESS & FASHION CAREERS
8 E 40th St   212/686-9040
Mon-Fri: 8:30-5:30; Sat: 10-3

When these people talk fashion, they mean business! Tobe Coller Davis and Julia Coburn were two of the top names in the fashion industry when they jointly founded the Tobe-Coburn school in 1937 as a training ground for careers in fashion marketing and management. Tobe was a personal friend of mine, and I had the privilege of attending many of her spectacular fashion clinics when I was in the retail business. She was an incredible person! Wood Tobe-Coburn students receive an intensive two-year course in all aspects of the garment industry. Even the liberal-arts courses are oriented to industry applications. Universal business-skills courses stress advertising and public-relations writing, and history courses deal with retailing and merchandising, as well as fashion trends. Over the years the school has established a better than 95% placement record and a reputation as one of the best schools for training in the merchandising, marketing, and management aspects of fashion. The school has co-op programs and internships with top names in the business. Also available: administrative assistant, accounting, travel and hospitality, graphic design, computer applications and programming, and medical assistant programs.

Formal Wear Rental and Sales

A. T. HARRIS FORMALWEAR
11 E 44th St (bet Madison and Fifth Ave, 2nd floor)   212/682-6325
Mon, Tues, Wed, Fri: 9-5:45; Thurs: 9-6:45
Sat: 10-3:45 by appointment

If ten U.S. presidents were fitted for formal attire at the same store, then it must be the place to go! A. T. Harris has been in business since 1892, selling and renting formal wear of the highest quality. You will find cutaways, tails, tuxedos, shoes, top coats, stud and cuff-link sets, and kid and suede gloves.

BALDWIN FORMALS
52 W 56th St (bet Fifth and Sixth Ave)   212/245-8190
Mon, Thurs: 8:30-7; Tues, Wed, Fri: 8:30-6; Sat: 10-4

If you are suddenly called to a state dinner at the White House or some similarly spiffy function, Baldwin will take care of all the dressing details. These folks rent and sell all types of formal attire: suits, overcoats, top hats, shoes, and more. They will pick up and deliver to many midtown addresses for free and for a slight charge to other addresses. Same-day service is guaranteed for orders received by early afternoon. Rapid alteration service (two or three days) is available.

Funeral Service

FRANK E. CAMPBELL FUNERAL HOME
1076 Madison Ave (at 81st St)   212/288-3500
Daily: 24 hours

In time of need it is good to know of a highly reliable funeral home. These folks have been in business since 1898, providing superior professional service.

Furniture Rental

CHURCHILL-WINCHESTER FURNITURE RENTALS
6 E 32nd St (bet Fifth and Madison Ave, 2nd floor)   212/686-0444
Mon-Thurs: 9-6; Fri: 9:30-4; Sun: 11-5

Mention Churchill, and you think of staid old England, right? Well, *this* Churchill is starkly contemporary, as well as traditional. They can fill any size order for business or residence, and they offer free interior-decorating advice and a lease-purchase plan. A customer simply selects what is needed from stock or borrows from the loaner program until special orders are processed. Churchill also offers a comprehensive package, including housewares and appliances, and they specialize in executive locations, both corporate and personal. They will rent out anything from a single chair to entire homes. Their clients include sports-team managers, executives on temporary assignment, and actors on short-term contracts.

CORT/afr (THE FURNITURE RENTAL PEOPLE)
711 Third Ave (bet 44th and 45th St)   212/867-2800
Mon-Sat: 9-6

CORT/afr is a furniture rental company providing furnishings for a single room, entire apartment, or business office. They show accessories as well, and all furnishings (including electronics) are available for purchase or rental with an option to purchase. An apartment-locator service is offered, free professional decorating is available, and a multilingual staff is at your service. A specialty part of their business is working with Japanese clients. The stock is large, delivery and setup can often be done within 48 hours, and all styles of furniture and accessories are shown in their 12,000-square-foot showroom, conveniently located near Grand Central Station.

INTERNATIONAL FURNITURE RENTALS
345 Park Ave (at 51st St)   212/421-0340
Mon-Thurs: 9-6; Fri: 9-5:30; Sat: 10-2

International Furniture Rentals is the largest firm that rents home and office furniture in the metropolitan area. They offer a free decorating and design specialist. The firm carries accessories to coordinate with furnishings, and all items are of executive quality. Quick delivery from their warehouse is a plus.

Furniture Repair and Restoration

ANTIQUE FURNITURE WORKROOM
210 Eleventh Ave (bet 24th and 25th St, 9th floor)   212/683-0551
Mon-Fri: 8-4

For years Antique Furniture Workroom was the traditional place of choice for French polishing, chair repair, and woodwork restoration. William Olsen added antique furniture restoration (especially American, English, Oriental, and continental originals), gold-leafing, building of furniture, and caning. Recreation of classic French art deco furniture is a new specialty. If a piece of furniture in your apartment or home needs special attention, this is a reliable place to go. Estimates are given in the home.

General Services

TOP SERVICE
845 Seventh Ave (bet 54th and 55th St)   212/765-3190
Mon-Fri: 8-6; Sat: 9-1

Shoe repair is the main business here, but there is much more. Dance shoes are a specialty, and Top Service is used by many Broadway theater groups. In addition, Top Service will make rubber stamps, cut keys, engrave anything, do luggage and handbag repair, and dye and clean shoes. They are great people to know in case of last-minute emergencies.

Gift Wrapping and Packaging Services

THE PADDED WAGON
1569 Second Ave (bet 81st and 82nd St)   212/570-5500
Mon-Sat: 9-7; Sun: 12-5

For gift-wrapping help, this is *the* place to visit. They have all sizes of boxes and paper, and can provide UPS and Federal Express service.

UNITED SHIPPING & PACKAGING
200 E 10th St (at Second Ave)   212/475-2214
Mon-Fri: 9-8; Sat: 10-5

United Shipping will ship anything, anywhere in the world. They also sell all kinds of packaging supplies and boxes. Additional services include faxing, mailboxes, office supplies, messenger services, and moves of relatively short distances (from New York to Boston or Washington, for instance).

Haircuts

Children

MICHAEL'S CHILDREN'S HAIRCUTTING SALON
1263 Madison Ave (at 90th St)   212/289-9612
Mon-Sat: 9-5; closed Sat in July, Aug

This place is totally dedicated to children. Since 1910, Michael's drawing card has been rapport with kids and consistency of personnel and style. Nick Di Sisto, the salon's owner, is living proof of this. He worked for Michael for years, and when Michael retired, he bought him out. Many of the hairstylists have worked under both owners. Appointments are unheard of, and lollipops, seats shaped like toy cars, and comic books are *de rigueur.*

SHORTCUTS
104 W 83rd St (bet Columbus and Amsterdam Ave)   212/877-2277
Tues-Sat: 10-6

Most kids do not relish going to the barber shop, but this outfit makes it easier for them and their parents. With fixtures from the old Gimbel store (remember that place?), kids are treated to quality haircuts. Among the features: beauty parties on Sunday, which involve crimping, curling, and braiding, along with nails and makeup. Your little princess will love them. By the way, they have done first haircuts on over 4,000 small fries from age six months up.

Family

ASTOR PLACE HAIR STYLISTS
2 Astor Pl (at Broadway)   212/475-9854
Mon-Sat: 8-8; Sun: 9-6

Does your hairstylist shop have a deejay on staff? They do here! Astor Place really doesn't need its address listed. Just follow the mob to the spot in Manhattan where getting a haircut is an event not unlike being admitted to the hallowed halls of the latest "in" nightspot. The personnel inside what was once a modest neighborhood barbershop give the trendiest, wildest, and most unusual haircuts on the scene. How did this all get started? It seems that the Vezza brothers inherited a barbershop from their father in the East Village at a time "when not even cops were getting haircuts." Enrico took note of the newly gentrified neighborhood's young trendies and their sleek haircuts and changed the name of the shop to "Astor Place Hair Stylists." Now, the shop is staffed with a resident manager, a doorman, a loft, and an ever-increasing number of barbers.

ATLAS BARBER SCHOOL
32 Third Ave   212/475-1360
Mon-Fri: 9-8; Sat: 9-5

This school offers students (and customers) general barbering and clippers and shaving techniques. They've been at it for half a century. High style it ain't; good value it is!

PAUL MOLE FAMILY BARBERSHOP
1031 Lexington Ave (at 74th St)   212/535-8461
Mon-Sat: 7:30-7; Sun: 9-4

This shop is just what it says: a family business. They will do both dad and the kids, with customer-friendly hours and pocketbook-friendly prices. The place is packed after school and on weekends, so appointments are suggested.

Men

Before getting into haircuts, a note about shaves. Yes, gentlemen, it is still possible to get shaved at a barber shop, even if the price has gone up a bit. Most hotel barbers will perform this luxury. You can also try **Astor Place Hair Stylists** (2 Astor Place, 212/475-9854), **Broadway Barber Shop** (2713 Broadway, 212/534-8043), **Paul Mole Family Barbershop** (1031 Lexington Ave, 212/535-8461), or **Feature Trim** (1108 Lexington Ave, 212/650-9746).

> **Sheer Luxury:** You can play billiards while waiting for a $25 hot-towel shave at the barber shop at **Harrison James** (5 W 54th St, 212/541-6870).

FEATURE TRIM
1108 Lexington Ave (bet 77th and 78th St)   212/650-9746
Tues-Fri: 11-7; Sat: 10-6

This neighborhood establishment maintains its standard of basic hair care for men, women, and children. Low maintenance is the key to Feature Trim's haircuts. Easy care, reasonable prices, friendly faces, and over 50 years combined experience keep the impressive clientele asking for proprietors Victor and Joe. Appointments are encouraged, but walk-ins are welcome. Feature Trim is a rare gem on Manhattan's Upper East Side—a barbershop for the 90's.

PEPPE AND BILL
Plaza Hotel (Fifth Ave and Central Park S), mezzanine   212/751-8380
Mon-Fri: 9-6; Sat: 9-2

When you pay the kind of prices charged here, you expect the best. That is exactly what you get with highly professional hairstyling by Jacques and first-rate manicure work by his wife, Marie. You can also be confident of the other personnel here.

Hardware Installation
F&J HARDWARE
15 Ave A (bet 1st and 2nd St)   212/473-6977
Mon-Fri: 9-7; Sat: 9-5

This store is a general housewares emporium with an emphasis on bathroom fixtures. Ceramic tile, medicine cabinets, shower doors, and hardware are house specialties, and they can install all of these items. They also have a good display of gates and locks. This store really shines in service. Mirrors and shower doors are hung with ease. Locksmith emergencies are answered routinely. They even stock and hang drapery hardware. Regular customers can get almost any kind of handiwork done. In this city, that's rare indeed.

Health and Fitness
With all the interest in keeping fit, health clubs have sprung up all over Manhattan. Some do not last long, and it is wise to be careful about making long-term financial arrangements with any but the largest and most secure operations. Prices and facilities vary. For those who live in the city, watch newspaper and television ads for special introductory offers. For visitors, many clubs honor reciprocal memberships or allow one- or two-day guest memberships. A number of hotels have excellent facilities, including the Peninsula, Holiday Inn Crowne Plaza, Four Seasons, Intercontinental, Parker Meridien, United Nations Plaza,

St. Regis, and RIHGA Royal. The New York Health and Racquet Club, the Vertical Club, and the New York Sports Club are the most highly recommended. Following are some of the better clubs, by district.

Downtown

Carmine Recreation Center (1 Clarkson St, 212/242-5228)
Crunch Fitness (404 Lafayette St, 212/614-0120; 54 E 13th St, 212/475-2018; 152 Christopher St, 212/366-3725)
David Barton Gym (552 Sixth Ave, 212/727-0004; 623 Broadway, 212/420-0507)
Equinox Fitness Club (897 Broadway, 212/780-9300)
Executive Fitness Center (New Marriott World Trade Center, 22nd floor, 212/466-9266)
Johnny Lat's Gym (7 E 17th St, 212/366-4426)
Lucille Roberts Health Club (80 Fifth Ave, 212/255-3999)
New York Health and Racquet Club (39 Whitehall St, 212/269-9800; 24 E 13th St, 212/924-4600)
New York Sports Club (30 Cliff St, 212/349-7700; 151 Reade St, at Greenwich St, 212/571-1000; Sheridan Square, 125 Seventh Ave S, 212/206-1500)

Midtown

Atrium Club (115 E 57th St, 212/826-9640)
Club La Raquette, Parker Meridien Hotel (119 W 56th St, 212/245-1144)
Manhattan Plaza Health Club (482 W 43rd St, 212/563-7001)
New York Health and Racquet Club (132 E 45th St, 212/986-3100; 20 E 50th St, 212/593-1500; 110 W 56th St, 212/541-7200; 115 E 57th St, 212/826-9650)
New York Sports Club (50 W 34th St, 212/868-0820; 380 Madison Ave, 212/983-0303; Holiday Inn Crowne Plaza, 49th St and Broadway, 212/977-8880; 59th and Park Ave, 212/308-1010; 614 Second Ave, 212/213-5999; 541 Lexington Ave, 212/838-2102; 404 Fifth Ave, 212/594-3120)
Prescriptive Fitness Gym (250 W 54th St, 212/307-7760)
Sports Training Institute (575 Lexington Ave, 212/752-7111)
Vertical Club (335 Madison Ave, 212/983-5320; 139 W 32nd St, 212/465-1750; 350 W 50th St, 212/265-9400)
YWCA (610 Lexington Ave, 212/735-9755) and **YMCA** (215 W 23rd St, 212/741-9210)

Upper East Side

Crunch Fitness (1109 Second Ave, 212/758-3434)
David Barton Gym (30 E 85th St, 212/517-7577)
Equinox Fitness Club (205 E 85th St, 212/987-8500)
Exude (47 E 68th St, 212/737-2870)
New York Health and Racquet Club (1433 York Ave, 212/737-6666)
New York Sports Club (151 E 86th St, 212/860-8630; 1470 First Ave, 212/744-7050; 349 E 76th St, 212/288-5700; 1635 Third Ave, 212/987-7200)
92nd Street Y Health and Fitness Center (1395 Lexington Ave, 212/415-5700)

Tower Tennis Courts (1725 York Ave, 212/860-2464): all-year indoor tennis club
Vertical Club (330 E 61st St, 212/355-5100)

Upper West Side

Crunch Fitness (160 W 83rd St, 212/875-1902)
Equinox (344 Amsterdam Ave, 212/721-4200; 2465 Broadway, 212/799-1818)
New York Sports Club (248 W 80th St, 212/873-1500; 61 W 62nd St, 212/265-0995)
Paris Health Club (752 West End Ave, 212/749-3500)
Reebok Sports Club (67th St and Columbus Ave, 212/362-6800): big, excellent
Riverbank State Park (679 Riverside Dr, 212/694-3600)
West Side YMCA (5 W 63rd St, 212/787-4400)
World Gym (1926 Broadway, 212/874-0942)

> **EXUDE**
> 47 E 68th St   212/644-9559
> 16 E 52nd St
> Mon-Sun: 6 a.m.-10 p.m.

Edward Jackowski is the founder of Exude, the largest motivational and one-on-one fitness consulting organization in the country. In addition to consulting, Exude offers a weight loss and control program, nutritional counseling, exercise therapy, cardiac rehabilitation, sports training (golf, tennis, and skiing), children's fitness programs, pre- and post-natal exercise, boxing, self-defense, home-gym design, and massage therapy. Services and seminars, including classes and training programs, are available for groups and corporate clients. Excude's fitness consultants can also come to your home, office, gym, or hotel room, with all programs arranged on an appointment basis. Prices are reasonable, and they work with men, women, and children.

Recommended personal trainers:

Bodysmith (212/249-1824: women only
Casa Specialized Private Fitness (212/717-1998)
Jonathan Urla (212/875-1777)
Rich Lettau (212/945-2525)

Massage:

Cynthia Bernardi (80 E 11th St, Room 625, 212/473-0760): Shiatsu
Great American Back Rub (958 Third Ave, 212/832-1766)
Healing Hands (851 Lexington Ave, at 64th St, 212/486-1122): home, hotel, and corporate services
Lewis Harrison (40 W 72nd St, 212/724-8782): also does hotel and home calls
Robert Lane (1727 Second Ave, at 89th St, 212/427-2635): house calls and Saturdays available
Robin Ehrlich-Bragdon (Eastside Massage Therapy Center, 351 E 78th St, 212/249-2927)

Help for Hire

A.E. JOHNSON EMPLOYMENT AGENCY
681 Lexington Ave (bet 56th and 57th St)   212/644-0990
Mon-Fri: 8:30-4:30

Dating from 1890, Johnson's is the oldest employment agency in the world dealing exclusively with household help. They specialize in providing affluent clients with highly qualified butlers, cooks, housekeepers, chauffeurs, valets, maids, and couples. Both temporary and permanent workers are available, many on a moment's notice. All employment references, criminal records, and driver's licenses are checked.

COLUMBIA BARTENDING AGENCY
212/854-4537
Mon-Fri: 9-5

The Columbia Bartending Agency uses students so apt at bartending that one wonders what profession they could possibly do as well after college. The service has been around a long time, and there is none better. Columbia also supplies waiters, waitresses, and coat checkers.

DIRTBURSTERS
20 W 64th St, #39N   212/721-4357
Daily: anytime

Boy, are these handy folks! They will clean apartments, residences, and small offices at hourly rates. Their staff, hours, and rates are flexible, and they are bonded. Dirtbursters can arrange upholstery and window cleaning, walk your dog, wax your floors, serve as party waiters, paint your rooms, and perform a homemaker's service for new mothers and invalids. They will also videotape the contents of your home for insurance purposes. A Dirtbursters' certificate makes a great gift.

LYNN AGENCY
250 W 57th St   212/582-3030
Mon-Fri: 9-5

The Lynn Agency has developed a child-care system division which offers on-site customized child-care programs for conventions, corporate facilities, meetings, and hotels. They are a full-service agency that can supply baby nurses, bartenders, butlers, geriatric care, chauffeurs, cooks, companions, couples, governesses, maids, nursing aides, and housekeepers. There is also a party-planning service. The agency can supply help for any kind of function, from a small dinner party to a formal corporate affair. The owners claim that Lynn's biggest virtue is its ability to mold its services to a client's needs. Rates are reasonable, personnel are reliable, and they will even serve outside Manhattan.

Hotels

Late hotel reservations: Stranded out-of-towners or those who don't want to go back home to the suburbs should call **Hotel Reservations Network** (800/96-HOTEL), or the **New York Convention & Visitors' Bureau** (800/846-ROOM).

Ripoffs (a few favorites)

- Carefully check to see if your in-room refrigerator is clean and working.
- Check the rate posted in your room against the quoted price.
- Leave your hotel key at the desk (keep the new plastic type key with you).
- Put an extra luggage tag (with name and address) inside your bag.
- Watch personnel put stamps on your letters and postcards.
- Don't change foreign currency at hotels; exchange rates are poor.
- Cash traveler's checks at banks, where there is no service charge.
- Leave your real jewelry at home; if you must bring along the family jewels, keep them in a room or hotel safe.
- Don't give out your room number to anyone you don't know.

Telephone Charges

Carefully examine the telephone charges at your hotel. Many outfits find this a handy way to pad the bill. A few hints:

- Don't bill calls to your room.
- Ask for your own long-distance carrier.
- Beware of the phrase "standard AT&T operator-assisted rates."
- Check your bill.
- Have friends and associates call you whenever possible.
- Don't hang up after completing a call; tap the pound sign and then make your next call.

Getting the Best Hotel Rate

- Contact a consolidator: **Quikbook** (800/789-9887), **Hotel Reservations Network** (800/964-6835), **RMC Travel** (800/245-5738), or **Express Hotel Reservations** (800/356-1123).
- Call hotel direct; do *not* call toll-free telephone line.
- Insist on the lowest rate and ask for a discount: senior, corporate, weekend, AAA, honeymoon, airline coupons, program member, etc.
- Consider a package; you may be surprised at the savings.
- Try a half-price program: **Entertainment Publications** (800/445-4137) or **Quest International** (800/742-3543).
- Stay at resorts during the week and business hotels on weekends.
- Check out all-suites hotels (like **Embassy Suites**) or extended-stay properties (like **Residence Inns by Marriott**).
- Consider college dorms, religious retreat homes, B&Bs, and other nontypical lodging options.
- Carefully check parking charges.

Ask:

- Is my room guaranteed after 6 p.m.?
- Is quoted price inclusive of service and tax charges?
- Is there a fee if I cancel or check out early?
- What is my reservation or voucher number?

Budget Lodging Guide: Over 3,000 listings (800/525-6633)

Hotel Lingo

All-suite hotels: lodging units are actually suites, often with a free breakfast and evening cocktails offered

American plan: room rate includes breakfast, lunch, and dinner

Corporate rate: room price set for employees of corporations

Double occupancy rate: price per person, two to a room

Double room rate: full price of a room shared by two

Economy hotels: good beds, basic rooms, and often a free continental breakfast for about half the price of traditional hotel rooms

European plan: breakfast included

Extended-stay hotels: fully equipped apartments in townhouse-style developments

Full-service hotels: top-of-the-line amenities for when you want to be pampered

Half-board/demi-pension: room rate includes breakfast and either lunch or dinner

Hotel broker: a service provider who gives price quotes on hotel rooms, finds out what's available, and makes confirmed reservations; fees paid by hotels

Hotel consolidator: acts as a centralized clearinghouse for unsold hotel accommodations

Limited-service hotels: oversized guest rooms with work spaces at prices about one-third below traditional hotel rates

Modified American Plan: room rate includes breakfast and dinner

Rack rate: retail price of a room, given in brochures

Service charge: fixed percentage automatically added to a room and meal bills (not taxes)

Reasonably Priced Digs

In the write-ups that follow are a number of places that give excellent value for money. In addition, there are several hotels that are not fancy but do provide clean and comfortable rooms at a good rate (usually less than $100/night):

Carlton Arms (160 E 25th St, 212/679-0680)
Excelsior (45 W 81st St, 212/362-9200)
Herald Square (19 W 31st St, 212/279-4017)
Mansfield (12 W 44th St, 212-944-6050)
Martha Washington (women only) (30 E 30th St, 212/689-1900)
Portland Square (132 W 47th St, 212/382-0600)
Roger Williams (28 E 31st St, 212/684-7500)
Stanford (43 W 32nd St, 212/563-1500)
Wolcott (4 W 31st St, 212/268-2900)

Concierge

A concierge is the handiest person in the hotel if you want special services: restaurant reservations, massage, car and driver, theater tickets, shopping hints. There is no charge for services, and any fees will be added to your hotel bill. Tipping is expected: $10 is about right for the average service, more if a request takes an unusual amount of time. For requests above and beyond the call of duty, 15% of the value of a service is a good guideline. If you are a regular guest, it is wise to keep on the good side of these helpful folks.

Hotels Near Airports

All of the following are conveniently located, provide transporation service to the airports, have restaurants, and are reasonably priced (ask for corporate rates). Some have recreation facilities such as fitness gyms and pools.

John F. Kennedy International: Hilton (328 rooms, Jamaica, Queens, 718/322-8700), Holiday Inn (359 rooms, Jamaica, Queens, 718/659-0200), Ramada Plaza (500 rooms, Jamaica, Queens, 718/995-9000)

LaGuardia: Holiday Inn Crowne Plaza (358 rooms, East Elmhurst, Queens, 718-457-6300), Marriott (437 rooms, East Elmhurst, Queens, 718/565-8900), Sheraton (173 rooms, Flushing, Queens, 718/460-6666)

Newark International: Courtyard by Marriott (146 rooms, Routes 1/9, 201/643-8500), Sheraton (258 rooms, Elizabeth, 908/527-1600), Radisson (502 rooms, Frontage Road, 201/690-5500)

Hotel Specialties:

Dancing, nightclubs: Carlyle, Kimberly, New York Hilton, Marriott Marquis, Paramount

Offbeat: Morgan's, Paramount, Royalton

Pets allowed: Dorset, Essex House, Gramercy Park, Holiday Inn Crowne Plaza, Plaza Athenee, Intercontinental, Lowell, Mayflower, New York Hilton, Marriott Marquis, New York Marriott World Trade Center, Pierre, Plaza, RIHGA Royal, Royalton, Sheraton Park Avenue, Westbury

---

Some of Manhattan's best restaurants are now in hotels—great rooms like **Lespinasse** (St. Regis), **Les Célébrités** (Essex House), **Le Cirque** (Palace), **Mark's** (Mark), **Adrienne** (Peninsula), and the **Edwardian Room** (Plaza). For more moderately priced hotel dining, try the **Sun Garden** (Grand Hyatt), the **Lobby Lounge** (Four Seasons), **Streeter's** (Sheraton New York), or **Sarabeth's** (Wales). Just a reminder to hotel guests: even if you are feeling lazy, it pays to dine at the hotel restaurant and not in your room. You pay through the nose with room service for food that is less than sensational!

New York Hotel Swimming Pools:

Holiday Inn Crowne Plaza (1605 Broadway, at 49th St): for exercise buffs
Millenium Hilton (55 Church St): gorgeous
Parker Meridien (119 W 56th St): visibly exciting
Peninsula (700 Fifth Ave, at 55th St): very classy
Sheraton Manhattan (790 Seventh Ave, at 52nd St): kid-friendly

Under Construction

Hotel Grand (141 E 44th St): 154 rooms, early 1998
Hotel Sofitel (44th St, bet Fifth and Sixth Ave): 400 rooms, early 1999
Marriott Courtyard (866 Third Ave): 320 rooms, early 1998
Mercer Hotel (Prince and Mercer St): 75-room boutique hotel, no opening date set
3 hotels in planning stages: (Eighth Ave/42nd St): 860 rooms, 2000, (Eighth Ave/42nd St): 800 rooms, no opening date set, (Battery Park City): 400 rooms, no opening date set

Where To Stay Downtown

Between 11th St and 27th St:
Gershwin (7 E 27th St, 212/545-8000): inexpensive, funky
Chelsea (222 W 23rd St, 212/243-3700): check room first; some are dingy
Gramercy Park (2 Lexington Ave, 212/475-4320): good location
Inn at Irving Place (56 Irving Place, 800/685-1447): charming townhouse
Larchmont (27 W 11th St, 212/989-9333): small rooms, good value, and new

Washington Square/Soho:
Soho Grand (310 West Broadway, 212/965-3000): big, new, modern decor

Wall Street:
Millenium Hilton (55 Church St, 212/693-2001): indoor pool, business center
Seaport Inn (33 Peck Slip, 212/766-6600): very tasteful
Marriott World Trade Center (3 World Trade Center 212/938-9100): good
fitness center and pool, restaurants, large

If it's a family vacation, the following hotels are favorites for the kids:

Days Hotel Midtown (Eighth Ave between 48th and 49th St, 212/581-7000)
Doubletree Guest Suites (1568 Broadway, 212/719-1600)
Drake (440 Park Ave, 212/421-0900)
Inn on 57th St (440 W 57th St, 581-8100

New York's Finest Hotels

ALGONQUIN
59 W 44th St (bet Fifth and Sixth Ave)   212/840-6800
Moderately expensive

The Algonquin is truly legendary; it was designated by the city of New York as a historic landmark in 1996. The elegance of years past is reflected in the property as the result of a $20 million restoration. This home of the famous Round Table—where Dorothy Parker, Harold Ross, Robert Benchley, and other literary wits sparred and dined regularly—now reflects the same charm and character as it did in the Roaring Twenties! There are 165 rooms, including 23 suites (some named after well-known personalities), and the atmosphere is intimate and friendly. The lobby is the best place in the city for people-watching, and the Oak Room still features renowned cabaret artists.

CHELSEA INN
46 W 17th St (bet Fifth and Sixth Ave)   212/645-8989
Moderate

In the true sense of the word *inn,* the Chelsea is a small, informal, European-style operation. Most rooms have kitchenettes. The two attached, refurbished townhouses offer studio rooms, guest rooms (with shared bath at a very modest price), and one and two-bedroom suites. For those with business in the Flatiron District, this is a handy destination.

DELMONICO
502 Park Ave (at 59th St)   212/355-2500
Moderately expensive

This all-suites hotel offers one- and two-bedroom suites with terraces, walk-in closets, and dining rooms. The location is right in the heart of things. A triplex health club and fitness center is at your disposal. The Delmonico Lounge is a popular bistro.

DRAKE SWISSOTEL
440 Park Ave (at 56th St)   212/421-0900
Moderate

A $33 million facelift—including the addition of a business and conference center, state-of-the-art fitness center, and complete renovation of all 485 guest rooms and suites—underscores the commitment of the Swissotel group to their superbly located Manhattan property. Special features include a multilingual concierge staff, valet parking, limousine service to the Wall Street area, and guest rooms equipped with all the latest electronics (computer outlets, fax/modem units). The Drake Bar serves fine wines and champagnes by the glass. This is a class operation!

ELYSEE
60 E 54th St   212/753-1066
Moderate

The Elysee is a comfortable 99-room European-style hotel in a very good neighborhood. It is within walking distance of Manhattan's best shopping, is very popular with business travelers, has a multilingual staff, and offers kitchenettes in some rooms and suites. Rooms are filled with attractive antique pieces, marble baths invite the visitor after a tough day, and rates include continental breakfast. The refurbished Monkey Bar downstairs is one of New York's hottest sipping and dining spots.

ESSEX HOUSE
160 Central Park S   212/247-0300
Moderately expensive to expensive

This 65-year-old architectural treasure has been completely restored to its original art deco grandeur. The restaurants (see "Restaurants" section) offer fine dining. The rooms feature classic Louis XVI and Chippendale decor, many with spectacular views of Central Park. All offer two-line speaker phones, voice mail and message retrieval, in-room fax, VCR, minibar, and safe. The all-marble baths come with robes, scale, hairdryer, and toiletries. A business center and health spa are added features.

FITZPATRICK MANHATTAN HOTEL
687 Lexington Ave (bet 56th and 57th St)   212/355-0100, 800/367-7701
Moderate

Have a bit of Irish nostalgia in your blood? Then head for this deluxe boutique hotel (92 units, half suites) located in the center of Manhattan shopping. There are Irish prints in the rooms, along with all modern conveniences. Round-the-clock room service is provided. Seven suites are named after past presidents of the Republic of Ireland. For those who long for a real Irish breakfast, take note: they serve it all day long, including goodies like Irish brown bread, oatmeal, bacon, sausage, and black-and-white pudding!

FOUR SEASONS HOTEL
57 E 57th St (bet Madison and Park Ave)   212/758-5700
Expensive

In the hotel world, no name elicits higher praise or wins more awards than Four Seasons. They are considered the best in the business. Now visitors to the Big Apple have an elegant 52-story limestone building to call their home away from home. The Four Seasons (designed by I.M. Pei and Frank Williams) provides 367 rooms and suites; several fine eating places (Fifty-seven Fifty-seven is top-notch), including a lobby lounge for light snacks and tea; a fully equipped business center, complete with freestanding computer terminals and modem hookups; a 5,000-square-foot fitness center with all the latest equipment; and numerous meeting rooms. The main attraction, however, is the size of the guest rooms. They average 600 square feet, offer spectacular views of the city, and feature huge, luxurious marble bathrooms with separate dressing areas. A classy staff is determined to make this another award-winning property for the the world's largest operator of luxury hotels and resorts. At the Fifty-seven Fifty-seven bar, a big choice of cigars is offered!

GRAND HYATT
109 E 42nd St (Park Ave at Grand Central Terminal)
212/883-1234, 800/233-1234
Moderate to expensive

This centrally located hotel provides safety and comfort for good value. The lobby, complete with a waterfall, is a popular meeting place. The hotel's Regency Club rooms feature a host of amenities like complimentary continental breakfast, afternoon tea and appetizers in the evening, terrycloth robes, and wall-mounted hair dryers. A penthouse health club is a special feature. Accessible rooms are provided for the physically challenged.

LARCHMONT
27 W 11th St (bet Fifth and Sixth Ave)   212/989-9333
Inexpensive

The Larchmont is a European-style accommodation located in the heart of Greenwich Village. There is breakfast service, TV, full kitchen for every seven rooms, and baths shared by three rooms. Furnishings are attractive, rooms are clean, and you can't beat the rates.

LOWELL
28 E 63rd St   212/838-1400
Moderate to expensive

This classy, well-located hotel features 44 suites and 21 deluxe rooms. Amenities include a 24-hour multilingual concierge service, at least two phones per room, VCRs and outlets for personal computers and fax machines, marble bathrooms, complimentary shoeshine service, fitness center, and all the rest that goes with a top operation. Thirty-three suites have wood-burning fireplaces, ten have private terraces, and one has a separate gym room with treadmill, stationary bicycle, weights, a Nautilus system, and a compact-disc stereo with built-in speakers. Oh, yes, the latter also has *seven* telephones! The Hollywood suite has all the latest entertainment facilities, plus a fully equipped kitchen.

MANHATTAN EAST SUITES HOTELS

Beekman Tower	
3 Mitchell Pl (at 49th and First Ave)	212/355-7300
Dumont Plaza	
150 E 34th St	212/481-7600
Eastgate Tower	
222 E 39th St	212/687-8000
Lyden Gardens	
215 E 64th St	212/355-1230
Lyden House	
320 E 53rd St	212/888-6070
Plaza Fifty	
155 E 50th St	212/751-5710
Shelburne Murray Hill	
303 Lexington Ave (37th and 38th St)	212/689-5200
Southgate Tower	
371 Seventh Ave (at 31st St)	212/563-1800
Surrey Hotel	
20 E 76th St	212/288-3700
Moderate	

These all-suites hotels are among the nicest, most reasonably priced and conveniently located in New York. Each features 24-hour attendants and modern kitchens in every apartment. Nearly 2,000 suites in all—studio suites, junior suites, and one- or two-bedroom suites—are available at very attractive daily, weekly, or monthly rates. These are particularly convenient accommodations for long-term corporate visitors and traveling families. Families can economize by putting the kids on the pull-out couches and by using the fully equipped kitchens. Additional attractions: fitness centers at most properties, recent renovations at Dumont Plaza, Plaza Fifty, Eastgate, Lyden Gardens, Lyden House, and Southgate Tower. Food facilities vary. The famous Daniel restaurant can be found at the Surrey. Women especially like these accommodations when they must travel and dine alone. A great buy!

MARK
Madison Ave at 77th St 212/744-4300
Moderately expensive

Here's a winner! An older residency building (the Hyde Park, built in 1926) has been converted into one of the most charming hotels in New York. There are 125 guest rooms, 26 junior suites, and 34 one- and two-bedroom suites, all decorated in exquisite taste. Every room has cable TV, fax capability, and two-line phones, and most have pantries. The suites (which I strongly recommend) have separate vanities and marble baths. Some even have libraries, wet bars, and terraces with views of Central Park. The location is terrific, and the personnel are extremely nice. Mark's, an excellent restaurant just off the lobby, serves all meals, plus tea and brunch. Everyone gets Frette linens, heated towel racks, down pillows, umbrellas, and Molton Brown of London soaps!

MARRIOTT MARQUIS
1535 Broadway   212/398-1900
Moderate to moderately expensive

The opening of this 50-story showplace at the center of Times Square in 1985 represented a major step in the rejuvenation of the area. The Marriott Marquis boasts over 1,800 rooms, huge meeting and convention facilities, and the largest hotel atrium in the world. In addition, guests can enjoy a 700-seat, three-story revolving restaurant and lounge at the top of the hotel; a revolving lounge overlooking Broadway on the eighth floor; a legitimate Broadway theater on the premises; a fully equipped health club; suites with walk-in wet bars and refrigerators; oversized rooms; and a sky lounge. There are *seven* restaurants and lounges in all! A concierge level offers special amenities, including 24-hour room service. Some rooms have recently been refurbished.

MAYFLOWER
15 Central Park W (at 61st St)   212/265-0060, 800/223-4164
Moderate

If you are coming to New York for cultural events at Lincoln Center or Carnegie Hall, this is an ideal place to stay. Overlooking Central Park, with most accommodations redecorated, this is a safe, comfortable hotel with spacious rooms. There are a number of two- and three-bedroom suites and several terraced penthouses, all with refrigerators. A fitness center and restaurant are on the property. Room service is available from 7 a.m. until midnight.

MILFORD PLAZA
Eighth Ave (bet 44th and 45th St)   212/869-3600, 800/221-2690
Moderate

Value is the key word here. The Milford Plaza, a Ramada operation located at the edge of the Theater District in midtown Manhattan, offers reasonable rates that are partially offset by its location. But the hotel has extremely tight security (electronic door locks), which lessens the need to be concerned. Rooms are small yet clean, and late-night dining is available. Very attractive rates are available on weekends and for groups. The Milford has been totally refurbished, with all new bathrooms, furniture, carpeting, and wall coverings.

MILLENIUM HILTON
55 Church St (bet Fulton and Dey St)   212/693-2001
Moderate to moderately expensive

For the traveler who has business appointments in downtown, the 55-story Millenium is a good bet. Most rooms are king-size. Nonsmoking accommodations are available, each room has two telephone lines, and every modern amenity (robes, umbrellas, etc.) is standard. The Taliesin restaurant features New American cuisine in an elegant atmosphere. Weekend packages, with reasonable parking fees, are featured. Additional attractions include an up-to-date fitness center with a swimming pool and business center. Various facilities have been upgraded in recent years.

NEW YORK MARRIOTT WORLD TRADE CENTER

3 World Trade Center   212/938-9100 or 800/228-9290
Moderate to moderately expensive

This is a big place, as befits the neighborhood. The 843-room hotel features a handy location, large meeting facilities, a first-rate rooftop fitness center with pool, spacious rooms, and several eating facilities.

NEW YORK PALACE

455 Madison Ave (between 50th and 51st St)   212/888-7000

Located close to Saks Fifth Avenue, one block off Fifth Avenue, the New York Palace (900 rooms) offers commanding views of the city skyline, which is particularly enchanting in the evening. The public rooms encompass the 115-year-old Villard Houses, a legendary New York landmark. The hotel has undergone a comprehensive renovation. New facilities include an expansive fitness center; an executive lounge; the two-floor Villard Center, with its selection of meeting and function rooms; and a casually elegant Mediterranean restaurant called Istana. The famous Manhattan restaurant Le Cirque has new quarters in the Villard Houses.

PENINSULA

700 Fifth Ave (at 55th St)   212/247-2200
Expensive

The name Peninsula is synonymous with quality. This is luxury at its very best. General Manager Niklaus Leuenberger makes sure it stays that way by expending millions to upgrade guest rooms and public facilities. The hotel has a prime location in the heart of the city's best shopping, right off Fifth Avenue. The state-of-the-art rooms are done in art nouveau style, featuring king-sized marble bathrooms. A superior staff, a great restaurant (Adrienne), and a lounge that serves afternoon tea and goodies are all pluses. Best of all, a trilevel, glass-enclosed fitness center offers a superb view and a swimming pool, making this one of the finest facilities in the city.

PIERRE

2 E 61st St (at Fifth Ave)   212/838-8000
Expensive

At a Four Seasons operation you expect top quality, and that is exactly what you get. The Pierre is quiet, modest, luxurious, and expensive. There are beautiful suites, excellent meeting and banquet facilities, and a three-to-one ratio of guests to staff. Some of the rooms and suites are part of a residential co-op. Even if you don't stay here, a meal in the elegant Cafe Pierre or tea in the Rotunda is a special experience.

PLAZA HOTEL

Fifth Ave and Central Park   212/759-3000
Expensive

In every city there is a perfect location. In New York it is the corner of Central Park and Fifth Avenue, home of the Plaza Hotel, now operated by Fairmont Hotels. Besides the prime setting, this grande dame of Manhattan exudes the physical charm and grace that has made it the center of activity in the city for decades. It is a historic landmark. The guest rooms and suites (many with fireplaces), public spaces, restaurants, and shops all have a look of comfort and convenience, along with a slight tinge of nostalgia for how it used to be. The result is a gorgeous matron with a world-class facelift. Magnificent floral arrangements adorn the lobby, gilded ceilings shine in lobbies and rooms, and fabulous chandeliers glitter in the famous Palm Court. Polite bellmen, some of whom have been here for a quarter of a century, guide you to your comfortable digs, where king-sized towels await in marble bathrooms. Special linens with the Plaza crest enhance the beds. If you really feel like celebrating, ask for an English suite. There are horse-drawn carriages at the front door, and Eloise, the Plaza's most famous inhabitant, still stares down from her lobby painting. If you do not want to jog in nearby Central Park, you can work out in the fitness center. The Sunday brunch is magnificent.

PLAZA ATHENEE
37 E 64th St (bet Park and Madison Ave)   212/734-9100
Expensive

This hotel is one of the tops in New York in several categories, including service. A renovation has spruced up most of the rooms; all have marble bathrooms. Some of the suites on the higher floors feature solariums and roof terraces. Additional amenities include a workout facility, 24-hour room service, and an outstanding restaurant, Le Régence.

RADISSON EMPIRE
44 W 63rd St (bet Broadway and Columbus Ave)   212/265-7400
Moderate

A $30 million renovation has injected new life into this 1923 building, located directly across from Lincoln Center. Special features include CD players, VCRs, two-line phones, and a voice-mail messaging service. West 63rd Street Steakhouse serves breakfast and dinner, there is 24-hour room service for guests, and a four-story health club is adjacent to the hotel.

RIHGA ROYAL HOTEL
151 W 54th St (bet Sixth and Seventh Ave)   212/307-5000
Moderately expensive

This is one special New York find! The RIHGA Royal is an all-suites residential-style hotel that is great for international travelers, as people on staff speak 54 languages between them! The hotel, located handy to New York's business and cultural institutions, offers a fully equipped 24-hour business center, a fitness center, complimentary newspapers, and a Wall Street-area limo shuttle. Their Pinnacle suites offer guests Town Car service from New York area airports, personalized business cards, cell phones, and more. The hotel restaurant, Halcyon, is a casual, elegantly appointed room serving contemporary American cuisine. A spectacular Sunday "Marketplace in the Sky Brunch" (53rd and 54th floors) is sensational. The RIHGA is one of Manhattan's best deals!

ROYALTON
44 W 44th St   212/869-4400
Moderate to moderately expensive

The refurbished Royalton is a historic hotel that's been reborn into a high-tech facility. It's sure to appeal to some modern travelers. A French designer has created stark rooms, furnished with low beds, new three-unit phone systems, VCRs, CD players, and finished with mahogany accents. Many of the rooms have working fireplaces, and the bathrooms are king-sized and very attractive. There is a lobby restaurant and an attractive small bar near the hotel entrance. The helpful staff offers 24-hour room service. Three penthouse suites are available.

ST. REGIS
Fifth Ave at 55th St   212/753-4500
Expensive

A three-year, $100 million restoration has made this historic hotel the crown jewel of the ITT Sheraton operation. With 222 oversized rooms and 91 suites, the hotel provides luxury accommodations with beautiful appointments. Each room has a classy bathroom, and all the fine extras you expect, including 24-hour room service. A private butler is assigned to each floor. Room service is outstanding. Gourmet French-Asian dining is available at Lespinasse, the showpiece restaurant. The King Cole bar is famous for its Bloody Marys. Old-timers will be pleased to learn that the St. Regis Roof, the only hotel-roof ballroom in the city, is available for private parties. With a superb location and a grand history, the St. Regis exudes class.

SALISBURY
123 W 57th St   212/246-1300
Moderate

The Salisbury has just over 300 rooms and suites, most of which have been redecorated. Many are outfitted with butler's pantries and refrigerators. Suites are large, comfortable, and reasonably priced. The walls are thick—really sound-proof! If you want to be in the vicinity of Carnegie Hall and other midtown attractions, this hotel is for you. If you've waited until the last minute for reservations, the Salisbury is a good place to call. Since it is not very well-known among out-of-towners, rooms are usually available. Rooms are also available for meetings and banquets.

SHERATON MANHATTAN HOTEL
790 Seventh Ave (at 52nd St)   212/581-3300, 800/325-3535
Moderate

Ideally located in midtown Manhattan, the Sheraton Manhattan is in one of the city's most prestigious corporate enclaves and within walking distance of the finest shopping, museums, theater, and musical venues. Following an extensive renovation and refurbishment, the property has reopened as an all "Corporate Club Room" hotel (joining the Sheraton Russell), with each guest room an efficient work environment. The 50-foot indoor swimming pool (a rarity in Manhattan) and the newly renovated health club are both special attractions of this 650-room West Side hotel.

SHERATON NEW YORK HOTEL AND TOWERS
811 Seventh Ave (at 52nd St)   212/581-1000, 800/325-3535
Moderate to moderately expensive

A great location, a nationwide referral service, and a wide selection of restaurants and lounges add up to a convenient and pleasant place to stay. The Sheraton Towers, the more expensive top two floors, offer exclusive digs for business or pleasure travelers, including private butler service. Corporate Club rooms offer business travelers a virtual office in each room, along with extra amenities. The Sheraton New York also has a wide selection of package deals and seasonal specials, and the price is right. One of New York's best!

SHERATON RUSSELL
45 Park Ave (at 37th St)   212/685-7676
Moderately expensive

Following an extensive renovation and refurbishment, this 146-room boutique hotel, formerly the Sheraton Park Avenue, reopened as the Sheraton Russell. It is ITT Sheraton's first all-business "Corporate Club Room" hotel in New York City. Designed traditionally in the style of a 19th-century English club, while keeping the needs of business travelers in mind, each guest room provides a "virtual office," with an oversized desk, ergonomic swivel chair, task lighting, in-room data ports, battery chargers, dual telephone lines, and Hewlett-Packard OfficeJet printer/fax/copier. Complimentary continental breakfast buffet and evening hors d'oeuvres are served in the new club lounge. Centrally located at Park Avenue and 37th Street in historic Murray Hill, the Sheraton Russell is a welcome retreat in busy midtown Manhattan. On weekends, the Sheraton Russell is ideal for those who want a stay with the charm and warmth of a country bed & breakfast in the heart of Manhattan.

SOHO GRAND
310 W Broadway   212/965-3000, 800/637-7200
Moderate

Finally a hotel in Soho! This one has 369 small rooms and four suites. It is rather high-tech, fitting in with the area's industrial past. Canal House restaurant is on the premises, and limited room service is available. A nice touch: bathroom toiletries from upscale Kiehl's. The minibar, unlike most others, is geared toward youngsters.

STANHOPE
995 Fifth Ave (at 81st St)   212/288-5800
Moderately expensive

The Stanhope is a quiet and refined hotel just right for those who are touring museums or wish to be away from the throngs. The hotel has about 140 rooms (70 of which are spacious and attractive suites), a health club, business center, and a wonderful park view from many rooms. An outside garden for tea and snacks (The Terrace) is pleasant.

WALDORF-ASTORIA
301 Park Ave (at 50th St)   212/355-3000
Moderately expensive

The Waldorf once more is a symbol of class in Manhattan. Hilton has invested more than $200 million to restore their flagship—and the work shows! The lobby, bedecked with magnificent mahogany wall panels and hand-woven carpets, is rich and impressive. In response to complaints about the size of some guest rooms, renovations created larger spaces by reducing the number of rooms. Oversize executive business rooms are available. All-marble bathrooms have been installed in some suites. There is a fitness center, a number of restaurants, and special deluxe rooms and suites in the Waldorf Towers. An event at the Waldorf is sure to be something special. Junior League members have access to rooms at very substantial savings.

WALES
1295 Madison Ave (bet 92nd and 93rd St)   212/876-6000
Moderate

The Wales is a small, European boutique hotel that has been restored to its original condition. It was built in 1901 as the Chastaigneray, and it is personally operated, which is unusual in this day of major chains. A free continental breakfast, complimentary video and CD library, and room service are provided. The uptown Madison Avenue address is good and safe for shoppers. Every Sunday night there is a chamber music concert. Busby's (a bistro) and Sarabeth's Kitchen (an excellent restaurant) are on the ground floor.

WESTBURY
Madison Ave at 69th St   212/535-2000
Moderate to expensive

The Westbury is ideal for the solo traveler. Rooms are comfortable, modern, and offer every convenience, including closet safes and refurbished bathrooms. There is 24-hour room service, a new health club with saunas and steam rooms, and state-of-the-art exercise equipment. Also, an excellent restaurant, Polo, is on the premises. The top-of-the-line suites are superbly tasteful and not a bit ostentatious. If you like refined living, check out this hotel.

WOLCOTT
4 W 31st St (bet Fifth Ave and Broadway)   212/268-2900
Inexpensive

This is one of Manhattan's better-kept hotel bargain secrets. Here you will find a good location (just south of midtown), clean rooms with private baths, good security, direct-dial phones, color TV, and individual air conditioners for under $100. It is no wonder that students and foreign travelers, along with savvy businessmen and women, are regular patrons.

WYNDHAM
42 W 58th St (at Fifth Ave)   212/753-3500
Moderate

This charming hotel is more like a large home in which the owners rent out rooms. Many guests regularly make the Wyndham their Manhattan headquarters. The advantages are numerous: great location, uniquely decorated rooms and suites, complete privacy, individual attention, and no business conventions. On the other hand, the hotel is always busy, and reservations for newcomers may be difficult. No room service is available; however, there is a restaurant, and the suites have cold pantries with refrigerators. John Mados has created a winner!

Looking out for your health, the **Casablanca Hotel** (147 W 45th St, 212/869-1212) serves free grape juice, based on new studies indicating that grape juice may prevent blood clots.

Alternative Housing

. . . AAAH! BED & BREAKFAST #1

212/246-4000

The principal market this outfit serves is the business person who is more interested in the comforts of home than a fancy address. They also have a following among tourists who like to have a host clue them in about what to do and what not to do in the big city. William Salisbury, the manager, was a butler for many years, and he knows the hospitality business. Hosted or unhosted apartments are available. It is desirable to contact the firm two to four weeks in advance of your stay.

ABODE

P.O. Box 20022, New York, NY 10021

212/472-2000, 800/835-8880 (outside tri-state area)

Mon-Fri: 9–5; Sat: 11–2

Do you have your heart set on staying in a delightful old brownstone? How about a contemporary luxury apartment in the heart of Manhattan? Abode selects their apartments with great care, and all homes are personally inspected to insure the highest standards of cleanliness, attractiveness, and hospitality. All apartments are nicely furnished. Rates begin at $100 for a studio, $325 for a three-bedroom apartment. Extended stays of one month or longer are available at a discounted monthly rate. There is a minimum stay of two nights.

BED AND BREAKFAST NETWORK OF N.Y.

134 W 32nd St, Suite 602   212/645-8134, 800/900-8134

Mon-Fri: 8-6

Would you like to stay in a million-dollar high-rise condo? Or are you more comfortable in an artist's loft? This outfit can fix you up with either for one night or several months. They offer over 300 accommodations, mostly in Manhattan. Guests can choose to stay with a host or have their own furnished apartment. Leslie Goldberg has been in business since 1986 and is sensitive to the needs and desires of guests.

BROADWAY BED & BREAKFAST INN

264 W 46th St (at Eighth Ave)   212/997-9200, 800/826-6300

This is the only European country-style inn in New York City. The 46 rooms are immaculate, the price is right, the atmosphere is homey, the location is safe, and the operation is family-owned. Additional features include a restaurant on the premises, continental breakfast, and a library with games and newspapers. The facility, built as a hotel in 1907, has been fully restored!

A HOSPITALITY COMPANY

580 Broadway (bet Houston and Prince St), Suite 1009   212/965-1102

Moderate

If you are looking for a reasonably priced, full-service, short-term furnished apartment in Soho, Greenwich Village, Chelsea, or the Theater District, this is a good number to call. They have over a hundred apartments in their inventory, offer free local phone calls, and feature discounts for extended stays.

HOSTELLING INTERNATIONAL NEW YORK
891 Amsterdam Ave (at 103rd St)   212/932-2300
Inexpensive

This facility is available to visitors of all ages. The hostel provides over 480 beds in a newly renovated, century-old landmark. They offer meeting spaces, cafeteria, coffee bar, airport shuttle, catering, tours, self-service kitchens, and laundry facilities to individuals and groups. Best of all, the price is right! The neighborhood can be tough, however.

INTERNATIONAL HOUSE
500 Riverside Dr   212/316-8436
Moderate

This is a community of over 700 graduate students, interns, trainees, and visiting scholars from nearly 100 countries. Occupants spend anywhere from a day to a few years in New York City. It is located on the Upper West Side near Columbia University and the Manhattan School of Music. There are all sorts of special features, including a low-budget cafeteria, a pub with dancing, a gymnasium, and a self-service laundry. Free programs include ballroom dancing, lectures, films, recitals, and organized sports. During the summer, single-room occupancy, with a shared bath on the floor runs $40 per night, but drops to $35 per night for a stay of 10-29 days. Rates are less still by the semester. Reasonably priced guest suites are also available with private bath, air conditioning, daily maid service, and cable television.

LEO HOUSE
332 W 23rd St   212/929-1010, 800/732-2438
Inexpensive

This is the answer to one of the major questions asked about New York: Where can a visitor find an inexpensive, safe, and clean place to stay in the city? You should have no qualms about the Leo House, a Catholic guest house. A secure, refined, and quiet place, it is still run by the Sisters of St. Agnes. Reservations are required and may be made as much as a year in advance. A small deposit must be placed; it is refundable if cancellation is made 24 hours prior to scheduled arrival. The maximum length of stay is two weeks. No smoking is allowed in guest and meeting rooms. Although the outside doors are locked at midnight, registered guests may still get in after that hour. Breakfast, featuring homemade bread, is available for a moderate price. It is a great place for the single student!

92ND ST Y (DE HIRSCH RESIDENCE)
1395 Lexington Ave
212/996-1100, 800/858-4692 (toll-free in USA and Canada)
Mon-Thurs: 9-7; Fri: 9-5; Sun: 10-5
Inexpensive

This facility offers convenient, inexpensive, and secure housing for men and women between the ages of 18 and 30. There are special discounts for Y health-club memberships, and both single and double rooms are available. Lengths of stay can range from three days to one year. Admission is by application, and it is nontransient.

PHILLIPS CLUB
Lincoln Square, 1965 Broadway (at 67th St)   212/835-8800
Moderate to moderately expensive

This 96-unit residential hotel near Lincoln Center is designed for long-term visitors. Minimum stay is 30 days. There is no room service, but other features are impressive: preferential memberships at the nearby Reebok Sports Club, suites with fully equipped kitchens, individually assigned telephone numbers, stereo systems in all living areas, 24-hour business center and concierge, garage, laundry and valet service, and a handy conference room. There are 22 deluxe rooms and 74 one- and-two-bedroom suites available.

SHORT TERM MANAGEMENT
862 Lexington Ave (at 64th St)   212/570-2288
Mon-Fri: 10-6; Sun: 1-5
Summer: Mon-Fri: 10-8; Sat, Sun: noon-5

While Short Term Management (formerly Short Term Housing) caters to the needs of business execs and well-heeled New York City visitors, it remains a good source for others who need help finding lodging when a hotel is not the answer. Short Term can sometimes find an apartment for as short a stay as one month, but the usual is two months to one year. (The shorter the stay, the harder it is to find suitable space.) Property owners contact Short Term when their apartment is available, but it is the lessee whom they represent and who pays to keep them in business.

URBAN VENTURES
P.O. Box 426, New York, NY 10024   212/594-5650
Mon-Fri: 8-5

Mary McAulay founded this service in 1979, modeling it after Britain's famous bed-and-breakfast rooms, because she felt something needed to be done about Manhattan's lack of reasonably priced lodging. After being carefully screened, 650 hosts — who live in apartments, townhouses, brownstones, and lofts — signed up with Urban Ventures. Hosts range from older people living in big apartments to young artists. Both groups need a little help with the rent, and they are friendly and interested in their guests. The spare bedrooms are found on the Upper West Side, in the Village, in midtown, on the East Side, in Soho and Tribeca, and even in Brooklyn. Security is good — after all, this is someone's home — and these B&B's are especially convenient for visiting parents, since their child's apartment may not be large enough for visitors. Accommodations ranging from studios to three-bedroom and three-bath apartments are available from two nights to two months or more without hosts. The price is right, and this is a first-rate chance to get a sense of what it's really like to live in Manhattan.

WEBSTER APARTMENTS
419 W 34th St (at Ninth Ave)   212/967-9000
Inexpensive

This place has to be one of the best buys in the city for working women with moderate incomes. It is *not* a transient hotel but operates on a policy developed by Charles B. Webster, a first cousin of Rowland Macy (of the department-store family). Webster left the bulk of his estate to found these apartments, which opened in 1923. Residents include college students, designers, actresses, secretaries, and other business and professional women. Facilities include dining rooms, recreation areas, a library, and lounges. The Webster also has private gardens for its guests, and meals can be taken outdoors in nice weather. Rates at press time were $142-$190 per week, which includes two meals a day, plus maid service. Visitors must be sponsored by a current guest. The Webster is a secret find, known mainly to residents and readers of this book.

Internet Service Provider: The best in a crowded, confused field is **Interport** (212/989-1128). They're not cheap or flashy, just reliable.

Interior Designers

AERO STUDIOS
132 Spring St (bet Wooster St and Greene St)   212/966-4700

Whether it is a design project for a major commercial space or just a little one at home, the Aero Studio staff is well equipped to handle the task. Be sure to visit their store for some special ideas.

DESIGNER PREVIEWS
212/777-2966

Having problems finding the right decorator? Designer Previews has information on over a hundred of Manhattan's most trustworthy and talented designers, architects, and landscaping experts, and they will present their work to you by way of slides and photographs. They will also discuss designers' fees. Karen Fisher, the genius behind this handy service, was the decorating editor at *Cosmopolitan* and the style editor at *Esquire*. She charges $100 for her services.

MARTIN ALBERT INTERIORS
9 E 19th St   212/673-8000, 800/525-4637
Mon-Fri: 9-6; Sat: 10-6; Sun: 12-6

Martin Albert specializes in window treatments, and they really know their business. They measure and install their products at prices that are considerably lower than most decorators. Any store has to be good to survive in this highly competitive field. Martin Albert offers 125,000 fabric samples, ranging from $8 to $400 a yard. Services include upholstery and slipcovers, a furniture shop and at-home service. A large selection of drapery hardware is also available, and they'll deliver to all 50 states.

NEW YORK METROPOLITAN CHAPTER OF THE AMERICAN SOCIETY OF INTERIOR DESIGNERS
212/685-3480
Mon-Fri: 9-3

This is not a decorating service; it's a self-monitoring professional association to which most ethical and qualified interior designers belong. After an interview—during which you must specify your needs, taste, and budget—ASID will recommend up to three members who would be suitable and available for the job. They are not snobbish, and they treat a small job just as seriously as a large one. Even if you don't go this route, be sure the interior designer you *do* choose is ASID-affiliated.

A Touch-Up Here . . . A Touch-Up There . . .

It is sometimes difficult, expensive, and exasperating to get even the smallest painting job done. Expect to wait longer than you want, and always get carefully crafted estimates. The really good people in the business will take special care in your home and should bring all of their own supplies. Here are some outfits that have been especially recommended to me:

Ira Smolin Painting (212/831-0205)
Master Craftsman Decorators (718/885-1807)
Robert Star Painting (212/737-8855)
Roth Painting (212/758-2170)

PARSONS SCHOOL OF DESIGN
66 Fifth Ave (at 13th St)   212/229-8940
Mon-Fri: 9-5

Parsons, a division of the New School for Social Research, is one of the two top schools in the city for interior design. Those who call will get their request posted on the school's board, and every effort is made to match clients with prospective decorators. Individual negotiations determine the price and length of a job, but it will be considerably less than what a not-so-recent student charges. The disadvantage is that most of these students don't have a decorator card. (One can always be borrowed.) This is a good place to contact if you just want a consultation.

RICHARD'S INTERIOR DESIGN
1390 Lexington Ave   212/831-9000
Mon-Wed, Fri, Sat: 10-6; Thurs: 10-7; Sun: 11-5

Here you will find over 10,000 decorator fabrics, including tapestries, damasks, stripes, plaids, silks, velvets, and floral chintzes. These are all first-quality, with competitive prices to boot. They will do upholstered furniture, reupholstery, slipcovers, draperies, top treatments, shades, bedroom ensembles, and wall coverings. Design services, in-home consultation, and installation are all available.

Decorating Advice, But No Bargains:

ABC Carpet and Home (888 Broadway, at 19th St, 212/473-3000)
Bloomingdale's (1000 Third Ave, at 59th St, 212/705-2590)
Crate and Barrel (650 Madison Ave, at 59th St, 212/308-0004)
Domain (938 Broadway, at 22nd St, 212/228-7450)

Jewelry Services
GEM APPRAISERS LABORATORY
608 Fifth Ave, Suite 403   212/333-3122
Mon-Fri: 9-5 by appointment

Robert C. Aretz, who owns Gem Appraisers Laboratory, is a graduate gemologist and a certified member of the Appraisers Association of America. He is a past officer and director who currently sits on the membership committee of the organization. He is entrusted with appraisals for major insurance companies, banks, and retail jewelry stores. His specialty is antique jewelry, precious colored stones, diamonds, and natural pearls. Appraisals and/or consultations can be done for many purposes, including estate, insurance, tax, and equitable distribution.

RISSIN'S JEWELRY CLINIC
4 W 47th St (at Fifth Ave)   212/575-1098
Mon, Tues, Thurs: 9:30-5; closed first two weeks of July

This is indeed a clinic! The assortment of services is staggering: jewelry repair and design, antique repair, museum restorations, eyeglass repairs, pearl and bead stringing, redoing of old necklaces, stone identification, and appraisals. Joe Rissin and his wife, Toby, now run the place. Joe's father was a master engraver, so the family tradition has been passed along for decades. *Honesty* and *quality* are bywords here, and customers can rest assured merchandise will be returned in excellent condition. Estimates are gladly given, and all work is guaranteed.

ZDK COMPANY
By appointment only   212/575-1262

Most of his work has been the creation of rare and original pieces for neighbors in the Diamond District, but in his free time Zohrab David Krikorian will do professional work for you, too. In addition to making jewelry, ZDK mends and fixes broken jewelry as only a professional craftsman and artist can. He makes complicated repairs look easy and has yet to encounter a job he can't handle. If he can't exactly match the stones in an antique earring, he'll redo the whole piece so it looks even better than before. He loves creating the latest designs from traditional materials, and his prices are reasonable.

Leather Repair
ARTBAG CREATIONS
735 Madison Ave (at 64th St)   212/744-2720
Mon-Fri: 9:30-5:45; Sat: 10-5:30; closed Sat in summer

Artbag will make, sell, or repair any type of handbag, and they do it well. The range goes from mounting needlepoint bags to relining heirloom bridal bags, as well as making leather, reptile, and beaded evening bags. The Moores, a father and son team, are highly trained craftsmen who modestly advertise themselves as "understanding, genteel, and good listeners [who] know their business." Any one of their customers could have said the same thing. Artbag is also known for its sense of style. They carry the latest and best designs, and they frequently refashion old handbags into chic trendsetters. It isn't every day you come across men who know more about handbags than women, but these gentlemen certainly keep up with the latest styles.

CARNEGIE LUGGAGE
1392 Sixth Ave (bet 56th and 57th St)   212/586-8210
Mon-Fri: 8:30-5:45; Sat: 9-5

It's a pleasure to do business with these people. Carnegie is handy to most major midtown and Central Park hotels. Service can be fast, if you let them know you're in a hurry. They are responsible, offer reliable work at competitive prices, and carry a complete line of luggage and travel accessories.

JOHN R. GERARDO
30 W 31st St (bet Broadway and Fifth Ave)   212/695-6955
Mon-Fri: 9-5; Sat: 10-2; closed Sat April-Aug

John Gerardo manages to dispense luggage and luggage repairs that rival Crouch and Fitzgerald's (minus the glamour). Gerardo carries the standard brands in almost all sizes and shapes. There are sample cases, overnighters, two-suiters, and drawers with seemingly endless spare parts. Zippers, handles, locks, and patches of fiber and material are available for emergency patching. Gerardo does quick, professional repair work. They also have a pickup and delivery service for a nominal fee.

SUPERIOR REPAIR CENTER
133 Lexington Ave   212/889-7211
Mon-Wed: 10-7; Thurs: 10-8; Fri: 10-6; Sat: 10-3;
Closed Sat in summer

Do you own a fine leather garment that's been damaged? Leather repair is the highlight of the service at Superior. Many major stores in the city use them for luggage and handbag work. They are experts in the repair or replacement of zippers on leather items and will work on sporting equipment, such as tents and backpacks. If there is a leather problem, Superior has the answer.

Locksmiths

AAA LOCKSMITHS
44 W 46th St (at Sixth Ave)   212/840-3939
Mon-Thurs: 8-5:30; Fri: 8-5

You can learn a lot from trying to find a locksmith in New York. For one thing, as a profession it probably has the most full-page ads in the Manhattan Yellow Pages. For another, this particular "AAA" is *not* the place to call about a dead battery. However, in an industry that has little company loyalty or recommendations, AAA Locksmiths has been in the business for over a half-century. That says a lot right there.

LOCKWORKS
212/736-3740

Locked out? Give Joel at Lockworks a call; he has been at the locksmith game for two decades, and there isn't anything he can't do. This gentleman does not put AAAAAAA in front of his name and does not even advertise, but he is highly regarded by some of the top businesses in Manhattan.

NIGHT AND DAY LOCKSMITH
1335 Lexington Ave (at 89th St)   212/722-1017
Mon-Sat: 9-6:30 (24 hours for emergencies)

In case you're ever locked out, Night and Day is a number you should carry close to your heart. New Yorkers, even those who are in residence for a short time, become experts on locks and cylinders. Cocktail-party conversation is frequently peppered with references to dead bolts, Medeco, and Segal. If you haven't the vaguest idea what all the talk is about, you obviously don't live in the city where a locksmith is as revered a professional as there can be. He's got to stay ahead of the cocktail-circuit fads, as well as the local burglar's latest expertise, and must be able to offer fast, on-the-spot service for a variety of devices designed to keep people out. (After all, no apartment has just *one* lock.)

Mena Sofer, Night and Day's owner, fulfills these rigid requirements. The company answers its phone 24 hours a day; posted hours are for the sale of locks, window gates, intercoms, car alarms, safes, and keys. Inside and outside welding is a specialty. If you buy a lock here, you can be sure they'll help you out (or *in,* as the case may be) when the time comes.

Marble Works

PUCCIO MARBLE AND ONYX
661 Driggs Ave, Brooklyn (factory warehouse showroom)
718/387-9778, 800/7-PUCCIO

The sculpture and furniture designs here range from traditional to sleekly modern. John and Paul Puccio show dining and cocktail tables, chairs, chests of drawers, buffets, desks, consoles, and pedestals. Custom-designed installations include foyer floors, complete bathrooms, kitchens, bars, staircases, fountains, and fireplaces. Retail orders are accepted. Work of the highest quality is a tradition with Puccio.

Matchmaking

FIELD'S EXCLUSIVE SERVICE
317 Madison Ave, Suite 1600   212/391-2233, 800/264-7539

The motto "New York lives by this book!" is a big challenge, but I can't let anyone down, so this edition even includes a hint on matchmaking. Dan Field's company has been playing Cupid for three quarters of a century. If Dan is successful for you, how about a testimonial for *Where to Find It, Buy It, Eat It in New York*—the Romance Edition, of course!

Medical Services

AMERICAN PREFERRED PRESCRIPTION
197 Eighth Ave (at 20th St)   212/691-9050
Mon-Fri: 9-8; Sat: 9-6; Sun: 11-3

APP provides home delivery of prescription medications, comprehensive claims management, and linkages to community resources and national support networks. Their specialties include HIV and transplantation prescriptions. All drugs are available, and an extensive line of vitamins, nutritionals, and homeopathic and holistic products. Many rare items can be provided in one-day service. They will bill insurance companies directly so that customers need not pay cash up front. Nationwide shipping is available.

DOCTORS ON CALL
718/238-2100

This service answers a real need in the city. In the past, hotels always had staff doctors on call. Medical and dental associations would arrange for doctors to cover the city during off hours, and, of course, hospital emergency rooms are open 24 hours a day. But private doctors have stopped making house calls, even to regular patients. Doctors On Call was created to take care of that problem. Most calls are to people who need a doctor to come to their home, but visitors as well as residents may use this service. The fee in Manhattan is $80–$125, which also covers the cost of transportation and parking, and most calls are completed within two hours of your phone call. All members of Doctors On Call are licensed, and further tests or treatments can be arranged, if necessary.

OLSTEN KIMBERLY QUALITY CARE
441 Lexington Ave (at 44th St)   212/856-0198
Mon-Fri: 9-5, on call 24 hours a day

Quality Care is a nationwide organization dedicated to providing temporary health-care personnel on all levels. It was created to meet the changing needs of medical care. Formerly, the sick were treated at home, but today they are sent to institutions. That isn't always what patients want, so there is a need for professionals who will work at a patient's home. Quality Care supplies registered and licensed practical nurses, home health aides, homemakers, companions, physical, occupational, and speech therapists, and just about every other kind of home-care specialist imaginable. These professionals will adapt their program to special needs, such as kosher cooking and small rooming accommodations, as well as providing health screening tests and guidance to clients. They also do IV therapy. Here's hoping you won't need them, but it's nice to know that Quality Care is there and that a national organization stands behind it.

UNION SQUARE DRUGS
859 Broadway (bet 17th and 18th St)   212/242-2725
Mon-Fri: 7:30-7; Sat: 9-4

This store consistently offers the best prices on prescription drugs, industrial first-aid supplies, and vitamins, and is equally well-known for its reliability. The service is so conscientious that the pharmacist will call — long-distance if necessary — to verify prescriptions. Union Square also fills union prescriptions.

Metal Work

RETINNING AND COPPER REPAIR
525 W 26th St (at Tenth Ave)   212/244-4896
Mon-Fri: 9-6

Jamie Gibbons has taken over a long-established Manhattan business whose specialty is retinning (which is basically tin plating). Gibbons, who has over a decade of experience in the field, restores brass and copper antiques; designs and creates new copperware (almost all copper pots in use today are heirlooms); restores lamps, chandeliers, and brass beds; and sells restored copper pieces.

Movers

BIG APPLE MOVING & STORAGE CO
83 Third Ave (bet Berger and Dean St), Brooklyn   718/625-1424
Mon-Sat: 9-5

This is a handy number to have, even though Big Apple is not located in Manhattan. They do all kinds of packing jobs, using special containers for valuable and hard-to-handle items; also on hand are packing supplies, including wood crates, and custom paper for wrapping antiques and fine furniture. Local, interstate, and international moving service is provided, with furniture fully wrapped and padded before removal from your residence. A high-security heated warehouse is available for storage. These folks get high marks from previous customers.

IKE BANKS
718/527-7505

Ike Banks breaks just about every rule for inclusion in this book. He's not bonded or licensed, nor is he a resident of Manhattan (he lives in Queens), but he never breaks anything, and I trust him more than anyone else. He was first recommended to me by an appliance store when a delicate and temperamental washing machine needed to be delivered. Since then, he has moved pianos, households, and dining rooms for friends. Ike will travel anywhere in the city, sometimes further, and will work odd hours.

MOISHE'S MOVING & STORAGE
800/266-8387

Moishe's grew from one man and a van to one of the largest independent moving and storage businesses in the New York area in just ten years. Moishe's does over 8,000 relocations annually, ranging from around the block to around the world. Moishe's storage facilities meet most any need.

Some helpful pointers in the moving game:
- Be wary of really low estimates; do not accept estimates over the phone.
- Get written confirmation of an estimate.
- Ask to see the mover's license, issued by the Department of Transportation.
- Packing charges should be per carton, not hourly.
- Take personal charge of valuables during moving.
- Inspect every item after unpacking.

MOVING STORE
644 Amsterdam Ave (bet 91st and 92nd St)   212/874-3800
Mon-Fri: 8-6; Sat: 9-4; Sun: 9-3

Steve Fiore started West Side Movers in the kitchen of his studio apartment more than 20 years ago. Business was so good that he soon moved into a storefront. He was happy there until he realized the magnitude of requests he was getting from people who wanted to rent and buy dollies and boxes of all sizes. A man who knows a good business opportunity when he sees one, Fiore moved into a brownstone storefront on Amsterdam Avenue in order to sell nothing but moving aids and paraphernalia. The main stock-in-trade is still boxes. They come in a multitude of sizes, including three different ones just for mirrors. He rents and sells dollies, in addition to moving pads. Since all items are built to the specifications of professional movers, they are durable.

WEST SIDE MOVERS
644 Amsterdam Ave (bet 91st and 92nd St)   212/874-3800
Mon-Fri: 8-6; Sat: 9-4; Sun: 9-3

We came to West Side Movers via their Moving Store. But such ecumenical and diverse groups as the Union Theological Seminary and Tiffany & Company came to West Side Movers by recommendation and have added their accolades to the file. A company with a subdivision that specializes in helping people move themselves (by selling boxes and moving supplies) has to be top-notch. West Side Movers pays particular attention to efficiency, promptness, care, and courtesy. Customer after customer has called their staff the most courteous they've dealt with—and they don't dent the furniture, either!

Office Services

PURGATORY PIE PRESS
19 Hudson St (bet Duane and Reade St), Room 403
212/274-8228
Mon-Fri: 10-2:30, by appointment only

Purgatory is ideal for a small printing job! They do typography designs, hand-letter press printing, and hand bookbinding. They'll also craft handmade envelopes, do logo and identity designs, and provide handmade paper with uniquely designed watermarks. Specialties include the full range of printings for weddings and parties, and limited edition post cards. They say that working with this firm is an *adventure,* and part of the fun will be learning how they got such a name for a business!

SEEFORD ORGANIZATION
75 Varick St (bet Canal and Watts St)   212/431-4000
Mon-Fri: 8:30-5

Not too many outfits can say they have dealt with one customer since the day they opened . . . over 49 years ago! Seeford does quality general commercial printing and advertising specialties of all kinds. They can handle printing jobs from concept and design right through printing, binding, and delivery. The boss, Sam Goldstein, is on the job himself, and the quality of the work and service shows that personal concern. Besides, he is one of the nicest individuals in New York.

WORLD-WIDE BUSINESS CENTRES
212/605-0200, 800/296-9922
Mon-Fri: 9-5:30; Sat, Sun: by request

Alan Bain, a transplanted English lawyer, has created a highly profitable business that caters to executives who need more than a hotel room when in New York on business. The operation grew out of Bain's own frustrations in trying to put together a makeshift office, write and get out reports, answer telephones, and still attend to matters that brought him to the city in the first place. Services by on-premises word processors and typists are available. Desk space, private offices, and conference rooms may be rented on a daily, weekly, monthly, or quarterly basis. The daily rate includes telephone answering, receptionists, and a private office. The company also operates a full-service travel agency that specializes in corporate travel and travel-management services to small and medium-sized companies, as well as corporate meeting planning.

Parenting Resources

EARLY CHILDHOOD DEVELOPMENT CENTER
163 E 97th St (at Third Ave)
212/360-7803 (mornings), 212/360-7755 (afternoons)

If you're a new parent in New York who's feeling a bit overwhelmed, this place may be the ticket. Becky Thomas and her team offer classes for parents from newborn to age three. Whether you're looking for something during the day or a class at night, the Early Childhood Development Center can accommodate your needs. The prices are reasonable, admission is rolling, and they offer groups for siblings. The Early Childhood Development Center has been working with Manhattan parents for 25 years, a fact that suggests to me they must be doing something right!

PARENTING CENTER AT THE 92ND STREET Y
1395 Lexington Ave (at 92nd St)   212/415-5611

Just about everything the 92nd Street Y does is impressive, and its Parenting Center is no exception. The Center offers just about every kind of class you can imagine: a newborn-care class for expectant parents, a baby massage and exercise class for new parents and their infants, a cooking class for preschoolers, and on and on. As this Y is a Jewish institution, Shabbat Get-Togethers and a Jewish heritage class for preschoolers are offered, along with workshops and seminars on a wide range of topics, from potty training to raising an only child as well as new parent get-togethers. On top of all that, the Parenting Center acts as a resource and support center for its members. Membership costs $150 a year, and benefits include priority in signing up for classes, as well as discounts. Non-members are welcome to take classes, too.

PARENTS LEAGUE
115 E 82nd St   212/737-7385

This nonprofit organization is a goldmine for parents in New York. In addition to putting together a calendar of events for children of all ages, the Parents League maintains extensive files on such topics as babysitters, birthday party places, tutors, summer camps, early childhood programs, and private schools throughout the city. For a $40 annual membership fee, you can get access to those files, as well as to workshops and other events throughout the year. If you are the parent of a child of three, you also get a copy of *The Toddler Book,* an invaluable list of more than 200 activities in New York for little ones.

Party Services

BALOOMS
147 Sullivan St   212/673-4007
Mon-Fri: 10-6; Sat: 12-6; Sun: available for parties

Balooms is a small balloon store that encourages browsing and spur-of-the-moment sales. In addition to the standard balloon bouquet, they offer party decorating and custom-designed bouquets with names, logos, and even portraits on each balloon. Balooms will deliver in Manhattan and the boroughs, and they will ship anywhere. The store also rents helium tanks. As befits this lighthearted business, owners Marlyne Berger and Raymond Baglietto are delightful.

BLAIR McMILLEN
212/579-6010
24-hour phone service

If you are looking for top-notch piano entertainment, look no further. Blair McMillen is an extremely talented concert pianist, having performed on some of the world's classiest cruise ships and at top events in Manhattan. McMillen is a Julliard School graduate (he still teaches there on weekends) and can work with other musicians in the area. He is very flexible in style, equally adept with Broadway, pop, New Age, Latin, and jazz standards, although classical piano is his first love. Besides, this gentleman is ultra-personable.

ECLECTIC ENCORE
620 W 26th St (at Eleventh Ave)   212/645-8880
Mon-Fri: 9-5

Do you need to rent an armoire or a zebra or anything in-between? If so, this outfit specializes in extremely hard-to-find props for a party at home, a set for motion pictures or television, or some novel product announcement. They have been in business since 1986 and are known for an extensive collection of 18th-, 19th- and 20th-century furniture and accessories. Looking for unusual items? How about the front half of a rhino or one of those cakes that scantily clad ladies pop out of?

HIGHLY EVENTFUL
11 Fifth Ave, Suite 17A   212/777-3565
Daily: 10-6

These folks take charge of everything, including food, liquor, equipment rentals, tents, flowers, lighting, music, and trained personnel. They offer prime locations, such as grand ballrooms, churches (like the Cathedral of St. John the Divine), museums (like the Metropolitan), or spacious yachts, if that is what you have in mind. In 1994, Highly Eventful began doing events not only in New York, but at locations throughout the world.

LINDA KAYE'S BIRTHDAYBAKERS, PARTYMAKERS
195 E 76th St (bet Lexington and Third Ave)   212/288-7112
Parties seven days a week

Big things happen from little ideas. Some 20 years ago, Linda Kaye needed some entertainment for her daughter's sixth birthday party. She came up with the idea of kids baking and decorating a birthday cake. The end result? One of the most unique party services in Manhattan. For kids there are party themes like "Bake-a-Cake" with a fairy-tale character, a party at the Central Park Zoo, a Gretel cookie-house party, and movie-making at FAO Schwarz. But the oldsters are not forgotten here: they have their own fun times, with fortune tellers, belly dancers, a four-foot pop-out cake for retirement or bachelor parties, caricaturists, and corporate family picnics, holiday parties, and karaoke.

McNABB & ASSOCIATES
121 W 27th St   212/989-7877
Mon-Fri: 9-7

Keep this number for future reference! For over a decade these folks have provided superior special events design planning and production, along with corporate program management and sponsorship. A specialty of their operation is expertise in the support of companies that have an interest in community and not-for-profit organizations. Their client list reads like a who's who: among them American Express, Cadillac Motor Cars, Cartier, General Electric, IBM, *Les Miserables,* NBC, *Rent,* Smith Barney, Plaza Hotel, World Wildlife Fund, and many others. Let them plan your next gala!

PARTY POOPERS
104 Reade St (bet West Broadway and Church St)   212/587-9030
Mon-Fri: 10-6 (hours may vary depending on party schedule)

Party Poopers are really entertainers who make sure they never do the same party twice. One of the few private party spaces for kids, Party Poopers' facility is 2,200 square feet, fully decorated, and packed with costumes, games, a moonwalk, and even a haunted house. They handle all the set-up, clean-up, and entertainment while parents sit back and relax. Themes include a carnival, fairy tale, superhero, game show, secret agent, and anything else you can dream up. Their parties are also available for takeout in other locations around the city.

PROPS FOR TODAY
121 W 19th St (bet Sixth and Seventh Ave)   212/206-0330
Mon-Fri: 8:30-5

This is the handiest place in town when you are preparing a party. Props for Today has the largest rental inventory of home decorations in New York. Whether you want everyday china and silver or unique antiques going back a hundred years, they have the goods in stock. There are platters, vases, tablecloths, and everything in between. There is a Christmas section, children's items, books, fireplace equipment, artwork, garden furniture, foreign items, and ordinary kitchenware. Over a million items are available, to give you an idea of the selection! Phone orders are taken, but it is a good idea to call for an appointment and see for yourself.

Pen and Lighter Repair

AUTHORIZED REPAIR SERVICE
30 W 57th St   212/586-0947
Mon, Tues, Thurs, Fri: 9-5; Wed: 9-6; Sat: 10-3:30

When a business' specialty is the repair of fountain pens and cigarette lighters in this day of disposable ball points and no-smoking campaigns, you might not think it would be a viable concern. But this outfit is incredibly busy after over four decades in business—perhaps because it is almost without competition. Those who use fountain pens or are interested in vintage pens or lighters are devoted customers. Authorized Repair sells and services nearly every brand, and the shop can refill lighters, as well as all kinds of ball point, cartridge, and fountain pens. Authorized also sells (at a discount), repairs, and services electric shavers. Tourists can pick up 220-volt appliances or adapter plugs, and the polite and helpful staff is well versed in the fine points of each brand.

FOUNTAIN PEN HOSPITAL
10 Warren St (across from City Hall)   212/964-0580
Mon-Fri: 8-6

This experienced establishment is one of the few in town that repairs fountain pens. The Fountain Pen Hospital sells and repairs pens of all types, as well as what is perhaps the largest selection of fine writing tools worldwide.

Personal Services

BIG APPLE GREETER
1 Centre St (at Chambers St)   212/669-8159
Office: Mon-Fri: 9:30-5:30;
Greeter appointments, daily, daytime (2-3 days prior notice)

More than 500 volunteers from all five boroughs will meet individuals and small groups and show them familiar neighborhoods. Notice is requested for those who need special language greeters. Greeters will come to a visitor's hotel and arrange a special itinerary for things that will be of interest. This is a wonderful way to get an inside view of a city that can be very intimidating. Tipping, home visits, and use of private transportation are considered inappropriate. Visitors are provided with transportation maps, site and attraction information, calendars of events, and arts and entertainment options. It is sort of like a new friend showing you the wonders of the city!

CATHERINE VAN ORMER
By appointment only   212/532-4446

Image-wardrobe-fashion consultant Catherine Van Ormer not only associates with diplomats, socialites, executives, and show-business personalities, but she also dresses them. As more people began demanding her fashion-shopping expertise, she closed her boutique and went into personal shopping full-time. She is quite simply the best in the business. Most of her clients have neither the time nor talent to put together a wardrobe, and they benefit from her close association with the city's top clothing designers. She scouts lines and then shows the best to her clients. Clothes can be purchased at Catherine's wholesale cost, which is roughly half of retail, and the fashions reflect her eye for couture lines and natural fibers. Her fee is a mere pittance for those who simply must have this service. Van Ormer offers a similar service for custom-made bridal gowns and accessories. The gowns are magnificent, and her one-hour consultation fee is included in the price. A full range of bridal planning is also available.

DIAL A SECRETARY
126 E 83rd St (bet Lexington and Park Ave)
521 Fifth Ave (bet 43rd and 44th St)   212/348-9575
Open every day

No secretary? Don't worry! If you need a resume written or reproduced, a book or screenplay processed, legal work or an audio tape transcribed, these folks will do it in a hurry—and do it well. Given notice, they will even send an assistant to your office. Their list of clients includes several movie stars. The business started in owner Natalie Parnass's apartment a quarter of a century ago with one electric typewriter. Now they have a staff of super-talented people, some of whom can type 160 words a minute.

Doula Agencies

Doula comes from a Greek word meaning "mothering the mother." These ladies, usually mothers themselves, are trained to provide all kinds of support for new mothers, including cooking, shopping, feeding, and emotional support. A few of the best:

In a Family Way (212/877-8112)
Motherlove (201/358-2703)
Mother Nurture (718/631-BABY)
N.Y. Nurse (212/989-3036)

EMILY CHO
212/289-7807, 201/816-8530
By appointment

Emily Cho is a lady whose job it is to make her clients "look and feel terrific!" She is a clothing psychologist and has been doing this kind of work for a quarter of a century. The process begins with an in-depth interview at your home or hotel, where your wardrobe is reviewed. She will organize and update your clothes, then escort you on a personal shopping tour. Emily finds new resources every year, and she promises to stay within her client's budget. Corporate services and an intensive two-day course in personal image consulting are also available. This talented professional has had prior experience at Bloomingdale's, *Seventeen* magazine, and the Ford Model Agency.

FASHION UPDATE
718/377-8873
Daily: 9-5

Sara Gardner is a mother of three who naturally wants to make sure she gets the best value out of every clothing dollar spent. Gardner found she could get apparel for her family at wholesale prices from some manufacturers, so she decided to share her discovery with others. Thus she started *Fashion Update,* a quarterly publication that uncovers over 200 bargains per season in women's, men's, and children's designer clothing and accessories available in the Garment District. She conducts special shopping expeditions to designer showrooms. Gardner also has teamed up with Elizabeth Arden's Fifth Avenue Salon; ask her about "Beauty and the Bargain."

> As a rule of thumb, personal shoppers usually pay at least 60% off retail price when buying from designers and manufacturers. Some are offered even better deals. They then add a surcharge that is usually 20%, but could vary according to how much you buy and how friendly you become with your shopper.

FLOOD'S CLOSET
212/348-7257
By appointment

Want to be pampered? Barbara Flood will shop for or with you. She can even bring things for you to choose from in your own home. She will help with clothes, jewelry, organizing closets, decor, and all those other things for which busy women just don't have time.

G. BRUCE BOYER
610/867-4582
Consultations available

Trying to find a gentleman who does personal and corporate image consulting is not easy! All paths led to Mr. Boyer, who was men's fashion editor of *Town and Country* magazine for 15 years and is author of three books on the subject. You can't do better, so if you want to spruce up your look, give this expert a call.

GLENN BRISTOW, CFP
218 W 10th St (at Bleecker St)   212/243-0571
Hours: by appointment

Glenn Bristow is a certified financial planner who claims she can demystify the process of managing money and paperwork, especially for the critically ill. Her clients include homemakers, dentists, designers, restaurant operators, and horticulturists. She has had over 25 years of experience in business administration, is computer literate, and comes highly recommended for bookkeeping and budgeting advice.

INTREPID NEW YORKER
1230 Park Ave (bet 95th and 96th St)   212/534-5071
Daily: 24 hours

Kathy Braddock, founder and owner of this service, is indeed "the Intrepid New Yorker." She was born, bred, and educated in the Big Apple. Like your author, she delights in trying to help folks unravel the hassles and confusion of this great city. She provides one of the most complete personal-service businesses in the area and is available at any time. A corporate relocation service for people moving into the tri-state area (especially New York City) is available. Kathy can take you on private guided tours and shopping expeditions, help you find a place to live, and take care of decorating or refurbishing needs.

IT'S EASY
30 Rockefeller Plaza   212/586-8880
Mon-Fri: 9-6

Some time ago, David Alwadish found himself trying to remain cool amid an angry crowd of people at the passport office in Rockefeller Center. When someone in line told him they would pay anything to get off that line, Alwadish took him literally, and a new business was born. Over the next decade Alwadish did so well as a stand-in and go-fer that he went national and branched out into doing research for attorneys and businesses, auto leasing, and even motor-vehicle inspection. His company can help with passports, visas, and "bureaucratic transactions." Indeed, if there is any occupation or line of work where someone else can wait in line for a client, then It's Easy will do it.

LET MILLIE DO IT!
212/535-1539
Daily: 10 a.m.

Millie Emory has been in business for nearly two decades as a professional organizer, saving people time, money, and stress. She especially likes working for theatrical folks but can help anyone with a broad variety of tasks. She will organize and unclutter apartments, desks, files, closets, libraries, attics, basements, garages, and storage rooms. She will also pay bills, reconcile checkbooks, and get your papers in order for a tax accountant or IRS audit. She can help with paper flow, time management, and space problems. Millie is also good at finding things: antiques, out-of-print books and records, and so on. She assists seniors in dismantling their homes before entering nursing facilities. When loss of a loved one strikes, she will handle estate liquidations, selling, donating, and leaving the space "broom clean." She is a real problem solver!

LEWIS/MORRIS ASSOCIATES
39 E 10th St (bet Broadway and University St)   212/877-6863
Mon-Fri: 9-6

Lewis/Morris have combined six services into one company, giving consumers the opportunity to do a sort of one-stop service shopping. They are able to take care of time management concerns, event planning, personal shopping, relocation problems, decorating advice, and visitor hospitality. The founders, Phyllis Morris and Renee Lewis, claim they have yet to encounter a problem that could not be solved.

LIGHTEN UP
254 W 98th St, Suite 3F   212/222-2488
By appointment

Michelle Passoff, the genius behind this operation, calls New York City "the clutter capital of the world." Lighten Up is a service for people who want to free themselves from all the stuff (papers, clothes, etc.) around them and to develop some new habits. Being very much of an "unclutterer" myself, I think Michelle offers a real service in handling trash flow and all that goes with it. She offers private consultations, classes, workshops, lectures, and an audio-cassette instructional program. Right on, Michelle!

Do you need two elephants for a birthday party? You might get help from personal concierge services like **New York Concierge** (212/319-5196) or **Your Personal Concierge, Inc.** (212/685-7607).

LSA
220 E 65th St, Suite 14K   212/935-5041

Lisa Applebaum has a unique specialty: she assists in acquiring artwork for personal or corporate use. This talented lady can advise on updating and appraising art for current market value. She can also arrange private tours of New York's best galleries, museums, and auction houses.

SAVED BY THE BELL
11 Riverside Dr   212/874-5457
Mon-Fri: 9-7 (or by appointment)

Susan Bell is the genius behind this organization. Her goal is to take the worry out of planning virtually any type of job for people who are too busy or disorganized to do it themselves. Bell says "doing the impossible is our specialty," and you can believe her. Specialties include weddings, fundraising and charity benefits, party planning, tag sales, relocations, shopping, delivery arrangements, and service referrals.

SMARTSTART
334 W 86th St   212/580-7365

There is always someone in New York alert enough to fill a special niche or need. Such a person is Susan Weinberg. By her own experience, she learned that many expectant mothers and fathers are too busy to plan for the arrival of the bundle from heaven. So she started Smartstart, a consulting service to aid folks in pulling everything together. Her service provides the basics of what the new arrival will need, as well as room design, birth announcements, thank-you cards, gifts, and personal shopping. In addition, Susan sells hand-painted children's furniture, from table and chair sets to coat hooks and toy chests. Custom cabinet work is a specialty. She is truly the stork's number one assistant.

SOMETHING TO TALK ABOUT/TALKPOWER
333 E 23rd St (bet First and Second Ave)   212/684-1711
Mon-Fri: 9:30-5:30

Do you know that speaking in front of a group is the single most feared experience? Well, if you suffer from this problem, here's a solution: give these folks a call. They are true professionals in their field, training clients to make public appearances just like an athlete would be trained. Personal or group sessions are available.

> **Is Your Closet a Mess?** If it is—and whose isn't?—you might want to call **Creative Closets** (364 Amsterdam Ave, at 77th St, 212/496-2473) or **Alternative Closet** (212/362-0428). Both do specialized work and come highly recommended. Their prices are reasonable compared to others in the field.

Photographic Services

A.A. IDENTIFICATION SERVICE
698 Third Ave (bet 43rd and 44th St)   212/682-5045
Mon-Fri: 8-6

A.A.'s main virtue is their ability to do passport and identification photos competently and quickly. This is no small matter, as some photo shops near passport offices can be very unreliable. A.A. has a good reputation for one-day business portraits, one-hour photo-lab services, and laminating.

DEVEREUX PHOTOGRAPHIC SERVICES
45 W 57th St, 7th floor   212/688-4555
Mon-Fri: 9-6

These folks were trained as commercial photographers, and now they have parlayed their experience into digital imaging and restoration of old and damaged photographs. It's amazing what they can do. They are pros at making a copy negative when the original is missing, retouching, and doing quantity work at special prices. Some work is hand-done while some is done on the computer.

GALOWITZ PHOTOGRAPHICS
50 E 13th St   212/505-7190
Mon-Fri: 8:15–5:30; Sat: 10–4

In a city that has two button shops, two seashell shops, and a dozen pet groomers, you would think there would be a number of photographic restoration establishments. No sir. This very exacting art is a rare bird, but I am happy to recommend Galowitz as a fine practitioner whose specialty is making old photos look presentable and worth more than sentimental value. One of their specialties is doing blowups that can be used for parties or business events. Galowitz is a quality, full-service photo lab. They do conservation, custom framing and matting, and they can restore or copy an old photo, frame and mat it.

PHOTOGRAPHICS UNLIMITED/DIAL-A-DARKROOM
17 W 17th St (bet Fifth and Sixth Ave), 4th floor   212/255-9678
Mon-Fri: 9 a.m.-11 p.m.; Sat: 10-7; Sun: noon-7

Here's another only-in-New York idea. Photographics Unlimited offers photographers a full range of photographic darkroom equipment and a place to work on a rental basis. The shop has everything from the simplest equipment to an 8x10 Saltzman enlarger, including all manner of printing paper and film supplies, as well as a lab for on-the-spot developing of black-and-white and color. They also do custom processing and printing. Ed Lee claims his center is a complete one for amateurs and advanced professional photographers alike. Darkrooms can be rented, and they come with advice and suggestions from the owner. A technical hotline is available to answer questions.

PROFESSIONAL CAMERA REPAIR SERVICE
37 W 47th St (bet Fifth and Sixth Ave)   212/382-0550
Mon-Fri: 8:30-5

Rush jobs are the specialty here, so there's no need to spoil your vacation because your camera is on the blink. Professionals work on still cameras from 35mm up. They can also perform modifications and adaptations for special camera equipment.

VISKO HATFIELD
212/979-9322
Mon-Fri: 9-5

Here is an opportunity to have a truly one-of-a-kind portrait done by a young photographer whose name you will be seeing in lights very soon. He possesses great talent and a magnetic personality. He has captured images of dozens of celebrities in the book, magazine, fashion, and art scenes around the world. You could be next!

One of the best deals in town for color copying is at **Clicks** (49 W 23rd St, 212/645-1971). You can do the work yourself at any hour of the day or night for $1/copy.

Planting and Gardening Assistance

COUNCIL ON THE ENVIRONMENT OF NEW YORK CITY
51 Chambers St, Room 228   212/788-7900
Mon-Fri: 9-5

It's a little-known fact that the city will loan tools to groups involved in community-sponsored open-space greening projects. Loans are limited to one week, but the waiting period is not long and the price (nothing!) is right. You can borrow the same tools several times a season, as long as no one is ahead of you on the list. A group can be as few as four people. The council will also design office-waste prevention and recycling programs for commercial businesses. They have a number of interesting free publications.

Want some gardening help? Try the **Window Box** (217 E 27th St, 212/686-5382). Maggy Geiger comes highly recommended.

Plumbing and Heating

JACK LICHTENBERGER & COMPANY
304 Spring St (bet Renwich St and Hudson St)   212/807-8811
Daily: 7:30-4:30 (24-hour emergency service available)

Plumbing problems should not be left to novices. Four generations of this family have run the business, so you know they have the credentials to do luxury alterations, repairs, and maintenance in all kinds of situations. The average person on staff has over 15 years experience.

KAPNAG HEATING AND PLUMBING
212/289-8847

A while ago, I was visiting a friend who was having a plumbing problem. She called Kapnag, but got no response. When she called a second time, Kapnag apologized profusely and came out immediately to fix it. There was even a follow-up call to make sure the problem had been completely corrected. Ask any New Yorker, and you'll learn what a rare virtue this story illustrates. Brett Neuhauser, Kapnag's president, is the impetus behind all this kindness and competence. Incidentally, Kapnag will also respond to heating problems.

Postal Services

MAIL BOXES ETC. USA
212/642-5000 (information on nearest facility)

Mail Boxes Etc. has over 30 locations in New York. They represent all major carriers and can do professional packaging and shipping. Handy services (not all of them available at every location) include faxing, stamps and envelopes, private mail boxes, mail forwarding, packing supplies, business cards, office stationery, notary and secretarial services, passport photos, laminating, key duplication, and computer letters.

Rug Cleaning

BESHAR'S
1513 First Ave (at 79th St)
212/288-1998 (gallery), 718/292-3301 (cleaning plant)
Mon-Wed, Fri: 10-5; Thurs: 10-8; Sat: 10-4

The Beshar family has run this rug and antique business for three generations. Their expertise and experience are the basis of the *Besharizing* cleaning process, developed by grandfather Arteen Beshar, which makes fine rugs last longer and cuts down on costly repairs. Beshar's will pickup and deliver. All rugs are cleaned by hand at the company's warehouse. Beshar's also has a large range of new and antique rugs.

Scissors and Knife Sharpening

HENRY WESTPFAL AND COMPANY
105 W 30th St   212/563-5990
Mon-Fri: 9-6

Henry Westpfal has been in business since 1874, with the same family in charge all that time. They do all kinds of sharpening and repair, from barber scissors and pruning shears to cuticle scissors, plus work on light tools. Tools for leather workers, cutlery, shears, and scissors are all for sale. They also sell those hard-to-find left-handed scissors!

Shoe Repair

B. NELSON SHOE CORPORATION
1221 Sixth Ave (McGraw-Hill Bldg, C-2 level)   212/869-3552
Mon-Fri: 7:30-5:15

When several luggage dealers recommend the same shoe-repair outfit, you know it must be pretty good. This is how I heard about B. Nelson. They are very good at repairing dress, leisure, or athletic shoes. Other B. Nelson outlets (which go under the name General Shoe Repair) are on the plaza concourse level at 30 Rockefeller Plaza (General Electric Building), 1285 Sixth Avenue (Paine-Webber Building), and 630 Fifth Avenue (International Building).

JIM'S SHOE REPAIR
50 E 59th St (bet Madison and Park Ave)   212/355-8259
Mon-Fri: 8-5:45; Sat: 9-3:45; closed Sat in summer

This operation offers first-rate shoe repair, shoeshine, and shoe supplies. The shoe-repair field is rapidly losing its craftsmen, and Jim is one of the few who upholds the tradition. Jim's owner is Joseph A. Rocco, who specializes in orthopedic work and boot alterations.

Silver Repair
BRANDT & OPIS
46 W 46th St, 5th floor   212/302-0294
Mon-Thurs: 8-5; Fri: 8-2

If it has anything to do with silver, Roland Markowitz can fix it. This includes silver repair and polishing, buying and selling estate silver, repairing and replating silver-plated items, and fixing silver tea and coffee services. They restore combs, brushes (dresser sets), and replace old knife blades. Gold-plating, lamp restoration, and plating antique bath and door hardware are other specialties. Brandt & Opis are, in short, complete specialists in metal restoration.

THOME SILVERSMITHS
49 W 37th St (bet Fifth and Sixth Ave), Room 605
212/764-5426
Mon-Fri: 8:30-5:30

Thome cleans, repairs, and replates silver, in addition to buying and selling some magnificent pieces. They have a real appreciation for the material, and it shows in everything they do. They will repair and polish brass and copper, and they also perform restorations of antique silver and *objets d'art,* silver and gold plating, pewter repair and cleaning, restoring the velvet backs of picture frames and velvet box linings, lacquering, and refining. Thome also specializes in brass and is one of the very few still engaged in that business.

Stained-Glass Restoration
A. VICTOR ROTHMAN FOR STAINED GLASS
212/255-2551, 914/776-1617

With over 20 years experience, this studio specializes in museum-quality stained-glass restoration, from residences to churches and public buildings. Consultation service is provided and specification reports written for professional and private use. New stained-glass windows can be designed and fabricated.

Tailors
BHAMBI'S CUSTOM TAILORS
14 E 60th St (bet Fifth and Madison Ave)   212/935-5379
Mon-Fri: 10-7; Sat: 10-5

One advantage of this firm is that they can cut suits in as little as two weeks, with advance notice. They have been in business for over a quarter of a century and have developed an excellent reputation. Next-day alterations are a specialty, as is hand-stitching on suits. Most of their fabrics come from England and Italy, so you can be assured of the quality of the materials used.

CLAUDIA BRUCE
140 E 28th St (bet Lexington and Third Ave)   212/685-2810
By appointment

You just can't part with that beautiful but outdated dress you got on your honeymoon in Paris? Or perhaps you don't want to send that gown you wore to your daughter's wedding to a dry cleaner to get a new look? Just call Claudia Bruce, a talented lady who has been taking care of such problems with finesse for over a decade. Not only will she repair and rejuvenate garments, she also will tailor made-to-order clothing. Home-fitting appointments and wardrobe consultations are also available.

MARSAN TAILORS
162 Fifth Ave (bet 21st and 22nd St), 7th floor   212/475-2727
Mon, Tues, Wed, Fri: 9:30-6:30; Thurs: 9:30-7:30;
Sat, Sun: 9:30-5:30

Before Moe Ginsburg—one of the biggest emporiums of men's clothing in Manhattan—established its own tailor shop, all of its alterations were done by Marsan. Any tailor who survives in the middle of the men's wholesale garment area must be good, and Marsan is among the best. All work is done by hand.

PEPPINO TAILORS
780 Lexington Ave (at 60th St)   212/832-3844
Mon-Sat: 8:30-6:30 (closed Sat in July, Aug)

Here you get the services of Mr. Peppino himself, a fine craftsman who has been in the tailoring field for over a quarter of a century. He will do custom tailoring for men and women at your home, office, or hotel. All types of garments, including evening wear, receive his expert attention.

SEBASTIAN TAILORS
767 Lexington Ave (at 60th St), Room 404   212/688-1244
Mon-Fri: 8:30-5:30; Sat 9-4:30

Tailors are a peculiar breed in New York. In a city that is the home of the garment industry, most professionals who repair garments build their trade as "custom alteration and design specialists," or else they're dry cleaners who incidentally mend whatever bedraggled outfit has been brought in for cleaning. Sebastian Tailors is one of the few places in the city that is exactly what it says it is: a tailor shop. Custom alterations for men and women are quick, neat, and reasonable. Sebastian also does reweaving. Best of all, everything is accomplished without the usual ballyhoo most such New York establishments seem to regard as their due.

Television Rental
TELEVISION RENTAL COMPANY
386 Park Ave S, 15th floor   212/683-2850
Mon-Fri: 9-5

Ted Pappas runs a rental service that is fast and efficient. He will rent televisions for long- or short-term periods and will happily deliver and pick up the sets. He also rents big-screen TVs, karaoke sing-a-long machines, beepers, fax machines, VCRs, camcorders, and other audio-visual aids. Prices are among the best in the city, and in a business like this, his solid reputation is a formidable recommendation in itself.

Translations

BERLITZ
257 Park Ave S   212/777-7878
Mon-Fri: 9-5

If you do business or travel overseas, this is a handy place to know. Berlitz provides translations of technical, advertising, legal, and commercial documents for (and on) software and audio-visual materials such as film, video, and slides. In addition, they operate more than 320 language centers in 31 countries where they teach people to speak new languages via live instruction. There are 12 such centers in Manhattan, and information about them can be obtained from this address.

Travel Services

MOMENT'S NOTICE
212/486-0500, 212/873-0908 (hotline)
Daily: 9-5:30

Moment's Notice is the place to call for last-minute travel arrangements. They are a clearinghouse for leading tour operators, airlines, and cruise lines that are often faced with undersold or canceled bookings. This outfit provides sizable discounts on all types of vacation destinations, including European air tickets, Caribbean packages, and international cruises. Discounts are offered for travel 30 days or less prior to departure. Membership is required. A hotline for members gives available last-minute travel bargains. Moment's Notice is not some fly-by-night outfit, but has been in the travel business for over 30 years.

PASSPORT PLUS
20 E 49th St, 3rd floor   212/759-5540, 800/367-1818
Mon-Fri: 9:30-5

Larry Marsiello was another person struck by inspiration while waiting in that infamous line at the passport office at Rockefeller Center. His passport-fetching was one of the first such services, and though he has expanded nationwide, he has remained a purist, concentrating on the procurement of travel documents. With the expansion, Passport Plus now offers a highly personalized and complete document service. They will take care of visas; birth, death, and marriage certificates; international licenses; passport photos (while you wait); and airline-ticket pickups.

TRAVEL COMPANION EXCHANGE
P.O. Box 833, Amityville, NY 11701   516/454-0880
Mon-Fri: 8:30-4:30

Tired of traveling alone? These folks can help. Now you can find a compatible travel companion or partner. They are a nationwide service that has been in business nearly 20 years, serving individuals from 20 to 80 years of age. (It's never too late!) A newsletter gives tips for solos, so you can make contacts with others in the same position in other cities. One of the nicest services is the opportunity to have company for a meal in New York. Although there are a number of good "single" places listed in the "Manhattan a la Carte" section at the front of this book, having someone to share the dining experience is a lot more fun. But plan ahead.

Travel Bargains

For discount fares, try:

Travel Bargains (800/872-8385)
Union Square Travel (212/675-4545): first-class and
  business-class discounts
Unitravel (800/325-2222)

Typewriter Repair

TYTELL TYPEWRITER COMPANY
116 Fulton St (bet William and Nassau St), 2nd floor   212/233-5333
Tues, Thurs, Sat: 10-3 and by appointment

Martin K. Tytell is a legend. Now in his 80s, he recently signed a new ten-year lease! This is the definitive place for any kind of typewriter service or repair, with antique restorations a specialty. Tytell claims to have the largest collection of type in the world: over 2 million pieces, in many languages. He is perhaps the United Nations of the typewriter business! They have also become a center for old and antique typewriters. With a 68-year-old collection of typewriters and parts, Tytell can restore virtually any machine. Free estimates, too!

Uniform and Costume Rental

ALLAN UNIFORM RENTAL SERVICE
121 E 24th St (bet Lexington and Park Ave), 7th floor   212/529-4655
Mon-Fri: 9-5; open Sat in Oct

Because you will probably use a costume only once, it is far less expensive to rent than buy. At this establishment you can rent contemporary, period, animal, Santa, or any number of other costumes. They also provide a uniform rental service.

Upholstering

RAY MURRAY INC
121 E 24th St (bet Park and Lexington Ave), 2nd floor   212/838-3752
Mon-Thurs: 8:30-5; Fri: 7:30-3:30

This is definitely an Olde World shop that does things the old-fashioned way. It is a very fine and very expensive drapery workroom that also does upholstery. Their specialty is creating classic custom-made furniture, and they can copy any design you want, including heirloom pieces.

VI. Where to Buy It: New York's Best Stores

The Limited. Crate & Barrel. Barnes & Noble. Starbucks. The Gap. The Disney Store. Burlington Coat Factory. Toys 'R' Us. And now Kmart! In recent years, the "superstore" invasion has made parts of New York feel like a suburban shopping mall without the climate control.

Don't get me wrong: I think very highly of some of these companies. Their New York stores are generally well run, well stocked, and in some cases they are the best source for a particular item (in which case I've listed them in the following pages). But they aren't the heart and soul of shopping in New York. They just aren't what makes shopping here special.

That's the subject of this chapter: what makes shopping in New York special. In the following pages, you'll find the names, addresses, and descriptions of several hundred very special stores you just can't find anywhere else. They are a diverse lot: a store devoted only to items with angels, another to buttons, another to things made of rubber, and still another to light bulbs. There's a fishing store in Chelsea (and a history lesson, too); a resale store exclusively for large-sized clothing; a UNICEF card shop that stocks collections that are otherwise only available overseas; and what can best be described as an anatomical supply company.

Just like the restaurant scene in New York, the retailing scene here is always changing. While some stores have been around for a century already and are preparing for the one ahead, others will open and close before this book even leaves the publisher. I take great pride in offering one of the most comprehensive, up-to-date lists available anywhere, but I nonetheless urge you to call first before setting out. And by all means don't let my suggestions keep you from wandering around a bit. You never know what you'll find!

How To Save Money!

1. Before you go, decide how much you can afford to spend.
2. Be careful when shopping for brand-name items, as they usually cost more.
3. Try to buy everything in the same color family or combinations that will work together.
4. Take advantage of seasonal sales.
5. Check out the thrift shops, where you can find some great bargains.

6. Don't be afraid to look at garage sales.
7. Don't buy impulsively.
8. Check factory outlet stores.
9. Shop alone.
10. Watch newspaper ads for special sales, and go early while selections are still good.

Best Times For Bargains

Monthly Sales

January: coats, white sales, jewelry, lingerie, cosmetics, electronics, luggage
February: furniture, kitchen appliances, hosiery, winter clothes
March: washers and dryers, silver, china, glassware
April: jewelry, lingerie, sleepwear, air conditioners
May: home furnishings, housewares, luggage
June: furniture, lingerie, sleepwear
July: garden and patio supplies, swimwear
August: garden furniture, fashion accessories, back-to-school items
October: coats
November: furniture (the day after Thanksgiving is the major shopping day!)
December: Christmas gifts

Bargain Outlet Lingo

As is: just that
Cancellation: item refused by major retailer
Closeout: no longer in fashion
Discontinued: item no longer made
First-quality: item could be sold in retail store
Irregular: minor imperfections
Open stock: pieces can be purchased separately later
Overrun: excess due to manufacturer's error
Overstocked: surplus first-quality items
Past season: last year's style
Sample: items made for showing to retailers
Seconds: easily detected major flaws

The Best (and Some Not So Good) Places to Find Specific Items in New York: An Exclusive List

(Note: Space limitations preclude detailed listings of some of these stores.)

Things for the Person (Men, Women, Children)

Albert Nippon apparel, discounted: Lea's (119 Orchard St)
Attitude-adjustment needed: Polo-Ralph Lauren (867 Madison Ave)
Baby gift ensembles: Ovations (World Financial Center)
Backpacks: Bag House (797 Broadway)
Bags, antique: Sylvia Pines Uniquities (1102-B Lexington Ave)
Boots, Western: PopCowBoy (285 Amsterdam Ave) and Lord John's Bootery (428 Third Ave)
Boots and shoes, men's, handmade: E. Vogel Boots and Shoes (19 Howard St)
Bridal gowns and accessories, expensive: Vera Wang Bridal House (991 Madison Ave, by appointment)
Bridal wear, non-traditional: Jane Wilson-Marquis (212/477-4408)

Briefcases: Per Tutti (37 Greenwich Ave) and Jobson's (666 Lexington Ave)
Buttons: Tender Buttons (143 E 62nd St)
Clothing, antique: Antique Boutique (712-714 Broadway and 227 E 59th St) and Alice Underground (481 Broadway)
Clothing, brand-name, discounted: Giselle (143 Orchard St)
Clothing, cancer survivors: Underneath It All (444 E 75th St)
Clothing, children's basics: Morris Bros. (2322 Broadway)
Clothing, children's French: Jacadi (787 Madison Ave and 1281 Madison Ave)
Clothing, children's French and Italian: Prince and Princess (33 E 68th St)
Clothing, children's funky and fun: The Chocolate Soup (946 Madison Ave) and Peanutbutter & Jane (617 Hudson St)
Clothing, children's party dresses: Spring Flowers (1050 Third Ave and other locations)
Clothing, children's resale: Second Act Children's Wear (1046 Madison Ave)
Clothing, custom-made men's clothing, shirts, and ties: Ascot Chang (7 W 57th St)
Clothing, designer, men's and women's: Showroom Seven (498 Seventh Ave, 24th floor)
Clothing, designer resale: Ina (101 Thompson St)
Clothing, high-priced infants: Wicker Garden (1327 Madison Ave)
Clothing, imported designer: India Cottage Emporium (1150 Broadway)
Clothing, maternity, discounted: Maternity Works (16-18 W 57th St)
Clothing, men's brand-name, discounted: L.S. Men's Clothing (19 W 44th St) and Century 21 (22 Cortlandt St)
Clothing, men's classic: Peter Elliot (1070 Madison Ave)
Clothing, men's custom-made: Alan Flusser (Saks Fifth Ave, 611 Fifth Ave, 6th floor)
Clothing, men's good value: Saint Laurie (895 Broadway, 3rd floor) and Gorsart (9 Murray St)
Clothing, men's resale: Exchange Unlimited (563 Second Ave)
Clothing, men's, ridiculously high prices: Bijan (699 Fifth Ave)
Clothing, party and wedding dresses: Mary Adams (159 Ludlow St; Wed-Sat: 1-6 and Sun: 1-5)
Clothing, school: Off Campus (1137 Madison Ave)
Clothing, unusual: Gallery of Wearable Art (34 E 67th St)
Clothing, vintage: Gene London's The Fan Club (22 W 19th St)
Clothing, women's (be careful of pricing): S&W (165 W 26th St)
Clothing, women's designer sportswear, discounted: PRG (307 Seventh Ave)
Clothing, women's, good prices: Miriam Rigler (14 W 55th St)
Clothing, women's trendy: Betsey Johnson (248 Columbus Ave, 251 E 60th St, 1060 Madison Ave, and 130 Thompson St)
Clothing, women's ultrasuede, discounted: Irving Katz (209 W 38th St)
Clothing, youth: TG-170 (170 Ludlow St)
Condoms: Condomania (351 Bleecker St)
Cosmetics, discounted: Kris Cosmetics (1170 Broadway)
Diamonds: Rennie Ellen (15 W 47th St; by appointment only, 212/869-5525)
Dresses, evening and wedding, made-to-order: Jane Wilson-Marquis (155 Prince St)
Dresses, knit sets and suits: Sam's Knitwear (93 Orchard St)
Earrings, custom-designed: Sheri Miller (578 Fifth Ave)
Eyewear, discounted: Quality Optical (50 W 34th St; by appointment, 212/239-5200)

Eyewear, elegant: Vision Fashion Eyewear (34 W 46th St) and Morgenthal-Frederics Opticians (944 Madison Ave and 685 Madison Ave)
Fabrics, couture and designer: Beckenstein Home Fabrics (130 Orchard St)
Fabrics, decorator, discounted: Harry Zarin (72 Allen St)
Fabrics, designer, discounted: B&J Fabrics (263 W 40th St)
Fabrics, discounted: A&N Fabrics (268 W 39th St)
Fabrics, Oriental: Oriental Dress Company (38 Mott St)
Footwear, women's, small sizes: Giordano's (1150 Second Ave)
Furs: G. Michael Hennessy (333 Seventh Ave, 5th floor)
Gifts, spiritual: Hero's Journey (2440 Broadway)
Gowns, couture, secondhand: Irvington Institute Thrift Shop (1534 Second Ave)
Handbags: Fine and Klein (119 Orchard St)
Handbags, magnificent (very expensive): Judith Leiber on Madison (987 Madison Ave)
Hats, custom fur: Lenore Marshall (235 W 29th St)
Hats, Hypnotic, and products: P. Chanin (152 Eighth Ave)
Hats, men's: Arnold Hatters (620 Eighth Ave), J. J. Hat Center (310 5th St), and Young's Hat Store (139 Nassau St)
Herbs: Meadowsweet Herbal Apothecary (77 E 4th St)
Jackets, leather: Arizona (91 Spring St)
Jeans: O.M.G. Inc (546 Broadway, 476 Broadway, 55 Third Ave, 217 Seventh Ave, and 850 Second Ave)
Jeans, antique 501: Antique Boutique (712-714 Broadway)
Jeans, vintage: What Comes Around Goes Around (351 West Broadway)
Jewelry: Fortunoff (681 Fifth Ave)
Jewelry, custom-made: Eurocraft Custom Jewelry (48 W 48th St, Room 303)
Jewelry, fine: Stuart Moore (128 Prince St)
Jewelry, Indian: David Saity (Trump Tower, 725 Fifth Ave, 5th floor and 450 Park Ave)
Jewelry, special designs: Eurocraft Custom Jewelry (48 W 48th St, Room 303)
Jewelry, vintage: Antique Addiction (436 West Broadway)
Jewelry, vintage costume: Norman Crider Antiques (Trump Tower, 725 Fifth Ave, Level D-5)
Kimonos: Kimono House (93 E 7th St)
Knit suits, sportswear: Sam's Knitwear (93 Orchard St)
Knitwear: Knit Couture (800-B Madison Ave)
Lingerie, fine: The Bra Smyth (905 Madison Ave)
Lingerie, sexy: Samantha Jones (996 Lexington Ave) and Victoria's Secret (34 E 57th St, 693 Madison Ave, and other locations)
Massage oils: Fragrance Shoppe (21 E 7th St)
Millinery, custom-made: Lola (2 E 17th St)
Outdoor wear: Eastern Mountain Sports (20 W 61st St and 611 Broadway)
Pearls: Sanko Cultured Pearls (45 W 47th St; 212/819-0585, Mon-Fri: 11-3, by appointment only)
Perfume: Warwick Chemists (1348 Sixth Ave)
Perfume copies: Essential Products Company (90 Water St)
Perfume, designer, discounted: Almaya Cosmetics (1214 Broadway, Room 208)
Perfume, discounted: R.S.V. Trading (49 W 27th St), Kris (1170 Broadway), Jay's Perfume Bar (14 E 17th St), and Hema Cosmetics (313 Church St)
Piece goods, men's: Beckenstein (121 Orchard St)

Police uniforms and equipment: Frielich Police Equipment (211 E 21 St)
Prescriptions: J. Leon Lascoff & Sons (1209 Lexington Ave)
Resale, women's designer: Kavanagh's (146 E 49th St) and New & Almost New (65 Mercer St)
Sandals: Barbara Shaum (60 E 4th St)
Sewing patterns: P&S Fabrics (355 Broadway)
Shawls: Patricia Pastor (212/734-4673, by appointment only)
Shirts, custom-made: Arthur Gluck Shirtmaker (47 W 57th St) and Seewaldt and Bauman (17 E 45th St)
Shirts, men's, great prices: Acorn Shirts (54 W 21st St, 4th floor; call first, 212/366-1185)
Shirts, sport: Sosinsky's (143 Orchard St)
Shoes, big sizes: Tall Size Shoes (3 W 35th St)
Shoes, bridal: Peter Fox (105 Thompson St)
Shoes, children's party, discounted: Trevi Shoes (141 Orchard St)
Shoes, children's upscale: Harry's (2299 Broadway) and Shoofly (465 Amsterdam Ave)
Shoes, discounted: Stapleton Shoe Company (68 Trinity Pl)
Shoes for millionaires: Susan Bennis/Warren Edwards (22 W 57th St)
Shoes, men's discounted: Statesman Shoes (6 E 46th St)
Shoes, women's custom-made: Oberle Custom Shoes/Mathias Bootmaker (17 E 45th St)
Sneakers, men's and women's, discounted: Shoe City (133 Nassau St)
Sportswear, name-brand discounted: Atrium (644 Broadway)
Sportswear, women's, good prices: Giselle (143 Orchard St)
Suits and dresses: Blue (125 St. Marks Pl)
Suits, European men's: Jodamo International (321 Grand St)
Sunglasses: Shades of the Village (33-D Greenwich Ave)
Sweaters, Austrian: Geiger of Austria (505 Park Ave)
Sweaters, cashmere, men's and women's: David Berk (781 Madison Ave)
Sweaters, college: Off Campus (1137 Madison Ave)
Sweaters, Coogi, discounted: Penn Garden (63 Orchard St)
T-shirts: Eisner Bros (75 Essex St)
Ties, discounted: Goidel (138 Allen St)
Tuxedo shirts and accessories, discounted: Ted's (83 Orchard St) and Allen Tie & Shirt Center (146 Allen St)
Umbrellas: Uncle Sam (161 W 57th St)
Uniforms: Dornan (653 Eleventh Ave) and Ja-Mil (92 Orchard St)
Used items, unusual: Out of the Closet Thrift Shop (220 E 81st St)
Vests, kimonos: Nicolina (247 W 46th St)
Watchbands: George Paul Jewelers (51 E 58th St)
Watches: Mostly Watches (200 W 57th St) and M.A.G. Time (60 W 22nd St)
Watches, discount: Yaeger Watch (578 Fifth Ave) and Foto Electric Supply Co. (31 Essex St)
Watches, vintage: Galleria Per Tutti (50 Central Park S), Aaron Faber (666 Fifth Ave), Time Will Tell (962 Madison Ave), and Fanelli Antique Timepieces (790 Madison Ave, Suite 202; by appointment)
Wigs: Theresa's Wigs (217 E 60th St) and Jacques Darcel International (50 W 57th St)
Yard goods: P&S Fabrics (355 Broadway)
Zippers: A. Feibusch (27 Allen St)

Things for the Home

Accents, bath and home: Collectania (49 Greenwich Ave and 1194 Lexington Ave)

Air conditioners: Elgot Sales (937 Lexington Ave)

Antiques, Chinese: Luxor Gallery (238 E 60th St) and Chinese Arts & Antiques (825 Broadway)

Antiques, decorative: Karen Warshaw (167 E 74th St)

Antiques, Early American: Coming to America (276 Lafayette St)

Antiques, imported: Cobweb (116 W Houston St)

Antiques, sterling and crystal: Alice Kwartler (123 E 57th St)

Antiques, Victorian: Somethin' Else Antiques & Needle Arts (182 Ninth Ave)

Appliances, discount: LVT Price Quote Hotline (516/234-8884), Dembitzer Bros. (5 Essex St), Kaufman Electrical Appliances (365 Grand St), Price Watchers (800/336-6694), and Bloom and Krup (504 E 14th St)

Appliances, kitchen: Gringer & Sons (29 First Ave) and Zabar's (2245 Broadway)

Appliances for overseas: Appliances Overseas (276 Fifth Ave, Suite 407)

Art, African: York's (319 and 321 Bleecker St)

Art, ancient European, Oriental, and pre-Columbian: Royal Athena Galleries (153 E 57th St)

Art, antique Oriental: Imperial Fine Oriental Art (790 Madison Ave)

Art deco, French: Maison Gerard (36 E 10th St)

Art, decorative: Susan Meisel Decorative Arts (133 Prince St)

Art, erotic: Erotics Gallery (41 Union Sq W, Suite 1011)

Art, North American Indian: Common Ground (19 Greenwich Ave)

Art, pop: Pop Shop (292 Lafayette St)

Art, primitive: Lands Beyond (1218 Lexington Ave) and Eastern Arts (365 Bleecker St and 107 Spring St)

Art, 20th century, American and European: Timothy Baum (212/879-4512)

Art, Western, 19th and 20th century: J.N. Bartfield Galleries (30 W 57th St)

Artifacts: Jacques Carcanagues Gallery (106 Spring St)

Bakeware, discounted: Broadway Panhandler (477 Broome St)

Baskets: Bill's Flower Market (816 Sixth Ave)

Baskets, custom scented: Bath Island (469 Amsterdam Ave)

Baskets, fruit: Macres (173 W 57th St)

Beds, brass and iron: Charles B. Rogers (899 First Ave)

Beds, Murphy: Murphy Bed Center (110 W 17th St, 2nd floor)

Beds, sofa: Avery-Boardman (979 Third Ave)

Bird cages: Lexington Gardens (1011 Lexington Ave)

Books, interior design: Morton Books (989 Third Ave)

Boxes, wooden: An American Craftsman Galleries (317 Bleecker St and other locations)

Cabinets, old lawyer: On Lafayette (325 Lafayette St)

Candles: Candleshtick (181 Seventh Ave and 2444 Broadway), Candle Shop (118 Christopher St), and Terra Verde Trading Company (120 Wooster St)

Candles, discount: Empire Restaurant Supply (114 Bowery)

Candles, illuminating: Imprescia (1407 Broadway)

Carpets, antique: Ghiordian Knot (212/722-1235, by appointment)

Carpets, Turkish: Beyond the Bosphorus (79 Sullivan St)

Chairs, folding, inexpensive: Crate & Barrel (650 Madison Ave)

Chairs, folding, quality: Coconut Company (129 Greene St)

China, Amari: Bardith (901 Madison Ave)
China and glass, discounted: Lanac Sales (73 Canal St)
China, bargain odds and ends: Fishs Eddy (889 Broadway and 2176 Broadway)
China, French hand-painted: Solanee (866 Lexington Ave)
China, Limoge: Prima Soho (478 West Broadway)
Christmas decorations, discounted (mid-November through Christmas): Kurt Adler's Santa's World (1107 Broadway)
Christmas ornaments: Matt McGhee (22 Christopher St)
Clocks, cuckoo: Alfry (48 W 46th St, 5th floor) and Time Pieces (115 Greenwich Ave)
Closet fixtures: Hold Everything (1311 Second Ave, 104 Seventh Ave, 2109 Broadway, and 231 Tenth Ave; the latter is an outlet store)
Coca-Cola merchandise: Coca-Cola (711 Fifth Ave)
Collectibles and display: Gargoyles, Ltd., of Philadelphia (200 Lexington Ave)
Comforters, down: Soho Mill Outlet (490 Broadway, 2nd floor)
Cookware, French: Lamalle (36 W 25th St, 6th floor)
Crafts, handmade American: Eclectic Energy (102 Christopher St)
Dinnerware, Chinese: Wing On Wo & Co. (26 Mott St)
Dinnerware, Fiesta (individual pieces): Mood Indigo (181 Prince St)
Dinnerware, porcelain: Bernardaud (499 Park Ave)
Displays, jewelry: Premier (33 W 46th St)
Domestics: Harris Levy (278 Grand St)
Ecological products: Terra Verde Trading Company (120 Wooster St)
Electronics, good values: The Wiz (726 Broadway and other locations) and Vicmarr (88 Delancey St)
Electronics, vintage: Waves (110 W 25th St)
Fans, ceiling: Modern Supply (19 Murray St)
Figurines, discounted: East Side Gifts and Dinnerware (351 Grand St)
Fixtures, impossible-to-find vintage: Carpe Diem Antiques (187 Sixth Ave)
Floor coverings: ABC Carpet and Home (888 Broadway)
Floral designs: Spring Street Garden (186-1/2 Spring St)
Frames, picture: Ready Frames (44 W 18th St) and Framed on Madison (740 Madison Ave)
Furnishings, traditional hand-carved: Devon Shops (111 E 27th St)
Furniture, custom-made: Navedo Woodcraft (179 E 119th St)
Furniture, department store: Bloomingdale's (1000 Third Ave)
Furniture, discounted: Knoll (105 Wooster St)
Furniture, fine mica: Room Plus (1555 Third Ave)
Furniture, foam, and mattresses: Dixie Foam (104 W 17th St)
Furniture, French Country: Pierre Deux Antiques (870 Madison Ave)
Furniture, handcrafted, 18th-century American reproductions: Barton-Sharpe (66 Crosby St)
Furniture, hardwood: Pompanoosuc (470 Broome St)
Furniture, high-quality children's: Kids' Supply Company (1325 Madison Ave)
Furniture, leather: Sofa So Good (106 Wooster St)
Furniture, modular: Room Plus Furniture (1555 Third Ave)
Furniture, one-of-a-kind: Props for Today (121 W 19th St, 6th floor)
Furniture, pine: Better Times Antiques (201 W 84th St) and Evergreen Antiques (1249 Third Ave)
Furniture reproductions: Foremost (8 W 30th St, 5th floor)
Furniture, Swedish antique: Eileen Lane (150 Thompson St)
Furniture, unusual children's: Wynken, Blynken & Nod's (306 E 55th St)

Furniture, vintage: Full House (133 Wooster St)
Gadgets: Brookstone (18 Fulton St)
Garden items: Lexington Gardens (1011 Lexington Ave)
Garden ornaments, antique: Foster & Feldman (219 E 60th St)
Glass: Simon Pearce (120 Wooster St and 500 Park Ave)
Glass, Venetian: Gardner & Barr (213 E 60th St)
Glass and tableware: Avventura (463 Amsterdam Ave)
Glassware, Steuben, used: Lillian Nassau (220 E 57th St)
Hardware: Barson Hardware (35 W 44th St)
Home accessories: Carole Stupell (29 E 22nd St)
Interiors, architectural, antique and reproduction: Frederick P. Victoria (154 E 55th St)
Judaica: Hecker Corporation (164 E 68th St) and J. Levine Co. (5 W 30th St)
Kitchens, custom: Regba Diran New York (1100 Second Ave)
Kitchenware, professional: Lamalle (36 W 25th St, 6th floor)
Lamp finials: Grand Brass (221 Grand St)
Lampshades: Just Shades (21 Spring St)
Lightbulbs: Just Bulbs (936 Broadway)
Lightbulbs, discounted: Wiedenbach-Brown (mail order, 800/243-0030)
Lighting fixtures: City Knickerbocker (781 Eighth Ave) and New York Gas Lighting Company (195 Bowery)
Linens, antique: Jean Hoffman (207 E 66th St) and Jana Starr (236 E 80th St)
Linens, Indian: Pondicherri (454 Columbus Ave)
Linoleum, vintage: Secondhand Rose (138 Duane St)
Locks: Lacka Lock (253 W 46th St)
Mattresses, good values: Town Bedding & Upholstery (205 Eighth Ave)
Movie-star photos: Movie Star News (134 W 18th St)
Perfume bottles, vintage: Gallery #47 (1050 Second Ave)
Pianos, grand, decorative: Maximiliaan's House of Grand Pianos (200 Lexington Ave)
Plants: Farm and Garden Nursery (2 Sixth Ave)
Plants, cactus: Grass Roots Garden (131 Spring St)
Plumbing parts: George Taylor Specialties (100 Hudson St)
Poster originals, 1880-1940: Philip Williams (60 Grand St)
Posters, best selection: Paris Images (170 Bleecker St) and Poster America (138 W 18th St)
Posters, international movie: Triton Gallery (323 W 45th St) and Jerry Ohlinger (242 W 14th St)
Posters, vintage: La Belle Epoque (280 Columbus Ave)
Prints, botanical: W. Graham Arader (29 E 72nd St)
Prints, contemporary wildlife and sporting: Holland & Holland (50 E 57th St)
Prints, Japanese: Japan Gallery (1210 Lexington Ave)
Quilt fabric: City Quilter (157 W 24th St)
Quilts: Down Quilt Shop (1225 Madison Ave and 518 Columbus Ave) and J. Schachter's (5 Cook St, Brooklyn)
Quilts, antique: Kelter/Malce (74 Jane St, 212/989-6760, by appointment) and Susan Parrish (390 Bleecker St)
Rugs, old: Doris Leslie Blau (724 Fifth Ave, 6th floor, 212/586-5511, by appointment)
Rugs, Oriental: Momeni International (36 E 31st St)
Screens, shoji: Miya Shoji (109 W 17th St)
Shelves: Shelf Shop II (1295 First Ave)

Signs, interior: De-Sign Letters of New York (15 E 18th St)
Silver and wedding gifts: Rogers and Rosenthal (2337 Lemoine Ave, Fort Lee, NJ 07024)
Silver, unusual: Jean's Silversmiths (16 W 45th St)
Silverware and Holloware, good values: Eastern Silver (54 Canal St)
Sofas: J. Mabley (355 West Broadway)
Software: Electronics Boutique (Manhattan Mall, Third Ave and 71st St, 901 Sixth Ave, and 687 Broadway)
Stairs and rails, replacement: Stairbuilders by B&A (516/432-1201)
Stationery, discounted home and office: Tunnel Stationery (301 Canal St)
Stationery, personalized: Jamie Ostrow (876 Madison Ave)
Stone pieces: Modern Stone Age (111 Greene St)
Strollers and other baby equipment: Schneider's (20 Ave A)
Tableware: Fishs Eddy (889 Broadway, 551 Hudson St, and 2176 Broadway)
Tapestries: Lovelia Enterprises (356 E 41st St, 212/490-0930, by appointment) and Saint-Remy (818 Lexington Ave)
Tiles, ceramic, and marble and wall coverings: Quarry Tile, Marble & Granite (128 E 32nd St) and Tiles (42 W 15th St)
Vacuum cleaners: Desco (1236 Lexington Ave and 131 W 14th St)
Wallpaper, discounted: Janovic (1555 Third Ave and other locations)
Wrought iron items: Morgik Company (20 W 22nd St)

Things for Leisure Time

Albums, out-of-print: Golden Disc (239 Bleecker St)
Art supplies: Pearl Paint Company (308 Canal St)
Athletic gear: Modell's (1535 Third Ave and 51 E 42nd St)
Athletic gear, team: Yankee Clubhouse (110 E 59th St and 393 Fifth Ave) and New York Mets Clubhouse (575 Fifth Ave)
Baseball cards, best selection: Card Collectors (mail order, 212/873-6999)
Bibles (in every language): International Bible Society (139 W 57th St)
Bicycles: Bicycle and Exercise Equipment Store (242 E 79th St) and Bicycle Habitat (244 Lafayette St)
Binoculars: Clairmont-Nichols (1016 First Ave)
Books, African-American history: Liberation Bookstore (421 Lenox Ave)
Books, art: Hacker Art Books (45 W 57th St)
Books, astrology: New York Astrology Center (350 Lexington Ave, 4th floor)
Books, children's: Barnes & Noble Jr. (120 E 86th St)
Books, children's and parents': Bank Street College Book Store (610 W 112th St)
Books, decorative arts: Archivia (944 Madison Ave)
Books, new and used discounted: Soho Books (351 West Broadway) and Bleecker Street Books (350 Bleecker St)
Books, exam-study and science-fiction: Civil Service Book Shop (89 Worth St)
Books, gay and lesbian: A Different Light (151 W 19th St)
Books, Japanese: Zakka (510 Broome St)
Books, mystery: Murder Ink (2486 Broadway and 1467 Second Ave) and Partners & Crime (44 Greenwich Ave)
Books, mystical and religious: Quest Bookshop (240 E 53rd St)
Books, old and rare: Imperial Fine Books (790 Madison Ave, 2nd floor)
Books, rare: Martayan Lan (48 E 57th St)
Books, readings: Shakespeare (1 Whitehall St, 939 Lexington Ave, and 716 Broadway)

Books, religious: Paraclete Book Center (146 E 74th St)
Books, tribal art: Oan-Oceanie-Afrique Noire (15 W 39th St, 2nd floor)
Books, used and review copies: Strand Book Store (828 Broadway)
Cameras: Grand Central Camera (420 Lexington Ave)
Camera and professional movie supplies: Cine 60 (630 Ninth Ave)
Cigarettes, luxury: Nat Sherman (500 Fifth Ave)
Cigars: Arnold's Tobacco Shop (323 Madison Ave)
Comic books: Village Comics (163 Bleecker St, 2nd floor)
Compact discs, discounted: Disc-O-Rama (40 Union Sq E)
Compact discs, rock and roll: Smash Compact Discs (33 St. Marks Pl)
Compact discs, used: NYCD (426 Amsterdam Ave) and St. Marks Sounds (20 St. Marks Pl)
Computer printers, discounted: TriState Computer (650 Sixth Ave)
Computers: Computrs (7 Great Jones St)
Dance-related items: World Tone Music (230 7th Ave)
Diving equipment: Pan Aqua Diving (460 W 43rd St) and Sea Horse Divers (1416 Second Ave)
Dogs, exotic breeds: International Kennel Club (1032 Second Ave)
Dolls: Bear Hugs & Baby Dolls (311 E 81st St)
Dolls, vintage: Manhattan Dollhouse Shop (236-A Third Ave)
Dollhouses: Tiny Doll House (1146 Lexington Ave)
Drums: Drummer's World (151 W 46th St, 3rd floor)
Films, videotape (classics): Evergreen Video (37 Carmine St)
Filofax, discounted: Altman Luggage (135 Orchard St)
Fishing tackle: Orvis (355 Madison Ave)
Fly-fishing equipment: Hunting World (16 E 53rd St)
Gambling gifts: Manhattan Gaming (Manhattan Mall, 901 Sixth Ave)
Games, war: Compleat Strategist (11 E 33rd St, 630 Fifth Ave, and 342 W 57th St)
Gifts: Mxyplyzyk (125 Greenwich Ave)
Globes, antique world and celestial: George Glazer Gallery (28 E 72nd St)
Golf accessories: Competitive Edge Golf (526 W 26th St)
Golf equipment, best selection: New York Golf Center (131 W 35th St)
Guitars: Rogue Music (251 W 30th St, 10th floor) and the Guitar Salon (45 Grove St; 212-675-3236, by appointment)
Guns: Beretta Gallery (718 Madison Ave)
Handicrafts and art, imported: Sam's Souk (979 Lexington Ave)
Holographs: Holographic Studio (240 E 26th St)
Home Entertainment: J&R (23 Park Row)
Horseback-riding equipment: Miller's Harness Co. (117 E 24th St)
Jazz albums and compact discs: Jazz Record Store (236 W 26th St)
Jukeboxes: Back Pages Antiques (125 Greene St)
Kaleidoscopes: After the Rain (149 Mercer St)
Kites: Big City Kite Company (1210 Lexington Ave)
Knitting supplies: Yarn Company (2274 Broadway)
Luggage, antique: Gargoyles (200 Lexington Ave)
Luggage, soft: Bag House (797 Broadway)
Magazines: Dina News Inc. (2077 Broadway), Eastern Newsstand (MetLife Building, 200 Park Ave, and many other locations), Magazine Store (30 Lincoln Plaza), and Universal News (977 Eighth Ave and 676 Lexington Ave)
Maps: Hagstrom Map Store (57 W 43rd St)

Maps and prints, antiquarian: Argosy Bookstore (1160 E 59th St) and E Greene (361 Bleecker St)

Marine supplies: E&B Goldberg's Discount Marine (12 W 37th St)

Movie memorabilia: Warner Bros. Studio Store (1 E 57th St)

Movie-star photos: Movie Star News (134 W 18th St)

Music (all publishers): Music Store at Carl Fischer (62 Cooper Sq)

Musical instruments: Music Inn (169 W 4th St) and Sam Ash Music Store (160 W 48th St)

Needlecraft: Yarn Company (2274 Broadway)

Newspapers, out-of-town: Hotalings News Agency (142 W 42nd St)

New York history: Museum of the City of New York (1220 Fifth Ave)

Novelties (5,000 types): Gordon Novelty (933 Broadway)

Outdoor gear: Tent & Trails (21 Park Pl)

Papers, elegant: Il Papiro (1021 Lexington Ave)

Paper, sheet: Kate's Paperie (561 Broadway and 8 W 13th St)

Pens: Arthur Brown & Brother (2 W 46th St) and Menash Signatures (213 W 79th St)

Pens, antique: Arthur Brown & Brother (2 W 46th St)

Pens, discounted: Altman Luggage (135 Orchard St)

Photo supplies: Ben Ness Camera & Studio (114 University Pl)

Pipes: Connoisseur Pipe Shop (Paine-Webber Bldg, 1285 Sixth Ave)

Postcards: Art Market (75 Grand St)

Records: Tower Records (692 Broadway and 1961 Broadway)

Records, Broadway show: Footlight Records (113 E 12th St)

Records (singles): Downstairs Records (35 W 43rd St)

Records, Japanese imports: Adult Crash (66 Ave A)

Records, old rock and roll: Strider Records (22 Jones St)

Science fiction: Forbidden Planet (840 Broadway)

Sci-fi and New Age gifts: Star Magic (745 Broadway, 274 Amsterdam Ave, and 1256 Lexington Ave)

Skateboards: Supreme (274 Lafayette St)

Skateboards, offbeat: Supreme (274 Lafayette St)

Skating equipment: Blades Board and Skate (120 W 72nd St, 160 E 86th St, 1414 Second Ave, 659 Broadway, and other locations)

Snorkeling equipment: Scuba Network (124 E 57th St and 175 Fifth Ave)

Soccer supplies: Soccer Sport Supply (1745 First Ave)

Software, computer: J&R Computer World (15 Park Row)

Soldiers, lead: Second Childhood (283 Bleecker St)

Soldiers, toy: Classic Toys (218 Sullivan St)

Sports cards: Alex's MVP Cards (256 E 89th St)

Sports photos, autographed: Future Sports & Memorabilia (659 Lexington Ave)

Sports video: Famous Sports Video (32 W 39th St)

Teddy bears: Bear Hugs & Baby Dolls (1184 Lexington Ave and 311 E 81st St)

Theater items: One Shubert Alley (1 Shubert Alley)

Tobacco: J.R. Tobacco (11 E 45th St and 219 Broadway)

Toys, handmade: Dinosaur Hill (306 E 9th St) and Geppetto's Toy Box (161 Seventh Ave S)

Toys, high-quality imports: Geppetto's Toy Box (161 Seventh Ave S)

Toys, museum quality (1900-1940): Bizarre Bazaar Antiques (130¼ E 65th St, by appointment)

Toys, vintage: Alphaville (226 W Houston St), Classic Toys (218 Sullivan St), and Darrow's Fun Antiques (1101 First Ave)
VCRs, discounted: Sound City (58 W 45th St)
Videos, foreign-film: Evergreen Video (37 Carmine St)
Videotapes, hard-to-find (for sale or rent): Evergreen Video (37 Carmine St)
Winemaking supplies: Milan Home Wine and Beers (57 Spring St)
Writing instruments, great selection: Rebecca Moss (510 Madison Ave)

Things from Far Away

African handicrafts: Craft Caravan (63 Greene St)
African jewelry: Schomburg Center Gift Shop (515 Malcolm X Blvd)
British imports: 99X (84 E 10th St)
Buddhas: Leekan Designs (93 Mercer St)
Chinese antiques: Chinese Arts & Antiques (825 Broadway)
Chinese goods: Pearl River Emporium (200 Grand St) and Chinese American Trading Company (91 Mulberry St)
Chinese sandals: Phoenix Import Corporation (51 Mott St)
Egyptian & Near Eastern antiquities: Royal-Athena Galleries (153 E 57th St)
European pottery: La Terrine (1024 Lexington Ave)
Hawaiian crafts: Radio Hula (169 Mercer St)
Himalayan craft items: Himalayan Crafts and Tours (2007 Broadway)
Indian imports: Sarajo (98 Prince St)
Indonesian art: Eastern Arts (107 Spring St and 365 Bleecker St)
Irish gifts: Grafton Gifts & Baskets (30 Rockefeller Plaza)
Irish imports: Shamrock Imports (Manhattan Mall, Sixth Ave and 33rd St, 4th level)
Italian clothing and shoes: Cellini Uomo (59 Orchard St)
Japanese books, records, and art: New York Kinokuniya Bookstore (10 W 49th St)
Japanese gift items: Katagiri (226 E 59th St)
Japanese pottery: Japanese Pottery (952 Lexington Ave)
Leather items, imported: Il Bisonte (72 Thompson St and 22 E 65th St)
Middle East caftans: Paracelso (414 West Broadway)
Scottish kilts and tartars: Scottish Products (141 E 44th St, Suite 311)
Tibetan treasures: Do Kham (51 Prince St), Tibetan Handicrafts (144 Sullivan St), and Vision of Tibet (167 Thompson St)

Other Things

Astrology items: New York Astrology Center (124 E 40th St)
Birds: Bird Jungle (401 Bleecker St)
Bottles, perfume: Gallery #47 (1050 Second Ave)
Butterflies: Mariposa, the Butterfly Gallery (South Street Seaport, Pier 17, 2nd floor)
Cat memorabilia: Just Cats (244 E 60th St)
Fire memorabilia: New York Firefighter's Friend (263 Lafayette St)
Flags and banners: Art Flag Co. (8 Jay St)
Fun shopping: Orchard Street on Sundays
Globes: George D. Glazer (28 E 72nd St)
Holographs: Holographic Studio (240 E 26th St)
Nursery items, garden: Farm and Garden Nursery (2 Sixth Ave)
Office furniture, discounted: Frank Eastern Company (599 Broadway, 6th floor)

Office supplies: MOMA Design Store (44 W 53rd St) and Seventh Avenue Stationers (470 Seventh Ave)
Optical instruments: Clairmont-Nichols (1016 First Ave)
Ornaments, antique garden: Foster & Feldman (219 E 60th St)
Parrots: Urban Bird (177 West Broadway)
Pet supplies, discounted: Petland Discounts (numerous locations)
Pharmacy, complete: Windsor Pharmacy (1419 Sixth Ave)
Plate books: George D. Glazer (28 E 72nd St)
Plexiglas & Lucite: Plexi-Craft Quality Products (514 W 24th St)
Quartz and minerals: Crystal Gardens (21 Greenwich Ave)
Stone items: Modern Stone Age (111 Greene St)
Store fixtures: Liberty Display & Supply (37 W 26th St)
Surveillance equipment, covert: Counter Spy Shop (444 Madison Ave)
Thrift Shop: Everybody's Thrift Shop (261 Park Ave S)
Travel items: Civilized Traveler (864 Lexington Ave, 2003 Broadway, and 2 World Financial Center)
Typewriter ribbons: Abalon Office Equipment (227 Park Ave)

Factory Outlet Centers in the Tri-State Area

Connecticut

Clinton Crossing Premium Outlets: Over 70 outlets, including: Anne Klein, Barney's New York Outlet, Bass, Brooks Brothers, Gap Outlet, Liz Claiborne, London Fog, Nautica, Off 5th (Saks Fifth Avenue Outlet), Polo/Ralph Lauren, Waterford Wedgewood, and more. (20 Killingworth Turnpike, Clinton, CT, 860-664-0700)
Factory Outlets at Norwalk: Bed Bath & Beyond, Carter's Childrenswear, Famous Footwear, Rascals Childrenswear, and more. (230 East Avenue, Norwalk, CT; 203-838-1349)

New Jersey

Flemington Area

Circle Outlet Center: Bed Bath & Beyond, Bugle Boy, Carter's Childrenswear, Dress Barn, Dress Barn Woman, Famous Brands Housewares, Toy Liquidators and more. (Hwy 202/31, Flemington, NJ; 908-782-4100)
Feed Mill Plaza Factory Outlet Center: Barbizon, Oneida, Roman Jewelers, and Swim & Sweat (Rte 12, Flemington, NJ; 908-788-0386)
Flemington Cut Glass: Asta Cookware, Bill Healy Crystal, Flemington Cut Glass, Flemington Mill Factory Outlet, Le Cruset, Main Street Antiques (156 Main Street, Flemington, NJ; 908-782-3017)
Heritage Place: Flemington's Coat World, Jockey, Levi's, Reebok (Rte 31 at Church St, Flemington, NJ; 908-782-3414)
Liberty Village Premium Outlets: Over 60 outlets, including: Anne Klein and Anne Klein Petites, Brooks Brothers, Calvin Klein, Capezio, Carole Little, Carter's Childrenswear, Donna Karan, Geoffrey Beene, Izod, Joan & David, Mondi, Sunglass World, Totes, Villeroy & Boch, Waterford Wedgewood, and more. (1 Church St, Flemington, NJ; 908-782-8550)

Secaucus Area

Castle Road Outlet Center: Collector's Emporium, Legg's/Hanes/Bali/Playtex, Light n' Up Cook n' Store, Male Ego Fashion Outlet, Marty's Wholesale

Shoe Outlet, Prato Menswear Outlet (600 Meadowlands Parkway, Secaucus, NJ)

Designer Outlet Gallery: Adolfo II, Calvin Klein Company Store, Joan & David, J.H. Collectibles, Jones NY, Jones NY Dress, Jones NY Woman, La Chine, Executive Suite (55 Hartz Way, Secaucus, NJ)

Harmon Cove Outlet Center: American Tourister Factory Outlet, Barbizon Lingerie, Carter's Childrenswear, Geoffrey Beene, G.H. Bass Company Store, London Fog, Oneida Factory Store, Perry Ellis, Welcome Home, and more. (20 Enterprise Ave N, Secaucus, NJ; 800-358-2373)

Outlets at the Cove: Calvin Klein Company Store, Evan Picone, Maidenform, National Luggage, Nine West, Van Heusen Direct (45 Meadowlands Parkway, Secaucus, NJ)

For a free comprehensive directory of all Secaucus outlet stores, including a map, contact the Hudson Reporter, 1400 Washington Street, Hoboken, NJ 07030; 201/798-7800. Request *The Secaucus Guidebook.*

Elsewhere in New Jersey

Circle Factory Outlets: Adolfo II, Bass, Brass Outlet, Bugle Boy, Carter's Childrenswear, Chaus, Corning Revere, Geoffrey Beene, Harry & David, Izod, Jones NY, Jones NY Sport, Nautica, and more. (Rte 35 at Manasquan Circle, Wall Township, NJ; 732-223-2300)

The Marketplace I and II: Basics for a Buck, Bon Worth, Carter's Childrenswear, L'eggs/Bali/Hanes, and New Vision (Hwy 34, Matawan, NJ; 732-583-8700)

Olde Lafayette Village: Bass, Capacity, Izod, Sneaker Factory, Van Heusen (Rte 15 & 94, Lafayette, NJ; 973-383-8323)

Princeton Forrestal Village Factory Outlet Stores: Carter's Childrenswear, Casual Corner Outlet, Charter Club Outlet, Corning Revere, Famous Brands Housewares, Fragrance Cove, Geoffrey Beene, Gerry Cosby Sporting Goods, Van Heusen, Welcome Home, WestPoint Pepperell, and more. (Rte 1 at College Rd W, Princeton, NJ; 609-799-7400)

Six Flags Factory Outlets: Bugle Boy, Claire's Accessories, Donna Karan, Dress Barn, Gap Factory Store, J. Crew, Florsheim Factory Outlet, London Fog, Nautica, OshKosh B'Gosh, Timberland, Sunglass Hut, and more. (Rte 537, Jackson, NJ; 732-833-0680)

New York

Apollo Plaza Outlet Center: Banister Shoe, Barbizon, Carter's Childrenswear, Fieldcrest Cannon, Hush Puppies, London Fog, Toy Liquidators, and more. (855 East Broadway, Monticello, NY; 914-794-2010)

Bellport Outlet Center: Adolfo II, American Tourister, Anne Klein, Chaus, Corning Revere, Galt Sand, Izod, Jones NY, Liz Claiborne, Maidenform, Naturalizer, Nike, Oneida, Van Heusen, and more. (Sunrise Highway at Exit 56, Bellport, NY; 516-286-3872)

Manufacturers Outlet Center: Bass Shoe, Casual Corner Outlet, Corning Revere, Farberware, Leather Loft, Levi's by Designs, Mikasa, Socks Galore, Welcome Home, and more. (195 North Bedford Rd, Mt. Kisco, NY; 914-241-8503)

Woodbury Common Premium Outlets: More than 150 outlets, including: A/X Armani, Adidas, Ann Taylor Loft, Anne Klein, Bally Shoe Outlet, Brooks Brothers, Chaus, Corning Revere, Danskin, Donna Kara, Espirit, Etienne Aigner, Jones NY, Joan & David, Kenneth Cole, Laura Ashley, Mark Cross,

Mikasa, Polly Flinders, Rodier Paris, Woolrich, and more. (Rte 32, Central Valley, NY; 914-928-7467)

Pennsylvania

Franklin Mills: Over 200 stores, including: Baby Guess?, Guess? Nordstrom Rack, Off 5th (Saks Fifth Avenue Outlet), Neiman Marcus Last Call, and others. (1455 Franklin Mills Circle, Philadelphia, PA; 800-336-MALL)

Looking for **famous** names? Here is where to find them:

American:

Calvin Klein (654 Madison Ave)
Disney (711 Fifth Ave)
Geoffrey Beene (783 Fifth Ave)
Levi Strauss (3 E 57th St, 750 Lexington Ave)
Liz Claiborne (650 Fifth Ave)
Niketown (2 E 57th St)
OshKosh B'Gosh (586 Fifth Ave)
Ralph Lauren (867 Madison Ave)
St. John (665 Fifth Ave)
Timberland (709 Madison Ave)

English, European, and Japanese:

Aquascutum (680 Fifth Ave)
Armani A/X (568 Broadway)
Bottega Veneta (635 Madison Ave)
Burberry's (9 E 57th St)
Celine (51 E 57th St)
Chanel (15 E 57th St)
Christian Dior (712 Fifth Ave)
Diego Della Valle (41 E 57th St)
Emanuel Ungaro (792 Madison Ave)
Emilio Pucci (24 E 64th St)
Emporio Armani (110 Fifth Ave and 601 Madison Ave)
Ermenegildo Zegna (743 Fifth Ave)
Escada (7 E 57th St)
Etro (720 Madison Ave)
Fendi (720 Fifth Ave)
Gianfranco Ferre (845 Madison Ave)
Gianni Versace (647 Fifth Ave)
Giorgio Armani/Armani Couture (754 Madison Ave)
Givenchy (954 Madison Ave)
Goldpfeil (777 Madison Ave)
Gucci (585 Fifth Ave)
Guy Laroche (36 E 57th St)
Hermes (11 E 57th St)
Issey Miyake (992 Madison Ave)
Jaeger (818 Madison Ave)
Kenzo (805 Madison Ave)
Krizia (769 Madison Ave)
La Perla (777 Madison Ave)
Laura Ashley (714 Madison Ave, 21 E 57th St, 398 Columbus Ave and South Street Seaport)

Laura Biagiotti (4 W 57th St)
Les Copains (801 Madison Ave)
Liberty of London (630 Fifth Ave)
Louis Feraud (3 W 56th St)
Louis Vuitton (49 E 57th St)
Missoni (836 Madison Ave)
Prada (45 E 57th St)
Rodier (610 Fifth Ave)
Romeo Gigli (21 E 69th St)
Salvatore Ferragamo (725 Fifth Ave)
Valentino (823 Madison Ave)
Yves St. Laurent (855 Madison Ave)

Some handy information for readers who may want to shop on the Internet from a place other than their home. Visit **Virtual Emporium** (www.virtualemporium.com) on Columbus Avenue between 80th and 81st streets. Nearly 200 on-line sites are available from 16 computers at this store.

Anatomical Supplies

EVOLUTION
120 Spring St. (bet Greene and Mercer St)   212/343-1114
Daily: 11-7

Evolution is one of the most unique stores in Manhattan. This Soho emporium offers mounted butterflies and beetles, seashells, fossils, skulls and skeletons (animal *and* human!), horns, feathers, jewelry, books, and more. You've gotta see it to believe it!

MAXILLA & MANDIBLE
451-455 Columbus Ave (bet 81st and 82nd St)   212/724-6173
Mon-Sat: 11-7; Sun: 1-5

Henry Galiano grew up in Spanish Harlem. On the days his parents weren't running their beauty parlor, the family often went to the American Museum of Natural History. His interest in things skeletal increased when Galiano got a job at the museum as a curator's assistant. He soon started his own collection of skeletons and bones. That, in turn, led to his opening Maxilla & Mandible (the scientific names for the upper and lower jaw, respectively), which is the first and only such store in the world. That's understandable. How many people need complete skeletons—or even a single maxilla? Apparently more than you might think. The shop started by supplying museum-quality preparations of skulls, skeletons, bones, teeth, horns, skins, butterflies, beetles, seashells, fossils, taxidermy mounts, and anatomical charts and models to artists, sculptors, painters, interior decorators, jewelry manufacturers, propmasters, medical personnel, scientists, and educators. They also carry natural-history books, African art, Papua New Guinea art, bronze skeletal models, and scientific equipment.

Animals, Fish, and Accessories

PACIFIC AQUARIUM & PET
46 Delancey St (bet Forsyth and Eldridge St)   212/995-5895
Daily: 10-8

Goldfish are the specialty of the house, but there is much more. Pacific Aquarium & Pet carries all types of freshwater and saltwater fish, parakeets and other exotic birds, and every kind of aquarium and supply you could imagine. With adequate notice they will even come to your home and maintain the aquarium.

PETLAND DISCOUNTS
85 Delancey St	212/477-6293
132 Nassau St	212/964-1821
7 E 14th St	212/675-4102
2708 Broadway	212/222-8851
304 E 86th St	212/472-1655
404 Third Ave	212/447-0739
976 Second Ave	212/755-7228
312 W 23rd St	212/366-0512
137 W 72nd St	212/875-9785
389 Ave of Americas	212/744-1913
530 E 14th St	212/228-1363

Hours vary from store to store

The folks at the New York Aquarium recommend this chain of stores for fish and accessories. Petland also carries birds and discount food and accessories for all types of pets, including dogs and cats.

Animation

ANIMAZING GALLERY - SOHO
415 West Broadway (bet Spring and Prince St, 2nd floor)
212/226-7374
Mon-Sat: 11-7; Sun: 12-6

Animation is one of the most captivating aspects of today's entertainment world. No one is better at showing animation than Animazing Gallery. They are New York City's largest authorized Disney Art Gallery. Vintage and contemporary cels and drawings from all major studios are featured. Specialties include appraisals, consignments, searches for special pieces, and autographed books; there are also monthly gala events, shows, and sales.

Antiques

Bleecker Street Area

Pierre Deux Antiques (369 Bleecker St): French Country
Susan Parrish (390 Bleecker St): quilts

Chelsea

Chelsea Antiques Building (110 W 25th St): 150 dealers
John Koch Antiques (514 W 24th St): furniture
Poster America (138 W 18th St): vintage advertising posters
Royal de Paris Antiques and Furniture (600 W 27th St): furniture
Showplace (40 W 25th St): 100 dealers

East 60th Street Area

A. Smith Antiques (235 E 60th St): European furniture
Antiques on 60th (207 E 60th St): Renaissance religious art
Darrow's Fun Antiques (1101 First Ave): fun antiques
Luxor Gallery (238 E 60th St): 18th- and 19th-century Chinese
Paris to Province (207 E 60th St): French, English furniture
Roy Anderson (212 E 47th St): American paintings
Stubbs Books & Prints (330 E 59th St, 6th floor): books
Victor Antiques (223 E 60th St): European furniture

Lexington Avenue Area

Antiques Salon (870 Lexington Ave): clothing
Evergreen Antiques (1249 Third Ave): furniture
James Hepner Antiques (130 E 82nd St): 17th-, 18th-, and 19th-century pieces
L'Art de Viere (978 Lexington Ave): early 20th-century
S. Wyler (941 Lexington Ave): silver, china
Sylvia Pines Uniquities (1102 Lexington Ave): diverse

Madison Avenue Area

Aaron Didier (32 E 67th St): 18th- and 19th-century pieces
Art of the Past (1242 Madison Ave): East Asian
Barry Friedman (32 E 67th St): art deco
Bernard & S. Dean Levy (24 E 84th St): American furniture and silver
DeLorenzo (958 Madison Ave): art deco
Eagles Antiques (1097 Madison Ave): English Country
Fanelli Antique Timepieces (790 Madison Ave, Suite 202): antique timepieces
Florian Papp (962 Madison Ave): furniture
Gorevic & Gorevic (635 Madison Ave): jewelry
Guild Antiques II (1089 Madison Ave): English Country
J.J. Lally (41 E 57th St): Chinese art
Leigh Keno (19 E 74th St): American furniture
Linda Horn Antiques (1015 Madison Ave): eclectic
Macklowe Gallery & Modernism (667 Madison Ave): Tiffany
Marco Polo (1135 Madison Ave): silver
Navin Kumar Gallery (212/734-4075, by appointment): Asian art
Orientation Gallery (802 Madison Ave): Japanese antiques
Stair & Company (942 Madison Ave): furniture
Time Will Tell (962 Madison Ave): watches
Ursus Books and Prints (981 Madison Ave): books
W. Graham Arader (29 E 72nd St): rare prints

Midtown/57th Street/Fifth Avenue Area

Á La Vielle Russie (781 Fifth Ave): Russian art
Ares Rare (608 Fifth Ave, 6th floor): jewelry
Dalva Brothers (44 E 57th St): French furniture
Doris Leslie Blau (724 Fifth Ave, 6th floor): rugs
Fanelli Antique Timepieces (790 Madison Ave, Suite 202): clocks, watches
Gotta Have It! (153 E 57th St): celebrity memorabilia
I. Freeman & Son (60 E 56th St): silver
James Robinson (480 Park Ave): silver flatware
Martayan Lan (48 E 57th St): 16th- and 17th-century maps and prints

Newel Art Galleries (426 E 53rd St): furniture
Ralph M. Chait Galleries (12 E 56th St): Chinese art
S.J. Shrubsole (104 E 57th St): English silver

Soho

Alan Moss (436 Lafayette St): furniture
Alice's of Soho (72 Greene St): iron beds
Antiquarian Traders (399 Lafayette St): desks, dining suites
Antique Addiction (436 West Broadway): eclectic
Art & Industrial Design Shop (399 Lafayette St): 1950s items
Back Pages Antiques (125 Greene St): classic Americana
Beyond the Bosphorus (79 Sullivan St): Turkish kilims and pillows
City Barn Antiques (269 Lafayette St): Heyword-Wakefield
Cobweb (116 W Houston St): imported furniture
Cranberry Hole Road (252 Lafayette St): furniture
Crosby Studio Decorative Arts (117 Crosby St): Venetian glass
Eileen Lane Antiques (150 Thompson St): refurbished art deco
Greene Street Antiques (65 Greene St): 19th and early 20th-century furniture
Historical Materialism (125 Crosby St): 19th-century collectibles
Lost City Arts (275 Lafayette St): architectural items
Portobello Antiques (190 Sixth Ave): eclectic
Rhubarb Home (26 Bond St): furniture
T&K French Antiques (200 Lexington Ave, Room 702): French furniture
Urban Archaeology (285 Lafayette St): architectural antiques

Tribeca

Wyeth (151 Franklin St): furniture

University Place/Village Area

Donzella (90 E 10th St): 30s, 40s, and 50s furnishings
George N. Antiques (67 E 11th St): mirrors
Howard Kaplan Antiques (827 Broadway): *belle époque*
Hyde Park Antiques (836 Broadway): English antique furniture
Karl Kemp & Associates (34 E 10th St): furniture
Kensington Place Antiques (80 E 11th St): furniture
Kentshire Galleries (37 E 12th St): English antiques
L'Epoque (30 E 10th St): armoires
Little Antique Shop (44 E 11th St): formal antiques
Maison Gerard (36 E 10th St): French art deco
Philip Colleck (830 Broadway): diverse
Proctor Galleries (824 Broadway): European antiques

Upper East Side

Antiquarium (948 Madison Ave): jewelry
Bizarre Bazaar (130 1/4 E 65th St): antique toys
Galleria Hugo (304 E 76th St): 19th-century lighting
Gardner & Barr (213 E 60th St): vintage Venetian glass
George D. Glazer (28 E 72nd St): prints
Hugo Ltd. (233 E 59th St): 19th-century lighting and decorative arts
Jean Hoffman Antiques (207 E 66th St): vintage wedding gowns and veils
Manhattan Art & Antiques Center (1050 Second Ave): 100 galleries
Naga Antiques (145 E 61st St): antique Japanese screens

Upper West Side

La Belle Epoque Vintage Posters (282 Columbus Ave): advertising posters

Art Supplies
CHARRETTE
215 Lexington Ave   212/683-8822
Mon-Fri: 8:30-7; Sat: 10-5; Sun: 12-5

This branch of a Massachusetts company is for serious architects, engineers, draftsmen, graphic designers, and artists. The stock includes more than 36,000 items, which means that a practitioner in any of these fields would be hard-put *not* to find what he or she needs. Charrette offers quality supplies and good advice. Professionals will be pleased; amateurs might study the catalog first.

LEE'S ART SHOP
220 W 57th St (nr Broadway)   212/247-0110
Mon-Fri: 9-7; Sat: 9:30-6:30; Sun: 12-5:30

Ricky, the very able boss, offers her customers expanded stock of all manner of materials for amateur and professional artists; a section for architectural and drafting supplies; lamps, silk screens, and art brushes; a large selection of paper goods, stationery, pens, cards, and gifts; plus much more. Same-day on-premises framing is available, along with catalog ordering and free delivery. Designer lighting equipment and good-looking furniture are available at Lee's other stores (1755 Broadway and Third Ave at 63rd St). This place is a must-visit!

NEW YORK CENTRAL ART SUPPLY
62 Third Ave (at 11th St)   212/473-7705
Mon-Sat: 8:30-6:30

Since 1905, artists have looked to this firm for fine-art materials, especially unique and custom-made items. There are two floors of fine-art papers: one-of-a-kind decorative papers in various designs and colors, and over a hundred Oriental papers from Bhutan, China, India, Japan, Thailand, Taiwan, and Nepal. Amateur and skilled artisans will find a full range of decorative paints and painting materials. Their collection of brushes is outstanding.

PEARL PAINT COMPANY
308 Canal St (bet Broadway and Church St)
212/431-7932, 800/221-6845
Mon-Wed, Fri, Sat: 9-5:30; Thurs: 9-7; Sun: 10-5:30

If you can't find it here, it probably doesn't exist! Thirteen retail selling floors contain a vast selection of art, graphics, and crafts merchandise. Selections and services include fabric paint, silk-screening and gold-leaf items, drafting and architectural goods, a fine-writing department, and custom framing. They provide every facet of fine-art supplies at some of the best prices in town and can ship overseas. The furniture and lighting sections have been expanded. And now The Custom Frame Factory is open for business selling wall, photo, and custom frames, as well as prints and posters at discount prices. A fine gift section carries items from all over the world.

SAM FLAX

425 Park Ave (at 55th St)   212/620-3060
12 W 20th St   212/620-3038
Mon-Wed: 8:30-6:30; Thurs: 8:30-7; Fri: 8:30-6:30;
Sat: 10-6; Sun (downtown only): 12-5

Sam Flax is one of the biggest and best in the art-supply business. The stock here is enormous, the service special, and the prices competitive. They carry a full range of art and drafting supplies, gifts, pens, drawing studio furniture, and photographic products. Framing services are offered at both stores, and one-day framing is available. The store on West 20th Street is primarily devoted to furniture, but also carries a full line of art supplies.

UTRECHT ART AND DRAFTING SUPPLIES

111 Fourth Ave (at 11th St)   212/777-5353
Mon-Sat: 9-6; Sun: 12-5

We once mused about the name of this art-supply outlet, and we received a letter from a reader who pointed out that Utrecht is a city in Holland with a long tradition of arts and crafts. Fair enough, but we initially raised the question because this shop used to be called Utrecht *Linens*. In any case, Utrecht is a major manufacturer of paint, art, and drafting supplies, with a large factory in Brooklyn. At this retail store, factory-fresh supplies are sold at discounts, and the Utrecht name stands behind every purchase. Quality and prices are superb. Utrecht also carries other manufacturers' lines at impressive discounts.

Autographs

ANNA SOSENKO

25 Central Park West (bet 62nd and 63rd St)   212/247-4816
By appointment

This lady is in love with the showbiz, music, and literary worlds, and it shows. She has assembled a fine collection of letters, photos, and autographs of leading figures in these fields, offering them for sale from her home. There are plenty of stories to go with the collections.

JAMES LOWE AUTOGRAPHS

30 E 60th St (bet Madison and Park Ave, Suite 304)
212/759-0775
Mon-Fri: 9-5

James Lowe is one of the nation's most established autograph houses. Catalogs, published several times a year, make visiting the gallery unnecessary, but in-person inspections are fascinating and invariably whet the appetite of autograph collectors. There is no one specialty; the gallery seems to show whatever superior items are in stock, though there is a particular interest in historic, literary, and musical autographs, manuscripts, documents, and 19th-century photographs. The offerings range from autographed pictures of Buffalo Bill to three bars of an operatic score of Puccini's.

KENNETH W. RENDELL GALLERY

989 Madison Ave (at 77th St)   212/717-1776
Mon-Sat: 10-6 or by appointment

Kenneth Rendell has been in the business for over 30 years. He offers a fine collection of pieces from famous personages in literature, arts, politics, and the sciences. Rendell shows autographed letters, manuscripts, documents, and signed books and photographs. All are authenticated, attractively presented, and priced according to rarity. Rendell evaluates collections for possible purchase.

TOLLETT AND HARMAN
175 W 76th St   212/877-1566
By appointment only

Autographs used to be a big business in New York, perhaps because of the number of celebrities in the city. Lately, however, there are less than a handful of reliable dealers. Tollett and Harman is one of the best. They carry or will try to obtain original autographs, manuscripts, signed books, maps, and vintage photographs. Collectors of specific items can leave requests with them. (I collect presidents of the U.S. and members of the Continental Congress.) When they come across an item, they will notify you. Each item is carefully authenticated. Ask for a catalog!

Baskets

BASKETFULL
1133 Broadway (at 25th St)   212/255-6800, 800/645-GIFT
Mon-Fri: 9-5:30

When you want a basket designed with unique and innovative ideas, this is the place to call. These designers custom-create gift collections year round for special occasions, events, and holidays. For example, you could send an Indulgence basket containing Belgian chocolate truffles and chocolate pralines! Or how about a New York-style basket that includes cheesecake, deli salami, bagel chips, and an egg cream? Bake shop, Tex-Mex, get well, sympathy, and baby baskets are other options. Same-day hand delivery is available in Manhattan, and arrangements can be made for shipment anywhere in the world.

Bathroom Accessories

A. F. SUPPLY CORPORATION
22 W 21st St (bet Fifth and Sixth Ave)   212/243-5400
Mon-Fri: 8-5 and by appointment

Some might argue that the bathroom is the most important room in the house, and the folks at A. F. Supply would definitely agree. They offer a great selection of luxury bath fixtures, whirlpools, faucets, bath accessories, door and cabinet hardware, saunas, steam showers, shower doors, medicine cabinets, and spas from top suppliers.

HOWARD KAPLAN BATH SHOP
831 Broadway (bet 12th and 13th St)   212/674-1000
Mon-Fri: 9-5

Howard Kaplan presents the largest assortment of top-quality antique bath items (1890-1920) in the country. Even the setting is special: an 1870 Napoleon III building! If the bathroom is an important part of your house, then you will want to inspect the unusual French, English, and American merchandise.

SHERLE WAGNER INTERNATIONAL
60 E 57th St (at Park Ave)   212/758-3300
Mon-Fri: 9:30-5

Sherle Wagner takes an often-skirted topic and places it in the most elegant location in the city, where it rubs elbows with silversmiths, art galleries, and exclusive antique shops. The luxurious bathroom fixtures are deserving of their 57th Street location. Fixtures come in every possible material, some so striking that they make a glass display case seem like a natural setting. Prices are high, as might be expected. One warning! The displays are in the basement, and what seems like the world's slowest elevator may make you feel claustrophobic.

Beads

GAMPEL SUPPLY
11 W 37th St (bet Fifth and Sixth Ave)   212/398-9222
Mon-Fri: 9-5

This is the kind of esoteric business New York does best. The sole stock-in-trade here is beads. Just make a request, and they'll invariably have it—at a cheap price, too. While single beads go for a dollar each at a department store one block away, Gampel sells them in bulk for a fraction of that price. Though they prefer to deal with wholesalers, individual customers are treated as courteously as institutions, and the wholesale prices are offered to all. As for the stock—well, a visit to Gampel is an education. Pearlized beads alone come in over 20 different guises, and they are used for everything from bathroom curtains to earrings and flowers. Since many of its customers are craftspeople, Gampel diverges slightly from its specialty to sell a few supplies for bead-related crafts. They stock needles, cartwheels, cord (in enough colors to match each bead), threads, glues, jewelry tools, jewelry findings, and costume-jewelry parts and pieces.

Books

Animal

DOG LOVERS BOOKSHOP
9 W 31st St (bet Fifth Ave and Broadway, 2nd floor)
212/594-3601
Tues-Fri: 12-6; Sat-Mon: by appointment

This is probably the only bookshop in the world devoted exclusively to dogs. They stock new and old books on the canine family, including foxes, wolves, and coyotes. Bring in your dog and let him or her browse (or enjoy the water bowl) while you shop.

Architecture

URBAN CENTER BOOKS
457 Madison Ave (bet 50th and 51st St)   212/935-3960
Mon-Thurs: 11-7; Fri, Sat: 10-6

The Municipal Art Society is a nonprofit organization dedicated to urban planning and historic preservation. Although best known for exceptionally diverse and well-conceived walking tours, the organization runs a gallery and a bookstore in its headquarters in the north end of the elegant Villard Houses. The bookstore is among the best sources in the country for books, magazines, and journals on such topics as urban and land-use planning, architecture, and interior design. It also carries a wide selection of guidebooks to New York City.

Art

HACKER ART BOOKS
45 W 57th St   212/688-7600
Mon-Sat: 9:30-6

There can only be one "largest" in any field, and Hacker is it in art books. You'll find books on fine arts, decorative arts, architecture, and much more. They have been in business for nearly half a century. If Hacker doesn't have it, it probably doesn't exist!

PRINTED MATTER
77 Wooster St   212/925-0325
Tues-Sat: 10-6

The name Printed Matter is almost a misnomer, since the store is the only one in the world devoted exclusively to artists books—a trade term for a portfolio of artwork in book form. They stock 6,000 titles by over 2,000 artists. The result is inexpensive, accessible art that can span an entire artist's career or hone in on a particular period or theme. The idea is carried further with a selection of periodicals and audio tapes in a similar vein. Nearly all featured artists are contemporary, so just browsing through the store will bring you up-to-date on what is going on in the art world. They sell wholesale and retail; a catalog is available.

Biography

BIOGRAPHY BOOKSHOP
400 Bleecker St (at 11th St)   212/807-8655
Mon-Thurs: 12-8; Fri: 12-10; Sat: 11-11; Sun: 11-7

Here's a New York specialty shop that specializes in books of a biographical nature. If you are researching a particular person or simply have an interest in someone's life story, this is the place to find it. There are biographies, books of letters, autobiographies, diaries, journals, and biographies for children. Even fiction, too!

Children's

BANK STREET BOOKSTORE
2875 Broadway (at 112th St)
212/678-1654, 800/724-1486 (outside New York State)
Mon-Thurs: 10-8; Fri-Sat: 10-6; Sun: noon-5

Adjacent to the Bank Street College of Education, a progressive graduate school for teachers, this bookstore is a marvelous source of books for children as well as books *about* children, education, and parenting. It also has a great selection of tapes, videos, and CDs and a small section of thoughtful, educational toys. While the store is a little cramped and not conducive to snuggling up with a good book, the sales staff knows its stock and cares enormously about quality children's literature. Make sure to ask about special readings and other events for children.

BARNES & NOBLE, JR.
86th St and Lexington Ave   212/427-0686
Mon-Sat: 9-9; Sun: 11-7

Although there are Barnes & Noble, Jr. locations in Barnes & Noble bookstores throughout the city (including a particularly friendly one on the second floor of the Broadway and 82nd Street location), this store is devoted entirely to kids. In addition to being a good source for just about any children's book (and book-related items), including ones in a variety of foreign languages, Barnes & Noble, Jr. is a great place to bring young children on a cold day to browse books and sit in on a story hour.

BOOKS OF WONDER
16 W 18th St   212/989-3270, 800/345-6665
Mon-Sat: 11-7; Sun: noon-6

Owners Peter Glassman and James Carey have moved their wonderful children's book store again, this time to a bustling area that is fast becoming the heart of the used and antiquarian book market. In so doing, they've increased their space by 30%. In addition to the largest selection of Oz (as in the *Wizard of*) books in the world, the store is known for its frequent "Meet the Author" events, a newsletter, and a story hour for young children on Sunday mornings. While they are still settling in to this new space, Books of Wonder remains an enchanting place.

TOOTSIE'S
554 Hudson Street (bet Perry and 11th St)   212/242-0182
Daily: 11-6

A newcomer to the children's book scene, this warm and inviting store was started by three mothers who felt a void in their neighborhood when Books of Wonder left the West Village. In addition to a large selection of books, Tootsie's carries a variety of toys, games, puppets, tapes, and videos—all obviously chosen with great care and thought. This is very much a neighborhood store, that's nonetheless worth a special trip no matter where you're from.

Comic

ACTION COMICS
1551 Second Ave (bet 80th and 81st St)   212/639-1976
Mon-Sat: 11-8; Sun: 12-6

Here you will find the best selection of comic books and more in the city. There are new comics from all publishers, collector's comics from the 1930s to the present, new and collector's sports (and non-sports) cards, new and collector's action figures, magic cards, posters, T-shirts, and collecting supplies.

ST. MARK'S COMICS
11 St. Mark's Pl (bet Second and Third Ave)   212/598-9439
Mon: 10 a.m.-11 p.m.; Tues-Sat: 10 a.m.-1 a.m.; Sun: 11-11

This unique store carries mainstream and licensed products, as well as small-press and underground comics that are difficult to find elsewhere. They have a large selection of back issues and claim, "If it's published, we carry it." The folks here are very service-oriented and will hold selections for you. The neighborhood will provide some comic relief, too!

SUPERSNIPE COMIC BOOK EUPHORIUM
P.O. Box 502-S, Plantarium Station, New York, NY 10024
212/580-8843
By appointment and mail order
Call Fri, Sat: 10-4:30

The ultimate comic-book emporium, Supersnipe now deals only by phone and mail order. It is worth your time, however, because their stock is unequaled.

VILLAGE COMICS
215 Sullivan St (bet Bleecker and W 3rd St)   212/777-2770
Mon, Tues: 11-8; Wed: 10:30-9; Thurs: 10:30-8:30; Fri, Sat: 10-9; Sun: 11-7

118 E 59th St (bet Lexington and Park Ave, 2nd floor)   212/759-6255
Mon-Sat: 11:30-7

If you're into comics, you must visit the Village Comics stores. Here you will find just about everything in the field for all tastes and age groups. There are collector items; old and new books; limited editions; collector's cards; a large and varied adult section; model kits of comic and horror figures in resin; vinyl, and plastic; hard-to-find items; and built-up display models. Check the stores for personal appearances by comic writers and rock and film stars!

Cookbooks

CHARLOTTE F. SAFIR
1349 Lexington Ave, Apt 9B   212/534-7933
Phone anytime

If you want to add to a book collection or find out more about a particular author, this lady can save you a lot of time and effort. Charlotte Safir provides a search service for out-of-print books by mail or phone only. She has a fantastic network of contacts and can locate any kind of book, although she specializes in cookbooks and children's books. Charlotte is efficient, persistent, and a pleasure to deal with.

KITCHEN ARTS & LETTERS
1435 Lexington Ave (at 94th St)   212/876-5550
Mon: 1-6; Tues-Fri: 10-6:30; Sat: 11-6;
closed Sat in July and Aug

Cookbooks traditionally are best sellers in bookstores, and with the renewed interest in health, fitness, and natural foods, that rule of thumb is more operative than ever. So it should come as no surprise that Nachum Waxman's Kitchen Arts & Letters should be an immediate success as a store specializing in books, literature, photography, and original art about food and its preparation. Imported books are a specialty. Waxman claims his store is the only one like it in the city and one of less than ten in the entire country. Waxman is a former editor at Harper & Row and Crown publishers, where he supervised several cookbook projects. Bitten with the urge to start a specialty bookshop, he identified a huge demand for out-of-print and original cookbooks. So while the tiny shop stocks more than 10,000 titles, as well as a gallery of photography and original art, much of the business consists of finding out-of-print and want-listed books.

Foreign

LIBRAIRIE DE FRANCE/LIBRERIA HISPANICA
Dictionary Store/Learn-A-Language Store
Rockefeller Center Promenade
610 Fifth Ave (bet 49th and 50th St)   212/581-8810
Mon-Sat: 10-6:15 (sometimes Sun)

A short stroll through Rockefeller Center Promenade takes you to this unique foreign-language bookstore which has been at this same location since 1934. Inside you will find an interesting collection of French magazines and newspapers, children's books, cookbooks, best sellers, greeting cards, and recorded French music. It is on the lower level, however, where most of the treasures are found. French books are available on seemingly almost every topic. There is a Spanish bookstore, as well as French and Spanish films on video, books on cassettes, a multimedia section, books and recordings for learning more than 100 foreign languages, and a specialized foreign-language dictionary section covering engineering, medicine, business, law, and dozens of other fields. You can even arrange to rent a car for your next European trip.

NEW YORK KINOKUNIYA BOOKSTORE
10 W 49th St (at Fifth Ave)   212/765-7766
Daily: 10-7:30

Kinokuniya is Japan's largest and most esteemed bookstore chain. An American branch, located in Rockefeller Plaza, has two floors of books about Japan. The atmosphere is the closest thing to Tokyo in New York. On the first floor are 20,000 English-language books, which leave no part of Japanese culture neglected. Art, cooking, travel, language, literature, history, business, economics, management techniques, martial arts—they're all here! The rest of the floor is rounded out with books on the same subjects written in Japanese. Comic books and Japanese stationery are sold on the second floor. Kinokuniya has the largest collection of Japanese books in the city and possibly anywhere outside of Japan.

General

BARNES & NOBLE
Branches throughout Manhattan   212/807-0099
Hours vary by store

For value and selection, you can't beat these folks! Barnes & Noble and their affiliated stores offer unexcelled opportunities for book buyers and browsers, no matter what area of the city. Generations of New York students have bought textbooks at the main store (105 Fifth Avenue). Now Barnes & Noble has opened a number of magnificent superstores with enormous stocks of staples and bargains, comfortable shopping conveniences (including cafes), and a large selection of discounted magazines. Best of all, they continue to offer discounts on best sellers and other popular titles. Barnes and Noble, Jr. stores appeal to youngsters with stocks that are similarly exciting and complete.

BORDERS BOOKS AND MUSIC
5 World Trade Center   212/839-8049

461 Park Ave (at 57th St)
Mon-Fri: 7 a.m.-8:30 p.m.; Sat: 10-8:30; Sun: 11-8:30

The book business has changed drastically in the past several years. Superstores are now the name of the game, and unless the small dealer has a special location or niche in book marketing, times are not easy. Borders is one of the major chains that has recently opened in Manhattan, offering books, records, periodicals, places to read, and a coffee bar. The stock at Borders is wide and deep. There is plenty of well-informed help, and personal visits by authors have brought crowds to their downtown location.

GOTHAM BOOK MART
41 W 47th St   212/719-4448
Mon-Fri: 9:30-6:30; Sat: 9:30-6

The Gotham is a New York institution founded in 1920 by the late Frances Steloff. In the early days, as is true today, there was a heavy emphasis on poetry, arts, and the theater, because those were Steloff's passions. Steloff, who could never understand how a book could be banned, once smuggled 25 first editions of Henry Miller's *Tropic of Cancer* into the country from Paris via Mexico. She developed a deep personal interest in authors and clients alike. Even as she grew older, Steloff would always make one daily visit downstairs to the shop around 2 p.m. Steloff lived to reach the century mark; her influence on this charming store will probably live on for another century. An exceptional search service is a special attraction.

McGRAW-HILL BOOKSTORE
1221 Sixth Ave (bet 48th and 49th St)   212/512-4100
Mon-Sat: 10-5:45

This huge shop, located downstairs in the McGraw-Hill Plaza (at Rockefeller Center), is limited in fiction and general titles, but for anything published by McGraw-Hill or written with a business, technical, or scientific bent, it is excellent. One-third of their books are about computers. This is a fine, well-run store, selling professional books of all publishers.

RIZZOLI
31 W 57th St (bet Fifth and Sixth Ave)   212/759-2424
454 West Broadway   212/674-1616
3 World Trade Center   212/385-1400

Mon-Sat: 9-8; Sun: 11-7

When you talk about class in the book business, Rizzoli is right on top of the list. They have maintained on elegant atmosphere that makes a patron feel he or she is browsing a European library rather than a midtown Manhattan bookstore. The emphasis is on art, literature, photography, music, dance (particularly ballet), and foreign languages. There is also a good selection of paperbacks. Upstairs you will find Italian books, a music department, and children's books. Art objects are shown throughout the store.

SPRING STREET BOOKS
169 Spring St   212/219-3033
Mon-Thurs: 10 a.m.-11 p.m.; Fri: 10 a.m.-12 midnight;
Sat: 10 a.m.-1 a.m.; Sun: 11-10

In addition to the fun of browsing an interesting bookstore, you'll enjoy the offbeat cast of characters who are your fellow customers! They ship anywhere, will do special ordering, and offer free gift-wrapping.

STRAND BOOK STORE
828 Broadway (at 12th St)   212/473-1452
Mon-Sat: 9:30-9:30; Sun: 11-9:30;

Strand Book Annex
95 Fulton St   212/732-6070
Mon-Fri: 8:30-8; Sat, Sun: 11-8

For book lovers, no trip to New York is complete without a visit to the Strand. This fabulous institution is the largest (over 2.5 million volumes) used bookstore in the world. For New Yorkers, the Strand is the place to start looking for that volume you must have. There are carts full of bargains outside. Inside, according to George Will, the only "eight miles worth saving in New York are the shelves at the Strand Book Store." These eight miles of books are tagged at up to 85% off list price. This enormous bookstore houses secondhand, out-of-print, and rare books at heavily discounted prices. In addition, the Strand offers thousands of new books at 50% off publisher's list price, plus a huge stock of quality remainders. In the rare book rooms, indivdual titles are priced from $10 to $100,000. There is also a fine selection of more moderately priced books, including 20th-century first editions, limited signed editions, fine bindings, and art books. The store imports English remainders, sells to libraries, sells books by the foot (supplying decorators, TV networks, and hotels), and does a booming mail-order business. In October 1996, Strand Book Annex opened, adding three more miles of books. It is located three blocks east of Broadway, has 15,000 square feet, features 20-foot ceilings, and is surprisingly sunny and organized. There's even a children's reading room. Owner Fred Bass is one of the nicest and most knowledgeable individuals in the book business.

TOWER BOOKS
383 Lafayette St (at 4th St)   212/228-5100
Daily: 11 a.m.-11 p.m.

The highly successful Tower chain has now gotten into the book business in a big way. Their first bookstore on the East Coast houses over 100,000 books and 1,200 periodicals, including national and international magazines. They specialize in hard-to-find literature, art, music, and pop culture. Best sellers are 30% off, while new release hardcovers are 20% off.

WALDENBOOKS
57 Broadway (at Exchange Pl)   212/269-1139
Mon-Fri: 8-6

Walden has chosen the Wall Street area for its major operation. And what an operation it is! The store literally overflows with titles in almost every category. Befitting its location, Walden offers one of the largest selections of computer, business, and investment books in the country. They also publish the *Walden Street Journal,* a free monthly newsletter featuring new and noteworthy business and investment titles. No matter what you are looking for, Waldenbooks can satisfy your needs from a vast selection of around 50,000 titles. In keeping with their reputation as a full-service bookstore, Walden will special-order, send merchandise anywhere in the U.S., and provide expert answers to readers' questions. They also specialize in corporate purchasing and bulk discounts.

Irish

THE IRISH BOOKSHOP
580 Broadway (bet Prince and Houston St, Room 1103)   212/274-1923
Mon-Fri: 11-5; Sat: 1-4

It's the written word with an Irish accent at this shop, which sells only new and used Irish books. They are offered in both Irish Gaelic and English.

Military

MILITARY BOOKMAN
29 E 93rd St   212/348-1280
Tues-Sat: 10:30-5:30

The inventory here is limited to books of a military nature. Proprieters Harris and Margaretta Colt specialize in out-of-print and rare books on military, naval, and aviation history. At any given time there are 10,000 such titles in stock. Topics run the gamut from Attila the Hun to atomic warfare. The Military Bookman also has a large mail-order business and maintains a subscription mail-order catalog.

Music

JUILLIARD BOOKSTORE
60 Lincoln Center Plaza (65th St and Broadway, plaza level)
212/799-5000, ext 237
Mon-Thurs: 9:30-7:30; Fri, Sat: 10-6

With over 20,000 sheet music titles and scores in stock, this bookstore claims to carry *every* classical music book in print! But there is more: imprinted stationery and apparel, souvenirs, and Juilliard music adventure software.

Mystery

MURDER INK®
2486 Broadway (bet 92nd and 93rd St)   212/362-8905
Mon-Sat: 10-7:30; Sun: 11-6

1467 Second Ave (bet 76th and 77th St)   212/517-3222
Sun-Thurs: 10-9; Fri, Sat: 10-10

Mystery fans: this is your place! In addition to mystery, suspense fiction, children's mysteries, and out-of-print paperbacks, Murder Ink® stocks a large section on true crime. Kids will love the secret door, and your mystery-loving friends will have sleepless nights with their great gift baskets.

MYSTERIOUS BOOKSHOP
129 W 56th St   212/765-0900
Mon-Sat: 11-7

Otto Penzler is a Baker Street Irregular, a Sherlock Holmes fan extraordinaire (an elementary deduction!), and the Mysterious Bookshop's owner. As a result, the shop is friendly, and spontaneous conversations among customers are the norm. Mysterious stocks new hardcover and paperback books that deal with all types of mystery. ("But not science fiction," says the store manager. "Science fiction is not mystery.") Upstairs, via a winding circular staircase, the store branches out to the width of two buildings and is stocked floor-to-ceiling with out-of-print, used, and rare books. Amazingly, they seem to know exactly what is in stock. If it is not on the shelves, they will order it. There is as much talk as business conducted here, and you can continue the conversation with authors who sign privately from time to time in the back room. Mysterious carries *thousands* of autographed books.

New York

CITYBOOKS
61 Chambers St (bet Broadway and Centre St)   212/669-8246
Mon-Fri: 9-5

This city government bookstore has access to more than 120 official publications, all of which are dedicated to helping New Yorkers cope with their complex lives. *The Green Book* is the official directory of the city of New York, listing phone numbers and addresses of more than 900 government agencies and 6,000 officials. It includes state, federal, and international listings, as well as courts and a section on licenses. There is also a unique collection of New York memorabilia: city-seal ties, pins, and more.

Out-of-Print

ACADEMY BOOK STORE
10 W 18th St (nr Fifth Ave)   212/242-4848
Mon-Sat: 10-8; Sun: 11-7

Academy Book Store houses one of New York's largest selections of used, rare, and out-of-print books. Its stock is carefully selected, and new collections are acquired weekly. Academy has been in business since 1977, offering secondhand and discounted scholarly books in all subject areas. Its stock is particularly strong in art, photography, decorative arts, architecture, philosophy, psychology, history, and music. The store also maintains a selection of antiquarian books and modern first editions. The quality and diversity of the stock offer rewards for the casual browser, scholar, and collector.

Photography

A PHOTOGRAPHER'S PLACE
133 Mercer St (at Prince St)   212/431-9358
Mon-Sat: 11-8; Sun: 12-6
Mail-order address: P.O. Box 274, Prince Street Station,
New York, NY 10012

There is no doubt that photography is an art form to Harvey Zucker and the staff who run A Photographer's Place. The shop is a temple to photographers, past and present. It is not a supply shop. Rather, it pays homage to great pictures of various eras and the people who took them. The owners claim to be "the only all-photographic book shop in the city and, perhaps, the country." The shop excels at offering history, advice, inspiration, and the latest technological advances. A super catalog is free for the asking.

Rare

ALABASTER BOOKSHOP
122 Fourth Ave (bet 12th and 13th St)   212/982-3550
Mon-Sat: 10-8; Sun: 11-8

There was a time when Fourth Avenue was known as "Bookshop Row," *the* place for used books in Manhattan. All that has changed with the advent of superstores and the demise of smaller entrepreneurs. Well, Steve Crowley has bucked the trend, offering a great selection of used and rare books in all categories, ranging from a $2 paperback to a $1,000 first edition. Specialties include New York City, photography, and modern first editions.

BAUMAN RARE BOOKS
Waldorf-Astoria Hotel, 301 Park Ave (at 50th St), lobby level
212/759-8300
Mon-Sat: 10-7

Bauman offers a fine collection of books and autographs dating from the 15th through the 20th centuries. Included are works of literature, history, economics, law, science, medicine, nature, travel, and exploration. They also provide services from designing and furnishing libraries to locating books for customers.

IMPERIAL FINE BOOKS
790 Madison Ave (bet 66th and 67th St, 2nd floor)   212/861-6620
Mon-Sat: 11-6

If you are in the market for books that look as great as they read, Imperial is the place to visit. Here you will find fine leather bindings, illustrated books, vintage children's books, unique first editions, and some magnificent sets of prized volumes. Their inventory includes literary giants like Twain, Dickens, Bronte, Churchill, and Shakespeare. There is also an outstanding Oriental art gallery, featuring Chinese, Japanese, and Korean ceramics and antiques. (They will purchase fine pieces.) Services include complete restoration and binding of damaged or aged books. A search office will locate specific titles and make appraisals.

J.N. BARTFIELD GALLERIES AND FINE BOOKS
30 W 57th St, 3rd floor   212/245-8890
Mon-Fri: 10-5; Sat: 10-3 (summer hours vary)

This shop is a spectacular hunting ground for lovers of fine paintings and rare books. Since 1937 they have specialized in masters of the American West and 19th- and 20th-century American paintings and sculptures. I have purchased outstanding collections of leatherbound books from them and can vouch for their expertise. First editions, sporting books, and high-quality antiquarian books are featured. Who wouldn't be excited to browse through elegantly bound volumes by famous authors that once graced the shelves of old family libraries?

PAGEANT PRINT AND BOOK SHOP
114 W Houston St (bet Thompson and Sullivan St)   212/674-5296
Mon-Thurs: 12-8; Fri, Sat: 12-10; Sun: 12-7

A holdover from the days when this area was the rare- and old-book capital of the world, this shop displays and sometimes sells antiquarian books, maps, prints, and first editions from the 15th to the 20th centuries. I doubt that anyone inside could readily tell me what year it is, but then again the shop is as timeless as its antiquarian attitude. Pageant carries virtually every kind of printed matter. There are etchings and early printed items; it would require several days just to admire the prints. But this is a print and book shop, and the emphasis is on the latter. In the old days, this would have been one of a dozen such shops. Today, it is one of the few places left where bibliophiles can have an authentic rare book-buying experience.

Religious

CHRISTIAN PUBLICATIONS BOOK STORE
315 W 43rd St (bet Eighth and Ninth Ave)   212/582-4311
Mon-Wed: 9:30-6:45; Thurs, Fri: 9:30-7:45; Sat: 9:30-5:45

This is the largest Christian bookstore in the metropolitan area. It has over 20,000 titles in stock, along with religious CDs, tapes, videos, and church and school supplies. A large number of these items are also available in Spanish, as befits the Latino neighborhood.

J. LEVINE BOOKS & JUDAICA
5 W 30th St
212/695-6888, 800/5-JEWISH (outside New York City)
Mon-Wed: 9-6; Thurs: 9-7; Fri: 9-2; Sun: 10-5 (except July)

The history of the Lower East Side is reflected in this store. Started back in 1902 on Eldridge Street, it was a fixture in the area for many years. Now things have changed, and J. Levine has moved uptown into expanded quarters, just off Fifth Avenue. Being one of the oldest Jewish bookstores in the city, Levine is a leader in the Jewish-book marketplace. They have added a second floor with many gift items, tapes, coffee-table books, and thousands of items of Judaica, though the emphasis is still on the written word. A 100-page catalog is available!

NEW YORK BIBLE SOCIETY
139 W 57th St   212/315-0230
Mon: 10-9; Tues-Fri: 10-6; Sun: 12-2

The New York Bible Society sells the world's most popular book in over 30 languages and in all kinds of editions. They can fill large church orders or special gifts. They have the greatest variety of low-cost New International Version scriptures in the city. There are all kinds of Bibles here, from pocket-sized and giant print to audio and videotapes. There's even a children's Bible storybook.

Science Fiction

FORBIDDEN PLANET
840 Broadway (at 13th St)   212/473-1576
Daily: 10-8:30

When Mike Luckman started a science-fiction bookstore-cum-toy shop in his native London, he quickly discovered that a good percentage of his customers were Americans clamoring for a similar shop at home. Now he has designed an even more unique shop that is a shrine of science-fiction literature and artifacts. While most stock is devoted to sci-fi comic books and publications, Luckman has learned that devotees are not catholic in taste. First-edition collectors love Chewbacca face masks and bookends, and Darth Vadar fans browse the vintage comic books and fantasy art. In between, there are enough videos, posters, T-shirts, cards, toys, and games to entertain the crew of Star Trek's Starship Enterprise. There is seemingly at least one copy of every science-fiction title ever published.

SCIENCE FICTION SHOP
214 Sullivan St, #2D   212/473-3010
Mon-Fri: 11:30-6:45; Sat: 11-6: Sun: 12-6

Sci-fi fans will rate this store tops on selection. The extensive stock includes rare and want-listed literature. They have now expanded to include horror and mystery volumes, and can provide mail-order service anywhere in the world!

Sports

SPORTSWORDS
1475 Third Ave (at 83rd St)   212/772-8729
Mon-Fri: 11-6; Sat: 11-5

Now sports fanatics have a bookstore to call their own. In well-organized shelving are books on baseball, cycling, golf, soccer, auto racing, hiking, martial arts, water skiing, roller-blading, and more. If you can't find it here, it probably does not exist in the world of sports books.

Theater

APPLAUSE THEATER & CINEMA BOOKS
212 W 71st St (at Broadway)   212/496-7511
Mon-Sat: 10-8; Sun: 12-6

Quite simply, this store offers the best selection of theater and cinema books in the world. There is great interest these days in theater literature, and these folks are on the cutting edge. They specialize in both new and out-of-print plays and film scripts.

DRAMA BOOK SHOP
723 Seventh Ave (bet 48th and 49th St), 2nd floor
212/944-0595, 800/322-0595
Mon-Fri: 9:30-7 (Wed: 9:30-8); Sat: 10:30-5:30; Sun: 12-5

This shop has been providing a valuable service to the performing arts community since 1923. Its stock includes a wide variety of publications dealing with theater, film, dance, music, puppetry, magic, and more. The Drama Book Shop is known for courteous and knowledgeable service in-store or by mail.

RICHARD STODDARD-PERFORMING ARTS BOOKS
18 E 16th St (bet Fifth Ave and Union Sq), Room 305
212/645-9576
Mon, Tues, Thurs-Sat: 11-6

Richard Stoddard runs a one-man operation dedicated to rare, out-of-print, and used books, and to memorabilia relating to the performing arts. Equipped with a Ph.D. from Yale in theater history and more than 20 years of experience as a dealer and appraiser of performing arts materials, Stoddard offers a broad range of items. So while there is an extensive collection of rare books, playbills, souvenir programs, original scenic and costume designs, and back issues of performing-arts magazines, Stoddard also stocks a case of paperback plays within the financial reach of the most impoverished actor. There is a similar table of bargain books. Stoddard's pride is his collection of scenic and costume designs. The sole agent for the estate of Jo Mielziner, an esteemed Broadway designer, Stoddard is also in possession of the drawings of a half-dozen other set designers. In fact, this is the only shop in the country that regularly sells such designs.

Travel

COMPLETE TRAVELLER ANTIQUARIAN BOOKSTORE
199 Madison Ave (at 35th St)   212/685-9007
Mon-Fri: 9-7; Sat: 10-6; Sun: 11-5

The largest collection of Baedeker Handbooks is but one feature of this store which deals exclusively in rare, antiquarian, and out-of-print books pertaining to travel. The 8,000-book collection includes volumes on polar expeditions, adventure travel, and 18th- and 19th-century maps.

TRAVELLER'S BOOKSTORE
22 W 52nd St (Time-Warner Bldg, 75 Rockefeller Plaza, bet Fifth and Sixth Ave), lobby level   212/664-0995, 800/755-8728
Mon-Fri: 9-6; Sat: 11-5

Folks who travel love to read, so it is only natural that Diana Wells has collected over 11,000 travel titles in her store. She also stocks an outstanding assortment of travel guides, maps, accessories, and international fiction and nonfiction books. Quarterly newsletters and a fall catalog are available.

Butterflies

MARIPOSA, THE BUTTERFLY GALLERY
South Street Seaport, Pier 17   212/233-3221
Daily: 10-9

At Mariposa, butterflies are regarded as art. Marshall Hill is a renowned designer in this unusual medium. Butterflies are unique, and Mariposa (the Spanish word for butterfly) displays them separately, in panels, and in groups. There are even butterfly farms, which breed and raise butterflies. They live their full one-month life span under ideal conditions for creating this art.

Buttons

GORDON BUTTON COMPANY
222 W 38th St (near Seventh Ave)   212/921-1684
Mon-Fri: 9-5

Peter Gordon's extensive collection of elegant, unusual, and antique buttons is fascinating, but I would mainly come to Gordon for its new buttons. The enormous stock is used by neighboring garment manufacturers. Gordon's quality, selection, and variety are that good! Belt buckles, components, chains, and brass rings are also sold at excellent discounts. Mail orders are accepted. Courtesy is the byword. Most garment-center manufacturers cannot be bothered with small retail customers, and their attention varies in direct proportion to the size of your order. But at Gordon, the size of the order is irrelevant.

TENDER BUTTONS
143 E 62nd St   212/758-7004
Mon-Fri: 11-6; Sat: 11-5:30

Owners Diana Epstein and Millicent Safro have assembled a retail button store that is complete in variety as well as size. One antique wooden display cabinet shows off Tender Buttons' selection of original buttons, many imported or made exclusively for them. There are buttons of pearl, wood, horn, Navajo silver, leather, ceramics, bone, ivory, pewter, and precious stones—many of them antique. Some are as valuable as artwork; a French enamel button, for instance, can cost almost as much as a painting! Unique pieces can be made into special cuff links—real conversation pieces for the lucky owner. They also have a fine collection of antique and period cuff links and men's stud sets. A cuff-link buff, I have purchased some of my best pieces from this shop.

Candles

CANDLE SHOP
118 Christopher St (bet Bleecker and Hudson St)   212/989-0148
Mon-Thurs: 12-8; Fri, Sat: 12-9; Sun: 1-7

Thomas Alva Edison's inventions haven't made a flicker of an imprint on the folks at the Candle Shop. They have assembled a collection of beeswax, paraffin, and stearin candles in an assortment of sizes and colors. It's positively illuminating to learn that candles are available in so many configurations! The shop also carries candle holders and accessories, oil lamps, and incense.

China, Glassware

Big Names in Tabletop:

Baccarat (625 Madison Ave)
Bernardaud (777 Madison Ave)
Buccellati (46 E 57th St)
Cartier (653 Fifth Ave)
Christofle (680 Madison Ave)
Daum (694 Madison Ave)
Lalique (680 Madison Ave)
Orrefors (58 E 57th St)
Puiforcat (811 Madison Ave)
Royal Copenhagen/Georg Jensen (683 Madison Ave)
Villeroy & Boch (974 Madison Ave)

CRATE & BARREL
650 Madison Ave (at 59th St)   212/308-0011
Mon-Fri: 10-7; Sat: 10-7; Sun: 12-6

Even if you aren't in the market for china, glassware, bedroom furnishings, or casual furniture, the way goods are presented here will make shopping hard to resist. First, the place is loaded with attractive, quality merchandise at sensible prices. Second, it is fixtured magnificently, with every item shown to its best advantage. Third, the lighting and signing are masterfully done. Finally, the store layout and number of check-out stands make for quick work in completing a sale. These folks are professional merchants in the best sense of the word.

FISHS EDDY

889 Broadway   212/420-9020
2176 Broadway   212/873-8819
Mon-Sat: 10-8; Sun: 11-7

Besides being a treasure trove for bargain hunters, Fishs Eddy is a fun place to browse for some of the most unusual china and glassware items available anywhere. Everything is made in America, and the stock changes on a regular basis. For young people setting up a new residence or a business looking for unique pieces, try here first.

LANAC SALES

73 Canal St (at Allen St)   212/925-6422
Mon-Thurs: 9-6; Fri: 9-2; Sun: 10-5

Lanac is a great source for chinaware, cut glass, silverware, and gifts at discount prices. They have a reputation for excellent discounts on everything in stock, and that stock includes some of the finest domestic and imported tableware and crystal in the city. They have a computerized gift registry. Lanac, incidentally, is Canal spelled backward!

Clothing and Accessories

Antique/Vintage

ANTIQUE BOUTIQUE

712-714 Broadway (at Washington Pl)
227 E 59th St (bet Second and Third Ave)
212/460-8830
Mon-Thurs: 11-10; Fri, Sat: 11 a.m.-12 midnight; Sun: 12-8

With a new, hip image, both vintage and new clothing are featured here! This is the place to find recently recycled clothing, as opposed to something from the Victorian period. You will see wedding dresses from the 1940s, a big selection of used Levi jeans, suede jackets, and incredible sweaters. Prices reflect the fact that these clothes are not one-of-a-kind antiques. In the "new" class are brand names like Diesel, Betsey Johnson, Pat Fields, Tripp, and AB Collections.

HARRIET LOVE

126 Prince St   212/966-2280
Tues-Sun: 11:30-7

Harriet Love is right on the front line in the field of "new with retrofeel" apparel and accessories. Her shop overflows with beautiful alligator purses, jackets, and jewelry. Harriet also buys from vendors who interpret vintage pieces to create new treasures that have a classic feeling.

JEAN HOFFMAN ANTIQUES

207 E 66th St   212/535-6930
Mon-Sat: 12-6 or by appointment

Jean Hoffman offers one of the best selections of quality vintage items in the city. She has laces and trims, parasols, shawls, linens, jewelry, and all kinds of vintage clothing. For the bride-to-be who wants something special, the stock of wedding gowns is without equal.

REMINISCENCE
74 Fifth Ave (nr 13th St)   212/243-2292
Mon-Sat: 11-8; Sun: 12-7

It's fun to go back to the 1960s and 1970s at this hip emporium which Stewart Richer created on lower Fifth Avenue. Although he is a child of this era, most of Richer's customers are between the ages of 13 and 30. The finds here are unusual and wearable, with large selections of colorful vintage clothing and attractive displays of jewelry, hats, shoes, gifts, and accessories. Richer's goods, although vintage in style, are mostly new, and the company has become a manufacturer that sells to outlets all over the world. Because of its large distribution, Richer is able to produce huge quantities and sell at low prices.

SCREAMING MIMI'S
382 Lafayette St   212/677-6464
Mon-Fri: 11-8; Sat: 12-8; Sun: 12-6

Laura Wills presides over this shop, which features styles from the 1950s, 1960s, and 1970s, as well as more current merchandise. There are vintage housewares, an excellent showing of handbags, shoes, lingerie, and a good selection of sportswear. Most everyone agrees this is a fun place to shop!

TRASH AND VAUDEVILLE
4 St. Mark's Pl (bet Second and Third Ave)   212/982-3590
Mon-Thurs: 12-8; Fri: 11:30-8; Sat: 11:30-9; Sun: 1-7:30

This place is hard to pin down, since the stock changes constantly and seems to have no boundaries. The store describes its stock as punk clothing, accessories, and original designs. "Punk clothing" means rock and roll styles from the 1950s to the 1990s, including some outrageous footwear. They also carry new clothing from Europe.

Bridal

I. KLEINFELD AND SON
8202 Fifth Ave	8209 Third Ave
Brooklyn, NY	Brooklyn, NY
718/833-1100	718/238-1500

Tues, Thurs: 11-9; Wed, Fri: 10-6; Sat: 9-6
(call for an appointment or Sun hours)

The bridal business has changed a great deal. Today there are very limited collections at some specialty stores (like Bergdorf and Saks), but there is only one true bridal complex. I use the word *complex* because two separate buildings are involved. The half-century-old operation is called I. Kleinfeld and Son. The bridal gown collection, which has 800 to 1,000 models in stock at all times, is located at 8202 Fifth Avenue in Brooklyn. Yes, I know this is a book about Manhattan, but there is no store anywhere that can match Kleinfeld. The mother of the bride will find a special section called Kleinfeld's P.M., that specializes in evening wear. Kleinfeld carries every major name in bridal wear, including Amsale, Caroline Herara, and Scassi. One-fifth of the collection is of international origin. A separate store for bridesmaids' gowns is located several blocks away at 8209 Third Avenue. The store operates by appointment; they can handle over a hundred a day with their specialized personnel. This is the place to come when wedding bells will soon be ringing.

VERA WANG
991 Madison Ave (at 77th St)   212/628-3400
Mon-Wed, Fri, Sat: 9-6; Thurs: 10-7
(Sat: 9-5 summer or by appointment)
   Vera Wang is considered one of the top bridal designers in the nation, and this is her only salon. Be prepared for beautiful styles and beautiful prices, starting at about $2,500 and with most gowns in the $3,000-$5,000 category. Exclusive evening-wear designs may be purchased off the rack.

SIZE COMPARISON CHART FOR CLOTHES

Children's clothing

						3	4	5	6	6x
American						3	4	5	6	6x
Continental						98	104	110	116	122
British						18	20	22	24	26

Children's shoes

American	8	9	10	11	12	13	1	2	3	
Continental	24	25	27	28	29	30	32	33	34	
British	7	8	9	10	11	12	13	1	2	

Ladies' dresses, coats and skirts

American	3	5	7	9	11	12	13	14	15	16	18
Continental	36	38	38	40	40	42	42	44	44	46	48
British	8	10	11	12	13	14	15	16	17	18	20

Ladies' blouses and sweaters

American	10	12	14	16	18	20
Continental	38	40	42	44	46	48
British	32	34	36	38	40	42

Ladies' stockings

American	8	8½	9	9½	10	10½
Continental	1	2	3	4	5	6
British	8	8½	9	9½	10	10½

Ladies' shoes

American	5	6	7	8	9	10
Continental	36	37	38	39	40	41
British	3½	4½	5½	6½	7½	8½

Men's suits

American	34	36	38	40	42	44	46	48
Continental	44	46	48	50	52	54	56	58
British	34	36	38	40	42	44	46	48

Men's shirts

American	14	15	15½	16	16½	17	17½	18
Continental	37	38	39	41	42	43	44	45
British	14	15	15½	16	16	17	17½	18

Men's shoes

American	7	8	9	10	11	12	13
Continental	39½	41	42	43	44½	46	47
British	6	7	8	9	10	11	12

Children's — General

AIDA'S & JIMI'S MERCHANDISING COMPANY
41 W 28th St (bet Broadway and Sixth Ave)   212/689-2415
Mon-Fri: 9-5; Sat: call for hours

The young ladies in your family will love this place, and so will their mothers! Aida and Jimi feature better girls' dresses from infant to preteen. You may also find boys' wear from toddler to size 7 and ladies' samples in sizes 5/6, 7/8, and 9/10. All merchandise is discounted.

BABY GAP
341 Columbus Ave (at 76th St)   212/875-9196
Mon-Sat: 10-9; Sun: 11-8

If you're one of the millions of parents, grandparents, aunts, and uncles who are making Baby Gap America's premier clothier of infants and toddlers, I've got good news: the only store in the country devoted exclusively to the Baby Gap line (as opposed to Gap Kids) is on the Upper West Side. Whether you're looking for hats, dresses, overalls, coats, or such nursery aceessories as crib sheets and quilts, this is the place to find them. Because Baby Gap turns its stock over quickly, last month's stock is almost always on sale.

BOMBALULU'S
101 W 10th St (just off Sixth Ave)   212/463-0897
Mon-Sat: 11-8; Sun: 11-7

332 Columbus Ave (bet 75th and 76th St)   212/501-8248
Daily: 11-7

Owned by the same people who make much of the cheerful and durable clothing sold here, these little stores are packed with wonderful, one-of-a-kind designs for infants and children. If batik rompers, colorful hand-knit sweaters, great hats, fun T-shirts, and snowsuits from Bali (yes, Bali) sound like your taste, look around or talk to the owners about placing a special order. Bombalulu's also has a good selection of well-made toys and puzzles.

CHOCOLATE SOUP
946 Madison Avenue (bet 74th and 75th St)   212/861-2210
Mon-Sat: 10-6

Madison Avenue is overrun with clothing stores for children, most of them ridiculously expensive and entirely unimaginative. Then there's the Chocolate Soup. This wonderful store has been around for 30 years, having created a real niche for itself in the area. "The theme is color," explained the manager (and one of the store's buyers). Indeed it is. For newborns through size 14, there are bright and lively dresses, swimming suits, shorts, sweaters, and more. The Chocolate Soup also has a small selection of fun toys.

JACADI
1281 Madison Avenue (at 91st St)   212/369-1616
Mon-Sat: 10-6 (Thurs to 7); Sun: 12-5

If you're in the market for upscale French clothing for infants and children, this is the most pleasant and welcoming of the many Madison Avenue boutiques. They carry beautiful, almost doll-like clothing for infants through size 12 (14 in some cases), and are especially known for coordinated outfits that include everything down to hats and tights. They also carry shoes and a full line of baby furniture. Look for particularly good sales in January and June.

KREINEN'S
301 Grand Street   212/925-0239
Sun-Thurs: 9-5: Fri: 9-4

There is nothing fancy or even particularly interesting about this longtime Lower East Side fixture, but it's a great place to stop if you're looking for really good prices on such basics as pajamas, underwear, jeans, and coats. Carter's, Levis, and OshKosh B'Gosh are just a few of the many brands Kreinen's carries at a discount. Sizes run from infant to 14 for girls and infant to 20 for boys. The store also carries some clothing, underwear, and hosiery for adults.

MARSHA D.D.
1324 Lexington Ave (bet 88th and 89th St)   212/534-8700
Mon-Fri: 10-6; Sat: 11-6; Sun: 12-5

Marsha D.D. is one of the hottest houses in town for cool preteen clothes. You'll find clothes, shoes, and accessories for girls and boys age 7-15, including items for hard-to-fit and sometimes self-conscious youngsters. This place is both fun and interesting.

MORRIS BROS.
2322 Broadway (at 84th St)   212/724-9000
Mon-Sat: 9:30-6:30; Sun: noon-5:30

You can't be a parent or kid on the Upper West Side and not know about Morris Bros. Whether you're looking for a backpack, hat, umbrella, tights, pajamas, jeans, underwear, or clothes for gym class, this is the place to go. It doesn't claim to be anything other than a good source for basic kids' clothing and accessories at decent prices. If you're in the market for the wildly popular children's slippers called Padders, Morris Bros has a particularly good selection of them at better prices than I've seen anywhere else in New York.

PEANUTBUTTER & JANE
617 Hudson St (at W 12th St)   212/620-7952
Mon-Sat: 10-7; Sun 12-6

This store is what a friend describes as "very Village." In addition to a varied and fun selection of clothing, it carries lots of funky things like ruby slippers for children, leather jackets for toddlers, and wonderfully imaginative dress-up clothes. Indeed, almost everything here is unique to the store. Unlike a lot of children's clothing stores that older children wouldn't be caught dead in, Peanutbutter & Jane appeals both to teenagers and their younger siblings.

SPRING FLOWERS
905 Madison Ave (bet 72nd and 73rd St)   212/717-8182
Mon-Sat: 10-6

410 Columbus Ave (at 79th St)   212/721-2337
1050 Third Ave (at 62nd St)   212/758-2669
Mon-Sat: 10-6, Sun 11-6

Spring Flowers, a newcomer to the Manhattan children's clothing scene, has taken the town by storm. The clothing is French and tends toward the formal (read: beautiful and quite expensive). In fact, Spring Flowers—especially the Third Avenue location—is fast becoming a leading source of party dresses for little girls. The heart of its stock is clothing for infants and toddlers, although you can find clothing for older children here, too. Spring Flowers also sells shoes and acccssories.

Children's — Used

GOOD-BYES
230 E 78th St   212/794-2301
Mon-Fri: 11:30-5:30; Sat: 10-5; summer hours may change

This comfortable, inviting little place is a relative newcomer to the children's consignment scene. In addition to clothing (up to size 8, although the focus is on infants), Good-Byes carries strollers, car seats, bassinets, toys, and the whole range of things that go along with having a baby or small children. Everything is in good condition, and the prices are a fraction of those at retail stores. If you're interested in selling clothing or equipment, call for an appointment. You get 40% of the selling price on clothing, 50% on equipment.

SECOND ACT CHILDREN'S WEAR
1046 Madison Ave (bet 79th and 80th St)   212/988-2440
Tues-Sat: 9-5

This is the dean of children's consignment shops! Don't be put off by the hard time you may have finding this store (it's on the second floor, and you must be buzzed in) or the dingy walk up to it, because the selection and bargains are well worth your effort. The mazelike rooms of Second Act are jammed with everything imaginable: shirts, pants, belts, suits, party dresses, shoes, boots, skates, sweaters, jackets, and even videos, toys, and books. Everything is at least a third to a half off its original price. If you're interested in selling clothes, call first for an appointment. You get 40% of the selling price.

Costumes

ABRACADABRA
10 Christopher St   212/627-5745
Mon-Sat: 11-7; Sun: 12-5 (extended hours in Oct)

19 W 21st St   212/627-5194

These two stores can transform you into almost anything! They rent and sell costumes, provide theme needs, offer costume accessories, and theatrical makeup, and stock props for magic tricks. It is a gagster's heaven!

Dance Wear

CAPEZIO
1650 Broadway (at 51st St)   212/245-2130

CAPEZIO EAST
136 E 61st St (at Lexington Ave)   212/758-8833

Open seven days a week

The Capezio stores are the definitive outlets for dance, theater, and fitness paraphernalia. The shop on Broadway is the largest dance-theater retail store in the world. There is a special section for men, in addition to departments for ballet companies and theatrical shows. Capezio East reflects the East Side neighborhood and includes a well-stocked children's area.

FREED OF LONDON
922 Seventh Ave (at 58th St)   212/489-1055, 800/835-1701
Mon-Sat: 10-6 (phone orders: 10-4)

The venerable English establishment Freed of London has landed in New York, bringing with it a tradition of supplying the best and finest dance supplies. There is virtually no piece of dance gear Freed does not stock or cannot order. The store has leotards, skirts, dresses, tutus, and leg warmers, as well as ballet, jazz, tap, ballroom, character, and flamenco shoes. A list of the shop's clientele reads like a who's who of stars who have danced internationally. The store carries, as a matter of course, the complete line of regulation wear for the Royal Academy of Dancing. For those who can't stop in, a measuring chart and mail-order catalog are available. For dancers, this store is a must.

Furs

FURS BY DIMITRIOS
130 W 30th St (bet Sixth and Seventh Ave)   212/695-8469
Mon-Fri: 9-6; Sat, Sun: 10-4

This store is the best source for men's fur coats at wholesale prices. The racks are shaggy with furs of all descriptions and sizes for both genders. Prices are wholesale but go up slightly if the garment has to be specially ordered. This shouldn't be necessary, though, since the high quality off-the-rack selection is the most extensive in the city.

G. MICHAEL HENNESSY FURS
333 Seventh Ave (bet 28th and 29th St), 5th floor   212/695-7991
Mon-Fri: 9:30-5; Sat: by appointment

Furs are one item you want to be very sure of when you buy. By this, I mean you want to be sure of the people from whom you are buying. They must be reliable, honest, knowledgeable, and have the proper stock. This firm strongly fits the mold. Michael Hennessy started as an international fur trader, ran a salon in Beverly Hills, and later became fur director of Bonwit Teller and president of Maximilian Furs. His talented and charming wife Rubye is a former editor at *Seventeen* magazine and the *Philadelphia Inquirer.* These folks manufacture high-quality designer furs for women that are sold to stores around the world. These same items are also available direct to the public at great values. Best prices are for in-stock furs, particularly mink, the house specialty. Wonderful buys are available for ladies who want a mink coat or fur-lined raincoat made to order. Hennessy has the only license in the world for Givenchy furs. European ladies on the best-dressed list come to this showroom for their Givenchys. If you are in the market for a sable, be sure to speak with G. Michael Hennessy, one of the world's top sable specialists. There are new specialties: large-size furs and cashmere-with-fur coats, exclusive shearlings for men and women, more classy men's furs, and fabulous lightweight mink coats and jackets. Hundreds of my readers have been well taken care of by Rubye and Michael.

GUS GOODMAN
345 Seventh Ave (bet 29th and 30th St), 16th floor   212/244-7422
Mon-Fri: 10-6; Sat: 10-2 (Sat by appointment in summer)

Since 1918 the Goodmans have been creating fine fur styles. Now father Gus and two sons, David and Mark, are carrying on the family tradition, offering a quality collection of fur-lined and reversible fur coats and jackets for both men and women. An unusually complete selection of outerwear fabrics is available: silk, poplin, microfiber, ultrasuede, leather, and cashmere. If you have a musty old fur coat in the closet that you never wear any more, these folks will bring it back to life with a trendy design. Goodman has a full-time designer on staff and specializes in custom designs.

HARRIS FURS
333 Seventh Ave (at 29th St), 2nd floor   212/563-0079, 212/563-0080
Mon-Thurs: 9-5:30; Sat: 9-4; Sun: 9-3 (closed July)

To be in business for nearly a hundred years means that you must be doing something people like. Harris does: their coats, suits, furs, and rainwear are all excellent quality items at very acceptable prices. One of the best reasons to shop here is that most every frame can be fitted, so don't worry if you are large or small, thin or plump. Harris also provides free alterations. (Note: they are not open on Fridays.)

HARRY KIRSHNER AND SON
307 Seventh Ave (bet 27th and 28th St)   212/243-4847
Mon-Fri: 9-6; Sat: 10-5

Kirshner should be one of your first stops for any kind of fur product, from throw pillows to full-length mink coats. They re-line, clean, alter, and store any fur at rock-bottom prices. They are neither pushy nor snobbish. Harry Kirshner offers tours of the factory, and if nothing appeals to a customer, a staff member will try to draw a coat to specifications. Often, however, the factory offers a collection of secondhand furs that have been restored to perfect and fashionable condition. Many customers come in for a new fur and walk out with a slightly worn one for a fraction of what they were prepared to spend.

RITZ THRIFT SHOP
107 W 57th St (bet Sixth and Seventh Ave)   212/265-4559
Mon-Sat: 9-6 (closed Sat in July); Sun: 11-5 (Nov-Jan only)

For luxurious furs at affordable prices, no one beats the Ritz! In business for over 50 years, famous for their great prices, the Ritz is New York's department store for fur. They offer an ever-changing variety of one-of-a-kind designer furs, luxurious shearlings, and fur-lined and fur-trimmed outerwear. In addition, the Ritz has one of New York's largest selections of previously owned luxury furs at good savings. Styles run from contemporary to classic, fun to funky, and include mink, sable, fox, lynx, and more. The Ritz will buy gently used furs outright or take them on consignment. The experienced multilingual sales staff offers personal service.

Hosiery

FOGAL
680 Madison Ave (bet 61st and 62nd St)   212/759-9782

510 Madison Ave (at 53rd St)   212/355-3254
Mon-Wed, Fri, Sat: 10-6:30; Thurs: 10-8

Before Fogal came to New York from Switzerland, the thought of a Madison Avenue boutique devoted to hosiery was, well, foreign. But since opening in 1982, it's hard to imagine Manhattan without it. If it's new, fashionable, and different leg wear you're after, Fogal has it. Plain hosiery comes in over 125 hues, at last count; the designs and patterns make the number of choices almost incalculable. You might say that Fogal's has a leg up on the competition! New at Fogal are lingerie and bodywear.

LOUIS CHOCK
74 Orchard St   212/473-1929
Sun-Thurs: 9-5; Fri: 9-1

It's hard to find a classification for this store. It seems to stock a little of everything, but perhaps the old-fashioned term "dry goods" sums up the stock sold here. Louis Chock sells dry goods for the home, school, and entire family from some of the nation's best: Berkshire, Burlington, Carters, Calvin Klein, Hanes, Duofold, and Munsingwear. They specialize in hosiery and underwear. Children's nightwear is available in a large choice of colors and sizes, and there is something in the hosiery section for every member of the family. Furthermore, everything in the store is sold at a discount that begins at 25%. There is an even larger discount on items bought in quantity. Louis Chock also has a mail-order department, offering a 25% to 30% discount on everything in stock. A catalog can be obtained for $2 (refundable with first order).

M. STEUER HOSIERY COMPANY
31 W 32nd St (nr Fifth Ave)   212/563-0052
Mon-Fri: 7:45-5:20

By walking one block from Herald Square, hosiery buyers can save a bundle. M. Steuer is a wholesale operation that treats each retail customer as a wholesaler, no matter how small the order. They even speak a half-dozen languages — the better to welcome visitors to New York. They stock a huge inventory of name-brand hosiery, socks, pantyhose, and dance wear, and will fill unusual requests with aplomb.

Jeans

CANAL JEAN COMPANY
504 Broadway (off Spring St)   212/226-1130
Sun-Thurs: 11-8; Fri, Sat: 10-9

From the moment you walk past the exciting window displays, you know Canal Jean is no ordinary store. Canal Jean buys and sells the latest Soho styles and has made itself a popular place. The looks are certainly casual. Even their best new clothing stretches the meaning of sportswear, but if it's motorcycle jackets, brightly colored pants, tops, and outfits you want, this is the place to shop. A large percentage of customers are Europeans and Japanese who stock up on as many pairs of jeans as they can hoard in their suitcases and backpacks. Other clothing items include outdoor outfits, beautiful new "vintage" clothing, and military surplus—all at low prices.

Leather

BARBARA SHAUM
60 E 4th St   212/254-4250
Wed-Fri: 1-8; Sat: 1-6

Barbara Shaum does magical things with leather. She's a wonder with sandals, bags, sterling-silver buckles, belts (with handmade brass, nickel-silver, inlaid wood, and copper buckles), jewelry, attache cases, and briefcases. Everything is designed in the shop, and Shaum meticulously crafts each item using only the finest materials. She is regularly featured in leading fashion magazines.

NORTH BEACH LEATHER
772 Madison Ave (at 66th St)   212/772-0707
Mon-Fri: 10-6:30; Sat: 10-6; Sun: 12-5

If leatherwear connotes "home on the range" or some biker bar on the Village waterfront, then you are obviously unaware that leather is the flip side of fur and can be just as elegant. If you need a leather ensemble for an outing in the Mercedes, then North Beach is the place to look. The emphasis is on jackets, coats, and outerwear, but there are also suits and even skirts and dresses for women. Their leather jackets for men are just the thing to round out an outfit. But they aren't cheap.

Men's and Women's—General

ORIGINAL LEVI'S STORE
1492 Third Ave (at 84th St)   212/249-5045
3 E 57th St   212/838-2188
Mon-Wed: 10-8; Thurs-Sat: 10-9; Sun: 12-7

Would you like to order a custom-made pair of Levi jeans at just $15 over the rack price? It can be done, but just for women. They are modeled after the 512 slim fit, with tapered or boot leg, and are available in 24-35 inch waist and 24-28 inch inseam. Six colors are offered. The store measures waist, hips, rise, and inseam to make sure the fit is sexy . . . and right!

New Clothing Bargain Opportunities in Manhattan!

Off-price discount clothing shopping for both men and women has recently gotten better in Manhattan! Wise shoppers can now roam the aisles of **Syms** (400 Park Ave and 32 Trinity Pl), **Loehmann's** (161 W 16th St), and **Old Navy Clothing** (10 Sixth Ave), where there are bargains galore! **Loehmann's** carries top labels at great prices, has a return policy, and takes credit cards. There is a huge selection (particularly for men) at **Syms**, and fantastic stocks of casual wear for the whole family (including kids) at **Old Navy**. It pays to visit these stores often, as the merchandise moves rapidly and new labels and styles are constantly being shown.

AVIREX, THE COCKPIT
595 Broadway (bet Houston and Prince St)   212/925-5455
Mon-Sat: 11-7; Sun: 12:30-6

This is a fascinating store for anyone interested in flying. A fabulous collection of flight jackets, varsity leather jackets, motorcycle jackets, T-shirts, coveralls, sweaters, insignias, watches, bags, flight suits, and gift items are displayed to create an attractive aviational atmosphere.

CASHMERE-CASHMERE
840 Madison Ave (bet 69th and 70th St)   212/988-5252
Mon-Sat: 10-6; Sun: 12-5

At this shop, every possible type of cashmere clothing from all over the world is available. Weights vary, making it possible to wear cashmere year-round. The styles vary as well, reflecting different lifestyles. There's clothing for men and women, as well as cashmere accessories for the home. A visit here will make cashmere a necessity in one's life!

Cashmere is hot!

Berk (781 Madison Ave)
Cashmere-Cashmere (595 Madison Ave and 840 Madison Ave)
Loro Piana (46 E 61st St)
Malo (791 Madison Ave)
Tse (827 Madison Ave)

CHARIVARI
18 W 57th St   212/333-4040
Mon-Fri: 9:30-8; Sat: 10-6:30; Sun: 12-6

These folks learned the hard way that you can't spread your operations so thin that you don't do anything very well. Now several decades old, after ups and downs in the fashion world, they have finally consolidated operations in one store that shows a wide range from casual to designer clothes. They continue to feature high-fashion items for both men and women, much of it from a hip, urban, avant-garde point of view. Favorite labels: Dries Van Noten, Ann Demuelemeester, Nartin Margiela, and Dolce Gabbana.

DAFFY'S
111 Fifth Ave (at 18th St)   212/529-4477
Mon-Sat: 10-9; Sun: 12-7

335 Madison Ave (at 44th St)   212/557-4422
Mon-Fri: 8-8; Sat, Sun: 10-6:30

1311 Broadway (at 34th St)   212/736-4477
Mon-Fri: 10-9; Sat: 10-8; Sun: 11-6

135 E 57th St (bet Lexington and Park Ave)
Mon-Fri: 10-8; Sat: 10-7; Sun: 12-6

Daffy's describes itself as a bargain clothing outlet for millionaires. Since a lot of folks got to be millionaires by saving money, perhaps they have something going for them. Great bargains can be found here in better clothing for men, women, and children. Fine leather items are a specialty. This is not your usual "off-price" store; they have done things with a bit of flair.

FILENE'S BASEMENT
2220-26 Broadway (at 79th St)   212/873-8000
Mon-Sat: 10-9; Sun: 11-6
18th St and Sixth Ave   212/620-3100
Mon-Sat: 9:30-9; Sun: 11-6

Everyone who has shopped in Boston knows the name Filene's Basement, recognized for many years for outstanding bargains. Well, now the most famous part of the famous store (a separate entity these days) has come to New York to offer the same great bargains in brand-name goods for misses and men. The store claims 30% to 60% savings. Sometimes they are not quite that good and sometimes they are better, but you can depend on the quality. The store is easy to shop in, and there are huge stocks of merchandise in every category.

MATSUDA
156 Fifth Ave   212/645-5151
Mon-Fri: 11-7; Sat: 11-6:30

Mitsuhiro Matsuda is one of Japan's most successful fashion designers. He designs lines of business, casual, and active sportswear for men and women. There is also a line of apparel and accessory basics, including bath items, nightwear, hats, glasses, jewelry, ties, gloves, belts, socks, and shoes. Madonna and Cher are customers, so you know the place is at the forefront of fashion.

OTTO PERL HOUSE OF MAURIZIO
18 E 53rd St, 5th floor   212/759-3230
Mon-Fri: 9-5

Tony Maurizio caters to women who like the functional and fashionable tailored look of suits. Although they can copy almost any kind of garment, this house is known for coats, two- to four-piece suits, and mix-and-match combinations. This look is favored by busy executives, artists, and journalists who have to look well-dressed but don't have hours to spend dressing. They create blazers or suits in a range of 2,000 fabrics, and those in silk, linen, cotton, and solid virgin wool are sensational. In addition to women's garments, Tony can design and create coats and suits for men in the same broad range of fabrics. He promises fast service, expert tailoring, and moderate prices on everything.

OUT OF OUR CLOSET
136 W 18th St (bet Sixth and Seventh Ave)   212/633-6965
Mon-Sat:12-7; Sun: 12-6

If you had your eyes on some designer outfit a favorite TV star wore, you might run down to Out of Our Closet and see if they have it hanging on their racks. If they do, the price will be about a third of what the star paid. This goes for men, too! A tailor is on the premises. A nice feature: all leftover goods go to the Housingworks Thrift Shop.

POLO-RALPH LAUREN
867 Madison Ave (at 72nd St)   212/606-2100
Mon-Sat: 10-6; Thurs: 10-8

Ralph Lauren has captured the mood of the times, and I admit to being a Ralph Lauren fan. He has probably done as much as anyone to bring a classic look to American fashion and furnishings. His showpiece store in Manhattan, housed in the magnificent remodeled Rhinelander mansion, is fabulous. There are four floors of merchandise for men, women, and the home, beautifully displayed and expertly accessorized. You will see a much larger selection here than in any of the many specialty Polo boutiques in department stores. There are several things to be aware of, however. One is an attitude problem. I'm sure that Ralph himself would not put up with the above-it-all way some of his people greet customers who don't look like they have big bucks to spend. Then again, although the clothes and furnishings are stylish and classy, one can find items of equal or better quality elsewhere at considerably lower price tags. But shopping elsewhere is not nearly as stylish as carrying your item out in one of those popular green bags. That little monogrammed horse says something about your taste and lifestyle! Polo Sport, also done with class and flair, is across the street.

REPLAY COUNTRY STORE
109 Prince St   212/673-6300
Mon-Sat: 11-7; Sun: 11-6

How about 25 different washings and fits in jeans? Or over 45 different shirt styles? You can find both at this very attractive Soho store that features outdoor clothing. There are stacks of jackets and overalls, too, and everything you might need for a Western party! Downstairs, a cafe will take care of any hunger pangs while you shop. This is one of the better-stocked stores in the area, and prices are as comfortable as the merchandise!

Don't miss the new **Shanghai Tang** (61st St and Madison Ave) for fabulous Oriental clothing and accessories.

Men's Formal Wear

JACK AND COMPANY FORMAL WEAR
128 E 86th St   212/722-4609
Mon-Fri: 10-7; Sat: 10-4

Jack and Company rent and sell men's ready-to-wear formal wear. They carry an excellent selection of sizes and names (After Six, Lord West), and they've had a good reputation for service since 1925. In sales or rentals, Jack's can supply head-to-toe formal wear. The people here are excellent at matching outfits to customers, as well as knowing exactly what is socially required for any occasion. Same-day service is available, and the full rental price will be applied toward purchase!

ZELLER TUXEDOS
Locations throughout Manhattan:
204 Broadway, at Fulton St (2nd floor)
201 E 23rd St, at Third Ave (2nd floor)
421 Seventh Ave, at 33rd St (2nd floor)
459 Lexington Ave, at 45th St (3rd floor)
201 E 56th St, at Third Ave
1010 Third Ave, at 60th St
212/355-0707 (store hours and information)

Zeller, with locations throughout the city, provides sales and rentals of ladies' and gentlemen's formal wear. There are tuxedos, formal shirts, dresses, and accessories for big-time occasions. Top names are featured: Canali, Bill Kaiserman, Bally, Valentino, Hugo Boss, Versace, and Giorgio Armani. A special made-to-order service is available.

Men's — General

CAMOUFLAGE
141 Eighth Ave (at 17th St)   212/741-9118
Mon-Fri: 12-7; Sat: 11-6; Sun: 1-5

At Camouflage you'll find men's clothing by Pendleton, New Republic, Reiss, Hartford Shirts, and Hanro, plus private-label trousers, shirts, ties, and accessories. Prices range from reasonable (their chinos are one of the best buys in the city) to good, considering those pricey designer names. Camouflage has the ability to dress customers with a dignified but unique look. Clothing from Camouflage definitely won't blend into the wallpaper!

EISENBERG AND EISENBERG
85 Fifth Ave, 6th floor   212/627-1290
Mon-Wed, Fri: 9-6; Thurs: 9-7; Sat: 9-5:30; Sun: 10-4

The Eisenberg and Eisenberg style is a classic one that dates from 1898, the year they opened. E&E consistently offers top quality and good prices on suits, tuxedos, coats, and sportswear. They also stock outerwear, slacks, name-brand raincoats, cashmere sport jackets, and 100% silk jackets. All are sold at considerable discounts, and alterations are available. London Fog coats are featured, and no label is better known for wet-weather needs.

FACONNABLE
689 Fifth Ave (at 54th St)   212/319-0111
Mon-Wed, Fri, Sat: 10-7; Thurs: 10-8; Sun: 12-6

I am very service conscious because that was the name of the game at my family's department store, Meier and Frank, in the Pacific Northwest. Well, Faconnable has a partnership with Nordstrom, and few provide personalized service like these master merchants. All of their employees are trained by Nordstrom personnel. You will find exceptionally stylish (but not flashy) men's items: sportswear, furnishings, tailored clothing, and shoes. The collection is designed in Nice, France, by Albert Goldberg, and the New York store is the only freestanding unit in this country.

GILCREST CLOTHES COMPANY
900 Broadway (at 20th St)   212/254-8933
Mon-Sat: 7:30-5:30; Sun: 9:30-4:30

These days buying a suit means laying out a lot of dough, so it is a good idea to shop around. Gilcrest provides savings on quality brands like Perry Ellis, Hugo Boss, Zegna, Mani, Jhane, Barnes, Ungaro, Andrew Fezza, Louis Feraud, and Baumler of Germany. Their own line of clothing is available at sensible prices. The sport-coat stock is worthy of inspection, and if you are in the market for a tux, the selection is enormous. No charge for alterations!

GORSART

9 Murray St   212/962-0024
Mon-Wed, Fri: 9-6; Thurs: 9-7; Sat: 9-5:30

If you find the style and quality of Brooks Brothers or Paul Staurt appealing but the prices appalling, head to this little-known jewel. In 1921, two brothers started catering to the financial community with what was then a new twist: quality merchandise at a discount. Moe Davidson and Neil Roberts purchased the store from its founders in 1975, and they carry on the same tradition. They offer classy suits made at prices that will make you smile. These are not seconds or markdowns. In addition to suits, there is a nice selection of sportswear and furnishings, all discounted. The reason for the great prices? Simple: low overhead. You can pick up a tux for about half the department-store price, and you don't pay for tailoring unless it's a complete restructuring. They have 35 in-house tailors on the job all the time. This is a special store, fellows. No high-pressure selling or gimmicks, just value and service.

Old . . . But Not Forgotten

With comfort the key word these days in men's dressing, either for casual wear or for the office, jeans are very much in the fashion forefront. Vintage jeans are even more popular, and top names include Levi's 501 and 505, Wrangler, Big E, Red Line, and old-time Double X. One of the best places to look is **What Comes Around Goes Around,** 351 West Broadway (212/343-9303).

J. PRESS

7 E 44th St (bet Fifth and Madison Ave)   212/687-7642
Mon-Sat: 9-6

As one of New York's classic conservative men's stores, J. Press prides itself on its sense of timelessness. Its salespeople, customers, and attitude have changed little from the time of Richard Press to J. Press today. Styles are impeccable and distinguished. Blazers are blue, and shirts are button-down and straight. Even in the days when button-down collars were out, Press was a bastion of support.

L.S. MEN'S CLOTHING

19 W 44th St, Room 403   212/575-0933
Mon-Thurs: 9-7; Fri: 9-4; Sun: 10-5

L.S. Men's Clothing bills itself as "the executive discount shop," but I would go further and call them a must for fashion-minded businessmen. For one thing, their midtown location precludes a trip downtown to Fifth Avenue in the teens, which is the main area for finding men's discount clothing. Better still, as owner Israel Zuber puts it, "There are many stores selling $200 suits at discount, but we are one of the few located in mid-Manhattan that discount the $475 to $975 suits." The main attraction, though, is the tremendous selection of executive-class styles. Within that category a man could almost outfit himself entirely at L.S. Natural. Soft-shoulder designer suits are available in all sizes. A custom-order department is now available with over 2,500 bolts of Italian and English goods in stock. Custom suits take about four to six weeks and sell for about $495. This is one of the top spots for top names. I would make it number one on the midtown shopping itinerary.

MOE GINSBURG
162 Fifth Ave (at 21st St)   212/242-3482
Mon-Fri: 9:30-7 (Thurs until 8); Sat, Sun: 9:30-6

Yes, Virginia, there was a Moe Ginsburg. Now even though he is history, the family carries on the tradition of providing brand-name men's clothing from American and European designers. You have to go upstairs, but the bargains are worth it! Alterations are available at a modest cost.

NAPOLEON
Trump Tower (Fifth Ave at 57th St)   212/759-1110
Mon-Sat: 10-6

Trump Plaza
1048 Third Ave (at 62nd St)   212/308-3000
Mon-Fri: 10-7; Sat: 10-6:30

Plaza Hotel Lobby
768 Fifth Ave   212/759-8000
Mon-Sat: 10-6:30

Napoleon carries clothes fit for a king—at kingly prices, too! You will find an extensive selection of handmade suits and jackets with high-fashion Italian tailoring in luxurious fabrics of cashmere and wool, many exclusive to this house. Great-looking shirts (they should be at those prices!) are done in the best Egyptian cottons. Leather goods by Zilli, handmade shoes of exotic skins and leathers, and a good showing of evening wear and accessories round out the appeal of this shop, where informed, professional service is the byword.

PAN AM SPORTSWEAR AND MENSWEAR
50 Orchard St (bet Grand and Hester St)   212/925-7032
Sun-Wed: 9-6; Thurs: 9-8; Fri: 9:30-3 (winter); 9-5 (summer)

With more stores like this, the Lower East Side could become synonymous with class as well as bargains. From the shiny glass windows (as opposed to the clutter of hangers that usually denotes an entrance) to the extremely fine stock (a big selection of Italian suits), Pan Am is distinctive enough to be on Madison Avenue, except for its prices. They are nothing short of super! Perry Ellis, Mani by Giorgio Armani, Polo by Ralph Lauren, and Andrew Fezza are but a few of the names that adorn the racks. Prices are at least a third off that of the uptown shops. What's more, styles are *au courant;* they often preview here first, and they're in classic good taste. Finally, the prompt and courteous sales help is a major exception to the Lower East Side norm.

PAUL STUART
Madison Ave at 45th St   212/682-0320
Mon, Tues, Wed, Fri: 8-6:30; Thurs: 8-7; Sat: 9-6; Sun: 12-5

This is the store for shoppers who don't really know what they want, have trouble putting things together to make a "look," and worry about quality. You would be hard-pressed to find a better selection of men's and women's fine apparel and accessories; however, there is little excitement here, either in the presentation or merchandise. The men's suits, ties, and sport jackets are first-class, as is the collection of handmade English shoes.

ROTHMAN'S
200 Park Ave S (at Union Sq)   212/777-7400
Mon-Wed, Fri: 10-7; Thurs: 10-8; Sat: 9-6; Sun: 12-5
(closed Sun in summer)

Forget your mental picture of the old Harry Rothman store. Harry's grandson, Ken Giddon, runs this classy men's store, which offers a huge selection of quality clothes at discounts of up to 40% in a contemporary and comfortable atmosphere. He carries top names like Canali, Hickey-Freeman, Corneliani, Joseph Abboud, Calvin Klein, and Valentino. Sizes at Rothman's range from 36 to 50 in regular, short, long, and extra long. Raincoats, slacks, sport jackets, and accessories are stocked at the same attractive prices, as are Kenneth Cole and Cable and Co. shoes.

SAINT LAURIE
350 Park Ave   212/473-0100
Mon-Fri: 9-6:30; Sat: 9:30-6

Big news here! Saint Laurie, one of the better priced clothing outlets in the city, has moved to a space just as unique as their former store on Broadway. They offer good-looking made-to-measure clothing for men and women at rack prices. Their new "Abbatte System" supposedly eliminates much of the trial and error typical of most custom clothiers. Saint Laurie buys directly from the weavers, thereby eliminating the markup of a fabric jobber. Shirts, haberdashery, and accessories are also available.

SOSINSKY'S
143 Orchard St (bet Delancey and Rivington St)   212/254-2307
Mon-Thurs: 10-5; Fri: 10-3; Sun: 9-5
(closed Fri in July and Aug)

Three generations of the Sosinsky family have been in business at this same location for nearly eight decades. This says something for the bargains offered on men's dress and sport shirts, sweaters, and robes by such famous names as Arrow and Alexander Julian. Unlike many of their neighbors, these folks are polite and helpful and will provide first-quality or irregular (always marked) merchandise at 25% to 50% or more off uptown prices. The Alexander Julian sport-shirt selection is especially complete, both in variety and value.

Men's Hats

J.J. HAT CENTER
310 Fifth Ave (at 32nd St)   212/239-4368, 800/622-1911
Mon-Sat: 8:45-5:45

If you can't find the hat you want here, it probably does not exist. This outfit stocks over 15,000 pieces of major-brand merchandise from all over the world. Founded in 1911, it is New York's oldest hat shop. Special services include free brush-up, and hat-stretching or tightening, as well as custom orders and a free catalog. Hats and caps up to size 8 are available.

VAN DYCK HATTERS
94 Greenwich Ave   212/929-5696
Mon-Fri: 7:30-6; Sat: 9-4

The quintessential hatter, Van Dyck is the first choice for anything that has to do with men's hats in New York. Since 1940, Van Dyck has been known for the quality of its own brand, which it manufactures and sells. Van Dyck also discounts Stetsons at a minimum of 25%. No matter what the brand, Van Dyck can also clean, block, re-style, re-band, or renovate any hat brought in.

Men's Shirts

MARK CHRISTOPHER
26 Broadway (at Wall St)   212/509-2355
Mon-Fri: 10-6; Sat by appointment

When it comes to custom shirts for well-dressed executives or upwardly mobile types aspiring to the big time, manager Mark Lingley is the guy to see. The classy shirts here are made of fine cotton and are hand-cut with superb tailoring. Of course you pay for this kind of special merchandise, but the service (he will make office calls) and the care (the usual shirt requires about 20 measurements for a fitting) are worth the extra bucks. Shirts are the foundation of the operation, but suits and ties are also available.

PENN GARDEN SHIRT CORP
63 Orchard St (at Grand St)   212/431-8464
Sun-Wed, Fri: 9-6; Thurs: 9-8

Penn Garden is the accessory store related to G&G International, which handles the men's clothing field. You'll find quality accessories here at 30% to 40% off normal retail.

SHIRT STORE
51 E 44th St (bet Vanderbilt and Madison Ave)   212/557-8040
Mon-Fri: 8-6:30; Sat: 10-5

The attraction here is that you buy directly from the manufacturer, with no middle man to increase the price. The Shirt Store offers all-cotton shirts for men, from the smallest (14x32) to the largest (18½x37). Although the ready-made stock is great, they will also do custom work and even come to your office with swatches. Imagine excusing yourself from the rest of the office crew to have your shirt-maker take some measurements! Additional services include mail-order, alterations, and monogramming.

VICTORY, THE SHIRT EXPERTS
125 Maiden Lane   212/480-1366, 800/841-3424
Mon-Fri: 8:30-6 (Sat, Sun in season)

Victory manufactures and retails their own all-cotton ready-to-wear and made-to-measure shirts. In their new facilities they will taper, shorten, alter, or monogram any shirt to individual specifications. Sizes run from 14x32 to 18½x36. There is also a good assortment of ties, cuff links, and belts. Periodic sales make their already reasonable prices even more attractive.

Men's Ties

GOIDEL NECKWEAR
138 Allen St (bet Rivington and Delancey St)   212/475-7332
Sun-Fri: 9-5 (9-3 on Fri)

Since 1935 this has been *the* place for bargains on ties, cummerbunds, men's jewelry, and accessories. They triple as manufacturers, wholesalers, and retailers, so the savings are passed on to customers. Special note to groups: these folks will match most items brought in, usually within a week or two.

Men's Underwear

UNDER WARES
210 E 58th St (bet Second and Third Ave)
212/838-1200, 800/237-8641
Mon-Fri: 10-7; Sat: 10-6; Sun: 12-5

It used to be that the average fellow couldn't tell you what kind of underwear he wore and probably didn't even buy it himself. All that changed when ads began featuring Jim Palmer and other celebrity jocks. These days men's underwear makes a fashion statement. Ron Lee's shop sells over a hundred styles of briefs and boxer shorts. It is the largest selection of men's undergarments in the world, many with top labels. There are also T-shirts, hosiery, robes, pajamas, workout wear, swimwear, and gift items. If you are shy about browsing all the sexy styles, call for one of their free catalogs.

Men's Western Wear

BILLY MARTIN'S
810 Madison Ave (at 68th St)   212/861-3100
Mon-Fri: 10-7; Sat: 10-6; Sun: 12-5

If Western wear is on your shopping list, head right to Billy Martin's, where you will find a great selection of deerskin jackets, shirts, riding pants, skirts, Western hats, and parkas. They also have one of the best collections of boots in the city for both men and women. Great accessory items like bandannas, jewelry, buckles, and belt straps complete the outfit. The items are well-tooled, well-designed, and priced accordingly.

Resale

ALLAN & SUZI
416 Amsterdam Ave (at 80th St)   (212/724-7445
Mon-Sat: 12-7

Now this is quite a store! Under one roof you'll find current designer and vintage clothing for men and women, old and new shoes, and accessories in what is called a "retro clothing store." There are some big names (like Galliano, Lacroix, Ungaro, and Versace) and some new ones you haven't heard of. Some outfits are discounted. They are proud of the fact that they dress a numher of Hollywood and TV personalities. Ask for Allan Pollack or Suzi Kandel.

DESIGNER RESALE
324 E 81st St (bet First and Second Ave)   212/734-3639
Mon-Wed, Fri: 11-7; Thurs: 11-8; Sat: 10-6; Sun: 12-5

Gently worn (whatever that means) is the byword here! Designer Resale offers previously owned ladies' designer clothing and accessories at moderate prices. Most major fashion names are represented; you might find Chanel, Armani, Hermes, or Valentino garments on the racks. If items do not sell, prices are further marked down. Call to find out what the latest bargains are.

ENCORE
1132 Madison Ave (bet 84th and 85th St, upstairs)   212/879-2850
Mon-Wed, Fri: 10:30-6:30; Thurs: 10:30-7:30; Sat: 10:30-6; Sun: 12-6
(closed Sun from July to mid-Aug)

Because it is so chic and select, Encore can honestly be billed as a "resale shop of gently worn clothing of designer/couture quality." When one sees the merchandise and the clientele at this shop, which is nearly a half century old, you'll see why. For one thing, it is a consignment boutique, not a charity thrift shop. Its donors receive a portion of the sales price, and according to owner Carole Selig, many of the donors are socialites and other luminaries who can't afford to be seen in the same outfit twice. Selig can afford to be picky, and so can you. The fashions are up-to-date and are sold at 50% to 70% off original retail prices. At any time, there are over 6,000 items in stock. Prices range from reasonable to astronomical, but just think how much more they sold for originally!

GENTLEMEN'S RESALE
303 E 81st St (bet First and Second Ave)   212/734-2739
Mon-Fri: 11-7; Sat: 10-6; Sun: 12-5

Now gentlemen who are interested in top-quality designer suits, jackets, and sportswear have a place where they can save a bundle of cash. Shopping here is like a treasure hunt, and that is half the fun. Isn't an Armani suit that originally sold for $1,000 and is now tagged at $200 worth the effort? You might also earn a few extra bucks by consigning some of your own current-style merchandise here.

KAVANAGH'S
146 E 49th St (bet Third and Lexington Ave)   212/702-0152
Mon-Fri: 11-7; Sat: 11-5 (closed Sat in summer)

Here is a designer resale shop for which I can vouch highly! It is owned by Mary Kavanagh, whom I had the pleasure of knowing and working with at Bergdorf. She has superb taste! As former director of personal shopping, she had access to the finest labels in the world. Here she carries many of those same labels: Chanel, Versace, Valentino, Ungaro, Armani, Galanos, Beene, Blass, Oscar de la Renta, and many more. Chanel clothes and accessories are a specialty. Mary describes her store as a sunny, happy spot filled with attractive antiques. You will describe it is as a classy shopping haven where customers come first. Moreover, she will open early, stay late, or open on Sunday for special groups.

PRETTY PLUS PLUS
1309 Madison Ave (bet 92nd and 93rd St)   212/427-4724
Mon, Tues, Fri: 11-6; Wed, Thurs: 11-7; Sat: 10-5

Do you often wonder what large-size models and opera stars do with clothing that is hardly ever used? It goes to this shop for resale. Pretty Plus Plus is the only resale store in Manhattan that caters solely to full-figured women. They will put a whole look together!

WHAT COMES AROUND GOES AROUND
351 West Broadway (bet Broome and Grand St)   212/343-9303
Daily: 11-8 (summer 11-11)

If you are looking for vintage clothing, here is a good place to start. This shop (with the clever name) offers one of the nation's largest collection of vintage clothing, with Levis, denim, and leather a specialty. They are also in the market to buy at all times.

Shoes — Children's

EAST SIDE KIDS
1298 Madison Ave (bet 92nd and 93rd St)   212/360-5000
Mon-Fri: 9:30-6; Sat: 9-6

Here's an answer for adults with small feet! East Side Kids stocks footwear items up to a woman's size ten and a man's size nine. They can accommodate older children and juniors, plus all the moms and dads who need smaller than standard sizes. Of course, there is also a great selection of children's shoes in both domestic and imported styles. Frequent-buyer cards are kept on file for special discounts. The store is known for helpful service.

LITTLE ERIC SHOES
1331 Third Ave (at 76th St)   212/288-8987
Mon-Fri: 10-7; Sat: 10-6; Sun: 12-6

1118 Madison Ave (at 83rd St)   212/717-1513
Mon-Sat: 10-6; Sun: 12-5

This is the place to find shoes for your small fry. They are comfy, with many lined in soft leather. You'll note that most of the "in" styles are made in Italy. The staff here are just as colorful as the shoes they sell!

RICHIE'S DISCOUNT CHILDREN'S SHOES
183 Ave B (bet 11th and 12th St)   212/228-5442
Mon, Tues, Thurs-Sat: 10-5; Sun: 10-4

Richie's offers your children's feet a one-of-a-kind experience. The decor is old, but the stock includes the latest shoes at a fraction of the prices found anywhere else. Brands include Stride Rite, Jonathan Bennett, Babybotte, Blue Star, Jumping Jacks, and Keds sneakers. You can rest assured that the fit will be extraordinary. Considerable time is spent with each customer. For each pair of shoes sold here, another sale is forfeited. Reasons include telling a customer that a child's old shoes are still good! The one drawback is the neighborhood. Gentrification hasn't yet reached this block of the East Village.

SHOOFLY
465 Amsterdam Ave (bet 82nd and 83rd St)   212/580-4390
42 Hudson St (bet Duane and Thomas St)   212/406-3270
Mon-Sat: 11-7; Sun: 12-6

Shoofly carries attractive and reasonably priced imported shoes for infants to 14-year-olds. But there are lots of women with tiny feet who have a difficult time finding an adequate selection of footwear. Look no further. Shoofly will take care of your needs with delightful styles and sizes, both funky and classic.

Shoes—Family

BUFFALO CHIPS BOOTERY SOHO
116-A Greene St (bet Spring and Prince St)   212/274-0651
Mon-Sat: 11-7; Sun: 12-6

The best of the West comes East! You'll be all set for a dude-ranch visit or plain old Western comfort and ambience with the wall art, Indian and contemporary Western jewelry, leather items, artifacts, pottery, rugs, and blankets from this attractive outlet. Best of all are the unique Western boots, all designed by store personnel. They can produce custom-made boots in about ten weeks.

E. VOGEL BOOTS AND SHOES
19 Howard St (one block north of Canal St, bet Broadway and Lafayette St)   212/925-2460
Mon-Fri: 8-4:30; Sat: 8-2
(closed Sat in summer and first two weeks of July)

The Vogels—Hank and Dean—and Jack Lynch are the third and fourth generations to join this family business (since 1879). They will happily fit and supply made-to-measure boots and shoes for any adult who can find the store. Howard is one of those streets that even native New Yorkers don't know exists. Many beat a path to Vogel for top-quality shoes and boots, personal advice, excellent fittings, and prices that, while not inexpensive, are reasonable for the service involved. The fit is not to be taken lightly, for made-to-measure shoes do not always fit properly. At Vogel, they do. Once you have a shoe pattern on record, they can make new shoes without a personal visit and will ship anywhere. For top craftsmanship, this spot is top-drawer. There are more than 600 Vogel dealers throughout the world, but this is the grandfather store and the people here are super.

KENNETH COLE
597 Broadway (at Houston St)   212/965-0283
353 Columbus Ave (bet 76th and 77th St)   212/873-2061
95 Fifth Ave (at 17th St)   212/675-2550
Mon-Sat: 11-8; Sun: 12-7

In addition to a hearty laugh at the expense of some well-known personalities (by signs), Kenneth Cole offers quality shoes, belts, scarves, watches, outerwear, and accessories, all at sensible prices.

LEACH-KALE
1261 Broadway (at 31st St), Suite 815-816   212/683-0571
Mon-Fri: 9-5

While some custom-shoe craftsmen are determined to prove that their product can and should be owned by every man, Andre S. Feuerman of the Leach-Kale Company is not among them. Perhaps he has been burned by too many bargain hunters who thought the gap between a high-class shoe salon and Leach-Kale couldn't be as great as it is, or by customers who think that at Leach-Kale's price a pair of shoes should cure all their orthopedic problems for life. Feuerman is careful to point out this is not the case. The business has customers who have been loyal patrons for 40 years, and these are the people Feuerman would rather court. They have neither unrealistic expectations nor impossible dreams but appreciate the quality items that Leach-Kale produces. They specialize in orthopedic work, which is probably why many customers pay the price without batting an eye. Shoes start at about $1200 for the first pair, but some first orders and all subsequent orders can be substantially less.

LORD JOHN'S BOOTERY
428 Third Ave (bet 29th and 30th St)   212/532-2579
Mon-Fri: 9-8; Sat: 10-7

John and son Mike Kyriannis operate Lord John's Bootery, which was originally founded by John's father over 40 years ago. Lord John's Bootery was renovated and expanded in the summer of 1994. They currently carry a wide selection of quality brand shoes and boots for men and women, discounted by 10% to 30%. Some of the well-known brands of casual and dress shoes offered are: Timberland, Rockport, Ecco, Bass, Sebago, 9 West, Kenneth Cole, Santana, Aerosoles, Clarks, Keds, Anna Clogs, Carlo Morandi, Birkenstock, Rieker, Theresia, Paul Green, and Minnetonka. Lord John's Bootery also carries a good selection of Western boots by Justin, Dan Post, Acme, and more.

T.O. DEY
9 E 38th St   212/683-6300
Mon-Fri: 9-5; Sat: 9-1

For years I have included T.O. Dey because they are a good, fancy, jack-of-all-trades operation. Though their specialty is custom-made shoes, they will also undertake repairs on any kind of shoe. These folks will create both men's and women's shoes based on a plaster mold of a customer's feet; their styles are limited only by a client's imagination. They make arch supports and cover shoes to match a garment, and they also sell sports shoes for football, basketball, cross-country, hockey, boxing, and running. Downhill ski boots, too!

If you have large feet, these outfits will cover them well:

Johnston & Murphy: men's to size 15 (115 Broadway and 351 Madison Ave)
Kenneth Cole: men's to size 16, women's to 11 (95 Fifth Ave, 597 Broadway, and 353 Columbus Ave)
Stapleton Shoe Co: men's to size 18 (68 Trinity Pl)

Shoes—Men's

CHURCH ENGLISH SHOES
428 Madison Ave (at 49th St)   212/755-4313
Mon-Fri: 9-6:30; Sat: 9-6; Sun: 12-5

Anglophiles have a ball here, not only because of the *veddy* English atmosphere but for the pure artistry and "Englishness" of the shoes. Church has been selling English shoes for men since 1873 and is known for classic styles, superior workmanship, and fine leathers. The styles basically remain unchanged year after year, although new designs are occasionally added as a concession to fashion. All are custom-fitted by shoe salesmen. If a style or size does not feel right, Church's will special-order what you want.

MCCREEDY AND SCHREIBER
213 E 59th St (bet Second and Third Ave)   212/759-9241
Mon-Sat: 9-7; Sun: 12-6

37 W 46th St (bet Fifth and Sixth Ave)   212/719-1552
Mon-Sat: 9-7; Sun: 11-5

How about a department store for shoes and boots? Here is one that features
Lucchese, Tony Lama, Frye, Justin, and Timberland boots, as well as Bass,
Alden, and Allen-Edmonds shoes. There are boots in large sizes (like 14 and
15), and prices are competitive.

STAPLETON SHOE COMPANY
68 Trinity Pl (at Rector St)   212/964-6329
Mon-Thurs: 8-6; Fri: 8-5

Their motto is "better shoes for less," but that doesn't begin to cover the
superlatives that Stapleton deserves. Gentlemen, here is *the* place to get Bally,
Alden, Allen-Edmonds, Cole-Haan, Timberland, Rockport, Johnston Murphy,
and a slew of other top names at a discount. Stapleton is located on the same
block as the American Stock Exchange, near the World Trade Center. There
probably isn't a better source for quality shoes anywhere. They are size
specialists, carrying 5-18 and A-EEE.

TO BOOT
256 Columbus Ave (at 72nd St)   212/724-8249
Mon-Sat: 12-8; Sun: 1-6

Bergdorf Goodman Men
Fifth Ave at 58th St (main floor)   212/339-3335
Mon-Wed, Fri: 10-7; Thurs: 10-8; Sat: 10-6

To Boot presents high-quality men's footwear for the sophisticated urban man.
They carry casual, dressy, and business shoes in fine leathers, suedes, and
exotics. Exclusive designer shoe collections from Prada, Gucci, and Dolce &
Gabbana are available at the Bergdorf-Goodman location.

Shoes — Women's

ANBAR SHOES
60 Reade St (bet Church St and Broadway)   212/227-0253
Mon-Fri: 9-6:30; Sat: 11-6

Bargain hunters rejoice! After years of searching through the dusty decor
at their former store, Anbar customers can find the same great bargains on brand-
name styles at discounts as high as 80%, but in a clean new setting! This is
a good place to save money.

GIORDANO'S SHOES
1150 Second Ave (at 60th St)   212/688-7195
Mon-Fri: 11-7; Sat: 11-6

Susan Giordano has a very special clientele. Giordano stocks a fine selection of women's designer shoes in small sizes (a range that is nonexistent in
regular shoe stores). If you're a woman with a shoe size in the 4 to 6 medium
range, you are probably used to shopping in children's shoe departments or
having shoes custom-made, either of which can cramp your style. For these
women, Giordano's is a godsend.

MARK JORDAN
23 W 36th St (bet Fifth and Sixth Ave)   212/714-2929
Mon-Fri: 10-6; Sat: 12-4

Ladies' shoes are very expensive these days, but here is a place that can save you big bucks on designer merchandise from Italy, France, and Spain. Popular names and bags can be discounted up to 85% (don't count on that figure for most) on names like Bruno Magli, Charles Jourdan, Anne Klein, and Calvin Klein. Sizes run from 5-10M and 7-9N.

PETER FOX SHOES
105 Thompson St (bet Prince and Spring St)   212/431-6359
Mon-Sat: 11-7; Sun: 12-6

806 Madison Ave (at 68th St)   212/744-8340
Mon-Wed, Fri, Sat: 10-6; Thurs: 10-7; Sun: 12-5

Peter Fox was the downtown trailblazer for women's shoes. Everything sold in the two shops is exclusive, limited-edition designer footwear. Perhaps because of the original Soho location, Fox's designs seem more adventurous than those of its competitors; the look is younger and more casual than it is with other designers. For those looking for shoes to be seen in, Sonny (Upper East Side) and Helga (downtown) are the people to see. Bridal and special-occasion shoes are available at both stores.

TALL SIZE SHOES
3 W 35th St (at Fifth Ave)   212/736-2060
Mon-Wed, Fri, Sat: 9:30-6; Thurs: 9:30-7

Finding comfortable shoes if you are a "tall size" is not easy. This store can solve the problem, as they carry a broad selection of shoes, sizes to 15, widths from 4A to extra-wide. There are custom-made shoes and designer names to choose from: Nichels, Via Spiga Vanelli, Sesto Meucci, Bandolino, Glacee, Evan Picone, and many more. They also have a Cinderella department with a wide selection of shoes in sizes 1 to 4-1/2. They will take phone orders and ship anywhere.

Sportswear

GERRY COSBY AND COMPANY
Madison Square Garden
3 Pennsylvania Plaza (at 32nd St and Seventh Ave)   212/563-6464
Mon-Fri: 9:30-7:30; Sat: 9:30-6; Sun: 12-5

There's a lot to like about this company. Located in the famous Madison Square Garden lobby, they are a professional business in an appropriate venue for "team sportswear"—as in what athletes wear. Gerry Cosby designs and markets protective equipment and is a top supplier to shoppers of professional licensed products. The protective equipment and bags are designed for professional use but are available to the general public as well. They accept mail and phone orders for all, including personalized jerseys and jackets.

GISELLE SPORTSWEAR
143 Orchard St (bet Delancey and Rivington St)   212/673-1900
Sun-Thurs: 9-6; Fri: 9-3

Women's designer sportswear, current season goods, at discount prices. This sums up the reasons Giselle is one of the more popular shopping spots on the Lower East Side. All merchandise is first quality only. It's worth a trip.

HOWARD SPORTSWEAR
295 Grand St (bet Eldridge and Allen St)   212/226-4307
Sun-Fri: 9-5

Howard was transformed from a typical Lower East Side shop into a fashionable boutique without sacrificing Lower East Side prices. They carry an excellent selection of men's sportswear and women's wear, including top names like Damon, Countess Mara, Members Only, and Pierre Cardin. For women, choose from Hanes, Bali, Wacoal, Vanity Fair, Warners, Maidenform, and Jockey.

NIKETOWN
6 E 57th St (bet Fifth and Madison Ave)   212/891-6453
Mon-Fri 10-8; Sat: 10-7; Sun: 11-6

Nike is an Oregon outfit, so of course I'm prejudiced in their behalf. They have created a mystique second to none in the athletic shoe and clothing business, and head honcho Phil Knight is a promotional genius. His new store in the heart of the high-rent district is different, to say the least; the effect is spectacular. In a building inspired by old school gyms, these folks show an immense line of shoes, numbering 1,200 in all, and hundreds of Nike clothing and accessory items on five selling floors. It's an experience!

Surplus

CHELSEA ARMY AND NAVY
110 Eighth Ave (bet 15th and 16th St)   212/645-7420
Mon-Wed, Sat: 10-6:45; Thurs, Fri: 10-7:45; Sun: 12-5:45

VILLAGE ARMY AND NAVY
328 Bleecker St (at Christopher St)   212/242-6665
Mon-Wed: 10-7:45; Thurs-Sat: 10-8; Sun: 1-6:45

These stores are among the best sources for camping supplies, durable clothes, and outdoor equipment at reasonable prices. They specialize in 501 Levis; sweat outfits; Timberland, Nike, and Rockport shoes; Schott leather jackets; and Champion and Russell athletic sportswear.

KAUFMAN SURPLUS
319 W 42nd St (bet Eighth and Ninth Ave)   212/757-5670
Mon-Wed, Fri: 11-6; Thurs: 11-7; Sat: 12-6

Kaufman's has long been a favorite among New Yorkers and visitors alike for its extensive selection of genuine military surplus from around the globe. Over the last half-century, Kaufman's has outfitted dozens of Broadway and TV shows and supplied a number of major motion pictures with military garb. The store is a treasure trove of military collectibles, hats, helmets, dummy grenades, uniforms, and insignias. Over a thousand military pins, patches, and medals from armies the world over are on display.

Sweaters

BEST OF SCOTLAND
581 Fifth Ave (bet 47th and 48th St, penthouse)   212/644-0403
Mon-Sat: 10-6

Two real pluses here: one of the largest collections of cashmere sweaters around and prices that are really competitive. There is a big difference between cashmere from Scotland and the Far East. Best of Scotland carries only the Scottish best in sweaters, scarves, mufflers, and blankets for both men and women. Ladies can find sizes up to 48; large gentlemen (those in the 6'6", 300-pound class) will find sweaters up to size 62! A variety of cableknit sweaters is an added attraction.

GRANNY-MADE
381 Amsterdam Ave (bet 78th and 79th St)   212/496-1222
Mon-Fri: 11-7:30; Sat: 10-6; Sun: 12-5

Granny Bert Levy's grandson, Michael Rosenberg, has assembled an extensive collection of sweaters for young people, from infants to size 14. Handmade cableknit sweaters from Uruguay sit beside ones that are hand-loomed right here at home. The selection of women's sweaters, knitwear, suits, dresses, skirts, slacks, and accessories is unique, as are the men's sweaters and novelty T-shirts. A new plus: moon and star cookies, from a recipe passed down through three generations! Granny must be looking down from heaven with pride!

Thrift Shops

East 20s:

Center Thrift Shop (124 E 28th St; 212/683-3070)
Everybody's Thrift Shop (261 Park Ave, at 20th St, 212/674-4298)
Goodwill Superstore (220 E 23rd St; 212/447-7270)
Gustavus Adolphus Thrift Shop (155 E 22nd St; 212/674-0739)
Help Line Thrift Shop (382 Third Ave; 212/532-5136)
Repeat Performance (220 E 23rd St; 212/684-5344)
Salvation Army Thrift Store (212 E 23rd St; 212/532-8115)
St George's Thrift Shop (61 Gramercy Park N; 212/260-0350)

East Side:

Arthritis Foundation Thrift Shop (121 E 77th St; 212/772-8816)
Bryn Mawr Book Shop (502 E 79th St; 212/744-7682)
Call Again Thrift Shop (1711 First Ave; 212/831-0845)
Cancer Care Thrift Shop (1480 Third Ave; 212/879-9868)
Council Thrift Shop (246 E 84th St; 212/439-8373)
Housing Works Thrift Shop (202 E 77th St; 212/879-4555)
Irvington Institute for Immunological Research Thrift Shop (1534 Second Ave; 212/879-4555)
Kavanagh's (146 E 49th St; 212/702-0152)
Memorial Sloan-Kettering Thrift Shop (1440 Third Ave; 212/535-1250)
Michael's (1041 Madison Ave, at 79th St; 212/737-7273)
Out of the Closet Thrift Shop (220 E 81st St; 212/472-3573)
Spence-Chapin Thrift Shop (1430 Third Ave; 212/737-8448)
Stuyvesant Square Thrift Shop (1704 Second Ave; 212/831-1830)
Thrift & Things (1871 Second Ave; 212/876-7223)

T-Shirts

EISNER BROS.
75 Essex St (bet Grand and Delancey St)
212/475-6868, 800/426-7700
Mon-Thurs: 9-6:30; Fri: 9-3; Sun: 9-5

Here you will find a full line of NBA, NFL, NHL, MLB, and other character and novelty products in T-shirts and sweat shirts. Major quantity discounts are offered; single pieces are also available. You will also find police, fire, emergency, and sanitation department logos, as well as Disney and Harley-Davidson. Personalizing is featured on all items. They are the largest source in the area of blank, printable, and embellishable sportswear.

Umbrellas

UNCLE SAM
161 W 57th St (bet Sixth and Seventh Ave)
212/582-1976
Mon-Fri: 9:30-6:15; Sat: 10-5

This is a New York specialty store at its very best. Uncle Sam sells canes and services, re-covers, and customizes umbrellas. There are umbrellas for children, golfers, photographers, fashion models, travelers, chauffeurs, doormen, and beachgoers. All are carved, sewn, and assembled by hand. Uncle Sam also sells umbrella accessories and remakes old umbrellas and canes.

Uniforms

DORNAN
653 Eleventh Ave (bet 47th and 48th St)
212/247-0937; outside New York State: 800/223-0363
Mon-Wed, Fri: 8:30-4; Thurs: 8:30-6

Dornan is the largest supplier of chauffeur uniforms in the country, and they carry many other lines of work uniforms as well. This includes outfits for butlers, maids, beauticians, hospital workers, doormen, bellboys, bartenders, chefs, flight attendants, pilots, firemen, police, doctors, nurses, and . . . you get the picture. They have been in the business for over seven decades, so they know what they are doing. Dornan is capable of setting up a uniform program, screenprinting, designing, customizing, and distributing outfits anywhere.

JA-MIL UNIFORMS
92 Orchard St (at Delancey St)   212/677-8190
Mon-Fri, Sun: 10-5

This is *the* bargain spot for those who wear uniforms and do not want to spend a fortune on work clothes. There are outfits for doctors, nurses, and technicians, as well as the finest domestic uniforms and chef's apparel. Dansks clogs and SAS shoes are available in white and colors. Mail orders are accepted.

Women's Accessories

FINE AND KLEIN
119 Orchard St (at Delancey St)   212/674-6720
Sun-Fri: 9-5

The finest handbag store for value and selection is not in Rome, Paris, or London. It is not even on Fifth Avenue in New York. It is on the Lower East Side, and the name is Fine and Klein. What a selection! There is a bag for every purpose, any time of day, in every fabric. Top labels are sold for a fraction of what you would pay uptown. Besides, shopping at Fine and Klein is fun. The crowds, especially on Sundays and holidays, are so great that the number of persons allowed to enter is controlled! My good friends Julius Fine and Murray Klein are the epitome of old-time merchants, and you will be delighted with their service. Tell them I sent you!

HYUK BAGS
39 W 29th St   212/685-5226
Mon-Thurs: 7:30-6; Fri: 7:30-5; Sat: 7:30-1

Hyuk K. Kim runs an importing company exclusively devoted to handbags. Importing and wholesaling companies are common in this area. What is uncommon is the courtesy and selection Kim gives individual retail customers. She has a knack for making everyone feel like a valued customer and does not take offense when a finicky lady picks through the entire stock in search of the right handbag. Besides, it shouldn't be too hard to find, within certain guidelines. "Imported" here usually refers to origins from points west rather than east. Hyuk seems to import every type of handbag—leather, vinyl, canvas, and nylon. Most of this is average, serviceable stuff. But there are a few stars in the line, and prices border on magnificent.

J.S. SUAREZ
450 Park Ave (bet 56th and 57th St)   212/753-3758
Mon-Fri: 9:30-6; Sat: 10-5:30

J.S. Suarez has been in business for nearly half a century (three generations). In that time, he has made his reputation by selling name-brand bags at a 30% to 50% discount. Copies of name-brand bags go for even better prices. For years, Suarez was *the* source for unlabeled Gucci bags that sold for less than half the price and were identical to the real thing (naturally, since they came from the same factory). He discounts name brands as well as "fake" (read "unlabeled") Bottega Veneta, Celine of Paris, Chanel, Fendi, and Hermes items. There is also a great selection of exotic skins. Suarez delivers top quality, great service, good selection, and excellent prices to all customers.

P. CHANIN
152 Eighth Ave (bet 17th and 18th St)   212/924-5359, 800/P CHANIN
Mon-Sat: 12-8; Sun: 2-6

Just one word describes this place: eclectic! There is a fascinating collection of unusual accessory items for men and women: fashion watches, Hypnotic hats (the largest selection in the country), jewelry, and attractive handmade items from local artisans. If you want raves from guests at a weekend party in the Hamptons, stop here first.

ST. REGIS DESIGNS
58 E 7th St (bet First and Second Ave)   212/533-7313
Daily: 9-7

From this unlikely spot in the East Village, Andrew Pelensky—who used to work for a top handbag designer—turns out handmade, original custom-designed handbags and belts from the finest leathers, including snake and alligator skins. The workmanship is magnificent, and items can be custom-ordered. For the quality, prices are downright cheap. It's the personal touch, like a final fitting before a belt leaves the premises, that makes St. Regis special.

Women's Evening Wear

TAMARA BOUTIQUE
15 E 71st St (bet Madison and Fifth Ave)   212/628-0902
Mon-Sat: 9:30-5:30 (closed Sat in July and Aug)

If you are looking for dinner, cocktail, evening, sportswear or business apparel that isn't carried in every other store in town, then Tamara is worth a try. Exclusive Italian knits are their specialty. Individual attention in the choice of garments and alterations is a tradition here. Naturally, you pay for the personal interest and the exclusive designs, but if it is a once-in-a-lifetime event, why not go for the best?

Women's — General

BETSEY JOHNSON
248 Columbus Ave (bet 71st and 72nd St)   212/362-3364
130 Thompson St (bet Prince and Houston St)   212/420-0169
251 E 60th St (at Second Ave)   212/319-7699
1060 Madison Ave (at 80th St)   212/734-1257
Hours vary by store

In the 1960s and 1970s, Betsey Johnson was *the* fashion designer. Her designs appeared everywhere, as did Betsey and her personal life. As an outlet for those designs not sold to exclusive boutiques, Betsey cofounded Betsey Bunky Nini, but her own pursuits led to more designing and ultimately a store in Soho. The Soho store proved so successful that Betsey moved first to larger quarters and then up and across town, as well as into such department stores as Bloomingdale's. While her style has always managed to be avant-garde, it has never been way-out. Johnson believes in making her own statement, and each store seems unique, despite the fact she has over 20 of them across the country. Prices, particularly at the Soho store (which started as an outlet), are bearable. Incidentally, it's hard to overlook the shops: pink, with neon accents and great windows.

BEVERLY M.
By appointment only   212/744-3726

The special edge here is that Beverly Madden will make and design clothing just for you, from skirts and blouses to jackets and evening pants. Delivery usually takes two to three weeks (depending on fabric availability), but the waiting time can be shortened if you are a Manhattan visitor. Personal interest and patience are the rules of the house.

CHELSEA ATELIER
128 W 23rd St (bet Sixth and Seventh Ave)   212/255-8803
Mon-Sat: 12-7; Sun: 12-5

This unusual store sells comfort in a big way. They design, make, and sell one-size-fits-all clothing for women. Best of all, their items have no buttons, zippers, or any other kind of closures. They carry great items in sizes 6-20 for maternity and post-maternity moms, and for those who just like to be able to expand a bit after a big dinner or a chocolate binge. Everything is made in natural fabrics, like crepe de chine silk, raw silk, silk velvet, Flax by Angelheart, cotton, rayon, and wool. You have to put on their clothes to grasp the appeal, because they don't show that well on hangers.

EILEEN FISHER
314 E 9th St   212/529-5715
521 Madison Ave (bet 53rd and 54th St)   212/759-9888
341 Columbus Ave (bet 76th and 77th St)   212/362-3000
103 Fifth Ave (at 18th St)   212/924-4777
1039 Madison Ave (at 79th St)   212/879-7799
Open every day; hours vary by store

For the lady who likes her clothes cool, loose, and casual, look no further than Eileen Fisher. This talented designer has put together a collection of easy-care, natural-fiber outfits that travel well and will be admired for their simple and attractive lines. The colors are earthy. From a small start in the East Village to five units all over Manhattan and space in some of the best stores, Eileen has produced a winner. The East Village store features discounted merchandise, plus first-quality goods.

FORMAN'S
82 Orchard St (regular sizes)
94 Orchard St (petite sizes)
78 Orchard St (plus sizes)   212/228-2500
Sun-Wed: 9-6; Thurs: 9-8; Fri: 9-4

59 John St (all sizes)   212/791-4100
Mon-Wed: 7:30-6:45; Thurs: 7:30 a.m.-7:45 p.m.; Fri: 7:30-5;
Sun: 11:30-5:30

145 E 42nd St (bet Lexington and Third Ave) (all sizes)   212/681-9800
Mon-Thurs: 8-7:30; Fri: 8-4:30; Sun: 10-5

Forman's has a well-deserved reputation for being the "fashion oasis of the Lower East Side." You'll find trendy sportswear, separates, and outerwear from such famous houses as Evan Piccone, Jones NY, Kasper, and Liz Claiborne at discount prices in sizes that will satisfy petites, normal figures, and plus-size women alike. The stock changes rapidly, so periodic visits are in order.

GALLERY OF WEARABLE ART
34 E 67th St   212/425-5379
Tues-Sat: 10-6 (closed Sat and open Mon in summer)

The best phrase to describe this innovative business is "anti-trendy." The Gallery of Wearable Art carries what is probably New York's largest collection of unusual clothing, jewelry, and accessories from all over the world. It is primarily a cottage industry, with a specialty in creating and designing special-occasion and bridal wear, plus all the accessories that go with the main item. If you are looking for unusual evening gowns, cocktail suits, bridal alternatives for nonclassic weddings, attractive jewelry, one-of-a-kind art jackets in antique textiles, and lace collage ensembles, make this your destination. You can even create your own gown. One thing is for sure: you won't see similar apparel on a friend or relative!

LAURA ASHLEY
398 Columbus Ave (at 79th St)   212/496-5110
Mon-Wed: 11-7: Thurs, Fri: 11-8; Sat: 11-7; Sun: 12-6

Laura Ashley has a new look . . . and it is a more contemporary one, mixed with the classic theme that has been so popular over the years. In trying to target a younger audience, she's designed some exciting new fashions. Dresses for infants and children are a sure grandma pleaser. There are also home furnishings, fabrics for wallpaper and curtains, and bolt fabrics.

LEA'S DESIGNER FASHION
119 Orchard St   212/677-2043
Mon-Fri: 9:30-5; Sun: 9-5

You don't have to pay full price for your Louis Feraud, Albert Nipon, or other famous designer dresses and suits if you head to this popular Lower East Side outlet. Lea discounts her merchandise up to 30% and sells the previous season's styles for 50% to 60% off. Don't expect much in the way of amenities, but you'll save enough here to afford a special dinner to show off your new outfit!

MENAGE A TROIS
799 Madison Ave (at 67th St), 2nd floor   212/532-3850
Mon-Fri: 9-5:30

Couture-to-go is the buy word here. Customers are treated to custom-fitted clothes that are cut, stitched, and sewn individually. There are beautiful cocktail dresses, silk jersey tops, handknit sweaters, and other one-of-a-kind pieces for the shopper who doesn't want to wait for her own stylish custom garment.

MIRIAM RIGLER
14 W 55th St   212/581-5519
Mon-Sat: 10-6 (Thurs: 10-7)

Miriam Rigler is the quintessential ladies' dress shop. They seem to have it all—personal attention, expert alterations, wardrobe coordination, custom designing (including bridal), and a large selection of everything from sportswear to knits to evening gowns, in sizes from 4 to 20. Also featured: custom headpieces, traditional and non-traditional bridal gowns, and mother-of-the-bride outfits. Despite the location, all items are discounted, including special orders that are not in stock. This store meets all of my criteria for the very best. Don't miss the costume jewelry!

NICOLINA OF NEW YORK
247 W 46th St   212/302-NICO
Mon-Sat: 10-8; Sun: 10-6

Theater people love this unique store, located in the midst of the Theater District, which features modern copies of old pieces made with charm and imagination. Vests and ties made of old kimonos and designed by the owner are a special feature of a stock that includes all manner of accessories and novelty ready-to-wear. An added incentive is the staff, who are as much fun and as consumer-friendly as the clothes.

PALMA
521 Broome St (at Thompson St)   212/966-1722
Tues-Sat: 12:30-7: Sun: 1-5

To have been in business in the Soho area for over two decades is a tribute to good retail practices. And that is exactly what you get at Palma, a store whose personnel design and make women's clothing from a large selection of styles and fabrics. Once your measurements are on file, you can easily reorder different items of clothing.

S&W
Coats:
287 Seventh Ave (at 26th St)

Bags, shoes, accessories:
283 Seventh Ave (at 26th St)

Dresses, sportswear:
165 W 26th St (at Seventh Ave)

212/924-6656
Mon-Wed: 10-6:30; Thurs: 10-8; Fri: 10-4; Sun: 10-6

Each location of S&W features a specialty, as indicated above. While the source of supply isn't entirely clear, S&W is one of the best places in the city for ladies' designer clothing. Clothing orders include elegant and top-of-the-line garments only. (The suedes and leathers in the coats and suits are magnificent.) Unlike so many other discount boutiques, S&W maintains a consistent level of quality. You won't uncover the buy of the year; the discount is a minimum of 40%, but 40% off a $300 suede suit still takes a bite out of a working girl's budget. On the down side, they would hardly win my "service with a smile" award.

SHULIE'S
175 Orchard St (bet Stanton and Houston St)   212/473-2480
Sun-Fri: 9:30-5:30

You probably don't think of Orchard Street as the place for designer clothes or shoes, but think again. Look uptown in some of the fancier shops for top-label clothing, shoes, and accessories, then phone or come down to Shulie's. The merchandise will be the same, but the shopping bag, ambience, and (most important) the price will be very different. A full line of Tahari designer clothing is available at comfortable prices. Special orders are taken, and service is above the norm for this area.

SPITZER'S CORNER STORE
101 Rivington St   212/477-4088
156 Orchard St   212/473-1515
Sun-Thurs: 9:30-5:30; Fri: 9:30-3:30

Spitzer's on Rivington is a Lower East Side landmark. There are two good reasons for shopping at these stores: excellent selection and terrific prices. On the down side, you have to put up with less than helpful salespeople, unmarked merchandise, and, at the Rivington store, three rooms jammed with goods. Be especially careful in any store that does not mark its merchandise; make sure you're getting the best price possible. A bit of "bargaining" may be necessary. Now that you know both sides of shopping here, you'll be able to get some great bargains and have a memorable shopping experience. Good luck.

TG-170
170 Ludlow St (bet Houston and Stanton St)   212/995-8660
Tues-Sun: 12-8

You won't see the clothes carried here in any other store. That is because most of the merchandise at TG-170 is from individuals who make small quantities especially for this store. This store started as a studio to make baseball hats and T-shirts, but has graduated into a retail showroom that displays really unique garments from young and emerging designers.

Women's Large Sizes

Large-Size Ladies, Take Note

You have finally come into your own with separate large-size clothing lines from some of the top names in the fashion world, including Ellen Tracy, Carol Little, Jones of NY, Liz Claiborne, and Eileen Fisher. Special departments can now be found at **Macy's, Bloomingdale's, Saks,** and (of course) the **Forgotten Woman** and **Ashanti.**

ASHANTI
872 Lexington Ave (bet 65th and 66th St)   212/535-0740
Mon-Wed, Fri, Sat: 10-6; Thurs: 10-8; Sun: 11-5

Its name is a throwback to the days when ethnic boutiques were popular in Manhattan, but Ashanti's current image couldn't be more in vogue. Today, Ashanti carries better dresses, clothing, and accessories solely for the larger woman. What they can't buy, they will have made to order. In fact, says Bill Michael, 75% of his merchandise is of Ashanti's own design and manufacturing. The craftsmen who work exclusively for Ashanti, adds Sandra Michael, are often supplied with patterns as well as designs, since the field is so new. There is more to large sizes than letting out seams or sewing up caftans in polka-dot polyester. For the first time, boutiques are operating on the belief that big ladies deserve a positive, stylish fashion image. Ashanti will do alterations and ship anywhere. It may be the only place that carries classic, quality clothing to size 28. There is even a bargain basement.

FORGOTTEN WOMAN
888 Lexington Ave (at 66th St)   212/535-8848
60 W 49th St   212/247-8888
Mon-Wed, Fri, Sat: 10-6; Thurs: 10-7:30

The Forgotten Woman was the first store in New York devoted exclusively to larger-size women. Over the years manufacturers have realized the possible market here, and this store stocks the best garments for the mature figure. Sizes range from 14 to 24. This is a store where "forgotten women" will really feel wanted!

Special New York Sale Information: Dial 212/55-SALES

Women's—Maternity

MADISON AVENUE MATERNITY AND BABY BOUTIQUE
1043 Madison Ave (bet 79th and 80th St), 2nd floor   212/988-8686
Mon-Fri: 10-7: Sat 10-6; Sun 11-5

The atmosphere here is definitely the worst of Madison Avenue, which is to say that the salesperson a female friend of mine encountered spent five minutes in a private, whispered conversation on a cellular phone before asking very disinterestedly if my friend had any questions. But the clothing, mostly a French line with lots of muted colors and luxurious fabrics that is exclusive to the boutique, is absolutely beautiful. If you're expecting and are willing to spend a lot of money on your wardrobe, you can't find a better place to shop.

MATERNITY WORKS
16-18 W 57th St, 3rd floor   212/399-9804
Mon-Wed: 10-7; Thurs: 10-8; Fri-Sat: 10-6; Sun: noon-6

Don't let the 57th Street address fool you: there are lots of good bargains to be had at this maternity outlet chain. It carries sportswear, career clothes, and even party dresses with such labels as A Pea in the Pod, Mimi Maternity, and MothersWork. (The folks at Mimi Maternity, by the way, swear that you won't find anything at Maternity Works with their label for less than it sells at their store, unless it's a second or returned item.) Things are a bit jumbled here and the elevator ride up is among the most claustrophobic in New York, but you can save a lot by visiting this store. Maternity Works also offers nursing bras and tops, sleepwear, and underwear.

MIMI MATERNITY
2005 Broadway (at 69th St)   212/721-1999
Other locations throughout Manhattan
Mon-Thurs: 10-8; Fri-Sat: 10-7; Sun: noon-5

This national chain is well-stocked with reasonably priced, good-quality maternity clothing for home and office. If you're looking at maternity clothes for the first time, rest assured that the salespeople know what you should be looking for and how to think about sizing. There's nothing particularly exciting at Mimi Maternity, but it's a good source for fashionable basics.

MOM'S NIGHT OUT
970 Lexington (bet 70th and 71st St)   212/744-MOMS (6667)

Ever wonder what pregnant women do when they need a formal dress for just one occasion? If you don't have the money or the inclination to spend hundreds or even thousands for that one special dress, call these folks. They advertise themselves as "New York's only store specializing in the rental of elegant evening and special occasion clothes for the stylish mom-to-be," and they do indeed have a tremendous selection for quite reasonable prices. One caveat: don't just wander into this place off the street without calling first for an appointment, lest you catch the staff unprepared to give you their full attention.

Women's Millinery
CARLOS NEW YORK HATS
By appointment   212/869-2207

Ladies will find unique and very specially designed handmade hats in this establishment, which is open by appointment only. Bridal party millinery is a specialty, and Carlos Lewis personally guarantees all work.

HAT SHOP
120 Thompson St (bet Prince and Spring St)   212/219-1445
Tues-Sun: 12-7 (special hours by appointment)

In case you haven't been following the fashion news, hats are "in" again! Why? First, they are stylish. Second, with all the concern about skin cancer, women want the top of their heads covered. This store has capitalized on the trend, offering custom sizing, a wide selection of colors and styles, and prices from $15-500, with a broad selection in the middle range. If you are looking for a full-service millinery outlet, this is it!

MANNY'S MILLINERY SUPPLY COMPANY
26 W 38th St   212/840-2235
Mon-Fri: 9-5:30; Sat: 9-4:30

Manny's is another New York institution. They carry millinery supplies, and that's an understatement. Row after row of drawers is dedicated to a particular aspect of head adornment. The section for ladies' hatbands alone takes up almost a hundred boxes and runs the gamut from thin pearl lines to wide leather Western-style belts. They have rhinestone banding and an enormous selection of artificial flowers and feathers. The center of the store is lined with tables displaying accumulated odds and ends, as well as several bins of larger items that don't fit in the wall drawers. At the front, hat forms can be found on hat-tree stands and sample hats are displayed in no particular order. Manny's will help fix up any hat with interchangeable decorations. Manny's also sells completed hats, close-outs, and samples, and they will even re-create an old hat.

PAUL'S VEIL AND NET
42 W 38th St (bet Fifth and Sixth Ave)   212/391-3822
Mon-Fri: 8:30-4; Sat: 8:30-2

The mob scene here is repeated up and down the block, and even that is a mere fraction of the bridal business nationwide. Unbelieveable! Despite the competition from its neighbors (or perhaps because of it), Paul's is my first-choice recommendation for any bride-to-be who wants to put together her own bridal headpiece. Although they deal in illusion (lace, that is), they are one of the few stores on the block that does not maintain the illusion that they are a wholesale-only outfit, doing the lowly retail customer a big favor by unbarring the doors. The staff at Paul's seems genuinely glad to see you—glad to share your joy and help create a truly unique bridal veil or crown. The store stocks all that's needed by the rest of the bridal party, as well as unusual accessories, bridal supplies, and a great collection of imported floral headpieces. The lucky bride will find both the selection and savings extraordinary.

Women's Undergarments

A. W. KAUFMAN
73 Orchard St (bet Broome and Grand St)   212/226-1629
Sun-Thurs: 10:30-5; Fri: 10-2

Trying to find that special someone a gift? A.W. Kaufman offers high quality lingerie at good values: elegant European and domestic lingerie, fine cottons, bra and panties, and stunning bridal sets. For three generations Kaufman has combined excellent merchandise with quality customer service. Among the many outstanding labels found here are Hanro, Lejaby, Christian Dior, Diamond Tea, Chantelle, Pluto, Valentino, and Natori.

Louis Chock (74 Orchard St) is another great underwear source.

IMKAR COMPANY (M. KARFIOL AND SON)
294 Grand St (bet Allen and Eldridge St)   212/925-2459
Sun-Thurs: 10-5; Fri: 9:30-2; Sun (summer): 10-3

Imkar carries pajamas, underwear, and shifts for women at about one-third off retail prices. A full line of Carter's infants' and children's wear is also available at good prices. The store has a fine line of women's lingerie, including dusters and gowns. Featured names include Model's Coat, Barbizon, Vanity Fair, Arrow, Jockey, Lollipop, and Munsingwear. Gold Toe Hosiery and Arrow shirts for men are also stocked.

MENDEL WEISS
91 Orchard St (at Broome St)   212/925-6815
Sun-Thurs: 9:30-5:30; Fri 9:30-4

Mendel Weiss is one of the stalwarts in the Lower East Side tradition of selling ladies' undergarments and lounge wear at sizable discounts. Depending on the dates of the merchandise, prices can range from wholesale (10% above cost) to markdowns of as much as 75%. Weiss includes T-shirts and bathing suits in his collection. Trained specialists are available to aid mastectomy fittings. This is not a glamorous shopping environment, but lingerie styles don't change much from season to season and you can save money here.

SAMANTHA JONES
996 Lexington (72nd St)   212/628-7720
Mon-Sat: 10:30-7; Sun: 1-5

Samantha Jones, the owner and operator of her own namesake boutique, specializes in contemporary and glamorous lingerie. Her collection consists of art-deco styling in robes, gowns, teddies, and camisoles. There are also interesting collections of undergarments, silk scarves and wraps, and Samantha Jones fragrances. This is the place to find something for a special lady!

SCHACHNER FASHIONS
95 Delancey St (bet Orchard and Ludlow St)   212/677-0700
Sun-Fri: 9-5:30

For over 35 years Schachner has been a Lower East Side institution, selling brand-name robes, sleepwear, underwear, and lounge wear at discount prices. They are still doing what they do best!

UNDERNEATH IT ALL
444 E 75th St (at York Ave)   212/717-1976
Mon-Thurs: 10-6

Underneath It All is a one-stop shopping service for women who have had any form of breast cancer or are undergoing chemotherapy. You can be assured of attentive, informed, and personal service, as all the staff are breast-cancer survivors. The store carries a large selection of breast forms in light and dark skin tones and in a variety of shapes, sizes, and contours. There is also a complete line of mastectomy bras and name-brand bras; mastectomy and designer swimwear; sleepwear, loungewear, and body suits; and wigs and fashionable head accessories.

VICTORIA'S SECRET
34 E 57th St (bet Park and Madison Ave)   212/758-5592
Mon-Sat: 10-7; Sun: 12-6

691 Madison Ave (at 62nd St)   212/838-9266
Mon-Fri: 10-8; Sat: 10-7; Sun: 12-6

This has to be one of the sexiest stores in the world, in terms of ambience. The beautiful lingerie and bedroom garb, bridal peignoirs, exclusive silks, and accessories are displayed against the most alluring backdrops. The personnel are absolutely charming as well.

Special note: If you want big-time shopping help, call **Marjorie Stokes** (212/753-0033). She is known as *the* person to get special prices on designer merchandise for elite shoppers (read: those with deep pockets). Be sure to ask about her commission, but be discreet!

Coins, Stamps

CHARLES G. MOORE GALLERIES
32 E 57th St (12th floor)   212/751-1900
Mon-Fri: 9:30-5; Sat by appointment

This gallery is one of America's leading auctioneers of Americana, antique glass, bottles, stoneware, general antiques, and pre-Columbian and classical antiquities. Gallery exhibits change monthly, and many of the top collections of American glass and stoneware are shown here. Collectors of antiquities can view and place bids at regularly scheduled auctions.

STACKS RARE COINS
123 W 57th St (nr Sixth Ave)   212/582-2580
Mon-Fri: 10-5

Stacks, established in 1858, is the country's oldest and largest rare-coin dealer. Specializing in rare coins, medals, and paper money of interest to collectors, Stacks has a solid reputation for individual service, integrity, and knowledge of the field. In addition to walk-in business, Stacks conducts ten public auctions a year. Both neophytes and experienced numismatists will do well at Stacks.

Computers
(See also "Electronics")

CompUSA
420 Fifth Ave (bet 37th and 38th St)   212/764-6224
Mon-Fri: 8:30-8; Sat: 10-7; Sun: 11-6

1775 Broadway (at 57th St)   212/262-9711
Mon-Fri: 9-8; Sat: 10-7; Sun: 12-6

If you are in computer mode, these are the best stops in Manhattan! They call them "computer superstores," and that's exactly what they are. There are over 5,000 computer products in stock, from modern desktop models to sophisticated software. The best part of the operation, besides the selection and competitive pricing, is the service. Even though the places are incredibly big and busy, the red-shirted sales staff are uniformly courteous and take time to answer the simplest questions.

COMPUTRS
7 Great Jones St (bet Broadway and Lafayette St)
212/254-9000
Mon-Fri: 10-6:30 (Thurs till 7); Sat: 11-6

This outfit has been in business since 1978—long before computers had become a way of life. They are now an authorized Apple/Macintosh dealer and are particularly expert in movie-industry software and CAD systems, as well as entry-level systems for beginners. A good selection of point-of-sale systems and software, desktop publishing systems and software, and audiovisual systems are offered. They also carry a large selection of computer magazines. Prices are competitive (frames are 30% off list prices), and repairs on personal computers are a specialty.

SOFTWARE, ETC.
Locations throughout Manhattan
Hours vary by store

Software, Etc. is the largest resource in the area for computer accessories, books, and software, with highly competitive prices and informed service. They will special-order any item that isn't stocked.

Other Reliable Computer Stores:

Computer City (Sixth Ave at W 41st St; 212/575-1751)
J&R Music World (15 Park Row, one block south of City Hall; 212/732-8600) (see "Electronics")
RCS Computer Experience (261 Madison Ave, at 39th St, and 575 Madison Ave, at 56th St; 212/949-6935)

Cosmetics, Drugs, Perfumes

BATH ISLAND
469 Amsterdam Ave (bet 82nd and 83rd St)   212/787-9415
Sun-Fri: noon-8; Sat: 10-8

The customer is queen here. Custom scenting of products and custom gift packages are offered at this shop, which offers highly personal service. Over a hundred essential perfume oils are available, plus a great variety of creams, cleansers, lotions, and hair and shaving products.

BOYD'S OF MADISON AVENUE
655 Madison Ave (at 60th St)   212/838-6558
Mon-Fri: 8:30-7:30; Sat: 9:30-7; Sun: 12-6

Boyd's is a drugstore in a city full of drugstores, so it has to have something special to be worthy of mention. In addition to a drug and prescription service, Boyd's carries a complete line of cosmetics, magnifying mirrors, soaps, jewelry, and brushes. The latter range from the common to the esoteric: i.e., nail brushes and mustache combs in a variety of sizes and shapes. Boyd's has one of the city's most complete selections of drugs, cosmetics, and sundries. A boutique department carries handbags, gloves, jackets, and hair accessories.

COSMETIC WORLD AND GIFT CENTER
393 Fifth Ave (bet 36th and 37th St, 2nd floor)   212/213-4047
Mon-Fri: 10-5 (Sat only during Christmas holidays)
Tour groups by appointment

Right in the heart of the city you can find cosmetics, crystal pieces, figurines, handbags, jewelry, ties, and men's and women's fragrances at discounts that range from 15% to 50%. You will not find every major brand in stock at all times, but there are excellent buys on such well-known names as Chanel, Christian Dior, Liz Claiborne, Ted Lapidus, Yves St. Laurent, and Calvin Klein. Cosmetic World has a multilingual staff, a corporate gift program, and telephone and mail-order facilities.

ESSENTIAL PRODUCTS
90 Water St (bet Wall St and Hanover Sq)   212/344-4288
Mon-Fri: 9-6

Essential Products has been manufacturing flavors and fragrances for over a hundred years. They know that an enormous percentage of the price of colognes and perfumes pays for advertising and packaging, so they set out to see how closely they could duplicate expensive scents at cheap prices. They describe their fragrances as "elegant interpretations" of designer names, sold at a fraction of the original's price. Essential features 49 sensual perfumes and 23 men's colognes, and they offer a money-back guarantee. If you send a self-addressed stamped envelope, they will send scented cards and ordering information.

JAY'S PERFUME BAR
14 E 17th St   212/243-7743
Mon-Fri: 9-6; Sat: 9-4; Sun: 10-3:30

Bargains, bargains, bargains! Perfumes, cosmetic bags, colognes, soaps, powders, and other great smells all sell for 10% to 95% off listed prices. Most are major brand names that you will recognize.

KAUFMAN PHARMACY
557 Lexington Ave (at 50th St)   212/755-2266
Daily: 7:30 a.m.-midnight

I hope Kaufman's is one New York phone number you will never need, but it's wonderful to know it's there. In addition to the usual drugstore operation—soda fountain, sundries, cigarettes, electrical goods, and traveling needs—Kaufman's has a prescription department. Should the nightmare of being ill in a New York City hotel room actually happen to you, it's nice to know that a pharmacy is open late and ready to deliver your prescription by cab. Bless them! (Incidentally, should you need a doctor to write that prescription, check this book's special telephone numbers.)

KIEHL'S
109 Third Ave (bet 13th and 14th St)
212/677-3171, 800/543-4571
Mon-Fri: 10-6:30; Sat: 10-6

Kiehl's has been a New York institution since 1851. It is a fourth-generation, family-owned company unlike any you have ever visited. Their special treatments and preparations are made by hand and distributed internationally. Natural ingredients are used in the full lines of cleansers, scrubs, toners, moisturizers, eye-area preparations, men's creams, masks, body moisturizers, bath and shower products, sports items, ladies' leg-grooming formulations, shampoos, conditioners, and treatments. Customers can also enjoy an unusual collection of memorabilia related to aviation and motorcycles—interests of the Aaron Morse family, which runs this famous shop.

Crafts

ALLCRAFT JEWELRY & ENAMELING CENTER
45 W 46th St, 3rd floor   212/840-1860
Mon-Thurs: 9-4:45; Fri: 9-4

If there is a definitive jewelry-making supply store, Allcraft is it. Allcraft's catalog is so all-inclusive that it's impossible to describe. There is a complete line of tools and supplies for jewelry making, silversmithing, metal smithing, lost-wax casting, and much more. Out-of-towners usually order from their catalog, but New Yorkers shouldn't miss an opportunity to visit this gleaming cornucopia. (For a catalog, write Allcraft Jewelry & Enameling Center at 666 Pacific Street, Brooklyn, NY 11217.)

CLAYWORKS
332 E 9th St (bet First and Second Ave)   212/677-8311
Mon-Wed: 3-7; Thurs, Fri: 3-8; Sat: 12:30-8; Sun: 2:30-8

For over a quarter of a century, talented Helaine Sorgen has been at work here! If you are interested in stoneware and porcelain, Clayworks is the place to come. True handmade American crafts (and craftspeople) are appreciated. All of Clayworks' pottery is lead-free and dishwasher- and microwave-safe. Small classes in wheel-throwing are given for adults. Everything here is individually produced, from teapots to casseroles, mugs, and sake sets. Decorative pieces include unique vases, goblets, platters, and bowls.

COMMON GROUND
19 Greenwich Ave   212/989-4178
Mon, Tues, Thurs, Fri: 11:30-7:30; Wed: 11-7; Sat: 11-7;
Sun: 12-7

55 W 16th St (bet Fifth and Sixth Ave)   212/620-3122
Wed-Sat: 1-6:30

Coming from Oregon, where a multitude of artifacts and crafts are made and sold by Native Americans, I can vouch that Common Ground has an excellent selection of American Indian jewelry, furniture, rugs, baskets, and the like. The folks in the shop are proud of their stock and will take time to explain the origin of each item. (Note that the address is Greenwich *Avenue,* not *Street.* Greenwich Avenue is a crosstown street in the Village, while Greenwich Street runs north-south from the Village into Tribeca.)

ERICA WILSON
717 Madison Ave (at 63rd St), 2nd floor   212/832-7290
Mon-Wed, Fri, Sat: 10-6; Thurs: 10-7

Erica Wilson is a lady of many talents. This British émigré not only writes books and newspaper columns about needlework, but also finds time to design needlepoint kits for the Metropolitan Museum of Art. Her store has a huge stock of knitting yarns, ranging from alpaca to cashmere, and you'll find the city's finest selection of hand-painted needlepoint patterns from London and elsewhere. You can select hand-knitted sweaters, finished pillows, hand-painted canvases, gifts, and beautiful accessories from Erica's stock. Her chintz bags are very special. Blocking, padding, mounting, finishing—as well as classes in these skills—are available.

LOVELIA ENTERPRISES
356 E 41st St (in Tudor City)   212/490-0930
Mon-Fri: 9:30-5 (by appointment only)

Lovelia F. Albright's establishment is one of New York's great finds. From a shop in Tudor City, overlooking the United Nations, she dispenses the finest European Gobelin, Aubusson, and Beauvais machine-woven tapestries at prices that are often one-third that of any other place. The tapestries are exquisite. Some of the designs depict the ubiquitous unicorns cavorting in a medieval scene; others are more modern. They come in all sizes. The latest additions include tapestries for upholstery, wool-pile miniature rugs for use as mats under objets d'art, and an extensive line of tapestry-woven borders. They're designed by Albright and made exclusively for her in Austria and France. Send $5 for her impressive mail-order catalog.

RADIO HULA
169 Mercer St (bet Houston and Prince St)   212/226-4467
Tues-Sat: 12-7

This is the only retail gift gallery on the East Coast dedicated to the native culture of Hawaii and the South Pacific. They carry traditional and contemporary arts and crafts, woodcarvings, weavings, clothing, gourmet foods, jewelry, and books, including vintage Hawaiiana and other unusual items.

WOMAN'S EXCHANGE
149 E 60th St (bet Lexington and Third Ave)   212/753-2330
Mon-Sat: 10-6

The Women's Exchange was started over a hundred years ago to provide a marketplace for the crafts of women widowed by the Civil War. Over the years it evolved into a source of income for women and men in need. In recent years it has regrouped and moved, but the tradition as a showcase for crafts continues. They are particularly known for their hand-smocking on children's clothing. Every item is one-of-a-kind. There are handmade sweaters, toys, dresses, quilts, whittled animals, paintings, decoupage, watering cans, flower pots, and delicious homemade jams, chocolates, and tea sugars. While prices are not cheap, they are certainly competitive. The consigners receive 60% of the sale, so you are supporting them while giving a special gift.

WOOLGATHERING
318 E 84th St (bet First and Second Ave)   212/734-4747
Tues-Fri: 10:30-6; Sat: 10:30-5

What is the Woolgathering? It is a unique oasis dedicated to the fine art of knitting! Featured here is a big selection of quality European woolen, cotton, and novelty yarns. There's free instruction for those of all skill levels. They carry many exclusive classic and contemporary designs, a complete library of knitting magazines and books, and European-made knitting implements and gadgets. Finally, they provide very professional finishing services.

Dance Items

BALLET COMPANY

1887 Broadway (bet 62nd and 63rd St)   212/246-6893, 800/219-7335
Mon-Sat: 10-7 (Thurs: 10-9); Sun: 11-6

This one-stop is a mecca for ballet fans. Half the display area is devoted to books, records, and other memorabilia, while the other half is devoted to wardrobing the dancer. There are leotards, tights, tutus, skirts, knitwear, and shoes for children and adults. Also available are gift and novelty items, T-shirts, rare and out-of-print books, limited editions, new books, albums, programs, posters, art, collector's items, ballet videotapes, and autographs of stars.

Department Stores and Malls

Be sure to check the listings at the start of this chapter for factory outlet centers in the tri-state area; you'll be able to do some excellent bargain shopping in the outfits listed on these pages.

The department-store scene in Manhattan has changed a great deal in the past several decades. No longer are famous names like **Gimbel's, Saks 34th Street, Alexander's, S. Klein, Ohrbach's, Bonwit Teller** or **B. Altman** a part of the picture. There have been bankruptcies, buyouts, and turmoil at the top in management. The principal survivors are described in this section.

Macy's and **Bloomingdale's** are the major players in the city. Both are owned by Federated Department Stores. Each has had financial problems, but both now seem to be on sound footing with improved operations. Macy's, in particular, has expanded stocks and a much better merchandising presentation. **Bloomingdale's** is not quite the exciting store it once was, but still offers vast selections of quality (and pricey) merchandise. Watch the newspapers for special sales events at both stores; you'll be able to pick up some bargains.

In the high-end fashion business, there are two contenders. **Saks Fifth Avenue** is a superb operation, showing quality merchandise for men and women in attractive surroundings. Sales help here are accommodating and experienced, and the best names in ready-to-wear, menswear, cosmetics, and accessories are all shown with vast assortments. **Bergdorf Goodman** has separate stores (across Fifth Avenue from each other) for men and women that specialize in top designer names, with top prices (in many cases) to match. Their home accessory floor is outstanding. If it's in the fashion magazines, you'll find the label here. Their men's operation has improved dramatically, but is not for bargain shoppers.

Henri Bendel is a fun store to shop; career women and youngish buyers will find attractive boutiques throughout the store. **Lord & Taylor** has a long history of catering to Manhattan shoppers. They specialize in American designers and carry on a tradition of appealing to budget and moderate-price shoppers.

And then there is **Barney's.** Once a great men's and boy's store downtown, younger owners let their egos run wild by expanding uptown and in other major cities. The result has not been a happy one. The Upper East Side Barney's (really two sections for men and women) is difficult to shop in and has overpriced merchandise in many categories, plus a certain unappealing attitude by many salespeople. Shoppers will find cutting-edge fashions in many sections, however. Unfortunately, the more appealing (and original) Chelsea location recently closed its doors.

Malls in Manhattan are not the huge bazaars we see elsewhere in the country. Major ones here include:

- **Trump Tower,** with a selection of high-end specialty stores
- **Herald Center,** a disaster from the start, now featuring Toys 'R' Us and Kids 'R' Us (and little more)
- **Manhattan Mall,** with **Stern's** as the major tenant, and a number of nationally-known shops, including a food fair
- the mall at the **World Financial Center** (Battery Park City), where the open-space Winter Garden is a magnificent setting for events and trendy stores add to the excitement
- **South Street Seaport,** not great shopping, but a fun place to visit for sightseers and young folks

Department Store Clearance Centers

Bloomingdale's: 155 Glencove Rd, Carleplace, Long Island, NY (516/294-3410): furniture

Lord & Taylor: 3601 Hempstead Turnpike, Levittown, Long Island, NY (516/731-5031) and 839-60 New York Ave, Huntington, NY (516/673-0009): clothing

Macy's: 155 Glencove Rd, Carleplace, Long Island, NY (516/742-8500): furniture and electronics

Department Stores

BARNEY'S
600 Madison Ave (bet 60th and 61st St)   212/826-8900
Mon-Fri: 10-8; Sat: 10-7; Sun: 12-6

World Financial Center (225 Liberty St)   212/945-1600
Mon-Fri: 9-7; Sat: 11-5; Sun: 12-5

Founder Barney Pressman would be distressed to see what has happened to the store that bears his name, a store that once was *the* place to buy clothing and accessories for men and boys. Third-generation family members borrowed money to expand rapidly throughout this country and overseas, and the results have spelled financial disaster. As this is being written, future ownership of the chain is still very much in doubt. The flagship store on Madison Avenue is a combination women's and men's operation. Merchandise is, in many cases, on the cutting edge of fashion, even though the store is slow-paying with some vendors. Prices are high and service can be less than accommodating. There is a good food operation at the uptown store. With so many fine department stores in New York, seasoned shoppers no longer make this their first choice.

BERGDORF GOODMAN
754 Fifth Ave (at 58th St)   212/753-7300

BERGDORF GOODMAN MEN
745 Fifth Ave (at 58th St)   212/753-7300
Mon-Wed, Fri, Sat: 10-7; Thurs: 10-8

Occupying a prime location on Fifth Avenue, just off the southwest corner of Central Park, Bergdorf is the epitome of class. The operation has broadened its appeal, reaching out to young and affluent customers scared away by the cold atmosphere of previous years. Many sections of the store have been redone into smaller boutiques. Lines have been expanded, and practically every major fashion name in the world is represented here. Dollar sales per square foot are among the highest in the nation. Bergdorf emphasizes top fashion names in all departments. Many of the styles shown are found exclusively in this store. Their windows usually display a fine selection of this apparel. The top floor presents an exciting array of home-accessory merchandise, carefully selected and beautifully displayed. Several trendy eating places entice shoppers to spend more time in the store. Personnel here are great if they know you; if not, don't appear in your grubbies. A much improved (in service and selection) men's store is located across the street. There you'll find top names, along with prices to match. If you're looking for a special men's gift, or if you are intent on appearing in the best-of-the-best, Bergdorf Goodman Men is the place to go.

BLOOMINGDALE'S
1000 Third Ave (at 59th St)   212/355-5900
Mon-Fri: 10-8:30; Sat: 10-7; Sun: 11-7

No visit to Manhattan is complete without a visit to the flagship Bloomingdale's store on the Upper East Side. Under one roof, in a building that has been added to and changed many times over the decades since 1879, you will find one of America's greatest showings of top brand names in clothing, accessories, and home furnishings. The fashion floors are filled with labels from top show American and foreign designers. The children's floors have a great selection! The men's furnishings section is complete, but the men's clothing department leaves a bit to be desired. Don't miss the great "Main Course" on six; it is a treasure trove for the home. The model rooms on the furniture floor are spectacular and change with the season. If you get hungry, Le Train Bleu is unique. Most every service imaginable is available; they will store packages, wrap gifts, and provide personal shopping companions.

CENTURY 21 DEPARTMENT STORE
22 Cortlandt St (bet Broadway and Church St)   212/227-9092
Mon-Wed: 7:45-7; Thurs: 7:45-8:30; Fri: 7:45-8; Sat: 10-7

This is a bargain palace! Ask anyone who works in the Wall Street area where they like to shop best, and the answer you will get most often is Century 21. Why? Because its 16 departments carry an amazing selection of quality merchandise for men, women, children, and the home at discounts that run from 25% to 75% off retail prices. Outstanding departments include housewares, women's shoes, and children's apparel, where the brand names are tops and prices comfortable. Don't expect fancy fitting rooms and special amenities. But the service is informed and courteous, and you will not be disappointed.

HENRI BENDEL
712 Fifth Ave (bet 55th and 56th St)   212/247-1100
Mon-Sat: 10-7 (Thurs: 10-8); Sun: 12-6

The Henri Bendel store on Fifth Avenue is one of the classiest stores around. Founded in 1896 as a millinery store, Bendel's was a fixture on 57th Street for years. In a boutique setting, the store catered to high-fashion women's apparel for the upwardly mobile New Yorker. The present store, in the former Coty Building, keeps the same boutique atmosphere but expands it into a series of shops that exude fashion, quality, and excitement. You will want to buy something in every section you visit; it is that colorful and attractive! Wood is used prominently throughout, and the magnificent original windows by Rene Lalique have been incorporated into the store design in a most appealing manner. The store re-creates the ambience of Paris in the 1920s. Don't miss the Gilded Cage (makeup), the Garren Hair Salon, and Salon de Thé (sandwiches, salads, pastries, and more by Les Delices Guy Pascal). Bendel's "stylists" can take you from boutique to boutique by oval staircases. (There are, happily, no escalators in the building!) Top billing is given to young, up-and-coming designers, and today's shopper will find a spectacular setting for wardrobe selections.

LORD & TAYLOR
424 Fifth Ave (at 39th St)   212/391-3344
Mon, Tues: 10-7; Wed, Thurs, Fri: 10-8:30; Sat: 10-7; Sun: 11-6

America's oldest specialty store, Lord & Taylor, is a retailing institution on New York's fashion front. The late Dorothy Shaver made it that way. The "L" and "T" could easily refer to Luxury and Tradition, because the store has been recognized for quality, service, and value since 1826. Now owned by the May company, Lord & Taylor on Fifth Avenue is the flagship of 63 stores nation-wide that display their allegiance to American designers in merchandise and advertising that touts "the Signature of American Style." Shoppers will find ten floors of famous-name options for everyone—from fashions to gifts for the home, plus special-size shops for the American Petite and the American Woman. There are three popular restaurants, including the traditional Soup Bar. During December, Lord & Taylor becomes one of New York's most special family attractions with the annual unveiling of its award-winning Christmas windows. On the down side, service is uneven, the men's sections leave much to be desired, the decor of the main floor is uninviting, and the store's phone system is abysmal.

MACY'S
151 W 34th St (at Herald Square)   212/695-4400
Mon-Sat: 10-8:30; Sun: 11-7

Macy's is billed as "the world's largest department store," and I doubt anyone would dispute that! Lots of changes have taken place recently in the retail field, and many of them have had a profound influence on this store. The retail giant Federated has taken over Macy's (who would have ever thought that Bloomie's and Macy's would be brothers?), and the new ownership shows. The store has renewed sparkle, more inventory, better service, and an increased showing of top names in clothing and accessories. The Cellar, a downstairs housewares and food carnival, is a highlight, as is their dazzling cosmetics department. You'll find a great selection of items for kids, an outstanding home furnishings section, and several fun places to rest and grab a snack. At Easter time, the flower show is magnificent.

SAKS FIFTH AVENUE
611 Fifth Ave (at 50th St)   212/753-4000
Mon-Wed, Fri, Sat: 10-6:30; Thurs: 10-8; Sun: 12-6

Situated across from the Channel Gardens in world-famous Rockefeller Center, Saks Fifth Avenue continues to be one of the ultimate destinations for the discerning shopper. The merchandise mix remains one of the city's best, offering the finest names in women's designer clothing from work to weekend. The Evening Boutique on the third floor is a favorite of New York women searching for the right outfit for a special occasion. Redesigned and substan-tially expanded, the Men's Store offers everything from Saville Row tailoring to the best names in sportswear. The Men's Store at Saks is home to the only Alan Flusser Custom Shop in the city. Shoppers will also find many amenities to help them restore body and soul: Cafe SFA (eighth floor) for a quick bite, and the Salon (ninth floor) for facials, massages, and haircuts. With their very helpful "One on One" complimentary shopping service, friendly associates truly personalize the shopping experience. Saks' premium credit-card program, SaksFirst, rewards shoppers for their yearly spending with a plethora of bonuses and perks. It truly is a great store.

TAKASHIMAYA
693 Fifth Ave (bet 54th and 55th St)   212/350-0100
Mon-Wed, Fri, Sat: 10-6; Thurs: 10-8

There is one thing you can say for sure about this new Manhattan store: it is different. Whether or not it will survive in Manhattan's hellbent-for-shopping atmosphere is another question. Located on prestigious Fifth Avenue, right in the middle of the Tiffanys and Guccis, this store is as much a museum and gallery as it is a retail establishment. Upstairs there are beautiful Japanese-made clothing and accessory items, home furnishings, and gifts. Gorgeous flower arrangements are featured on the first floor. Downstairs is a Japanese cafe for rest and meditation.

Display Accessories
NIEDERMAIER DISPLAY DIVISION
120 Wooster St (showroom)   212/343-8751
By appointment

Niedermaier designs and creates all kinds of displays, and they are considered the best. Although most of the business is conducted at trade shows, if you ask nicely (and mention this book) they will take care of individual customers.

Domestics
AD HOC SOFTWARES
410 West Broadway (at Spring St)   212/925-2652
Mon-Sat: 11-7; Sun: 11:30-6

The name of this store means just what it says: soft textures for modern living. There are sheets and towels, blankets, table linens, robes, dressing gowns, and pajamas. You will also see luggage, table-top items (china, glassware), gifts, shower curtains, bathroom hardware, and furniture. You'll have a soft spot in your heart for this unusual establishment after you visit!

D. PORTHAULT
18 E 69th St   212/688-1660
Mon-Fri: 10-5:30; Sat: 10-5

Porthault, the French queen of linens, needs no introduction. Custom-made linens are available in a range of 600 designs (more if you count custom designs), scores of colors, and weaves of luxurious density. Wherever the name Porthault appears—e.g., some fancy hotels—you know you're at a top-notch operation. Their printed sheets seem to last forever and are passed along from one generation to another. Porthault can handle custom work of an intricate nature for odd-sized beds, baths, and showers. Specialties include signature prints, printed terry towels, unusual gift items, and decorative accessories like trays, wastebaskets, tissue-box covers, and room sprays.

HARRIS LEVY
278 Grand St (nr Forsyth St)   212/226-3102
Mon-Thurs: 9-5; Fri: 9-4; Sun: 9-4:30

Harris Levy is the dominant store on the Lower East Side for bed and table linens, pillows, comforters, bath and closet accessories, and towels. They have been in business since 1894 and offer good values and custom services, such as monogramming on sheets and towels and special embroideries for tablecloths. Customers will find dozens of patterns from leading American and European manufacturers at a fraction of the prices paid in uptown stores. This is a true family operation, with fourth-generation family members right on the job.

J. SCHACHTER'S
5 Cook St, Brooklyn 718/384-2732, 800/INTOBED
Mon-Thurs: 10-5; Fri: 10-1:30; Sun: by appointment

J. Schachter's is the foremost purveyor of quilts in the New York area and perhaps on the entire continent. Schachter's is the oldest quilting firm in New York, and they know everything there is to know about quilts and their making. They also do work in polyester, lamb's wool, and cotton. The talented staff can make a quilt in any size and in 20 different quilting patterns from any fabric given to them. Baby ensembles are a specialty. Schachter's has a complete line of linens as well. Some of their bed linens come from Europe and are offered at discount prices. Custom pillows can be made while you wait. Entire bedrooms and bathrooms—from rugs to ceiling and wall coverings—can be coordinated. A catalog is available.

PONDICHERRI
454 Columbus Ave (at 82nd St)   212/875-1609
Mon-Sat: 11-7; Sun: 11-7

This is one of those stores some people pass right by because the beautiful window displays make you think you'll never be able to afford anything inside. However, if you like exotic cotton prints and are looking for pillows, pillowcases, bags, trays (from Hong Kong), handicrafts and furniture (from Indonesia), tablecloths, quilts, clothing, and the like, by all means go in—both the selection and the prices are excellent! You'll find items from Tibet, India, Africa, and other exotic spots. Keep an eye out for unusual pottery and interesting knickknacks, too. Because the selection is large and most things are folded on shelves, you might want to ask for help.

PORTICO BED & BATH
139 Spring St (at Wooster St)   212/941-7722
Mon-Sat: 11-7; Sun: 12-6

Portico is located in a turn-of-the-century factory loft—a suitable background for their showing of a highly unusual collection of bath and body-care products, cast- and wrought-iron beds, and fine domestic and imported linens. This is not a store for bargain hunters; rather, Portico is for discerning shoppers who take pride in making home a very special place.

PRATESI LINENS
829 Madison Ave (at 69th St)   212/288-2315
Mon-Sat: 10-6

Pratesi says it carries the best linens the world has to offer, and they're right.

Families hand them down for generations. Customers who don't have affluent ancestors will wish to avail themselves of the new collections that come out in spring and fall. The Pratesi staff is unexcelled in coordinating linens to decor or creating a custom look. Nearly all of the linens are of natural fibers, although some easy-care versions are carried. The three-story store boasts a garden, which sets the mood for the luxurious linens. Towels are made in Italy exclusively for Pratesi and are of a quality and thickness that must be felt to be believed. Bathrobes are magnificent, plush, and quietly understated. (So are the price tags.) There is also a baby boutique.

Electronics, Appliances, Fax Machines

When visiting the numerous electronics, camera, and office-supply stores along Fifth Avenue and in the 50s along Sixth Avenue, don't be misled by the discounts quoted off the marked retail figure. In many cases, those prices are grossly inflated. It is a wise idea to shop around at reputable stores before deciding on a purchase. Don't say I didn't warn you!

BERNIE'S DISCOUNT CENTER
821 Sixth Ave (bet 28th and 29th St)   212/564-9431
Mon-Fri: 9:30-6; Sat: 11-4; closed in July, Aug

Bernie's stocks appliances, TVs, video games, answering machines, refrigerators, washers, dryers, radios, tape recorders, and air conditioners from the finest names in the business (e.g., Mitsubishi, Sony, Panasonic, and Norelco). The discount may be better at some other stores mentioned in this section, but Bernie's is more conveniently located. Besides, Bernie's also services what it sells. If you want first-class treatment, ask for George Vargas.

DEMBITZER BROS.
5 Essex St (at Canal St)   212/254-1310
Mon-Thurs: 10-5; Fri: 10-2; Sun: 10-5

Dembitzer was one of the first discount appliance stores on the Lower East Side, and it was so successful that it spawned many imitators. This is good for the consumer. With a host of competitors nearby, Dembitzer is alert to keeping the business it has garnered so far. They specialize in appliances that work in 220-volt, 50-cycle applications for overseas use. However, they also have appliances for domestic use. Dembitzer's motto is, "If it plugs in, we have it," but even that doesn't do justice to the stock. Left out of that description are pens, luggage, soda makers, cameras, film, ad infinitum. Dembitzer also breaks the Lower East Side rudeness code. Between them, the brothers speak 8 or 11 languages (depending on whom you ask). While they clearly don't have time to traffic with people who are "just looking" or comparing prices, they can be charming to real customers in any of those languages.

HARVEY ELECTRONICS
2 W 45th St (nr Fifth Ave)   212/575-5000
Mon-Fri: 9:30-6 (Thurs: 9:30-8); Sat: 10-6

Not everyone understands all the fine points of the new technologies flooding the markets these days. For those who need professional advice and individual attention, Harvey's is the place to shop for state-of-the-art consumer electronics. They offer the whole spectrum of quality audio/video components, with home theater being their specialty. Harvey has an in-home design and installation division that will fully integrate both studio and video systems into new and existing residences.

J&R MUSIC & COMPUTER WORLD
Park Row (one block south of City Hall)
212/238-9000, 800/221-8180
Mon-Sat: 9-6:30; Sun: 11-6

These folks bill themselves as one of the nation's most complete single computer, electronics, and home-entertainment department store, and I believe them. They carry cameras, radios, televisions, speaker systems, VCRs, cassette and CD players, personal electronics, records, tapes, compact discs, computer systems, telephone answering machines, telephones, typewriters, microwave ovens, and even breadmakers. The place is well organized, but gets rather hectic at times. Prices are very competitive, and all merchandise is guaranteed.

PHONE BOUTIQUE
828 Lexington Ave (at 63rd St)   212/319-9650
Mon-Fri: 10:30-6:30; Sat: 12-6

In my opinion, the breakup of Ma Bell was one of the saddest episodes in American corporate history. The confusion with the phone system since then has overwhelmed nearly everyone. Fortunately, there is a place in Manhattan where you can buy or rent new and antique-style phones; have them repaired; browse answering machines, fax machines, and telephone-related accessories; and even have your phone painted. They also rent cellular phones and beepers to visitors in New York.

SHARPER IMAGE
4 W 57th St (at Fifth Ave)   212/265-2550
900 Madison Ave (at 73rd St)   212/794-4974
Mon-Fri: 10-7; Sat: 10-6; Sun: 12-5

Pier 17, South Street Seaport   212/693-0477
Mon-Sat: 10-9; Sun: 11-8

If you are a gadget freak (like me), you'll go wild at the Sharper Image. This is truly a grown-up's toy store! The very latest electronic gadgets, household helpers, sports items, games, novelties, and clothing make browsing this fascinating emporium a unique experience.

SONY PLAZA
550 Madison Ave (bet 55th and 56th St)   212/833-8830
Mon-Sat: 10-7; Sun: 12-6

You'll delight in this mixture of two Sony retail stores and a consumer-friendly atrium. Sony is usually at the cutting-edge of new developments in consumer electronics, so periodic visits here will reveal the latest in radios, television, home entertainment, cameras, clocks, and all the rest. You'll find most of the sales personnel to be patient and knowledgeable, despite a somewhat overbearing security atmosphere.

SPECTRA AUDIO RESEARCH
903 Madison Ave (bet 72nd and 73rd St)
212/744-2255, 800/342-0456
Mon-Sat: 10-6

It's always best to deal with the experts, and Spectra definitely fits that description. Don't be taken in by the low-price come-ons at the Fifth Avenue electronics stores; many times you will pay more and receive outdated merchandise. Spectra has a one-price policy and offers state-of-the-art items that include surveillance equipment, night-vision devices, phone accessories, and home-theater equipment. Oh, if you want to phone someone in the middle of an African rain forest, these guys sell and rent satellite phones!

VICMARR STEREO AND TV
88 Delancey St   212/505-0380
Sun-Fri: 9-6

In the middle of famed Delancey Street on the Lower East Side, Mal Cohen presides over a treasure house of electronics, including stereo and hi-fi equipment, multi-voltage items, telephones, answering machines, and camcorders, as well as such items as microwave ovens, organs, sunglasses, and fans. Unlike many electronics outfits, this place has everything well organized, marked, and displayed, with none of the high-pressure selling that's often encountered. Best of all, the prices are right, and you can be assured of not getting secondhand merchandise. Vicmarr is one of the largest JVC outlets in the area; they also carry Sony, Alpine, Kenwood, and Panasonic products. Save yourself some time by calling ahead for prices.

WAVES
110 W 25th St, Suite 1005   212/989-9284
Mon-Fri: 12-6; Sat, Sun: 10-6

The past lives on at Waves, and Bruce and Charlotte Mager are trying to make it last forever with their collection of vintage record players, radios, receivers, and televisions. They have scorned the electronics age in favor of the age of radio. Their shop is a virtual shrine to the 1930s and before. Here you'll find the earliest radios (still operative) and artifacts. There are radio promotion pieces, such as a radio-shaped cigarette lighter. Gramophones and anything dealing with the radio age are available, and Waves is capable of repairing instruments. Waves also rents phonographs, telephones, and neon clocks. They make appraisals and will answer any questions on repair, sales, or rental.

THE WIZ
Locations throughout Manhattan
Hours vary by store

There is a tendency to think twice about shopping at chain electronics stores. Service can be irregular. Prices may not be the lowest. Fortunately in Manhattan there is one chain that can be depended on for excellent customer relations, huge inventories, and a real concern for your satisfaction. I would recommend a stop at any of the Wiz stores. Their prices are extremely competitive. They claim "Nobody Beats the Wiz," and I'd be the first to agree.

Environmental and Natural Items

EARTH GENERAL
147 Eighth Ave (bet 17th and 18th St)   212/929-2340
Mon-Wed: 11-8; Thurs-Sat: 11-9; Sun: 11-7

If concern for the environment is your thing, then Earth General is your store! Here you will find items for every part of your life: housewares, body care, clothing, bedding, pet food, and garden merchandise, all friendly to planet Earth. To show the concern these folks have for their surroundings, the entire store has been constructed and designed with eco-friendly building materials like soybean paste countertops and recycled cork floors.

Fabrics, Trimmings

A.A. FEATHER COMPANY
(GETTINGER FEATHER CORPORATION)
16 W 36th St, (bet Fifth and Sixth Ave), 8th floor   212/695-9470
Mon-Thurs: 9-6; Fri: 9-3

Suppose you've made a quilt and want to stuff it with feathers? What if your latest outfit simply has to have an ostrich plume, feather fan, or feather boa? Well, you're in luck with A.A. Feather (a.k.a. Gettinger Feather Corporation). The Gettingers have been in the business since 1915 and have passed the trade down to Dan Gettinger, who is the first grandson. There aren't many family businesses around now, and there are even fewer sources for really fine-quality feathers. This is a find!

A. FEIBUSCH—ZIPPERS & THREADS
27 Allen St   212/226-3964
Mon-Fri: 9-5; Sun: 9-4 (closed Sun in summer)

Would you believe a large store dedicated entirely to zippers? Well, in New York, nothing is impossible. One of the many amusing aspects of my visit here was hearing the boast, "We have one of the biggest selections of zippers in the U.S.A." It's as if they really think there are zipper stores throughout the country! Feibusch does have zippers in every size, style, and color (hundreds of them), and if it's not in stock, they will make it to order. I saw one woman purchase tiny zippers for doll clothes! Feibusch carries matching threads to sew in a zipper as well. A selection of threads rivaling the zippers is available in all varieties. Eddie Feibusch assured me that no purchase is too small or large, and he gives each customer prompt, personal service.

ART MAX FABRICS
250 W 40th St   212/398-0755
Mon-Fri: 8:30-6; Sat: 9-5

The Fabric Wholesale District is conveniently adjacent to the Garment District, and the usual retail-shopper traditions of that area apply here. Some stores welcome retail customers, some don't, and some fluctuate with the market. Art Max is dedicated to the retail customer. Many languages are expertly spoken. The three floors are filled to overflowing with outstanding fabrics for clothing. They now carry full lines of fabric for everyday wear: linens, English all-wool suitings, domestic and imported wools, cotton prints, solids, wool and cashmere coatings, and silks. The really striking brocades, metallics, and laces require an experienced touch; it would be a shame for a novice to ruin such beautiful fabrics. The real specialty here, however, is bridal fabrics. When the fabrics mentioned above are made into gowns, the wedding party could rival a *Vogue* layout. There are a dozen different types of nets for bridal veils and infinite combinations of heavier materials. Try to get a peek at the basement, which looks like the catacombs!

B&J FABRICS
263 W. 40th St (bet Seventh and Eighth Ave)   212/354-8150
Mon-Fri: 8-5:45; Sat: 9-4:45

B&J started in the fabric business in 1940 and is now run by the second and third generations of the Cohen family. There are three complete floors of fashion fabrics, many imported directly from Europe. Specialties of the house: natural fibers, designer fabrics, bridal fabrics, and silk prints. There are over a thousand of the latter in stock! Swatches are sent free of charge, upon request.

BECKENSTEIN MEN'S FABRICS
121 Orchard St   212/475-6666, 800/221-2727
Sun-Fri: 9-6

Simply put, this is the finest men's fabric store in the nation. Proprietor Neil Boyarsky has been called "the fabric czar of the U.S." These folks sell to about 90% of all custom tailors in the country, and also to many of the top manufacturers of men's clothing, so you know the goods are best quality. Their customer list reads like a who's who: Warren Beatty, Al Pacino, all three *Godfather* movies, Robert DeNiro, diplomats and politicians, Magic Johnson, Wayne Gretsky, and on and on. You will find every kind of fabric, from goods selling for $10 a yard to fabulous pieces at $1,000 a yard. There are pure cashmeres, fine English suitings, pure silks, camel hair, and more. This professional operation is not typical of most Lower East Side stores. Don't miss it!

BUTTONHOLE FASHIONS
580 Eighth Ave (bet 38th and 39th St)   212/354-1420
Mon-Fri: 8-5:30

For nearly half a century these folks have been offering bound buttonholes and buttonhole eyelets, plus straight and curved pockets with cords in all lengths and sizes.

CINDERELLA FLOWER AND FEATHER CO.
60 W 38th St   212/840-0644
Mon-Fri: 9-5:15; Sat: 9-4:15

A few years back, in the midst of a particularly cold and dreary winter, Seventh Avenue fashions began to blossom with artificial flowers as the "in" look for spring. The department stores quickly got the message, and in just a few weeks, people were removing their fur-lined gloves to hand $10 over the counter for a single flower for their lapel. Many of these transactions were made along 34th Street or Fifth Avenue, and only a few wise New Yorkers walked an extra two blocks to the "trimmings district," where they could buy an identical flower for 75 cents. There were even buyers of the $10 variety who knew of the district and assumed they couldn't get in! Cinderella Flower and Feather Company is for them. They have the country's largest selection of feather trimmings, decorations, craft supplies, and conversation pieces, as well as silk and other artificial flowers. You can also find ribbons, shoulder pads, veiling, netting, and feather boas in many colors.

HANDLOOM BATIK
214 Mulberry St (at Spring St)   212/925-9542
Wed-Sat: 12-7; Sun: 1-6

At Handloom you'll find one of the largest and best collections of batik outside a crafts museum. Carol Berlin runs Handloom Batik with near reverence for her merchandise. All of the fabrics are handmade, and she is quick to show how each can be set off to best advantage. Imported hand-woven and hand-batiked fabrics (primarily from India and Indonesia) are sold by the yard as fabric or are made up as clothing, napkins, tablecloths, and handiwork. Handloom Batik will also use its own fabrics for custom-made shirts and other garments. In addition, a gift selection features handicrafts of wood, stone, brass, and paper from the aforementioned countries. Pillows, bed covers, curtains, and napkins can be custom-made from the store's cotton ikat and batik.

HARRY ZARIN
318 Grand St   212/925-6112
Daily: 9-5:30

Imagine a city block full of upholstery- and drapery-fabric and window treatment bargains! Harry Zarin has been in business for over a half century and shows one of the largest selections in the area at this expanded outlet on the Lower East Side. Many of Manhattan's top decorators use this source. Another operation is worth knowing about: BZI Distributors (105 Eldridge St), a full building of drapery rods and Levolor blinds at great prices.

HYMAN HENDLER AND SONS
67 W 38th St (bet Fifth and Sixth Ave)   212/840-8393
Mon-Fri: 9-5:30; Sat: 10-3 (closed Sat in July and Aug)

Although Hyman Hendler has passed away, the store that proudly bears his name is in the capable hands of his sons and niece. In the middle of the trimmings center of the world, Hyman Hendler is one of the oldest businesses (established in 1900) and the crown head of the ribbon field. This organization manufactures, wholesales, imports, and acts as a jobber for every kind of ribbon. It's hard to believe as many variations exist as are jammed into this store.

LEATHER FACTS
262 W 38th St (bet Seventh and Eighth Ave)   212/382-2788
Mon-Fri: 9:30-5; Sat by appointment

Francois George dispenses all manner of leather, suede, and exotic skins. He concentrates upon custom-made clothing.

LONG ISLAND FABRIC WAREHOUSE
406 Broadway (bet Canal and Walker St)   212/431-9510
Mon-Wed, Fri: 9-6; Thurs: 9-7; Sat, Sun: 10-5

Island Fabric Warehouse has one huge floor of every imaginable kind of fabric and trimming. Since it is all sold at discount prices, it's one of the best places to buy fabrics. Some of the attractions include an extensive wool collection and such dressy fabrics as chiffon, crepe, silk, and satin. Most amazing are the bargain spots, where remnant and odd pieces go for so little it's laughable. They sell an excellent selection of patterns, notions, and trimmings at the same low prices, so that customers won't have to make several stops. Dollar-a-yard fabrics are also available.

M&J TRIMMING CO.
1008 and 1014 Sixth Ave (bet 37th and 38th St)   212/391-9072
Mon-Fri: 9-6; Sat: 10-5

These folks say they have the largest selection of trims at one location in the entire country. After visiting the store, I'm inclined to believe them! You will find imported trims, buttons, decorator trims, and various fashion accessories. One store specializes in clothing and fashion trims; the other features interior decor trim. They have over a half century of experience in this business.

PARON FABRICS
56 W 57th St (bet Fifth and Sixth Ave)   212/247-6451
Mon-Sat: 9-5:45

PARON II
56 W 57th St (bet Fifth and Sixth Ave), 2nd floor
Mon-Sat: 9-5:15

PARON EAST
855 Lexington Ave (bet 64th and 65th St)   212/772-7353
Mon-Sat: 9-5:45 (Thurs until 7)

PARON WEST
206 W 40th St (at Seventh Ave)   212/768-3266
Mon-Sat: 9-5:45

At Paron, you will find an excellent selection of designer fabrics uptown at discount prices. Paron carries the very latest, and many of the goods are available only in their stores. This is a family operation, so personal attention is assured. (Note: Paron II and Paron West are their 50%-off outlets.)

PIERRE DEUX-FRENCH COUNTRY
870 Madison Ave (at 71st St)   212/570-9343
Mon-Sat: 10-6

Pierre Deux, the French Country home-furnishings company, specializes in authentic, handcrafted products from the provinces of France. Everything from 18th-century antique and reproduction furniture to fabrics, brightly colored pillows, faience, pewter, lighting, table linens, and glassware can be found here. A personalized bridal registry and custom orders are also available.

SILK SURPLUS/TOWNHOUSE
THE ANNEX
249 E 59th St (at Second Ave)   212/753-6511
Mon-Fri: 10-6; Sat: 10-5

Silk Surplus is the exclusive outlet for Scalamandre close-outs of fine fabrics, trimmings, and wallpaper, as well as its own line of imported and domestic informal fabrics and trimmings. Scalamandre is sold for half off retail price, and there is a choice selection of other equally luxurious fabrics at similar savings. There are periodic sales, even on fabrics already discounted, at this elegantly run fabric store.

TINSEL TRADING
47 W 38th St   212/730-1030
Mon-Fri: 10-5; Sat: call for hours

The personnel at Tinsel Trading claim it is the only firm in the United States specializing in antique gold and silver metallics from the 1900s. They have everything from gold thread to lamé fabric. Tinsel Trading offers an amazing array of tinsel threads, braids, fringes, cords, tassels, gimps, medallions, edging, banding, gauze lamés, bullions, tinsel, fabrics, ribbons, soutache, trims, and galloons. All are genuine antiques, but many customers buy them for accenting modern clothing. The collection of military gold braids, sword knots, and epaulets is unexcelled anywhere.

TOHO SHOJI (NEW YORK)
990 Sixth Ave (at 36th St)   212/868-7466
Mon-Fri: 9-6; Sat: 10-5

Ever hear of a trimmings supermarket? Only in New York will you find an establishment like this. Toho Shoji stocks all manner of items that will allow you to design and make your own custom jewelry: earring parts, metal findings, chains, and every kind of jewelry component. Items are well displayed for easy selection.

Fireplace Accessories

DANNY ALESSANDRO
223 E 59th St (bet Second and Third Ave)   212/421-1928
Mon-Fri: 10-5 (open weekends seasonally)

New Yorkers have a thing for fireplaces, and Danny Alessandro caters to that infatuation. Just as New York fireplaces run the gamut from antique brownstone to ultramodern blackstone, Danny Alessandro's fireplaces and accessories range from antique pieces to a shiny new set of chrome tools. The shop also stocks antique marble and sandstone mantelpieces, andirons, and an incredible display of screens and tool kits. In the Victorian era, paper fans and screens were popular for blocking fireplaces when not in use. Alessandro's collection of surviving pieces is great for modern decorating. Danny Alessandro will also custom-order mantels, mantelpieces, and accessories. This is primarily a fireplace accessory source, however; neither advice nor information is given on how to put a fireplace in working order. Alessandro has been in business for over 40 years, and they assume every New Yorker who has a fireplace knows how to use it.

WILLIAM H. JACKSON
210 E 58th St   212/753-9400
Mon-Fri: 9:30-5

"WBFP" in the real-estate ads stands for "wood-burning fireplace," and they are the rage in New York. William H. Jackson is reaping the harvest of this resurgence in fireplace usage. In business since 1827, the company is familiar with the various types of fireplaces in the city. In fact, many of the fireplaces were originally installed by the company. William H. Jackson has hundreds of mantels on display in its showroom. The variety ranges from antique and antique reproductions (in wood or marble combinations) to stark modern. There are also andirons, fire sets, screens, and excellent advice on enjoying your own fireplace. Jackson does some repair work (removing and installing mantels is a specialty), but is better known for selling fireplace paraphernalia. A handy item: a reversible hanging sign that reads "Damper is open"/"Damper is closed."

Flags

ACE BANNER AND FLAG COMPANY
107 W 27th St   212/620-9111
Mon-Fri: 7:30-4

If you need a flag, Ace is the place. Established in 1916, Ace prides itself on having the flags of every country in the world readily available; other kinds of flags can be ordered. They range in size from lapel pins to bridge-spanning banners. (The largest flag flown in the world is the Stars and Stripes that hangs from the New Jersey side of the George Washington Bridge every holiday.) For those who are not flag-waving types, Ace also sells custom banners, buttons, pins, patches, and pennants. If you're running for any kind of office, campaign paraphernalia can be ordered with a promise of quick delivery. Carl Calo, Ace's owner, does not subsist on flags and campaigns alone, however. A large part of his business consists of outfitting grand openings and personalizing equipment with such items as boat flags.

Floor Coverings

BEYOND THE BOSPHORUS
79 Sullivan St (bet Spring and Broome St)   212/219-8257
Tues-Sun: 12-6

Ismail Basbag, the owner of this establishment, was a kilim dealer for 12 years in Istanbul's grand bazaar before opening his shop in Soho in 1985. Anyone who can survive at that colorful, crowded, and noisy marketplace can certainly do business in Manhattan! Here you will find hand-woven Turkish kilim rugs and pillows in a variety of sizes, patterns, and colors. The owner travels to Turkey several times a year and will try to pick up special pieces ordered by customers. Cleaning and repair for rugs purchased here or elsewhere is available.

CENTRAL CARPET
426 Columbus Ave (bet 80th and 81st St)   212/787-8813
81 Eighth Ave (at 14th St)   212/741-3700
Mon-Fri: 10-7 (Thurs: 10-8); Sat: 10-6; Sun: 11-6

Imagine over 20,000 rugs in stock! Central Carpet carries new, antique, and handmade semi-antique Oriental rugs from Persia, China, India, and Tibet; machine-made rugs from Belgium and Egypt; and hand-hooked rugs from China. Also featured are needlepoints, kilims, area rugs, and items suitable for children's rooms. A large selection of broadloom, as well as sisal carpeting and rug padding, is shown. Everything is at discount prices! All rugs are displayed on racks for easy viewing.

COUNTRY FLOORS
15 E 16th St   212/627-8300
Mon-Fri: 9-6 (Thurs: 9-8); Sat: 9-5 (closed Sat in summer)

Country Floors is one of New York's biggest success stories, probably because they offer a magnificent product. Begun in 1964 in the tiny, cramped basement under the owner's photography studio, Country Floors has grown to include huge stores in New York, Philadelphia, Miami, Los Angeles, and 35 other affiliates nationwide. Customers from across the country have learned that

Country Floors carries the finest in floor and wall tiles and stone. Their sources include a wide variety of styles and artisans from all over the world. All are unique, and a visit—or at least a look at their catalog—is really necessary to appreciate the fineness and intricacy of each design. Even the simplest solid-color tiles are beautiful.

ELIZABETH EAKINS
21 E 65th St   212/628-1950
Mon-Fri: 10-5:30

If you are looking for a first-class source for hand-woven rugs, look no further. Elizabeth Eakins custom-designs and makes hand-woven and hand-hooked rugs in standard and hand-dyed colors. She also offers beautiful pillows made of antique fabrics.

I.J. PEISER'S SONS
475 Tenth Ave (bet 36th and 37th St)   212/279-6900
Mon-Fri: 9-5

In business for nearly a century, these folks specialize in furnishing and installing new hardwood flooring. They work with top-end architects, designers, and general contractors who are impressed with their flawless reputation. A large showroom displays various types of wood that may be installed in both residential and commercial spaces.

MOMENI INTERNATIONAL
36 E 31st St (2nd floor)   212/532-9577
Mon-Fri: 9-5

The people here will tell you they are wholesale only, but don't let the stated policy scare you away. Those who do visit will be rewarded by what may be the single best source for Oriental rugs in the city, because Momeni is a direct importer. Since they don't officially suffer individual retail customers, their prices reflect wholesale rather than retail business. That doesn't make them cheap (good Oriental rugs never are), but it does assure top quality at a fair price.

PASARGAD CARPETS
105 Madison Ave (at 30th St)   212/684-4477
Mon-Sat: 9-6; Sun: 11-5

Pasargad is a fifth-generation family business, established in 1904. They know what they are talking about when it comes to antique, semi-antique, and new Persian and Oriental rugs. They have one of the largest collections in the country, and they provide decorating advice, repair and cleaning, and a pickup and delivery service. Pasargad will also buy or trade quality antique rugs.

PARVIZ NEMATI ANTIQUE RUGS & TAPESTRIES
510 Madison Ave (at 53rd St)   212/486-6900
Mon-Fri 9-6; Sat: 10-4 (or by appointment)

Parviz Nemati comes highly recommended for those who are interested in high-end antique Oriental rugs and 15th- to 19th-century tapestries. They claim to have the largest selection in the country, and they will be glad to come to a client's home for consultation. This is no fly-by-night outfit; Nemati has been in the area for over 30 years and is a published author in his field of expertise.

PILLOWRY
132 E 61st St   212/308-1630
Mon-Fri: 11:30-5:30; Sat: by chance or appointment;
closed Aug

Marjorie Lawrence specializes in an eclectic collection of antique and semi-antique pillows, Oriental rugs, and kilims. She has been doing so since 1971 and is one of the best in the business. The name of the shop derives from the pillows made out of fragments of Aubusson tapestries and old rugs and textiles on the premises. Customers can select fabric from the kilims, knotted rugs, and Oriental carpets lying around the shop, or they can have them made to order. Her fabrics are authentic and come from all parts of the world. The Pillowry does expert rug restoration, as well as pillow creations from old textiles, needlepoints, and rugs. You might say Lawrence has the subject covered!

RUG WAREHOUSE
220 W 80th St (nr Broadway)   212/787-6665
Mon-Sat: 10-6 (Thurs: 10-8); Sun: 11-5

One of the largest collections of antique and semi-antique Oriental rugs in the city is available at the Rug Warehouse. The current owners come from a family tradition of five decades in the rug business. A huge inventory of over 5,000 antique and contemporary rugs includes creations from 13 countries. Modern premises provide an attractive setting for rugs that are often offered at good discounts).

SAFAVIEH CARPETS
153 Madison Ave (at 32nd St)   212/683-8399
238 E 59th St (at Second Ave)   212/888-0626
Mon-Fri: 9-6; Sat: 10-6; Sun: 11-5

902 Broadway   212/477-1234
Mon, Thurs: 10-8; Tues, Wed, Fri: 10-7; Sat, 10-6; Sun: 11-6

There was a time when it was possible to visit the teeming markets of Tehran and find some real bargains in rugs. No more. But one is still able to see a vast selection of these beautiful works of art, even if the setting is a little less glamorous. Safavieh has one of the finest collections of Persian, Indian, Pakistani, and Chinese rugs in this country. They're displayed in a showroom spacious enough for you to visualize how the prized pieces would look in your own home or place of business. These rugs are truly heirlooms, and you will want to spend time hearing about these exotic products. Prices, although certainly not inexpensive, are competitive for the superior quality represented. (It doesn't hurt to do a little haggling.)

Flowers, Plants, Gardening
CHELSEA GARDEN CENTER NURSERY
205 Ninth Ave (at 22nd St)   212/929-2477
Daily: 9-6:45

There's no shortage of stock here. That is one of the big advantages of Chelsea, as you will be able to compare dozens of varieties. There are big selections of plants, shrubs, trees, and pots, and prices are competitive. The sales personnel are reasonably helpful. Be sure to get on their mailing list.

FARM AND GARDEN NURSERY
2 Sixth Ave (bet White and Walker St)   212/431-3577
Daily: 9-6 (Jan, Feb: Tues-Sat: 10-5)

This is one of New York's most unusual enterprises. First, a little background. The towering buildings in this neighborhood are the two spires of the World Trade Center. However, the surrounding area used to be made up of 50-year-old buildings housing government offices, while the site of the future trade center was occupied by tiny and dirty electronics, job-lot, and gardening shops. When construction began on the World Trade Center, the small businesses were dislocated. Some retired. Many vanished. Those that relocated have done remarkably well. Of the garden centers, Farm and Garden Nursery was the only one to remain in the area. It operates like a suburban nursery, dispensing landscape designs, grass seed, fruit trees, vegetables, and sprays. Its nursery is an outdoor lot, while its customers' lawns are usually six-foot terraces. Oblivious of this fact, the nursery blissfully sells all manner of garden plants, indoor tropical plants, and trees under the assumption that they will grow anywhere. One holdover from the old days is the prices, which are cheaper than uptown.

GARDEN CRAFTERS (THE SOHO GARDEN)
37 Grand St   212/268-0530
Tues-Fri. 10-7; Sat, Sun. 11-8
Hours vary by season; call ahead

A garden oasis amid the cast-iron columns of Soho? Everything for the garden can be found at Garden Crafters, from the finest plants to the largest selection of planters, garden furniture, and ornaments. Here you'll find the leading edge in planters: lightweight fiberglass in metallic antique finishes, bronze verdigris, and rusted cast iron. All of the fiberglass and distinctive gift items can be shipped anywhere in the country.

GRASS ROOTS GARDEN
131 Spring St (bet Wooster and Greene St)   212/226-2662
Tues-Sat: 9-6; Sun: 12-6

Larry Nathanson's grass-roots movement began more than a quarter of a century ago when he turned his hobby into a full-time vocation. The possessor of a genuine green thumb, Nathanson couldn't understand why city pavement had to be an inhibiting factor for would-be urban farmers. So he blithely set up his Grass Roots Garden, paying no mind to the boutique atmosphere or cutesy merchandising that marked the shops of his peers. Every square inch in Nathanson's shop is crammed with a sprouting green plant. The business primarily stocks indoor plants, but they also design, install, and maintain outdoor rooftop, backyard, and terrace gardens. If having to prune and water plants infringes on your happiness, Grass Roots can handle that, too. In addition to soil, plants, lighting units, insecticides, fertilizers, gardening tools, and equipment, garden furniture, and a consulting business, Grass Roots makes house calls all over town and runs a plant-maintenance service. They also show one of the largest stocks of pottery in Manhattan.

PRESTON BAILEY FLORAL & EVENT DESIGN
88 Lexington Ave (bet 26th and 27th St), Room 16C   212/683-0035
By appointment

For over 15 years Preston Bailey has been a leader in the floral design world.

He is used by some of the top names in the city, like Tiffany, Christie's, Time-Warner, and Disney. Bailey's work is not inexpensive, but for theme weddings, corporate events, stage and film decoration, and other big-time activities, you can't do better.

SIMPSON & COMPANY
852 Tenth Ave (at 56th St)   212/772-6670
Mon-Fri: 9-6

Simpson offers unusual flowers, plants, and beautiful freeze-dried arrangements of flowers, fruits, and vegetables. These are very lifelike; you can only tell the difference from fresh flowers by touching them. The fourth floor houses an orchid greenhouse, which is the only one of its kind in the city. These folks can handle gatherings of all sizes, and their prices are very competitive.

SPRING STREET GARDEN
186½ Spring St (bet Thompson and Sullivan St)   212/966-2015
Tues-Sat: 11:30-7 (closed Aug)

You'd never know you were in the bowels of Manhattan in this store. The service is highly personalized, and there is a great selection of cut flowers and plants. They do everything to order and will deliver all over Manhattan. You'll also enjoy the picturesque 19th-century building.

TREILLAGE
418 E 75th St (nr York Ave)   212/535-2288
Mon-Fri: 10-6; Sat: 10-5 (closed weekends in July, Aug)

People forget that New Yorkers have gardens, too, although they are small. Many times they are just patios, but still they add a special dimension of charm to city living. Along comes Treillage to help make an ordinary plot of outside living into something special. There are all sorts of garden items, including furniture and accessories for indoors and outdoors, with a great selection of unusual pieces that will set your place apart. They sell everything except plants and flowers! The prices are not exactly inexpensive, but why not splurge and enjoy the blue sky when you get a chance?

VSF
204 W 10th St (bet 4th and Bleecker St)   212/206-7236
Mon-Fri: 10-6; Sat: 11-5 (summer: Mon-Fri: 10-5)

Those who want a special English country garden look when it comes to fresh-cut flowers or dried creations know that you can't do any better than this outfit. They have a *primo* list of clients who take advantage of their talents for weddings, office flower arrangements, and other special events. Ask for owners Jack Follmer or Spruce Rodens.

ZEZÉ FLOWERS
398 E 52nd St (bet First Ave and East River)   212/753-7767
Mon-Fri: 8-6 (and holiday weekends)

Zezé came to New York several decades ago from Rio, a city known for its dramatic setting, and he brought a bit of that drama to the flower business in Manhattan. Zezé's windows reflect his unusual talent. Their exotic orchid selection is outstanding. Here you will find the ultimate in personalized service: same-day deliveries, cards written in calligraphy, unusual containers.

Furniture, Mattresses

General

ARISE FUTON MATTRESS COMPANY
265 W 72nd St (bet Broadway and West End Ave)   212/496-8410
Mon-Sat: 11-7; Sun: 12-5

Futons are thick sleeping mats popular in Japan. They look like upholstered cushions with cotton batting and unbleached muslin casings. Arise claims to have introduced them in 1970, and their success has been substantial. There are four styles currently available, ranging from the standard futon to the "Living Health Imperial" models. So while the classic futon has all-cotton batting, Arise's other models incorporate cores of various fibers for greater resiliency. In addition, the adaptation to New York has been made with the introduction of folding futon beds and even convertible sofas. These don't pull out; they simply drape the furniture. Frames are also available. All products are American-made.

CHARLES P. ROGERS BRASS & IRON BED COMPANY
899 First Ave (bet 50th and 51st St)   212/935-6900, 800/272-7726
Mon-Fri: 11-7; Sat: 10-6; Sun: 12-5

Are you hunting for a real antique piece? Rogers has been in the bed business for a century and a half and knows everything about good looks and comfort. Rogers shows over 50 models in four-posters, contemporary, canopied, and hand-painted styles. There are replicas of original designs and old-time beds, and all sizes are available in stock or on order. These folks sell factory-direct, so prices are competitive.

DEUTSCH WICKER
200 Lexington Ave, Suite 1101   212/683-8746, 800/223-4550
Mon-Fri: 9-5:30; Sat: by appointment

Wicker and rattan became popular in the mid-1970s, but Deutsch had been in the business for 20 years by that time. They originally sold to interior designers, furniture stores, and large businesses, but now the public (as well as commercial customers) can benefit from this high-quality merchandise. All of it is imported, and there are no cheap weaves here. Roger Deutsch is rightfully proud of his position in the field, and you should seek him out for advice when shopping here. Also available are leather and rattan chairs.

FOREMOST FURNITURE SHOWROOMS
8 W 30th St (at Fifth Ave), 5th floor   212/889-6347
Mon-Fri: 10-6; Sat: 9-5; Sun: 11-5

Decorators recommend Foremost to friends who want to avoid decorator commissions because it's a good place to get quality furniture at a 20% to 50% discount. Foremost has five full floors of furniture, laid out by floor and room plans. The personnel are friendly and helpful, making this an excellent source. Comparison- and window-shopping are difficult here. Though the values are indeed very good, it isn't obvious unless you've shopped around. So make this one of your last stops.

FRANK EASTERN COMPANY
599 Broadway (at Houston St)   212/219-0007
Mon-Fri: 9-5; Sat: 11-3:30 (closed Sat in summer)

For business and computer furniture, Frank Eastern Company should be a first choice. They are capable of completely furnishing a business or home office with tables, desks, chairs, files, bookcases, partitions, and a full line of computer work stations. Frank Eastern Company specializes in advanced ergonomic chairs that prevent backache and premature fatigue. The company president has conducted 27 years of extensive research in this field. He has personally tested over 2,200 different chairs from all over the world in an ongoing attempt to find the ultimate chair for the person who works at a desk or a computer. All of it is sold at a discount; free catalog on request.

GRANGE
200 Lexington Ave (at 32nd St), 2nd floor   212/685-9057
Mon-Fri: 9-6 or by appointment

Superb French furniture and accessories dominate the selling floor of this very attractive showroom. The goods are all French-inspired, and the furniture is clean-lined, functional, and in great taste. What the Italians have contributed to the classy look in ready-to-wear, the French have achieved in home collections. Note, however, that this is not a place for bargain hunters.

JENSEN-LEWIS
89 Seventh Ave (at 15th St)   212/929-4880
Mon-Wed, Fri, Sat: 10-7; Thurs: 10-8; Sun: 12-5

Jensen-Lewis had its origins in the late 19th-century sailmaking business of Charles Jensen and the canvas-awning business of Edward Lewis. In 1932, the two businesses united to become the premier canvas-awning dealer in the country. In 1964, they expanded to include canvas furniture. In very short order, the canvas furniture took off, and Jensen-Lewis now concentrates on canvas products and accessory pieces. There are bunk beds and bedroom sets, wardrobes in two heights and four sizes, home and office furniture, leather furniture, sofabeds, dining-room tables, lamps, and kitchen accessories. There's loads more, too—and we haven't even touched on such basic items as canvas chairs, bags, pillows, and futons! Not all of this is canvas, but it does fit the Jensen-Lewis look. You'll recognize it when you see it. It's relaxed, updated, practical, and very comfortable.

J. MABLEY CUSTOM FURNITURE
355 West Broadway (bet Grand and Broome St)   212/966-3930
Tues-Fri: 10-6; Sat: 11-6; Sun: 12-5

If you are looking for handcrafted fine-quality upholstered sofas, chairs and ottomans at reasonable prices, this is a good place to start. Fabrics range from high-end printed linens from England to simple cottons. J. Mabley also offers kilims and Persian rugs, custom pillows, accessory tables, and side chairs. Each frame is hand-assembled from fine California hardwoods; most deliveries are made within three to five weeks.

KENTSHIRE GALLERIES
37 E 12th St (bet University Pl and Broadway)   212/673-6644
Mon-Fri: 9-5; Sat: 10:30-3 (Oct-April)

Kentshire presents eight floors of English furniture and accessories, circa 1690-1870, with particular emphasis on the Georgian and Regency periods. This gallery has an excellent international reputation, and the displays are a delight to see, even if the price tags are a bit high. There is also a collection of 18th- and 19th-century English jewelry. A Kentshire boutique at Bergdorf Goodman features antiques, accessories, and antique jewelry.

KLEINSLEEP

962 Third Ave (at 58th St)   212/755-8210
874 Broadway (at 18th St)   212/995-0044
2330 Broadway (at 84th St)   212/501-8077
Mon-Fri: 10-9; Sat: 10-8; Sun: 11-7

Kleinsleep is a chain of stores specializing in bedding needs. At each store, the byword is discount, and at their three New York locations, prices are reduced even further. Kleinsleep showrooms feature mattresses from Stearns & Foster, Sealy Posturepedic, Simmons Beautyrest, Serta Perfect Sleeper, Kingsdown Sleeping Beauty, and their newest handcrafted line of Aireloom products. The Aireloom models feature an eight-way hand-tied box spring at prices you'd normally pay for a regular mattress and box spring. At Kleinsleep, customers get advice, expertise, and discounts up to 65% off department-store prices.

NORTH CAROLINA FURNITURE SHOWROOM

12 W 21st St (at Fifth Ave), 5th floor   212/260-5850
Mon-Sat: 10-6 (Thurs 10-8); Sun: 12-5

You'll find 409 famous name brands in furniture here, and most everything is at discount prices. There are items for living rooms and bedrooms, dinettes and dining-room tables and chairs, sofa beds, recliners, platform beds and bedding, and things for children's rooms. For space-conscious New Yorkers, who must make every square inch of apartment count, this place is a must-visit.

OAK-SMITH & JONES

1510 Second Ave (bet 78th and 79th St)   212/327-3462
Daily: 10-8

There is a distinct foreign accent in the furniture and accessories carried here. Unique original and reproduction antiques and accessories from all over the world are shown next to an outstanding collection of antique pine items and brass and iron beds. Upholstery and decorating services are available.

OFFICE FURNITURE HEAVEN

22 W 19th St, 7th floor   212 989-8600
Mon-Fri: 9-6

Have you used up all the extra bucks opening a new office? Relax. This place has bargains in first-quality contemporary pieces. Some are manufacturer's close-outs, others are discontinued items. You'll find the big boys of the industry represented: Knoll, Bernhardt, Herman Miller, and Oxford. There are conference tables, chairs, bookcases, file cabinets, accessories, and much more.

OSBORNE & OSBORNE

508 Canal St   212/431-7075
Sat-Sun: 1-6 or by appointment

Since 1975, Kipp and Margot Osborne have been building custom-made hardwood furniture for private and corporate clients. Each of their pieces is signed, dated, and numbered, marking both the continuing evolution of their work and the unique nature of each piece. They are shown in an 1827 landmark rowhouse in Tribeca. Traditional, time-proven cabinetmaking techniques and joinery provide the quality basis for Osborne furniture. Using these methods in conjunction with a careful process of wood selection and matching of wood grain, the Osbornes have created a body of work that numbers more than 1,800 pieces.

PHILIP ENGEL
220 E 54th St (at Third Ave)   212/759-9595
Mon-Sat: 10-6; Sun: 12-5

They like to call themselves the "world's greatest leather stores," and indeed they do have outstanding pieces of furniture in leather; sofas, dining-room tables and chairs, sectionals, sofa beds, and reclining chairs from all over the world. The company has been in business since 1967 and has five stores throughout the metropolitan area. Prices are reasonable, delivery is quick, pieces may be custom-ordered, and free in-store design service is available.

Infants and Children

ABC CARPET AND HOME
888 Broadway (at 19th St)   212/473-3000
Mon-Fri: 10-8; Sat: 10-7; Sun: 11-6:30

ABC has a baby department filled with whimsical, unusual, and well-designed furniture and other items. Cribs and bassinets, handmade quilts, bumper sets, and infant clothing, chairs that Goldilocks would no doubt find "just right," and lots of wood toys are among the highlights here. From an iron bassinet that carries a $795 price tag to a line of high-quality terry-cloth bathrobes for toddlers and children, nothing in this department is a bargain. But if you're looking for good-quality furnishings for infants and small children, put ABC at the top of your list.

ALBEE'S
715 Amsterdam (at 95th St)   212/662-5740
Mon-Wed, Fri, Sat: 9-5:30; Thurs: 9-7:30

This place makes me crazy. It's got one of the city's best selections of basics for infants and toddlers—everything from strollers and car seats to cribs and rocking chairs—and the staff can be very helpful. But the place is a disaster area, and it's hard to get anyone's attention in the chaos, particularly on weekends. That said, Albee's is very popular with Manhattan parents (and grandparents!), and it's worth a trip if you're expecting. For the record, prices aren't the best in town, but they *are* the best north of 23rd Street.

BABY DEPOT
Sixth Ave and 23rd St, 3rd floor   212/229-2247
Mon-Sat: 8-9; Sun: 10-6

As part of Burlington Coat Factory, this is exactly the kind of place that has some New Yorkers bemoaning the "malling" of their city. The service stinks, the stock is poorly presented, and the selection is spotty . . . but prices on baby furniture and accessories are great. If you know what you want and are willing to put up with what I consider to be the worst face of retailing to save a couple bucks, I regretfully recommend this perpetually crowded place.

BEN'S FOR KIDS
1380 Third Avenue (bet 78th and 79th St)   212/794-2330
Mon-Fri: 9:30-5 (Thurs to 8); Sat: 10:30-5

If you aren't willing to leave the East Side and yet want a good selection of basic baby and toddler furniture, clothing, toys, and accessories at relatively reasonable prices, this is the place to go. One real price-saver: Ben's doesn't charge for delivery or setup. The store's good organization and helpful staff make it easy to look around and try out different options.

CHILDREN'S ROOM
140 Varick St (at Spring St)   212/627-2006
Mon-Fri: 10-5:30; Sat 10-5

The name says it all. While there is absolutely nothing fun or fancy about this longtlme (23 years uptown, 5 at this location) children's furniture store, it does have all the basics at good prices. If you're looking for beds (particularly the bunk beds that are so popular in this space-starved city), bookcases, dressers, desks, and the like for your children and don't want to spend their college tuition, take a trip down here.

KID'S SUPPLY COMPANY
1325 Madison Ave, 2nd floor (bet 93rd and 94th St)   212/426-1200
Mon-Sat: 10-6; Sun: 12-5

This newcomer to the children's-furniture scene advertises itself as an "elegant but reasonable resource for antique and contemporary furuishings." (Read: You have really good taste and a lot of money to spend on your child's room.) I highly recommend a visit with these talented folks in their beautiful but jam-packed showroom. From bunk beds and desks to rugs and other accessories, the owners of Kid's Supply Company have really put together a classy operation. A worthwhile extra if you're tight on space and want to make the most of what you have: for $150, they'll visit your home and work up a floor plan.

SCHNEIDER'S
20 Ave A (at 2nd St)   212/228-3540
Mon-Sat: 10-6

If you are in the market for baby furniture and accessories, this little-known store (at least to "uptown" people) often has the very best prices in Manhattan. On top of that, the staff knows its stock, and there's enough space in the store to take a stroller for a test drive. Whether you're looking for cribs, car seats, strollers, backpacks, cribs or anything else for little ones, Schneider's is well worth a visit. They carry juvenile furniture as well.

WICKER GARDEN'S BABY
1327 Madison Avenue (at 93rd St)   212/348-1166
Mon-Sat: 10-6 (call for special hours in July and Aug)

There are no two ways about it: Pam Scurry has a great sense of style. If you like wicker furniture, handpainted detail and unusual, often whimsical designs, you'll love the baby and juvenile furniture on the second floor of this store. You'll also no doubt be quite taken with the extensive selection of beautiful and almost quaintly formal infant and children's clothing on the first floor. (The infant clothing is heavy on pink, blue, and white.) That's the good news. The bad news is that everything at Wicker Garden is incredibly expensive, and the staff are among the haughtiest I've encountered in New York.

Good Places to Bargain Shop!

The 16th-floor clearance center at the **New York Design Center** (200 Lexington Ave; 212/679-9500) has furniture and gift items. There are exceptional values on showroom samples, available for immediate delivery. Hours: Mon-Fri: 9-5 p.m.

For furniture overstocks, canceled orders, and slow-moving items, try **Macy's Clearance Center** (155 Glen Cove Rd, Carleplace, Long Island, 516/742-8500) and **Bloomingdale's Clearance Center** (same building, different entrance, 516/294-3410). These centers are open seven days a week. (See page 416)

Games—Adult

COMPLEAT STRATEGIST
11 E 33rd St (at Fifth Ave)   212/685-3880
Mon-Wed, Fri, Sat: 10:30-6; Thurs: 10:30-9

320 W 57th St (bet Eighth and Ninth Ave)   212/582-1272
Mon-Sat: 11-8; Sun: 12-5

630 Fifth Ave (Rockefeller Center)   212/265-7449
Mon-Fri: 10:30-5:30

The Compleat Strategist was established as a fortress for military games and equipment. As the only such place in the city, it became an overwhelming success and was soon overrun with military strategists. As time went on, the store branched into science fiction, fantasy, and murder-mystery games, as well as adventure games and books. When this, too, captured the imagination of the public, the Compleat Strategist opened two more outposts. Today people who are fighting the Civil War all over again can browse alongside Dragon Masters at three locations in the city! The stock is more than ample for any military or Dungeons and Dragons addict, and the personnel are knowledgeable and friendly. For the less feisty, they have chess and backgammon sets—even good old Monopoly! These are adult games with no sneering or innuendo— unless, of course, you're playing the villain.

GAME SHOW
474 Sixth Ave (bet 11th and 12th St)   212/633-6328
Mon-Sat: 12-7 (Thurs: 12-8); Sun: 12-5

1240 Lexington Ave (bet 83rd and 84th St)   212/472-8011
Mon-Sat: 11-6 (Thurs 11-7); Sun: 12-5

If you can't find a kid's or adult's game or puzzle at Game Show, it probably doesn't exist. This store is crammed with the best of the lot, and the folks here love to talk to customers about their stock.

MARION & COMPANY
147 W 26th St   212/727-8900
Mon-Fri: 8-5:30; Sat: 10-4 (except July, Aug)

When you think of casino and game equipment, think of Marion! This outfit has been in business for nearly a century and is still presided over by a family member, Ed Weinstein. Marion distributes a large selection of chess, back-gammon, and dominoes items, plus plastic cards and casino equipment for home or professional use. They also make personalized poker chips and offer a wide range of gaming tables and roulette wheels. Marion is both a wholesale and retail operation.

VILLAGE CHESS SHOP
230 Thompson St (bet Bleecker and 3rd St)   212/475-9580
Daily: noon-midnight

People who enjoy chess can play at the Village Chess Shop for about a dollar an hour. Those who are searching for really unique chess pieces would be wise to patronize this shop as well. Chess sets are available in pewter, brass, ebony, onyx, and more. Many boards can be flipped over for backgammon. Village Chess has outstanding sets for that game as well. In short, this should be the first stop when you're moving chess pieces—whether from one square to another or from their store to your home!

Gifts, Accessories

BERTABRASIL BUTIK
151 W 46th St (bet Sixth and Seventh Ave), 7th floor   212/354-9616
Mon-Fri: 9-5:30; Sat: 9-2

This is a loft discount boutique featuring a number of well-known names in watches, sunglasses, electronics, cosmetics, and some clothing items. Don't expect to find depth in any classification, but good bargains exist if you don't mind disinterested salespeople and zero ambience.

BE-SPECKLED TROUT
422 Hudson St (at St. Luke's Pl) 212/255-1421
Mon-Sat: 10-10; Sun: 11-7

Here is a turn-of-the-century general store that features unique items for fishermen and anyone else with good taste. There is folk art, many tea-related antiques, English bone china from the 1920s and 1930s, and handmade chocolates, plus the owner's collection of angling antiquities and eccentricities. Craig and Charlotte Bero's grandfather owned the shop's original fixtures. You can try homemade American pies on what used to be a real fishing ground—the place is on the site of Minetta Creek, which still flows under the Village.

BIZARRE BAZAAR
130-1/4 E 65th St (bet Lexington and Park Ave)   212/517-2100
Gallery hours by appointment

Some people collect baseball cards, others find political buttons fascinating. One friend of mine, Judi Hofer, has one of the greatest doll collections in the world. I collect "Do Not Disturb" signs from hotels I have stayed at! For the discerning and serious collector, Bizarre Bazaar offers antique toys, aviation and automobilia, vintage Louis Vuitton luggage, enamel glassware, French perfume bottles, Lalique pieces, artist mannequins, architectural miniatures, and much more of good quality. This is a place for browsing and buying!

CAROLE STUPELL
29 E 22nd St   212/260-3100
Mon-Sat: 10-6

Imagine the fun of being able to set a table with the most beautiful accessories available. The first place anyone who has such a yen should visit is Carole Stupell. In my opinion, this is the finest home-accessory store in the country. The taste and thought that has gone into the selection of merchandise is simply unmatched. Keith Stupell, a second-generation chip-off-the-old-block, has assembled a fabulous array of china, glassware, silver, and gift treasures, and he displays them in spectacular settings. In addition, the store offers a large selection of china and glassware replacement patterns that date back over 30 years. The prices are not in the bargain range, but the quality is unequaled.

CERAMICA GIFT GALLERY
1009 Sixth Ave (bet 37th and 38th St)   212/354-9216, 800/666-9956
Mon-Fri: 9:30-6; Sun: 12-5

We've been looking for a place that has good bridal-registry giftware at discount prices, as it's been one of the most frequent requests from readers. We've found just the place, and the convenient midtown location is a bonus. At Ceramica Gift Gallery, you'll find all major brands of china, crystal, tableware, and collectibles, including Waterford, Royal Doulton, Gorham, Minton, Wedgwood, and Lenox. In addition, they ship anywhere in the country and will accept mail and phone orders. Discounts can go as high as 50%, and they will quote prices over the phone.

CURACAO
20 W 57th St, 4th floor   212/581-6970
Mon-Fri: 9-6; Sat, Sun: 9-2

This is a special find, but only for those with non-U.S. passports. There is a great selection of pens, electronics, perfumes, gifts, and some clothing at considerable savings. For visitors from overseas, Curacao is a bonanza. For New York residents, go with someone who has a foreign passport and share in the savings.

EVERYTHING ANGELS
9 W 31st St (bet Fifth Ave and Broadway), 2nd floor   212/564-6950
Mon-Sat: 12-6 or by appointment

Everything Angels is just brimming with heavenly gifts from all over the world. There is jewelry, artwork, clothing, books, and much more. The sky is the limit! They also work with special groups and do corporate, bridal, and wholesale gift business.

FELISSIMO
10 W 56th St   212/247-5656
Mon-Wed, Fri-Sat: 10-6; Thurs: 10-8

Felissimo is a highly unique gift store with an emphasis on tabletop merchandise. The four-story building, a turn-of-the-century townhouse, has eight rooms displaying beautiful merchandise like jewelry, scarves, cashmeres, outdoor living items, and plants and flowers, as well as things to make your dining table extra special. They are known for their *furoshiki* gift wrap: beautiful fabric squares that are a longstanding Japanese tradition. On the fourth floor are bimonthly exhibits featuring the work of renowned and up-and-coming artists. Afternoon haiku tea (sandwiches, scones, sweet bits) is served in the store's tearoom.

FLIGHTS OF FANCY
1502 First Ave (bet 78th and 79th St)   212/772-1302
Mon-Fri: 12-7 (Wed until 8); Sat: 10-6; Sun: 12-6

Flights of Fancy exudes charm, presenting soft music and an array of American treasures arranged in a Victorian parlor setting beckoning passers-by. Many of the gifts are handmade and exclusive to the shop, and the window display (which changes weekly) often showcases only one item in a line. That item is often so unusual and special that orders pour in from around the country. Prices range from $2 to $2,000, so there is something for every kind of gift-giving. July is the month to save 15% on holiday items. Suggestions? It's hard to be specific, since the stock is always changing. But a handmade American theme runs through one of the largest selections of one-of-a-kind gifts in the city.

GOLDMAN'S TREASURES
655 Sixth Ave (at 20th St)   212/924-4900
Mon-Thurs: 10-9; Fri: 10-3; Sun: 11-6

Goldman's moved from the Lower East Side in 1994 to this rather unusual-looking store, which provides a unique shopping experience. You'll find brand-name china and crystal, lighting fixtures, furniture, paintings, home decor, and a huge selection of gift items, all at discount prices. They have been in the gift business since 1907.

L. S. COLLECTION
765 Madison Ave (at 66th St)   212/472-3355
469 West Broadway   212/673-4575
Mon-Fri: 11:30-7; Sat: 11;30-8; Sun: 12-6

Even if you have no intention of buying a thing, you'll get a thrill out of this superb collection. Seldom have I seen home- and office-accessory items done in such superb taste. Each piece is almost museum-quality. You'll find dishes, vases, glassware, tea and coffee sets, desk pieces, and leather goods that would be just the thing for your dream home. Prices are not low, but are not out of line for the quality represented.

MARION DESIGN FOR DINING
401 E 58th St (at First Ave and Sutton Pl)   212/888-0894
Tues-Sat: 11-6:30; Sun: 1-5; (closed Sun and Mon in Aug)

Doing some fancy entertaining? Marion Johnson can be a big help! In her 1870s carriage house in the Sutton Place area you will find some very classy items, like beautiful service plates and European china, vintage sterling service pieces, great chocolates, and hand-dipped tapers. The owner is an interior designer, assuring that the mixture of antique, vintage, and current tableware and accessories is unique and attractive.

MICHAEL C. FINA COMPANY
3 W 47th St (at Fifth Ave)   212/869-5050
Mon-Fri: 9:30-6 (Thurs: 9:30-7); Sat: 10:30-6

A New York tradition for over 60 years, Michael C. Fina is a popular bridal-registry firm with an extensive selection of sterling silver, china, crystal, and housewares. Prices are attractive, quality is top-notch, and the place is well organized.

ONLY HEARTS
386 Columbus Ave (at 79th St)   212/724-5608
Mon-Sat: 11-8; Sun: 12-7

This is one of the most fun shops in New York! Helena Stuart offers the romantic in the family a fascinating array of intimate apparel and lingerie, heart-shaped or printed jewelry, balloons, boudoir pillows, soaps, tissues, and even plungers decorated with heart-shaped tops.

OPHELIA & MAYA SCHAPER
Cheese & Antiques/Furniture & Paté
106 W 69th St (at Columbus Ave)   212/873-2100
Daily: 10-8

Maya Schaper is one of those special personalities who knows what she likes and wants to share her interest, which pertains to cheese and food-related antiques. Granted, this is an unusual combination. But Maya is an unusual person. You'll find interesting gifts, gift baskets, imported dried flower arrangements from France, freshly baked pies, hand-painted furniture, and a willingness to locate special items for customers.

SUSAN P. MEISEL DECORATIVE ARTS
133 Prince St (bet West Broadway and Wooster St)   212/254-0137
Tues-Sat: 10-6

Meisel is really a toy store for nostalgic adults. You will find the area's largest selection in certain specialized categories: pond sailboats, pinup originals, and airplanes of all sorts. It strikes me as a rather unusual combination, but if the mentioned items are on your want list, this is the place to visit!

WOLFMAN-GOLD & GOOD COMPANY
116 Greene St (bet Prince and Spring St)   212/431-1888
Mon-Sat: 11-6; Sun: 12-5

This Soho shop is described as a "marriage of contemporary and antique table settings," and that says it best. There are linens that would look classy in a Park Avenue penthouse and a series of white-on-white tableware that would blend with the starkest Soho loft. Some of the tableware is imported from France, Italy, and England; the rest is domestic. But all of it is elegant. The store also stocks baskets, birdhouses, cutlery, glasses, linens, home accessories, lamps, and slip-covered couches. This is a first-choice source for an exquisite house gift.

WORKS GALLERY
1250 Madison Ave (bet 89th and 90th St)   212/996-0300
Mon-Thurs: 10-7; Fri, Sat: 10-6; Sun: 12-5 (closed Sun in summer)

Sometimes we all need a very unique gift for a special person or occasion. If so, this is a place to visit. At Works Gallery you will find unusual one-of-a-kind jewelry and art-glass items handmade by talented artists. You can even have a personal piece made up from your own stones. Their reliability is attested to by the fact they have been in business for over 20 years.

YELLOW DOOR
1308 Avenue M, Brooklyn, NY   718/998-7382
Mon-Fri: 10-5:45; Sun: 11-5

Brooklyn is renowned for a number of famous people who were born there:

Mary Tyler Moore, Sandy Koufax, Woody Allen, Barbra Streisand, and Larry King, to mention a few. Another famous thing about Brooklyn is a discount gift store on Avenue M in Flatbush, off the promenade of Ocean Parkway. It is run by a native-born entrepreneur by the name of Sallee Bijou. For over 30 years the Yellow Door has been providing "Madison Avenue style at Brooklyn prices." The store carries an unparalleled selection of the finest name brands (Lalique, MacKenzie-Childs, Waterford, Lenox, Orrefors, Alessi, Towle) in 14- and 18-carat gold jewelry, gifts, china, table accessories, and bath items. Many prices are at least 20% to 30% below suggested retail. Services include free local delivery, a bridal registry, and phone orders.

Greeting Cards

UNICEF CARD & GIFT SHOP
3 United Nations Plaza (44th St bet First and Second Ave)
212/326-7054
Mon-Fri: 10-6; Sat: 10-2

For half a century the United Nations Children's Emergency Fund (UNICEF) has been devoted to improving the lives of the world's children. One way this tremendous organization raises money for its life-saving projects and programs is through the sale of cards and gifts. If you've never seen UNICEF products before, you're in for a treat at this well-planned and friendly store. In addition to greeting cards, stationery, books and games for children, and a fascinating assortment of Nepalese paper products, this store sells cards chosen for sale in Asia, Africa, Europe, and South America. In fact, it's the only store in the U.S. that does sell those exotic cards.

UNTITLED
159 Prince St (at West Broadway)   212/982-2088
Mon-Sat: 10-10; Sun: 11-7

The Metropolitan Museum and the Louvre each have approximately 1,500 art cards. Untitled, by contrast, has 4,000-plus cards in stock at any given moment. Those cards include modern-art postcards, greeting cards, and note cards. The postcards are filed as either pre- or post-1945, and they're further ordered within those classifications by artist's names. There are also postcards of famous photos and depictions of every possible type of art. Some of these items are good for gags, while others are suitable for framing. Untitled also sells art magazines; books on art, design, typography, architecture, and photography; and boxed cards.

Hearing Aids

EMPIRE STATE HEARING AID BUREAU
31 W 43rd St   212/921-1666
Mon-Fri: 9-5:30 (Wed until 6)

If President Reagan left no other legacy, he set a shining example of not being ashamed to wear a hearing aid. The new aids are so small that most people are not even aware of their use. Empire State has been in the business for over 40 years and carries the top names in the field: Siemens, Starkey, Bosch, Danavox, and the lastest in digital hearing aids by Widex. They have mature and skilled personnel who will test and fit quality hearing aids in a quiet, unhurried atmosphere.

Hobbies

AMERICA'S HOBBY CENTER
146 W 22nd St   212/675-8922
Mon-Fri: 8:45-5:30; Sat: 8:30-3:30

While hobbies and models are serious business here, there's also a lighthearted touch evident everywhere in the shop. Marshall Winston introduces himself as the "known authority on vehicular hobbies," which include model airplanes, boats, ships, trains, cars, radio-controlled materials, model books, helicopters, model rocketry, tools, and everything for model builders. They also sell wholesale to dealers and by mail order to retail customers, as well as doing export business. Ask for a catalog to see what they have in your field of interest.

JAN'S HOBBY SHOP
1557 York Ave (bet 82nd and 83rd St)   212/861-5075
Mon-Sat: 10-7; Sun: 12-5

Jan is one of my favorite examples of New York retailing! When Fred Hutchins was young (he's now in his 30s), he was obsessed with building models and dioramas, particularly on historical themes. Eventually, it became economically viable for his parents to buy his favorite source of supply. Now he runs the shop. So while the front of the store is still a hobby shop, the star of the show is clearly the grown-up Fred, who keeps Jan's stocked with everything a serious model builder could possibly want. The store has a superb stock of plastic scale models, model war games, paints, books, brushes and other paraphernalia, toys, trains, planes, ships, and tank models. It also has remote-controlled cars, ships, and tanks. In the meantime, Fred himself has gone professional. He creates models and dioramas to order for television, advertising, and private customers. In addition to his craft skills, he is noted for his accurate historical detail. There is yet a third business: showcase building. Because any hobbyist likes to show his wares, Fred builds custom-made wood and plexiglass showcases for that purpose.

Home Furnishings–General

Of interest in the **NoLiTa** area are several small home furnishings stores worthy of a visit when you are out exploring:

Gates of Marrakesh (8 Prince St): This is a Moroccan-style bazaar, with fabrics, lighting fixtures, and other exotics.

Just Shades (21 Spring St at Elizabeth St): There are over 4,000 lamp shades in stock. If you can't find it here they will order it.

Michael Anchin (250 Elizabeth St): Beautiful one-of-a-kind hand-blown glass vases, shades, and drinking glasses are displayed here.

ABC CARPET & HOME
881 and 888 Broadway (at 19th St)   212/473-3000
Mon-Fri: 10-8; Sat: 10-7; Sun: 11-6:30

If you had time (and money) to visit just one store in Manhattan, this should be it! What started in 1897 as a pushcart business has grown and expanded into one of the most unique, exciting, and well-merchandised emporiums (actually two buildings, which are across the street from each other). ABC is the Bergdorf Goodman of home furnishings. There are floors of great-looking furniture, dinnerware, linens, gifts, accessories, antiques and everything in between. You will see many one-of-a-kind pieces as you explore corner after corner. There is an entire floor of fabrics by the yard and a carpet and rug selection you won't believe at great prices. The Parlor Cafe on the main floor helps out hungry shoppers.

BED BATH & BEYOND
620 Sixth Ave (bet 18th and 19th St)   212/255-3550
Mon-Sat: 9:30-9; Sun: 10-6

I've been in the business for a long time, and I have never seen an operation like this! It is an absolute must if you are in the market for anything for the apartment or home. In a huge store of over 80,000 square feet on lower Sixth Avenue, these home-furnishings experts show stocks as far as the eye can see. There are sheets, blankets, rugs, kitchen gadgets, hangers, towels, dinnerware, hampers, cookware, kiddie items, pillows, and much more, with hundreds of choices in each category. Best of all, prices are discounted, the personnel are friendly and helpful, checkout is well organized, and carts are available so you can pile up purchases.

Home Furnishings in Soho

These stores, with goods from the generic to the unique, help make Soho a home-furnishings mecca:

Ad Hoc Softwares (410 West Broadway; 212/925-2652)
Broadway Panhandler (477 Broome St; 212/966-3434)
Dialogica (484 Broome St; 212/966-1934)
Interieurs (114 Wooster St; 212/343-0800)
Knoll (105 Wooster St; 212/343-4000)
Lechter's Housewares and Gifts (536 Broadway; 212/274-0890)
Moss (146 Greene St; 212/226-2190)
Platypus (126 Spring St; 212/219-3919)
Poltroniafrau (145 Wooster St; 212/777-7592)
Portico Bed and Bath (139 Spring St; 212/941-7722)
Portico Home (379 West Broadway; 212/941-7800)
Pure Madderlake (478 Broadway; 212/941-7770)
Terra Verde (120 Wooster St; 212/925-4533)
Williams-Sonoma Grande Cuisine (580 Broadway, 212/343-7330)
Wolfman Gold and Good Company (117 Mercer St; 212/431-1888)
Zona (97 Greene St; 212/925-6750)

Housewares, Hardware

AMERICAN STEEL WINDOW SERVICE
108 W 17th St (bet Sixth and Seventh Ave)   212/242-8131
Mon-Fri: 7:30-4:30

Peter Weinberger has one of the most esoteric businesses in the city—

one that his family has been in for over 75 years. What he does is sell window hardware. If you need a lock, latch, handle, or bracket, American undoubtedly has it. The store is actually a tiny office, but the warehouse is right next door. It resembles a garage crammed full of window hardware. How he stays in business is beyond comprehension.

APPLIANCES OVERSEAS
276 Fifth Ave, (at 30th St), 4th floor   212/545-8001
Mon-Fri: 8:30-5

For nearly 40 years Appliances Overseas has been a valuable resource for folks traveling or living overseas. This firm offers a full range of large and small appliances for use in every country of the world (110-220 volt). If purchased overseas, these same items are significantly more expensive. Besides, all appliances sold here have American features, are larger in capacity, and often have dual-voltage capability. Enzo Borges, formerly of Thor Export, has joined Allen Sausen in providing superior service. They distribute over 4,000 international appliances and electronics. Mention this book and they will give a 5% discount on orders over $250.

BARSON HARDWARE
35 W 44th St (bet Fifth and Sixth Ave)   212/944-8181
Mon-Fri: 8:30-6; Sat: 10-5

Can you imagine a hardware store in the middle of Manhattan that is well organized and competitively priced? Founder Barney Rubin's daughter Anita and David Schneiderman operate a store that carries everything from first-aid kits to drill bits, 29 sizes of scissors, hair curlers, and fire extinguishers. They specialize in travel needs, unique kitchen and housewares items, tools, and plumbing needs. The personnel know their stock and can come up with the right item to fix that "whatjamagig" in the bathroom. The staff is fluent in six languages: Hebrew, Yiddish, Chinese, Italian, Spanish, and English.

BLACK AND DECKER FACTORY OUTLET STORE
50 W 23rd St (bet Fifth and Sixth Ave)   212/929-6450
Mon-Fri: 9-5:30; Sat: 10-4

Black and Decker is a name well known for power tools. At this location, the company sells tools, appliances, and accessories at prices that are hard to beat. Everything is sold with a two-year guarantee. Imagine buying a power saw on your trip to ultra-urban New York!

BRIDGE KITCHENWARE
214 E 52nd St   212/688-4220
Mon-Fri: 9-5:30; Sat: 10-4:30

Bridge Kitchenware is a unique-to-New York store that supplies almost every restaurant and institution within 500 miles. Bridge carries bar equipment, cutlery, pastry equipment, molds, copperware, cast-iron ware, woodenware, stoneware, and kitchen gadgets. All goods are professional quality and excellent for home gourmets. Be sure to see the line of imported copperware from France, as well as the professional knives and baking pans. After trying them, people use no other. By the way, Bridge takes its name from founder Fred Bridge, not from the nearby 59th Street Bridge.

BROADWAY PANHANDLER
477 Broome St (at Wooster St)   212/966-3434
Mon-Fri: 10:30-7; Sat, Sun: 11-7

In new and expanded quarters, thousands of cutlery, bakeware, tabletop items, and cookware pieces are available at sizable savings. Guest chefs make periodic appearances here, and a fine selection of professional items is offered to walk-in customers as well as restaurant and hotel buyers.

CK&L SURPLUS
307 Canal St (at Broadway)   212/966-1745
Mon-Sat: 8:30-5:45; Sun: 9:30-5:30

In New York, a shopping trip for hardware wouldn't be complete without a trip to Canal Street. On Canal Street, CK&L is the oldest and best. Years ago, these very same stores dealt in industrial and war surplus. With the passing demand for military supplies and an influx of electronics, the Canal Street surplus stores turned to areas best described as "hardware and whatever." All of the stores do business the same way. Sawed-off cardboard boxes containing an assortment of homogeneous but totally implausible merchandise are "displayed" in front. The junk at the front is there to draw customers inside, where the real merchandise is sold. There are power tools, simple tools, plumbing and electrical goods, accessories, and supplies. Prices are much lower than those at retail stores uptown. When you see the place, you'll understand why the overhead is so low.

CLOSET KING
415 E 72nd St (bet First and York Ave)   212/717-6110
Mon-Sat: 10-6

Living quarters in the city have always been notoriously tight, but people tend to stay put and small apartments are measured for every inch of usable space. Frequently, closets – if they exist at all – are the first things to go. They are reincarnated as nurseries, bars, bathrooms, eating areas, and even at-home offices. It was inevitable that experts would specialize in organizing closet space, and Don Constable and his Closet King staff do just that. The overall aim is to provide maximum storage space, tailored to a customer's needs. Since the store exists to sell components, they encourage do-it-yourselfers. A customized system can be planned and purchased here, then self-installed at a fraction of the cost a professional closet organizer would charge.

GARBER HARDWARE
49 Eighth Ave (bet Horatio and Jane St)   212/929-3030
Mon-Fri: 8-5; Sat: 8-3

This is another unique family business that has become a New York institution. The Garbers have been in business for over 116 years at the same location with the appealing motto "Either We Have It, or We Can Get It For You." You will find a complete inventory of paints, hardware, plumbing and electrical supplies, housewares, locks, tools, and building materials. Same-day or next-day free delivery, locksmith service, custom window shades, instant lamp repair, and pipe cut to size are just a few of the many handy services offered here.

GARRETT WADE
161 Sixth Ave (at Spring St)   212/807-1155
Mon-Fri: 9-5:30; Sat: 10-3

The Garrett Wade customer uses and appreciates fine woodworking tools, for the store prides itself on offering only the best-made tools from all over the world. The main business is mail-order, and the catalog is all-encompassing. It lists every imaginable woodworking aid and explains each piece's function and advantage over its peers. It reads like a how-to guide! Garrett Wade assumes that anyone can put together a rocker or, at the very least, appreciate the function of a lightweight spokeshave. After a visit here, you may become a believer, too!

GEORGE TAYLOR SPECIALTIES
100 Hudson St (bet Franklin and Leonard St)   212/226-5369
Mon-Wed: 7:30-5; Thurs: 7:30-6; Fri: 7:30-4

Taylor stocks plumbing replacement parts to fit all faucets, and custom faucets can be fabricated via special order. There are also reproduction faucets and custom designs of fittings for unique installations. Antique towel bars, bath accessories, and pedestal sinks are a specialty. Founded in 1869, Taylor remains a family-run operation. Ask for Chris, his daughter Valerie, or son John.

GRACIOUS HOME
1217 and 1220 Third Ave (bet 70th and 71st St)
212/988-8990, 212/517-6300
Mon-Fri: 8-7; Sat: 9-7; Sun: 10-6

For over 30 years Gracious Home has been a local New York-style hardware store. Run with a personal style, its products and services are geared for New York life. They sell appliances, wall coverings, brass hardware, decorative bath accessories, lighting, china, casual furniture, bedding, shelving, pots and pans . . . you get the picture. Full-scale kitchen and bathroom remodeling is a specialty. Services include cooking demonstrations, tool rental, and repairs. They will special-order items and deliver in Manhattan.

LAMALLE KITCHENWARE
36 W 25th St, 6th floor   212/242-0750
Mon-Fri: 9-6; Sat: 10-6

Since 1927 this has been the definitive shop for fine-quality French cookware. (It is the oldest cookware business in the country.) Now Chip Fisher has made it even better! Lamalle is both an importer and manufacturer of copperware, stainless-steel stovetop and ovenware, pastry tools, and molds. All are available at reasonable prices. They re-tin copper and have a bridal-registry department, as well as a great cookbook section. Ask to go through their stockroom, as many treasures lie hidden in the stacks.

LEESAM KITCHEN AND BATH CENTER
124 Seventh Ave (at 17th St)   212/243-6482
Daily: 9:30-6 (Thurs: 9:30-8); Sat: 12-5

For over a half-century these folks have been fixing up kitchens and bathrooms. Whether it is a medicine cabinet, kitchen cabinets, faucets, shower enclosures, or counters, you will see one of the largest selections of top brands from both domestic and foreign suppliers. There's no excuse not to remodel your old, cluttered, dysfunctional kitchen using one of their computer-designed plans.

LUDLOW HARDWARE AND VARIETY
246 Broome St (at Ludlow St)   212/673-1642
Mon-Thurs, Sun: 9:30-5

This is one of the last mom-and-pop hardware stores in the city, and the ambience and prices reflect its advantages. Ludlow has some of the lowest prices around on hardware, housewares, paint, and tools. They also make keys and speak several languages.

NEW CATHAY HARDWARE CORPORATION
49 Mott St (nr Canal St)   212/962-6648
Daily: 10-7:15

In the heart of Chinatown, this gem of a shop has been dispensing Chinese cooking items, utensils, knives, hardware, small appliances, and restaurant equipment since 1928. There's no more authentic place to get your woks, chopsticks, steamers, or eggroll rollers, and prices and quality are geared for professionals. This is also a great place to find an unusual housewarming or shower gift.

P.E. GUERIN
23 Jane St (bet Greenwich St and Eighth Ave)   212/243-5270
Mon-Fri: 9:30-4:30 by appointment only
(closed first two weeks of July)

Andrew F. Ward, P.E. Guerin's current president, is the fourth generation of the oldest decorative hardware firm in the country and the only foundry in the city. What's more, they've been on Jane Street for 105-plus years of the firm's existence. In that time, though, the firm has grown into a worldwide operation. The main foundry is now in Valencia, Spain (although work is still done at the Village location), and there are branches and showrooms across the country and in Puerto Rico. The Jane Street location is still headquarters for manufacturing and importing decorative hardware and bath accessories. Much of it is done in brass or bronze, and the foundry can make virtually anything in those materials, including copies and reproductions. The Guerin table has garnered design and production awards and enjoys a worldwide reputation. No job is too small for this firm, which operates like the hometown industry it thinks it is. They offer free estimates and help with such hardware problems as locks. Their work is impressive!

PULL CART
31 W 21st St (bet Fifth and Sixth Ave), 7th floor   212/727-7089
Mon-Thurs: 12-9; Fri-Sun: 11-6
(summer: Mon-Thurs: 12-9; Fri: 12-6)

This is the largest ready-to-decorate ceramic-housewares company in the country. Customers can decorate ceramic dinnerware and other tabletop and houseware items with their own designs and imagination. Pull Cart will glaze the finished product, and the designer may pick it up within two to four days. There are over 200 shapes and 60 colors to choose from. You need not be an expert to have a fun and productive time here. This is also a great place for an unusual catered party or shower.

SIMON'S HARDWARE & BATH
421 Third Ave (bet 29th and 30th St)   212/532-9220
Mon-Fri: 8-5:30 (Thurs until 7); Sat: 10-5

This is really a hardware supermarket. Customers take numbers just as they would at a bakery counter. No one minds waiting, because Simon's offers one of the city's finest selections of quality decorative hardware items, bath and kitchen fixtures and accessories, plus marble, stone, and tile. The personnel are patient, even if you just need something to fix a broken handle on a chest of drawers.

WILLIAMS-SONOMA
1175 Madison Ave (at 86th St)   212/289-6832
110 Seventh Ave (at 17th St)   212/633-2203
20 E 60th St (bet Madison and Park Ave)   212/980-5155
1309 Second Ave (at 69th St)   212/288-8408
580 Broadway (bet Prince and Houston St)   212/343-7330

Hours vary by store

WILLIAMS-SONOMA OUTLET STORE
231 Tenth Ave (bet 23rd and 24th St)   212/206-8118
Mon-Fri: 11-6; Sat, Sun: 10-5

From humble beginnings in the wine country of Sonoma, California, these stores have expanded over the nation and now are referred to as the "Tiffany of cookware stores." The serious cook of the kitchen will find a vast display of quality cookware, bakeware, cutlery, kitchen linens, specialty foods, cookbooks, small appliances, kitchen furniture, glassware, and tableware. The stores also offer a gift and bridal-registry service, cooking demonstrations, free recipes, gift baskets, and shopping assistance for corporations or individuals. Ask for their very attractive catalog, which includes a number of excellent recipes. Note that the Broadway location is the largest in the chain.

Imports

Afghan

NUSRATY AFGHAN IMPORTS
215 W 10th St (at Bleecker St)   212/691-1012
Sun-Fri: 1-9; Sat: 1-11

Abdul Nusraty has transformed a corner of the Village into a corner of Afghanistan that is fascinating and free of politics. Nusraty is probably the best source of Afghan goods on the continent. There are magnificently embroidered native dresses and shirts displayed alongside semiprecious stones mounted in jewelry or shown individually. One part of the store features carpets and rugs, while another displays antique silver and jewelry. Nusraty has an unerring eye; all of his stock is of the highest quality and often is unique as well. The business operates on both a wholesale and retail level.

Arctic

ALASKA ON MADISON
937 Madison Ave   212/879-1782
Tues-Sat: 11:30-6 or by appointment

This store and gallery is New York's most complete source for Eskimo art.

Rare antiquities and artifacts of centuries-old Arctic cultures are displayed next to sculptures of Indians of the Northwest. Periodic shows highlight different aspects of Northern culture. A number of contemporary Eskimo artists whose works have been shown here have gained international acclaim.

Central America

BAZAAR SABADO
54 Greene St (bet Broome and Grand St)   212/941-6152
Mon-Sat: 11:30-6:30; Sun: 12-5:30

How about some Mexican or Central American artwork and furnishings to jazz up your abode? This is the place! Assembled in one spot is a great collection of silver jewelry, religious pieces, textiles, pottery, frames, wood carvings, glassware, and furniture from the 1940s to the present. Suzanne Rubin, the owner, travels extensively throughout the region, selecting unique pieces. She also places special orders, and repairs and restores items.

Chinese

CHINESE PORCELAIN COMPANY
475 Park Ave (at 58th St)   212/838-7744
Mon-Fri: 10-6; Sat: 11-5 (closed Sat in summer)

Khalil Rizk and his partners opened this store in 1985 as a source for Chinese decorative arts, with a particular emphasis on porcelain and furniture. They show Chinese export porcelain, ancient Asian sculptures, Chinese scholars' works of art, snuff bottles, and European furniture and accessories. You will also find a good selection of hardwood and lacquer furniture, cloisonné, woodcarvings, prints, and watercolors.

WING-ON TRADING
145 Essex St   212/477-1450
Mon-Sat: 9-6

No need to go to Hong Kong to get your set of Chinese porcelain or earthenware. Even though it is located on the disorganized Lower East Side, Wing-On has a clean and complete stock of household goods. One of their specialties is Chinese teas sold at low prices.

General

BACK FROM GUATEMALA
306 E 6th St (bet First and Second Ave)   212/260-7010
Mon: 1-9:30; Tues-Thurs: 12-10:30; Fri, Sat: 12-11:30; Sun: 2-10:30

Back from Guatemala shows a unique collection of clothing, jewelry, and artifacts from over 30 countries. Included are musical instruments, masks, hats, scarves, sweaters, deities, puppets, wall hangings, ornaments, and much more.

UNIQUE TABLEWARE
340 E 6th St (bet First and Second Ave)   212/533-8252
Tues-Sun: 3-11

Unique Tableware features china, crystal, ceramics, glassware, and jewelry from all over the world at discount prices.

JACQUES CARCANAGUES
106 Spring St (at Mercer St)   212/925-8110
Daily: 11:30-7

After a stint in the diplomatic service, Frenchman Jacques Carcanagues decided to assemble and sell the best artifacts he had run across in his world travels. So while the store is mostly Southeast Asian, it is, in Jacques own words, "a complete ethnic department store, not a museum." Yet it is all of museum quality. Textiles and *tansus* (dressers) are everywhere, as is a considerable stock of jewelry and lacquerware. It is also very appealing to Soho shoppers who can choose among Indian, Burmese, and Thai sculptures of many periods and unusual household objects not likely seen elsewhere in New York. The overall effect is like an Eastern marketplace; all that is lacking are water pipes and music.

KATINKA
303 E 9th St (at Second Ave)   212/677-7897
Daily: 2-6 (call, as hours may vary)

This is an import paradise, with jewelry, natural-fiber clothing, shoes, scarves, belts, hats, musical instruments, incense, and artifacts from India, Thailand, Pakistan, Afghanistan, and South America. The most popular items are colorful shoes from India and embroidered silk skirts that look like they just came out of the Taj Mahal. The place is small, as are the prices. Jane Williams and Billy Lyles will make you feel like you have embarked on a worldwide shopping expedition!

KNOBKERRY/SARA PENN
211 West Broadway (at Franklin St)   212/925-1865
Mon-Tues: by appointment; Wed-Sat: 12-7; Sun: 1-6

Sara Penn is the kind of world shopper with whom you would like to travel! She knows all about textiles, furniture, jewelry, and clothing from Africa, Asia, and the Americas. With nearly 40 years experience, she is an expert on such things as kimonos, saris, ethnographic art, and some of the most compelling textiles you have ever seen.

PIER ONE IMPORTS
461 Fifth Ave (at 40th St)   212/447-1610
Mon-Fri: 9-8; Sat: 10-8; Sun: 11-7

71 Fifth Ave (at 15th St)   212/206-1911
Mon-Fri: 9-9; Sat: 10-7; Sun: 11-7

1551 Third Ave (at 87th St)   212/987-1746
Mon-Sat: 10-9; Sun: 12-7

No need to spend your time or money running off to distant places; just come to Pier One. Here you will find imported dining-room sets, occasional furniture, bathroom accessories, picture frames, brassware, china and glassware, floor coverings, bedding, pillows, and much more. The goods come from exotic lands throughout Asia and the rest of the world. The selections are inviting, the prices are right, and the places are fun to visit. Besides, the chain's head honcho, Marvin Girouard, is one of the best merchants in the business!

PUTUMAYO
147 Spring St   212/966-4458
Mon-Sat: 11-7; Sun: 12-6

The merchandise is mostly designed by Putumayo and imported from India and Indonesia. The emphasis is on fashions and accessories, but there are also music and crafts from around the world. In the fall, Putumayo displays a variety of hand-knit virgin-wool sweaters and jackets inspired by tradtional cultures. For summer, there are sun dresses, skirts, and loose-fitting pants – all of them cool, comfortable, and practical.

Indian

HANDBLOCK
487 Columbus Ave (bet 83rd and 84th St)   212/799-4342
860 Lexington Ave (bet 64th and 65th St)   212/570-2775
Mon-Fri: 10-8; Sat: 10-7; Sun; 11-7

Handblocking, an ancient art of India, gives this store both its name and wares. Two partners divide their time overseeing production in India and merchandising at this store and other ones in Canada. There are linens, place mats, napkins, tablecloths, bedcovers, and dish towels, all created in India of cotton, tinted in brilliant colors, and handblocked in designs that range from traditional to contemporary. One can also find rugs, dishes, jewelry, and pottery. The merchandise is distinctive and fashionable.

HIND INDIA COTTAGE EMPORIUM
1150 Broadway (at 27th St)   212/685-6943
Mon-Fri: 9:30-6:30; Sat: 10-5

Hind India Cottage Emporium features clothing, jewelry, handicrafts, and gifts imported directly from India. Moti R. Chani has a sharp eye for the finest details, and the saris and other Indian clothing he sells reflect his taste and expertise. The clothing is prized by Indian nationals and neighborhood residents for its sheer beauty. The garments are made of cotton and feature unique madras patterns. Pay particular attention to the leather bags and jewelry.

Irish

GRAFTON GIFTS & BASKETS
30 Rockefeller Plaza   212/489-7029
Mon-Fri: 8:30-6:30; Sat: 10-6

Grafton Gifts & Baskets is a delightful touch of Ireland in the middle of the hustle and bustle of New York. Stop by in the afternoon for a cup of tea with Bernadette Ryan. On the way out, pick up some beautiful Irish imports, including sweaters, capes, blouses, hats, scarves, jewelry, crystal, and china. They also make gift baskets for all occasions. There's even Irish food!

MATTIE HASKINS SHAMROCK IMPORTS
Manhattan Mall (901 Sixth Ave at 32nd St, 4th floor)   212/564-7474
Mon-Sat: 10-8; Sun: 11-6

This delightful bit of Old Ireland is famous for hospitality and Irish goods like tapes, candies, tweed caps, Irish china, glassware, and pewter and brass gifts. It is like St. Patrick's Day every day at this spot!

Italian

CAROSELLO MUSICALE COMPANY (PENTAGRAMMA)
119 Mulberry St (nr Canal St)   212/925-7253
Mon-Sun: 11-11

Every section of New York with a concentrated ethnic population has a group of stores that serve its specific needs. Usually the group will include a bakery, coffee shop, bookstore, and import shop featuring various items of the homeland. There is often one shop devoted to a distinctive characteristic of that nationality. What could be more natural than a shop in Little Italy dedicated to recordings and music? Carosello is primarily a music shop specializing in Italian recordings and operas, but it is also a bookstore, import store, and gift shop. One can find perfumes, Italian newspapers, magazines, and gifts, as well as Caruso recordings. The atmosphere is informal but proud, and frequently customers can be heard humming an aria while checking record labels.

Japanese

THINGS JAPANESE
127 E 60th St, 2nd floor   212/371-4661
Mon-Sat: 11-5 (Tues: 11-6)

Things Japanese believes the Japanese "things" most in demand are prints. So while there are all sorts of Japanese artworks and crafts, prints highlight the selection. They know the field well and recognize that the market, while almost exhausted for high-priced established artists, is just beginning for less well-known artists. The store will help would-be collectors establish a grouping or assist decorators in finding pieces to round out the decor. There are also original 18th- to 20th-century Japanese woodblock prints, porcelains, baskets, chests, lacquers, and books. Prices range from ten dollars to several thousand, and everything is accompanied by a certificate of authenticity. Things Japanese claims you need to appreciate both the subject matter and the artistry in the works it sells, and that's not a difficult or unpleasant task at all.

Middle Eastern

PERSIAN SHOP
534 Madison Ave (bet 54th and 55th St)   212/355-4643
Mon-Sat: 10-7

This outfit has been in business since 1940, featuring unusual Middle Eastern items including end tables, chairs, frames, mirrors, and brocades sold by the yard or made up into magnificent neckties for men. There are also Chinese vases, garden stools, Russian and Greek icons, and planters that will add a special air of interest to any setting. The jewelry selection is especially noteworthy. There, you'll find precious and semiprecious items, silver and gold cuff links, rings, earrings, bracelets, necklaces, belts, and heirloom pieces.

Russian

VICTOR KAMKIN
925 Broadway (at 21st St)   212/673-0776
Mon-Fri: 9:30-5:30; Sat: 10-5

Fluency in the Russian language is increasingly prized in business and government, and Victor Kamkin can be of great help in this area. His store features books in Russian, translations from Russian, guidebooks, art albums and reproductions, textbooks, and dictionaries. There is also an excellent stock of Russian recordings and souvenirs (like lacquer boxes and dolls). An added feature is a subscription service for Russian magazines and newspapers.

Ukrainian

SURMA (THE UKRAINIAN SHOP)
11 E 7th St (nr Third Ave)   212/477-0729
Mon-Sat: 11-6

Since 1918, Surma has conducted business as the "general store of the Slavic community in New York City." My only quarrel with the description is that it should not be limited to the city, since it seems capable of serving the entire hemisphere. More than a store, Surma is a bastion of Ukrainianism. Once inside, it is difficult to believe you're still in New York. Fortunately, language is not much of a problem. The clothing here is ethnic opulence. There are dresses, vests, shirts, blouses, hand-tooled and soft-soled leather dancing shoes, and accessories. All are hand-embroidered with authentic detailing. For the home, there are accent pieces (including an entire section devoted to Ukrainian Easter-egg decorating), brocaded linens, and Surma's own Ukrainian-style honey (very different and very good). Above all, Surma is known for its tapes (learn conversational Ukrainian for your next travels to Kiev), stationery, and books. (Not surprisingly, the business is also known as the Surma Book and Music Company.) Pay particular attention to the paintings and the stationery, which feature modern-day depictions of ancient Ukrainian glass painting.

Jewelry

Pearls are very "in." Make sure you fully understand what you are buying. Practically all pearls on the market these days are cultured, which means that a mother-of-pearl bead is implanted in an oyster to start the pearl-coating process.

Akoya pearls: These come from Japan. The best ones are round and white, with high luster and a slight rose tint.
South Sea pearls: very large, from the South Pacific
Black pearls: grown in black-lipped oysters in Tahiti
Baroque pearls: less expensive, unusual shapes
Mabe pearls: Grown as a blister on the inside of an oyster shell, these can be brittle and break easily. Prices have become inflated.
Dome pearl: Grown in Tennessee, these are more durable.
Freshwater pearls: Inexpensive and attractive, these are grown by a type of mollusk that produces many pearls simultaneously.

Gems of the Month

January: garnet
February: amethyst
March: aquamarine
April: diamond
May: emerald
June: pearl, moonstone
July: ruby
August: peridot, sardonyx
September: sapphire
October: opal
November: topaz
December: turquoise, zircon

BILL SCHIFRIN
National Jewelers Exchange
4 W 47th St (Booth 86)   212/221-1873
Mon-Fri: 10-5

From a booth in the National Jewelers Exchange—better known for its diamond engagement rings than its plain wedding bands—Bill Schifrin and son-in-law Herman Rotenberg preside over a collection of nearly 2,000 unusual wedding bands. Prices range from a few dollars to several thousand, depending upon the complexity of the work and the stones used. If you have the time, there's a story behind each ring. Bill's been doing this for over 40 years, and after all this time you might think he'd be cynical. But he's just "cautious," and his stories, prices, and selection draw customers from all over the world.

DAVID SAITY/SAITY JEWELRY
450 Park Ave (bet 56th and 57th St)   212/308-6570
Mon-Sat: 10-6

David Saity's magnificent store creates a great showcase for his renowned collection of authentic Native American jewelry. In this collection are numerous rare and breathtaking turn-of-the-century collector's items, such as watchbands, belt buckles, bolo ties, squash-blossom necklaces, chokers, bracelets, rings, hair accessories, cuff links, earrings, and concha belts. Over 10,000 original masterpieces, handcrafted by artisans of the Zuni, Navajo, Hopi, and Santa Domingo tribes, are shown here. The collection spans over 50 years, featuring sterling silver, turquoise, coral, jet, and mother-of-pearl gemstones.

FORTUNOFF
681 Fifth Ave (at 54th St)   212/758-6660
Mon-Wed, Fri, Sat: 10-6; Thurs: 10-8

This is one of the best stores in Manhattan devoted to quality merchandise. Prices on all items are very competitive, and the store has a reputation for meeting or beating any legitimately quoted price in town. There is a crystal and clock department, but it is in the jewelry area (especially antique silver) that the store really shines. There is a jeweler in residence at all times. Fortunoff shows one of the largest and finest collections of 14-, 18-, and 24-karat gold jewelry in the city, as well as a fine selection of precious and semiprecious stones and brand-name watches.

GALERIA CANO
Trump Tower
725 Fifth Ave (at 57th St), Level C-4   212/751-0946
Mon-Sat: 10-6

Galeria Cano is a third-generation jewelry and accessory business with items made from 24K gold-plated brass. If you want to attract some attention at the next big party, put on one of their dramatic, handcrafted reproductions of original pre-Columbian artifacts. If you mention this book, they will smile upon you with some special prices for 18K jewelry!

JADED JEWELRY
1048 Madison Ave (at 80th St)   212/288-6631
Mon-Sat: 10:30-6:30; Sun: 12-5; closed Sat in summer

If you have a costume jewelry design in mind, then head to Jaded, where your vision can become reality. They design and make 75% of their jewelry, bringing to their craft an expertise of over 35 years in this country and Italy.

MAX NASS
118 E 28th St (bet Park Ave S and Lexington Ave)   212/679-8154
Mon-Fri: 9:30-6; Sat: 9:30-4

The Shah family members are jewelry artisans; Arati is the designer and Parimal ("Perry") is the company president. Together they make and sell handmade jewelry, and also service, repair, and restore antique jewelry. At Max Nass, they deal in virtually any type of jewelry: antique (or merely old), silver, an expanded gold selection, and semiprecious stones. Two special sales each year bring their low prices down even lower. One occurs during the last three weeks in January (33% discount), and the other runs for two weeks in July (25% discount). In between, Arati will design pieces on a whim or commission. The necklaces are particularly impressive; his work is often one-of-a-kind. The store also restrings and redesigns necklaces.

MURREY'S JEWELERS
1395 Third Ave (bet 79th and 80th St)   212/879-3690
Mon-Sat: 9:30-6

I heartily recommend this one! Murrey's, family jewelers since 1936, sells fine jewelry and giftware. In the service area, they do fine-jewelry repair, European clock repair, engraving, stringing, and watch repair. They have three talented goldsmiths for custom-designed pieces and three talented watchmakers.

MYRON TOBACK
25 W 47th St (bet Fifth and Sixth Ave)   212/398-8300
Mon-Fri: 8:30-5 (closed first two weeks in July and Dec 25-Jan 1)

Myron Toback is ostensibly a refiner of precious metals with a specialty in findings, plate, and wire. Not very exciting or helpful to the average customer, you might think. But you'd be wrong. Note the address. Toback is not only in the heart of the Diamond District, but he is a bonafide landlord of a new arcade crammed full of wholesale artisans of the jewelry trade. Taking their cue from Toback, they are open and friendly to individual retail customers. So note Toback as a source of gold, gold-filled, and silver chains sold by the foot at wholesale prices. And don't overlook the gold and silver earrings, beads, and other jewelry items sold at prices that are laughably less than those at establishments around the corner on Fifth Avenue. Even though most of the customers are professional jewelers or wholesale organizations, Toback is simply charming to do-it-yourselfers, schools, and hobbyists. They now carry tools and other materials with which to string beads and pearls.

PEDRO BOREGAARD
18 E 53rd St, 15th floor   212/826-3660
Mon-Fri: 10-5:30 by appointment

Unusual rings, earrings, and bracelets—all handmade and each a true work of art—are hallmarks of this very talented designer, who features items for men and women. Boregaard's credentials are impressive: apprenticeship and professional work in Germany; a jewelry workshop in England; and work with Tiffany for designers such as Angela Cummings, Elsa Peretti, and Paloma Picasso.

RENNIE ELLEN
15 W 47th St, Room 401   212/869-5525
Mon-Fri: 10-4:30 by appointment only

Rennie Ellen is a wholesaler offering the sort of discounts the city's wholesale businesses is famous for. She was the first woman diamond dealer in the male-dominated Diamond District. Ellen personally spent so much time and effort to keep the Diamond District straight and honest that she earned the title "Mayor of 47th Street." Ellen's reputation is impeccable. Her diamond-cutting factory deals exclusively in diamond jewelry. There are pendants, wedding bands, engagement rings, and diamonds to fit all sizes, shapes, and budgets. All sales are strictly confidential and are made under Ellen's personal supervision. There is a $2 catalog for mail orders.

SAVAGE UNIQUE JEWELRY
267 Columbus Ave (at 72nd St)   212/724-4662
Mon-Sat: 12-9:30; Sun: 1-6

Outrageous is the word here! Very unusual and unique watches, flamboyant accessories, and spectacular earrings will dazzle your eye. This is not a place for conservative matrons, but the fashion-conscious will find themselves rubbing shoulders with soap-opera actors and rock stars. Be sure to check out the large assortment of gold rings, cookie jars, and salt and pepper shakers. As a special service, they will make appointments afterhours for out-of-town visitors.

Ladders

PUTNAM ROLLING LADDER COMPANY
32 Howard St (bet Lafayette St and Broadway)   212/226-5147
Mon-Fri: 8-4:30

This is a great, esoteric shop on an esoteric street! What, you might ask, would anyone in New York do with those magnificent rolling ladders used in traditional formal libraries? Could there possibly be enough business to keep a place like this running all those years? The answer is that Putnam has been in existence since 1905. Clever New Yorkers turn to Putnam for designing access to their lofts (especially sleeping lofts). Here's a partial list of ladders, which come in many different hardwoods: rolling ladders (custom-made, if you want), rolling work platforms, telephone ladders, portable automatic ladders, scaffold ladders, pulpit ladders, folding library ladders, library stools, aerial platforms, library carts with steps, steel warehouse ladders, safety ladders, electric stepladders for industrial use, and mechanics' stepladders. Then there are Alpine, Crosby, Peerless, Durable, twin, and dual-purpose stepladders, plus extension ladders, window cleaners' ladders, sectional ladders, shelf ladders, extension trestle ladders, custom ladders, and more.

Leather Goods, Luggage

ANANIAS
Manhattan Mall (Sixth Ave at 32nd St), 2nd floor   212/947-0323
Daily: 10-8

The owners of Ananias—one from Germany and the other from China—fell in love with the beautiful island of Crete and decided to bring back a bit of that culture to our country. They have a large selection of handmade sandals, purses, knapsacks, school bags, belts, briefcases, and wallets made from cowhide. The tanneries in Crete date back to the 16th century and produce some of the most durable goods around. I have been using cowhide suitcases that were purchased a half century ago. They have made dozens of trips around the world and are still very serviceable.

BETTINGER'S LUGGAGE SHOP
80 Rivington St   212/475-1690, 212/674-9411
Sun-Fri: 10-6

This tiny shop, established in 1914, can be located by keeping an eye peeled for trunks (both vintage wardrobes and new camp trunks) crowding the sidewalk in front of the store. Inside, it is even more crowded, but amazingly the staff can put their hands on almost any piece of luggage in only a few minutes. Bettinger's merchandise includes Samsonite, Lark, Zero Halliburton, Travelpro, Briggs N'Riley, and Andiamo luggage, all of it sold for at least 30% off uptown prices. They also carry a huge inventory of leather garment bags, briefcases, portfolios, litigation bags, attachés, and vintage and retro luggage.

JOBSON'S LUGGAGE
666 Lexington Ave (bet 55th and 56th St)
212/355-6846, 800/221-5238
Mon-Sat: 9-6; Sun: 11-5

Apparently, the key to a successful luggage store in New York is to offer a vast selection at discount prices. With the exception of a store such as T. Anthony, which depends on quality and service to offset its high prices, most of the stores I've listed offer good variety and discounts. At Jobson's, they claim to have the largest selection of brand-name luggage, attaché cases, and small leather goods in the metropolitan area. (Their stock is enormous.) Their sales volume enables them to sell at guaranteed low prices that are close to wholesale. While there must be a dozen other stores that make similar claims, Jobson's sales staff and personal attention set it apart. They also offer free monogramming, a repair service, and free delivery in Manhattan.

ORIGINAL LEATHER STORE
176 Spring St (bet Thompson St and West Broadway)   212/219-8210
Mon-Sat: 11-8; Sun: 12-8

171 W 4th St (bet Sixth and Seventh Ave)   212/675-2303
Mon-Wed: 11-8; Thurs-Sat: 11 a.m.-12 p.m.; Sun: 12-8

This is one of those special smaller stores whose craftspeople make all the products shown. There are beautiful leather jackets, pants, belts, classy briefcases, bags, and luggage. The styles are current, and the prices are competitive. If you enjoy the aroma of a good leather store, you'll love these outlets.

T. ANTHONY
445 Park Ave (at 56th St)   212/750-9797, 800/722-2406
Mon-Fri: 9:30-6; Sat: 10-6

T. Anthony handles luxurious luggage of distinction. Anything purchased here will stand out in a crowd as being of really fine quality, and that is what T. Anthony customers expect and receive. Every person who comes into the store receives courteous attention. Luggage ranges in size from small overnight bags to massive pieces that just fall short of being steamer trunks. The wallets, key cases, and billfolds make terrific gifts, individually or in matched sets. Don't come looking for discount prices, but the quality and service are well-established New York traditions. Exclusive T. Anthony products are also available through the store's catalog.

Lighting Fixtures and Accessories

CITY KNICKERBOCKER
781 Eighth Ave (bet 47th and 48th St)   212/586-3939
Mon-Fri: 8-5

The fourth generation of the Liroff family operates this outfit, which has been in business since 1906. If it has anything to do with lighting—including quality antique reproductions, glassware, and even first-rate repair—then be assured these folks are completely reliable. In addition to a large sales inventory, there is a rental service. Not all of the inventory is vintage; their art-glass lamps, for instance, are all new.

JUST BULBS
936 Broadway (bet 21st and 22nd St)   212/228-7820
Mon-Fri: 9-6 (Thurs until 7); Sat: 10-5

From a practical point of view, this is probably the only shop in the world that can supply certain types of bulbs. In addition to the obvious ones, Just Bulbs has a collection for use in old fixtures. The staff boasts that the store stocks almost 25,000 types of bulbs. It's hard to imagine that many exist! The shop looks like an oversized backstage dressing-room mirror, and everywhere you look there are bulbs connected to switches that customers are invited to flick on and off.

JUST SHADES
21 Spring St   212/966-2757
Thurs-Tues: 9:30-4

This store specializes in lampshades. They are experts on matching shades to lamps, and they'll willingly share their expertise with retail customers. They have lampshades of silk, hide, parchment, and just about any other material imaginable. Interestingly, they say their biggest peeve is customers who "neglect" (a polite way of putting it) to take the protective cellophane off their shades. When left on, the shade actually collects ruinous dust.

LIGHTING BY GREGORY
158 Bowery (bet Delancey and Broome St)   212/226-1276
Daily: 9-5:30

No false modesty here. This full-service discount lighting store claims to be the most technically knowledgeable such outfit in the country. I'll take them at their word and pass on that they are major dealers of Lightolier and Casablanca ceiling fans, as well as being experts in track lighting.

LIGHTING PLUS
676 Broadway (bet 2nd and 3rd St)   212/979-2000
Mon-Sat: 10-7; Sun: 11-7

Few things are more annoying than not having that special electrical gadget you need to fix a lamp, computer, hair dryer, or whatever. Running around from one store to another to find an elusive item is even more frustrating. Save yourself some trouble and go straight to Lighting Plus. In this well-organized store, you can find just about anything connected with electricity, and the personnel are eager to help.

NEW YORK GAS LIGHTING COMPANY
195 Bowery   212/226-2840
Mon-Fri: 9-5; Sat, Sun: 10:30-5

The definitive source for quality lighting, New York Gas Lighting Company is mentioned repeatedly by decorators. Consumers will find a wide array of tranditional and elegant merchandise for all lighting applications at good prices. Go through all the rooms, as there's lots to see!

ROSETTA LIGHTING & SUPPLY CO.
21 W 46th St (bet Fifth and Sixth Ave)   212/719-4381
Mon-Fri: 9-6; Sat: 9-5

Right in the middle of Manhattan, under one roof, you can buy top-name lighting fixtures like Lightolier, Stiffel, and Kovacs, and also find a great selection of electrical supplies. Rosetta has been a reliable electrical-goods store for over 60 years. Special orders are taken, delivery is available, and prices are in the discount category. This is a personalized, boutique-style operation carrying merchandise not usually found in a larger "home center" outlet.

TUDOR ELECTRICAL SUPPLY
222-226 E 46th St (bet Second and Third Ave)   212/867-7550
Mon-Thurs: 8:30-5; Fri: 8:30-4:30

Although you may feel like you need an engineering degree to enter Tudor Electrical, the staff is trained to explain everything in stock. Light bulbs are the store's forte. They are cataloged by wattage, color, and application by a staff who can quickly locate the best bulb for your needs. For instance, quartz, tungsten, and halogen bulbs offer undistorted light, while incandescent and fluorescent lamps are best for desk work. Tudor discounts at least 20% off list prices.

UPLIFT
506 Hudson St   212/929-3632
Daily: 12-8

This uplifting store mainly sells art-deco and Victorian lighting fixtures. Uplift has one of the largest collections of original American art-deco chandeliers in the country. They also carry some less expensive reproductions and a full line of fantasy figures, like wizards and dragons made of pewter. Uplift has accessories for lighting fixtures: lamps, wiring, bases, glass bowls, and shades.

Lighten up! Some of the more interesting lamp shops:

Aero (132 Spring St): shadeless pieces
Lee's Studio (1755 Broadway, at 56th St, and 1069 Third Ave, at 63rd St): great selection
1950 (440 Lafayette St): French pieces from the 1950s
Stephen McKay (225 Lafayette St): new classics

Magic

FLOSSO AND HORNMANN MAGIC
45 W 34th St, Room 607   212/279-6079
Mon-Fri: 10:30-5:30; Sat: 10:30-4

Harry Houdini is one of a score of professional magicians who have owned this shop since its creation in 1856. Flosso and Hornmann is proof that magic is timeless. Its clientele spans all ages, and the store seems unchanged since Houdini's day. In part, that's due to the dim light and dust, but mostly it's because the stock is so complete. It's hard to think of a trick that's *not* stocked here. The staff will gladly show you what's new. In addition to magic acts, the shop carries books, manuals, historical treatises, and photographs. They'll even create stage sets. Ask for a catalog, in which many of the tricks are explained in detail.

LOUIS TANNEN/TANNEN MAGICAL DEVELOPMENT COMPANY
24 W 25th St, 2nd floor   212/929-4500
Mon-Fri: 10-5:30; Sat: 10-4

This is a magical place! Tony Spina or one of his helpful associates will spend time with both amateur and professional magicians. A fabulous catalog is available for a modest price, and classes are offered each week. The quality here is first-rate, as they produce many pieces in their own machine and wood shops. There are over 8,000 individual items and 350 books in their inventory.

Maps

HAGSTROM MAP AND TRAVEL CENTER
57 W 43rd St (at Sixth Ave)   212/398-1222
Mon-Fri: 8:30-5:45; Sat: 11-3

The staff here are experts when it comes to maps and travel information. They are the only complete map and chart dealer in the city, highlighting the maps of most every major manufacturer and five branches of the U.S. government. There are also nautical, hiking, global, and travel guides, as well as globes and world atlases.

Memorabilia

COLLECTOR'S STADIUM
17 Warren St (bet Church St and Broadway)   212/353-1531
Mon-Fri: 10-6; Sat: 10-5

Collectors will have a field day here! Manhattan's largest sports card and memorabilia store has a nice selection of new and vintage comic books. They carry a huge inventory, but if they don't have the piece you want, they will try to track it down. It's a good idea to fax them your want list before appearing at the door.

GOTTA HAVE IT! COLLECTIBLES
153 E 57th St (bet Lexington and Third Ave)   212/750-7900
Mon-Fri: 10-7; Sat: 11-6

Do you have a favorite sports star? Hollywood personality? Musical entertainer? Political figure? If you are a collector or are looking for a gift for someone who is, this store features original and unique products in these categories. There are signed photos, musical instruments, baseball bats, used sports uniforms, documents, and movie props.

LOST CITY ARTS
275 Lafayette St (bet Prince and Houston St)   212/941-8025
Mon-Fri: 10-6; Sat, Sun: 12-6

Are you looking for a special old Coca-Cola advertising piece or a souvenir from the New York World's Fair? Lost City specializes in such items, with an emphasis on architectural antiques, old advertising fixtures, and a great collection of vintage New York souvenirs. They also carry classic furniture and lighting from the 1930s to 1960s.

MOTION PICTURE ARTS GALLERY
133 E 58th St, 10th floor   212/223-1009
Tues-Fri: 12-5

The Motion Picture Art Gallery displays original posters and lobby cards from motion pictures as artwork and sells them. Ira Resnick's customers include film buffs and vintage poster collectors and investors. A *Casablanca* poster that could be had for a couple of dollars in the early 1960s fetches upward of $4,500 today! There are over 15,000 items in stock here.

MOVIE STAR NEWS
134 W 18th St (bet Sixth and Seventh Ave)   212/620-8160
Mon-Fri: 10-6; Sat: 11-6

In what is becoming the movie memorabilia center of the city, Movie Star News claims to have the world's largest collection of movie photos. Stars past and present still shine brightly in this shop, which offers posters and other cinema publicity materials. The selection is arranged like a library. The Kramers, who run Movie Star News, do a lot of research for magazines, newspapers, and the media. This may be the closest thing to Hollywood on the East Coast!

NEW YORK FIREFIGHTERS FRIEND
265 Lafayette St (bet Prince and Spring St)   212/226-3142
Mon-Sat: 10-6

Firemen and fire buffs from all over the world find this the most fascinating store in all of Manhattan! You'll find alarms, boots, bumper stickers, door knockers, earrings, extinguishers, fire engines, hydrants, nozzles, patches, posters, T-shirts, toys, turnout coats, work shirts, and other items all related in some way to the fire theme. Firefighters' jackets for kids are a big hit!

ONE SHUBERT ALLEY
1 Shubert Alley (bet Broadway and Eighth Ave)
212/944-4133, 800/223-1320 (mail order only)
Mon-Sat: 9 a.m.-11:30 p.m.; Sun: 12-7:30

Shubert Alley is a narrow alleyway in the Broadway Theater District often used as a shortcut between theaters. One Shubert Alley is the only retail establishment in the alley, and it's a fascinating place to browse. You will find T-shirts, posters, recordings, buttons, and other paraphernalia from current shows on and off-Broadway. They have a mail-order catalog and a special number for telephone orders.

SILVER SCREEN
124 W 36th St (nr Broadway), 5th floor   212/967-2419
Mon-Fri: 9:30-4:45

Are early 20th-century movies your passion? Ken, Carol, and Irma sell posters, autographs, movie magazines, and other theatrical memorabilia. In addition, they rent old photographs in black-and-white or color. The place is jammed with memories of movie and stage personalities and events, evoking tears and thrills of glamorous yesteryears. Clients must write or phone in their wants. No browsing!

Mirrors

SUNDIAL-SCHWARTZ
1582 First Ave   212/289-4969
Mon-Fri: 8-4:30; Sat: 10-4

The people at Sundial claim they supply "decorative treatments of distinction," and anyone who has ever seen a cramped New York apartment suddenly appear to expand with the strategic placement of a few mirrors will understand that claim. Sundial deals with professional decorators as well as do-it-yourselfers, and both benefit from the staff's years of experience. They carry mirrors for home, office, and showroom. In addition, Sundial will remodel, re-silver, and antique mirrors. Sundial also custom-designs window treatments, blinds, shades, draperies, and more.

Museum and Library Shops

As anybody on a mailing list knows, scores of museums across the country now produce catalogs that allow people to browse their gift shops from a great distance. In New York, however, you can browse in person at more than four dozen museums. Even at museums that charge an admission fee, you need not pay it if you're only there to shop. Rather than simply listing all the museum gift shops in New York in the following section, I've chosen particularly large or unique ones. Indeed, whether you're looking for a one-of-a-kind gift, a poster for your college dorm room, or unusual books, I highly recommend shopping in the following places. Instead of Empire State Building salt-and-pepper shakers, expect to find classy, well-made items. In most cases, at least some of the wares in these shops directly relate to current and past exhibits or the museum's permanent collection. If you plan to do Christmas or birthday shopping at one of these stores, find out whether you would save money by becoming a member and taking advantage of discounts.

AMERICAN CRAFT MUSEUM
40 W 53rd St (bet Fifth and Sixth Ave)   212/956-3535
Tues: 10-8; Wed-Sun: 10-5

Although quite small, this sales desk in the lobby of the American Craft Museum is worth a visit if you're interested in contemporary crafts. Much of the selection changes with the exhibits, but you will always find exhibition catalogs and postcards, as well as interesting jewelry and other original work by contemporary artists.

AMERICAN MUSEUM OF NATURAL HISTORY
Central Park West (bet 77th and 81st St)   212/769-5100
Sun-Thurs: 10-5:45; Fri, Sat: 10-8:45
Junior Shop: Mon-Fri: 10-4:45; Sat, Sun: 10-5:45

Hooray! For years I've been visiting the shops at this grand institution and coming away disappointed by cramped spaces and poor presentation. Not anymore! The main store for adults on the first floor has always been a great source for interesting jewelry, minerals, books and videos on natural history and related subjects, and beautifully made items from around the world. But now it's also a pleasant place to browse. The various shops throughout the museum, including one set in a turret on the third floor and the "Dinostore" on the fourth floor, all have a specialty and are well worth a visit. If your child simply cannot leave without a souvenir but you don't want to break the bank, check out the Junior Shop on the lower level. (Be forewarned that it closes much earlier than the museum itself, especially on weekends.)

ASIA SOCIETY
725 Park Ave (bet 70th and 71st St)   212/288-6400
Mon-Fri: 10-6:30; Sat: 11-6; Sun: noon-5

Off the Asia Society's main lobby is an exceptional book and gift store that's a little-known treat for anyone interested in Asiana. Its collection of books by American and Asian authors on Asian religions, philosophy, art, culture, history, and other topics is among the largest in the nation. The store also carries a wide range of children's books, language books, and coffee-table books. Inside the bookstore to the left is a rather small but wonderful gift store full of games, dolls, prints and posters, jewelry, scarves, wrapping paper, T-shirts, stationery, and other imports from all over Asia. They even carry chopsticks!

BROOKLYN MUSEUM
787 Seventh Ave (bet 51st and 52nd St)   212/554-4888
Mon-Fri: 11-6

This tiny shop in a corner of the Equitable Center's soaring atrium specializes in what the Brooklyn Museum is best known for: Egyptian art and artifacts. Whether you're looking for jewelry, picture frames, textiles, cards, or books on the subject, this is a great place.

CATHEDRAL CHURCH OF ST. JOHN THE DIVINE
Amsterdam Ave (at 112th St)   212/222-7200
Daily: 9-5

Known as the Cathedral Shop, this eclectic gift shop and bookstore is tucked off the left side of the main sanctuary about halfway between the main entrance and the altar. It specializes in stained glass, antique, and other kinds of crosses. They also carry Christian books, creches, and Christmas tree ornaments from all over the world. You can find a little bit of a lot of things here. Pressed flowers in glass, wrapping paper, wind chimes, mobiles, jewelry, Ghanaian *kente* cloth, note cards and stationery, jams, spices, and children's books are just a sampling. Make sure to ask about "adopting" an organ pipe if you're looking for a unique gift for a music lover. The atmosphere is very pleasant and browsing is encouraged, although the sales staff is strangely disinterested.

THE CLOISTERS
Fort Tryon Park   212/650-2277
Tues-Sun: 9:30-4:30 (summer); Tues-Sun: 9:30-4:15 (winter)

The Cloisters gift shop is actually one of the Metropolitan Museum's satellite gift shops. It's smaller and less crowded than the ones inside the Metropolitan, however, and stocked mostly with items related to the museum's medieval collection. The gift shop closes half an hour earlier than the museum.

COOPER-HEWITT NATIONAL MUSEUM OF DESIGN
2 E 91st St (bet Fifth and Madison Ave)   212/860-6868
Tues: 10-8:45; Wed-Sat: 10-4:45; Sun: noon-4:45

Housed in what was once the music room of the elegant Carnegie Mansion, this terrific store offers an eclectic mix of items that relate to the museum's extensive collection or reflect its dedication to design excellence and innovation. Whether you're looking for pens or other things for the office, tea cups, silverware, plates, or an unusual wedding present, this is a good place to start. And for those who remember this shop as a place to be afraid of turning around and bumping into something, it has been redesigned and now is easy to move around in. The store also sells books relating to the museum's collection. The gift shop closes 15 minutes earlier than the museum.

EL MUSEO DEL BARRIO
1230 Fifth Ave (near 105th St)   212/831-7272
Wed-Sun: 11-5

This unique museum gift shop was added to the museum during its 1994 renovation. In addition to housing a small collection of books about such topics as Caribbean culture and the Puerto Rican experience in New York, the shop sells children's books in both English and Spanish. The shop also sells carnival masks made in Puerto Rico and a variety of crafts from throughout the Caribbean and Latin America.

FRICK COLLECTION
1 E 70th St (bet Fifth and Madison Ave)   212/288-0700
Tues-Sat: 10-5:45; Sun: 1-5:45

The Frick's gift shop makes the most of its small space by concentrating on exquisite cards, stationery, and a few books. You will also find an assortment of maps, guidebooks, and art books here. Be forewarned that the gift shop closes 15 minutes earlier than the museum.

GUGGENHEIM MUSEUM STORES
1071 Fifth Ave (bet 88th and 89th St)   212/423-3615
Fri, Sat: 10-8; Sun-Wed: 10-6; Thurs: 10-4

575 Broadway (at Prince St)   212/423-3867
Sun-Fri: 11-6; Sat: 11-8

Although many of the things for sale in these stores are ordinary—scarves, T-shirts, prints and posters, tote bags, umbrellas, note cards and stationery, jewelry, and children's toys—the designs and craftsmanship are anything but ordinary. If you're looking for an unusual clock, a great wedding present, or the right pair of earrings to set you apart from the crowd, look here. Be warned, however: the prices are often through the roof (look for the $315 mobile!). Both shops also carry books on modern art and exhibition catalogs.

INTERNATIONAL CENTER FOR PHOTOGRAPHY
1130 Fifth Ave (at 94th St)   212/860-1777, ext 102
1133 Sixth Ave (at 43rd St) 212/768-4684
Tues: 11-8; Wed-Sun: 11-6

These two shops (really museums with a museum store) are definitely places to look if you're shopping for a photography buff with high-quality gifts in mind. They are both relatively small but have excellent collections of books about the history and technology of photography and photojournalism. You can also find coffee-table books of collected works by specific photographers, as well as prints, picture frames, and unusual postcards.

INTREPID SEA-AIR-SPACE MUSEUM
Pier 86 (at 46th St and the Hudson River)   212/245-0072
Daily: 10-5 (summer); Wed-Sun: 10-5 (winter)

This museum's gift shop has all sorts of junk, but it's also a great source for books on military history, space exploration, and aircraft and weapon systems. This is a good place to look for model airplanes and ships, as is the Intrepid Museum itself. The gift shop is open every day between Memorial Day and Labor Day but only Wednesday through Sunday the rest of the year.

JEWISH MUSEUM
1109 Fifth Ave (at 92nd St)   212/423-3200
Sun: 10-5:45; Mon, Wed, Thurs: 11-5:45; Tues: 11-8; Fri: 11-3

This relatively large store is an excellent source for both Jewish literature and decorative art. Its selection of menorahs, for example, is among the classiest in the city. The store also sells cards, coffee-table books, and a wide selection of children's books with Jewish themes and characters. Although the museum is closed on Friday, the store is open abbreviated hours.

LOWER EAST SIDE TENEMENT MUSEUM
90 Orchard St (at Broome St)   212/431-0233
Tues-Fri: noon-5; Sat, Sun: 11-6

This is one of the most interesting museums in all of Manhattan, but its tiny gift shop is generally disappointing and clearly not among the management's priorities. I've included it here, however, because the shop sells some of the most compelling black-and-white prints I've ever seen. The photographs all relate directly to the museum or the experiences of those who have passed through the Lower East Side.

METROPOLITAN MUSEUM OF ART
Fifth Ave (bet 80th and 84th St)   212/535-7710
Sun, Tues-Thurs: 9:30-5:15; Fri, Sat, 9:30-8:45

Macy's Herald Square (34th St and Sixth Ave, mezzanine)
212/268-7266

Rockefeller Center (15 W 49th St, bet Fifth and Sixth Ave)
212/332-1360

Soho (113 Prince St, bet Wooster and Greene St)   212/614-3000

The two-floor store inside the Metropolitan Museum of Art is the grandfather of all museum gift shops. It specializes in reproductions of paintings and other pieces in the Met's incredible collection, as well as museum collections around the world. You can find jewelry, statues, vases, scarves, ties, porcelain, prints, rugs, napkins, silver serving dishes, and scores of other beautiful gift ideas, as well as books relating to special exhibits and the museum's extensive holdings. They also carry umbrellas, tote bags, and other things with the Metropolitan's name emblazoned on them. There's even a bridal-registry department! Prices range from very reasonable to wildly expensive, and the salespeople are usually as patient as they are helpful. Satellite gift shops are located inside the museum itself (there's a beautiful one specializing in jewelry across the main entrance hall to your right) and throughout Manhattan. The hours of those satellite shops outside the Met vary. The second floor of the main store in the Met and the second floor of the satellite shop in Rockefeller Center have particularly good children's sections.

METROPOLITAN OPERA SHOP
Metropolitan Opera House (at Lincoln Center)   212/580-4090
Mon-Sat: 10 a.m. through second intermission; Sun: noon-6

This is an opera lover's heaven. In addition to operas on video, compact disc, and other media, you'll find books, mugs, umbrellas, stationery, T-shirts, and pillows for the opera buff. It even has opera-buff hours: the store does not close on weekdays and Saturday until the second intermission of the evening's performance. Be sure to check out the Performing Arts Shop on the lower concourse, too. And if you're looking for posters and prints from various seasons, visit the Gallery, also on the lower concourse.

MUSEUM FOR AFRICAN ART
593 Broadway (bet Houston and Prince St)
212/966-1313, ext 115
Tues-Fri: 10:30-5:30; Sat, Sun: noon-6

Anybody interested in African art—either books about the subject or the actual work of African artists and artisans—ought to make a stop at this relatively small but unusual gift shop. You can't miss it: the shop begins the moment you walk in the door and runs around the right side of the main desk. In addition to beautiful coffee-table books and a wonderful collection of children's books, the shop carries art and artifacts from throughout the continent.

MUSEUM OF AMERICAN FOLK ART
2 Lincoln Sq (Columbus Ave bet 65th and 66th St)   212/496-2966
Mon: 11-6; Tues-Sat: 11-7; Sun: noon-6

62 W 50th St (bet Fifth and Sixth Ave)   212/247-5611
Mon-Sat: 10:30-5:30

Like the small galleries at the museum's Lincoln Square location, these shops offer a wide range of Americana—innovative toys and books for children, quilts, cookbooks, picture frames, and lots of unusual handcrafted knicknacks you would expect to find in an upscale country cottage. These stores are also an excellent source for books on folk and decorative arts. The Lincoln Square location is adjacent to the museum, while the midtown location is across 50th Street from Radio City Music Hall.

MUSEUM OF THE CITY OF NEW YORK
Fifth Ave (bet 103rd and 104th St)   212/534-1672, ext 227
Wed-Sat: 10-5; Sun: 1-5

What a pleasure it is to find someone who cares so passionately about her store as manager Ann Goldsmith. In the past several years, she has transformed this little gem from a perfectly pleasant but uninspired shop into a wonderous reflection of the city itself and its history, present, and future. Whether you're looking for a black-and-white prints from the museum's extensive archives, videos on such subjects as the construction of the subway system, books on the so-called outer boroughs, thoughtful and imaginitive children's toys and books, or selections relating to the museum's permanent and changing exhibitions, this is a really exciting place to shop. (One caveat: the museum itself is in the process of an enormous expansion and may temporarily move from this location before reopening here in 2001, so call before going.)

MUSEUM OF MODERN ART BOOKSTORE
11 W 43rd St (bet Fifth and Sixth Ave)   212/708-9480
Tues-Sun: 11-5:45 (Thurs until 8:45)

Most of the things in this two-story shop relate to the museum's incredible modern-art collection and its exhibitions. Its selection of books on the subject is second to none, but you'll also find stationery, prints, wrapping paper, children's books, toys, CD-ROMs, videos, and calendars.

MUSEUM OF MODERN ART DESIGN STORE
44 W 53rd St (bet Fifth and Sixth Ave)   212/767-1050
Mon-Wed, Sat: 10-6; Thurs, Fri: 10-8; Sun: 11-6

Across the street from the museum, this magnificent store is dedicated to what the curators consider to be the very best in modern design. Furniture, vases, ties, kitchen gadgets, silverware, picture frames, watches, lamps, and toys and books for children are just a few of the things you'll find here. One of my favorite items is a set of architectural cookie cutters that includes such buildings as the Guggenheim Museum and the Sydney Opera House. You can even buy wall-to-wall carpeting for your home! These items are not cheap (keep your eye out for a great summer sale), but they are of the highest quality.

MUSEUM OF TELEVISION AND RADIO
25 W 52nd St (bet Fifth and Sixth Ave)   212/621-6800
Tues, Wed, Fri-Sun: noon-6; Thurs: noon-8

This shop, across the main lobby from the information desk, is so small that I would almost describe it as a cubby hole, but a stop here is a must for any fan of television or radio. Aficionados of such popular shows as *M*A*S*H*, *Star Trek*, *Star Trek: The Next Generation* and *Quantum Leap* will be particularly excited. Postcards, posters, books, T-shirts, videos, tapes of radio shows, and relatively inexpensive knicknacks like key chains and magnets are among the things they've managed to squeeze into this tiny space.

NATIONAL MUSEUM OF THE AMERICAN INDIAN
1 Bowling Green (at the foot of Broadway)
Museum Shop   212/825-8093
The Gallery   212/825-8094
Daily: 10-4:45 (Thurs until 7:45)

Like everything else about the museum, its two gift shops are classy operations. The Gallery, on the main floor to the right of the entrance, has a wide selection of books and high-quality Native American weavings, jewelry, and other handicrafts. The Museum Shop, down the grand marble staircase from the main entrance, is focused more on kids and families. Children's books, videos, toys, craft kits, and the obligatory arrowheads are for sale here, along with T-shirts and some moderately priced jewelry. Both stores close 15 minutes before the museum. Because the museum is part of the Smithsonian Institution, both stores also offer discounts to Smithsonian Associates.

NEW YORK PUBLIC LIBRARY SHOPS
New York Public Library (Fifth Ave bet 41st and 42nd St)
212/930-0641
Mon-Sat: 11-6

New York Public Library Midtown Branch (Fifth Ave and 40th St)
212/340-0849
Mon-Fri: 10-7; Sat: 10-6; Sun: noon-5

If ever there were a perfect gift shop for intellectuals (and those who fancy themselves as such), this is it. The original one is located just off the main lobby of the New York Public Library's main branch,while the other is across the street, where one of the Metropolitan Museum's satellite shops used to be. They feature everything from magnets with sayings like "I Think, Therefore I'm Dangerous" and "Think for Yourself, Not for Me" to books about the library's history. In addition to stocking an unusual, high-quality selection of merchandise, the staff people are particularly pleasant and helpful.

NEW YORK TRANSIT MUSEUM
Boerum Pl and Schermerhorn St, Brooklyn   718/243-8601
Tues-Fri: 10-4 (Wed until 6); Sat, Sun: noon-5

Grand Central Station   212/682-7572
Mon-Fri: 8-8; Sat: 10-4:30

Pennsylvania Station
Mon-Fri: 10-7; Sat:10-4

Run by the Metropolitan Transit Authority, these three shops are enough to make train and subway buffs downright giddy. Items for sale include books, conductor's caps, clever T-shirts, replicas of old station signs, banks for children in the shape of city buses, giant chocolate subway tokens, jewelry made from old tokens, and even old token boxes. Bus and subway maps and other MTA information are also available. The store in Grand Central Station used to be far superior, but the folks responsible for the newly reopened store at the museum itself deserve a round of applause for creating a stop worthy of that marvelous place.

PERFORMING ARTS SHOP
Metropolitan Opera House (Lincoln Center, lower concourse)
212/580-4356
Mon-Sat: 10 a.m. until second intermission; Sun: noon-6

This store is lots of fun for anyone interested in opera, classical music, and the performing arts. It is much like the Metropolitan Opera Shop on the floor above it but with a wide selection of things for children and an even wider selection of recordings. It stays open weekdays and Saturdays until the end of the second intermission of the evening's performance. If you're interested in prints and posters from past seasons, walk a little further down the hall and visit the Gallery.

PIERPONT MORGAN LIBRARY SHOP
29 E 36th St (at Madison Ave)   212/685-0008, ext 358
Tues-Fri: 10:30-4:45; Sat: 10:30-5:45; Sun: noon-5:45

This elegant shop is housed in a beautiful room once used by J.P. Morgan as a dining room. You'll find all sorts of books about medieval and renaissance art, master drawings, current and past exhibitions, and related subjects. There's also unusual china, clocks, painted trays, boxes, and other gifts. The shop sells cards and postcards with pictures of paintings and other pieces from the library's remarkable collection. The shop closes 15 minutes before the museum.

SOUTH STREET SEAPORT MUSEUM SHOPS
Fulton St and the East River   212/669-9455
Mon-Wed: 10-6; Thurs-Sun: 10-8

South Street Seaport is full of stores, and merchants in the surrounding area sell souvenirs, too, but the Seaport Museum itself runs two gift shops. The main store is by the bookstore and Visitor's Center at 12-14 Fulton Street. It carries the sorts of basic souvenirs that kids eat up—T-shirts, mugs, magnets, and the like—as well as some impressive jewelry and handmade boxes with images from the Museum's Seamans Bank collection. A smaller version of this store is located on Pier 16, right next to the water.

STUDIO MUSEUM
144 W 125th St (bet Malcolm X and
Adam Clayton Powell, Jr Blvd)   212/864-4500, ext 237
Wed-Fri: 10-4:45; Sat, Sun: 1-5:45

Just inside the museum's entrance on the right, this store sells a wide and generally high-quality selection of jewelry, textiles, crafts, notecards, and calendars created by African and African-American artists. It also sells an unusually broad selection of cookbooks, fiction, biographies, and children's books by and about Africans and African-Americans. Be forewarned that the store closes 15 minutes before the museum.

UKRAINIAN MUSEUM
203 Second Ave (bet 12th and 13th St), 5th floor   212/228-0110
Wed-Sun: 1-5

This unique little place is not exactly on the main tourist path, but it's a real gold mine for anyone interested in Ukrainian eggs (already made and kits), embroidery, and other crafts.

UNITED NATIONS
First Ave bet 45th and 46th St   212/963-4465
Mon-Sun: 9-5:15 (March-Dec);
Mon-Fri: 9-5:15 (January and February)

On the lower level of the main UN building you'll find a bookstore, a post office (a real treat for stamp collectors), a small UNICEF shop, and an even smaller shop run by the UN Women's Guild. That's in addition to the main gift shop, also on the lower level. The bookstore features calendars, postcards with the flags of all member nations, holiday cards in dozens of different languages, and a wide variety of books about the UN and related issues. The main gift shop features a wonderful array of carvings, jewelry, scarves, dolls, and other items from all over the world. The better imports can get pricey, but it's definitely going to a good cause! One final thought: if you are interested in UNICEF cards and gifts but find the selection at the UN itself rather thin, then visit the store in the lobby of the nearby UNICEF House (44th St bet First and Second Ave). Note that the UN stores are closed on weekends in January and February.

WHITNEY MUSEUM'S STORE NEXT DOOR
943 Madison Ave (bet 74th and 75th St)   212/606-0200
Tues-Sat: 10-6 (Thurs: 10-8); Sun: 11-6

Although there is a small and rather perfunctory book shop in the lobby of the Whitney Museum itself, any fan of modern art looking for unusual gifts ought to stop by the Store Next Door. In addition to creative toys and games for children, you'll find a changing collection of jewelry, T-shirts, scarves, ties, and offbeat things created for the museum's exhibitions. The latter include the "Popular Bridges and Tunnels of New York" notepad and pencils inscribed with Jack Kerouac's "List of Essentials." Some items are pricey and the staff can be a bit haughty, but the store is a hit with area residents and visitors alike. It is quite narrow, and its street entrance—to the right of the Whitney itself—is easy to miss. Thanks to the Whitney's recent renovation, however, you can now get to the store through the museum as well.

Wow! The largest retail music and entertainment complex in the world is at Times Square. **Virgin Megastore** is a $15 million complex. There are over one million CDs in stock, more than a thousand listening and viewing stations, a huge selection of CD-ROMS, a Virgin travel shop for flight and holiday bookings, a 12,000-square-foot classical-music section, and the broadest selection of laserdisc and video titles in the world! When you decide to buy, there are 45 cash registers ready to ring up your sale!

Music, Musical Instruments
ACADEMY RECORDS & CDs
12 W 18th St (nr Fifth Ave)   212/242-3000
Mon-Sat: 9:30-9; Sun: 11-9

Academy Records & CDs has Manhattan's largest stock of used, out-of-print, and rare classical, jazz, and rock LPs and CDs. Their classical stock—emphasizing opera, contemporary classical, and early music—has an international reputation. Prices are low, while a catalog of rarer classical records is issued occasionally. Academy has built one of the finest secondhand selections of CDs. The rock and jazz holdings, while less extensive than the classical, are strong and steadily growing.

BLEECKER BOB'S GOLDEN OLDIES RECORD SHOP

118 W 3rd St (bet MacDougal St and Sixth Ave)   212/475-9677
Sun-Thurs: noon-1 a.m.; Fri, Sat: noon-3 a.m.

Let us sing the praises of Bleecker Bob, who is nothing if not perverse. (Name another store that's open till 3 a.m. on Christmas Day!) For one thing, although there is a real Bob (Plotnik, the owner), the store isn't on Bleecker Street. For another, Bleecker Bob is an institution to generations of New Yorkers who have sifted through his selection of virtually every rock record ever recorded. With a stock that includes old rock and soul records (plus some rare jazz), autograph parties for rock stars, and a boast that they can fill any wish list from their stock, Bleecker Bob's is much more than a punk-rock store. It is also *the* gathering place in the wee hours of the morning in the Village. But above all, it's one great source for out-of-print, obscure, and imported compact discs.

DETRICH PIANOS

211 W 58th St (nr Broadway)   212/246-1766
Mon-Fri: 10-6; Sat: 10-4

Kalman Detrich fled Hungary for the United States many years ago, bringing his love and knowledge of pianos with him. His shop, within earshot of Carnegie Hall, ministers to any of the myriad needs a piano player might have. Detrich will tune, repair, polish, rent, buy, sell, and even buy back a piano with all the finesse of his Old World training. His specialty is antique and Steinway pianos. He lovingly restores them, and the few he can't restore are polished to a gloss and sold as furniture. The small shop is jammed with the cream of whatever is being revitalized at the moment, and passers-by cannot help but understand Detrich's pride when viewing the finished results. The Museum of the American Piano is also at this location.

DRUMMERS WORLD

151 W 46th St   212/840-3057
Mon-Fri: 10-6; Sat: 10-4

This is a great place unless the patron is your teenager or an upstairs neighbor. Barry Greenspon and his staff take great pride in guiding students and professionals through one of the best and well-rounded percussion stores in the country. Inside this drummer's paradise you'll find everything from commonplace equipment to one-of-a-kind antiques and imports. All of the instruments are high-quality symphonic percussion items, and customers receive the same attention whether they are members of an orchestra, rock band, or rap act. The store also offers instructors and how-to books. There are esoteric ethnic instruments for virtuosos who want to experiment. Drummers World has a catalog and will ship anywhere in the country.

FOOTLIGHT RECORDS

113 E 12th St (bet Third and Fourth Ave)   212/533-1572
Mon-Fri: 11-7; Sat: 10-6; Sun: 12-5

In keeping with this outfit's passion for rare and unusual records, the emphasis is on show tunes, film soundtracks, and jazz. Their prices are among the best around, and many of their records just aren't available anywhere else. If an original cast album was made of a Broadway show, you can bet Footlight has it. The store's personnel know at a glance what is available. They have one of the most comprehensive collections of film scores in the country, whole collections of artists from the 1920s through the 1960s, an impressive showing of European and Japanese imports in related fields, and a large selection of big-band and early jazz.

FRANK MUSIC
250 W 54th St (bet Broadway and Eighth Ave), 3rd floor
212/582-1999
Mon-Fri: 10-6

Founded in 1938, this professional business has never advertised, relying instead on word of mouth. They sell classical sheet music from European and American publishers. There is a corridor for voice and violin, another for piano, and so on. Frank Music gladly fills mail orders. Ask for Heidi Rogers, the helpful owner, or Dean Streit, her assistant.

GRYPHON RECORD SHOP
251 W 72nd St, 2nd floor   212/874-1588
Mon-Sat: 11-7; Sun: 12-6

Gryphon is one of a handful of stores specializing in rare and out-of-print LPs. They're world-famous for their collection. Raymond Donnell knows his business; he's able to help customers search out the most elusive LP, be it classical (the main area of emphasis), jazz, Broadway, pop, or spoken word.

GUITAR SALON
45 Grove St (nr Seventh Ave and Bleecker St, at Sheridan Sq)
212/675-3236
By appointment only

Beverly Maher's Guitar Salon is a unique one-person operation located in a historic brownstone in Greenwich Village. Here you will find handmade classical and flamenco guitars for serious students and professionals priced from $2,000. The shop buys and sells fine instruments, giving outstanding personal service from a talented guitarist and guitar teacher. The salon specializes in 19th- and 20th-century vintage instruments. Appraisals are available, and lessons are given on all styles of guitars. Maher appraised Segovia's guitars, which he donated in 1987 to the Metropolitan Museum. Even the Rolling Stones shop here!

HMV U.S.A.
1280 Lexington Ave (at 86th St)   212/348-0800
57 W 34th St   212/629-0900
2081 Broadway (at 72nd St)   212/721-5900
565 Fifth Ave (at 46th St)   212/681-6700
Call individual stores for hours; all open Sun

This is truly a musical supermarket! There are separate departments for rock and pop, classical, dance, jazz, and video. Listening booths are available, and a discount club is offered to regular patrons. This outfit is nearly a century old, with outlets all over the world. They know their business. If you are looking for CDs, cassettes, records, VHS tapes, laserdiscs, or accessories, HMV is a good place to visit.

JAZZ RECORD CENTER
236 W 26th St, Room 804   212/675-4480
Tues-Sat: 10-6 (Sept-May); Mon-Fri: 10-6 (June-Aug)

This is the only jazz specialty store in the city. They deal primarily in out-of-print jazz records, but there are also CDs, videos, books, posters, photos, periodicals, postcards, and T-shirts on the topic. The center buys collections, runs a search service, fills mail orders, and offers appraisals. Every two years it holds a jazz rarities auction. All of this is run by Frederick Cohen, a world-famous specialist in jazz records. Cohen is a charming guy who really knows his business.

JOSEPH PATELSON MUSIC HOUSE
160 W 56th St   212/582-5840
Mon-Sat: 9-6 (closed Sat in summer)

Located behind Carnegie Hall, Joseph Patelson is a shop known to every student of music in the area. From little first-graders to artists from Carnegie Hall wanting an extra copy of sheet music, everyone stops here first because of the fabulous selection and excellent prices. The stock includes music scores, sheet music, music books, and orchestral and opera scores. All are neatly cataloged and displayed in open cabinets. One can easily browse his or her section of interest—be it piano music, chamber music, orchestral scores, opera scores, concerts, ethnic scores, or instrumental solos. Sheet music is filed in bins the way records are elsewhere. There are some musical accessories, like metronomes and pitch pipes, as well. Patelson is an unofficial meeting place for the city's young artists. Word goes out that "we're looking for a violinist," and meetings are often arranged in the store. Mail and phone orders are accepted.

LYRIC HIGH FIDELITY
1221 Lexington Ave (bet 82nd and 83rd St)   212/439-1900
Mon, Fri, Sat: 10-6; Tues-Thurs: 10-7

Lyric is a favorite among sound fanatics known as audiophiles. As owner Michael Kay says, Lyric caters to those with a passion for recorded music and the cash to indulge their wildest audio fantasies. You can buy a basic music system at Lyric for under $1,000, but you can also part with a six-figure sum for an exotic component ensemble. Kay has owned Lyric since 1959, selling equipment to people who want the best, and he's very particular about the lines he carries.

MANNY'S
156 W 48th St (bet Sixth and Seventh Ave)   212/819-0576
Mon-Sat: 10-6

Manny's is a huge discount department store for musical instruments. "Everything for the musician" is their motto, and it is borne out by a collection of musical equipment so extensive that each department has its own salespeople. There is an emphasis on modern music, as evidenced by the hundreds of autographed pictures of contemporary musicians on the walls and the huge collection of electronic instruments. This does not, however, preclude classical instruments; there is a good collection of them as well. All of the musical instruments, keyboards, accessories, electronic equipment, and supplies are sold at discount prices. They also have a large computer department for musical software needs.

MUSIC STORE AT CARL FISCHER
62 Cooper Sq (at 7th St and Fourth Ave)   212/777-0900
Mon-Sat: 10-5:45

Outside of the Carnegie Hall area, the Music Store at Carl Fischer offers the best selection of sheet music from all publishers and categories, including pop, jazz, folk, rock, and classical. Everything is reasonably priced, with real bargains to be found in the older music. The store also has extensive research facilities and background information for piano, vocal, instrumental, band, orchestral, and choral music.

NOSTALGIA . . . AND ALL THAT JAZZ
217 Thompson St (bet Bleecker and 3rd St)   212/420-1940
Mon-Thurs: 1-8; Fri: 1-9; Sat: 1-10; Sun: 1-7:30

Recorded nostalgia—especially jazz, original cast, and soundtrack recordings—is sold here. All are very reasonably priced. The shop has a sideline in photography, with Kim Deuel and Mort Alavi doing a healthy business producing, cataloging, and reproducing photos. Nostalgia will reproduce any photograph, in any size or quantity, up to 30" x 40". They also have a good collection of posters, sports photos, movie and jazz stills, and large (16"x 20") showbiz photos in black-and-white and color.

RITA FORD
19 E 65th St (at Madison Ave)   212/535-6717
Mon-Sat: 9-5

George and Nancy Wright and Joseph and Diane Tenore collect antique music boxes. In the process they have become experts in all aspects of the business. Stock consists of valuable old music boxes, as well as some not-so-valuable old pieces, including ones in various states of disrepair. The main stock-in-trade is expertise; having been in business for half a century, these people know all there is to know about the music-box business. They are acknowledged experts on music box scores, workings, and outer casings. Some pieces are rare antiques, and they are priced accordingly. Somewhat more reasonable are the contemporary pieces, which are based upon original antiques. The store also does repairs.

TOWER RECORDS AND VIDEO
Locations throughout Manhattan (see below)
Hours vary by store

692 Broadway, at 4th St (212/505-1500): records, tapes, CDs
Trump Tower, 75 Fifth Ave (212/838-8110): records, video
383 Lafayette St, at 4th St (212/228-5100): book and video sales
   and rentals
2107 Broadway (212/799-2500): records and video sales and rentals
20 E 4th St, at Lafayette St (212/228-7317): clearance outlet

These stores are busy, well-stocked, and noisy.

VENUS RECORDS
13 St. Mark's Pl (bet Second and Third Ave)   212/598-4459
Mon-Thurs: 12-8; Fri, Sat: 12-11; Sun: 12-8

For the rock and roll enthusiast, Venus offers one of New York's finest selections of 1950s and 1960s reissues and original editions, plus punk, alternative, and other new and used rock records not usually found in the Top Forty. They also carry imported and independent releases, many out-of-print items, and a large selection of 45s. You can bring in used LPs, CDs, and cassettes for cash or trade. A mail-order service is available, and they will place special orders.

VINYL MANIA RECORDS
60 Carmine St   212/924-7223
Mon-Fri: 11-9; Sat, Sun: 11-7

Vinyl Mania Records, about two decades old, is New York's specialty shop for DJs. Its business is still 80% vinyl, as they primarily cater to the dance, hip-hop, and rap community. They also carry a small but unique selection of CDs and CD singles, both imported and domestic.

Looking for some hard-to-find vinyl records? These shops might be of help:

Housing Works Used Book Cafe (126 Crosby St, 212/334-3324)
Salvation Army Warehouse (536 W 46th St, 212/664-8563)
Thrift & New Shoppe (602 Ninth Ave, bet 43rd and 44th St, 212/265-3087)
Tower Records Clearance Outlet (20 E 4th St, 212/228-7317)

Newspapers, Magazines

HOTALINGS NEWS AGENCY
142 W 42nd St   212/840-1868
Mon-Fri: 7:30 a.m.-9 p.m.; Sat, Sun: 7:30 a.m.-8 p.m.

As every homesick out-of-towner should know, hometown newspapers can be picked up at Hotalings for the regular price plus the cost of shipping. Domestic and foreign newspapers are sold on the day of issue (or soon thereafter). Many non-natives keep in daily contact with their hometowns through these papers. Hotalings also carries a full line of domestic magazines.

Occult

MAGICKAL CHILDE
35 W 19th St (bet Fifth and Sixth Ave)
Mon-Sat: 11-8; Sun: 12-6

I asked the late proprietor Herman Slater how to best describe this incredible place to readers of a book on New York. He answered that his shop was an "occult emporium," and I guess that is the best formal description. You have to see Magickal Childe to believe it. There are shelves and bins of quartz crystals, gemstones, books, ritual accessories, videos, herbs, oils, powders, incense, curios, tarot cards, jewelry, and anything else that fits the occult image. The aisles are filled with readers and lookers, and they are as fascinating as the merchandise. Oh, yes, there are skulls, too.

Optical

THE EYE MAN
2266 Broadway (bet 81st and 82nd St)   212/873-4114
Mon, Wed: 10-7; Tues, Thurs: 10-7:30; Fri, Sat: 10-6;
Sun: 12-5 (closed Sun in summer)

There are dozens of places in Manhattan to find eyeglasses, but not many that take special time and care with children. The Eye Man carries a great selection of frames for young people, as well as specialty eyewear for grownups.

GRUEN OPTIKA
1225 Lexington Ave (bet 82nd and 83rd St)   212/628-2493
599 Lexington Ave (bet 52nd and 53rd St)   212/688-3580
1076 Third Ave (bet 63rd and 64th St)   212/751-6177
740 Madison Ave (at 64th St)   212/988-5832
2382 Broadway (at 88th St)   212/724-0850
10 Main St (East Hampton, Long Island)   516/324-5441
Mon-Fri: 9:30-6:30; Sat: 10-5; open Sun at Third Ave,
Madison Ave and Broadway: 12-5

Gruen Optika boasts the same faces and personal quality care year after year. The firm enjoys a reputation for excellent service, be it emergency fittings or one-day turnaround, and there's a super selection of specialty eyewear. Their sunglasses, theater glasses, sport spectacles, and party eyewear are particularly noteworthy.

JOEL NAME OPTIQUE DE PARIS
65 W Houston St (at Wooster St)   212/777-5888
Mon-Fri: 11-7; Sat: 11-6; Sun: 12-5

When ordering glasses, I always feel more comfortable knowing the people who are helping me are true professionals. Service is the name of the game here. Owner Joel Nommick and his crew stock some of the most fashionable specs in town.

MORGENTHAL-FREDERICS OPTICIANS
685 Madison Ave (bet 61st and 62nd St)   212/838-3090
Mon-Fri: 9-7; Sat: 10-5:30; Sun: 12-6 (Oct-May)

944 Madison Ave (bet 74th and 75th St)   212/744-9444
Mon-Fri: 10-7; Sat: 10-5:30; Sun: 12-6 (Oct-May)

If you are looking for state-of-the-art creative and elegant eyewear, this is the place. Owner Richard Morgenthal is a knowledgeable and helpful gentleman. He features his own designs, manufactured in Europe and created in-house. As an added service they will make appointments with some of New York's best-known ophthalmologists. The fact that they have been in business in the city for eight decades says something about the caliber of products and service.

Photographic Equipment and Supplies

ADORAMA CAMERA
42 W 18th St (bet Fifth and Sixth Ave)   212/741-0052
Mon-Thurs: 9-6:45; Fri: 9-1:45; Sun: 9:30-6

These people operate one of the largest photographic mail-order houses in the country. They carry a huge stock of photographic equipment and supplies, telescopes, video paraphernalia, and digital equipment. All is sold at discount.

ALKIT CAMERA SHOP
866 Third Ave (bet 52nd and 53rd St)   212/832-2101
222 Park Ave S (at 18th St)   212/674-1515
Mon-Fri: 8:30-6:30; Sat: 9-5

If you want to go where the photographers of the Elite and Ford modeling agencies shop, Alkit is the place. But don't feel like you have to be a professional to come here. While most establishments that deal with the real pros have little time for amateurs, nothing gives Edward Buchbinder, the store's owner, more pleasure than introducing the world of photography to neophytes. Few stores are better equipped to do so. Alkit maintains a full line of cameras, film, and equipment, as well as stereos, TVs, VCRs, and electronics, and they have a one-hour professional processing lab on-premises. The shop repairs and rents photographic equipment, and it also maintains a professional catalog full of praise and gripes about particular models.

KEN HANSEN PHOTOGRAPHIC
509 Madison Ave (at 53rd St)   212/317-0923
Mon-Fri: 9-5:30

This is a classy, upscale headquarters for photographic equipment. There is a vast selection of merchandise and a great showing of unique cameras not found elsewhere. Equipment is available for rent, and you will find Ken and his crew to be professional and well-informed.

LAUMONT/NEWMAN PHOTOGRAPHICS
333 W 52nd St   212/245-2113
Mon-Fri: 9-5:30 (evenings and weekends by appointment)

Professional or amateur, Laumont/Newman can take care of your photographic needs. They do excellent work producing Cibachrome and Iris prints, all of them exhibition-quality. They are patient and understanding with those who need counseling and advice. They are also experienced digital retouchers and duplicators, and can repair damaged originals or create brand-new images on state-of-the-art computers. Lamination and print-mounting are done on-premises.

WILLOUGHBY'S CAMERA STORE
136 W 32nd St (bet Sixth and Seventh Ave)
212/564-1600, 800/378-1898
50 E 42nd St (bet Park and Madison St)   212/681-7844
Mon-Fri: 8:30-8; Sat, Sun: 10-7

Established in 1898, this is the largest camera shop in the world, boasting a huge stock, an extensive clientele, and a good reputation. Willoughby's can handle almost any kind of camera order. For those in doubt, there is a mail-order division. Ask for something really esoteric, and Willoughby's can probably fill it without a problem. In addition to selling cameras, Willoughby's services them, supplies photographic equipment, and recycles used cameras. A large computer division has been added, and they also sell video cameras and cellular phones.

Pictures, Posters, Prints

ARGOSY BOOK STORE
116 E 59th St   212/753-4455
Mon-Fri: 9-6; Sat: 10-5 (closed May-Sept)

Argosy is the largest out-of-print, secondhand, and rare-volume bookstore in New York. The six-story building houses a stock of books from the 15th through the 20th centuries, including modern first editions and regional American-history volumes, as well as others on art, science, and medicine. There is a separate autograph section with pieces from a number of well-known personalities. Their print department is famous for its large collection of antique maps from all over the world, prints of every conceivable subject, and vintage posters. The stock is undeniably great, but their personnel could lower their noses a degree or two!

JERRY OHLINGER'S MOVIE MATERIAL STORE
242 W 14th St   212/989-0869
Daily: 1-7:45 p.m.

How about a Bonnie and Clyde poster for the guest bedroom? Jerry Ohlinger has a huge selection of movie posters, plus movie and television photographs, and he will gladly provide a catalog to help with your selection. He also does research for these kinds of items.

OLD PRINT SHOP
150 Lexington Ave (bet 29th and 30th St)   212/683-3950
Tues-Sat: 9-4:30 (closed Sat in summer)

Glancing at the Old Print Shop while strolling down Lexington Avenue, one might think that time was suspended in the 19th century. Established in 1898, the shop exudes an old-fashioned charm, and its stock only reinforces the impression of timelessness. Kenneth M. Newman specializes in Americana. That includes original prints, paintings, town views, Currier and Ives prints, and original maps that reflect America as it used to be. Most of the nostalgic bicentennial pictures that adorned calendars and stationery were copies of prints found here. Amateur and professional historians have a field day in this shop. Kenneth Newman also does "correct period framing," and prints in his custom frames are striking. Everything bought and sold here is original, and Newman purchases estates and single items.

POSTER AMERICA
138 W 18th St (bet Sixth and Seventh Ave)   212/206-0499
Tues-Sat: 11-6; Sun: 12-5 (except summer)

You've never seen a poster gallery more interesting than this one! Poster America features original posters circa 1905-1965, nearly all of which are lithographs. But, ah, the setting! Poster America, one of the oldest galleries in the country devoted to vintage poster art, is in a former stable and carriage house that used to serve the department stores on Ladies' Mile in the 1880s. The magnificent mahogany-and-glass storefront still catches the eyes of passers-by, luring them into a huge, well-appointed gallery. Poster America is known for brilliant graphics and the magnitude of its rare and unusual posters.

TRITON GALLERY
323 W 45th St (bet Eighth and Ninth Ave)   212/765-2472
Mon-Sat: 10-6

Theater posters are the show here, and Triton presents them like no one else. The list of current Broadway posters is but a small part of what's available, and it's balanced by an almost equally complete range of older show posters from here and abroad. Show cards, the most readily available items, are the standard 14"x22" size. Posters range in size from 23"x46" to 42"x84" and are priced according to rarity, age, and demand. None of these criteria, incidentally, has much to do with the actual success of the show. Often hundreds of posters were printed for shows that lasted less than a week and for which no one has any use. At the same time, some hits produced more posters than anyone could use, so their show cards cost no more than the obscure ones. The collection is not limited to Broadway or even American plays, and some of the more interesting pieces are of plays from other times. Triton also does custom-framing. Much of the business is conducted via mail and phone orders. Ask for Triton's catalog.

Plastics

INDUSTRIAL PLASTICS
309 Canal St (bet Mercer St and Broadway)   212/226-2010
Mon-Sat: 9-5:30

Industrial Plastics is a large loft dedicated to plastics—both the Lucite and soft plastic variety. Their line includes waterproofing material, Lucite cubes, and sheets of plastic. They are particularly accommodating to do-it-yourselfers.

PLEXI-CRAFT QUALITY PRODUCTS
514 W 24th St   212/924-3244
Mon-Fri: 9:30-5

Plexi-Craft offers anything made of Lucite (and Plexiglas) at wholesale prices. If you can't find what you want among the pedestals, tables, chairs, shelves, and cubes, they will make it for you. The personnel are extremely helpful at pointing out various styles of cocktail tables, shelves, magazine racks, television stands, and chairs. A catalog is available for $2.

Religious Arts

GRAND STERLING SILVER COMPANY
345 Grand St (bet Essex and Ludlow St)   212/674-6450
Sun-Thurs: 10:30-5:30

Ring the bell and you will be admitted to a stunning collection of silver religious art. You'll also find almost anything from silver toothpick holders to baroque candelabra over six feet tall. Grand Sterling will repair and re-silver any silver item, be it religious or secular. They are manufacturers and importers of fine sterling holloware, and silver is revered with unmatched dedication.

Rubber Goods

CANAL RUBBER SUPPLY COMPANY
329 Canal St (at Greene St)   212/226-7339
Mon-Fri: 9-5; Sat: 9-4:30

"If it's made of rubber, we have it" is this company's motto, and that sums up the supply at this wholesale-retail operation. There are foam mattresses, bolsters, cushions, pillow foam, pads cut to size, hydraulic hoses, rubber tubing, vacuum hoses, floor matting, tiles, stair treads, sheet-rubber products of various kinds, and much more.

Security Devices

CCS COUNTER SPY SHOP
444 Madison Ave (at 49th St)   212/688-8500
Mon-Fri: 9-6; Sat: 11-4; Sun and evenings by appt

Waldorf Astoria Hotel, 301 Park Ave   212/750-6645
Same hours as above, plus Sun: 12-2

With security high on many people's minds these days, the CCS Counter Spy Shop provides relief for worriers. These folks supply all manner of security items for business and private use. There is bulletproof clothing—everything from T-shirts to safari outfits. Other items include covert video systems, night-vision equipment, debugging devices, phone or fax scramblers, voice-stress analyzers, lie detectors, and even bulletproof cars. It's all here, and confidential consultations can be arranged.

EMPIRE SAFE COMPANY
433 Canal St (at Varick St)   800/543-5412
Mon-Fri: 9-5; Sat: 10-3 (closed Sat in July, Aug)

Empire has one of the largest safe showrooms in the country, with safes and vaults for all types of businesses and offices. They also carry a complete selection of burglary protection safes for apartments and private homes, most with digital locks. Empire delivers and installs across the country. It is worth a visit just to see the exhibit of rare, antique, and art-deco safes!

QÜARK SPY CENTRE
537 Third Ave (at 36th St)   212/889-1808, 800/343-6443
Mon-Fri: 9-6; Sat: by appointment

Qüark is Manhattan's most exclusive and extensive countersurveillance showroom. With more than 400 items on display, and on-staff specialists in the field of protection, Qüark is able to service all personal and professional security needs, no matter how unique. Products offered include night-vision equipment, bug detection and telephone security items, audio devices, body armor, voice scramblers, long-play recording devices, and alarm briefcases.

Sexual Specialties

COME AGAIN
353 E 53rd St (at First Ave)   212/308-9394
Mon-Fri: 11-7:30

Come Again is a one-stop shopping center for all your sexual needs. There are vibrators, bondage equipment, exotic lingerie for men and women, adult books and magazines, oils and lotions, gift baskets, party gifts, and favors. They boast an X-rated shop-at-home adult-toy and lingerie video catalog.

CONDOMANIA
351 Bleecker St   212/691-9442
Sun-Thurs: 11-11; Fri, Sat: 11 a.m.-midnight

Yes, this is a store that specializes in condoms: all shapes, sizes, colors, and what-have-you. Mixed in are suggestive postcards and the like. The place seems to be as popular with the ladies as the gentlemen. I guess it was inevitable someone would capitalize on the trend to make these items more easily available. Your author is just keeping up with the times!

EVE'S GARDEN
119 W 57th St, 4th floor   212/757-8651
Mon-Sat: 12-7

One of the real pleasures of the "New York Is Book Country" fair each September on Fifth Avenue is the opportunity to meet and exchange views with readers and business folk who are (or would like to be) featured in this book. During one such fair, Dell William, who runs Eve's Garden, suggested I visit her unusual emporium. The descriptive line in her literature is, "We grow pleasurable things for women." Well, you get the picture. It may not be a must-see place on your shopping list, but this is a book designed for every type of reader, and women will find a unique selection of merchandise at this liberated garden. Gentlemen are welcome only if accompanied by a woman.

Signs

LET THERE BE NEON
38 White St   212/226-4883
Mon-Fri: 8:30-5:30; Sat by appointment

Though the image of neon is modern, it harks back to Georges Claudes' capturing of it (from oxygen) in 1915. And while the flashing neon sign is perhaps the ultimate urban cliché, Rudi Stern has turned neon into a modern art form. Let There Be Neon operates as a gallery. At any given moment there is an assemblage of sizes, shapes, functions, and designs to entice the browser. Almost all of Let There Be Neon's sales are custom-made, commissioned pieces. Stern claims that even a rough sketch is enough for them to create a literal or abstract sculpture.

Silver

EASTERN SILVER COMPANY
54 Canal St, 2nd floor   212/226-5708
Sun-Thurs: 9:30-5; Fri: 9:30-1 (showroom closed Fri)

Prepare to enter a floor-to-ceiling wonderland of silver. Not all of it is clean or polished, but it has the potential of becoming as beautiful as only silver can be. The stock includes virtually any product made of silver or pewter, and Robert Gelbstein seems able to put his hand on any desired item almost immediately. Eastern has a large collection of Jewish ceremonial silver and secular silver items, such as candlesticks and wine decanters. However, most of the collection would look perfect gracing any home. Prices are extremely reasonable, and the quality is A-1.

JEAN'S SILVERSMITHS
16 W 45th St (at Fifth Ave)   212/575-0723
Mon-Thurs: 9-4:30; Fri: 9-3:30

Having a problem replacing a fork that went down the garbage disposal? No worry. Proceed directly to Jean's, where you will find over a thousand discontinued, obsolete, and current flatware patterns. They specialize in antique and secondhand silver, gold, and diamond jewelry, and they also sell watches.

ROGERS AND ROSENTHAL
201/346-1862
Mon-Fri: 10-4

Rogers and Rosenthal is one of the very best places in the area, if not the best, for silver, china, and crystal. Nearly all of their business is done by mail. This shop features major brand names and a 25% or more discount on every piece by mail. They will send price lists upon request, and what isn't in stock will be ordered. They are very accommodating.

TIFFANY AND COMPANY
727 Fifth Ave (at 57th St)   212/755-8000
Mon-Wed, Fri, Sat: 10-6; Thurs: 10-7

What can you say about a store that's such an institution it has appeared in plays, movies, books, and even slogans? Almost nothing, except that the store really isn't that formidable or forbidding, and it can be an exciting place to shop. Yes, there really is a Tiffany diamond, and it can be viewed on the first floor. That floor also houses the watch and jewelry departments. While browsing is welcome, salespeople are quick to approach lingering customers. The second floor has clocks, silver jewelry, sterling silver, bar accessories, centerpieces, leather accessories, scarves, and knickknacks. The third floor highlights china, crystal, flatware, and engraved stationery. The real surprise is that Tiffany has an excellent selection of reasonably priced items. Many come emblazoned with the Tiffany name and are wrapped in the famed Tiffany blue box – all at prices less than some neighborhood variety stores.

Sporting Goods
Bicycles and Accessories

BICYCLE & EXERCISE STORE
242 E 79th St (at Second Ave)   212/249-9344
Mon-Fri: 9:30-8; Sat, Sun: 9-7

This is *the* bike shop in New York. They feature children's bikes, racing bikes, tour bikes, mountain bikes, and BMX bikes – all made by leading manufacturers. Names like Raleigh and Peugeot are represented in quantity, and all kinds of accessories are available. The store will repair or rent any kind of bike. A big selection of exercise equipment is offered, including aerobic bikes, treadmills, and home gyms. They also guarantee to meet or beat any competitor's price. The service is good, the personnel knowledgeable, and the selection tremendous.

BICYCLE RENAISSANCE
430 Columbus Ave (at 81st St) 212/724-2350
Mon-Fri: 10-7:30; Sat, Sun: 10-5; summer: 10-7:30 daily

Biking is a way of life here. Services include custom-building bikes, and their mechanics aim for same-day service on all makes and models. They carry all manner of racing and mountain bikes; in stock are Trek, Cannondale, and Specialized, as well as custom frames for Campagnolo, Shimano, and many others. Prices are on par with the so-called discount shops.

LARRY & JEFF'S SECOND AVENUE BICYCLES PLUS
1690 Second Ave (at 87th St) 212/722-2201
Daily: 10-7; (summer: 10-8:30)

Larry started young (age 15) fixing bicycles, so you can bet he knows all about them. He then taught the art to Jeff, and together they have been operating this unique shop since 1977. You can find bikes here ranging in price from $200 to $5,000, with parts and accessories to boot. Lots of special services: five years of free tune-up with purchase of a new bicycle, rental of bikes to ride through Central Park, and free delivery.

Billiards

BLATT BILLIARD
809 Broadway (bet 11th and 12th St) 212/674-8855
Mon-Fri: 9-6; Sat: 10-4 (closed Sat in summer)

Blatt is outfitted from top to bottom (15 floors) with everything for billiards. You can also get friendly pointers from a staff that seems, at first glance, to be all business.

Darts

DART SHOPPE
30 E 20th St (bet Park Ave S and Broadway) 212/533-8684
Mon-Fri: 12-6; Sat: 11-5

Most towns have sporting goods shops, but few have a department or even a display for darts. In New York, things are different. Dart Shoppe is an emporium dedicated solely to darts and darting equipment. Their collection of darts, dartboards, accessories, and English darting equipment is impressive. (England's pubs are where it all started, you know.) Indeed, darts is largely a neglected game in America. That is a shame, since it's so good for channeling aggression!

Exercise Equipment

GYM SOURCE
40 E 52nd St (bet Park and Madison Ave) 212/688-4222
Mon-Fri: 9-6; Sat: 10-5

This is the largest exercise-equipment dealer in the Northeast. They carry treadmills, bikes, stair and weight machines, rowers, and more. Over 300 top brands at good prices are available here, and their skilled technicians provide competent service. They will rent equipment or provide a visitor with an item to be used in a hotel room while in Manhattan.

Fishing

CAPITOL FISHING TACKLE COMPANY
Chelsea Hotel, 218 W 23rd St (nr Seventh Ave)
212/929-6132
Mon-Fri: 9-6; (Thurs until 7); Sat: 10-5

Historical records show that over a hundred years ago the 42nd Street Library and the adjacent Bryant Park were once a cemetery and later a reservoir—an indication of just how distinct and countrified their location was in relationship to the rest of the city. In 1897, when Capitol Fishing Tackle Company was established, its present location would have justified a store dedicated to fishing. Today, in the hustle and bustle of Chelsea, the store is totally incongruous and yet is typical of New York. Where else could one find a fishing store so totally landlocked that a subway roars beneath it, yet one that offers bargains unmatched at seaport fishing stores? Capitol features a complete range of fishing tackle with such brand names as Penn, Shimano, Tycoon Finnor, Garcia, and Daiwa at low prices. There is a constantly changing selection of fantastic specials and close-outs. Capitol buys up surplus inventories, bankrupt dealers, and liquidations. Almost nothing in the store was purchased at full wholesale, and those savings are passed on to customers.

Game Equipment

V. LORIA AND SONS
178 Bowery (bet Kenmare and Spring St)   212/925-0300
Mon-Fri: 11-6; Sat: 11-4 (closed Sat in summer)

This family business, established in 1912, is a mecca for indoor sports enthusiasts. One can find a complete line of bowling and billiards items, pool tables, and such supplies as cues and chalk, plaques, and awards—not to mention ping-pong and poker tables. Winner's trophies can be ordered from Loria as well. Vernon Loria doesn't mind if you try out some of the equipment right on the premises.

General

EASTERN MOUNTAIN SPORTS (EMS)
20 W 61st St (bet Broadway and Columbus Ave)   212/397-4860

611 Broadway (at Houston St)   212/505-9860
Mon-Fri: 10-9; Sat: 10-6; Sun: 12-6

This is the place to go for authentic outdoor clothing and gear, although prices can be bettered elsewhere. Still, for one-stop shopping it's an excellent source, and the merchandise is of better quality than that found in department stores. Incidentally, EMS covers virtually all outdoor sports, including mountain climbing, backpacking, skiing, hiking, tenting, kayaking, camping, and more.

G&S SPORTING GOODS
43 Essex St   212/777-7590
Mon-Fri, Sun: 9:30-6

If you have a sports buff in the family and are looking for a place to buy him or her a birthday or Christmas gift, I'd recommend G&S. They have a large selection of brand-name sneakers, in-line skates, boxing equipment, balls, gloves, toys and games, sports clothing, and accessory items. The prices reflect a 20% to 25% discount.

MODELL'S
280 Broadway   212/962-6200
200 Broadway   212/964-4007
243 W 42nd St   212/575-8111
51 E 42nd St   212/661-4242
Manhattan Mall, Sixth Ave at 33rd St (lower level)
212/594-1830
Hours vary by store

You can't beat this outfit for quality and value! Founded in 1889, Modell's is America's oldest family-owned and -operated sporting goods chain. The stores specialize in menswear, sporting goods, footwear, luggage, and sundries. Prices are right, especially on shoes.

PARAGON SPORTING GOODS
871 Broadway (at 18th St)   212/255-8036
Mon-Sat: 10-8; Sun: 11-6:30

This is truly a sporting goods department store, with over 100,000 square feet of specialty shops devoted to all kinds of sports equipment and apparel. There are separate departments for skis, team equipment, athletic footwear, skateboards, ice skates, racquet sports, aerobics, swimming, golf, hiking, camping, diving, biking, sailing, and whatever else you might want to do in the great outdoors. There are also gift items, and the stock is arranged for easy shopping. It is a pleasure to shop in this vast wonderland of fun!

SPIEGEL'S
105 Nassau St (at Ann St)   212/227-8400
Mon-Fri: 10-6; Sat: 12-5

You wouldn't expect to find a good place to buy sporting goods in this neighborhood, but Spiegel's (established in 1916 and not to be confused with the catalog company) would be top-notch in any location. The most advantageous point is their discount prices, which are as good as any in the city. In addition, the selection is ample, the sales help is excellent, and the supply is amazing for a store of its size. Call ahead to find out if they have what you are looking for. The golf department has been expanded and now includes a hitting net.

Golf

NEW YORK GOLF CENTER
131 W 35th St (nr Broadway)   212/564-2255
Mon-Fri: 10-8; Sat: 10-7

This shop is the ultimate hole-in-one for the golfer! In premises that provide the largest selection of quality brand-name golfing merchandise in the area, they offer goods at prices that average 20% below list. There are clubs, bags, clothing, shoes, accessories, and novelties . . . everything except one's own hard-won expertise. In short, this is a great place to shop for gifts for the golfing enthusiast. Besides, the folks here couldn't be nicer or more helpful.

Guns

JOHN JOVINO GUN SHOP
5 Centre Market Pl (at Grand St)   212/925-4881
Mon-Fri: 9-6; Sat: 8-3

These folks have been in business since 1911 and are recognized leaders in the field. They carry all major brands of handguns, rifles, shotguns, and accessories, including ammunition, holsters, bulletproof vests, knives, and scopes. Major brands include Smith & Wesson, Colt, Ruger, Beretta, Browning, Remington, Walther, Glock, Winchester, and Sig Sauer. Jovino is an authorized warranty repair station for all gun manufacturers, with two licensed gunsmiths on the premises.

Horseback Riding Equipment

MILLER HARNESS CO.
117 E 24th St   212/673-1400
Mon-Sat: 10-6 (Thurs:10-7)

The Miller's symbol (two boots) is displayed in hundreds of shops across North America. The exclusive Miller line covers a horse rider from head to hoof. Sizes suit men, women, children, stallions, mares, and foals. The haberdashery offers proper English riding gear and saddles. Hermes' saddles, incidentally, are registry-numbered and sell for $3,400 and up! There are boots, helmets, riding shirts, breeches, and riding potpourri. Miller's is a super place to find gifts for both horses and owners.

Marine

E&B/GOLDBERGS MARINE
12 W 37th St (at Fifth Ave)   212/594-6065
Mon-Sat: 9-6; Sun: 10-6 (closed Sun in winter)

Goldbergs sells marine supplies as if it were situated in the middle of a New England seaport rather than the heart of Manhattan. The staff sometimes looks like a ship's crew on leave in the Big Apple, and they are actually that knowledgeable. They carry marine electronics, sailboat fittings, big-game fishing tackle, lifesaving gear, ropes, anchors, compasses, clothing, clocks, barometers, and books. Many items—ropes and compasses, for example—are of professional quality. Foul-weather suits are a star attraction, and there is also a line of clothes for yacht owners.

Outdoor Equipment

TENT AND TRAILS
21 Park Pl (bet Broadway and Church St)
212/227-1760, 800/237-1760
Mon-Wed, Sat: 9:30-6; Thurs, Fri: 9:30-7; Sun: 12-6

Whether you are buying for a weekend camping trip or an expedition to Mt. Everest, Tent and Trails is ready for the outfitting! In the urban canyons near City Hall you will find a 6,000-square-foot store devoted to camping. The staff is experienced and knowledgeable. There are boots from Asolo, Merrill, Vasque, Hi Tec, and Nike, and camping gear from Madden, Patagonia, Fabiano Clothing, Camp Trails, Moonstone, Jansport, Gregory Packs, Mountainsmith

Packs, Eureka Tent, Coleman, Moss Tent, Timberland, and NorthFace. You'll find backpacks, sleeping bags, tents, down clothing, and much more. Tent and Trails also rents camping equipment.

Running

ATHLETIC STYLE
118 E 59th St (bet Park and Lexington Ave)   212/838-2564
Mon-Wed, Fri, Sat: 10-6; Thurs: 10-6:30; Sun: 12:30-5:30

ATHLETIC STYLE AT BLOOMINGDALE'S
1000 Third Ave   212/705-3968
(same hours as Bloomingdale's)

Athletic Style was originally a running-shoe shop owned by avid joggers. The store has grown and prospered, and it is now one of the top outlets in the city in terms of quality, value, and service. The 59th Street store has evolved into a custom job outlet. Owners Vic and Dave are always on the job. Bloomingdale's was so impressed that they opened a branch in their store. Footwear includes many famous names. They also carry a good stock of clothing items, including logo merchandise and personalized T-shirts, caps, and sweats.

SUPER RUNNERS SHOP
1337 Lexington Ave (at 89th St)   212/369-6010
360 Amsterdam Ave (at 77th St)   212/787-7665
1246 Third Ave   212/249-2133
Mon-Fri: 10-7 (Thurs until 9); Sat: 10-6; Sun: 12-5

416 Third Ave (at 29th St)   212/213-4560
Mon-Fri: 11-8 (Thurs until 9)

Here you'll get informed service by salespeople who are themselves runners. Co-owner Gary Muhrcke was the winner of the first New York City Marathon in 1970. Entry blanks for local races are available in the stores. Merchandise selection includes a superb collection of men's and women's running and racing shoes, in addition to performance running clothes. The crew here believes that each person should be fitted individually in terms of sizing and need.

Skating

BLADES WEST/EAST
120 W 72nd St   212/787-3911   Chelsea Piers, Pier 61   212/336-6299
160 E 86th St   212/996-1644   Sky Rink   212/336-6199
128 Chambers St   212/964-1944   441 Columbus Ave   212/579-3700
659 Broadway   212/477-7350   Sixth Ave and 32nd St   212/563-2448
1414 Second Ave   212/249-3178
Mon-Sat: 10-8; Sun: 10-6

Here you will find all kinds of skates, skateboards, ice-hockey equipment, and snowboards for rent and sale. Classy apparel and accessories are also available. A repair shop is on the premises, and party rentals are a specialty.

ISLAND SPORTS
1623 York Ave (bet 85th and 86th St)   212/744-2000
Mon-Fri: 10-8; Sat: 9:30-6:30; Sun: 10-6

This is in-line skating and windsurfing headquarters! They have a windsurfing school in Southampton, give skating lessons, do service work, rent in-line skates and videos on a number of sports, and will special-order any item not in stock. A full selection of in-line skates, windsurfing racks, swim fins, snowboards, wet suits, car racks, bathing suits, and goggles is in stock. The staff here is eager to help out both amateurs and professionals.

PECK AND GOODIE
917 Eighth Ave (bet 54th and 55th St)　　212/246-6123
Mon-Sat: 10-8; Sun: 10-6

Skating is a popular means of summer transportation in Manhattan, so there are plenty of skate shops. But Peck and Goodie has been around for a good long while, offering equipment and apparel to skaters who need the best with minimum fuss. The store offers a complete stock of roller and ice skates, in-line skates, skateboards, and accessories. With faddish skates costing a hundred dollars a pair or more, it's wise to go to an expert. Boot-fitter Mike, who works there, is a self-proclaimed skate doctor!

Skiing

SCANDINAVIAN SKI SHOP
40 W 57th St (bet Fifth and Sixth Ave)　　212/757-8524
Mon-Sat: 10-6 (Thurs until 6:30); Sun: 11-5

Despite its name, this shop is really an all-around sporting-goods store with an emphasis on skiing in the winter and in-line skating in the summer. They stock a full range of goods, from skis and skiwear to skates. They also offer repairs and advice, as well as outfitting.

Soccer

SOCCER SPORT SUPPLY COMPANY
1745 First Ave (bet 90th and 91st St)
212/427-6050, 800/223-1010
Mon-Fri: 10-6; Sat: 10-3

Max and Hermann Doss, the proprietors of this half-century-old soccer and rugby supply company, operate as if they were located in England instead of New York. Indeed, they are international; half their business involves importing and exporting equipment around the world. Soccer Sport obtains the finest rugby and soccer equipment available and ships it to customers. Visitors to the store have the advantage of seeing the selection in person, as well as receiving guidance from a staff that knows the field (excuse the pun) completely.

Tennis

MASON'S TENNIS MART
911 Seventh Ave (bet 57th and 58th St)　　212/757-5374
Mon-Fri: 10-7; Sat: 10-6

Mason's is the only tennis specialty store left in Manhattan. Mark Mason offers a superb collection of clothing with all the best brand names: Fila, Nike, Le Coq Sportif, Bogner, Prince, Reebok, Fred Perry, and more. U.S. Open products are carried from May to December. Besides clothing, you will find ball machines, bags, and every other kind of tennis paraphernalia. They will match any authorized dealer on racquet prices and will special-order any tennis product a customer may want. Same-day stringing services are offered, and twice-yearly half-price clothing (except children's) sales take place in mid-August and mid-January.

Stationery

HUDSON ENVELOPE
111 Third Ave (bet 13th and 14th St)   212/473-6666
611 Sixth Ave (at 18th St)   212/255-4593
1100 Second Ave (at 58th St)   212/980-1999
Open 7 days a week

These folks have become the largest single paper and envelope store in the city and perhaps the world! You can purchase as little as a 100 sheets of paper and 25 envelopes. Their inventory of paper stocks includes recycled merchandise. Over 150 different kinds of paper, with matching card stock and envelopes, are available. They also have a vast selection of presentation folders. Closeouts and discounted items provide excellent bargains. Ask for their free catalog!

JAMIE OSTROW
876 Madison Ave (bet 71st and 72nd St)   212/734-8890
Mon-Sat: 10-6

For contemporary personalized stationery and invitations, you can't do better than Jamie Ostrow. They design and manufacture their own items to the specifications of individual customers, and they also carry Crane stationery and wedding invitations. A good selection of boxed Christmas and holiday cards is shown, and personalized Christmas cards are a specialty.

KATE'S PAPERIE
561 Broadway (bet Prince and Spring St)   212/941-9816
Mon-Fri: 10:30-7; Sat: 10-6; Sun: 12-6

8 W 13th St (at Fifth Ave)   212/633-0570
Mon-Fri: 10-7; Sat: 10-6; Sun: 12-6

Here you will find one of the largest selections of decorative and exotic papers in the country. Kate has 8,000 kinds of papers, including papyrus, hand-marbled French paper, Japanese lace papers, handmade paste papers, and just about anything else you can think of in the paper classification. But that isn't all that's available at this unique store. There are leather-bound albums and journals, classic and exotic stationery, boxes, rubber stamps, rice-paper lamps, and desk accessories. They will do custom printing and engraving, personal and business embossing, and custom and corporate gift wrapping.

MRS. JOHN L. STRONG
699 Madison Ave (bet 62nd and 63rd St), 5th floor
212/838-3848
Mon-Fri: 10-5 and by appointment

Why anyone would want to steal stationery is beyond me, but several barriers must be crossed to reach this high-end stationery establishment in a fifth-floor room. First, a claustrophobic elevator. Then a locked door. When you are buzzed in, the atmosphere is strictly high-altitude, as are the noses of some of the salesladies. But when you are selling very high-quality papers, invitations, and announcements—with very high prices to match—I guess you have a right to impart a regal touch. If you are looking for the best, this is as good a place as any to splurge.

REBECCA MOSS
510 Madison Ave (at 53rd St)   212/832-7671
Mon-Fri: 10-6; Sat: 10-5:30

If you are in the market for pens, this is the place! They carry the largest selection and the latest items from Montblanc, Parker, Waterman, Aurora, Pelikan, Omas, Lamy, Sheaffer, and all the other big names. Moreover, the personnel are informed and friendly. It is a family-owned business, and customers are treated as part of the clan. The late grandmother, Rebecca Moss, would be pleased at what her grandson is doing!

Tiles

IDEAL TILE
405 E 51st St   212/759-2339
Mon-Fri: 9-5:30; Sat: 10-5

Ideal Tile imports ceramics, porcelain, marble, granite, and terra cotta from Italy, Spain, Portugal, and Brazil. They have absolutely magnificent hand-painted Italian ceramic pottery as well. This outfit guarantees installation of tiles by skilled craftsmen. They also offer marble and granite fabrication for fireplaces, countertops, window sills, and tables.

TILES - A REFINED SELECTION
42 W 15th St (bet Fifth and Sixth Ave)   212/255-4450
Mon-Fri: 9:30-6; Thurs: 9:30-8; Sat: 10-5

If you are in the market for quality tiles, try Tiles' "refined selection." There are American art tiles, slate, granite, molded tiles, marble and limestone mosaics, glass tiles, and a large assortment of handmade tiles. Design services are available, and the selection is tops.

Tobacco and Accessories

BARCLAY-REX
7 Maiden Lane (nr Broadway)   212/962-3355
Mon-Fri: 8-6

70 E 42nd St (bet Madison and Park Ave)   212/692-9680
Mon-Fri: 8-6:30; Sat: 9:30-5:30

570 Lexington Ave (at 51st St)   212/888-1015
Mon-Wed: 8-6:30; Thurs, Fri: 8-7:30; Sat: 9:30-5:30

This is a tobacco connoisseur's shop, and a specialty shop at that. The specialty is pipes (cigars are anathema and cigarettes more so), and third-generation owner Vincent Nastri knows the field inside-out. His shop is prepared to create a pipe from scratch, fill it with any imaginable type of tobacco (including a good house brand), repair the pipe if it should break, and offer advice on proper pipe care and blending of pipe tobacco. Nastri has a good reputation for prompt quality repairs and reasonable prices. It might pay to buy a new "irregular" pipe, which can be had for a surprisingly low price. As with most specialties, esoteric models are available at astronomical prices. If you have $1,000 to send up in smoke, Nastri will come up with something extraordinary.

CONNOISSEUR PIPE SHOP
1285 Sixth Ave, concourse level   212/247-6054
Mon-Fri: 10-6

Edward Burak is an artist. At his shop he has assembled a beautiful collection of hand-carved pipes that range in price from $27 to over $3,500. His store features natural unvarnished pipes, custom-made pipes, custom-blended tobacco, and expert repair of all kinds of pipes. Burak will also do appraisals for insurance purposes. Although you have to be careful about where pipes are smoked these days, if yours came from Connoisseur you'll get admiring glances from those who know quality.

J.R. TOBACCO
11 E 45th St (at Madison Ave)   212/983-4160
Mon-Fri: 7:45-5:45; Sat: 9-3:45

219 Broadway (at Vesey St)   212/233-6620
Mon-Fri: 7:45-5

For years Lew Rothman has claimed to offer the world's largest selection of cigars and pipe tobacco at the world's lowest prices. The cigars come in over 3,000 different brands—and, as we all know, they are very "in" right now. Prices are 20% to 70% off regular retail.

Choosing the Right Cigar
  A wrapper ties an entire cigar together and gives it character. Cigar wrappers come in six basic colors:

Double Claro: green
Claro: tan, neutral in flavor, often from Connecticut
Colorado Claro or Natural: light brown to brown leaf
Colorado: reddish-brown color and rich flavor
Maduro: dark brown, oily, with a rich and strong flavor
Oscuro: dark brown or black, grown in Connecticut, Mexico, Nicaragua, and Brazil

---

Toys, Trains
General

B. SHACKMAN AND COMPANY
85 Fifth Ave (at 16th St)   212/989-5162
Mon-Fri: 9-5; Sat: 10-4; Sun: 12-6

In the midst of the wholesale toy district, B. Shackman has been playing house since 1898. But their form of play is a very serious business that's devoted to manufacturing, importing, and selling toys, novelties, and miniatures. Though a large portion of their business is still on the wholesale level, it is run by people who obviously enjoy what they are doing. They are willing to take time to share their vocation with amateurs and single retail customers. Shackman carries a full line of aforementioned specialties. However, the items of interest to retail customers are their miniatures and a striking collection of Victoriana. Again, this is not at all in keeping with its neighbors, but Shackman excels in Victorian postcards, Christmas tree decorations, old-fashioned greeting cards, and children's books. There are also Steiff toys, lead hand-painted soldiers, dolls, contemporary stuffed toys, and paper dolls.

CLASSIC TOYS
218 Sullivan St (bet Bleecker and 3rd St)   212/674-4434
Tues-Sun: noon-6:30

Now three times their former size, Classic carries old and new toys that have proven popular with generations of youngsters. It is also a haven for collectors and those (like your author) who just like to browse in toy shops. Here you will find the largest selection of die-cast vehicles in New York, with pieces of old Matchbox, Dinky, and Corgi that go back to the 1930s. Over a hundred years of miniature figures are on display, as well as soft toys, Christmas tree ornaments from Europe, and a great selection of antiques that will charm both parents and children. They thoughtfully maintain a list of stores for shoppers who can't find what they want here!

DINOSAUR HILL
306 E 9th St   212/473-5850
Daily: 11-7

At Dinosaur Hill you can travel the world through toys! There are marbles from England, tin windups from China, papier-maché masks from Mexico, wooden pull toys from Greece, and solid wooden blocks made right here in the U.S.A. In addition, there is hand-made clothing in natural-fiber fabrics for infants through four years and a wonderful expanded assortment of hats, music boxes, monkeys, moons, and mermaids!

ENCHANTED FOREST
85 Mercer St (bet Spring and Broome St)   212/925-6677
Mon-Sat: 11-7; Sun: 12-6

The Enchanted Forest physically and philosophically matches its name. David Wallace and Peggy Sloane, a husband-and-wife team of owners, hired theatrical set designer Matthew Jacobs to create an enchanted-forest backdrop for a collection of toys, whimsies, and artwork. The shop purports to be a "gallery of beasts, books, and handmade toys celebrating the spirit of the animals, the old stories, and the child within." The emphasis is on the gallery aspect. One can enter a crystal cave that transforms into an old wooden wardrobe through which one passes into a small Victorian room. Other featured items include a fine selection of fairy tales, mythologies, children's stories, and various eclectic gems. This truly is an enchanted place!

F.A.O. SCHWARZ
767 Fifth Ave (bet 58th and 59th St)   212/644-9400
Mon-Wed: 10-6; Thurs-Sat: 10-7; Sun: 11-6

Ask any kid where he or she wants to go in New York, and the answer will likely be F.A.O. Schwarz! It is on the cutting edge of the toy business, because most manufacturers want to get their items in this store first. But it is more than just a retail establishment. Groups of youngsters grow wide-eyed at the enormous selection and exciting demonstrations. The store now has three levels, arranged into small shops that specialize in stuffed animals, bears, games, electronics, dolls, soldiers, Star Wars, Barbie, and all the other things that you'd expect in a first-rate toy emporium. There is even a counter by the door where those in a hurry can pick up a last-minute gift to take home. Just don't expect bargains. We're talking top-of-the-line!

GEPPETTO'S TOY BOX
161 Seventh Ave S (bet Waverly Pl and Perry St)   212/620-7511
Mon-Thurs: noon-8; Fri, Sat: noon-10; Sun: 1-7

One of the great pleasures of New York is walking into a store because of its window display and having it turn out to be a special place like this magical new West Village toy store. I simply can't say enough good things about the exceptionally high-quality teddy bears, jack-in-the-boxes. snow globes, marionettes, and other whimsical toys and games this store offers or the passion and care with which it's run. You'll also find a variety of interesting items made by local artists and a small but carefully chosen selection of books. If you're a toy collector, someone with a child in your life, or simply like a store with class and grace, make a visit to Geppetto's a top priority.

KIDDING AROUND
60 W 15th St   212/645-6337
Mon-Fri: 10-7; Sat. 11-7; Sun: 11-6

68 Bleecker St   212/598-0228
Mon-Sat: 11-7; Sun: 11-6

Amid a rather routine selection of Ambi toys, Ravensberger puzzles, and the like, you'll find some of the most interesting riding and rocking toys I've ever seen at the 15th Street location. While that store is bigger and brighter, however, I prefer the coziness of the Bleecker Street store. Both stores carry an unusual and fun selection of natural-fiber clothing for infants and small children, as well as lots of things for Curious George fans.

Specialty and Novelty

ALPHABETS
115 Ave A   212/475-7250
Mon-Sat: noon-10; Sun: noon-7

This crowded littte place is really not so much a toy store for kids as a novelty shop and a bit or a stroll down memory lane for grown-ups. If you're looking for a Desi Arnaz wristwatch, a Gumby and Pokey piggy bank, some particularly kitschy ceramics, or a T-shirt with the Velveeta logo on it, this is the place to come. It's also a great source for moderately risqué greeting cards, pasta in the shape of human anatomy parts, and other R-rated novelty items. That's not to say that Alphabets doesn't have some great toys for children—the kit for making balloon animals, for example—but most younger kids wouldn't understand much of what's in here and most parents wouldn't want them exposed to it.

BEAR HUGS & BABY DOLLS
311 E 81st St (bet First and Second Ave)   212/717-1514
Mon-Sat: 10-6; Sun: 12-5 (closed Sun, Mon in summer)

"Beary" novel is the best description for this unique store, which features teddy bears and collectible dolls. They have over 300 different teddies, including an array of handmade artist originals. You'll find many famous names: Steiff, the Muffy Vander Bear collection, and Madame Alexander dolls. They even have a seamstress who can custom-make doll and bear outfits.

BIG CITY KITE COMPANY
1210 Lexington Ave (at 82nd St)   212/472-2623
Mon-Fri: 11-6:30 (Thurs: 11-7:30); Sat: 10-6;
Sun (seasonally): 12-5

You would expect New York to have a store dedicated totally to kites, and it is a great one. Big City's David Klein sells kites for people's houses: i.e., mobiles and wall hangings. He sells custom-made specialty kites and brilliantly colored fighter kites made of tissue paper. He also offers a kite-repair service. Prices begin at about $2 and go as high as $300. The staff's genuine devotion is most evident in the community programs it sponsors. There are kite festivals and exhibitions, even "kite-ins." They also carry a full line of darts, dartboards, and accessories for recreational and competitive throwers.

BURLINGTON ANTIQUE TOYS
1082 Madison Ave (at 82nd St)   212/861-9708
Mon-Sat: 10-6; Sun: 12-5

Anyone who has been to Forbes Gallery knows that toy soldiers are not just for children. At Burlington Antique Toys, the toy soldiers are serious antiques, as is virtually everything else in the store. That roll call includes toy cars, airplanes, boats, and other tin toys. There is a "used car lot" specializing in out-of-production, die-cast car models. Best of all, Burlington proves that not only fabulously rich men can play with toy soldiers or float their own armadas. This is a place for everyone, and the folks here couldn't be nicer. Crawford Doyle Booksellers is upstairs.

CHILDREN'S GENERAL STORE
2473 Broadway (at 92nd St)   212/580-2723
Mon-Sat: 10-6; Sun: 12-5 (closed Sun in summer)

Located in the lobby of Playspace, an indoor playground for children, this store specializes in classic wooden toys that encourage imaginative play by young folks. Don't come looking for space-age wizardry or battery-operated gizmos here—just good old-fashioned toys that are plenty exciting in their own way. The store also obliges customers with a baby-shower registry, custom stationery, and party bags.

DISNEY STORE
Seventh Ave and 42nd St   212/221-0430
Mon-Thurs:10-9; Fri, Sat: 10-1 a.m.; Sun: noon-6

Fifth Ave and 55th   212/702-0702
Mon-Sat: 10-8; Sun: 11-6

34th St (bet Fifth and Sixth Ave)   212/279-9890
Mon-Sat: 10-8; Sun: 11-6

Columbus Ave and 66th St   212/362-2386
Mon-Sat: 10-9; Sun:11-6

If the "malling" of New York hasn't gotten you down, these stores—particularly the one on 42nd Street—can be pleasant and fun places to shop. Unlike the staff at a lot of the huge, mall-like stores that have been popping up all over New York in recent years, the folks here really know their stock and are personable besides. If you don't have a Disney Store back home and are looking for luggage with Mickey Mouse on it, backpacks for kids in the shape of Winnie the Pooh, or any other Disney-related item you can imagine, by all means visit one of these locations.

DOLLHOUSE ANTICS
1343 Madison Ave (at 94th St)   212/876-2288
Mon-Fri: 11-5:30; Sat: 11-5

Dollhouse Antics, a shop dedicated to miniatures, is straight out of childhood dreams. Dollhouse-making is serious business here. The most popular orders are for replicas of ancestral homes, and you can bet your made-to-order miniature needlepoint rug that these dollhouses aren't made for eager little children. Dollhouses come in kit form, but if money is no object — or when the fun of assembling it yourself wanes — the store will put it together for you. But be wary: like real houses, these models need to be furnished. I just hope you can afford the scaled-down Oriental rugs, custom upholstery, special wallpaper, electrical supplies, and made-to-order furniture!

E.A.T. GIFTS
1062 Madison Ave (bet 80th and 81st St)   212/861-2544
Mon-Sat: 10-6; Sun: noon-5

It's impossible to sum up what this store offers in a few sentences. E.A.T. Gifts is a wonderland of imaginative party favors and stocking stuffers that must be seen to be believed. From the tiny tea sets, party supplies, and invitations to the piñatas on the ceiling and seasonal holiday items, you'll want to inspect each square foot of this store! As the Madison Avenue address suggests, there's nothing inexpensive about what you'll find here. But if you want to put together a really fun party bag or special stocking, this is *the* place to go.

MANHATTAN DOLL HOUSE
236-A Third Ave   212/253-9549
Mon-Fri: 11-6; Sat: 10-5

Edwin Jacobowitz operates the Manhattan Doll House, which boasts the city's largest collection of dolls (including Madame Alexander), dollhouses, dollhouse furniture, and doll paraphernalia.

RED CABOOSE
23 W 45th St, basement level   212/575-0155
Mon-Fri: 11-7; Sat: 11-6

Owner-operator Allan J. Spitz will tell you that 99% of his customers are not wide-eyed children but sharp-eyed adults who are dead serious about model railroads. Since these are the people Spitz serves, it is rather difficult for a Christmas-morning engineer to adequately describe his stock, but I'll try. The Red Caboose claims to have 100,000 items on hand. That includes a line of 300 hand-finished, imported brass locomotives alone. It doesn't begin to cover the tracks or track gauges available. Spitz claims that the five basic sizes — 1:22, 1:48, 1:87, 1:161, and 1:220, in a ratio of scale to life size — will allow a model railroader to build layouts sized to fit into a desk drawer or a basement. They also carry an extensive line of plastic kits.

TOY BALLOON
204 E 38th St   212/682-3803
Mon-Fri: 9-5:30

The Toy Balloon sells balloons individually or in multitudes of up to 50,000. They are so varied that there are graduations in diameter, thickness, style, and type (including Mylar balloons). Sizes range from peewees to blimps, while shapes include dolls, rabbit heads, hearts, dachshunds (they're often used to advertise hot dogs), and extra-long shapes. Most of this whimsical business is done for advertising campaigns.

WARNER BROTHERS STUDIO STORE
Fifth Ave and 57th St   212/754-0300
Mon-Sat: 10-7; Sun: 11-6

I experience sensory overload whenever I walk through this place, but it must have something going for it: tourists, especially ones from foreign countries, flock to it. So do children. If you're a Warner Brothers fan, you'll be hard pressed not to find something here: hats with Daffy Duck, infant clothing with Porky the Pig, mugs with Bugs Bunny . . . you get the idea. If the character originated at Warner Brothers, there are at least a dozen items with him or her on it for sale here. For more serious collectors, original animation production cels are also available. Recently the store more than doubled its size to 75,000 square feet, adding such things as the Moving Pictures Cafe (on the fifth floor) and a space for birthday and other private parties (on the ninth floor). As this goes to press, a new location is being planned for One Times Square.

Accessories and Gifts

LITTLE EXTRAS
550 Amsterdam Ave (bet 86th and 87th St)   212/721-6161
Mon-Fri: 10:30-6:30 (Thurs until 7); Sat: 10:30-6; Sun: 11-5
(closed Sun in July and Aug)

Whether you're looking for a personalized bathrobe, the perfect picture frame, a baby present, or hand-painted furniture, this cheerful store is teeming with gifts and accessories for infants and children. Owner Terry Seigel's great taste shows in everything you'll find here. Make sure to look up at the mobiles and other things hanging from the ceiling! An added bonus: Little Extras offers a wide selection of reasonably priced birth announcements and will deliver them to your doorstep (in Manhattan) when they're ready.

WYNKEN, BLYNKEN & NOD'S
306 E 55th St   212/308-9299
Mon-Thurs: 11-6; Fri: 11-5; Sat: 10:30-5; and by appointment

Retailing ought to count itself lucky that the owner of this little gem left the practice of law to open up shop here in the quiet east side of midtown. Wynken, Blynken & Nod's is a celebration of Deborah Kleman's eclectic, whimsical, and tremendously good taste. From the unique children's furniture (much of it antique) to the clever puppets, games, and other toys, this relatively small shop is filled to the brim with something for every budget. Kleman buys stock from local artists. So much of what you'll find here—including some beautiful clothing for infants and small children—is unique.

Travel Goods

CIVILIZED TRAVELER
864 Lexington Ave   212/288-9191

2003 Broadway (bet 68th and 69th St)   212/875-0306
Mon-Sat: 10-9; Sun: 12-7

2 World Financial Center   212 786-3301
Mon-Fri: 10-7; Sat: 10-6; Sun: 12-5

For the person on the go, these stores are the most helpful places around! Books, maps, and videos are the specialties of the house, but you will also find unique and handy travel items like personal grooming pieces, pocket tailors, shoe kits, water purifiers, packable rainwear, slippers, travel-size games, travel alarm clocks, world-time calculators and clocks, translators, doorknob burglar alarms, and automobile tool kits.

Variety, Novelty

DANSE MACABRE
263½ Lafayette St (bet Prince St and Spring St)   212/219-3907
Sun-Thurs: 12-6; Fri, Sat: 12-8

One thing is for sure about this book: we cover New York life in all aspects. Now we cover death! Danse Macabre is a unique gift shop dedicated to multicultural death in art! And what does that mean? Well, you'll find things like vampires, gargoyles, death masks, and small-sized guillotines, electric chairs, gallows, and tombstones . . . if those are items you happen to be looking for! There are items from around the world, like Mexican Day of the Dead figurines, Indonesian wood crafts, and English pewter all having to do with death crafts. Oh yes, they have CDs, too . . . requiems, of course!

ODD JOB TRADING
390 Fifth Ave (bet 35th and 36th St)
66 W 48th St (bet Fifth and Sixth Ave)   212/575-0477
149 W 32nd St (bet Sixth and Seventh Ave)   212/564-7370
10 Cortlandt St (west of Broadway)   212/571-0959
465 Lexington Ave (bet 45th and 46th St)   212/949-7401
Mon-Fri: 8-7; Sat, Sun: 10-6
(Cortlandt St store closed Sun)

Odd Job has been around for awhile and seems to consistently come up with good buys on quality merchandise. What differentiates Odd Job from other stores of its type is that its stock is more current. Anything from book racks to perfume may turn up, but it's always interesting. It's also the perfect place to buy gifts for the folks back home; they'll never know how little it cost unless you tell. Odd Job is perhaps the most aggressive of the close-out stores and has a reputation as the best of its kind.

STAR MAGIC
745 Broadway (bet 8th St and Astor Pl)   212/228-7770
275 Amsterdam Ave (at 73rd St)   212/769-2020
1256 Lexington Ave (bet 84th and 85th St)   212/988-0300
Mon-Sat: 10-10; Sun: 11-9

Step through Star Magic's door, and you step through a time warp into the future. From its midnight-black ceiling with suspended galactic spheres to its spacecraft-like walls, Star Magic is designed to make a visitor forget contemporary New York and enter a timeless universe. The setting is inducement enough to pay a visit. Star Magic's theme is "Yesterday's magic is today's science," and that perhaps is the only way to describe the eclectic selection that owner Shlomo Ayal calls "space-age gifts." There are toys and items for children of all ages with a scientific bent. There are books chosen for their ability to make a reader "ponder the cosmos." Star Magic offers minerals and prisms, scientific instruments with which to explore the universe, high-tech toys, and new-age music that is positively futuristic.

Videotapes

BLOWOUT VIDEO
1521 Broadway (at 45th St)   212/764-7070
Daily: 10 a.m.-midnight

The big news here is large selection and low prices. You'll find a stock of new and used movies that will make your pocketbook happy.

EVERGREEN VIDEO
37 Carmine St (at Bleecker St)   212/691-7362
Mon-Thurs: 10-10; Fri: 10 a.m.-11 p.m.; Sat: noon-11; Sun: noon-10

Here you will find New York's largest rental collection of silent films; films of the 1930s, 1940s and 1950s; and foreign-language titles and documentaries. There are over 10,000 titles in their rental collection. Evergreen is particularly popular with folks involved in the arts and media.

PALMER VIDEO STORE
470 Hudson St   212/463-9377
Mon-Thurs, Sun: 11 a.m.-midnight; Fri, Sat: 10 a.m.-midnight

The nice thing about this store is that the titles are all displayed in a neat and orderly way. Palmer carries popular titles, as well as unusual and out-of-print ones. There is a membership plan, reservation privileges, and a deep stock of titles. No deposit is required of members. A five-day rental of all releases is offered at $3.50 or less.

STEREO EXCHANGE
627 Broadway (at Houston St)   212/505-1111
Mon-Fri: 11-7:30; Sat: 10:30-7; Sun: 12-7

You can't do better for high-end audio-video products than this outfit! They carry top names, there is an on-site service department, and customer installation is available. Personnel here really seem to care about their products.

VIDEO ROOM
1487 Third Ave (at 84th St)   212/879-5333
Mon-Thurs: 10-10; Fri-Sat: 10 a.m.-11 p.m.; Sun: 12-10

Two distinct advantages here: first, a large selection of foreign films and classics; and second, a highly competent staff of film students who seem motivated to help inquiring customers. There is also an in-depth selection of new releases, home pickup and delivery service, and a special order department for hard-to-find films.

Visually Impaired Person's Help

SPECTRUM (THE LIGHTHOUSE STORE)
111 E 59th St (bet Park and Lexington St)   212/821-9384
Mon-Fri: 10-6; Sat: 10-5

This is a wonderful place for the visually impaired and the blind. They also carry items for the hard-of-hearing and for seniors who may have mobility problems. Over 200 articles are displayed, including reading and writing supplies, large print books, talking appliances, and electronic devices to enhance vision.

Wall Coverings

SHEILA'S INTERIORS
323 Grand St (at Orchard St)   212/966-1663
Sun-Thurs: 9-5; Fri: 9-4

Bucking the trend on the Lower East Side, Sheila's has expanded into larger quarters, showing fashion- and budget-conscious home-furnishings buyers how to save time and money. You'll find top-quality wallcoverings, furniture, trimmings, fabrics, drapes, bedspreads, window treatments, and coordinated accessories. These folks also do floor coverings and reupholstery.

Watches

Don't be taken by the watch peddlers who will tackle you along Fifth Avenue, near Bloomingdale's, and on side streets in midtown. Most of what they sell is fake, and you have no recourse if there are problems.

YAEGER WATCH CORPORATION
578 Fifth Ave (at 47th St)   212/819-0088
Mon-Sat: 10-5

Some attractive discounted watches are carried here. Choose from name brands retailing from $100 to $150,000 in a store that has been in the same family since 1970. Watch repair and guarantees on purchases are offered.

New York's best watch stores include **Cellini Fine Jewelry** (509 Madison Ave, at 52nd St; 212/888-0505), **Kenjo** (40 W 57th St; 212/333-7220), **Tourneau** (500 Madison Ave, at 52nd St, and 57th St and Madison Ave; 212/758-3265), and **Wempe** (700 Fifth Ave, at 55th St; 212/397-9000).

VII. Where to "Extras"

Since I started publishing this book almost two decades ago, I've been asked thousands of questions that have nothing to do with restaurants, stores, museums, or any other topics I originally included. When do the Christmas windows go up? Which Santa is the best? What can I do with my kids in New York? Where should I think about having my wedding reception? How can I get a plot summary of the shows playing on Broadway?

Questions like these are why I include this special "Extras" chapter. It's packed with useful information that just doesn't fit anywhere else: a calendar of annual events, information on the club scene in New York, a list of places that are open 24 hours (or almost), tips on where to take the kids for a fun meal, ideas for planning a free (or close to it) itinerary, and even a list of clean public restrooms. And, by the way, the answers to the questions in the preceding paragraph are as follows:

- the week before Thanksgiving
- the one at Macy's Herald Square
- with a couple of noted exceptions, just about anything
- choose from among several beautiful spaces, assuming you're planning ahead and are willing to spend several thousand dollars for an evening's rental
- by calling NYC/Onstage at 212/768-1818.

Annual Events

While stores, museums, restaurants, and so forth are open all year, some special events are held only during certain seasons or once a year. (The "Resources" section in this chapter tells where to look for what's happening at any given time and the "Telephone Numbers and Web Sites" section gives the numbers of most venues listed below.) You'll find a brief list of special events in the front section of the Manhattan Yellow Pages. In addition to shows, fairs, and festivals, I've included several particularly big or worthwhile sales in the following list.

JANUARY – All of the city's Christmas decorations come down in early January, but there's still time to catch the last few performances of the annual Christmas Spectacular at Radio City Music Hall. Check out the ice skating at

Rockefeller Center and in Central Park's two rinks, or go see the Ice Capades at Madison Square Garden toward the end of the month. On New Year's Day, the Polar Bear Club takes a dip in the Atlantic out on Coney Island. The National Boat Show is held at the Jacob K. Javits Convention Center in the middle of the month, and the prestigious Winter Antiques Show at the Seventh Regiment Armory (Park Avenue and 66th Street) begins at the end of the month. Golden Gloves boxing begins at Madison Square Garden and runs through March. Depending on the lunar calendar, the Chinese New Year falls anywhere between the middle of January and the middle of February. Chinatown is definitely the place to be for the celebration. January is also winter sale time. One of the best is at Saks Fifth Avenue.

FEBRUARY – February is Black History Month, and New York has all sorts of official and unofficial celebrations of it. Keep an eye out for announcements on the street and in newspapers. In early February, the Westminster Kennel Club's Dog Show moves into Madison Square Garden for two days, while the National Antiques Show moves in later in the month. Look for the New York International Motorcycle Show at the Jacob K. Javits Convention Center. On Valentine's Day, the chapel on the Empire State Building's 80th floor is the site of a giant wedding ceremony for all comers. In the middle of the month, some of the city's more energetic people participate in the Empire State Building Run-Up (that's right – *up* the stairs, from the lobby to the 86th floor!), an invitational event sponsored by the New York Road Runners Club. Snow or no snow, there's a wonderful Winter Festival on Central Park's Great Lawn in the middle of the month. President's Day, the third Monday in February, is a huge sale day at department stores, electronics stores, clothing stores, and just about everywhere else. The Art Dealers Association of America holds an exhibition for its member galleries at the Seventh Regiment Armory (Park Avenue and 66th Street) late in the month.

MARCH – The most famous New York event this month is the March 17th St. Patrick's Day Parade, although this 200-year-old march up Fifth Avenue from 44th to 86th streets has been the center of great controversy in recent years. The Greek Independence Day Parade is held a week later, also on Fifth Avenue. The International Cat Show is held at Madison Square Garden early in the month, as is the Spring Armory Antiques Show held at the Seventh Regiment Armory (Park Avenue and 66th Street). The circus comes to town in March – the Ringling Brothers and Barnum & Bailey Circus, that is – immediately preceded by a hush-hush march of the biggest animals into Manhattan from Long Island City via the Queens-Midtown Tunnel in the middle of the night. Cirque du Soleil, an unusual and innovative circus with no animals and lots of contortionists, begins its run in Battery Park City late this month, as well. The Golden Gloves boxing finals are held at Madison Square Garden in March, as is the Big East college basketball tournament. The New York Flower Show is held at Pier 92 (51st Street at the Hudson River) in the middle of the month. The Film Society of Lincoln Center and the Museum of Modern Art co-sponsor the New Directors/New Films series this month as well. Depending when Easter falls, you can also visit the Easter-egg exhibit at the Ukrainian Museum or the Easter-lily display in the Channel Gardens at Rockefeller Center and the Winter Garden at the World Financial Center. The Macy's Spring Flower Show is held at Macy's at Herald Square for several weeks beginning around Palm Sunday, and the Greater New York Orchid Show opens this month at the World Financial Center's Winter Garden. An Easter-egg roll and other events for children are held in the East Meadow in Central Park on the Saturday before Easter, and an informal Easter parade is held on Easter Day on Fifth Avenue around St. Patrick's Cathedral, beginning at 11 a.m. You can catch the annual Easter Show at Radio City Music Hall throughout the Easter season.

APRIL – The month opens with the International Auto Show at the Jacob K. Javits Convention Center. April also means the beginning of baseball season, so check out the home schedules for the Mets and the Yankees. The year's first outdoor festival is held on the third Sunday in April at Stuyvesant Park, on both sides of Second Avenue from 15th to 17th streets. You can browse rare autographs, manuscripts, and first editions at the New York Antiquarian Book Fair at the Seventh Regiment Armory (Park Avenue and 66th Street). Also check out the beautiful spring flower displays at Rockefeller Center, the World Trade Center, and the Winter Garden at the World Financial Center.

MAY – At the beginning of the month, the Little Red Schoolhouse (196 Bleecker Street) holds its annual international fair. The Ninth Avenue International Food Festival is held the third weekend in May along Ninth Avenue, from 37th to 57th streets; the Ukrainian Festival on 7th Street, between Second Avenue and Bowery, is usually held the same weekend. The American Ballet Theater begins its nine-week season this month at the Metropolitan Opera House in Lincoln Center. The Martin Luther King, Jr. Parade is held along Fifth Avenue this month, and the Spanish and Portuguese Synagogue on the Upper West Side holds a Sephardic Fair on a Sunday in the middle of the month. The Coast Guard and Navy sail into town the week before Memorial Day for Fleet Week. Look for festivities at the Intrepid Sea-Air-Space Museum. Over Memorial Day weekend and into early June, look for the Washington Square Outdoor Art Exhibit at the foot of Fifth Avenue in Greenwich Village. And keep an eye out for the Lower East Side Jewish Festival, held on a Sunday late in May.

JUNE – A number of cultural events that last all summer and are free to the public begin in June: Shakespeare in the Park at the Delacorte Theater in the southwest corner of Central Park's Great Lawn; performances by the Metropolitan Opera Company and New York Philharmonic in Central Park and other parks throughout the city; the Midsummer Night Swing concerts at Lincoln Center Plaza; Central Park SummerStage performances; and Monday night movies in Bryant Park are some of the highlights. Although many museums along Fifth Avenue's Museum Mile offer free admission one night a week all year, almost all of them offer free admission one evening in mid-June during the Museum Mile Festival. Half the city turns out as Fifth Avenue between 82nd and 102nd streets becomes a pedestrian mall. An Italian street fair to commemorate the Feast of St. Anthony of Padua is held in Little Italy during two weeks in June, and street performers show up en masse for the Lower Manhattan Cultural Council's Buskers Fare in the middle of the month. The annual Salute to Israel parade is held along Fifth Avenue above 59th Street in the middle of the month, and one of the nation's largest gay and lesbian marches is held on the last Sunday of the month to commemorate the 1969 raid on the Stonewall Inn in Greenwich Village. The JVC Jazz Festival opens this month with events at Bryant Park, Carnegie Hall, and other locations throughout the city. Both the Lesbian and Gay Film Festival at the Public Theater and the Human Rights Watch Film Festival at the Walter Reade Theater are held this month.

JULY – The Fourth of July goes off with a bang at the Macy's Fireworks Display, launched from barges on the East River. FDR Drive from 14th to 51st streets is closed to traffic, so you can get really terrific views. Get ready for the fireworks at the Fourth of July Festival, held all day on Water Street from Battery Park to John Street in lower Manhattan. Lincoln Center Plaza, on Columbus Avenue between 62nd and 65th streets, comes alive with the American Crafts Festival during the first two weekends of the month. You'll also find free concerts galore in July: Metropolitan Opera Company and New York Philharmonic performances in Central Park and other parks throughout the city; jazz in the Museum of Modern Art's Sculpture Garden; concerts on Thursday and Friday evenings at South Street Seaport; and chamber music in Washington Square Park at the foot of Fifth Avenue in Greenwich Village every Tuesday night. Also look for the enormously popular Mostly Mozart concerts at Avery Fisher Hall in Lincoln Center, and the Midsummer's Night Swing in Lincoln Center Plaza.

AUGUST—August has never been New York's best month. It's usually hot and humid, and piles of garbage on the city's streets make the whole island smell. The city is relatively quiet, particularly on weekends, because a lot of New Yorkers head for summer homes or pick this month to go on vacation. That said, however, there's still lots to do. In early August, the Uptown Chamber of Commerce sponsors a week-long salute to Harlem's past, present, and future. There are outdoor performances throughout the month in Lincoln Center Plaza, off Columbus Avenue between 62nd and 65th streets. A big crafts fair is held there on weekends at the end of the month and the beginning of September. Look for the Festival Latino's concerts, films, and other events at the Public Theater and other locations. As any tennis fan knows, the U.S. Open begins in late August and runs through Labor Day weekend. It's lots of fun, though traffic is hell!

SEPTEMBER—Labor Day weekend is the last breath of summer, and roads in and out of the city are a nightmare on Monday evening. If you're in the city that weekend, check out the art fair in and around Washington Square at the foot of Fifth Avenue in Greenwich Village. My favorite event is the New York Is Book Country fair on the third Sunday of September. I haven't missed one yet, and we've made a tradition of releasing new editions of this book there! Fifth Avenue is closed to traffic between 48th and 57th streets, and there's something for just about everybody. The Third Avenue Festival, on Third Avenue between 68th and 90th streets, is usually held the same day. Little Italy comes alive with the Feast of San Gennaro. For 11 days beginning in mid-September, there's food, fun, and family reunions. Alice Tully Hall at Lincoln Center is home to the New York Film Festival beginning the third week of the month. The New York Philharmonic begins its long season this month in Avery Fisher Hall in Lincoln Center. Look for lots of "Back to School" sales at the end of the month.

OCTOBER—The NBA's Knicks and the NHL's Rangers open their seasons this month at Madison Square Garden, and there are three big parades: the Columbus Day Parade, the Polish Day Parade, and the Hispanic Day Parade. Look for the Soho Arts Festival in early October, when more than 100 galleries host open houses. Keep an eye out for the Fall Antiques Show at Pier 92 (52nd Street and the Hudson River), arguably the most prestigious antique show in the country. Get a jump on winter as ice skating begins in Rockefeller Plaza. Finally, there's a Halloween Parade in Greenwich Village, for which participants line up at Sixth Avenue just north of Houston Street in the early evening. Don't expect much else for Halloween, however, since concerns about safety and a lack of space mean that most kids in Manhattan wander through their apartment buildings rather than neighborhoods. The sporting event that draws more spectators than any other in the world (well over 2.5 million at last count) is the New York Marathon, held on a Sunday in late October or early November. The 26-mile course runs through all five boroughs, starting on the Staten Island end of the Verrazano Narrows Bridge and ending at Tavern on the Green on West Drive in Central Park. Call the New York Road Runners Club for the exact date and viewing suggestions.

NOVEMBER – Christmas is still more than a month away, but you wouldn't know it from the way Manhattan gets decked out in November. The first sure sign is the annual Radio City Music Hall Christmas Show, beginning in the middle of the month. The Christmas windows in major department stores start to go up the week before Thanksgiving. Saks Fifth Avenue (Fifth Avenue at 50th Street) is just one of the many more conventional ones worth seeing along Fifth Avenue. Santa Claus arrives at Macy's at Herald Square the day after Thanksgiving and stays through Christmas Eve. Of all the Santas to visit in Manhattan, this is one of the best, year in and year out. Check out the crafts and antiques at the Triple Pier Show on Piers 88, 90, and 92 (along the Hudson River between 48th and 55th streets). Look for the annual Home Show at the Jacob K. Javits Convention Center early in the month; the Corel/WTA Women's Tennis Tournament at Madison Square Garden in the middle of the month; and the Margaret Meade Film Festival at the American Museum of Natural History. Of course, it wouldn't be November without the Macy's Thanksgiving Day Parade. The parade starts on Central Park West at about 79th Street and winds down to Columbus Circle; from there, it heads down Broadway to Macy's at Herald Square. For a real treat, let the kids stay up to watch the giant balloons being inflated on Central Park West the night before!

DECEMBER – December means Christmas in New York, and it's hard to turn around without seeing advertisements for performances of Handel's *Messiah* and the *Nutcracker* ballet. The best of the former is the "Messiah Sing-In" at Avery Fisher Hall, while the best *Nutcracker* is staged at the New York State Theater. They're both in Lincoln Center. The famed Christmas tree at Rockefeller Center, just off Fifth Avenue between 49th and 50th streets, is lit the late afternoon of the first Monday in December, and Fifth Avenue in midtown is closed off on two Sunday afternoons this month for holiday shoppers. Other great trees can be found in the Plaza at Lincoln Center, in front of the New York Stock Exchange, and on Friday and Saturday nights at the Metropolitan Museum of Art. The Chorus Tree, made from tiers of carolers, is at South Street Seaport throughout the month. The Brick Presbyterian Church has caroling accompanied by an organ and brass quartet early in the month, Central Presbyterian Church offers a blessing of pets on Christmas Eve, and the Church of the Heavenly Rest on East 90th Street has an enormous Christmas Pageant on Christmas Eve. Check out the crafts fair in Ferris Booth Hall at Columbia University on (Broadway at 115th Street), and look for the wares of a lot of the city's museum shops to be on display at a Christmas bazaar in Grand Central Station. You can do some shopping (window and otherwise) in midtown – assuming you can stand the crowds, which seem overwhelming even by New York standards on the weekends leading up to Christmas. Peek at the shops at Citicorp Center for a wonderful model-train exhibit. The eight nights of Chanukah are commemorated with the lighting of candles on a giant menorah at sundown in Grand Army Plaza (Fifth Avenue and 59th Street). Both the Jewish Museum and the 92nd Street YMHA host lots of Chanukah events. Kwanza is celebrated at the end of the month with a variety of events throughout the city, including storytelling at the Museum of African Art. Finally, if you must go to the annual New Year's celebration in Times Square, crowds begin to gather around 7 p.m. If you want to celebrate in a more family-friendly atmosphere, try the very popular series of events during the day and evening associated with First Night New York at locations throughout Manhattan; the Concert for Peace at the Cathedral Church of St. John the Divine (Amsterdam Avenue at 112th Street); or fireworks, a midnight run, and other events in Central Park.

Atriums and Other Public Spaces

If the hustle and bustle of the city makes you want to rest your weary feet for a couple of minutes, Manhattan has lots of beautiful atriums and public sitting areas. Indeed, it sometimes seems that the lobby of every big building in midtown has a waterfall and tables. Some, including the Equitable Center and the Phillip Morris Building, are also home to small galleries. Others, including the Ford Foundation, offer magnificent flowers and plants. Still others, such as Citicorp Center and the World Financial Center's Winter Garden, always seem to be the site of concerts, special events, and family workshops. I've put together the following list of some of my favorite atriums, public spaces, and popular sitting areas in midtown and other parts of the city.

Citicorp Center, 53rd St and Lexington Ave (indoors)
Conservatory Garden, in Central Park, just off Fifth Ave at 105th St (outdoors)
Crystal Pavilion, 50th St bet Second and Third Ave (indoors)
Equitable Center, Seventh Ave bet 51st and 52nd St (indoors)
Ford Foundation Gardens, 42nd and 43rd St bet First and Second Ave (indoors)
Galleria, 57th and 58th St bet Park and Lexington Ave (indoors)
Grace Plaza, Sixth Ave and 43rd St (outdoors)
IBM Garden Plaza, Madison Ave at 56th St (indoors)
Margaret Mead Green, Columbus Ave bet 79th and 81st St (outdoors)
Metropolitan Museum of Art steps, Fifth Ave bet 80th and 84th St (outdoors)
Museum of American Folk Art, Columbus Ave bet 65th and 66th St (indoors)
New York Public Library steps, Fifth Ave bet 40th and 42nd St (outdoors)
Olympic Tower, 51st St off Fifth Ave (indoors)
Paley Park, 53rd St bet Fifth and Madison Ave (outdoors)
Park Avenue Plaza, 52nd and 53rd St bet Madison and Park Ave (indoors)
Parker Meridien Hotel, 56th and 57th St bet Sixth and Seventh Ave (indoors)
Philip Morris Building, Park Ave at 42nd St (indoors)
St. Luke's-in-the-Fields, at Hudson and Grove St (outdoors)
Sony Plaza Arcade, Madison Ave at 56th and 55th St (indoors)
Strawberry Fields, in Central Park, near Central Park West and 72nd St (outdoors)
Sutton Place Park, Sutton Place at 57th St (outdoors)
Trump Tower Gardens, Fifth Ave bet 56th and 57th St (outdoors on levels 4 and 5)
UN Plaza, First Ave bet 45th and 46th St (outdoors)
Vivian Beaumont Theater Plaza, in Lincoln Center, off 65th St bet Broadway and Amsterdam Ave (outdoors)
Vietnam Veterans Memorial Plaza, off Water St north of Broad St (outdoors)

Winter Garden, World Financial Center, bet West St and Hudson River (indoors)
World Trade Center, various plazas throughout the complex (outdoors)

Book Talk

Despite dire predictions of its demise over the last decade, the written word is alive and well. Books are selling briskly, bookstores (at least the chains) are thriving, and book talks and reading groups are hot, hot, hot. That's probably more true in New York than anywhere else. After all, this is the publishing capital of the world, and almost every author shows up here sooner or later.

If you want to sit in on a book talk or find others who share your interests, the following places all have much going on along the literary lines. You might also try various museums (the Museum of the City of New York, for example, sponsors a group that meets at sites complementing a given book's theme!), societies, and churches throughout Manhattan. In addition, *Time Out New York* has an excellent day-by-day list of book talks, poetry readings, and the like in its "Books & Poetry" section. Most events are free, or inexpensive.

Barnes & Noble—The literary equivalent of the Gap in terms of number of stores, this bookstore chain of longstanding offers a diverse range of authors, discussions, and panels. Locations are scattered throughout the city, but the Barnes & Noble Events Line (212/727-4810) will let you know what is going on where.

Borders—This nationwide chain attracts interesting authors, most of them on book tours. New York's branch is located in 5 World Trade Center, at the corner of Vesey and Church streets. (212/839-8049)

Fred's—Speaking of hot, hot, hot . . . the monthly breakfast panel discussion at this restaurant inside the East Side Barney's has become a place to see and be seen. (It's the exception to my comment about such events being free or relatively inexpensive.) Fred's (and Barney's) is on 61st Street near Madison Avenue. (212/940-7480)

New York Public Library Center for the Humanities—All sorts of interesting and erudite discussions take place at the library's main branch on 42nd Street and Fifth Avenue. (212/254-9628)

92nd Street YMHA—This amazing community resource consistently attracts leading authors for its lecture series. The 92nd Street Y is at 1395 Lexington Avenue. (212/996-1100)

Partners & Crime—There are meet-the-author events and other fun things going on at this mystery bookstore on Greenwich Avenue at Charles Street. (212/462-3027)

Look for poetry readings and discussions at the **Knitting Factory Poetry Series** (212/219-3055) and the **Poetry Project at St. Mark's Church-in-the-Bowery** (212/674-0910).

Dancing and Other Clubs

Whether you want to go out for an evening of elegant dining and dancing, spend the wee hours bopping to rock music, drop in on a set of jazz, or catch some stand-up comedy, New York's club scene offers plenty of choices. For descriptions of places to go and information about who is playing where, look under "Night Life" in the front of *The New Yorker* or under specific listings in the back of *New York* magazine and throughout *Time Out New York*. I've listed several of the most popular places in each category to get you started. Most levy a cover charge, many offer at least a light menu, and some require reservations and jackets for men. As with so many other things, it is wise to call in advance.

Dancing

Cafe Pierre—In the Pierre Hotel, at 63rd Street and Fifth Avenue, this elegant place features music from the 1930s, 1940s, and 1950s. There's a cover charge for people who aren't dining here. There's dancing from 9 until after midnight on Thursday, Friday, and Saturday nights. Call 212/940-8185 for more information.

Denim & Diamonds—This upscale country-and-western dance club doubles as a Texas barbecue restaurant. It's located at 511 Lexington Avenue. Call 212/371-1600 for more information.

Rainbow Room—This world-famous restaurant has a revolving floor and its own orchestra every night except Monday. Both the Rainbow Room and Rainbow & Stars, an intimate and classy supper club, are located on the 65th floor of 30 Rockefeller Plaza. Call 212/632-5000 for more information.

Roseland—This enormous place has faded a bit but remains quite popular for rock music and ballroom dancing (obviously not on the same nights). It's located at 239 West 52nd Street. Call 212/247-0200 for more information.

S.O.B.—The letters stand for "Sounds of Brazil and Beyond," and this enormous club at 200 Varick Street (at Houston Street) is a favorite eating and dancing club for New York University students and those who favor Latino, Caribbean, and other international forms of music. Call 212/243-4940 for more information.

Supper Club—An older, more elegant crowd comes here for dinner and dancing in a pre-war atmosphere complete with big bands on weekend nights until midnight. The club is located at 240 West 47th Street. Call 212/921-1940 for more information.

The Tunnel—If your idea of fun is becoming hot and going deaf in the company of 3,000 other people, this club near the entrance to the Holland Tunnel (220 Twelfth Avenue, at West 27th Street) is just the place for you. Call 212/695-4682 for more information.

Windows on the World—This recently reopened restaurant on top of 1 World Trade Center has dancing every Thursday, Friday, and Saturday night in the bar. Call 212/938-1111 for more information.

Finally, if you're a fan of swing dancing, try calling the **New York Swing Dance Society** to find out about their Sunday night dances and other events (212/696-9737).

Cabaret Rooms

Bemelman's Bar, at the Carlyle Hotel (35 E 76th St, 212/744-1600)
Cafe Carlyle, at the Carlyle Hotel (35 E 76th St, 212/744-1600)
Danny's Skylight Room (346 W 46th St, 212/265-8133)
Don't Tell Mama (343 W 46th St, 212/757-0788)
Eighty-Eight's (228 W 10th St, 212/924-0088)
Michael's Pub, at the Parker Meridien Hotel (119 W 56th St, 212/758-2272)
Oak Room, at the Algonquin Hotel (59 W 44th St, 212/840-6800)
Rainbow & Stars (30 Rockefeller Plaza, 212/632-5000)

Jazz and Other Music

Birdland – One of the few jazz clubs outside Greenwich Village, this restaurant and bar is a favorite among older and more mellow fans. It recently moved from the Upper West Side down to 315 West 44th Street but hasn't lost one bit of its class and style. Call 212/581-3080 for more information.

Bitter End – A longtime showcase for soon-to-be-discovered folk-rock musicians, this club is located at 147 Bleecker Street (between Thompson Street and Laguardia Place). Call 212/673-7030 for more information.

Blue Note – You'll find two and sometimes three sets a night of great jazz at this supper club. It's located at 131 West 3rd Street, just off Sixth Avenue. Call 212/475-8592 for more information.

Bottom Line – Depending on the night, this perennially popular cabaret club offers rock, jazz, soul, folk, and country music. It's located at 15 West 4th Street. Call 212/228-7880 for more information.

Iridium – A newcomer to the jazz scene, it's nonetheless among the best. The club is beneath Merlot, a restaurant at 44 West 63rd Street across the street from Lincoln Center. Call 212/582-2121 for more information.

Knitting Factory – An alternative rock and jazz club with a basement space (the AltaKnit Room) for all sorts of interesting experimentation, the Knitting Factory is in Tribeca at 74 Leonard Street. Call 212/219-3055 for more information.

Metropolitan Museum of Art – The Met started a big trend at New York museums by offering live music on Friday and Saturday evenings. The Great Hall Balcony Bar Classical Quintet performs at a wonderful space in the Great Hall balcony. Drinks are available. The museum is on Fifth Avenue between 80th and 84th streets. Call 212/535-7710 for more information.

Museum of Modern Art – The museum's Garden Cafe plays host to a variety of jazz musicians on Friday evenings. A menu and drinks are available. The museum is at 11 West 53rd Street, between Fifth and Sixth avenues. Call 212/708-9480 for more information.

Small's – Another newcomer that rank's among the best jazz clubs in New York, this one is down among the giants in the Village at 183 West 10th Street. Call 212/929-7565 for more information.

Solomon R. Guggenheim Museum – The Guggenheim offers live jazz (with an international flavor) in its rotunda on Friday and Saturday evenings. A light menu and drinks are available. The museum is on Fifth Avenue at 88th Street. Call 212/423-3500 for more information.

Sweet Basil – This club is among the elite for serious jazz fans. It's in the West Village at 88 Seventh Avenue South. Call 212/242-1785 for more information.

Village Gate – Despite the name, this jazz institution recently moved to 240 West 52nd Street. For information about dinner and shows, call 212/307-5252.

Village Vanguard – A Greenwich Village institution for well over half a century, this jazz showcase for the famous and up-and-comers is located at 178 Seventh Avenue South. Call 212/255-4037 for more information.

Comedy Clubs

Caroline's Comedy Club – The site of the Arts and Entertainment channel's *Caroline's Comedy Hour* series, this popular place attracts such comedians as Jerry Seinfeld and Billy Crystal. An Italian restaurant as well as a comedy club, it's located at 1626 Broadway. Call 212/757-4100 for more information.

Comedy Cellar—Known for its relaxed atmosphere, this place sometimes finds established comedians trying out new jokes. It's located at 117 MacDougal Street (between Bleeker Street and Third Avenue). Call 212/254-3480 for more information.

Dangerfield's—As in Rodney. This magnet for suburban comedy fans is located at 1118 First Avenue. Call 212/593-1650 for more information.

Gay and Lesbian Clubs

A Different Light—A cafe and bookstore that specializes in gay and lesbian literature, videos, and the like, this is also a very informal and popular meeting place. It's located at 151 West 19th Street between Sixth and Seventh avenues. Call 212/989-4850 for more information.

The Boiler Room—An East Village institution, the crowd here is very mixed. It's at 86 East 4th Street between First and Second avenues. Call 212/254-7536 for more information.

Bowery Bar—A big favorite of the fashion (and fashionable) crowd, this bar is at 358 Bowery (at 4th Street). Call 212/475-2220 for more information.

g—A newcomer to the Chelsea bar scene, this gay bar seems to be a big hit. It's at 223 West 19th Street between Seventh and Eighth avenues. Call 212/929-1085 for more information.

Meow Mix—A very popular lesbian bar in the East Village, this one is at 269 Houston (at Suffolk Street). Call 212/254-1434 for more information.

Holidays

1998

January 1	New Year's Day
January 19	Martin Luther King's birthday (observed)
February 14	Valentine's Day
February 16	Presidents' Day
March 17	St. Patrick's Day
April 5	Palm Sunday
April 10	Good Friday
April 11	Passover begins (eight days)
April 12	Easter Sunday
May 10	Mother's Day
May 25	Memorial Day (observed)
June 21	Father's Day
July 4	Independence Day
September 7	Labor Day
September 21	Rosh Hashana begins (two days)
September 30	Yom Kippur
October 12	Columbus Day (observed)
October 31	Halloween
November 3	Election Day
November 11	Veterans Day
November 26	Thanksgiving
December 14	Chanukah begins (eight days)
December 25	Christmas Day

1999

January 1	New Year's Day
January 18	Martin Luther King's birthday (observed)
February 14	Valentine's Day
February 15	Presidents' Day
March 17	St. Patrick's Day
March 28	Palm Sunday
April 1	Passover begins (eight days)
April 2	Good Friday
April 4	Easter
May 9	Mother's Day
May 31	Memorial Day (observed)
June 20	Father's Day
July 4	Independence Day
September 6	Labor Day
September 11	Rosh Hashana begins (two days)
September 20	Yom Kippur
October 11	Columbus Day (observed)
October 31	Halloween
November 2	Election Day
November 11	Veterans Day
November 25	Thanksgiving
December 4	Chanukah begins (eight days)
December 25	Christmas Day

Manhattan at Night

New York bills itself as "the city that never sleeps," and a sizable number of people who live here are night people. They include not only actors and artists but also those who maintain and clean the huge office buildings; who work for answering services; who put together morning newspapers and newscasts; who work the night shift at hospitals and other businesses that never close; and secretaries, transcribers, and editors who must make sure paperwork is ready overnight.

The following list includes an array of emergency services and other places that are open at night. **Unless otherwise noted, they are open 24 hours a day, seven days a week.** This list is not intended to be inclusive but rather to give you some choices throughout Manhattan. In general, stores and restaurants in Soho, Tribeca, and Greenwich Village stay open later than ones in the rest of the city. The restaurants and mom-and-pop operations on Broadway in the Upper West Side, and on both Lexington and Third avenues in the Upper East Side, also tend to keep late hours. As with everything else, I suggest calling before setting out for any of these places to make sure that they keep the same hours.

BANKS—Assuming you have a compatible card, thousands of automated teller machines (ATMs) are open at all hours of the night. Look on the back of your bank card for a phone number you can call to find the ATM nearest you. **Western Union** (212/354-9750), at 1440 Broadway, near 40th Street, is open 24 hours a day on weekdays (Friday until 11:30 p.m.), from 7 a.m. to 11:30 p.m. on Saturday, and from 8 a.m. to 11:30 p.m. on Sunday.

BOOKSTORES—The following bookstores stay open until at least 11 p.m.

(some close earlier on Sunday): **B. Dalton Bookstore,** at 396 Sixth Avenue, at 8th Street (212/674-8780), and other locations; **Barnes & Noble,** 2289 Broadway, at 82nd Street (212/362-8835) and other locations; and **Tower Bookstore,** at 383 Lafayette Street (212/228-5100).

CAR RENTALS—All major car rental companies have offices in New York. Different locations, however, often have varying hours. The **Avis** office at 217 East 43rd Street (800/331-1212) is open 24 hours; the **Hertz** office at 222 East 40th Street (800/654-3131) is open until midnight; and the **National** office at 219 West 77th Street (800/328-4567) is open until 10:45 p.m. All of these companies have locations at Kennedy and LaGuardia airports that stay open all night.

CLEANERS—Although it's located in Long Island City, **Midnight Express Cleaners** (212/921-0111) will pick up and deliver in Manhattan, can turn things around in a day, and costs a fraction of what the hotels charge. Midnight Express can pickup and deliver between 9 a.m. and around 11 p.m. on weekdays (depending on your location) and between 9 a.m. and 3 p.m. on Saturday. **Meurice Garment Care** (212/475-2778) will pick up, deliver, and turn clothes around in two hours at any time of the day or night for $200. And the **Videotown Launderette** (212/721-1706)—A video store and laundermat at 217 West 80th Street, between Broadway and Amsterdam Avenue—is open from 7 a.m. until midnight, seven days a week. The last load of wash goes in at 10:30 p.m.

DELIVERY AND MESSENGER COMPANIES—If it "absolutely positively has to be there" at any time of day or night, call **Moonlight Courier** (212/473-2246). You can also try **Able Motorized Deliveries** (212/687-5515).

DENTIST—For late-night referrals, call the **Emergency Dental Service's** referral line (212/679-3966). The **Beth Israel Medical Center** at First Avenue and 16th Street also can handle dental emergencies.

DOCTORS—If you need to find a doctor who makes house calls at all hours of the night, call **Doctors on Call** (212/737-2333). Also see the listings under "Emergency Rooms."

ELECTRICIANS—If you need an electrician in the middle of the night, try **Altman Electric** (212/744-7372).

EMERGENCY ASSISTANCE—The citywide emergency number to call an ambulance, the police, or to report a fire is 911. The number for the city's **Victims' Services Hotline** is 212/577-7777. To find out the location of the nearest police precinct, call 212/374-5000. And if you smell gas, call Consolidated Edison's 24-hour emergency number at 212/683-8830.

EMERGENCY ROOMS—The citywide emergency number is 911. An ambulance called through 911 will take you to the nearest hospital—which may or may not be the one you want. If you want to be taken to a private hospital, if it's not a life-threatening emergency, and if you are willing to pay for the service, call **Keefe & Keefe** at 800/479-1600. If you are well enough to get to an emergency room under your own power, the following are some of the city's major hospitals that offer 24-hour service:

Bellevue Hospital: First Ave at 27th St (212/562-4141)
Beth Israel Medical Center: First Ave at 16th St (212/420-2000) and 170 East End Ave, at 87th St (212/870-9000)
Columbia Presbyterian Medical Center: 622 West 168th St, nr Fort Washington Ave (212/305-2500)

Lenox Hill Hospital: 100 East 77th St, nr Park Ave (212/434-2000)
Mount Sinai Medical Center: Madison Ave at 99th St (212/241-6500)
New York Hospital/Cornell Medical Center: 510 East 70th St (212/746-5454)
St. Luke's-Roosevelt Medical Center: Ninth Ave at 58th St, and Amsterdam
Ave at 114th St (212/523-4000)

ENTERTAINMENT—For clubs that stay open all night or close to it, look
in the "Dancing and Other Clubs" section of this chapter. Here are some other
suggestions:

Billiards: Chelsea Billiards (212/989-0096), at 54 West 21st Street, between
Fifth and Sixth Avenue, is open all night.
Bowling: Bowlmor Lanes (212/255-8188), at 110 University Place, near 12th
Street, is open from 10 a.m. until 1 a.m. on Sunday through Thursday and
until 4 a.m. on Friday and Saturday.
Chess: The Chess Shop (212/475-9580), at 230 Thompson Street, near West
3rd Street, is open until midnight every night.

FOOD (EAT-IN)—With few exceptions, you aren't going to find an elegant
dining experience at four in the morning. But you will find a surprising number
of decent places open, including:

Around the Clock Cafe: 8 Stuyvesant St, nr Third Ave (212/598-0402)
Azure: 830 Third Ave, at 51st St (212/486-8080)
Big Nick's: 2175 Broadway (212/362-9238)
Chelsea Square Restaurant: 368 W 23rd St (212/691-5400)
Coffee Shop: 29 Union Sq W (212/243-7969)
Cooper Square II: 87 Second Ave, at 5th St (212/420-8050)
Cosmos Diner: 395 Second Ave, at 23rd St (212/679-1290)
Empire Diner: 210 Tenth Ave, at 22nd St (212/243-2736)
French Roast: Sixth Ave at 11th St (212/533-2233) and Broadway at 85th St
(212/799-1533)
Kiev: 117 Second Ave, at 7th St (212/674-4040)
McDonald's: 39th St and Second Ave; 56th St and Eighth Ave; 71st St at
Amsterdam Ave (weekends only); and Broadway bet 95th and 96th St
(weekends only)
Moondance Diner: Sixth Ave at Grand St (212/226-1191
Morning Star Restaurant: 401 West 57th St (212/246-1593)
Odessa: 119 Ave A (212/253-1470)
Restaurant Florent: 69 Gansevoort St (212/989-5779)
Sarge's: 548 Third Ave, bet 36th and 37th St (212/679-0440)
Silver Star: 1236 Second Ave, at 65th St (212/249-4250)
Skyline Coffee Shop: 1055 Lexington Ave, at 75th St (212/861-2540)
Tick-Tock Diner: Eighth Ave at 34th St (212/268-8444)
Tivoli: 515 Third Ave (212/532-3300)
Tramway Coffee House: 1143 Second Ave, at 60th St (212/758-7017)
Washington Square Coffee Shop: 150 West 4th St, at Sixth Ave (212/533-9306)
Woo Chon: 8-10 W 36th St (212/695-0676)

FOOD (TAKEOUT) In addition to many mom-and-pop operations along Broadway on the Upper West Side and Lexington and Third avenues on the East
Side, you can try:

Bagels On the Square: 7 Carmine St (212/691-3041)

Columbia Hot Bagels: 2836 Broadway, at 110th St (212/222-3200)
Crown Gourmet Deli: Broadway and 52nd St (212/956-8410)
Delmonico Gourmet Food Market: 55 East 59th St, bet Park and Madison Ave (212/751-5559)
Gray's Papaya: 2090 Broadway, at 72nd St (212/799-0243)
H&H Bagels: 2239 Broadway, at 80th St; and 639 West 46th St, at Twelth Ave (212/595-8000)
Jumbo Bagel and Bialys: 1070 Second Ave, bet 56th and 57th St (212/595-6185)

GAS STATIONS—Like everything else, the price of gas in Manhattan is outrageous. If you possibly can, fill the tank elsewhere. If you have no choice, try:

Amoco: Broadway at East Houston St
Citgo: Bowery at 3rd St
Getty: Eighth Ave between Horatio and 13th St, and Tenth Ave at 20th St
Gaseteria: West End Ave at 59th St
Mobil: Eleventh Ave at 51st St, and Eleventh Ave at 57th St

GROCERY STORES—Although Manhattan does have chain supermarkets that vaguely resemble the kind found in the suburbs, the shortage of space in the city and exorbitant rents mean that Manhattan is full of mom-and-pop grocery stores. Sometimes you'll find as many as three on one block—and chances are at least one will be open all night or close to it.

The chain supermarkets in Manhattan include **Food Emporium, Sloan's,** and **D'Agostino** (or **Dags,** as New Yorkers call it). Most are open seven days a week, from early in the morning until at least 11 p.m. Some are open 24 hours. Many people in New York feel strongly that one chain is far superior to the others, but I've found that the quality of each depends more on the individual stores and their management than on the chain.

GYMS—If you need to work out in the middle of the night, try **World Gym** at Broadway and 64th Street (212/874-0942). Crunch Fitness on Lafayette Street between East 4th Street and Astor Place (212/614-0120), or the decidedly downscale and relatively cheap **Johnny Lat's Gym** at East 17th Street just off Fifth Avenue (212/366-4426).

HAIR SALONS—If you need a late-night haircut, try **Heads and Tales Hair-cutting** (212/677-9125), at 22 St. Mark's Place, between Second and Third avenues anytime before midnight.

LOCKSMITHS—Three things can be said of most locksmiths in Manhattan: they stay open all night, they put a lot of "A"s before their name so they'll be near the top of the list in the Manhattan Yellow Pages, and they probably won't give you a good deal. If you're really desperate, try **Manhattan Locksmiths** (212/877-7787), **AAA Locksmiths** (212/840-3939), or **Night and Day Lock-smith** (212/840-3939) for reputable service. Make sure you get an estimate!

NEWSSTANDS—Although there are some newspaper boxes in Manhattan, most people who don't get home delivery buy their newspapers and magazines at newsstands, which are all over the city. In addition to local newspapers, these newsstands sell a wide range of magazines and cigarettes. (Try not to be put off by the fact that many of them display pornographic magazines right alongside *The New Yorker* and *Newsweek.* It's hard to miss them.) These days, even New York's newstands are being "gentrified," but they're usually on corners. The vast majority are open seven days a week and late into the evening, but you can find some open all night on:

- Second Ave and St. Mark's Place
- Sixth Ave and 8th St
- Broadway at 42nd St (the first dropoff spot for the *New York Times*)
- Eighth Ave at 42nd St (Port Authority Bus Terminal)
- Broadway and 50th St
- First Ave and 63rd St
- Broadway and 72nd St
- Columbus Ave and 81st St
- Broadway and 116th St

NOTARY PUBLICS—If you need to have something notarized in the middle of the night, call **West Side Stationers** (212/662-3151), at 2620 Broadway, in advance to arrange an after-hours house call.

PLUMBERS—Read what I said about locksmiths: the same holds true here. But you can try **Kapnag Heating and Plumbing** (212/289-8847) for honest, reliable service. All plumbers must be licensed by the city's Department of Buildings. Make sure anybody who shows up to fix your sink has a license, and call 212/312-8217 if you have problems. (Unfortunately, you can't call that number in the middle of the night.) Make sure to get a written estimate before any work is done.

PHARMACIES—Manhattan now has two pharmacies that can fill prescriptions 24 hours a day, seven days a week: **Kaufman Pharmacy** (212/755-2266), off the lobby of the Beverly Hotel at Lexington Avenue and 50th Street, and **Duane Reade** (212/541-9708), at the corner of Broadway and 57th Street. Several other Duane Reade stores are open 24 hours day, including those at 2465 Broadway (212/799-3172) and 378 Sixth Avenue (212/674-5357).

PHOTOCOPYING AND COMPUTER RENTALS—Part of a national chain, **Kinko's** stays open all night and offers photocopying services, Macintosh computer rentals (you use them there), and basic office supplies. Manhattan locations include: 2872 Broadway, between 112th and 113th streets (212/316-3390); 16 East 52nd streets, off Fifth Avenue (212/308-2679); 191 Madison Avenue, between 34th and 35th streets (212/685-3449); and 24 East 12th Street, between Fifth Avenue and University Place (212/924-0802).

PHOTO DEVELOPING—Try **K&L Custom PhotoGraphics** (212/661-5600), at 222 East 44th Street, between Second and Third avenues, or **Duggal** (212/242-7000), at 3 West 20th Street, off Fifth Avenue.

POST OFFICE—Although money orders cannot be purchased between 6 p.m. on Sunday evening and Monday morning, you'll find windows open all night long, seven days a week, at the main post office on Eighth Avenue between 31st and 33rd streets.

RECORD, TAPE, AND CD STORES—The **Virgin Records Superstore** at 1540 Broadway between 45th and 46th streets (212/921-1020) is open from 9 a.m. until 1 a.m. Sunday through Thursday, and until 2 a.m. Friday and Saturday. **Tower Records** stores at Broadway and 4th Street (212/505-1500) and Broadway and 66th Street (212/799-2500) are open daily until midnight.

VETERINARIAN – Emergency services for pets are available at the **Animal Medical Center** (212/838-8100), at 510 East 62nd Street.

VIDEO STORES – More hotels are putting VCRs in their rooms. If you have one, check with the front desk to see if the hotel has a video library. Otherwise, you can become a member at a local video store with a credit card. **Blockbuster Video,** a huge national chain open nightly until midnight, has become a dominant force even in Manhattan. Look for it on the corners of Lexington and 85th Street (212/439-0960), Amsterdam Avenue and 69th Street (212/787-0300), Third Avenue and 24th Street (212/686-0022), Eighth Avenue and 17th Street (212/924-4771), or check the phone book for the location nearest you. **Tower Video,** at Lafayette and East 4th streets, (212/505-1166) is open until midnight also.

Manhattan for Children

When I first began writing this book, I did so from the perspective of a businessman who comes to New York without children. I quickly learned, however, that many people bring kids to New York, whether they're coming for business or pleasure. New York can be a little overwhelming at first for kids (the same is true for adults!), but it can also be a wonderland if you know where to go.

The "Kids" pages in the back of *New York* magazine and *Time Out New York,* and the "For Children" column in the Friday *New York Times* Weekend section are great places to look for upcoming events and activities for children in and around New York City. Another good source of information is the seasonal schedule of cultural events for children put out by the Alliance for the Arts (212/947-6340). Pick up a copy of their schedule at the New York Convention and Visitors' Bureau (2 Columbus Circle, near the southwest corner of Central Park). Finally, call the Arts and Festivals Hotline (212/765-2787) and listen to its children's selection.

I've listed the best places for kids in several categories: birthday parties; entertainment; museums and sights; play spaces, art centers and classes; restaurants; and toy and bookstores. (If you are a New Yorker with children or bring children here often, I urge you to look under "Parenting Resources" in Chapter IV as well.) *When a specific place is described in another part of the book, in many cases I've simply included the address and phone number and marked the entry with an asterisk (*).* When the place isn't described elsewhere, however, I've provided a little more information. Of course, different children are interested in different things, so I've included places that one child might love and another might find boring. I'll let you be the judge of that!

Birthday Parties

Chelsea Piers – Whether you want in-line skating, rock-climbing, or gymnastics at your next birthday party, the amazing Chelsea Piers facility at the far west end of 23rd Street can probably accommodate you. Call 212/336-6666 for more information.

Central Park Wildlife Conservation Center – Throw a party for children between 4 and 12 amid the animals in Central Park, off Fifth Avenue at 64th Street. Call 212/439-6538 for more information.

Children's Museum of the Arts – This child-centered art exploration and play space is available for children's birthday parties. It's located in Soho at 72 Spring Street, between Crosby and Lafayette streets. Call 212/274-0986 for more information.

*Linda Kaye's Birthdaybakers and Partymakers – A mom turned birthday-party genius, Linda Kaye has been putting on unique parties for children since I first began writing this book. Call 212/288-7112 for more information.

New York Transit Museum – For surprisingly reasonable prices, you can have a party for as many as 50 children in what can only be described as a train-lover's heaven. Activities include train videos for preschoolers, workshops for older kids, and ice cream for everyone from Peter's Ice Cream Parlor. Call 718/243-3060 for more information.

Party Poopers – These folks had a private party space for kids long before such things became trendy. They do theme parties at their place or yours. Call 212/587-9030 for more information.

*Serendipity 3 – You can have your child's birthday party for up to 70 guests in this perennially popular and decidedly upscale East Side ice cream parlor. Rates are high but the food is great. Call 212/838-3531 for more information

Screening Room – The birthday boy or girl can sit in an Alice in Wonderland-inspired throne at the head of a banquet table while watching a favorite movie or television show in this popular restaurant-cum-movie theater's new party room. Rates are surprisingly affordable and catering is available. Call 212/334-2100 for more information.

Tortoise and the Hare – If your little girl likes to have her hair done and her nails painted, this East Side Salon for children puts on "glamour parties" for girls aged five and up. The price tag is a bit much, but partygoers get to be in a fashion show and are given a bag of hair accessories. Call 212/472-3399 for more information.

Warner Brothers Studio Store – Birthday parties for children on the ninth floor of this in-your-face Warner Brothers wonderland include a film, party favors and a cake. There's nothing cheap about them, but they do seem to be a great hit with kids. The space is also available for private functions and parties for grownups. Call 212/754-0300 for more information.

Entertainment

*ARTime – Run by two art historians, this organization offers tours of Soho and Chelsea art galleries geared for elementary schoolchildren and their families.

*Bryant Park – Assuming warm weather, kids (and adults) can rent such games as Scrabble and checkers for $4 an hour and sailboats to sail in the fountain for $2 an hour.

*Central Park – Particularly during the spring and summer months, Central Park is full of events and activities for children. In addition to the marvelous Wildlife Conservation Center, there are activities for children on Saturday and Sunday afternoons at Belvedere Castle (212/772-0210), inside the park near West 79th Street; a puppet theater on weekday mornings near the 62nd Street playground inside the park (call the Dairy at 212/794-6564 to make reservations); a marionette theater near West 81st Street (212/988-9093); and story readings at the Hans Christian Anderson Statue, at the Conservatory Water near East 74th Street, on Saturday at 11 a.m. Make sure to call ahead, as some of the events require reservations and/or a small fee, and the hours and locations may vary. You might also stop by the Charles A. Dana Discovery Center (212/860-1370), in the northeast corner of the park near Fifth Avenue and 110th

Street, to borrow fishing poles or attend a family workshop. Every day from 10 to 7 (except Saturday) in warmer months, you can rent a small sailboat to sail in the Conservatory Water Pond (north of the park's 72nd Street entrance, off Fifth Avenue). If you're looking for an unusual way to see the park, try a two-hour bicycle tour ($25 for adults and $20 for kids, bicycle included). Call Bite of the Apple Tours at 212/541-8759 for more information. You can find out what is happening on any given day in Central Park and other parks throughout Manhattan by calling 212/360-3456.

*Circle Line Sightseeing Yachts–Pier 83, at Twelfth Avenue and 43rd Street (212/563-3200). For more information, see the "Tours" section in Chapter III.

Donnell Library Center–Another branch of the New York Public Library, this one houses a special room for children with more than 100,000 books, magazines, and recordings. It's also home to the Nathan Straus Young Adult Center. The Donnell Library is located at 20 West 53rd Street, between Fifth and Sixth avenues. Call 212/621-0636 for information about the children's room and 212/621-0633 for information about the Young Adult Center.

IMAX Theater–Inside the American Museum of Natural History on Central Park West between 77th and 81st streets, this theater shows films on such topics as African animals and tornados. The screen is enormous, and the films are consistently well conceived. Call 212/769-5034 for more information.

Kaye Playhouse–As in Danny Kaye. Home of the perennially popular (with young children) Paper Bag Players. this theater always has something fun going on. It's located on East 68th Street between Park and Lexington avenues. Call 212/772-4448 for ticket and show information.

Movies–The Museum of Modern Art (212/708-9805) has a weekly family film series, the Walter Reade Theater (212/875-5610) sometimes has movies and other programs for children, and the Donnell Library Center (621-0618) actually shows kids movies for free! (For specific movies intended for tourists, see other listings below.)

New Amsterdam Theater–Part of the revitalization of 42nd Street, this renovated theater is part of the Disney operation. Once home to the Ziegfeld Follies, it's located on 42nd Street west of Seventh Avenue. Call (212/282-2900) for more information.

New Victory Theater–This theater at 209 West 42nd Street (between Seventh and Eighth avenues) is entirely devoted to productions for children and families. Call 212/564-4222 to find out what's playing and when.

Show Me New York–Although it may be a bit much for younger children (and is not recommended for children under five), this wild introduction to New York is a 22-minute ride above and through New York via two high-definition screens. The price seems outrageous ($11.50 for adults, $9 for children up to 12), but the film is both amazing and educational. Actors in the lobby share tidbits of New York trivia and history. You can't miss the theater on East 58th Street, east of Madison Avenue. Call 212/888-5200 for more information.

Sony IMAX Theater–This eight-story, 3-D movie screen is located on the top floor of Sony's wildly popular theater at Broadway and 67th Street, north of Lincoln Center. Among its offerings is *Across the Sea of Time,* a sentimental but surprisingly educational movie about the experience of generations of

New York immigrants. Kids and adults alike will enjoy it. Call 212/336-5000 for more information.

Story Hours – Several children's bookstores – including Books of Wonder (on Sunday at 11:45 a.m.), Barnes & Noble, Jr. (Tuesday at 10:30 a.m. and Thursday at 5:30 p.m.), the children's section of the Upper West Side Barnes & Noble (Tuesday at 10:30 a.m.), and Tootsie's (Saturday at 10 a.m.) – have story hours for young children. There's also a daily story hour at 3 p.m. at the Wildlife Conservation Center in Central Park. Check the times and age requirements before setting out.

Theaterworks/USA – This is the nation's largest theater company dedicated to children and family audiences. Look for its productions at the Promenade Theater (2162 Broadway, near 76th Street). Call 212/677-5959 for current schedule and ticket information.

Museums and Sights

*Abigail Adams Smith Museum – 421 East 61st St, between First and York Ave (212/838-6878).

*American Museum of Natural History – Central Park West between 77th and 81st St (212/769-5100). The hands-on Discovery Room is open on weekend afternoons, and tickets are handed out on a first-come, first-serve basis in late morning.

*Central Park Wildlife Conservation Center – Central Park behind the Arsenal, off Fifth Ave at 64th St (212/861-6030).

*Children's Museum of Manhattan – 212 West 83rd St, between Broadway and Amsterdam Ave (212/721-1234).

*ConEd Energy Museum – 145 East 14th Street, between Irving Place and Third Ave (212/460-6244).

*Ellis Island – In New York Harbor, off Battery Park (212/363-7620).

*Empire State Building Observation Deck – Fifth Ave between 33rd and 34th St (212/736-3100).

*Fraunces Tavern Museum – 54 Pearl St, at Broad St (212/425-1778).

*Intrepid Sea-Air-Space Museum – Pier 86, at Twelfth Ave and 46th St (212/245-0072).

*Metropolitan Museum of Art – Fifth Ave between 80th and 84th St (212/535-7710). Although not everything here is for children, and *strollers are not admitted on Sunday,* the Egyptian mummy exhibit and the gallery full of arms and armor will be big hits. Call the Education Department (212/570-3756) for information about films and other special events for children.

 *Museum of the City of New York – 1220 Fifth Ave, between 103rd and 104th St (212/534-1672).

*Museum of Television and Radio – 25 West 52nd St, between Fifth and Sixth Ave (212/621-6600).

*National Museum of the American Indian – 1 Bowling Green, at the foot of Broadway (212/668-6624).

*New York City Fire Museum—278 Spring St, between Hudson and Varick St (212/691-1303).

*New York Transit Museum—Boerum Place at Schermerhorn St in Brooklyn (718/243-3060).

*Police Academy Museum—235 E 20th St (212/477-9753).

*Roosevelt Island Tram—The tram leaves from a station on Second Ave, between 59th and 60th St.

Skyride—An overpriced tourist attraction inside the Empire State Building. Thanks to a lot of bells, whistles, and computer technology, you "fly" through the entire city in less than an hour. It's open daily between 10 a.m. and 10 p.m. Tickets are sold in the basement of the Empire State Building, along with tickets to the building's observation deck. Call 212/564-2224 for more information.

*Sony Wonder Technology Lab—Madison Ave at 56th St (212/833-8100).

*South Street Seaport—Located at the eastern end of Fulton St (212/669-9400), Seaport produces a seasonal schedule of activities for children and families, and has a special center for children.

*Statue of Liberty—On Liberty Island in New York Harbor, just off Battery Park.

*United Nations—The visitors' entrance is on First Ave, between 45th and 46th St (212/963-7713). *Be forewarned that strollers are not allowed on the grounds and children under five cannot go on the tour.*

World Trade Center Observation Deck—Top of 1 World Trade Center (212/435-7377).

Play Spaces, Art Centers, and Classes

Arts Connection—This wonderful place at 120 W 46th St devotes Saturday mornings to creative and thoughtful art workshops for children and Saturday afternoons to storytelling. Reservations are required and parents must stay with their children, but prices are reasonable and the quality is extremely high. Call 212/302-7433 for more information.

Children's Museum of the Arts—This friendly Soho spot is a big favorite with children who like to create and explore with their hands. Designed for children between 18 months and 10 years, this child-centered museum (there is a small gallery) has various work spaces where children can explore different media. Workshops for children of different ages are held throughout the day and sometimes cost an additional dollar. Singalongs are usually held at noon and 4. The museum is open Tuesday through Friday from 11 a.m. until 5 p.m. and weekends from noon until 6 p.m. It's located at 72 Spring St, between Crosby and Lafayette St. Admission is $4 per person on weekdays and $5 per person on weekends. Call 212/274-0986 for more information.

*Children's Museum of Manhattan—The museum, at 212 West 83rd St, between Broadway and Amsterdam Ave, has a well-designed play space for preschoolers in its basement.

Craft Studio—A fun place for kids who like crafts to create, this relative newcomer is at 1657 Third Ave, between 92nd and 93rd St (212/831-6626).

Field House at Chelsea Piers—You name it and Chelsea Piers teaches it to kids. Classes for children six months and up are offered. The field house is near the entrance of the Chelsea Piers complex, at the far west end of 23rd St. Call 212/336-6500 for more information.

Little Hands Playcafe—Once a part of the city I steered tourists and New Yorkers alike away from, the East Village has been cleaned up in recent years and is now home to one of the city's most innovative and fun play spaces for toddlers and preschoolers. It doubles as a restaurant that actually welcomes kids (and feeds them healthy, delicious fare) and a wonderful set of spaces for the kind of play that nurtures youthful creativity and enthusiasm. If you're feeling claustrophobic in your apartment or hotel room, make a trip 433 E Sixth St. Call 212/388-0957 for more information.

Little Shop of Plaster—These stores allow children to paint, glitter, and varnish pre-made plaster shapes. They're located at 431 E 73rd St (212/717-6636) and 106 W 90th St (212/877-9771).

My Favorite Place—A big hit with little ones, this relative newcomer to the Upper West Side's "Play space" scene combines a low-key toy store with a safe play room for toddlers and studio space for toddler and preschool art, movement, and music classes. It's in an old Red Apple supermarket at 265 W 87th St, west of Broadway. Call 212/362-5320 for more information.

92nd Street YMHA—This amazing institution offers classes for infants and children beginning at two months through its Parenting Center. Prices are a bit high, but the quality and new-mom networking opportunities are great. The Y is on 92nd St at Lexington Ave. Call 212/415-5611 for more information.

Outdoor playgrounds—Manhattan has lots of safe, relatively clean, and imaginative public playgrounds. Look in Central Park along Central Park West and Fifth Ave or call the Manhattan Department of Parks and Recreation at 212/360-8111 to find out the location of a playground near you.

PlaySpaces—Part of a new trend in New York and elsewhere, this is a safe, indoor free-play areas for children between six months and six years old located at 2473 Broadway, at 92nd St (212/769-2300).

Pull Cart—At this drop-in art studio, children can paint on ceramic bisqueware and then have their pieces fired in a kiln. It's located at 31 W 21st St, between Fifth and Sixth Ave. Call 212/727-7089 for more information.

WonderCamp—Designed for children between one and ten, this 20,000-square-foot facility is designed to be a summer camp of sorts. It's located at 27 W 23rd St, between Fifth and Sixth Ave. Call 212/243-1111 for more information.

Restaurants

All Star Cafe—For sports fans in the family, this restaurant in Times Square (212/840-8326) is one of the many "theme" restaurants now taking over New York. People like Andre Agassi. Shaquille O'Neal. and Joe Montana all have a stake in it, and sports stars do indeed show up periodically. A myriad of screens showing every sport imaginable make conversation difficult, but that's hardly the point of a visit here.

*America—A big restaurant at 9 E 18th St with large portions and lots of French fries. Call 212/505-2110 for more information.

*American Festival Cafe—Pretty upscale for small kids, but it's next to the ice-skating rink at Rockefeller Plaza (off 50th St, west of Fifth Ave) and the views can't be beat. The food is pretty good, too. Call 212/246-6699 for more information.

*Brooklyn Diner—Another one of many new theme restaurants in midtown (212 W 57th St, to be exact), this one has lots of the kinds of basic foods that will make parents nostalgic. Call 212/977-1957 for more information.

*Carnegie Delicatessen and Restaurant—Huge portions, rude waiters, and bench seats at 854 Seventh Ave (between 54th and 55th St). It can be a bit touristy, but it's a real New York institution. Call 212/757-2245 for more information.

*Cowgirl Hall of Fame—Small children can be entertained for hours looking at the walls of this low-key spot at 519 Hudson St (at 10th St) in the West Village. Call 212/633-1133 for more information.

*EJ's Luncheonette—A friendly neighborhood place on Amsterdam Ave and 81st St with basic food at good prices. Call 212/873-3444 for more information.

Food Fair Foodcourts—There's nothing particularly special about the food courts at Manhattan Mall (at Herald Square) and South Street Seaport's Pier 17, but kids love them anyway.

Gray's Papaya—Cheap and delicious hot dogs and other such foods are served at this downscale, hurried spot at the corner of Broadway and 72nd St. Call 212/799-0243 for more information.

*Hard Rock Cafe—This place isn't exactly my speed, but kids and teenagers eat it up. This popular location is part of a wildly successful international chain. Look for the line to get into this one at 221 W 57th St. Call 212/459-9320 for more information.

*Jackson Hole Burgers—You'll get great, juicy hamburgers and lots of thick fries and onion rings at this restaurant with several locations, including 232 E 64th St (212/371-7187).

Jekyll and Hyde—There's usually a long line, but that's because kids love to dine in this not-too-scary haunted house, complete with talking heads, at 1409 Ave of the Americas. Call 212/541-9505 for more information.

*John's Pizzeria—Many New Yorkers swear this is the best pizza around. The original John's is at 278 Bleecker St (at Jones St) in the West Village, but locations are popping up all over the city. Call 212/243-1680 for information on the Bleecker Street location, or look in the phone book for the one nearest you.

McDonald's—Kids love McDonald's, and this one certainly lives up to all generic expectations. But it also has a store inside selling Ronald McDonald dolls and things with the McDonald's logo. They also offer table service on the second floor in the back. The store is open seven days a week from 11 a.m. to 7 p.m. Look for the familiar golden arches at 160 Broadway, between Cortlandt and Liberty St.

Motown Cafe—Yes, another theme restaurant. And yes, it's wildly popular. Look for the lines at 104 W 57th St or call 212/581-8030 for more information.

*Peppermint Park Cafe—This favorite spot for sweet tooths is at 1225 First Ave (between 66th and 67th St). Call 212/288-5054 for more information.

*Planet Hollywood—This is the grandfather of all theme restaurants. Stars come out nightly, as do tourists. Look for the long lines at 140 W 57th St (212/333-7827).

*Serendipity 3—The East Side's favorite ice cream parlor is Serendipity 3, at 225 E 60th St. It is the home of Frozen Hot Chocolate and other wondrous deserts, as well as good but overpriced meals. Call 212/838-3531 for more information.

*Tavern on the Green—The chef at this beautiful spot in Central Park (off Central Park West at 67th St) has five children of his own and has put together a terrific children's menu. Reservations are usually necessary. Call 212/873-3200 for more information.

Two Boots—A favorite pizza place that loves kids (and vice versa). The original location is at 37 Ave A (212/505-2276), but locations are popping up all over the city.

Toy Stores and Bookstores

*Bank Street Bookstore—Not much fun to cuddle up in, but a tremendous source for children's books, as well as resources for parents and teachers. Up near Columbia University at 2875 Broadway, at 112th St (212/678-1654).

*Barnes & Noble, Jr.—86th St and Lexington Ave (212/427-0686) and locations in Barnes & Noble stores throughout the city.

*Books of Wonder—A legend among children's bookstores, known especially for its *Wizard of Oz* collection. 16 W 18th St (212/989-3270).

*Classic Toys—For people who believe that good toys don't need to change every ten minutes (or even every generation). 218 Sullivan St (212/674-4434).

*Disney Store—The one on the corner of 42nd St and Seventh Ave is the best (212/221-0430).

*FAO Schwarz—The grandfather of all toy stores at Fifth Ave at 58th St. Crowded and overpriced, it's nonetheless a fantasyland.

*Geppetto's Toy Box—A special place run by people who really care about toys and children, young and old. 161 Seventh Ave S (212/620-7511).

*Tootsie's—A warm and inviting store owned by three mothers. 554 Hudson St, in the West Village (212/242-0182).

*Warner Brothers Studio Store—A store, tourist attraction, and theme park rolled into one. On the corner of Fifth Ave and 57th St (212/754-0300).

Just as there are some things that are all the more fun done with kids, there are others that you *shouldn't* do with them. Museums like the Frick Collection, the Grolier Club's gallery, and the Pierpont Morgan Library, for example, are not places to bring small children. Indeed, children under ten are not allowed in the Frick, children under six can't go on the NBC Studio Tour, children under five are not welcome on the tour of the United Nations, and children under two are not permitted in the Hayden Planetarium. If you're going shopping at a perpetually crowded place like Zabar's or Fairway, don't take the kids along or make sure you keep a firm grip on their hands if you do. The latter holds true just about everywhere in New York—it's very easy to get lost in a crowd! And remember that kids tire more quickly than adults. Chances are you'll be doing a lot of walking, and they're taking two or three steps for every one you take! (As the *New York Times* recently put it, "Baby miles are like dog years"!) Finally, a word of warning: it's a real challenge to tote along an infant or toddler in New York. While hundreds of thousands of children are born and raised in the city, visitors who are accustomed to carting their children through malls in strollers and around town in car seats may have trouble here. Many places, including the subway system, are not exactly stroller-accessible. A few, including the United Nations and the Metropolitan Museum of Art on (Sundays), ban them altogether. Taxis with functioning seatbelts are few and far between, while ones with car seats simply don't exist. Very few public restrooms have changing tables, and I've yet to hear of a store that has followed the Nordstrom chain's example and set aside space for nursing mothers. The Mama Bear Room at F.A.O. Schwarz and the ladies' lounges at Bloomingdale's and other large department stores are about as close as New York comes to offering such thoughtful accommodations to motherhood.

Manhattan for Free

There's no way to get around it: New York is expensive. Even the most frugal and resourceful visitors often feel like they're bleeding money ("Didn't we just get $100 out of the cash machine yesterday!?") after a couple of days here. Still, you can find some good deals and do a lot of sightseeing for free. Look in *Time Out New York's* tremendous weekly listings of events throughout the city for boxes denoting ones that are free. You can also try some of the following:

Book Talks – If you're a reader, don't forget you're in the publishing capital of the world. Look for free lectures and discussions with all sorts of authors at bookstores and libraries including Barnes & Noble (121/727-4810), Borders (212/839-8049), the New York Public Library (212/254-9628), Posman Books (212/533-BOOK), and Shakespeare & Company (212/570-0201).

Concerts and Other Performances – On Monday nights in summer, Bryant Park hosts (and HBO sponsors) free movies. Also in the summer, Central Park comes alive with free concerts by the New York Philharmonic (212/875-5700), operas by the Metropolitan Opera (212/362-6000), Shakespeare in the Park (212/598-7100), and all sorts of performances on the SummerStage (212/360-2777). Call 212/360-3456 for recorded information about events in Central Park and other parks throughout the city. You'll also find the Midsummer Night Swing concerts at Lincoln Center Plaza (212/875-5400), concerts on Thursday and Friday evenings at South Street Seaport (212/669-9400), and chamber music in Washington Square Park, at the foot of Fifth Avenue in Greenwich Village, every Tuesday night. Thanks to a pay-what-you-wish admission policy at the Museum of Modern Art on Friday night, you can enjoy an evening of live jazz in the museum's Sculpture Garden and cafe throughout the year without paying a dime. For information about concerts and other performances at the Winter Garden in the World Financial Center, call 212/945-0505.

If you're interested in discount tickets for concerts, the theater, and other performances, make sure to look in the "Tickets" section of Chapter III.

Museums and Sights – In alphabetical order, the free museums and sights in Manhattan include the American Bible Society's gallery, the American Numismatic Society, the Americas Society gallery, the Cathedral Church of St. John the Divine, the Commodities Exchange, the ConEd Energy Museum, Dyckman Farmhouse, the Equitable Center Gallery, Federal Hall National

Monument, the Forbes Magazine Galleries, the Ford Foundation Gardens, Grant's Tomb, the Grolier Club's gallery, the Hispanic Society of America, the Municipal Art Society's Urban Center Gallery, the Museum of American Folk Art, the Museum of American Illustration, the National Museum of the American Indian, the New York Public Library, the New York Public Library for the Performing Arts, the New York Stock Exchange, New York Unearthed, the Nicholas Roerich Museum, the PaineWebber Gallery, the Police Academy Museum, the Rose Museum at Carnegie Hall, the Schomburg Center for Research in Black Culture, the Sony Wonder Technology Lab, Trinity Church's small museum, and the Whitney Gallery and Sculpture Garden at Philip Morris. Some of these places accept donations, but none pressures visitors for them.

Several other museums are technically free but make a point of telling you that they expect a "suggested contribution." These museums include the Alternative Museum, the American Museum of Natural History, the China House Gallery, and the Museum of the City of New York.

It used to be that the museums along Museum Mile offered free admission to everyone one night a week. Unfortunately, that tradition lives on only one night a year in late June. Some museums in the city do offer pay-as-you-wish admission on different evenings throughout the year, however. They include the Cooper-Hewitt (Tuesday between 5 p.m. and 9 p.m.), both branches of the International Center of Photography (Tuesday between 6 p.m. and 8 p.m.), the Jewish Museum (Tuesday between 5 p.m. and 8 p.m.), the Museum of Modern Art (Thursday and Friday between 5:30 p.m. and 8:30 p.m.), the National Academy of Design (Friday between 5 p.m. and 8 p.m.), the New Museum of Contemporary Art (Saturday between 6 p.m. and 8 p.m.), and the Whitney (Thursday between 6 p.m. and 8 p.m.).

Finally, children under 12 are admitted to a lot of places for free. Smithsonian Associates are admitted without charge to the Cooper-Hewitt, and art students with identification are admitted free to the National Academy of Design on Wednesday. Although it isn't free, you can go to both the Cloisters and the Metropolitan Museum of Art on the same day and pay only one admission price. You can also buy a seven-day pass to both branches of the Guggenheim for $15 (as opposed to $17 for one-day admission if you pay separately at both places). For more information about these museums, see the "Museums" section of Chapter III.

Tours – The very best bargain in this category is the personalized tour offered free of charge by the city through its Big Apple Greeters program. A close runner-up is the marvelous free tour of Grand Central Station offered every Wednesday at 12:30 p.m. by the Municipal Art Society. Other free tours include ones of the neighborhood around Grand Central Station, the Federal Reserve Bank, the New York Public Library, the New York Public Library for the Performing Arts, the New York City Police Department's headquarters and its academy, the Schomburg Center for Research in Black Culture, Times Square, the area on and around 34th Street, the Lower East Side, and Trinity Church. The Urban Park Rangers also conduct a variety of free tours in the city's parks. For more detailed information about tours, see the "Tours" section of Chapter III.

Views – The best bargain on a view of the New York skyline is a trip on the Staten Island Ferry (718/390-5253). The trip is free to walk-on passengers and the ferry leaves nearly continuously from the end of Whitehall Street in Battery Park. Another bargain view of the city is from the west side of Roosevelt Island. A trip on the tram (Second Ave between 59th and 60th St) costs $1.50 each way. For $2, you can climb the 22-story bell tower at Riverside Church (212/222-5900) and gaze down on the Hudson and the city to your south. And for nothing at all, you can walk the 1.2 miles of the Battery Park Esplanade.

Walking—It doesn't cost a dime to just walk around. Some of the more pleasant walking areas include Fifth Avenue in midtown, Soho (on Saturday afternoon and early evening), South Street Seaport and Central Park (particularly on weekends), Fifth and Madison avenues on the Upper East Side, the Lower East Side (on Sunday), the Lincoln Center area, and Greenwich Village (particularly on weekends). Take a look at the "Flea Markets" section of Chapter III—most of them cost nothing to browse and can be lots of fun!

Who says there's no free lunch? You can spend hours listening to music and playing with CD-ROMs at the Virgin Music superstore in Times Square, read a book in a comfortable chair at Barnes & Noble on Broadway at 82nd Street (or just about any bookstore in town these days), park for up to four hours in lots maintained by the Lower East Side Business Improvement District at the foot of the Williamsburg Bridge, or ride around lower Manhattan on one of the Alliance for Downtown New York's buses without paying a cent. You can also take free classes about how to use the Internet at the New York Public Library's new Science, Industry and Business Library. For $25, you can join one of the city's recreation centers (there are 29 of them) for a year. For $3, you can see a first-run movie at the Cineplex Odeon's Worldwide Cinema (50th St between Eighth and Ninth Ave). For $2, you can swim in the clean, beautiful pool at Riverbank State Park (Riverside Drive at 145th St). And for the price of a token, you can get to LaGuardia Airport (on the M60 bus) or Kennedy Airport (on the A train).

Manhattan for Lovers

Whether you're falling in love for the first time or celebrating your golden anniversary, New York can be one of the most romantic places in the world. If you're in the mood or want to create one that's just right, try the following:

- A getaway weekend swaddled in the first-class luxury of the Four Seasons Hotel, at 57 East 57th St.
- Warming up by your own fireplace in one of the suites at the Lowell, a small hotel at 28 East 63rd St.
- A night at the always-elegant Plaza Hotel, overlooking Central Park from its southeast corner.
- An intimate dinner at the small and sophisticated Sonia Rose, at 132 Lexington Ave (between 28th and 29th St).
- Dinner and dancing in the Rainbow Room, on the 65th floor of 30 Rockefeller Center, or at the more intimate Rainbow & Stars down the hall.
- Dinner amid the flowers in the French elegance of La Grenouille, at 3 East 52nd St.
- Drinks by the fireplace followed by dinner at the hard-to-find One If By Land, Two If By Sea, at 17 Barrow St (between Seventh Ave and 4th St).
- A summertime dinner in the garden at Barbetta, 321 West 46th St (between Eighth and Ninth Ave).
- Dinner in at the discreet and classy March, at 405 East 58th St (between First Ave and Sutton Pl).
- Dinner in Tavern on the Green's sparkling Crystal Room, in Central Park just off W 67th St.

- Dinner at a window table in Columbia University's excellent Terrace restaurant, at 400 W 119th St.
- A late-night visit to the Empire State Building Observation Deck, on Fifth Ave between 33rd and 34th St.
- A picnic lunch looking out over the Hudson River from the Cloisters.
- Listening to jazz great Bobby Short in the Carlyle Hotel's intimate Cafe Carlyle.
- A stroll through the splendid lobby of the Waldorf-Astoria.
- A weekend evening spent listening to classical music in the Metropolitan Museum of Art's Great Hall balcony.
- A wintertime visit to the warm, lush greenery of the Ford Foundation's Gardens, at 320 E 43rd St (between First and Second Ave).
- A Friday evening of jazz in summer at the Museum of Modern Art's sculpture garden.
- A nighttime sail around Manhattan.
- A stroll through Central Park in the springtime on some of its less traveled paths.
- A picnic dinner gazing at the Manhattan skyline from Lighthouse Park on Roosevelt Island.
- Cozying up in a love seat to watch a movie at the Screening Room, 54 Varick St (between Canal and Laight St).
- A rowboat or gondola ride on Central Park Lake, followed by drinks at the Boathouse Cafe.
- An evening carriage ride through Central Park in the winter, just after a fresh snow has fallen.
- A visit to the "Kissing Gallery" in Grand Central Station, in what is now the basement of the Bank of America building on 43rd St (directly across Vanderbilt Ave from the station).

Manhattan on the Water

Although it's easy to forget, Manhattan is an island surrounded on all four sides by water. Boat trips around the island (or even part of it) not only help convey a better sense of how the city is laid out but can also be lots of fun. Look for a special "Boat and Yacht" section in the back of *New York* magazine if you're interested in chartering a private boat. Otherwise, I suggest one of the following:

Atlantic Kayak Tours—If you have a lot of courage and a bit of skill, this company offers kayaking tours of New York Harbor and even a paddle around the island of Manhattan. It's not my cup of tea, but the views must be stunning! The company also offers lessons for students at all skill levels. Call 914/246-2187 for more information.

Circle Line—One of the most pleasant ways to see the city (and to cool off on a hot summer afternoon), the standard Circle Line sightseeing cruise lasts three hours and circumnavigates the entire island. See the listing under "Tours" in Chapter III, or call 212/563-3200 for more information.

Seaport Liberty Cruises—A refurbished Circle Line ship (this outfit is part of the same company), sails several times a day (except January, February, and early March) from Pier 16 at South Street Seaport. You can buy drinks and refreshments on board, and the tour of New York Harbor takes roughly · an hour and a half. Tickets cost $12 for adults, $6 for children. A one-hour twilight cocktail cruise and an evening music cruise are also offered. For information about tickets and times, call 212/630-8888.

Spirit Cruises—If you're interested in a two-hour buffet lunch cruise or a three-hour buffet dinner cruise on the Hudson River in warmer months, those folks at the Chelsea Piers complex have numerous scheduled sailings. Prices are higher on weekends and for dinner. All have cash bars. Call 212/727-2789 for more information or reservations.

Staten Island Ferry—There are two great bargain ferries left in the world, and this is one of them. (The other is the Star Ferry in Hong Kong.) It runs 24 hours a day, seven days a week, all year round—and now, thanks to a decision in 1997 to get rid of the 50-cent fare for walk-on passengers, is totally free!) The loading terminals (in Battery Park at the foot of Whitehall Street in Manhattan and at the end of Bay Street on Staten Island) aren't very nice and can get smelly in the summer, but the views from the water during the 22-minute trip are spectacular. Call 718/390-5253 for more information.

World Yacht—This is the upscale cousin of the Circle Line sightseeing trips. (Again, they're owned by the same company.) You can have lunch, brunch, or dinner on board, and there is dancing at night. Some trips last longer than others, and prices vary accordingly. The World Yacht cruises leave every day except Christmas from Pier 81, at 41st Street and the Hudson River. Call 212/630-8100 for more information.

New York for New Yorkers

Although New Yorkers often think there can't be anything an outsider can tell them about their city, I've yet to meet one who has done all of the following things. Culled from years spent buying it, finding it, and eating it in New York, this list represents what I believe to be the very best, most interesting, and most important experiences this magnificent city has to offer:

◄ Riding the tram to Roosevelt Island and strolling along its west side.
• Climbing the seemingly endless set of stairs inside the bell tower at Riverside Church to reach one of the city's prettiest views.
• Going to Ellis Island and retracing the steps taken by many of our brave ancestors.
• Enjoying a quiet afternoon at the Cloisters.
• Gazing around the Rockefeller Rooms, on the fifth floor of the Museum of the City of New York, and perusing Mr. Morgan's Library at the Pierpont Morgan Library.
• Spending an evening listening to Bobby Short at Cafe Carlyle.
• Taking the vertical tour of the Cathedral Church of St. John the Divine.
• Walking the length of Central Park on a spring weekend.
• Exploring the ins and outs of Grand Central Station on the Municipal Art Society's free tour.
• Wandering through the Lower East Side Tenement Museum and the Eldridge Street Synagogue on a Sunday afternoon.
• High tea at the Stanhope Hotel.
• Lingering over a glass of wine on an afternoon in the early fall at the Roof Garden atop the Metropolitan Museum of Art.

New York Is Always in a Hurry!

If you've got just an hour to get to a meeting, to catch a plane, or to meet at a restaurant, here are some quick tips:

* To get clothing cleaned and pressed: One Hour Martinizing, 232 Ninth Ave, near 24th St (212/255-7317).
* To get fed and out in one hour, guaranteed: Hour Glass Tavern, 373 W 46th St (212/265-2060).
* To get photos developed: New York Film Works, 928 Broadway, at 21st St (212/475-5700).
* To get a button sewn on or a zipper fixed: Mr. Tony, Inc., 120 W 37th St (212/594-0930).
* To get shoes repaired: Jim's Shoe Repair, 50 East 59th St, bet Madison and Park Ave (212/355-8259)
* To get your New York State driver's license renewed: License X-Press, 300 W 34th St.

New York-ese

"The City," "the Island," "the Village," and "the Garden." I have a friend from Oregon who spent the first several weeks after she moved to Manhattan wondering what city, what island, what village, and what garden everyone was talking about! Anyone who has spent time here knows the answers: New York City, Long Island, Greenwich Village, and Madison Square Garden. But to the uninitiated, it often seems that New Yorkers are speaking in tongues. So that you aren't caught off-guard, here's a quick list of "New York-ese":

* **B&T Crowd:** Bridge and tunnel crowd, often used rather disparagingly by New Yorkers to describe people from New Jersey
* **Bloomie's:** Bloomingdale's
* **The City:** New York City, specifically Manhattan
* **Coffee regular:** coffee with milk but not sugar
* **The FDR:** Franklin D. Roosevelt Drive, an expressway running the length of Manhattan's East Side, next to the East River
* **The Garden:** Madison Square Garden
* **The Island:** Long Island
* **Houston:** a street in lower Manhattan (pronounced HOUSE-ton)
* **The Met:** Depending on the context, it can be either the Metropolitan Museum of Art or the Metropolitan Opera
* **MoMA:** the Museum of Modern Art
* **Noho:** the area immediately north of Soho
* **Slice:** a piece of pizza
* **Soda:** any carbonated beverage
* **Standing on Line:** nobody in New York seems to stand *in* line!
* **Upstate:** anywhere in New York north of the Bronx
* **The Village:** Greenwich Village (If you want to sound like a native, call it "the Village," "the East Village," or "the West Village," but definitely *not* Greenwich Village)
* **Zagat's:** a pocket-sized restaurant guide many New Yorkers rely on

Resources

If you're planning in advance, I suggest doing a couple things before packing your bags and heading for New York. First, call the New York State Division of Tourism (800/342-3810) and ask for a copy of the *Big Apple Visitors Guide* and whatever other free information they have about New York City. (For $4.95, they'll guarantee delivery in a week and a half and include discount coupons for a variety of museums and other sights.) Second, look through both the "Tours" and "Tickets" sections of Chapter III to see if any of the things you want to do require advance reservations. Finally, write to the New York City Transit Authority (Customer Services, 370 John Jay Street, Brooklyn, NY 11201) for maps and brochures about the public transportation system so you'll be ready to go from the moment you hit town. Make sure to ask for the wonderfully useful "Token Tips," a brochure that lists information about how to get to scores of the city's cultural institutions using public transportation.

Whether you're planning a trip in advance or are sitting in your hotel room trying to figure out what to do tomorrow, get copies of *The New Yorker*, *New York* magazine, *Time Out New York*, the *New York Times*, and the *Village Voice*. All but *Time Out New York* are generally available throughout the country (although the various national editions of the *New York Times* are smaller and less comprehensive than the metropolitan one). *The New Yorker* (in the front), *New York* magazine (in the back), and *Time Out New York* (throughout) have detailed information about current theater, movies, gallery and museum exhibitions, concerts, dance, and New York nightlife. The third section of the metropolitan edition of the *New York Times* always has a current calendar, as well as information on movies, new shows, the theater, and even television and radio highlights (except on Sunday, that is, when you should look in the Arts and Leisure section—*the* definitive guide for the week ahead). Friday's Weekend section is particularly useful. The *Village Voice* is published weekly on Wednesday and is a particularly good source for the younger set and for less conventional events and places. Be forewarned that the free magazines in hotel rooms are paid for by advertisers and are not particularly reliable (although the maps can be useful).

If you don't have everything planned when you arrive, you ought to stop at one of the city's several visitor information centers. The biggest and best is the New York Convention and Visitors' Bureau at Columbus Circle, but all of them have brochures, maps, subway and bus information, "twofer" coupons for discount theater tickets, and at least a bilingual if not a multilingual staff. Macy's and Bloomingdale's operate visitor information centers for their customers, but ones for the general public can be found at:

2 Columbus Circle: In the lobby of an unusually ugly building across from the southwest corner of Central Park, at 59th Street, this one is run by the New York Convention and Visitors' Bureau. In addition to a multilingual staff of "counselors" who can offer suggestions and answer questions about hotels, events, and just about everything else you might need to know, it has literally hundreds of brochures on museums, tours, stores, and sights throughout the city. It's open weekdays from 9 a.m. to 6 p.m. and weekends from 10 a.m. to 3 p.m. (assuming, that it hasn't moved as part of the city's planned sale of the building).

Lower East Side: This one is run by the Lower East Side Business Improvement District and stocks information about sightseeing, shopping, dining, and various events in the neighborhood and throughout the city. Located at 261 Broome St between Orchard and Allen St, it's open Sunday through Friday from 9 a.m. to 5 p.m.

Pennsylvania Station: Inside the main waiting area of Penn Station near the exit at Eighth Ave and 31st St, this small but well-supplied center has lots of a brochures on cultural events and institutions, as well as information on transportation. It's open weekdays from 8:30 a.m. to 5:30 p.m. and weekends from 9 a.m. to 6 p.m.

Times Square: At 229 West 42nd St, under the quite obvious marquee on the north side of the street, between Seventh and Eighth Ave, this one is also well-supplied and well-staffed. It's open every day from 9 a.m. to 6 p.m.

2 World Trade Center: At the top of the escalators on the mezzanine level, this makeshift center is rather small and has somewhat spotty hours. If you've come down here for a trip up to the World Trade Center Observation Deck or a visit to the TKTS outlet, however, definitely stop by to see what they have.

The front section of the Manhattan Yellow Pages is a good place to look for information and ideas. In addition to useful telephone numbers, it includes diagrams of major concert halls and sports stadiums. It also includes a short calendar of major annual events and maps of both the subway and bus systems.

Finally, the one-stop phone number for information on current events in New York is the Convention and Visitors' Bureau's Event Line (212/397-8222). If you have access to the Internet, take a look at the Bureau's Website (www.nycvisit.com). You also can call the city's recording for upcoming events in Central Park and other parks throughout the city (212/360-3456) and the Visitors Center in Central Park (212/794-6564). Other potentially useful information numbers and websites are listed at the end of this chapter.

Restrooms

Nothing can ruin your trek around New York (or anyplace else for that matter) more quickly than needing to use a bathroom and not being able to find one. By law, public buildings are required to have public restrooms. They are not, however, required to have clean and safe public restrooms.

The city has been debating and experimenting with public pay toilets for what seems like an eternity. There's even an "I'll-believe-it-when-I-see-it" plan to build more than 30 public toilets in Manhattan within the next few years. If you're interested in the latest in public toilet technology, take a look at the one behind City Hall, just off the corner of Centre and Chambers St. For a quarter, you can use it for up to 20 minutes (after which, the door automatically opens). Made by a German company, it is wonderfully clean and efficient (and wildly popular).

The following list ought to give you some ideas of bathrooms in specific areas that I've found to meet at least a minimum standard of safety and cleanliness. You may need to ask for directions or a key at some of them, but all are free to the public. As a general rule, however, try major hotel lobbies, busy restaurants (if you act like a patron, you can probably get away with it), department stores, schools, theaters, churches, libraries, and even hospitals. Of course, if you have small children in tow, the manager of just about any store or restaurant is likely to take pity and let you use even otherwise private facilities.

Wherever you end up, be sure to follow a few safety tips. Leaving anything on the floor in a public restroom is a mistake: purses, packages, and everything else have a bad habit of disappearing while you're otherwise occupied! The same is true of items left hanging on the back of the stall door. It's also a good idea to stay away from otherwise deserted bathrooms. No matter how badly you need to go, avoid bathrooms in parks (except the ones listed below) and most subway stations.

Below 14th Street

- **National Museum of the American Indian** (1 Bowling Green)
- **World Trade Center**
- **World Financial Center**
- **McDonald's** (160 Broadway, bet Cortlandt and Liberty St)
- **Federal Hall National Memorial** (Wall St, at Nassau St)
- **South Street Seaport**
- **City Hall** (Broadway at Chambers St)
- **Lower East Side Visitors Center** (261 Broome St, bet Orchard and Allen St)
- **Kmart** (770 Broadway, at 8th St)
- **Strand Bookstore** (828 Broadway, at 12th St)

Between 14th Street and 42nd Street

- **Barney's** (Seventh Ave, at 17th St)
- **Supreme Court of the State of New York** (25th St, bet Madison and Park Ave)
- **Manhattan Mall** (33rd St, at Sixth Ave)
- **Macy's Herald Square** (Broadway, at 34th St)
- **Science, Industry, and Business Library** (Madison Ave, at 34th St)
- **Sheraton Park Avenue Hotel** (Park Ave and 37th St)
- **Grand Hyatt Hotel** (42nd St bet Park and Lexington Ave)
- **New York Public Library** (Fifth Ave bet 40th and 42nd St)
- **Bryant Park** (42nd St bet Fifth and Sixth Ave)

Midtown

- **United Nations** (First Ave bet 45th and 46th St)
- **Waldorf-Astoria Hotel** (301 Park Ave, bet 49th and 50th St)
- **Rockefeller Center** (bet Fifth and Sixth Ave and 49th and 51st St)
- **Olympic Tower** (bet Fifth and Madison Ave and 51st and 52nd St)
- **Park Avenue Plaza** (55 E 52nd St, bet Madison and Park Ave)
- **Trump Tower** (Fifth Ave bet 55th and 56th St)
- **Henri Bendel** (712 Fifth Ave, nr 55th St)
- **Omni Park Central** (870 Seventh Ave, bet 55th and 56th St)
- **Sony Wonder Technology Lab** (56th St, nr Madison Ave)
- **Warner Brothers Studio Store** (57th St, at Fifth Ave)

Upper East Side

- **McDonald's** (Third Ave bet 57th and 58th St)
- **Bloomingdale's** (1000 Third Ave, at 59th St)
- **Hunter College Student Center** (Lexington Ave at 68th St)
- **Asia Society** (725 Park Ave, at 71st St)
- **92nd Street YMHA** (1395 Lexington Ave, at 92nd St)
- **Museum of the City of New York** (Fifth Ave bet 103rd and 104th St)
- **Charles A. Dana Discovery Center** (Central Park, nr Fifth Ave and 110th St)

Upper West Side

- **New York Visitors Bureau** (Columbus Circle, across from the southwest corner of Central Park)
- **Avery Fisher Hall at Lincoln Center** (in Lincoln Center, nr 64th St)
- **New York Public Library for the Performing Arts** (in Lincoln Center, nr 65th St)
- **Museum of American Folk Art** (Columbus Avenue bet 65th and 66th St)
- **Barnes & Noble** (Broadway and 82nd St)
- **Cathedral Church of St. John the Divine** (Amsterdam Ave at 112th St)
- **Hispanic Society** (Audubon Terrace, off Broadway bet 155th and 156th St)

Special Events

If you're looking for the perfect spot to hold a wedding reception, bar mitzvah, or gala event for thousands, New York inevitably has the right place . . . and the people to put it together for you. The trick, of course, is finding them. (The other trick is paying them!)

Note that you will not find museums, restaurants, or hotels in the following list. Many museums, including the Abigail Adams Smith Museum and the Roosevelt Rotunda of the American Museum of Natural History (complete with its dinosaur display), do rent space for parties and other events. Many restaurants have spaces for private parties, as do most hotels. Some of my favorite private party rooms in New York are **Adrienne** (at the Peninsula Hotel, 700 Fifth Ave); **Chez Josephine** (414 W 42nd St); the **Four Seasons** (99 E 52nd St); **Fraunces Tavern Restaurant** (54 Pearl St); **Gramercy Tavern** (42 E 20th St); **Hard Rock Cafe** (221 W 57th St); the **Hudson River Club** (World Financial Center); **La Reserve** (4 W 49th St); **Le Cirque** (Palace Hotel); **Le Perigord** (405 E 52nd St); **Lutece** (249 E 50th St); **Montrachet** (239 Broadway); **One If By Land, Two If By Sea** (17 Barrow St); **Primavera** (1578 First Ave); the **Rainbow Room** (Rockefeller Center, 65th fl); **Serendipity 3** (225 E 60th St); **Seventh Regiment Armory** (643 Park Ave); **Sign of the Dove** (1110 Third Ave); **Tavern on the Green** (Central Park W at 67th St); and the **Tribeca Grill** (375 Greenwich St, at Franklin St). If you want to throw a party at your favorite museum, restaurant, or hotel, by all means ask. (Look for a list under "Party Room" in Chapter I.)

Before you jump ahead with planning a party here, be forewarned: it's going to cost a great deal of money. I'm talking *really* big bucks. You can save some money by avoiding Saturday evenings, keeping your numbers down, and throwing your party in the off months of July and August or between January and early April. Some places and services will negotiate on their prices. But don't expect any great or even particularly good deals.

In the following section, I've tried to give some idea of what's available rather than provide a comprehensive list. I've divided the information between spaces to rent (to be done at least six months and as many as two years in advance, by the way) and all the details.

Spaces to Rent

Burden Mansion—It was once given to a Vanderbilt as a wedding present. Rental costs run between $3,500 and $4,500. It's located at 7 E 91st St, just off Fifth Ave. Call 212/722-4745 for more information.

Glorious Food—A converted 1903 garage, complete with a terrace and open-air roof space, this place is run by very fashionable caterers and can accommodate up to 200 in warmer months. It's located at 522 E 74th St. Call 212/628-2320 for more information.

Lincoln Center—There are many different spaces to choose from, but they're all hard to get. For information about Alice Tully Hall, call 212/875-5009. For information about the Metropolitan Opera House, call 212/799-3100. For information about the New York State Theater, call 212/870-5567.

Loeb Boathouse—In the middle of Central Park at about 74th St, this indoor-outdoor cafe and garden pavilion looks out on the lovely Central Park Lake. Rental costs with catering start at $100 per person. Call 212/517-3623 for more information.

Museum Club at Bridgewaters—This club in the Fulton Market Building at South Street Seaport has stunning views of the Brooklyn Bridge and New York Harbor. It can accommodate up to 2,000. Call 212/608-8823 for more information.

New York Botanical Garden—A new building complete with ballroom and outdoor terrace at this wonderful spot in the Bronx rents for somewhere between $80 and $200 per person, if catering is included. Call 718/220-0300 for more information.

New York Public Library—The magnificent main branch of the New York Public Library, on Fifth Avenue between 40th and 42nd streets, has several different spaces available for up to a thousand people (half that for dinner). Call 212/930-0730 for more information.

Pratt Mansion—You can't ask for a better location: across the street from the Metropolitan Museum of Art, at 1026 Fifth Ave. It's going to cost somewhere in the neighborhood of $4,000 to rent the space or $125 per person if they take care of the details. Call 212/717-1130 for more information.

Puck Building—One of the hottest properties in New York, Saturday nights at this elegant building on Lafayette St (at Houston St) are booked at least a year in advance. It will cost between $3,500 and $4,500 to rent, and that's just for the space. Call 212/274-8900 for more information.

Radio City Music Hall—It's hard to get, but the Great Hall of this magnificent place can accommodate up to a thousand for cocktails. Radio City can also be used for premieres, press conferences, and other big events. It's on the corner of 50th St and Sixth Ave. Call 212/632-4244 for more information.

Studio 450—This renovated industrial building overlooks the Hudson River from 450 W 31st St (between Ninth and Tenth Ave). The rental cost is around $4,000. Call 212/290-1400 for more information.

The Terrace—There's a glass greenhouse for relatively small parties at this wonderful and little-known restaurant on the 16th floor of Columbia University's Butler Hall, at 400 W 119th Street. Call 212/666-9490 for details.

Whitehall Club—A Victorian club founded by John D. Rockefeller, Jr. (among others), it's decorated with nautical memorabilia and art. The club is located at 17 Battery Place in the Financial District. Call 212/425-1960 for more information.

The Details

Caterers

To learn more about most of the caterers listed below, consult the "Delis, Catering, Food to Go" section of Chapter IV.

Abigail Kirsch: The business is in Tarrytown, but they do functions in Manhattan (914/631-3030).
Charlotte's: They can take care of music and flowers, too (212/732-7939).
Flavors Catering: Great prices for full service (212/647-1234).
Glorious Food: Well-established and perennially popular (212/628-2320).
Great Performances: Another full-service caterer with a great personal touch (212/727-2424).

Flowers

To learn more about most of the florists listed below, consult the "Flowers, Plants, Gardening" section of Chapter VI.

Chelsea Wholesale Flower Market: A newcomer with good prices (212/620-7500).
Preston Bailey Floral & Event Design: High-class arrangements for high-class clients (212/683-0035).
Simpson & Company: Unusual arrangements at competitive prices (212/772-6670).
Sura Kayla: One of the great floral talents in Manhattan (212/941-8757).
VSF: English country garden looks for primo clients (212/206-7236).

Music

A Touch of Jazz: Just what the name suggests (212/642-5441).
Blair McMillen (212/579-6010)
Ken Gross Orchestra: Whatever kind of music you want (212/688-4480).
New York Edge Orchestra: Almost everything (212/749-2364).
Sounds Perfect: Ditto (212/691-5044).
Sterling Music Ensembles: Classical solos and ensembles (212/481-7697).

Photographers

Rob Fraser (212/941-0433)
David Gordon (212/989-9329)
Events Filmworks (212/252-4045)
Visko Hatfield (212/979-9322)
Karen Hill (212/874-4468)
Mary Hilliard (212/879-7839)
Sharon Schuster (212/734-0927)

Staying in Touch

Thanks to the explosion of cellular phones, fax machines, modems, and other telephone-based technologies, the demand for phone numbers in New York and throughout the country has risen dramatically in recent years. In fact, New York City's area codes have been adjusted half a dozen times since I started writing this book to accommodate the increased demand!

For the time being, all Manhattan phone numbers have a 212 area code (except pagers and cellular phones, which are being assigned a 917 area code). As this edition goes to the publisher, however, Nynex (the New York telephone company) is warning that Manhattan is about to run out of telephone numbers again. When that happens, sometime in late 1997 or early 1998, Manhattan will get another area code (probably 646) to supplement 212. The bottom line is that telephone numbers in New York are about to get confusing! Beware: you may need to dial an area code just to call a neighbor across the street or a museum down the block.

All impending changes aside, there are a couple things you ought to know about making telephone calls in New York. Pay phones charge 25 cents for a three-minute local call, but local directory assistance is free (as is a call to 911, the police and fire emergency number). Pay phones on the street are almost impossible to find anymore, so look in the lobbies of office buildings or hotels. You can also make calls from the AT&T Public Calling Center on the main concourse of Grand Central Station (42nd St, at Park Ave) between 7 a.m. and 9 p.m. on weekdays.

If you're going to be in New York for more than a few days and need a mailing address, you can use the main post office. People can send things to you c/o General Delivery, 390 Ninth Avenue, New York, NY 10001. Your mail will be held for ten days, and you can pick it between 10 a.m. and 1 p.m., Monday through Saturday, with some form of photo identification. Call 212/330-3099 to verify the address, hours, and other details.

Telephone Numbers and Web Sites

Emergencies and Hotlines

AIDS hotline..212/447-8200
Alcoholism Council Hotline...........................212/979-1010
Ambulance 911
Domestic Violence Hotline...........................800/942-6906
Electricity Outages and Steam Leaks (Con Ed)..........212/683-0862
Fire 911
Gas Leaks (Con Ed)...................................212/683-8830
Narcotics Anonymous..................................718/929-6262
Poison Control.......................................212/764-7667
Police 911
Police (precinct locator)............................212/374-5000
Police (sex-crimes hotline)..........................212/267-7273
Runaway Hotline...........................   .800/246-4646
Suicide Help Line... .   . .   . ..212/532-2400
Travelers' Aid Society...............................212/944-0013
Victim Services Hotline 212/577-7777

Entertainment

Central Park Visitors Center.........................212/794-6564
Department of Parks and Recreation
    (permits and information)........................ 212/360-8111
    (recording of special events)....................212/360-3456
Information..411
Javits Convention Center (recording of upcoming events)...212/216-2000
Lincoln Center (recording of upcoming events)............212/546-2656
Macy's Herald Square (recording of upcoming events)......212/494-4495
Madison Square Garden (recording of upcoming events)....212/465-6741

Movie Locator.......................................212/777-3456
NYC/Onstage 212/768-1818
Restaurant Locator.................................212/888-3663
Rockefeller Center (recording of upcoming events).........212/632-3975
World Trade Center (recording of upcoming events)....... 212/435-4170
World Financial Center (recording of upcoming events).... 212/945-0505

Information and Complaints

Hospital Audiences, Inc. Hotline
   (access information for people with disabilities)..........888/424-4685
Lesbian and Gay Community Service Center............. 212/620-7310
Manhattan Borough President.........................212/669-8300
Marriage Licenses (City Clerk's office)................... 212/669-2400
Mayor's Office for People with Disabilities..............212/788-2830
New York City Board of Elections......................212/886-3800
New York City Department of Consumer Affairs
   (complaints division)...............................212/487-4444
New York City Department of Health (complaints line).... 212/442-9666
New York Public Library (branch information)...........212/340-0849
Post Office (general informnation)......................212/967-8585
U.S. Customs (regional office).........................212/466-4547

Transportation

Airports
Air-Ride (transportation information)....................800/247-7433
Kennedy Airport
   (general information)...............................718/244-4444
   (lost and found)...................................718/244-4225
LaGuardia Airport
   (general information)...............................718/533-3400
   (lost and found)...................................718/533-3988
Newark Airport
   (general information)...............................201/961-2000
   (lost and found)...................................201/961-6230

Mass Transit
Metropolitan Transit Authority
   (general information on buses and subways).............718/330-1234
   (general information in foreign languages). 718/330-4847
   (general information for people with disabilities).........718/596-8585
   (lost and found)...................................718/625-6200

Taxis
Taxi and Limousine Commission
   (general information and complaints)..................212/221-8294
   (lost and found)...................................212/840-4732

Trains and Buses
Amtrak...800/872-7245
Grand Central Station
   (general information)...............................212/340-3000
   (lost and found)...................................212/340-2555
Greyhound 212/231-2222

Long Island Railroad.................................718/217-5477
Metro North Railroad...............................212/532-4900
New Jersey Transit..................................201/762-5100
PATH...800/234-7284
Port Authority Bus Terminal
    (general information)..............................212/564-8484
    (lost and found)..................................212/435-2611

Miscellaneous
Bridge and Tunnel Construction Information............. 800/221-9903
On-street Parking Information........................ 212/442-7080
Towing (involuntary)................................212/971-0774
Vehicle Registration and Licenses..................... 212/645-5550

Web Sites

Central Park.................................www.centralpark.org.
League of American Theatres and Producers.........www.broadway.org
Lincoln Center.............................www.LincolnCenter.org
New York Convention and Visitors' Bureau ....www.nycvisit.com
New York Nightlife..........deck.com/entertain/nightmap/ny/indie.html
Mayor's Office and City Services.....www/ci/nyc/ny/us/html/mayor.html
Ticketmaster...............................www.ticketmaster.com

INDEX

(Note: Bold face numbers signify main entry.)

NOTES

NOTES

NOTES

NOTES